2007 LECTURES

PROCEEDINGS OF THE BRITISH ACADEMY · 154

2007 LECTURES

Published for THE BRITISH ACADEMY
by OXFORD UNIVERSITY PRESS

Oxford University Press, Great Clarendon Street, Oxford OX2 6DP

Oxford New York
Auckland Cape Town Dar es Salaam Hong Kong Karachi
Kuala Lumpur Madrid Melbourne Mexico City Nairobi
New Delhi Shanghai Taipei Toronto

© The British Academy 2008
Database right The British Academy (maker)
First published 2008

British Library Cataloguing in Publication Data
Data available

ISBN 978–0–19–726435–5
ISSN 0068–1202

Typeset in Times
by J&L Composition, Filey, North Yorkshire
Printed in Great Britain
on acid-free-paper by
CPI Antony Rowe
Chippenham, Wiltshire

The Academy is grateful to Professor Ron Johnston, FBA
for his editorial work on this volume

Contents

Palace or Powerstation?
Museums Today

DUNCAN ROBINSON
University of Cambridge

IN 1965 ISAIAH BERLIN delivered the A. W. Mellon Lectures at the National Gallery of Art in Washington DC on 'Sources of Romantic Thought'. According to his faithful editor, Henry Hardy, he suggested 'The Roots of Romanticism' as a title for the series, but agreed to change it, no doubt with a wry smile, when it was pointed out to him that he had been pipped to the post, because the eponymous hero of Saul Bellow's novel *Herzog*, published a year earlier in 1964, was a Jewish academic of a certain age undergoing a crisis of confidence as he struggled to deliver a course of adult-education lectures not simply on the same subject, but with the very same title.[1]

As I stand here this evening in the British Academy, to give a lecture in the name of one of its most distinguished past presidents, who was also for many years a devoted Trustee of the National Gallery, you will forgive me, I hope, if I empathise for a moment with his fictional counterpart!

However, I want to make a more serious point. By giving a course of lectures in which he identified, in his own words, 'a radical shift of values (that) occurred in the latter half of the eighteenth century', a shift so radical that it 'has affected thought, feeling and action in the western world',[2] Berlin lent his authority to the idea of the museum as a place for discourse. He was not, apparently, in sympathy with that younger generation of

---

Read at the Academy 2 May 2007.

[1] Isaiah Berlin, *The Roots of Romanticism*, ed. Henry Hardy (London, 2000), p. x.
[2] Quoted by Hardy from Berlin's notes, ibid., p. xii.

Proceedings of the British Academy, **154**, 1–27. © The British Academy 2008.

European philosophers whom he thought of as café intellectuals, but I like to think that he would have been willing, at least, to entertain Michel Foucault's definition of museums as heterotopia, or sites designated 'to enclose in one place all times, all epochs, all forms, all tastes, . . . the idea of constituting a place of all times that is itself outside time and inaccessible to its ravages . . . this whole idea belongs to our modernity'.[3] My only quibble is with that last clause; for while it is true that the word we use in English, *museum*, gained currency as late as the seventeenth century, as private cabinets of curiosities, such as the one formed by the Tradescants, father and son, began to enter the public domain, we also need to remind ourselves of the word's much earlier, classical derivation—from the Museum (with a capital M) at Alexandria, that seat of learning which flourished under the Ptolemies from the third century BC onwards. The association between collections and academic pursuits (scientia literarum) is therefore, I would argue, definitive. It is also one which, by that same definition, assigns a particular importance to university museums. This was recognised explicitly by the founder of the one where I work; in the will he signed shortly before he died in 1816, Richard, Viscount Fitzwilliam bequeathed his collections to the Chancellor, Masters and Scholars of the University of Cambridge 'for the increase of learning'.

But let me turn now to one or two examples of museum architecture. I would like to do so for the obvious reason that the shape and size of buildings are bound to reflect not only their purpose but also the cultural assumptions of the period in which they were created, or recreated. Form may not always follow function, but to the informed eye it rarely fails to reveal it.

The Louvre is, of course, the *palace par excellence*. However, we are concerned not with its original purpose, to accommodate the household and offices of a highly centralised absolute monarchy, but with its recreation as a museum during the French Revolution. Ten years later, in 1803, enlarged by loot from his conquests, it was renamed for the emperor, Musée Napoléon. Notwithstanding Napoleon's defeat, and the subsequent repatriation of some of his more egregious spoliations, by the third decade of the nineteenth century the Louvre was established as one of Europe's outstanding national museums; a reproach, in a word, to Regency London and the British Museum, with its muddle of collections,

[3] Michel Foucault, 'Texts/Contexts: of other spaces', *Diacritics*, 16/1 (Spring 1986), 22–7.

from Sloane's curiosities to the Elgin Marbles, all crammed into the barely modified rooms of Montagu House.

Smirke's original plans date from those very years and, looking at the British Museum as it was rebuilt between 1823 and 1846, it is easy to see the influence of what were rapidly becoming assumptions about museum architecture; the relationship to royal palaces and to their original contents, those 'princely goods' that formed the basis of so many national collections, but also an equally strong association with classical temples. Schinkel's Altes Museum in Berlin of 1823 was, of course, one of the first to invoke antiquity directly, with its central rotunda emulating the Pantheon in Rome. In London, the emphasis was on Greece; not only because of the Elgin purchase, made in 1816, but also because of Charles Towneley's and other collections formed in the late eighteenth century by a generation of antiquarians and connoisseurs for whom, to quote one of them, Richard Payne Knight, 'the prodigious superiority of the Greeks over every other nation, in all works of real taste and genius, is one of the most curious moral phaenomena in the history of man'.[4]

Turning from exteriors to interiors: I think we can see that here too there were distinct assumptions about the display of art. Johann Zoffany's painting of Grand Tourists among cognoscenti and British residents in Florence, informally assembled in the Tribuna of the Uffizi, was painted for Queen Charlotte in the 1770s.[5] Setting aside as we must the degree of artistic licence he employed in this elaborate conversation piece, it reproduces quite faithfully the way in which paintings were hung in European palaces, from the High Renaissance onwards. And when the last of the Medici, the Electress Palatine Anna Maria Luisa de Medici, entrusted the Uffizi and its contents to the city of Florence in 1743 'to benefit the public of all nations', it would not have occurred to anyone that there was anything inappropriate in the way that the pictures were arranged. Lord Northwick's Picture Gallery at Thirlestaine House, which was painted by Robert Huskisson in 1846, provides one example among many of the persistence of this fashion.[6] Even today, one or two delightful examples of

---

[4] Richard Payne Knight, *Specimens of Antient Sculpture*, 1 (London, 1809); quoted by Nicholas Penny, 'Collecting, interpreting, and imitating ancient art', in *The Arrogant Connoisseur: Richard Payne Knight, 1751–1824*, ed. Michael Clarke and Nicholas Penny (Manchester, 1982), p. 79.

[5] See Oliver Millar, *The Later Georgian Pictures in the Collection of Her Majesty the Queen*, 2 vols. (London, 1969), 1. p. 154, no. 1211; 2. plates 40–2.

[6] Robert Huskisson, *Lord Northwick's Picture Gallery at Thirlestaine House*, Yale Center for British Art, Paul Mellon Collection, oil on canvas, 81.4 × 108.5 cm.

Duncan Robinson

Figure 1. The Fitzwilliam Museum Cambridge: Founder's Building, 1848, designed by George Basevi (1794–1845) and completed after his death by C. R. Cockerell (1788–1863).

these aristocratic interiors survive: the Palazzo Doria Pamphili in Rome, for instance.

Moving closer to home, as far as I am concerned, the 'good, substantial, museum repository' George Basevi designed to fulfill one of the stipulations made in Lord Fitzwilliam's will, opened to the public in 1848 (Fig. 1). Its exterior bears a family resemblance to Smirke's British Museum, completed at the same time and already the hallmark for art museums in Victorian Britain. The interior was, quite naturally, arranged according to those time-honoured conventions we have already examined (Fig. 2). However, by the middle of the nineteenth century there were murmurings against hanging on, above and below the line. They began, I suspect, among artists who were dismayed when their paintings were 'skied' in exhibitions at the Royal Academy and elsewhere. They were certainly voiced by at least one reviewer of the new galleries in Cambridge. Writing in the *Cambridge Chronicle and Huntingdonshire Gazette* on 1 July 1848, he observed that

> the first coup d'oeil must convince the beholder how cleverly the pictures have been marshalled according to their *sizes*. This grouping, we must confess, has been most successful in its way. He must not, therefore, be offended at a few special effects produced in consequence. Companionship in subject or style, having been made a secondary point, there must occur some few violations, perhaps rather harsh, of other harmonies . . .

> One group embraces a piece of fish, and flesh, and fowl, with landscape delineations of almost all the elements.

> Another group contains a portrait of Hone, a Holy Family, and a cattle market.

Further on in the article, the reviewer cannot resist the inevitable quip that the viewer 'may wish to have a ladder to help him to a fair view of a few inviting works'. But there are also two more serious criticisms, one veiled, the other levelled more directly. First:

> Until . . . they (the Syndics) shall . . . mark out the boundaries between the dominions of purity and indecency, and draw the fine line which excludes a work of art of a certain kind from the immoral, it is to be feared that many . . . will condemn the present display . . .

Secondly:

> not a few will, till better informed, lament the non-adoption, in a place of science, of a scientific arrangement for such a collection.

Both of these comments are, I believe, signs of the times. The lack of 'scientific arrangement' remained a problem for decades, to judge not only

Figure 2. Gallery 3, The Fitzwilliam Museum, photographed in the nineteenth century.

from the surviving photographic records but also from the guide to the collections written at the turn of the century. On the other hand, in 1856 the university's vice-chancellor 'thought it his duty to make considerable changes in the FITZWILLIAM MUSEUM during the Christmas vacation'. As he explained in a flysheet dated January,

> the exhibition of nude figures in a public gallery is always a matter of some embarrassment. Even where the gallery is visited by those only who are habituated to regard merely the pictorial interest of such objects, they ought not, it would seem, to be obtruded on the eye of the visitor. But since, in recent times, we have opened the Fitzwilliam Gallery to the public indiscriminately, and to very young persons of both sexes, it appears to be quite necessary, for the credit of the University, that it should be possible to pass through the Gallery without looking at such pictures:

We smile, but we also need to remind ourselves that although the goal posts have moved, in terms of what is, and what is not, acceptable, the museum is still a sensitive site in which the question of censorship remains open. Twenty years ago, when I was working in the United States of America, I remember the very varied fortunes of a touring exhibition of photographs by Robert Mapplethorpe. In Washington it was scheduled to appear at the Corcoran, a few hundred yards from Capitol Hill. Such was the outcry against its homoerotic content that the Trustees declined to open it and the director resigned. Questions of a threatening kind were asked in Congress about the use of public money via the Arts and Humanities Endowments to support such controversial art. Six months later, however, the same exhibition opened at the Wadsworth Atheneum in Hartford, Connecticut; a State Capitol this time, in the heart of puritan New England. There, ironically, it was a runaway success, earning valuable dollars for the museum and accolades for the director and his board.

In the case of the Fitzwilliam, it took rather longer to address the second criticism, until 1924 in fact, and the completion of the first of the museum's twentieth-century extensions, the Upper Marlay Gallery. In what was seen as a highly innovative approach to the display of art, Sydney Cockerell, director from 1908 to 1937, installed the early Italian schools in more or less chronological order, hanging the pictures at or near to eye level and interspersing them with appropriate sculpture, furniture and ceramics (Fig. 3). But if Cockerell's installation owes a great deal to the new science of connoisseurship derived from Morelli and applied particularly to the fourteenth and fifteenth centuries in central Italy by that most passionate of all sightseers, Bernard Berenson, it also

Figure 3. Upper Marlay Gallery, The Fitzwilliam Museum, designed by A. Dunbar Smith and Cecil C. Brewer, 1915–24.

descends from another late nineteenth-century tradition, one associated with both Arts and Crafts and the Aesthetic Movement, the 'Haus eines Kunstfreundes', the collector's domestic paradise in which he could dwell in a tastefully constructed world surrounded by his most cherished possessions. It was, of course, a deliberate construct, both illuminated and exploded by the image of the dealer William Agnew posing in his Bond Street Gallery.[7] This, the *fin de siècle*, was the era of collectors, connoisseurs and marchand-amateurs, and sometimes, as in the case of Charles Fairfax Murray, a blend of all three. Berenson too, with I Tatti, his beloved *casa colonica* in the hills above Florence where he supported himself by writing opinions and advising other collectors on their purchases; Berenson who wrote towards the end of his life that 'rereading Pater's Marius, I am surprised to discover to what extent it is my own spiritual biography'.[8]

Looking more closely at the disposition of works of art throughout the Upper Marlay Gallery (Fig. 4), André Malraux's famous dictum springs to mind: 'A Romanesque crucifix was not regarded by its contemporaries as a work of sculpture; nor Cimabue's Madonna as a picture'. But whereas he attributes this metamorphosis as he calls it—of the devotional image into an object of aesthetic contemplation—to the museum, which he characterises as an institution which 'divests works of art of their functions', it is clear, I think, that this process of transformation began at least a generation earlier, with those collectors who rehabilitated the discarded fragments of late medieval altarpieces into icons of their own taste. Simone Martini's three separate panels, as they have been presented with minor modifications to their framing ever since they emerged from the Charles Butler collection in 1893, make no sense at all iconographically. It is only when we use our art-historical knowledge to take them apart and to rearrange them mentally around the missing central image, with its subjects of the saints' eternal devotion, that we begin to appreciate their original function.

To go further, beyond the walls of the museum, in search of the historical contexts for Simone's altarpieces, we have to look for evidence of a different kind; evidence which can be derived from archival, documentary, or visual sources. One example of the last is a small painting by Sassetta,

[7] Edward Salomons (d. 1906), *William Agnew in his Gallery*, c.1880, Thos. Agnew & Sons, London.
[8] Quoted by John Pope-Hennessy, 'Portrait of an Art Historian' in *Essays on Italian Sculpture* (London and New York, 1968), p. 206.

Figure 4. Detail of the Upper Marlay Gallery, showing Simone Martini's three panels of Saints Geminianus, Michael and Augustine, each 59.7 × 35.8 cm. The Fitzwilliam Museum, purchased 1893.

another Sienese artist, active in the fifteenth century, who faithfully depicted this Miracle of the Eucharist in what were for him the familiar surroundings of a late medieval church interior.[9]

This is not the place or time to elaborate upon a single art-historical detective story, although it provides a good example of the kind of museum-based research to which we owe our knowledge, in this instance of Simone's commission to paint an altarpiece for the church of Sant Agostino in the Tuscan hill-town of San Gimignano, and the where-abouts of the other surviving fragments of the polyptych.[10] What I wish to emphasise instead is the general point; that the relationship between museum collections and scholarship is one which has to be maintained and, if possible, strengthened. Personally, I have no objections to anyone constructing their own myths around surviving fragments of material culture; in fact doing so has been one of the main preoccupations of artists and writers during the past century, but I am convinced that by careful research we can recover something at least of the original meanings of the works of art we have inherited from the past. Think back for a moment to Palma Vecchio's *Venus and Cupid*, or consider Titian's great allegory of the five senses summarised in his painting of *Venus, Cupid and a Lutenist* (Fig. 5). No one in the western world objects today to the display of naked flesh; indeed, it is hard to avoid exposure to it, in paint and on the screen, not to mention it being served up in gigantic portions on bill-boards, but to attribute our acceptance of Renaissance art to our more permissive attitudes is to miss its point just as completely as our repressed Victorian counterparts did. Our appreciation is based not on toleration but on knowledge, on a far greater understanding of the artistic and intel-lectual milieu from which those idealised images of sacred and profane love arose.[11] This brings me back to the importance of collections-based scholarship and to the expression of one of my serious concerns about the status of research in museums today.

Fifty years ago and for much of the second half of the twentieth century, scholar-curators set new standards for the cataloguing of public collections in our national and regional museums: for example, Martin

[9] Sassetta, (Stefano di Giovanni) c.1400–50, 'The Miracle of the Eucharist', Bowes Museum, Barnard Castle.

[10] J. W. Goodison, *Catalogue of Paintings: The Fitzwilliam Museum, Cambridge*, 2. *Italian Schools* (Cambridge, 1967), pp. 158–62.

[11] See, for example, Erwin Panofsky, 'The Neoplatonic Movement in Florence and North Italy', in *Studies in Iconology: Humanistic Themes in the Art of the Renaissance* (Oxford, 1939; repr. New York, 1962), pp. 129–69.

Figure 5. Titian (Tiziano Vecellio) (? 1477–1576), Venus, Cupid with a Lute Player, oil on canvas, 150.5 × 196.8 cm. The Fitzwilliam Museum, Founder's Bequest

Davies, Assistant Keeper, Keeper and then Director of the National Gallery; John Pope-Hennessy, Assistant Keeper, Keeper of Sculpture and then Director of the Victoria and Albert Museum. Their catalogues remain indispensable tools for any serious student of the areas and periods they covered. Contrast today, when far too many curators have far too little time to work on the permanent collections in their care, because their roles have widened and diversified. Of course there are honourable exceptions—but what I find disturbing is that although the national museums (and where they lead, presumably others will follow) are gaining analogue status with institutions of higher education, and thereby qualifying for funding by the Arts and Humanities Research Council, they have a tendency to buy in research, to regard it as an add-on, to be carried out by independent scholars or temporary staff, paid for by external funding, as opposed to treating it as a core function of the permanent staff or establishment.

For me the curatorial function remains crucial, and it must certainly not be underestimated. To return to Foucault's notion of the museum as a heterotopia, a place where different cultures can be both represented and contested, simultaneously, side by side; in such a context, the curator wields enormous power, simply by selecting the exhibits and less simply by arranging them. To illustrate the point, I offer a comparison of two photographs taken at different times of the same paintings in the same space (Figs. 6 and 7). The gallery was designed in the 1930s by the architects A. Dunbar Smith and Cecil C. Brewer. The earlier photograph shows the gallery as Cockerell installed it initially, applying the somewhat austere aesthetic of the Arts and Crafts movement including truth to materials. The more recent one shows it after it was refurbished by another of my predecessors, Michael Jaffé, in 1975. His aim was to increase the impact of these three great masterpieces from the founder's collection by suggesting the opulence of their original settings—in the emperor's palace in Prague for instance, or the Palais d'Orleans. Once again, this is not so much an attempt at accurate, historical reconstruction, as an act of empathy and evocation.

The process continues, and I take my share of the responsibility. In 1975 the Adeane Gallery opened as a temporary exhibition gallery, a use to which it was dedicated until it was made over, on my watch, to provide a gallery for our permanent collection of the arts of the late twentieth century. I am fully aware of the fact that this action not only extended the museum's narrative chronologically, but also that it did so in a particular way, giving priority within that narrative to a certain type of art produced

Figure 6. Detail of the Courtauld Gallery, Fitzwilliam Museum, photographed *c.*1970.

Figure 7. Detail of the Courtauld Gallery, Fitzwilliam Museum, photographed after 1975.

in the last three decades of the last century. In other words, decisions taken within the museum about both the design and the content of the galleries will inevitably influence the way in which art is received and perceived. The text is unwritten, and perhaps all the more persuasive for being so.

In trying to understand the place and importance of museums today, it is worth recalling the outlook a hundred years ago. Marinetti's call to 'Burn the Museums' was echoed by avant-gardes all over Europe, impatient with the claustrophobic constraints of the nineteenth century. Museums, with their dinosaurs' bones and dusty cases of stuffed birds, became the antithesis of modernity, of progress, of the machine age. Wyndham Lewis led the charge in England; his *Blasts* were directed against those individuals and institutions he held responsible for the repressions of the Victorian era. I hesitate to mention it, but on one page of *Blast* a predecessor of mine at Magdalene College, A. C. Benson, shares the honours of excoriation with the British Academy![12]

How did museums, along with academies, survive this assault? The reason is, I suggest, that museums have proved adept, over the past century or so, at reinventing themselves. Twenty years ago, when I read the table of contents of the American journal, *Museum News*,[13] I was struck by the way in which the titles of the articles provided a series of highly relevant cues: here, under four headings, are the reasons why the futurists, among other cultural iconoclasts of the early twentieth century, were proved to be wrong.

Museums have modernised. The first heading was 'The Selling of the Museum', indicating the importance we now attach to marketing and promotion as well as the needs of our different audiences. The second, provocatively headed 'Serving up Culture', featured the expansion of the Whitney Museum of American Art to off-site locations, in a conscious attempt to create a *different* kind of 'museum without walls' from the one envisaged by Malraux. The third caption read 'Showplace, Playground or Forum', to indicate the way in which museums are increasingly seen as sites for a variety of discourses; why should they not serve all three of those functions, not least as fora for the kind of intellectual debate the A. W. Mellon lectures were designed to stimulate in Washington? Finally, 'Investing in Conservation' as one of our most urgent priorities.

---

[12] Wyndham Lewis (ed.), *Blast: Review of the Great English Vortex*, 1. 20 June 1914 (London, New York and Toronto), p. 21.

[13] *Museum News*, 64/4, April 1986.

Museums have in many ways anticipated in microcosm several of our global concerns, and by doing so they have attracted public attention, support, and respect for technical art history, that branch of the discipline in which academic art historians, conservators and curators confer and combine their skills and experience.

Another reason why the museum today has not only survived but has also achieved unprecedented levels of attendance is surely attributable to the iconoclasm within the sector itself. The decision was taken in the late 1960s to break from tradition in the museum capital of Europe, and to rehouse the French national collection of twentieth-century art in a building which could not have presented a greater contrast with the Beaux-Arts idiom derived from the Louvre. That decision, taken at a time of considerable social unrest in Paris, and indeed elsewhere in the world, was both political and cultural. It combined urban renewal with democratisation, utilising high-tech allure to demystify high art and to make it both more accessible and more inviting. The approach to the opening hours of the Pompidou Centre was, initially at least, as radical as its architecture, replacing office hours, when the vast majority of the population is at work, with extended openings into the evenings and at weekends.

As you know, one of the most successful recent additions to the Parisian art scene was not originally an art gallery at all. The Gare d'Orsay (Fig. 8) was one of the last railway stations to be built in nineteenth-century Paris. Commanding a highly sensitive, riverside site, clearly visible from the Tuileries, it was obliged to rise to the occasion and succeeded to the point that when it opened in 1900 one commentator exclaimed 'mais c'est un véritable palais des beaux-arts'. Less than a hundred years later, his prophecy was fulfilled, when an unsuccessful railway station, with platforms that were too short to accommodate the increasingly long commuter trains bringing workers to the centre of Paris from its southern suburbs and satellite towns, was converted into the highly successful Musée d'Orsay (Fig. 9).

One reason the Musée d'Orsay works so well is that it was designed originally to deal with large numbers of people. Like the commuters of yesteryear, today's visitors are keen to get on with their journey and to do so with a maximum of comfort and efficiency. What I hope my illustrations show is how little had to be done to convert the central hall into an art terminal, with clear sight-lines and self-explanatory signals to direct those passing through towards a whole network of cultural destinations. In many ways, I think the comparison itself is worth emphasising, for practical as well as metaphorical reasons. Museums today receive more

4074.- PARIS.— La Gare d'Orsay
Construite en 1900   Architecte Laloux

Figure 8.   The Gare d'Orsay, Paris, designed by Victor Laloux, 1900.

Figure 9.   Le Musée d'Orsay, Paris, remodelled by ACT Architecture, 1986.

visitors than ever before. We read in a recent *Manifesto for Museums* that 'the 2,500 museums in the UK receive more than 100 million visits each year, more than all the country's live sporting events combined'.

Today's museum architecture needs to reflect this dramatic increase in public interest. And museums must also consider and provide for the rising expectations of their users as they embark on their journeys of discovery, or take a break, halfway through, to visit the buffet car. I illustrate two recent interventions within museums to improve the kinds of provisions I have alluded to; Rick Mather's courtyard at the Wallace Collection, completed in 2000 (Fig. 10), and John Miller's for the Fitzwilliam Museum, which opened in 2004 (Fig. 11). The *Manifesto* I referred to above points out that 'museums make important contributions to urban, economic and social regeneration'. It cites different examples, but I would like to highlight the success of the Tates. Tate North, or Tate Liverpool, to be more precise, was one of the first UK museum essays in urban renewal; moreover one which, instead of clearing the industrial wasteland, recognised the value of retaining old buildings and refashioning them. Like their counterparts in Paris, Tate's planners realised that existing structures were not only fit for purpose, but ideally suited; in their case, the shell of an abandoned warehouse in Liverpool's docklands offered the kind of wide-open, unordered and flexible space which a great deal of contemporary art requires. After that, the treatment of Bankside should have been a foregone conclusion, but we all remember the debate in which there was vociferous support for new architecture as a corollary of new art. Eventually we may have both, but in the meantime few now disagree with the decision that was taken, to remodel the redundant powerstation. The redundant machinery, rusting away in the Turbine Hall, has been superseded by a different kind of power generation and energy. Once again, I make no apology for what is, I think, an effective metaphor for the museum today, one supported by the unprecedented success of the Tate Modern. After only one year of operation, it had become the third most visited tourist attraction in Britain and, according to the McKinsey consultancy, it had by then already generated £100 million of economic activity and 3,000 new jobs.[14]

---

[14] *A Manifesto for Museums: Building Outstanding Museums for the 21st Century*, issued on behalf of the Directors of the National Museums, the Chairman of the Museums, Archives and Libraries Council, the Chairman of the Association of Independent Museums, the Convenors of the Group for Large Local Authority Museums, the President of the Museums Association and the Chief Executives of the Regional Agencies (2007), n.p.

Figure 10. Wallace Collection, Hertford House, London. Courtyard designed by Rick Mather Architects, 2000.

Duncan Robinson

Figure 11. Fitzwilliam Museum. Courtyard development designed by John Miller + Partners, 2004.

I have to admit that, in many ways, I am more interested in the reasons for this achievement than in the outcomes themselves. Free admission, flexible opening hours and effective publicity have all played their parts, as has the quality of the exhibitions programme. Beyond those factors, however, I would like to suggest that there are at least two less tangible ones, ones that neither McKinsey nor Mori are likely to tease out with their surveys and samplings. Like the Pompidou Centre, the Bankside development was the right thing at the right time. It struck the right notes socially and politically in London at the millennium—in contrast with that contemporary disaster downstream, the meaningless Dome.

My second point is that Tate Modern shares its success with the sector as a whole; a success which I believe owes much to the increasing emphasis on visual communications within our culture generally. Wherever we look, the evidence is incontrovertible. Take the newspaper for instance, and compare *The Times* of 1957 with its successor today. The obvious difference can be summarised in a single sentence: the photographer has displaced the journalist. The impact of television is, justly in my view, the topic of widespread concern, . . . but setting aside the whole issue of broadcasting standards, about which I suspect we all have strong views, what we cannot deny is that one of television's greatest legacies is the *screen*—an invention which, like many others, is susceptible to misuse as well as use. So we have violent videogames on the one hand and information technology on the other. In terms of the World Wide Web, the screen has become the page, and no one bats an eyelid at the usage of 'web page', although it represents a considerable act of verbal appropriation considering the precise, single side of a single leaf, hard copy definition of the second of its syllables. But this cavalier attitude to language as our principal means of communication pervades the internet. Where images once illustrated words, they have now replaced them. And of course in our shrinking world where the difficulty of communicating in different languages is a daily occurrence, there is a growing tendency to rely on signs and symbols. Road signs are an obvious example, as are identifiers for public lavatories. Trivial as these instances are, the point I am trying to make is that generation by generation we are learning to see more, and that our growing dependence on non-verbal communication is just one indication of an increasingly visual culture in which we now refer to 'reading' images and objects.

To state the obvious—all of this has serious implications for museums and their visitors. In last January's issue of *Research Horizons,* the

University of Cambridge's research magazine, there was an article on 'using technology in cultural spaces'. In it, the author pointed out that

> Already digital technology is beginning to find a place in museums in the form of eguides and digital information points which augment the glass cases and printed labels . . . The rise of ubiquitous computing and increased affordability of digital technologies will doubtless see further developments in the integration of smart-media in the museum context.[15]

In March a series of workshops was held, sponsored by the AHRC Museums and Galleries Research Programme, to explore some of the wider issues—of place, narrative and digitality—in the museum of the future.

Which brings me to the last point I want to make about museums today. They are, fundamentally, about images and about objects. There is always a temptation to define them in terms of what they do, socially and economically, and I hope I have said enough about those effects to persuade you that I take them seriously, but we must not confuse cause and effect: what museums are, with what they can achieve. *Collections* differentiate museums from all other public institutions, and I have tried to demonstrate how the art museum as we know it has evolved from those private collections of 'princely goods', as well as 'cabinets of curiosities'. Acquisitions are, by the same token, the life-blood of collecting institutions. They come in all shapes and sizes, from a variety of sources including gifts, bequests and purchases. At times acquiring them can be difficult, expensive and also controversial. Take for instance that incomparable painting by Raphael, 'The Madonna of the Pinks', purchased by the National Gallery in 2004. I did not envy the director as he shouldered the particularly difficult task of raising public money to pay for a very small, very expensive, cult object—by that I mean a picture of a subject unfamiliar to many and offensive to some. But of course history will side with the director and trustees, because they took the lead in saving for the nation a pre-eminent work of art, an object of enduring beauty which will inspire and uplift visitors to the National Gallery from all over the world for years to come. It takes courage to declare that works like these are literally priceless—worth far more than even the hideously inflated prices their owners sometimes demand.

[15] Tamsin Pert, 'Guiding muses—using technology in cultural spaces', *Research Horizons*, University of Cambridge research magazine, Spring 2007, 24–5.

Two years ago in Cambridge we faced a similar, though in some ways easier, challenge. The *Macclesfield Psalter* was seen as a national treasure not least because it was produced in this country. On the other hand, because it was small and bound, it was difficult to answer all of those questions about accessibility and impact that are now considered to be of such crucial importance by the funding bodies. It is, I am afraid, a feature of the current climate, one consistent with my fears about defining museums in terms of their utility, that funders tend to place more emphasis upon the immediate, measurable benefits to be derived from their investments in objects, than upon their intrinsic qualities, or the long-term benefits they hold in store for future generations. The same is true, I might add, in the case of the conditional exemption of pre-eminent works of art from capital taxation. However, in the case of the *Macclesfield Psalter* I need not have worried as much as I did. The response to the museum's efforts, and to the national appeal launched on its behalf by the Art Fund, demonstrated a surprising level of public support; sufficient, in the end, to convince the Trustees of the National Heritage Memorial Fund to commit to the purchase. And in what seemed at the time to be a vindication of the museum's efforts, when the psalter finally returned to the east of England, its region of origin, and was placed on display, for several days thousands of people queued to catch a glimpse of this rare treasure of medieval art. So much for presuppositions about wall-power.

Allow me to offer one more example of a recent acquisition, of Barbara Hepworth's three figures from her 'Family of Man', to make a related point, albeit about an object acquired by a different route. The group was standing on the salt marshes next to the Maltings at Snape in 2000 when it was accepted by HM Treasury in lieu of capital taxes. The figures were placed there originally to mark the bonds of mutual respect and friendship that united the sculptor with the musicians Benjamin Britten and Peter Pears, the *genii loci* so to speak. So, while the sculptures are not site-specific in the strict sense, their present siting adds meaning as well as resonance to them. In allocating them to the Fitzwilliam Museum, the Department of Culture, Media and Sport therefore stipulated that they should remain *in situ*, unless some overriding consideration arose to necessitate their removal to the museum. Let us hope it will not, for here I suggest we have a clear demonstration of one way in which museums can play important regional roles *fuori le mure*, or museums without walls again!

To retain the regional focus for a moment, there have been two highly positive developments during the past decade; the 'designation' of collections as being of national importance irrespective of their ownership and location; and 'Renaissance in the Regions', an initiative designed to build regional museums services not as free-standing entities but as museum-based networks throughout the country. With only three of the nine regional hubs fully funded, and the other six capacity-building and in waiting, it is already clear that renaissance works, that it delivers in terms of government's priorities, socially and economically. In his fore-word to *Understanding the Future: Priorities for England's Museums*, published last October, Arts Minister David Lammy writes about museums as 'community spaces, as mediators between the past and the present, and as agents in a dialogue about who we are and what we might become or achieve'. For those of us within these heterotopia, we could not wish for a more ringing endorsement of our aims and ambitions. On the other hand I do think that we have to be careful to maintain that distinction I have already emphasised, between what museums are—collections-based institutions devoted to the study and appreciation of the past through material culture surviving into the present—and what they can achieve.

To summarise: I think we have come a long way in the last 100 years. The museum today looks outward, not inward, and in spite of the problems they face in terms of resources, museums have succeeded in moving closer to the centre of the stage of public life. As I have hinted, that incurs risks, of increasing regulation for example, and the growing expectation on the part of governments that museums will earn their keep by promoting specific social agendas. While not for one moment denying the importance of those, what museum professionals have to do is remind our funders and stakeholders, tactfully but persistently, that people do not visit museums in order to comply with public policies. As we know from our visitor surveys, their pretexts differ: from schoolchildren following the national curriculum to members of the University of the Third Age; through life-long learners, united in their personal and above all pleasurable pursuit of that 'increase of learning' which is integral to the definition of the museum; to local residents from across the social spectrum, regular visitors for whom '*their*' museum is a source of pride and joy; and tourists from near and far for some of whom at least their visit is a once-in-a-lifetime experience. I could go on expanding this list, but for all of the above there is one common cause: palace or powerstation, or ideally a combination of the two, unlike so many museologists who cannot see the wood for the trees, millions of museum visitors every year know that the museum is what it is. And here, at last I know that I am on firm ground with that distinguished scholar whom we commemorate this evening, the philosopher who championed 'common humanity' above all differences of age, race or gender. In his essay on 'Two concepts of liberty' Isaiah Berlin abbreviated one of his favourite quotations from the eighteenth-century divine, Bishop Butler, to read, quite simply, 'Everything is what it is'.[16]

---

[16] Isaiah Berlin, 'Two concepts of liberty' [1958], in *The Proper Study of Mankind: An Anthology of Essays* (London, 1997), p. 197.

Architectural Politics in Renaissance Venice

DEBORAH HOWARD

St John's College, Cambridge

WHAT IS THE ROLE OF ARCHITECTURE in the self-definition of a political regime? To what extent are the ideologies of state communicated in public space? Can public confidence be sustained by extravagant building initiatives—or be sapped by their failures? These issues are, of course, as relevant today as they were in the Renaissance. Venice, in particular, seems closer to our own times than most other Early Modern states because of its relatively 'democratic' constitution, at least within the ranks of the ruling oligarchy. It was a democracy only for noblemen, since voting rights and eligibility for important committees and councils were limited to members (men only, numbering about 2,000) of a closed, hereditary caste. Nevertheless, many of the problems over decision-making ring true to modern ears. Indeed, it could be argued that the continual revision of public building projects during their execution is an essential characteristic of the democratic process.

It has been claimed by architectural historians over the past few decades that ambitious programmes of building patronage in Renaissance Venice helped to communicate political ideals to the public.[1]

Read at the Academy 10 May 2007.

[1] See, for example, Manfredo Tafuri, *Jacopo Sansovino* (Padua, 1969; 2nd edn., 1972); Deborah Howard, *Jacopo Sansovino: Architecture and Patronage in Renaissance Venice* (New Haven & London, 1975; rev. edn., 1987); Manfredo Tafuri, '"Renovatio urbis Venetiarum": il problema storiografico', in M. Tafuri (ed.), *'Renovatio urbis': Venezia nell'età di Andrea Gritti (1523–1538)* (Rome, 1984), pp. 9–55; Manfredo Tafuri, *Venezia e il Rinascimento* (Turin, 1985; English edn., trans. Jessica Levine, Cambridge, MA and London, 1989).

Proceedings of the British Academy, **154**, 29–67. © The British Academy 2008.

Historians have suggested that the remodelling of Piazza San Marco reinforced the power of the ruling nobility by framing its elaborate programmes of public ceremonial.[2] Scholars have sought to identify political affiliations in both executed and unexecuted designs.[3] Meanwhile, the role of print culture in controlling the ideological meaning of public iconography has been highlighted. This lecture seeks to reinforce some of these views, but at the same time to show how unpredictable the processes of government could be. It will become evident that, as the sixteenth century progressed, religious perplexities on the one hand, and an increasing respect for technical expertise on the other, came to frustrate the ambitions of those who wanted to glorify the state with grand classical buildings. The argument relates specifically to architectural issues, but similar political processes governed the whole range of government policy.

Background to the constitution

The uniqueness of the Venetian constitution was continually reiterated: for example, in 1581 the elderly Doge Nicolò da Ponte declared that 'the form of our government is extraordinarily different from every other government and state in the whole world'.[4] In the same year, the first comprehensive guidebook to the city by Francesco Sansovino declared the constitution to be 'fortified by its laws with marvellous prudence, founded on justice, and rooted in the solid ground of religion, for the salvation and preservation of liberty and of the honour that has been almost lost in [the rest of] poor Italy'.[5] This rhetoric of state, known to historians as 'The Myth of Venice', helped to sustain the Republic as its

---

[2] Edward Muir, *Civic Ritual in Renaissance Venice* (Princeton, NJ, 1981); *idem*, 'Manifestazioni e cerimonie nella Venezia di Andrea Gritti', in Tafuri (ed.), '*Renovatio urbis*', pp. 59–77; Deborah Howard, 'Ritual Space in Renaissance Venice', *Scroope: Cambridge Architecture Journal*, 5 (1993–4), 4–11.

[3] Especially Tafuri, *Venezia e il Rinascimento, passim.*

[4] '. . . la forma del nostro governo è diversissima da tutti gli altri governi, et stati del mondo'. Address of the Doge to the Collegio, Archivio di Stato di Venezia (henceforth ASV), Collegio, Esposizioni Roma, registro 2, ff. 28v–32r, 9 Feb. 1581, cited in Silvio Tramontin, 'La visita apostolica del 1581 a Venezia', *Studi veneziani*, 9 (1967), 453–533, at p. 476.

[5] 'Fortificato dale leggi con maravigliosa prudenza, fermato su la giustizia, & stabilito su la saldissima base della religione, per salvezza, & per conservatione della libertà, & dello honor quasi perduto affatto della misera Italia.' Francesco Sansovino, *Venetia città nobilissima et singolare* (Venice, 1581), f. 174v.

real power waned, both politically and economically, over the course of the sixteenth century.[6]

The mechanisms of decision-making in the public realm of Renaissance Venice were extremely complex. Whereas a dynastic ruler could employ his own court artists to fulfil his personal commands, in Venice every major decision had to pass through the Senate or Council of Ten, or even, in the case of a crucial policy initiative, through the whole adult male nobility in the Greater Council.[7] Elected magistracies were given day-to-day executive responsibilities for specific building projects, but had to solicit funding from the relevant council.

Debates in the Venetian assemblies, the Greater Council, the Senate, the Council of Ten and the Collegio, were not recorded verbatim; the proceedings, beautifully inscribed in humanistic script on parchment by the council secretaries, only summarised the motions and recorded voting figures. We have to rely on the testimony of diarists and chroniclers to recover more fully the debates about architectural matters. Most of the projects to be discussed below were directed by the Senate and managed by its delegated committees. As originally constituted, the Senate consisted of sixty members elected by the Greater Council, but by the sixteenth century it also included the Council of Forty (the 'Quarantia Criminale'), as well as an addition (or *zonta*) of sixty elected by the outgoing Senators. In addition, many high-ranking holders of government posts had ex-officio membership, making a potential total voting membership of around 230, although the average number of votes was about 180. The existence of the *zonta* ensured a stable core of experienced statesmen, many of them renowned for their eloquence. Sometimes discussions were so heated that they had to be adjourned for a cooling-off phase. Nevertheless, powers of oratory, however much they were praised at the time, were often resisted by the machinery of government when it came to the decisive vote.

---

[6] Muir, *Civic Ritual*, pp. 13–61. On the historiography of the 'Myth of Venice' see especially James S. Grubb, 'When myths lose power: four decades of Venetian historiography', *Journal of Modern History*, 58 (1986), 43–94.
[7] For a simple summary of the Venetian constitution see Frederic C. Lane, *Venice: A Maritime Republic* (Baltimore & London, 1973), pp. 95–117, 250–73. On modifications to the constitution in the Early Modern period, see M. J. C. Lowry, 'The Reform of the Council of Ten 1582–3: An unsettled problem', *Studi Veneziani*, 13 (1971), 275–310; Giuseppe Gullino, 'L'evoluzione constituzionale', in Alberto Tenenti and Ugo Tucci (eds.), *Storia di Venezia*, vol. 4 (Rome, 1996), pp. 345–78.

Deborah Howard

The executive powers of the doge in the patronage of public buildings, as in other areas, were strictly circumscribed. Like popes, doges were often elected at a very advanced age, after a lengthy conclave. Nicolò da Ponte, for example, was 87 when he took the ducal throne in 1578 and he remained in office until his death at the age of 94. As Francesco Sansovino explained, the doge was the head (*capo*) of the body politic (*quel corpo*): 'a prince in name and appearance, created not by hereditary succession or violence, but by the legal elective process'.[8] Although direct ducal participation in government was prevented by strict constitutional measures, there can be no doubt that individual doges could make their mark on the face of the city through influence and charisma. Unlike dynastic rulers, doges rarely travelled outside the city, except occasionally in times of plague, but relied on experienced ambassadors chosen from the elite of the nobility. Thus the Doge's presence on the ducal throne in government assemblies was always visible and his personality palpable, even if, like Nicolò da Ponte, he tended to doze off during long speeches.[9]

Architectural context

Sixteenth-century Venice was the scene of one of the most ambitious programmes of urban renewal in Early Modern Europe. The large-scale renovation of most of the buildings around Piazza San Marco, the so-called *renovatio urbis,* has been associated with the impetus of Doge Andrea Gritti.[10] The main elements of this campaign are now very familiar. The designer was the Florentine sculptor and architect Jacopo Sansovino who was appointed *proto,* or chief building superintendent, to the Procuratia de Supra at the instigation of Doge Gritti in 1529. The eminent body of nobles known as the Procuratia di San Marco administered the church of St Mark's and owned most of the buildings around the Piazza, apart from the Doge's Palace.[11] Membership of the Procuratia di San Marco was the

---

[8] 'Nel nome, & nell'apparenza esteriore, forma di capo & di vero Principe, creato, non per soccessione di heredità, o per violenza, ma per ordine di leggi ciò disponenti.' Sansovino, *Venetia*, f. 174v.

[9] Because of his tendency to fall asleep during sessions of the Collegio, a special padded wooden support was added to the throne to prevent Doge Nicolò da Ponte from falling over. See Andrea da Mosto, *I Dogi di Venezia* (Venezia, Ongania, 1939), p. 197.

[10] Howard, *Jacopo Sansovino*, pp. 2–6; Tafuri, 'Renovatio urbis', pp. 31–5; Manuela Morresi, *Jacopo Sansovino* (Milan, 2000), pp. 443–51.

[11] On the Procuratia de Supra, see below, pp. 48–50.

highest office of state apart from the doge himself—as the architect's son Francesco remarked, the Doge usually emerged from the 'lap' of the Procurators.[12]

Sansovino's designs for three new buildings, begun in successive years, the Zecca (Mint), Library and Loggetta, created a coherent hierarchy of function, from the industrial (the minting of coins), through the intellectual (the Library of St Mark's with its rich collection of Greek and Latin codices), to the representational (culminating in a rich marble triumphal arch opposite the main entrance to the Doge's Palace).[13] In the Piazza, Sansovino combined the role of architect with that of the traditional Venetian *proto,* or superintendent of buildings. As we shall see, however, following his death in 1570, these roles—*proto* and architect—once again became separated. The lecture focuses on four major state building initiatives of the later sixteenth century, in an attempt to track the political background to the architectural decisions. Two of these revived dormant schemes, and two were new projects provoked by unforeseen disasters.

The church of the Redentore

The decade following Sansovino's death in 1570 was the scene of a seemingly endless series of catastrophic events, which eventually drove the Republic to address its building programme directly to God Almighty. After a disastrous fire in the Arsenal in 1569, there followed the loss of Cyprus in 1573, a fire in the Doge's Palace in 1574, and a major flood in the same year, culminating in the great plague of 1575–6 which was to kill about a third of the population of the city.[14] When practical medical precautions imposed by the Magistrato della Sanità failed to halt the terrifying mortality, the Venetian Senate resolved on 4 September 1576 to erect

---

[12] 'Ellegendosi nel creare il Principe il piu meritevole, è necessario che il Doge esca le piu uolte dal grembo de Procuratori.' Sansovino, *Venetia,* f. 107v.

[13] The Zecca was begun in 1536, the Library in 1537 and the Loggetta in 1538. See Howard, *Jacopo Sansovino,* pp. 14–47; Bruce Boucher, *The Sculpture of Jacopo Sansovino,* 2 vols. (New Haven and London, 1991), 1. 73–88; 2. cat. no. 27, pp. 334–5; Morresi, *Jacopo Sansovino,* cat. nos. 30–2, pp. 182–227.

[14] For eye-witness accounts of these disasters, see Biblioteca Marciana di Venezia (henceforth BMV), cod. Marc. it. VII 2585 (=12477), Stephano Tiepolo, 'Cronaca veneta, 1546–1576', ff. 224–55; BMV, cod. Marc, It. VII, 553 (=8812), 'Memorie del N.H. S. Francesco da Molin', ff. 11–80; BMV, cod. Marc. it, 134 (=8035), 'Cronaca veneta di Girolamo Savina sino al MDCXV', ff. 343–52.

a votive church dedicated to Christ the Redeemer.[15] The new church was to be visited by the Doge and his successors annually in perpetuity on the anniversary of the day when the city would be declared free of the plague.

In the debates over the choice of model for the new church, the two opposing factions in the nobility known as the 'giovani' and the 'vecchi' began to crystallise.[16] These were never formal political parties, and they did not correspond with the traditional division between 'case vecchie', the oldest Venetian noble families, and the 'case nuove', those almost as old but admitted soon afterwards. Allegiances shifted constantly, and from the point of view of architectural debates their respective stances seem contradictory. The 'giovani' were both politically radical and culturally conservative, while the 'vecchi' were politically conservative yet culturally ambitious. The 'giovani' were puritanical in their tastes, yet opposed to any kind of Protestantism as well as to the Papacy and deeply attached to local traditions, while the 'vecchi', sometimes called 'papalisti', had closer links with the church of Rome and their cultural horizons were broader. Reforms to the Council of Ten in 1582–3 attempted to control the power of the rich and powerful 'vecchi', although in practice they continued to be elected, with impressive regularity, to the highest magistracies of state.[17]

The decision-making process was both heated and long drawn-out. The first decision concerned the site of the new votive church, and in the climate of public guilt after such a painful series of divine 'punishments' the interests of splendid ducal ceremonial hardly entered the discussion. A proposed site at the nunnery of Santa Croce at the upper end of the Grand Canal was rejected in three successive ballots of the Senate, without mention of a possible processional route through the heart of the city. Meanwhile, reluctant support was given by just 39 votes to 35 to a site at San Vidal, on which a church and college would be built for the Jesuits.[18] As frequently occurred in the case of controversial issues, the debate was adjourned.

---

[15] ASV, Senato Terra, registro 51, f. 111v. The document has been published in Flaminio Corner, *Ecclesiae Venetae*, 18 vols. (Venice, 1749), 11. 37–8; Giangiorgio Zorzi, *Le chiese e i ponti di Andrea Palladio* (Vicenza, 1967), pp. 130–1, doc. 1; and Wladimir Timofiewitsch, *La chiesa del Redentore* (University Park and London, 1971), p. 65, doc. 1.

[16] For a very brief introduction to these factions see Lane, *Venice*, pp. 393–5. A fuller account is given by Gaetano Cozzi, *Il doge Nicolò Contarini: Ricerche sul patriziato veneziano agli inizi del Seicento* (Venice and Rome, 1958), pp. 2–52.

[17] The fundamental study of these reforms is Lowry, 'The Reform'.

[18] ASV, Senato Terra, registro 51, f. 133v. The document is transcribed in Zorzi, *Le chiese*, p. 132, document no. 5. For recent accounts of the Redentore debates, see Deborah Howard, 'Venice between East and West: Marc'Antonio Barbaro and Palladio's church of the Redentore', *Journal*

After a week of reflection and lobbying, the debate was resumed, and once again the Santa Croce site was rejected. The account of the Senate speeches by Agostino Valier, Bishop of Verona, allows us to sense the mood of the debate. Two eminent senators, Paolo Tiepolo and Marc'Antonio Barbaro, both regarded as 'vecchi', eloquently supported the site at San Vidal. Tiepolo extolled the virtues of the Jesuits as defenders of the true Catholic faith and as exemplary teachers of the young.[19] On the other hand, Barbaro's concerns focused on the form of the church rather than on religious doctrine. As a patron of Palladio and an amateur stuccoist of some renown, he had well-informed artistic views.[20] Barbaro supported the architect Palladio's preference for a centralised design 'because buildings commissioned by the full Senate should be magnificent and reflect the dignity of the Republic'.[21] This overt defence of *magnificenza* as a mirror of the virtues of the state directly follows in the tradition established in Doge Gritti's *renovatio urbis* of the 1530s.

of the Society of Architectural Historians, 62 (2003), 307–25; Vittorio Pizzigoni, 'I tre progetti di Palladio per il Redentore', *Annali di Architettura*, 15 (2003), 165–77; Tracy E. Cooper, *Palladio's Venice* (New Haven and London, 2005), pp. 229–39.

[19] Agostino Valerio (Valier), *Dell'utilità che si può ritrarre dale cose sperate dai Veneziani: libri XIV*, trans. Antonio Giustiniani (Padua, 1787), pp. 393–4. See also the extract from the same speech in Latin in Corner, *Ecclesiae venetae*, 11. 15. A brief account of the life of Paolo Tiepolo (1523–85) is given in Eugenio Alberì, *Le relazioni degli ambasciatori veneti al Senato durante il secolo decimosesto*, series II, vol. 10 (Florence, 1857), pp. 163–4. According to Alberì, Tiepolo was universally regarded as a 'gran senatore, uomo veramente di fino giudizio, di matura prudenza, di perfetta intelligenza delle dottrine, di eloquenza distinta'.

[20] The classic biography of Marc'Antonio Barbaro is Charles Yriarte, *La vie d'un patricien de Venise au seizième siècle* (Paris, 1874). See also Angelo Ventura, 'Marc'Antonio Barbaro', *Dizionario biografico degli italiani*, 6 (Rome, 1964), pp. 110–13. In 1648, Ridolfi recorded that the stucco figures in the Nymphaeum at Maser were made 'per ricreatione' by Marc'Antonio Barbaro. See Carlo Ridolfi, *Le meraviglie dell'arte*, 2 vols. (Venice, Gio. Battista Sgava, 1648), 1. 289–90. In her posthumous study of the stucco sculptures of the Nymphaeum of the Villa Barbaro at Maser, Carolyn Kolb attributed the execution of all the statues to Marc'Antonio Barbaro himself, and the authorship of the iconographic program to his brother Daniele. See Carolyn Kolb, 'The Sculptures on the Nymphaeum Hemicycle of the Villa Barbaro at Maser', *Artibus et Historiae*, 35 (1997), 15–33. (The stuccoes, like the villa itself, are datable to *c.*1554–8.) Marc'Antonio Barbaro's design for a cantilever spiral stair with curved treads was illustrated by Andrea Palladio, *I quattro libri dell'architettura* (Venice, Domenico de' Franceschi, 1570), Book I, Chap. XXVIII, pp. 61–2.

[21] Valerio, *Dell'utilità*, p. 394: 'Marc'Antonio Barbaro procuratore di S. Marco egli ancora diffusamente procurò di persuadere il Senato, che questo Tempio fosse fatto in forma rotonda, dovendo le fabbriche decretate dall'amplissimo Senato essere magnifiche, e farvi risplendere la dignità della Repubblica; ed a lui pure, come a molti altri, piaceva il luogo vicino a S. Vitale, purchè non si differisca, e sia in nobile rotonda forma'. See also the Latin rendering in Corner, *Ecclesiae venetae*, 11. 16.

It fell to Leonardo Donà, a generation younger and then just 40 years old, the most outspoken of the 'giovani', to put the opposing view.[22] Donà adopted a deliberately extreme position: 'Why are you looking for magnificent buildings? There is no need of a Temple, whether round or not. I think God would not support this. All that is needed is your obedience, to please God with your devotions.'[23] Since the vow had already been taken to build a church, this was obviously a ridiculously provocative statement. But Donà went on to attack the Jesuits, not for their papal connections (although this was surely a sub-text, for the 'giovani' were bitterly opposed to Roman intervention) but for the extravagance of having to build a Jesuit college, even though it was to house only four priests and two lay-brothers.[24] Instead he defended a third site, newly proposed by the Collegio (the doge's closest advisory body), on the Giudecca, at the friary of the austere Franciscan Capuchins. The Giudecca site was duly chosen, but it is worth remembering that the Jesuits did not yet fall from favour.[25] A year later they were allowed to take over half of the upper part of the Republic's salt warehouses in order to extend their accommodation, right opposite the site of the new Redentore church, because of their contribution 'to Venice and to all Christianity'.[26]

Three months were to pass before the matter of the Redentore was again raised in the Senate in February 1577.[27] By now the Giudecca site

---

[22] On the life of Leonardo Donà, see, in particular, Federico Seneca, *Il Doge Leonardo Donà: la sua vita e la sua preparazione politica prima del dogado* (Padua, 1959); Gaetano Cozzi, 'Leonardo Donà' in *Dizionario biografico degli italiani*, vol. 40 (Rome, 1991), pp. 757–71.

[23] Valerio, *Dell'utilità*, pp. 394–5 (in Latin in Corner, *Ecclesiae venetae*, 11. 16–17): '[Per]che cercate fabbriche magnificentissime? Non si cerca qui un Tempio, il quale sia di forma rotonda, o no: penso che Iddio nol curi: cercasi soltanto la vostra ubbedienza, si compiace Dio del vostro ossequio.'

[24] ASV, Senato Terra, registro 51, ff. 133v–134r. The letter from the Jesuits referred to 'il carico di mettergli sacerdoti no. 4 et fratelli no. 2' (ASV, Senato Terra, filza 70, 17 Nov. 1576). As Cooper has pointed out, Donà tactically went on to declare his respect for the Jesuits (Cooper, *Palladio's Venice*, pp. 232–3).

[25] ASV, Senato Terra, registro 51, f. 134r. The document is published in Zorzi, *Le chiese*, p. 132, doc. 5, and a short extract is in Wladimiro Timofiewitsch, *The Chiesa del Redentore* (University Park and London, 1971), p. 66, doc. 4. A copy of the motion of the Senate is transcribed in ASV, Collegio, Cerimoniale, registro I, ff. 48v–49r. The Jesuits were expelled from Venice after the papal interdict of 1606, during the *dogado* of Leonardo Donà, and were not allowed to return until 1657.

[26] ASV, Consiglio dei Dieci, Parti comuni, registro 33, f. 106v–107r, 21 Dec. 1577. On the early history of the Jesuits in Venice, see Silvio Tramontin, 'Le nuove congregazioni religiose', in Giuseppe Gullino (ed.), *La chiesa di Venezia tra riforma protestante e riforma cattolica* (Venice, Edizioni Studium cattolico veneziano, 1990), pp. 113–30, at pp. 100–1.

[27] ASV, Senato Terra, registro 51, ff. 155v–156r, 9 Feb. 1576 m.v. (=1577); transcribed in Zorzi, *Le chiese*, pp. 132–3, doc. 6, and in part in Timofiewitsch, *The Chiesa*, doc. 5, p. 67.

had been decided, but Barbaro was still pressing for a centralised design. Three options were considered: the longitudinal plan gained 103 votes, while the centrally planned alternative attracted only half as many adherents. Just nineteen senators supported the compromise solution to make three-dimensional models and costings of both options. It was only at this point that the commission was formally awarded to Palladio, but no evidence suggests that any other architect was considered for the design.

The remarkable feature of this intense and protracted debate is that, although Barbaro was praised for the eloquence of his speeches, the Senate did not succumb to oratory. In a personal memoir Leonardo Donà dismissed the value of rhetoric as a political tool in the Greater Council and the Senate; instead, he claimed, speakers should employ 'charity and truthfulness, not fine words which are useless, but with an opening of the heart, with genuine and sincere ideas, and with devotion to the public good and the happiness of all'.[28] Donà detested pomp and finery. Having taken a vow of chastity in his youth, he presented a public image of semi-religious austerity, apparently modelling himself on ancient stoics such as Cato.[29]

The anomaly of the Redentore project is that controls fell away once the work began and even after Palladio's death in 1580 expenditure was never questioned. Because the commitment was intended to display the religious devotion of the state and to protect the city against the plague, funds could not be refused. Even though two nobles, Agostino Barbarigo and Antonio Bragadin, both 'vecchi' and Palladio supporters, were put in charge of the project, controls on site were few (Fig. 1).[30] The original pledge resolved to build a 'solid building without ornament or marbles, as befits a votive church', but it is well-known that the budget for the

---

[28] '. . . con charità et con verità più d'una volta, non con bellezza di parole, che non servono a nulla, ma con apertura di cuore, con concetti veri et sinceri, et con pietà verso il pubblico bene et la contentezza di tutti.' Cited in Cozzi, *Il doge*, pp. 27–8, from Mario Brunetti, 'Da un carteggio di Leonardo Donà ambasciatore in Roma col fratello Nicolò (1581–1583)', in *Miscellanea di studi storici in onore di Alessandro Luzio*, 2 vols. (Florence, 1933), 1. 135.

[29] Cozzi, *Il doge*, pp. 32–3, 37–40.

[30] The two Provveditori sopra la fabbrica were elected on 18 Sept. 1576 (ASV, Senato Terra, registro 51, f. 114v, published in Zorzi, *Le chiese*, pp. 131–2, doc. 3; Timofiewitsch, *The Chiesa*, p. 66, doc. 3). See Angelo Ventura, 'Agostino Barbarigo', in *Dizionario biografico degli italiani*, VI, Istituto dell'Enciclopedia Italiana, Rome, 1964, pp. 49–50; and Ugo Tucci, 'Antonio Bragadin', in *Dizionario biografico degli italiani* (Rome, Enciclopedia Italiana, 1971), 8. 663–4; Cooper, *Palladio's Venice*, pp. 230–1. By 1591, both men had died, so the final stages of completion of the church were entrusted to the three Provveditori in charge of the restoration of the Palazzo Ducale. See Senato Terra, registro 61, f. 75r, 10 Sept. 1591.

Deborah Howard

Figure 1. Andrea Palladio, Venice, Church of the Redentore, begun 1577, interior. (Photograph: Cameraphoto, Venice.)

Redentore exceeded the estimated cost of 10,000 ducats by more than seven times.[31] Although the estimate was soon raised to 12,000 ducats, by November 1579 this sum had already been exceeded by 3,000 ducats.[32] From that point on, twice a year the Senate voted sums of 4,000 ducats until the building was finished.[33]

Palladio's design was infused with just the sort of classicising *magnificenza* that both the Capuchins and Donà detested. Paradoxically, though, once he was elected Doge in 1606, Donà was to show a surprising enthusiasm for Palladio's work, asking for the removal of the buildings that obscured his view of the church of San Giorgio Maggiore from the Palazzo Ducale, and erecting his own funerary monument on the entrance wall of the same church.[34]

Restoration of the Palazzo Ducale[35]

Whereas funds for the Redentore came from the state treasury, the Palazzo Ducale, like the commercial buildings at the Dogana and the Rialto, was

[31] '. . . sia speso fino alla summa de ducati dieci mille' in ASV, Senato Terra, registro 51, f. 111v, 4 Sept. 1576; published in Corner, *Ecclesiae Venetae*, 11. 37–8; Zorzi, *Le chiese*, p. 130–1, doc. 1; Timofiewitsch, *La chiesa*, p. 65, doc. 1. On 26 April 1577, it was explained that the funds should be routed through the Salt Office; by this time the estimated cost had risen to 12,000 ducats. See ASV, Provveditori al Sal, busta 10, fascicolo 12, Restauri di fabbriche pubbliche 1571–92, Parti del Consiglio dei Dieci, f. 17v.

[32] ASV, Senato Terra, reg. 52, f. 217r., 7 Nov. 1579. The original sum of 10,000 had been raised to 12,000 by a motion of the Council of Ten on 26 April 1577; see ASV, Provveditori al Sal, busta 10 (reg. 12), Restauri di fabbriche pubbliche 1571–92, Parti del Consiglio di X, f. 17v.

[33] Sums of 4,000 ducats each, to be paid to the Redentore's budget from the treasury through the Salt Office, were authorised by motions of the Senate as follows: ASV, Senato Terra, registro 52, f. 217r, 7 Nov. 1579; Senato Terra, registro 53, f. 20v, 30 May 1580; f. 76r, 12 Nov. 1580; f. 163v, 28 Sept. 1581; f. 200v, 20 Jan 1581 *m.v.* (=1582); Senato Terra, registro 54, f. 19v, 21 Apr 1582; f. 40, 11 Aug. 1582; ff. 80v-81r, 10 Jan. 1582 *m.v.* (=1583); f. 127v, 24 June 1583; ff. 167v–168r, 11 Nov. 1583; Senato Terra, registro 55, f. 62r, 23 July 1584; Senato Terra, registro 56, f. 4r, 9 Mar. 1585; f. 108v, 19 Dec. 1585; Senato Terra, registro 57, f. 48v, 22 Dec. 1586; f. 231v, 15 Dec. 1587. In 1588 smaller payments were authorised for the completion of the decoration: e.g. Senato Terra, registro 55, f. 30v–31r, 400 ducats on 8 Apr. 1588; f. 54r, 600 ducats on 16 May 1588; f. 57r, 600 ducats on 28 May 1588. 4,000 ducats was granted on 3 March 1589, Senato Terra, ref. 59, f. 1v; and again on 24 March 1590 for the floor, two bronze statues for the high altar, and 'alcune altre poche cose', Senato Terra, registro 60, f. 7r. Further small payments followed: 500 ducats for the floor and other costs on 11 Nov. 1591, Senato Terra, registro 61 f. 98r; and 1,000 ducats on 21 May 1592, Senato Terra, registro 62, f. 24r.

[34] Tracy E. Cooper, 'La facciata commemorativa di S. Giorgio Maggiore', in André Chastel & Renato Cevese (eds.), *Andrea Palladio: nuovi contributi* (Milan, 1990), pp. 136–45, at pp. 140–2.

[35] Subsequent to my British Academy lecture I discussed the restoration of the Palazzo Ducale in my paper 'Attitudes to the Gothic in Renaissance Venice' at the conference *Le Gothique de la*

funded by the Salt Tax, which enjoyed an annual income of around 200,000 ducats.[36] When a second disastrous fire struck the Doge's Palace in 1577, once again vigorous public debate ensued over how to proceed. Like the recent plague, the calamity was attributed to 'the wrath of God', a view reinforced by strange astronomical phenomena including a comet that remained visible for two months and a bolt of lightning in the form of a torch which struck the Campanile.[37] After the fire, tearful spectators lamented the erasure of public memory, especially the loss of the cycles of history painting and the destruction of the chancery's notarial archives.[38] Luckily, however, although the roof of the Sala del Maggior Consiglio had been destroyed, the external walls were left standing (Fig. 2).

In contrast to the Redentore project, a decision on how to proceed had to be taken urgently. This time a different procedure came into action. Whereas at the Redentore Palladio had been selected as architect from the outset, in the case of the Palazzo Ducale an elaborate process of consultation was put into motion, involving the widest possible range of technical experts.[39] The Salt Office, the body that funded works in the palace, had its own *proto* or superintendent of buildings, Antonio da Ponte, but he was just one of a series of fifteen *periti* or experts who were interrogated by a special committee of three advisors or *Provveditori* established by the Senate.[40] These included not only Venetians but also

---

Renaissance, Institut National de l'Histoire de l'Art, Paris, Quatrième rencontre d'architecture européenne du Centre André Chastel, Paris/Sorbonne-Paris IV), 12–16 June 2007.

[36] The net income of the Salt Office in 1587 was 190,982 ducats; and in 1594 252,074 ducats. See David Chambers and Brian Pullan, *Venice: A Documentary History 1450–1630* (Oxford and Cambridge, MA, 1992), p. 150.

[37] BMV, Cod. Marc. it. VII, 553 (=8812), 'Memorie del N.H. S. Francesco da Molin', f. 68 (referring to 'l'ira del Signor Dio'); Cod. Marc. it. VII, 134 (=8035), Cronaca Savina, f. 354 (on comet and lightning).

[38] BMV, Cod. It. VII, 134 (=8035), Cronaca Savina, f. 354v.; Cod. Marc. it. VII, 553 (=8812), 'Memorie del N.H. S. Francesco da Molin', f. 65.

[39] For fuller accounts of the process leading up to the post-fire restoration, see Antonio Foscari, 'Un dibattito sul foro marciano allo scadere del 1577 e il progetto di Andrea Palladio per il palazzo ducale di Venezia', in *Saggi in onore di Guglielmo De Angelis d'Ossat*, special issue of Quaderni dell'Istituto di Storia dell'Architettura, NS 1/10 (Rome, 1987), 323–32; and Cooper, *Palladio's Venice*, pp. 205–11, with further bibliography.

[40] The three Provveditori were Alvise Zorzi, Giacomo Foscarini and Piero Foscari, elected on 20 Jan. 1578. (This was the second committee of three elected in the post-fire period, replacing the three elected in Dec. 1577 to choose a temporary site for the meetings of the Greater Council. In the initial phase of consulation, just five *periti*, including both Palladio and Antonio da Ponte, had been consulted.) The reports were published, with some biographical details of each *proto*, by Giuseppe Cadorin (ed.), *Pareri di xv architetti e notizie storiche intorno al Palazzo Ducale di Venezia* (Venice, 1838). Cadorin added the opinion of Francesco Sansovino from his *Del Segretario libri vii* (Venice, 1584), pp. 215–18. Several of the reports were published in

Figure 2. Ludovico Toeput, called 'il Pozzoserrato', *Fire in the Palazzo Ducale, Venice, 1577*. (Treviso, Museo Civico.)

prominent masons, builders, *proti*, and architects from elsewhere in the Veneto, Palladio among them.

Those who were literate wrote their own reports, while others were interrogated and their replies transcribed in detail. There were various points of agreement. Most noticed that the 'paradise wall', that is to say, the east wall of the Sala del Maggior Consiglio, was cracked, and that many of the capitals of the arcades had split open, although opinions diverged over whether these cracks were recent and whether they mattered. Those who thought the damage was of little significance used graphic analogies—the architect and treatise-writer Giovanni Antonio Rusconi compared the damage to the old walls to the effect of 'an insect bite on an elephant'.[41] Because the fire had destroyed the roof, the walls were in danger of leaning outward, but even on this question some experts thought the walls leaned out and others that they leaned in. Some complained that the upper walls were thicker than the lower walls, and others disagreed, their views depending on whether the wall thickness was taken to be the width of the capitals or the width of the columns (Fig. 3). Some, including Andrea Palladio, criticised the excessive thickness of the upper walls by comparing the structure unfavourably to the natural world, where tree trunks are thicker at the bottom.[42] Others, by contrast, noted that men, who are obviously superior to trees, have thin legs and stouter bodies, but Palladio dismissed this argument on the grounds that men have to be mobile.[43] Cristoforo Sorte, the celebrated map-maker, totally rejected the very idea of restoration of the old building because he could not contemplate the idea of this most serene government occupying a palace 'built in the air'.[44]

Giambattista Lorenzi, *Monumenti per servire alla storia del Palazzo Ducale di Venezia*, part I (Venice, 1868), docs. 851–3, 856, pp. 423–38. The opinions of the *proti* have also been discussed by Wolfgang Wolters, 'Riflessioni sulla riconstuzione di edifici gravemente danneggiati', in Giandomenico Romanelli (ed.), *Palazzo Ducale: Storia e restauri* (Verona, 2004), pp. 195–204, previously published in German in V. von Flemming and S. Schütze (eds.), *Festschrift für Matthias Winner* (Mainz am Rhein, 1996), pp. 327–33.

[41] '. . . sarà conforme alla beccadura di una mosca fatta ad un elefante', Rusconi in Cadorin (ed.), *Pareri*, pp. 20–32, at p. 21.

[42] Palladio in Cadorin (ed.), *Pareri*, pp. 52–61, at p. 57. Palladio's writings on the restoration are discussed in detail by Giangiorgio Zorzi, *Le opere pubbliche e i palazzi privati di Andrea Palladio* (Vicenza, 1965), pp. 151–67.

[43] Palladio in Cadorin (ed.), *Pareri*, pp. 52–61, at p. 58, supported by Francesco Sansovino, in ibid., pp. 111–16, at p. 114.

[44] '. . . dice, che non lauda per alcun modo di metter questo Serenissimo Dominio in tanto pericolo d'habitar un palazzo fabricato in aria', Sorte in Cadorin (ed.), *Pareri*, pp. 103–4, at p. 104.

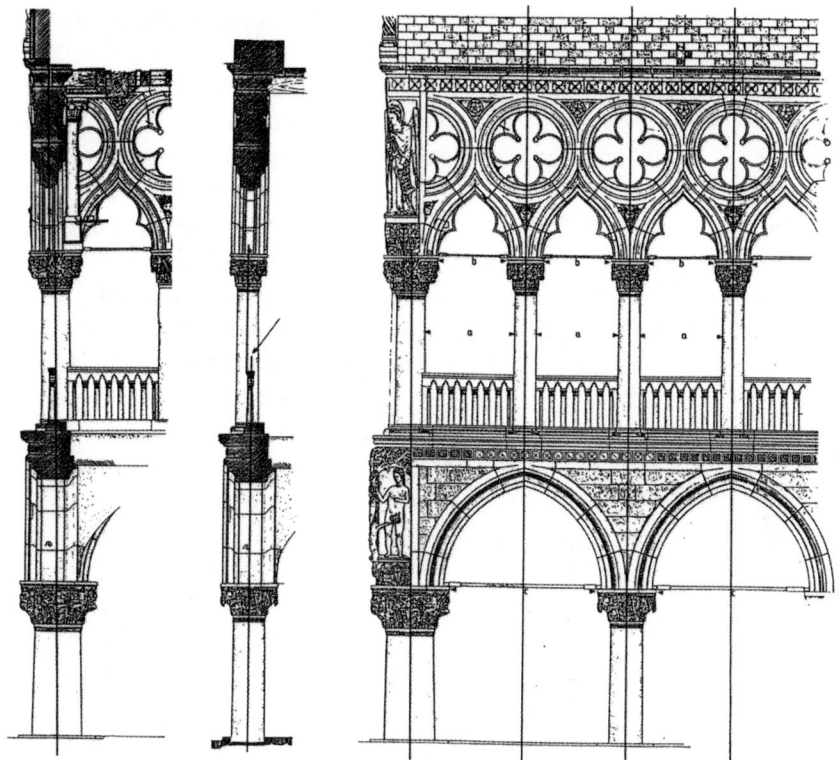

Figure 3. Venice, Palazzo Ducale, (left) section through south facade, begun 1341, taken through the central balcony of 1404; (right) detail of elevation. From Manfred Schuller, 'Il Palazzo Ducale di Venezia: Le facciate medioevali', in Francesco Valcanover and Wolfgang Wolters (eds.), *L'architettura gotica veneziana* (Venice, Istituto Veneto di Scienze, Lettere ed Arti, 2000), p. 430, fig. 92.

Some bold and radical solutions were proposed. One consultant, Guglielmo Grandi, the deputy *proto* to the Magistrato alle Acque (the magistracy responsible for the management of the lagoon and its waterways), suggested wrapping the lower columns in a row of square piers with Ionic capitals. His second alternative was to add a second Corinthian order above, and his third most ambitious proposal was to rebuild both the two outer facades with round arches according to his own design, in order to provide a building that was not only 'safe but also decorated as befits a Serenissima Repubblica' such as Venice.[45] In other

---

[45] '. . . nel quale appare una forma et un modo di fabricare sicuro et ornato come appartiene ad una Serenissima Repubblica, tale quale quella della sublimità vostra'. Grandi in Cadorin (ed.), *Pareri*, pp. 37–40, at pp. 39–40.

words, he considered a classical design to be more fitting to the dignity of the Republic.

At the other extreme, Francesco Zamberlan from Bassano was eloquent about the merits of Gothic vaulting, which, he claimed, exerted a downward force rather than an outward one. He went on to make an ingenious defence of the structural merits of the tracery on the *piano nobile:* 'the roundels rest in the upper curve of the arches, and they cannot spread sideways because then the arch would have to become narrower, which would squeeze the top upwards, which is obviously impossible, since a wall cannot rise, and therefore they [the roundels] can carry a greater load'.[46] His suggestion was simply to reinforce the structure by adding an extra pier between each of the ground-floor columns. He advised against rebuilding the Gothic facades because this would require a classical design 'with all those proportions and measurements that good architecture requires and all the other rules'.[47] A surprising supporter of the structural strength of Gothic architecture was Francesco Sansovino, son of the architect Jacopo who had master-minded Doge Gritti's *renovatio.* Francesco pointed out that over the centuries the structure had resisted earthquakes and explosions, remaining 'uncorrupted by the fury of past accidents'.[48]

Palladio's report did not offer a constructive alternative, but a drawing at Chatsworth attributed to his hand has been identified by Howard Burns as the proposal for the complete renewal of the Palazzo Ducale (Fig. 4).[49] Although the identification of the intended site has been contested, it may yet be Palladio's project, since one contemporary chronicler noted that Palladio planned to 'demolish and move' the whole building.[50] It is worth

---

[46] 'Che li occhi, che sono sopra le colonne dell'ordine secondo sono parimenti fortissimi, et non possono a niuna banda allargarsi, perchè li piedi di essi sono la cima delli volti, et l'allargarsi per il peso essi occhi, saria un stringer li volti, nè possono stringersi essi volti senza alzarsi, et l'alzarsi è molto contro la natura del peso, perchè non può star che la muraglia vada all'insù, et perciò stanno per forza nel suo loco, et sono atti a portar molto maggior peso.' Zamberlan in Cadorin (ed.), *Pareri*, pp. 96–9, at p. 97.

[47] '. . . poichè ruinando le fazzade bisogna metterse in obbligo di farle con tutte quelle proporzioni, et misure che seco apporta la buona architettura allegando altre ragioni in tal proposito.' Zamberlan in Cadorin (ed.), *Pareri*, pp. 96–9, at p. 98.

[48] '. . . incorrotto dalla furia di tanti accidenti passati', Francesco Sansovino in Cadorin (ed.), *Pareri*, pp. 111–16, at p. 116.

[49] Howard Burns, Lynda Fairbairn and Bruce Boucher, *Andrea Palladio 1508–1580: The Portico and the Farmyard*, exh. cat. (London, 1975), pp. 158–60.

[50] '. . . sol Andrea Paladio [*sic*] celebre e famoso Architetto teneva conclusione che non vi era restata cosa niuna di sicuro, et che la facciata verso S. Giorgio tutta si dovesse distruggere, e spianare, e in sostanza muovere tutta la Fabbrica.' BMV, MS Marc. it, VII, 110 (=8612), 'Memorie del N.H. S. Francesco da Molin', f. 67r. Tafuri claimed that the drawing is intended to represent a new ducal residence on the site of the present prisons. See Manfredo Tafuri, 'Il disegno

considering this design in its European context. The most prominent recent town-hall was that of Antwerp, completed just over a decade earlier in 1565 (Fig. 5).[51] Although Palladio cannot have known the Flemish precedent at first-hand, the design of a grand facade with three superimposed triumphal arches in the centre may indeed represent his attempt to rival the greatest northern European seaport, visited regularly by Venetian galleys on the Flanders convoy.

Historiography has devoted a great deal of attention to the ideological reasons for the rejection of Palladio's arguments, but the consultation process revealed a clear majority of the 'experts' in favour of restoration of the existing structure, which was both quicker and cheaper.[52] With the entire male nobility forced to assemble in temporary accommodation in the Arsenal, this was not the time for ambitious displays of magnificence.[53] Once again, oratory fell on deaf ears. The diary of Francesco da Molin records that Palladio's principal supporter in the Senate was once again Marc'Antonio Barbaro, 'most valiant Procurator of St Mark's and most renowned orator, who even though the whole Senate thought the idea [of rebuilding the Palace] to be excessively extravagant, remained on his feet for days bravely arguing [his case]'.[54] Interestingly, it seems that the Chatsworth drawing was acquired by Lord Burlington at the Villa Barbaro at Maser, which was then in the hands of Marc'Antonio Barbaro's heirs, the Nani

di Chatsworth (per il palazzo Ducale di Venezia?) e un progetto perduto di Jacopo Sansovino', in André Chastel and Renato Cevese (eds.), *Andrea Palladio: nuovi contributi* (Milan, 1990), pp. 100–11; Tafuri, *Venezia e il Rinascimento*, pp. 272–8. For a summary of recent views on this drawing see Douglas Lewis, *The Drawings of Andrea Palladio*, rev. edn. (New Orleans, 2000), pp. 262–3, cat. 121.

[51] See Christa de Jonge and Konrad Ottenheym, *Unity and Discontinuity, Architectural Relations between the Southern and Northern Low Countries 1530–1700* (Turnhout, 2007), pp. 45, 226–9.

[52] The six most trusted experts were asked for further reports: see Cooper, *Palladio's Venice*, pp. 208–9. On the unanimity of the group's recommendation of the restoration of the old palace, despite variations of detail, see Molin, who stresses the isolation of Palladio's position. BMV, MS Marc. it, VII, 'Memorie del N.H. S. Francesco da Molin', 110 (=8612), ff. 67r–67v.

[53] A great deal of debate in the immediate aftermath of the fire focused on where the temporary accommodation for the Maggior Consiglio assemblies should be located. A range of sites was considered, including the state Granary at the Terra Nova, on the Bacino to the west of the Zecca, the interior of San Marco, the Palazzo Patriarcale, and the oar-makers' building at the Arsenal. Cooper, *Palladio's Venice*, p. 208, mistakenly locates the Terra Nova warehouses at the Dogana.

[54] '. . . [Palladio] era fomentata cosi questa sua opinione da Marc'Antonio Barbaro Procurator di San Marco valentissimo et principalissimo Oratore, che ancor che a tutto il Senato parese stravagantissima, pure col suo valore disputando per molti giorni la sostenne in piedi.' BMV, MS Marc. it, VII, 110 (=8612), 'Memorie del N.H. S. Francesco da Molin', f. 67r.

Deborah Howard

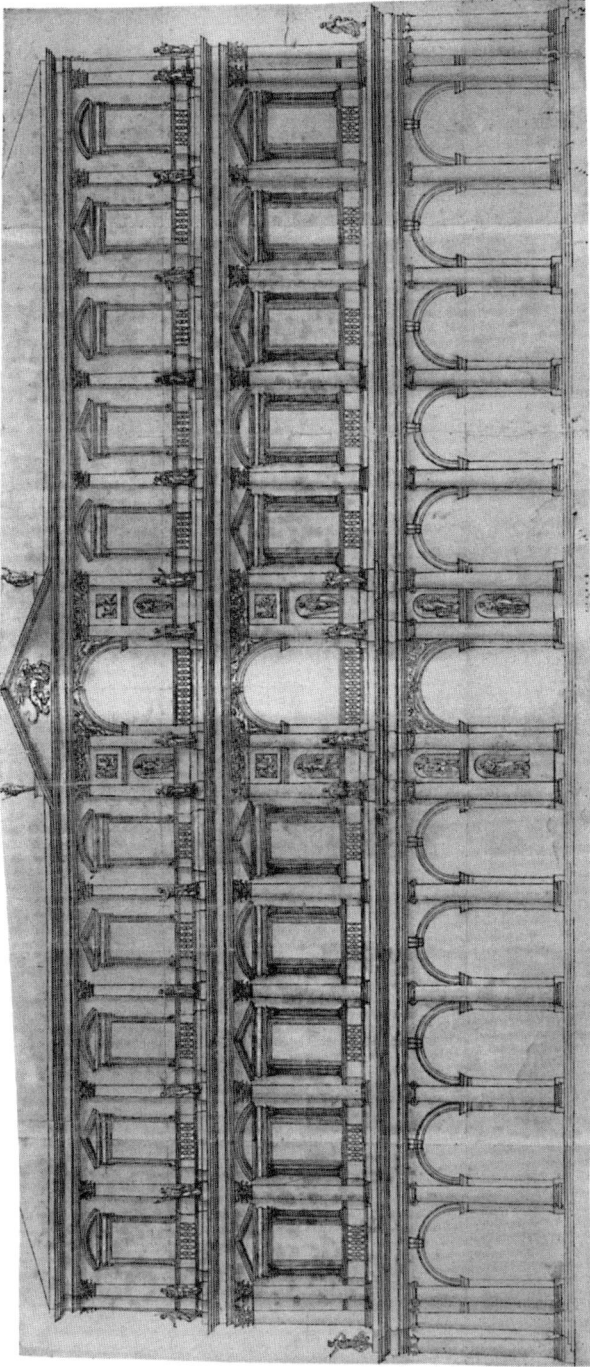

Figure 4. Andrea Palladio (attrib.), *Elevation drawing of a public palace, possibly for the Palazzo Ducale, Venice, c.1577 (?)*. (Chatsworth, the Devonshire Collection, SOS/B.)

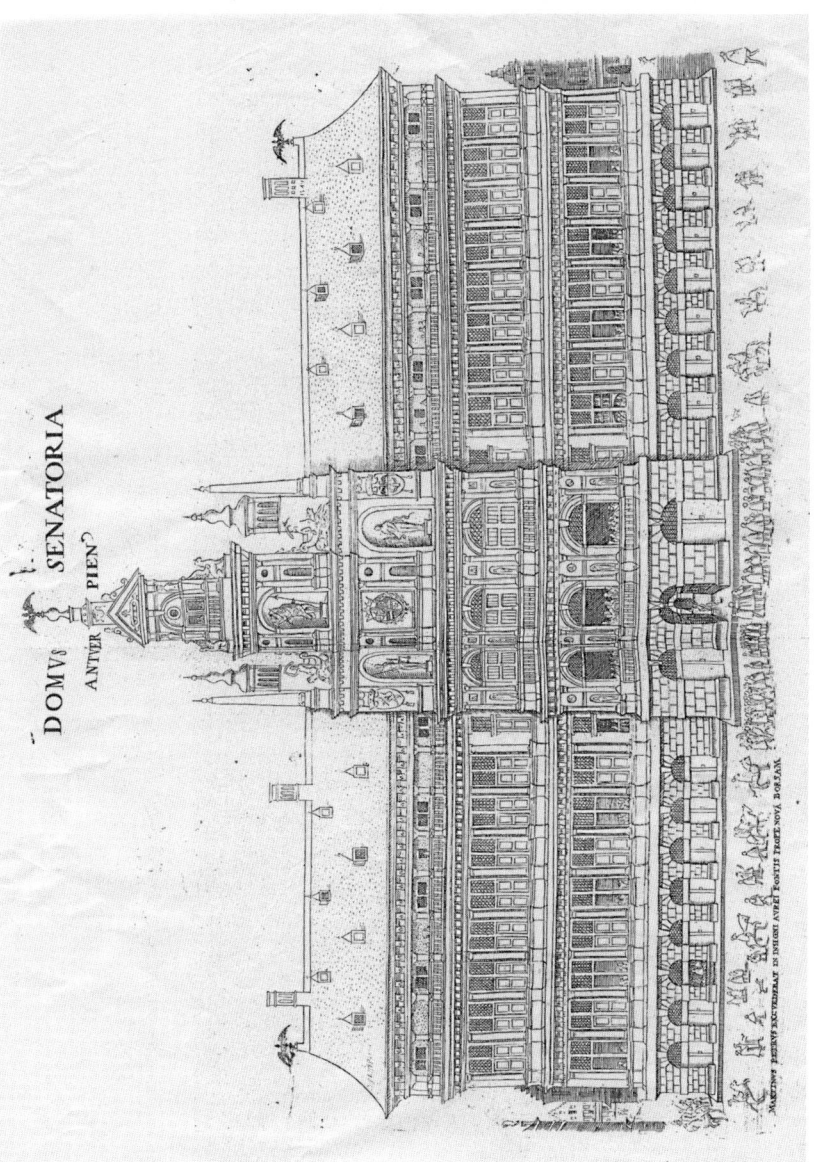

Figure 5.   Cornelis Floris de Vriendt, Antwerp Town Hall, 1561–5, from L. Guicciardini, *Descritione di tutti i Paesi Bassi*, Antwerp, 1567. (British Library, 568.k.5, plate before f. 82. © The British Library. All rights reserved.)

family.[55] Despite Barbaro's filibustering efforts, the decision to restore and re-roof the old palace 'no more and no less than it was before' was approved overwhelmingly by the Senate in 1578 by the huge majority of 146 votes to 6, with 38 undecided.[56]

If Barbaro and Palladio considered a classical design imperative for the glory and international reputation of the Republic, the arguments for the restoration of the old palace rested not on any attachment to the symbolic or sentimental value of the medieval building, but on the speed and economy of a simple restoration. The restoration of the old palace duly began under the supervision of the experienced *proto* to the Salt Office, Antonio da Ponte. From this time on, funds were provided from the Salt Office chest by order of the Senate and the Council of Ten until the restoration and redecoration was completed.

The Procuratie Nuove

The conspicuous exception to this process of decision making in elected assemblies was the Procuratia de Supra, the branch of the Procuratia de San Marco responsible for most of the buildings in Piazza San Marco, apart from the Doge's Palace. Income flowed in from centuries of endowments and the rents of valuable properties in the Piazza, providing generous funding for building initiatives.[57] The Procurators were elderly patricians chosen for their long and distinguished record in public service, and unlike most elected magistrates, they held office for life.[58] (The two other divisions, 'de Citra' and 'de Ultra', administered private trust funds on either side of the Grand Canal.)

---

[55] John Harris, 'Three unrecorded Palladio designs from Inigo Jones's collection', *Burlington Magazine*, 113 (1971), 34–7, at p. 34 and n. 4.

[56] 'non più ne meno com'era avanti' in BMV, MS Marc. it, VII, 110 (=8612), 'Memorie del N.H. S. Francesco da Molin', f. 67v. For the Senate resolution and vote see Senato Terra, filza 72, 21 Feb. 1577 *m.v.* (=1578). Barbaro is recorded as absent, and Foscarini, though named as a 'Consiglier', is also declared absent 'per indispositione'.

[57] Sanudo commented on the sacks of ducats protected in strong-rooms in the Procurators' offices. See Marin Sanudo il Giovane, *De origine, situ et magistratibus urbis Venetae ovvero La città di Venezia*, ed. A. Caracciolo Aricò (Cisalpino, 1980), pp. 104–5; English translation in Chambers and Pullan, *Venice*, pp. 51–2.

[58] The best introduction to the Procuratia di San Marco is still Reinhold C. Mueller, 'The Procurators of San Marco in the thirteenth and fourteenth centuries: a study of the office as a financial and trust institution', *Studi veneziani*, 13 (1971), 106–220.

In times of war, however, Procurators could also be elected for money in an attempt to refill the public coffers, and in such cases much younger, less experienced figures could enter the Procuratia. For example, during the Turkish wars, Federico Contarini, a member of one of the city's wealthiest families, began his political career at the top when he was elected to the Procuratia de Supra in 1571 at the age of just 33, in return for a payment of 20,000 ducats.[59] Similarly, Andrea Dolfin, scathingly described by a contemporary as 'a new man in government and the richest man in the city', was elected to the Procuratia de Supra in 1573 at the even younger age of 32, again for 20,000 ducats.[60]

Such appointments could even be used to raise funds for public building. In 1580, Doge Nicolò da Ponte proposed the election of a new Procurator in order to raise funds for the reconstruction of the Procurators' houses on the south side of Piazza San Marco 'because our very wise ancestors have always been vigilant in adorning the public places of this city with important buildings, as we see in our church of San Marco, the Palazzo [Ducale], the Campanile and other most distinguished buildings nearby, which do not achieve their full splendour on account of the age and unsightliness of the dwellings of the Procurators'.[61] This measure allowed the election of his young grandson of the same name to the Procuratia de Ultra for the huge sum of 22,000 ducats, thus, in effect, making a direct gesture of ducal sponsorship, as well as ensuring a dignified office for his chosen heir.[62]

Over the past half-century, historians have extolled the Procuratia de Supra as a selfless body of erudite and distinguished nobles, dedicated to

[59] ASV, Misc. Cod., Serie I, no. 47, Cronica de' procuratori veneziani dall'an. 812 sin all'an. 1689, 14 Jan. 1570 *m.v.* (=1571). See Gaetano Cozzi, 'Federico Contarini', *Dizionario biografico degli italiani*, 28 (Rome, 1983), pp. 158–60. On Contarini's collection of works of art, see Michel Hochmann, *Peintres et commanditaires à Venise* (Rome, 1992), pp. 183–5.

[60] ASV, Misc. Cod., Serie I, no. 47, 'Cronica de' procuratori veneziani dall'an. 812 sin all'an. 1689', unnumbered ff., 15 Nov. 1573. See Gino Benzoni, 'Giovanni Dolfin', *Dizionario biografico degli italiani*, 40 (Rome, 1991), pp. 504–11, at p. 510. The comment on 'Andrea Dolfin procurator, nuovo nel governo et in ricchezza primo della città' is taken from Nicolò Contarini's 'Problemi monetari della Repubblica', published in Cozzi, *Il doge*, Appendix III, pp. 351–60, at p. 354.

[61] 'Hanno sempre invigilato li nostri sapientissimi Progenitori di adorner li lochi publici di questa città con fabriche de importantia, come si vede nella chiesa nostra di San Marco, del Palazzo, Campaniel, et altre fabriche honoratissime che vi sono, le quali tutte mancano del compito suo spendor per la vecchiezza et brutto veder che fanno le case dove habitano li Procuratori nostri'. ASV, Senato Terra, registro 53, ff. 84r–84v, 10 Dec. 1580; copy in Senato Terra, filza 81, 10 Dec. 1580.

[62] ASV, Misc. Cod., Serie I, no. 47, 'Cronica de' procuratori veneziani dall'an. 812 sin all'an. 1689', unnumbered ff., 11 Dec. 1580.

the service of state, but at least in the later sixteenth century, this myth does not stand up to close scrutiny.

Sansovino's unfinished Library building in the Piazzetta, begun under Doge Andrea Gritti in 1537, had to be continued in two directions.[63] Towards the Bacino to the south, offices were to be built, while along the south side of Piazza San Marco new dwellings for the Procurators were planned. The first moves towards the building of the new Procurators' houses began in 1581, when, once again, discussions were held with a series of unnamed 'architects and experts' (Fig. 6).[64]

Any project of this kind needed firm supervision. In theory, all the Procurators were supposed to live in Piazza San Marco, and should therefore always be at hand to supervise the building work, but in practice the houses were old and many of them preferred to live elsewhere.[65] The Procurator Giacomo Foscarini, for example, had built a magnificent palace at the Carmini, some distance from Piazza San Marco, where his close friend and fellow Procurator de Supra, Marc'Antonio Barbaro, occupied the upper floor.[66]

Scholars have assigned to Barbaro a crucial role in the project for the extension of Sansovino's buildings. At the end of May 1581 he was, indeed,

---

[63] There has been some confusion in the secondary literature between these two linked but separate projects, especially in Tafuri, *Venezia e il Rinascimento*, pp. 252–71. A similar approach to the present argument is found in Tracy E. Cooper, 'Expert opinion: *proto* and *perizia* in the case of the Libreria Marciana and the Procuratia Nuova', *Annali di architettura*, 7 (1995), 111–24. See also Gabriele Morolli, 'Vincenzo Scamozzi e la fabbrica delle Procuratie Nuove', in *Le Procuratie Nuove in Piazza San Marco* (Rome, 1994), pp. 11–116; Andrew Hopkins, 'Completamento della libreria sansoviniana (1581–1588) e portale e atrio della Zecca (1582–1588)', and 'Procuratie Nuove in piazza San Marco (1581)', in Franco Barbieri and Guido Beltramini (eds.), *Vincenzo Scamozzi 1548–1616*, exh. cat. (Venice, 2003), cat. nos. 11–12, pp. 202–20.

[64] ASV, Procuratia de Supra: Chiesa, Atti, registro 135, ff. 24v–25r, 15 Jan. 1580 *m.v.* (=1581).

[65] Decrees of the Senate on 5 Nov. 1562 and 22 Sept. 1569 attempted to persuade the Procurators to inhabit their houses in the Piazza. See ASV, Senato Terra, registro 44, f. 68, 5 Nov. 1562; Procuratia de Supra, Restauro Stabile, busta 65, processo 142, 'Scritture pella costruzione delle Procuratie nuove et altre fabbriche in Piazza dal 1574 al 1686', ff. 7r, 8r. In 1580 and 1581 the Procuratia itself tried to improve the adherence to this requirement. See ASV, Procuratia de Supra: Chiesa, Atti, registro 135, f. 10r, 30 July 1580; and ff. 24v–25r, 15 Jan. 1580 *m.v* (=1581).

[66] Foscarini's testament confirms that the house at the Carmini was 'da me fabricata'. See ASV, Archivio Notarile, Testamenti, Nicolò Doglioni, busta 344, no. 399, drawn up on 8 March 1595, at f. 4r. He states more than once that Marc'Antonio Barbaro lived on the upper of the principal two living floors (ff. 1v., 4r). The house must have been built by 1574 when a reception was held there for the entertainment of the visiting king Henry III of France. See BMV, MS Marc. it, VII, 'Memorie del N.H. S. Francesco da Molin', 110 (=8612), f. 46v. On Foscarini's life, see Bartholomeo Ridolfi Sforza, *Vita di Giacopo Foscarini, Cavaliere e Procuratore di S. Marco* (Venice, 1624; translation of Latin edn. of 1623); R. Zago, 'Giacomo Foscarini', *Dizionario biografico degli italiani*, 49 (Rome, 1997), pp. 365–70.

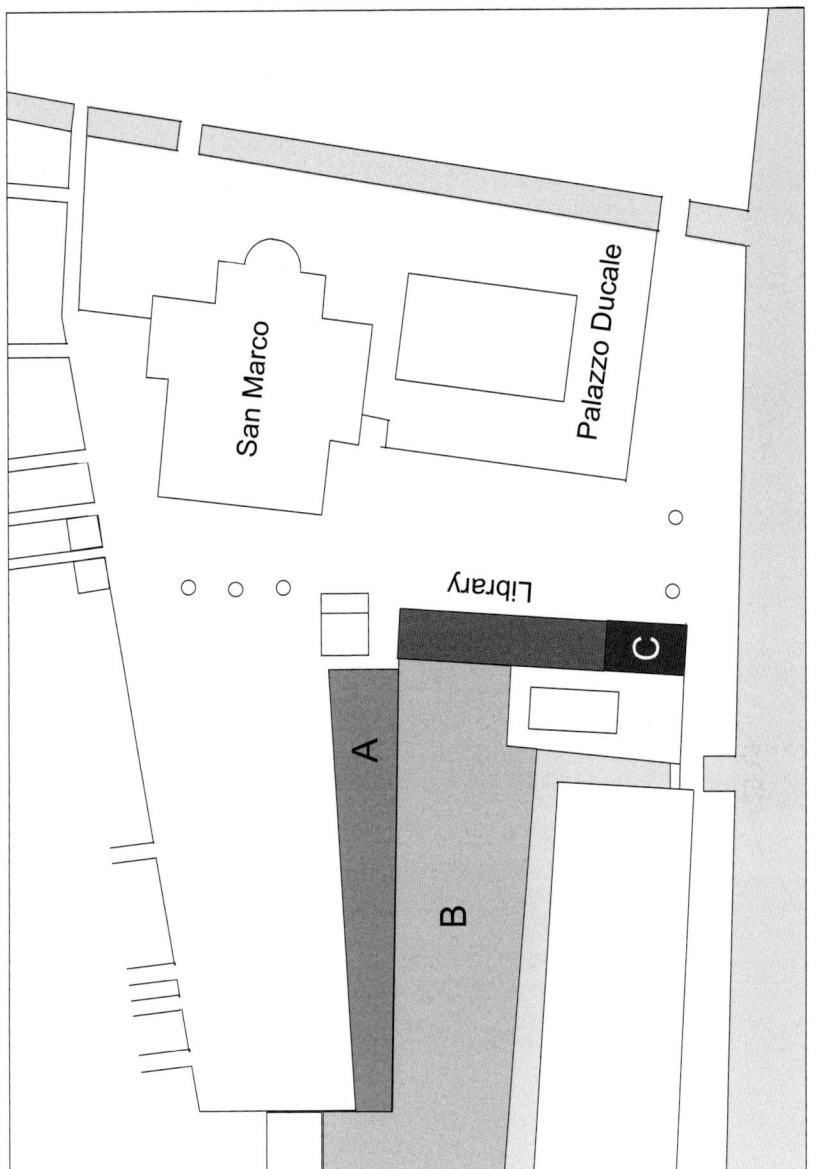

Figure 6. Sketch-plan of Piazza San Marco, Venice, showing (A) the areas to be demolished, (B) the site of the new Procurators' houses, now known as the 'Procuratie Nuove', and (C) the extension to the Library.

appointed the sole Procurator responsible for the work.[67] Significantly, however, it has been overlooked that Barbaro was appointed in his absence. He was still absent when a few days later his two much younger colleagues, Andrea Dolfin and Federico Contarini, were elected to join him to form the small executive committee to administer the construction of the new buildings.[68] As early as January in the following year, Barbaro asked to be excused from the committee, and he was replaced by his friend Giacomo Foscarini, who, in turn, resigned a year later in March 1583.[69] There seems to have been little enthusiasm for direct involvement in the task.

A meeting to consider the three designs submitted for the continuation of the buildings was held on 5 April 1582.[70] As is well known, Barbaro and Foscarini persuaded their colleagues to select the model by the young Vincenzo Scamozzi, who had inherited their support after the death of Palladio in 1580. As a native of Palladio's adopted home town, Vicenza, Scamozzi presented the academic credentials of a scholar–architect rather than a mere *proto*. His design was chosen in preference to those by two local *proti,* the Procuratia de Supra's own *proto* Simon Sorella, and Francesco Fracao, also known as Smeraldi. In contrast to the situation in the time of Sansovino, who had been both *proto* and architect, design and execution were once again separated. Although Scamozzi was paid for his drawings and models, Sorella was put in charge of the building site.[71] Nonetheless, the procedure of broad consultation of local *proti* was once again put into action in 1582 when concern arose over whether Sansovino's Library could support a third storey on top, as recommended by Scamozzi.[72] Even a relatively autonomous body such as the Procuracy of St Mark's relied on continual recourse to outside consultants.

Still there was reluctance to take responsibility. Andrea Dolfin and Giacomo Foscarini both resigned from the building committee in 1584, and one of the Procurators appointed to succeed them, Giacomo Soranzo, declined on the grounds of ill-health.[73] Late in 1586 the three

[67] ASV, Procuratia de Supra: Chiesa, Atti, registro 135, ff. 41v–42r., 30 May 1581.

[68] ASV, Procuratia de Supra: Chiesa, Atti, registro 135, ff. 42r–42v, 4 June 1581.

[69] ASV, Procuratia de Supra: Chiesa, Atti, registro 135, f. 64v., 17 Jan. 1581 *m.v.* (=1582), with marginal note dated 9 March 1583.

[70] ASV, Procuratia de Supra: Chiesa, Atti, registro 136, f. 5v, 5 April 1582. The selection of Scamozzi's design was confirmed on 10 April 1582 (ibid., f. 6v). Copies of these documents are contained in ASV, Procuratia de Supra, Restauro Stabile, busta 65, processo 142, ff. 18r, 19r.

[71] Sorella was given a salary rise on 31 May 1582. See ASV, Procuratia de Supra: Chiesa, Atti, registro 136, f. 13v.

[72] Tafuri, *Venezia e il Rinascimento*, pp. 257–8; Hopkins, 'Completamento', p. 202.

[73] ASV, Procuratia de Supra: Chiesa, Atti, registro 136, f. 104v, 15 Jan. 1583 *m.v.* (=1584), and f. 105v, 29 Jan. 1583 *m.v.* (=1584).

Provveditori in charge of the new Procurators' houses finished their term and suggested the election of a single commissioner to succeed them. The election, however, was a tie between Foscarini and Barbaro, so no election was made.[74] Barbaro was absent for most of the spring of 1587, but in September he made his now famous speech urging his fellow Procurators to accept the addition of a third storey.[75] Four of his fellow Procurators urged caution, and once again technical experts were consulted. Whereas Sorella asserted with conviction that the foundations were inadequate, Scamozzi marshalled more representational arguments for the opposite view, claiming that the aim was to complete this masterpiece both to enhance the image of the Republic and to create a timeless example worthy of respect throughout the world.[76]

The arguments between Sorella and Scamozzi and their respective supporters dragged on during 1588, with further consultations of other *proti*.[77] In the end the dispute was resolved only with a motion of the Senate, which imposed on the Procurators the decision that the Library elevation in the Piazzetta should be continued without the third storey, but that the new Procurators' houses in the Piazza should have three storeys.[78] By May 1589 the office accommodation in the Piazzetta was ready for occupation, and Federico Contarini was put in charge of the erection of the new Procurators' houses in recognition of his excellent service in the earlier phase, recorded by an inscription on the building dated 1581.[79] Yet again, however, in 1590 the Senate asserted its authority over the

[74] The three Procurators who had finished their term were Francesco di Priuli, Federico Contarini and Girolamo da Mula. They wished to elect 'un solo clarissimo Procuratore' to succeed them. Barbaro and Foscarini each received five votes in favour and one against; Andrea Dolfin received four in favour and two against; while Girolamo Emo received two in favour and four against. ASV, Procuratia de Supra, busta 65, Restauro Stabile, processo 142, f. 25r, 9 Dec. 1586. Because of the stalemate, it was decided not to record the motion in the Atti of the Procuratia dei Supra.

[75] ASV, Procuratia de Supra: Chiesa, Atti, registro 137, f. 118, 27 Sept. 1587; copy in ASV, Procuratia de Supra: Chiesa, busta 65, Restauro Stabili, processo 142, f. 26r.

[76] ASV, Procuratia de Supra: Chiesa, busta 65, Restauro Stabili, processo 142, ff. 28r–28v, 13 Oct. 1587 (Sorella's report); ff. 30r–31r, 6 Dec. 1587 (Scamozzi's report). Two *proti* from the building site at San Giorgio Maggiore were brought in to support Scamozzi, but contrary to Tafuri's assertion, they only addressed technical issues and did not discuss the recondite question of the correct heights of the friezes. ASV, Procuratia de Supra: Chiesa, busta 65, Restauro Stabili, processo 142, ff. 32r–32v, 6 Dec. 1587.

[77] Further opinions were taken from a range of *proti* from Jan. to April 1588. See ASV, Procuratia de Supra: Chiesa, busta 65, Restauro stabili, processo 142, ff. 34r–45r.

[78] Senato Terra, registro 58, ff. 110r–111r, 7 Sept. 1588.

[79] ASV, Procuratia de Supra: Chiesa, Atti, registro 137, ff. 179v–190r, 10 Sept. 1589; Procuratia de Supra: Chiesa, busta 65, Restauro stabili, processo 142, ff. 48r–48v, 1 Oct. 1589.

Procuratia de Supra, complaining of poor accounts and incompetent site supervision. Almost certainly these accusations were entirely justified, although they must be seen in the context of factional power struggles within the ruling oligarchy.[80] In 1591 Barbaro and Foscarini were once again put in charge of the work, but both asked to be excused a few months later.[81] Despite his strong support for Scamozzi, Barbaro had no desire to be in charge of the detailed site supervision, and on at least two occasions he asked to skip his turn as chief treasurer.[82]

The Procuratia de Supra, as constituted, represented the elite of the Venetian patriciate, whether through experience or wealth. Thus their arguments tended to reflect the cultural affiliations of the *vecchi*: that is to say, they preferred erudite classicism and the display of magnificence to represent the public face of the Venetian state. But even within their ranks, internal disagreements and reluctant management characterised their patronage in the later sixteenth century, and their independence was increasingly reined in by the elected assemblies.[83]

The Rialto Bridge[84]

While the heated polemic about the continuation of Sansovino's Library raged in the Procuratia de Supra, a very different debate in the full Senate focused on the decrepit state of the old wooden Rialto Bridge. The issue of the bridge had remained unresolved ever since the idea of rebuilding it in stone had first been suggested in 1507.[85] Since 1554 a magistracy of

[80] ASV, Senato Terra, registro 60, ff. 142r–142v, 16 Nov. 1590.

[81] ASV, Procuratia de Supra: Chiesa, Atti, registro 138, f. 52r, 15 Dec. 1591; and f. 59r, 6 April 1592.

[82] ASV, Procuratia de Supra: Chiesa, Atti, registro 137, f. 71, 13 July 1586; and registro 138, f. 62v, 3 May 1592.

[83] Tafuri has credited Andrea Dolfin, the one Procurator who urged restraint, with 'giovani' politics but the 'giovani' themselves had little respect for Dolfin. See Tafuri, *Venezia e il Rinascimento*, pp. 258–62. For Nicolò Contarini's opinion of Andrea Dolfin, see Cozzi, *Il doge*, p. 354. Dolfin certainly had enemies, for he was murdered in 1602. See Benzoni, 'Giovanni Dolfin', p. 510.

[84] This section is based on my paper 'The Great Rialto Bridge Debate', given at the conference *Bâtiments publics aux XVIe–XVIIIe siècles. I: Le gouvernement, la justice et l'économie/Public Buildings in early Modern Europe (16th–18th Century), part I: Government, Justice and Economy* (Troisième rencontre d'architecture européenne du Centre André Chastel, Paris/Sorbonne-Paris IV), at the Catharijneconvent, Utrecht, 28–30 June 2006 (proceedings in press, ed. Konrad Ottenheym).

[85] Marin Sanudo (Sanuto), *I diarii*, 58 vols., ed. R. Fulin *et al.* (Venice, 1879–1903), vol. 7, column 168, 22 Oct. 1507. See also Donatella Calabi and Paolo Morachiello, *Rialto: le fabbriche e il Ponte 1514–1591* (Turin, 1987), p. 195.

three nobles had been elected annually to address the problem, but because of the constant rotation of magistrates no coherent policy had emerged.[86] In December 1587, the Senate re-opened the discussion, focusing on two main issues: the alignment of the bridge and whether it should have one arch or three.[87] At this point Leonardo Donà, as outspoken as ever, opposed the very idea of a new bridge and suggested restoring the bridge in wood to save money for the defence budget. One chronicler complained of Donà's tiresome propaganda outside the Senate which 'wore everyone out, referring to the affairs of the whole world and the danger of war'.[88]

In December 1587 three new Provveditori (commissioners in charge of the building project) were elected, and this time they were to remain in office until the bridge was finished. Two of them, Giacomo Foscarini and Alvise Zorzi, had already served on the body of three Provveditori or commissioners responsible for the post-fire rebuilding of the Doge's Palace. The third, yet again, was Foscarini's close friend and fellow Procurator de Supra, Marc'Antonio Barbaro. It must already have been evident from the experience of the Palazzo Ducale repairs that Zorzi and Foscarini held diametrically opposite political views. Zorzi, like Donà, was a puritanical, anti-aesthetic adherent of 'giovani' policies, and it may not be insignificant that he suffered from very poor eyesight.[89] Foscarini, on the other hand, generally sympathised with Barbaro's preference for monumental classicism as a representation of the state.

By 7 January it had already been decided to rebuild the bridge with two rows of shops like the old wooden structure, but with additional

---

[86] The resolution to elect the magistracy had been taken in the Senate in 1525, but it was not revived until 1551, when the first three Provveditori, Vettor Grimani, Antonio Cappello and Tomaso Contarini were elected. ASV, Senato Terra, registro 37, ff. 88r–88v, 17 Jan. 1550 *m.v.* (=1581). From 1554 onwards, except in the years 1568–77, the three magistrates were re-elected regularly, but with the constant rotation of officers little progress was made. The annual elections are recorded in ASV, Segretario alle Voci, Elezioni Senato, registro 2, 1554–9, f. 53; registro 3, 1559–67, f. 50; registro 4, 1568–77, no elections listed; registro 5, 1578–88, ff. 113v–114. See also Zorzi, 1966, docs. 5–10, pp. 248–9.

[87] The debate is recorded in the chronicle of Alvise Michiel, Biblioteca Correr di Venezia (henceforth BCV), cod. Cic. 2556, 'Annali delle cose della Repubblica di Venezia 1587–8', unnumbered ff., 2 Jan. 1587 *m.v.* (=1588).

[88] BCV, cod. Cic. 2556, Alvise Michiel, 'Annali delle cose della Repubblica di Venezia 1587–8', unnumbered ff., 2 Jan. 1587 *m.v.* (=1588).

[89] On Alvise Zorzi, son of Benedetto (1515–93), see Tafuri, *Venezia e il Rinascimento*, pp. 247–8, n. 7. Zorzi's poor eyesight was mentioned as an excuse when he declined the position of Proveditor in Zecca on 23 April 1585 'per la molta debilità della sua vista'. ASV, Senato Terra, registro 56, f. 26r.

walkways on the outer sides 'so that, to enhance its beauty, it will be possible to view the [Grand] Canal, as the drawing shows'.[90] Who made the drawing is unclear. Already a detailed procedure of consultation was under way, and over thirty technical experts had already been consulted. Between late December and mid January a series of questions drawn up by the Provveditori was put to seventeen *proti* from different building sites in and around Venice. Some replied in writing, and others dictated their responses to a chancery secretary.[91] On 12 January the three commissioners put their views to the Senate. Barbaro (with Foscarini's support) spoke vigorously (*gagliardamente*) and at length in favour of the three-arched proposal, recommending a grandiose classicising scheme by Scamozzi, while Zorzi passionately defended the single-arched option (Fig. 7).[92] As in the case of the Redentore, the debate was so heated that it had to be adjourned. A week later they resumed their polemic, but when it came to the vote Barbaro received just eight votes from the 174 Senators present.[93] Instead, it was decided to base the decision on the views of the 'experts'.[94] As Table 1 shows, their views were equivocal about the number of arches, but everyone agreed that the single arch would cause less obstruction to the Grand Canal and, above all, would cost less (Table 1).

Barbaro's sense of public duty obliged him to accept the decision to choose the single-arched option, but he was alarmed by the casual procedures. First of all, he asserted, 'there must be a firm and solid resolution of the form of the bridge, with its measurements of length, height, width, foundations and so on', in order to avoid expensive errors.[95] Secondly, 'it is necessary to appoint the most intelligent person possible to take charge

[90] '. . . accioche per maggior bellezza possa scoprir esso canale come nel disegno si vede.' ASV, Senato Terra, registro 56, f. 246r, 7 Jan. 1587 *m.v.* (=1587), published in Zorzi, *Le chiese*, pp. 250–1, doc. 14.

[91] ASV, Provveditori sopra la fabbrica del ponte di Rialto, busta 3, Pareri, fasc. 1. Published in Roberto Cessi and Annibale Alberti, *Rialto: L'isola—il ponte—il mercato* (Bologna, 1934), doc. XIX, g–s, pp. 352–71, and docs. bb–ii, pp. 376–85. See Calabi and Morachiello, *Rialto*, pp. 244–50.

[92] BCV, cod. Cic. 2556, Alvise Michiel, 'Annali delle cose della Repubblica di Venezia 1587–8', unnumbered pp., 12 Jan. 1587 *m.v.* (=1588).

[93] BCV, cod. Cic. 2556, Alvise Michiel, 'Annali delle cose della Repubblica di Venezia 1587–8', unnumbered pp., 19 Jan. 1587 *m.v.* (=1588). ASV, Senato Terra, registro 57, ff. 256r–256v, 20 Jan. 1587 *m.v.* (=1588) does not give the full voting figures cited by Michiel. See also Cessi and Alberti, *Rialto*, pp. 201–2.

[94] See above, note 91.

[95] ASV, Provveditori sopra la fabbrica del ponte di Rialto, busta 3, Pareri, fascicolo 2, 28 Jan. 1587 *m.v.* (=1588): 'si deve fare ferma e salda resolutione della forma di esso ponte con le sue misure di grandezza, altezza, largezza, fondamento et altro'. The document is published in Cessi and Alberti, *Rialto*, pp. 205–6; and in Calabi and Morachiello, *Rialto*, p. 259.

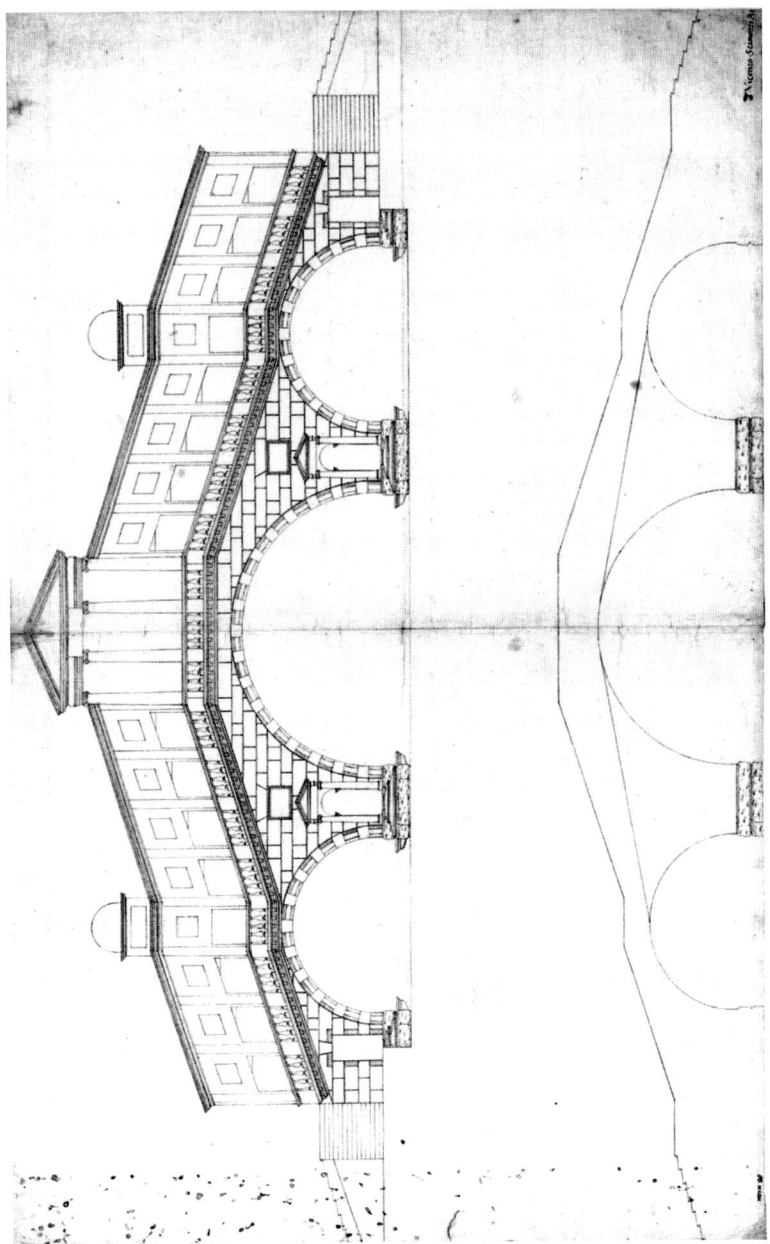

Figure 7. Vincenzo Scamozzi, project for the Rialto Bridge, 1587. (London, Royal Institute of British Architects, VIII/10.)

Table 1. Rialto Bridge, Venice: consultation process, January 1588.

Name	Description	Should there be a single- or triple-arched construction?	Which would be safer?	Which would involve more ascent for the pedestrian?	Which would have a greater total height?	Which would be more economical?	Which would obstruct the Grand Canal less during building?	Which is more convenient for shipping?	Which would block the flow of water less?	Which would silt up the Canal less?	Which would be more beautiful?
Felice Brunello		1	=	=	1						1
Paolo dal Ponte	proto di Padova	∞	∞	=	=	1	1	1	1	1	1
Ottavio Fabri	invited by M. A. Barbaro	3	3	1	1			3	3	3	
Zuan Alvise Boldù	nobil huomo	3	3	=	=	1	1	3	=	3	
Antonio da Marchò	detto Paliari	3	3	=	=	1	1	1	3	3	
Cristoforo Sorte	perito ai Beni Inculti	3	3	?	?	?	1	3	3	3	
Zuan Loredan & Iseppo della Fontana		3		1	1	1					
Antonio da Ponte	Proto al Sal	1	3	=	=	1	1	1		1	
Dionisio Boldù	Bresciano	1	3	=	=	1	1	1	1		
Vincenzo Scamozzi	architetto da Vicenza	3	3	3		3			3		
Marchesin di Marchesini	Proto	3	3	1	1	=	3	=	3		
Zuane de Hironimo	da Venezia	1	=	=	1	1	1	1			
Guglielmo di Grandi	Proto alle Acque	1	3	1	1	1	1	∞			
Simon Sorella	Proto alla Procuratia de Supra	3	3	1	1	1	1	1	3		
Tiberio Zorzi		1	1	=	=	1	1	1	1		
Giacomo di Guberni	Proto dei Lidi	1	∞	=	=	1	1	1	1		
Bonaiuto Lorinip		1	1	=	1	1	1	1	∞		

Notes: ∞, it depends; =, both alternatives equal.
Source: Archivio di Stato di Venezia, Provveditori sopra la fabbrica del ponte di Rialto, busta 3, Pareri, fascicolo 1.

of the execution of the project, so that the work will be administered and carried out as it should be'.[96]

Work had already begun on sealing the site for laying piles at the market end of the bridge and when problems arose the elderly *proto* to the Salt Office, Antonio da Ponte, then 78 years old, came to the rescue, promising to secure the site at his own expense. With this ostensibly public-spirited gesture, he seized full control.[97] Da Ponte was almost illiterate, and was completely agnostic about the architectural language: he simply stated 'Above these streets [on the bridge] put some decoration that befits the site.'[98] His one surviving drawing for the bridge, in an eccentric mixture of plan, section and elevation, reveals his lack of a classical training in draughtsmanship (Fig. 8), but its ingenious format conveyed all the necessary information on a single sheet. What is more, his successful direction of the restoration of the Doge's Palace had already gained the confidence of Zorzi and Foscarini. And he had produced the fullest and most convincing budget, always a confidence-inspiring move.

The pile-driving at one end of the site went ahead through the spring and summer, until doubts began to arise over the unprecedented system of piles on three different levels (Fig. 9).[99] At this point Barbaro requested an investigation into the technical merits of this solution. Once again stormy sessions in the Senate ensued, and a committee of five more Senators was appointed to advise the original committee of three.[100] Their

[96] ASV, Provveditori sopra la fabbrica del ponte di Rialto, busta 3, Pareri, fasc. 2, 28 Jan. 1587 *m.v.* (=1588): 'e nesesario di far eletion di persona quanto piu inteligente sia posibele per asister continuamente all'operation che sia conduta et fatta come si deve' (transcribed in Cessi and Alberti, *Rialto*, pp. 205–6). Barbaro presumably hoped Scamozzi would be appointed to this role.
[97] ASV, Senato Terra, registro 58, f. 7v, 12 March 1588, published in Zorzi, *Le chiese*, doc. 26, p. 254. See also Calabi and Morachiello, *Rialto*, pp. 261–2, 266. On Antonio da Ponte's career see T. Temanza, 'Vita di Antonio da Ponte architetto', in *Vite dei piu celebri architetti e scultori veneziani che fiorirono nel secolo decimosesto* (Venice, 1778), pp. 499–518; Brigida Balboni and Paola Martinelli, 'Antonio dal Ponte Proto al Sal: "l'acconciar" e le nuove "fabbriche", Ponte di Rialto e Prigioni', unpublished *tesi di laurea* (*relatore* P. Morachiello), Istituto Universitario di Architettura di Venezia, anno academico 1982–3, approved 1984; M. Petrecca, 'Antonio da Ponte', *Dizionario biografico italiano*, 32 (Rome, 1986), pp. 701–6.
[98] ASV, Provveditori sopra la fabbrica del ponte di Rialto, busta 3, Pareri, fasc. 1, no. 5, 20 Dec. 1587: 'E di sopra a deto strade farli qualche adornamento che ricercha deto liogo'.
[99] William Barclay Parsons, *Engineers and Engineering in the Renaissance* (Cambridge, MA and London, 1939), pp. 516–18; Cessi and Alberti, *Rialto*, p. 208; Calabi and Morachiello, *Rialto*, pp. 269–70.
[100] ASV, Senato Terra, registro 58, ff. 95v–98r, 6–9 Aug. 1588; ff. 100r–100v, 13 Aug. 1588 (documents partially cited in Zorzi, *Le chiese*, docs. 31–2, pp. 256–7); Secretario alle voci, Elezioni in Senato, registro 5, ff. 113v–114r, 9 Aug. 1584. The debates are recounted in BCV, cod. Cic. 2556, Alvise Michiel, 'Annali delle cose della Repubblica di Venezia 1587–8', unnumbered pp., 6–9 Aug. 1588.

Deborah Howard

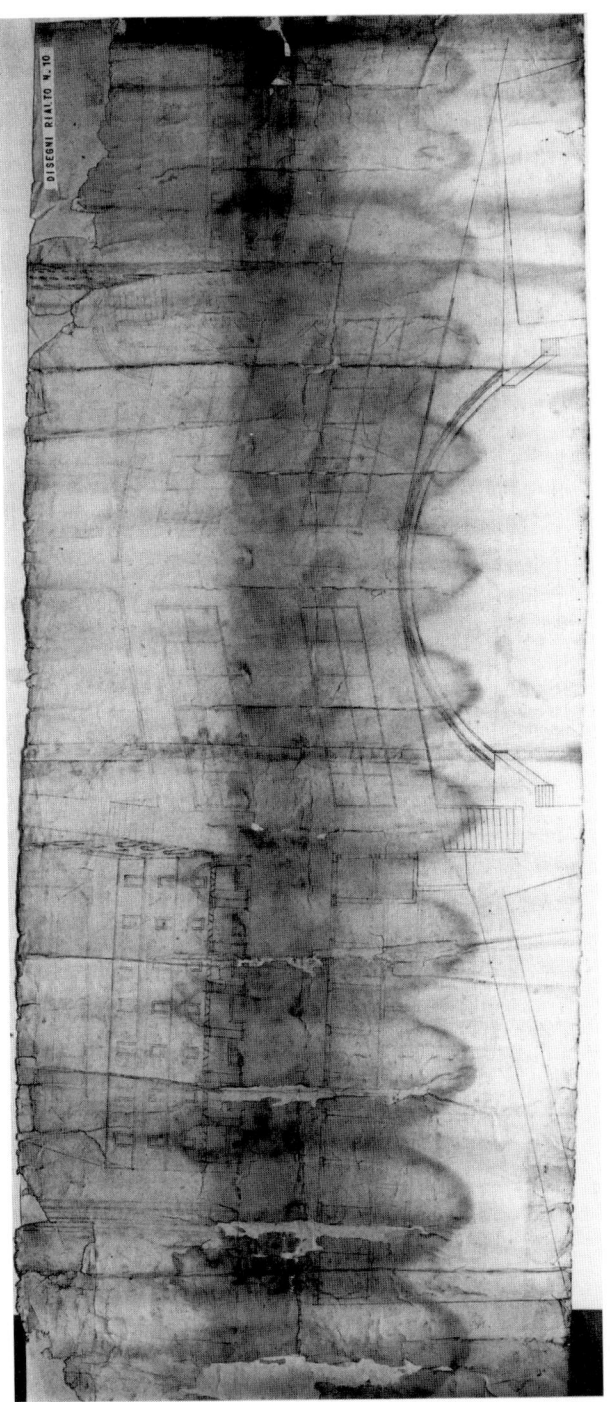

(a)

(b)

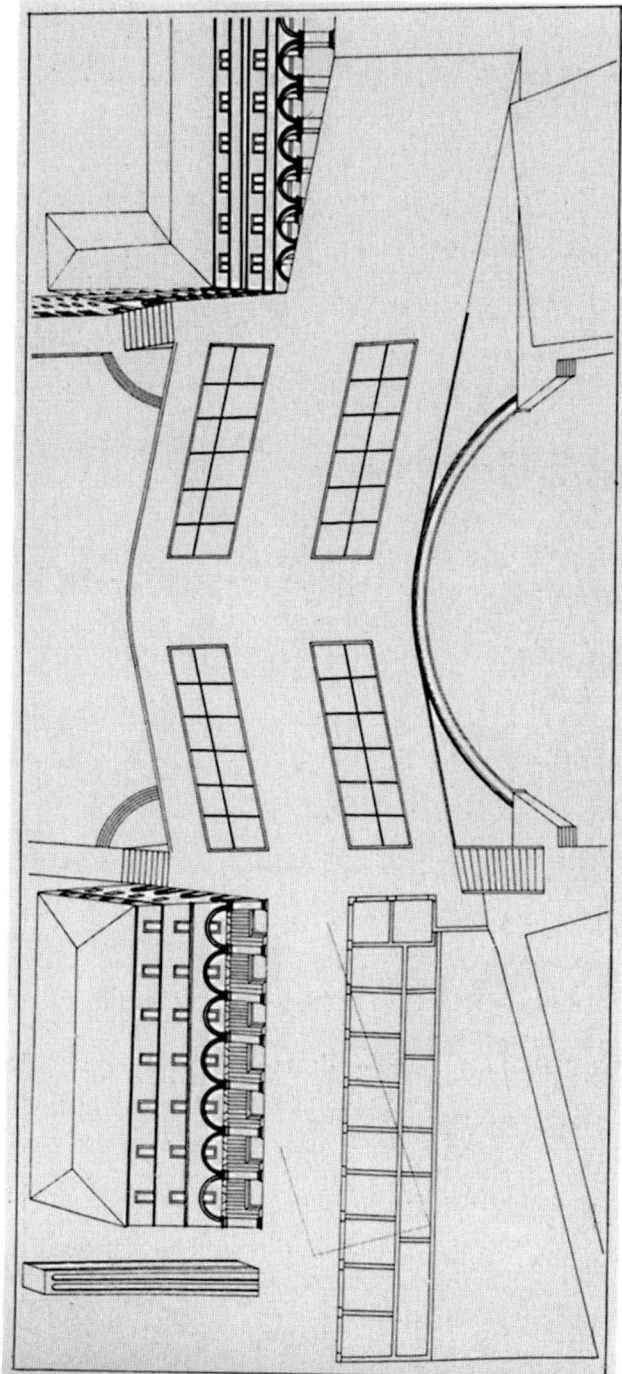

Figure 8.– (*a*) Antonio da Ponte, project for Rialto Bridge, Venice. (Archivio di Stato di Venezia, Provveditori sopra la fabbrica del ponte di Rialto, disegni, no. 10); (*b*) as re-drawn by Paolo Rossi in Calabi and Morachiello, 1987, fig. 93. (Photograph: Istituto Universitario di Architettura di Venezia, diateca del DSA.)

Deborah Howard

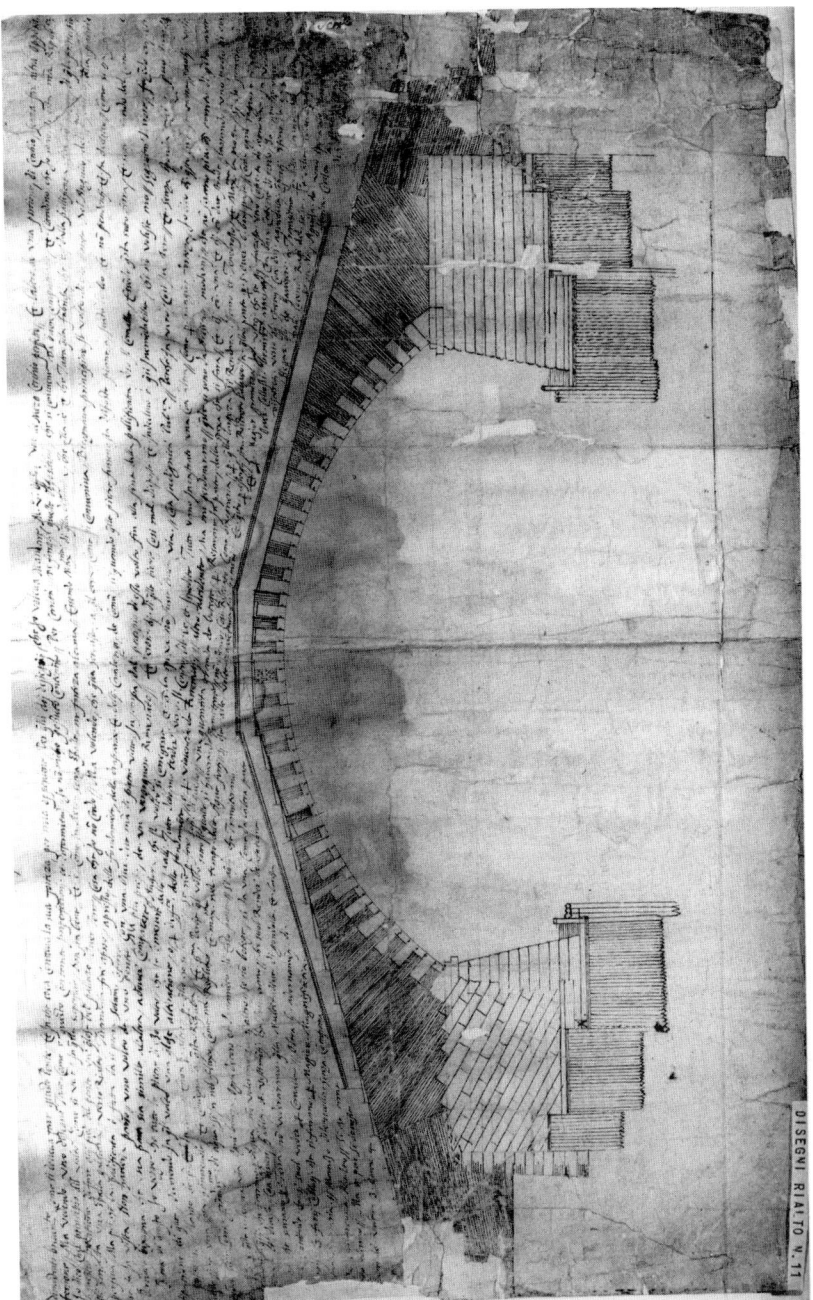

Figure 9. Rialto Bridge, Venice, section showing structure as built (left) and as recommended by the anonymous draughtsman (right). (Archivio di Stato di Venezia, Provveditori sopra la fabbrica del Ponte di Rialto, disegni, no. 11.)

solution was the same as before, to put the matter out to public consultation. Surprisingly, the committee not only interrogated *proti,* but even canvased opinions from bystanders and stall-holders including a sausage-maker, a wine-merchant and two fruit sellers, all of whom gave their views on the pile-driving process.[101] A brandy-seller claimed that the sinking of some piles had taken three hours: 'In my judgment it is impossible that these foundations should be defective, and I can assure you that the pile-driving has been done properly; [I say this] as confidently as I know how to taste a glass of *malvasia,* and tell whether it is good or bad, which is my profession.'[102]

Meanwhile the *proti* were invited to give their views to the committee on the stepped foundations and the diagonal bedding of the stone-work, which in reality were the secret to the success of the design, effectively preventing outward slippage of the foundations.[103] Once again, the *proti* were far from unanimous, as Table 2 demonstrates, but the majority view supported the continuation of the work as begun. Finally in September another series of six questions about the alignment was put to the *proti,* for even after nine months the actual route of the bridge was still undecided.[104]

The dynamics within the group of three Provveditori were uneasy. In the first summer (1588), Zorzi tried to resign when his wife was ill, but his resignation was not accepted by the Senate.[105] The three commissioners had to sign every contract for every stage of the work, including

[101] The interrogation was carried out in the Collegio in front of Ottaviano Valier, Giacomo Contarini, Lorenzo di Priuli and Caterino Corner and the Provveditori supra il Ponte di Rialto, and transcribed by a secretary. See Provveditori supra la Fabbrica del Ponte di Rialto, busta 3, Pareri, no. 4; BMV, cod. Marc. it. Z, 29 (=4796), 'Difficoltà sopra la fabbrica del ponte di Rialto', ff. 15r–17r, 12 Aug. 1588. See also Cessi and Alberti, *Rialto,* pp. 403–5; Calabi and Morachiello, *Rialto,* p. 273.

[102] BMV, cod. Marc. it. Z, 29 (=4796), 'Difficoltà sopra la fabbrica del ponte di Rialto', ff. 16r–17r: 'Et a mio giudicio de mi non è possibile che quel fondamento mai manca, et fece io cosi buon giudicio di quella fondamenta, havendola fatto fabrichar come faria, à saver gustar un bichier de Malvasia, se l'è buona, ò cattiva, che s'è mia profession.' This evidence is discussed by Parsons, *Engineers,* p. 520, remarking that: 'This is what a modern commission would do— listen to both reason and gossip.'

[103] BMV, cod. Marc. it. Z, 29 (=4796), 'Difficoltà sopra la fabbrica del ponte di Rialto', ff. 5r–14r.

[104] ASV, Provveditori sopra la fabbrica del ponte di Rialto, busta 3, Pareri, fasc. 2, nos. 14–25; also contained in BMV, cod. Marc. it. Z, 29 (=4796), 'Difficoltà sopra la fabbrica del ponte di Rialto', ff. 35v–49r, 1–2 Sept. 1588, transcribed in Cessi and Alberti, 1934, doc. XXII, pp. 418–32.

[105] ASV, Provveditori sopra la fabbrica del ponte di Rialto, busta 3, Pareri, fasc. 2, no. 3, 8 Aug. 1588.

Deborah Howard

Table 2. Rialto Bridge, Venice: consultation process, August 1588.

Name	Role	Are the new stepped foundations secure?	Are the diagonally laid stones satisfactory?	Should the water-edge of the foundations be reinforced with a *coronella*?	Should the buttressing be reinforced?	Has there been any subsidence so far?
Ottavio Fabris		N	N	Y		
Francesco de Piero	murer (bricklayer)	N	Y	Y	Y	Y
Francesco de Fermo	proto ala Procuratia di Citra	Y	Y	Y	Y	Y
Tiberio Zorzi		Y	Y	N	N	
Cesare de Franco			N	Y	Y	
Martin Rigotti	gastaldo della Scuola di S. Marco	N	Y	Y	Y	
Simon Sorella	Proto alla Procuratia de Supra	Y	Y	Y	Y	N
Antonio da Marcò	Muraro dell chiesa di San Giorgio	Y	Y	Y	N	
Antonio di Marchesi	ditto Bozzettoi	Y	Y	Y	Y	N
Zuan Manca de Piero	proto	Y	N	Y	Y	N
Marchesin di Marchesini	Proto (del Ponte delle Guglie)	Y	N		Y	N
Giacomo dei Guberni	Proto dei Lidi	Y	Y	N	Y	N
Cristoforo Sorte	perito ai Beni Inculti	N	N	N	N	
Dionisio Boldù	Bresciano	Y	Y		N	
Francesco Zamberlan		N	N	Y	Y	
Guglielmo di Grandi	Proto alle Acque	N	N	N	Y	

Notes: N, no; Y, yes.
Source: Biblioteca Marciana di Venezia, cod. Marc. it. Z, 29 (=4796), 'Difficoltà sopra la fabbrica del ponte di Rialto', ff. 5r–14r.

those for boatmen, pile-drivers, masons, bricklayers. Barbaro was often absent from their meetings, and in reality it was Zorzi who provided the most dedicated support for the day-to-day execution of the project. All the technical drawings and templates were provided by Antonio da Ponte, but the design details of the superstructure were prepared by Benedetto Banelli, the on-site deputy of the second *proto al Sal,* Antonio Contin.[106] (The second *proto al Sal* was needed because of da Ponte's great age and numerous commitments.) The fact that the masons had to go to Foscarini's house to collect the templates strongly suggests that Barbaro and Foscarini kept close control over the classical details.

There were undoubtedly problems, too, with the on-site supervision — when challenged, da Ponte admitted that he was often too busy with other work, while Contin declared that he could not remember if he had supervised the workers properly.[107] Considering that a budget of 250,000 ducats was spent on the project, such loose site management is surprising. Nonetheless, da Ponte was so proud of the design that he was granted a patent for its invention by the Senate in October 1590, forbidding anyone to sell views of the bridge or images of its foundations for twenty years.[108]

Technologically, scenographically and functionally the bridge was a triumphant success. (Fig. 10). By contrast the classical details were super-ficial additions — the central arch plucked from Serlio's treatise, the balustrade from Scamozzi's rejected design, and the rustication of the shops from the arena in Verona.[109] Here the inherently dynamic — and sometimes erratic — process of decision-making through consultation with experts in local building practice ensured that the image of the Republic was conveyed by technical innovation rather than by coherent classical erudition.

---

[106] The specifications awarded to the various *maestri,* are contained in ASV, Provveditori sopra la fabrica del ponte di Rialto, busta 4, Contratti. On the next stages of the building work see Cessi and Alberti, *Rialto,* 218–21; Calabi and Morachiello, *Rialto,* pp. 283–99.

[107] ASV, Provveditori sopra la fabbrica del Ponte di Rialto, busta 4, fascicolo 8, parte 3, Processi, 13 Aug. 1591 and 1 Sep. 1591. Contin was probably the nephew of Antonio da Ponte, as first suggested by Temanza, *Le vite,* p. 518.

[108] ASV, Senato Terra, registro 60, ff. 130r–130v, 27 Oct. 1590.

[109] Sebastiano Serlio, *Tutte l'opere d'architettura et prospettiva* (Venice, Giacomo de' Franceschi, 1619 edn.), Book III, f. 74v.

Deborah Howard

Figure 10. Antonio da Ponte, Rialto Bridge Venice, erected 1588–91. (Photograph: author.)

Conclusion

As we have seen, in later sixteenth-century Venice the utopian ideals of the 'vecchi' and their favourite architects, Palladio and Scamozzi, were repeatedly thrust aside by the democratic processes of government. Architectural classicism, by now diffused across Europe through printed architectural treatises, held little sway in the decision-making processes. In Venice, by contrast, the rigid academic approach seemed old-fashioned and impractical, while an ever-increasing regard was given to technical expertise. In a patrician oligarchy it is perhaps surprising that the views of mere *proti* and even (as in the case of the Rialto) members of general public were held in such high regard. Yet the number of patents granted by the Venetian Senate in this period for inventions of all kinds reminds us of the Republic's enthusiasm for technological expertise.[110] By the second half of the sixteenth century, any coherent attempt to refine the Roman identity introduced by Sansovino in the time of Doge Gritti faded beneath the more pragmatic, technologically orientated cultural programme of the 'giovani'. The lengthy and elaborate consultation processes could have been paralysing, but in reality they played a crucial role in winning political acceptance for ambitious adventures in public building.

Note. This lecture was written while I was the Robert Lehmann Visiting Professor at Harvard University's Villa I Tatti near Florence in the Spring Semester of 2007. The support of the Director Joseph Connors and the kind assistance of the Library staff, as well as the friendship of the other Visiting Professors and Fellows, made this the ideal place to undertake the work. Brian Pullan kindly read the whole text and made numerous helpful and perceptive suggestions. I am most grateful to John Law, Malcolm Longair, Sarah Longair and Laura Moretti for advice, information and support.

Note on transcriptions. The original spelling has been retained, but abbreviations have been expanded and the punctuation and capitalisation modernised. Where appropriate, 'u' has been rendered as 'v', and 'j' as 'i', both in documents and in early printed sources.

Dating. According to the Venetian dating system, the year began on 1 March. Thus dates in January and February are given both in *more veneto* (*m.v.*) and in modern dating.

---

[110] See for example, the 30-year patent granted in 1578 to the Florentine architect Bernardo Buontalenti for three machines: two for milling grain with and without water, and one for raising water (ASV, Senato Terra, reg. 51, f. 96v, 20 Sept. 1578; renewed reg. 52, f. 161v., 23 Apr. 1579); and the 30-year patent granted in 1580 to the Venetian *proto* Francesco Zamberlan for a new method of spinning fine woollen thread (ASV, Senato Terra, reg. 52, f. 246r, 6 Feb. 1579 m.v. (=1580)).

Anthropology is *Not* Ethnography

TIM INGOLD
Fellow of the Academy

Acceptable generalisation and unacceptable history

THE OBJECTIVE OF ANTHROPOLOGY, I believe, is to seek a generous, comparative but nevertheless critical understanding of human being and
knowing in the one world we all inhabit. The objective of ethnography is
to describe the lives of people other than ourselves, with an accuracy and
sensitivity honed by detailed observation and prolonged first-hand experience. My thesis is that anthropology and ethnography are endeavours of
quite different kinds. This is not to claim that the one is more important
than the other, or more honourable. Nor is it to deny that they depend on
one another in significant ways. It is simply to assert that they are not the
same. Indeed this might seem like a statement of the obvious, and so it
would be were it not for the fact that it has become commonplace—at
least over the last quarter of a century—for writers in our subject to treat
the two as virtually equivalent, exchanging anthropology for ethnography
more or less on a whim, as the mood takes them, or even exploiting the
supposed synonymy as a stylistic device to avoid verbal repetition. Many
colleagues to whom I have informally put the question have told me that
in their view there is little if anything to distinguish anthropological from
ethnographic work. Most are convinced that ethnography lies at the core
of what anthropology is all about. For them, to suggest otherwise seems

Read at the University of Edinburgh 12 March 2007, and at the Academy 14 March 2007.

Proceedings of the British Academy, **154**, 69–92. © The British Academy 2008.

almost anachronistic. It is like going back to the bad old days—the days, some might say, of Radcliffe-Brown. For it was he who, in laying the foundations for what was then the new science of social anthropology, insisted on the absolute distinction between ethnography and anthropology.

He did so in terms of a contrast, much debated then but little heard of today, between *idiographic* and *nomothetic* inquiry. An idiographic inquiry, Radcliffe-Brown explained, aims to document the particular facts of past and present lives, whereas the aim of nomothetic inquiry is to arrive at general propositions or theoretical statements. Ethnography, then, is specifically a mode of idiographic inquiry, differing from history and archaeology in that it is based on the direct observation of living people rather than on written records or material remains attesting to the activities of people in the past. Anthropology, to the contrary, is a field of nomothetic science. As Radcliffe-Brown declared in his introduction to *Structure and Function in Primitive Society*—in a famous sentence that, as an undergraduate beginning my anthropological studies at Cambridge in the late 1960s, I was expected to learn by heart—'comparative sociology, of which social anthropology is a branch, is . . . a theoretical or nomothetic study of which the aim is to provide acceptable generalisations' (Radcliffe-Brown 1952: 3). This distinction between anthropology and ethnography was one that brooked no compromise, and Radcliffe-Brown reasserted it over and over again. Returning to the theme in his Huxley Memorial Lecture for 1951 on 'The comparative method in social anthropology', best known for its revision of the theory of totemism, Radcliffe-Brown insisted that 'without systematic comparative studies anthropology will become only historiography and ethnography' (1951*a*: 16). And the aim of comparison, he maintained, is to pass from the particular to the general, from the general to the more general, and ultimately to the universal (ibid.: 22).

The distinction between the idiographic and the nomothetic was first coined in 1894 by the German philosopher–historian Wilhelm Windelband, a leading figure in the school of thought then known as neo-Kantianism. Windelband's real purpose was to lay down a clear dividing line between the craft of the historian, whose concern is with judgements of value, and the project of natural science, concerned as it is with the accumulation of positive knowledge based on empirical observation. But he did so by identifying history with the documentation of particular events and science with the search for general laws. And this left his distinction wide open for appropriation by positivistic natural science to denote not its opposition to history but the two successive stages of its own programme: first, the systematic collection of empirical facts; and secondly, the organisation of these facts within an overarching framework of general principles. It was left to Heinrich Rickert, a pupil of Windelband and co-founder with him of the neo-Kantian school, to sort out the confusion by pointing out that there are distinct ways, respectively scientific and historical, of attending to the particular, to each of which there corresponds a specific sense of the idiographic (Collingwood 1946: 165–70). One way treats every entity or event as an objective fact, the other attributes to it some meaning or value.[1] In so far as a geologist setting out to reconstruct the history of a rock formation, or a palaeontologist seeking to reconstruct a phylogenetic sequence on the basis of fossil evidence, necessarily deals in particulars, the reconstruction could—in the *first* of these senses—be deemed idiographic. Moreover the same might have been said (and indeed was said) of attempts, predominantly by North American scholars and going under the rubric of ethnology, to reconstruct chronological sequences of culture on the evidence of distributions of what were then called 'traits'.

It was in this sense that Radcliffe-Brown could set aside North American ethnology, which he associated primarily with the work of Franz Boas and his followers, as an idiographic enterprise wholly distinct from his nomothetic social anthropology conceived as a search for general laws governing social life (Radcliffe-Brown 1951*a*: 15). But while Boasian ethnology was thus being portrayed in Britain as historical rather than scientific, on the other side of the Atlantic it was being criticised for being scientific rather than historical. This critique came from Alfred Kroeber. Thoroughly conversant with the writings of the neo-Kantian school, Kroeber called for an anthropology that would be fully historical and therefore idiographic in the *second* sense. It must, in short, attend to particulars in terms of their value and meaning. Yet no particular—no thing, or happening—can have value and meaning in itself, cut out from the wider context of its occurrence. Each has rather to be understood by way of its positioning within the totality to which it belongs. Thus while preserving its phenomena rather than allowing them to be dissolved into laws and generalisations, the historical approach—in Kroeber's words—'finds its intellectual satisfaction in putting each preserved phenomenon into a relation of ever widening context within the phenomenal cosmos' (Kroeber 1952: 123). He characterised this task, of preservation through

---

[1] Contemporary readers will immediately recognise in this a forerunner of the so-called etic/emic distinction.

contextualisation, as 'an endeavour at descriptive integration' (Kroeber 1935: 545). As such, it is entirely different from the task of theoretical integration that Radcliffe-Brown had assigned to social anthropology. For the latter, in order to generalise, must first isolate every particular from its context in order that it can then be subsumed under context-independent formulations. Kroeber's disdain for Radcliffe-Brown's understanding of history, as nothing but a chronological tabulation of such isolated particulars awaiting the classificatory and comparative attentions of the theorist, bordered on contempt. 'I do not know the motivation for Radcliffe-Brown's depreciation of the historical approach,' he remarked caustically in an article first published in 1946, 'unless that, as the ardent apostle of a genuine new science of society, he has perhaps failed to concern himself enough with history to learn its nature' (in Kroeber 1952: 96).

The sigma principle and the totality of phenomena

Though I am not sure that the terms are the best ones, the distinction between descriptive and theoretical integration is of great importance. For the two modes of integration entail entirely different understandings of the relation between the particular and the general. The theoretician operating in a nomothetic mode imagines a world that is, by its nature, particulate. Thus the reality of the social world, for Radcliffe-Brown, comprises 'an immense multitude of actions and interactions of human beings' (1952: 4). Out of this multitude of particular events the analyst has then to abstract general features that amount to a specification of form. One of the strangest attempts to spell out this procedure appears in a book ominously entitled *The Theory of Social Structure* by the great ethnographer and anthropologist Seigfried Nadel, posthumously published in 1957. Introduced by his friend and colleague Meyer Fortes (in Nadel 1957: xv) as a work 'destined to be one of the great theoretical treatises of twentieth-century social anthropology', it was soon forgotten. Its peculiarity lay in its author's use of notation drawn from symbolic logic in order to formalise the move from the concreteness of actually observed behaviour to the abstract pattern of relationships. Let us suppose, Nadel postulated, that between persons A and B we observed diverse behaviours denoted by the letters a, b, c . . . n, but that all index a condition of 'acting towards'—of A acting towards B and of B acting towards A. We denote this condition with the colon (:). It then follows that a formal relationship (r) exists between A and B, under which is subsumed the behavioural series a . . . n. Or in short:

$$A \, r \, B, \text{ if}$$
$$A \, (a, b, c \ldots n): B, \text{ and } \textit{vice versa}$$
$$\therefore r \supset \Sigma \, a \ldots n$$

My purpose in recovering this formulation from the rightful oblivion into which it quickly fell is only to highlight the sense of integration epitomised in the last line by the Greek 'sigma', the sign conventionally used in mathematics to denote the summation of a series. The abstract relation, here, takes the form of a covering statement that encompasses every concrete term in the series.

When Kroeber spoke of 'descriptive integration', however, he meant something quite different: more akin, perhaps, to the integration of an artist's picture on the canvas as he paints a landscape. To the artist's gaze, the landscape presents itself not as a multitude of particulars but as a variegated phenomenal field, at once continuous and coherent. Within this field, the singularity of every phenomenon lies in its enfolding—in its positioning and bearing, and in the poise of a momentarily arrested movement—of the entangled histories of relations by which it came to be there, at that position and in that moment. And as the artist tries to preserve that singularity in the work of the brush, so, for Kroeber, does the anthropologist in his endeavours of description. This is what he meant when he insisted that the aim of anthropology, as of history, must be one of 'integrating phenomena as such' (1935: 546). The integration he was after is one of a world that already coheres, where things and events occur or *take place*, rather than a world of disconnected particulars that has to be rendered coherent, or joined up after the fact, in the theoretical imagination. Thus what Kroeber called the 'nexus among phenomena' (ibid.) is there to be described, in the relational coherence of the world; it is not something to be extracted from it as one might seek the general features of a form from the range of its concrete and particular instantiations. For precisely that reason, Kroeber thought, it would be wrong to regard the phenomena of the social world as *complex* (ibid.). Contemplating the landscape, the painter would be unlikely to exclaim 'What a complex landscape this is!' He may be struck by many things, but complexity is not one of them. Nor is it a consideration in the regard of the historically oriented anthropologist. Complexity only arises as an issue in the attempt to reassemble a world already decomposed into elements, as a picture, for example, might be cut up to make a jigsaw puzzle. But like the painter, and unlike the puzzle-builder, Kroeber's anthropologist seeks an integration 'in terms of the totality of phenomena' (1935: 547) that is ontologically prior to its analytical decomposition.

Yet if the anthropologist describes the social world as the artist paints a landscape, then what becomes of time? The world stands still for no one, least of all for the artist or the anthropologist, and the latter's description, like the former's depiction, can do no more than catch a fleeting moment in a never-ending process. In that moment, however, is compressed the movement of the past that brought it about, and in the tension of that compression lies the force that will propel it into the future. It is this enfolding of a generative past and a future potential in the present moment, and not the location of that moment in any abstract chronology, which makes it historical. Reasoning along these lines, Kroeber came to the conclusion that time, in the chronological sense, is inessential to history. Presented as a kind of 'descriptive cross-section' or as the characterisation of a moment, a historical account can just as well be synchronic as diachronic. Indeed it is precisely to such characterising description that anthropology aspires. 'What else can ethnography be', asked Kroeber rhetorically, 'than . . . a timeless piece of history?' (1952 [1946]: 102). The other side of this argument, of course, is that the mere ordering of events in chronological succession, one after another, gives us not history but science. Boas, whose painstaking attempts to reconstruct the lines of cultural transmission and diffusion over time had been dismissed by Kroeber as anti-historical, was perplexed. He confessed to finding Kroeber's reasoning utterly unintelligible (Boas 1936: 137). Back in Britain, however, Kroeber's understanding of what a historical or ideographic anthropology would look like fell on the more sympathetic ears of E. E. Evans-Pritchard.

In his Marett Lecture of 1950, 'Social anthropology: past and present', Evans-Pritchard virtually reiterated what Kroeber had written fifteen years previously about the relation between anthropology and history. These were his words:

> I agree with Professor Kroeber that the fundamental characteristic of the historical method is not chronological relation of events but descriptive integration of them; and this characteristic historiography shares with social anthropology. What social anthropologists have in fact chiefly been doing is to write cross-sections of history, integrative descriptive accounts of primitive peoples at a moment in time which are in other respects like the accounts written by historians about peoples over a period of time . . . (Evans-Pritchard 1950: 122)

Returning to this theme over a decade later, in a lecture on 'Anthropology and history' delivered at the University of Manchester, Evans-Pritchard roundly condemned, as had Kroeber, the blinkered view of those such as Radcliffe-Brown for whom history was nothing more than 'a record of a succession of unique events' and social anthropology nothing less than 'a set of general propositions' (Evans-Pritchard 1961: 2). In practice, Evans-Pritchard claimed, social anthropologists do not generalise from particulars any more that do historians. Rather, 'they see the general in the particular' (ibid.: 3). Or to put it another way, the singular phenomenon opens up as you go deeper into it, rather than being eclipsed from above. Yet Evans-Pritchard was by no means consistent in this view, for hardly had he stated it than he asserted precisely the opposite: 'Events lose much, even all, of their meaning if they are not seen as having some degree of regularity and constancy, as belonging to a certain type of event, all instances of which have many features in common' (ibid.: 4). This is a statement fully consistent with what, following Nadel, we might call the sigma principle of comparative generalisation, and flies in the face of the Kroeberian project of descriptive integration, or preservation through contextualisation.

In defence of Radcliffe-Brown

The problem is that once the task of anthropology is defined as descriptive integration rather than comparative generalisation, the distinction between ethnography and social anthropology, on which Radcliffe-Brown had set such store, simply vanishes. Beyond ethnography, there is nothing left for anthropology to do. And Radcliffe-Brown himself was more than aware of this. In a 1951 review of Evans-Pritchard's book *Social Anthropology*, in which the author had propounded the same ideas about anthropology and history as those set out in his Marett lecture (see Evans-Pritchard 1951: 60–1), Radcliffe-Brown registered his strong disagreement with 'the implication that social anthropology consists entirely or even largely of . . . ethnographic studies of particular societies. It is towards some such position that Professor Evans-Pritchard and a few others seem to be moving' (Radcliffe-Brown 1951*b*: 365). And it was indeed towards such a position that the discipline moved over the ensuing decade, so much so that in his Malinowski Lecture of 1959, 'Rethinking Anthropology', Edmund Leach felt moved to complain about it. 'Most of my colleagues', he grumbled, 'are giving up in the attempt to make comparative generalisations; instead they have begun to write impeccably detailed historical ethnographies of particular peoples' (Leach 1961: 1). But did Leach, in regretting this tendency, stand up for the nomothetic social anthropology of Radcliffe-Brown? Far from it. Though all in favour of generalisation, Leach launched an all-out attack on Radcliffe-Brown for having gone about it in the *wrong way*. The source of the error, he maintained, lay not in generalisation per se, but in comparison.

There are two varieties of generalisation, Leach argued. One, the sort of which he disapproved, works by comparison and classification. It assigns the forms or structures it encounters into types and subtypes, as a botanist or zoologist, for example, assigns plant or animal specimens to genera and species. Radcliffe-Brown liked to imagine himself working this way. As he wrote in a letter to Lévi-Strauss, social structures are as real as the structures of living organisms, and may be collected and compared in much the same way in order to arrive at 'a valid typological classification' (Radcliffe-Brown 1953: 109). The other kind of generalisa-tion, of which Leach approved, works by exploring a priori—or as he put it, by 'inspired guesswork'—the space of possibility opened up by the combination of a limited set of variables (Leach 1961: 5). A generalisa-tion, then, would take the form not of a typological specification that would enable us to distinguish societies of one kind from those of another, but of a statement of the relationships between variables that may operate in societies of *any* kind. This is the approach, Leach claimed, not of the botanist or zoologist, but of the engineer. Engineers are not interested in the classification of machines, or in the delineation of taxa. They want to know how machines work. The task of social anthropology, likewise, is to understand and explain how societies work. Of course, soci-eties are not machines, as Leach readily admitted. But if you want to find out how societies work, they may just as well be compared to machines as to organisms. 'The entities we call societies', Leach wrote, 'are not natu-rally existing species, neither are they man-made mechanisms. But the analogy of a mechanism has quite as much relevance as the analogy of an organism' (ibid.: 6).

I beg to differ, and on this particular point I want to rise to the defence of Radcliffe-Brown who, I think, has been grievously misrepresented by his critics, including both Leach and Evans-Pritchard. According to Leach, Radcliffe-Brown's resort to the organic analogy was based on dogma rather than choice. Not so. It was based on Radcliffe-Brown's commitment to a philosophy of process. On this he was absolutely explicit. Societies are *not* entities analogous to organisms, let alone to machines. In reality, indeed, there are no such entities. 'My own view', Radcliffe-Brown asserted, 'is that the concrete reality with which the social anthropologist is concerned ... is not any sort of entity but a process, the process of social life' (1952: 4). The analogy, then, is not between society and organism as entities, but between social *life* and organic *life* understood as processes. It was precisely this idea of the social as a life-process, rather than the idea of society as an entity, that Radcliffe-Brown drew from the comparison. And it was for this reason, too, that he compared social life to the functioning of an organism and *not* to that of a machine, for the difference between them is that the first is a life-process whereas the second is not. In life, form is continually emergent rather than specified from the outset, and nothing is ever quite the same from one moment to the next. To support his processual view of reality, Radcliffe-Brown appealed to the celebrated image of the Greek philosopher Heraclitus, of a world where all is in motion and nothing fixed, and in which it is no more possible to regain a passing moment than it is to step twice into the same waters of a flowing river (Radcliffe-Brown 1957: 12).

What his critics could never grasp, according to W. E. H. Stanner (1968: 287), was that in its emphasis on continuity through change, Radcliffe-Brown's understanding of social reality was thoroughly historical. Thus we find Evans-Pritchard, in his 1961 Manchester lecture, pointing an accusing finger at Radcliffe-Brown while warning of the dangers of drawing analogies from biological science and of assuming that there are entities, analogous to organisms, that might be labelled 'societies'. One may be able to understand the physiology of an organism without regard to its history—after all, horses remain horses and do not change into elephants—but social systems can and do undergo wholesale structural transformations (Evans-Pritchard 1961: 10). Yet a quarter of a century previously, Radcliffe-Brown had made precisely this point, albeit with a different pair of animals. 'A pig does not become a hippopotamus ... On the other hand a society can and does change its structural type without any breach of continuity' (Radcliffe-Brown 1952 [1935]: 181). This observation did not escape the attention of Lévi-Strauss who, in a paper presented to the Wenner-Gren Symposium on Anthropology in 1952, deplored Radcliffe-Brown's 'reluctance towards the isolation of social structures conceived as self-sufficient wholes' and his commitment to 'a philosophy of continuity, not of discontinuity' (Lévi-Strauss 1968: 304). For Lévi-Strauss had nothing but contempt for the idea of history as continuous change. Instead, he proposed an immense classification of societies, each conceived as a discrete, self-contained entity defined by a specific permutation and combination of constituent elements, and arrayed on the abstract co-ordinates of space and time (Lévi-Strauss 1953: 9–10). The irony is that it was from Lévi-Strauss, and not from Radcliffe-Brown, that Leach claimed to have derived his model for how anthropological generalisation should be done. Whereas Lévi-Strauss was elevated as a mathematician among the social scientists, the efforts of Radcliffe-Brown were dismissed as nothing better than 'butterfly collect-ing' (Leach 1961: 2–3). Yet Lévi-Strauss's plan for drawing up an inven-tory of all human societies, past and present, with a view to establishing their complementarities and differences, is surely the closest thing to butterfly collecting ever encountered in the annals of anthropology. Unsurprisingly, given its ambition, the plan came to nothing.

I do not pretend that Radcliffe-Brown's approach was without con-tradictions of its own. On the contrary, it was mired in contradiction from the start. Much has been made of Radcliffe-Brown's debt to the sociology of Durkheim (1982 [1917]), and for Durkheim, of course, soci-eties *were* self-contained entities, each with its own individuality, which could nevertheless be classified in terms of the possible combinations of their constituent parts.[2] But where Lévi-Strauss took this principle of dis-continuity to its logical extreme, Radcliffe-Brown—influenced as much by Whitehead's (1929) philosophy of organism as by Durkheim's socio-logy—moved in the opposite direction, to re-establish the principle of continuity. This attempt to refract the process ontology of Whitehead through the classificatory epistemology of Durkheim, though brave, was bound to fail. Inevitably, social life reappeared as the life of society, emer-gent form as pre-existent structure, the continuity of history as the alter-nation of stability and change (Ingold 1986: 153–4). Indeed there was no way in which Durkheim's first rule of sociological method, *to consider social facts as things*, could be squared with Radcliffe-Brown's idea of social life as a continuous and irreversible process. Nevertheless, I have

---

[2] Starting from the premises (*a*) that every society is a structured combination of parts, and (*b*) that these parts can combine in only a limited number of possible ways, Durkheim thought that it should be possible in theory to construct a table of essential social types prior to seeking out their empirical manifestations in the form of particular societies. 'Thus', Durkheim concluded, 'there are social species for the same reason as there are biological ones. The latter are due to the fact that organisms are only varied combinations of the same anatomical unity' (Durkheim 1982 [1895]: 116). Durkheim was alluding here to the biology Georges Cuvier. A firm believer in the fixity of species, Cuvier had proposed—under his principle of the 'correlation of parts'—that each and every naturally existing organism manifests one of the total set of logically possible working combinations of basic organs.

found more inspiration in this idea of the social as a life-process than in all the criticisms that have been levelled against it put together. Divested of the dead-weight of Durkheim's sociologism, I believe it is an idea that we can and should take forward from Radcliffe-Brown in forging a conception better suited to our times of what a genuinely open-ended and comparative anthropology could be. Quite simply, it would be an inquiry into the conditions and possibilities of social life, at all times and everywhere. To be more precise, I need to explain what I mean by both 'social' and 'life'.

Social life and the implicate order

In a series of seminars presented at the University of Chicago in 1937, subsequently transcribed and published under the title *A Natural Science of Society*, Radcliffe-Brown dwelt at some length on the distinction between social science and psychology (Radcliffe-Brown 1957: 45–52). The matter was for him absolutely clear-cut. Psychology studies the mind, and mind is a system of relations between states internal to the individual actor. They are, so to speak, 'under the skin'. Social science, however, deals with relations between individuals, not within them. 'The moment you get outside the skin of the individual', Radcliffe-Brown declared, 'you have no longer psychological, but social relations' (1957: 47). The deep-seated assumption that mind is an internal property of human individuals that can be studied in isolation from their involvement with one another or with the wider environment continues to reverberate within the field of psychology. It has however been widely challenged. One of the first to issue such a challenge was the great pioneer of psychological anthropology, A. Irving Hallowell. In an extraordinarily prescient paper on 'The self and its behavioral environment', published in 1954, Hallowell concluded that no physical barrier can come between mind and world. 'Any inner-outer dichotomy', he maintained, 'with the human skin as boundary, is psychologically irrelevant' (Hallowell 1955: 88). Fifteen years later, Gregory Bateson made exactly the same point. Mind, Bateson insisted, is not confined within individual bodies as against a world 'out there', but is immanent in the entire system of organism–environment relations within which all human beings are necessarily enmeshed. 'The mental world', as he put it, 'is not limited by the skin' (Bateson 1973: 429). Rather, it reaches out into the environment along the multiple and ever-extending sensory pathways of the human organism's involvement in its surroundings. Or as Andy Clark has observed, still more recently, the mind has a way of leaking from the body, mingling shamelessly with the world around it (Clark 1997: 53).

I invoke the word 'social' to signify this understanding of the essential interpenetrability or commingling of mind and world. Far from serving to demarcate a particular *domain* of phenomena, as opposed, say, to the biological or the psychological, I take the word to denote a certain ontology: an understanding of the constitution of the phenomenal world itself. As such, it is opposed to an ontology of the particulate that imagines a world of individual entities and events, each of which is linked through an external contact—whether of spatial contiguity or temporal succession—that leaves its basic nature unaffected. In the terms of the physicist David Bohm (1980), the order of such an imagined world would be *explicate*. The order of the social world, by contrast, is *implicate*. That is to say, any particular phenomenon on which we may choose to focus our attention enfolds within its constitution the totality of relations of which, in their unfolding, it is the momentary outcome. Were we to cut these relations, and seek to recover the whole from its now isolated fragments, something would be lost that could never be recovered. That something is life itself. As the biologist Paul Weiss put it, in a 1969 symposium on the future of the life sciences, 'the mere reversal of our prior analytical dissection of the Universe by putting the pieces together again . . . can yield no complete explanation of even the most elementary living system' (Weiss 1969: 7). That is why, to return to my earlier criticism of Leach, a mechanical analogy can offer no account of social *life*. A machine can be constructed from parts, but machines do not live. And this brings me from the meaning of the social to the second of my key terms, namely 'life'. By this I do not mean an internal animating principle that is installed in some things but not others, distinguishing the former as members of the class of animate objects. Life, as Weiss observed, 'is process, not substance' (1969: 8), and this process is tantamount to the unfolding of a continuous and ever-evolving field of relations within which beings of all kinds are generated and held in place. Thus where Radcliffe-Brown drew an analogy between organic life and social life, I draw an identity. Organic life *is* social, and so for that matter is the life of the mind, because the order to which it gives rise is implicate.

In this distinction between explicate and implicate orders lies an echo of the contrast I drew earlier between theoretical and descriptive modes of integration. To recapitulate: the theoretical mode works through the summation of discrete particulars, according to the sigma principle, so as to arrive at covering statements of the general form of social relations. The descriptive mode, on the other hand, seeks to apprehend the relational coherence of the world itself, as it is given to immediate experience, by homing in on particulars each of which brings to a focus, and momentarily condenses, the very processes that brought it into being. Though both modes of integration aspire to a kind of holism, their respective understandings of totality are very different. The first is a totality of *form*: it implies the closure and completion of a system of relations that has been fully joined up. The second, however, is a totality of *process* which, since it is forever ongoing, is always open-ended and never complete, but which is nevertheless wound up in every moment that it brings forth. Now as I mentioned earlier, I am not convinced that the terms 'theoretical' and 'descriptive' are entirely appropriate for these two approaches. The trouble is that the very notion of description as a task that is somehow opposed to the project of theory has its roots in the first of the two modes. It harks directly back to Radcliffe-Brown's division between ethnography and anthropology: respectively idiographic and nomothetic, descriptive and theoretical. Yet in the opposition between descriptive data and theoretical generalisation the act of description is itself diminished, reduced to a mechanical function of information pick-up. The second mode, on the other hand, refuses this reduction, recognising—as the first does not—that any act of description entails a movement of interpretation. What is 'given' to experience, in this mode, comprises not individual data but the world itself. It is a world that is not so much mapped out as taken in, from a particular vantage point, much as the painter takes in the landscape that surrounds him from the position at which he has planted his easel.

It follows that any endeavour of so-called descriptive integration, if it is to do justice to the implicate order of social life, can be neither descriptive nor theoretical in the specific senses constituted by their opposition. It must rather do away with the opposition itself. What then becomes of my initial distinction between ethnography and anthropology? Have I not argued myself out of the very position from which I began? I have certainly argued against the simple alignments of ethnography with data collection and of anthropology with comparative theory. If there is a distinction between ethnography and anthropology, then it must be drawn along different lines. Let me return for a moment to Radcliffe-Brown. In his 1951 lecture on 'The comparative method in social anthropology', he had a word or two to say about armchairs. It is told that long ago, in the days before fieldwork had become established practice in anthropological research, scholars sat in their libraries, ensconced in comfortable armchairs, as they carried out their comparative work. By the middle of the twentieth century, however, the 'armchair anthropologist' had become a figure of fun, whose airy speculations were brushed aside by a new generation for whom fieldwork was paramount. For Radcliffe-Brown this was a matter of regret. A social anthropology that aspires to systematic comparison, and that is not content to rest on its ethnographic laurels, must, he thought, allow space for the armchair (Radcliffe-Brown 1951*a*: 15). Now whether our anthropological ancestors actually sat in armchairs as they worked, I do not know. But the reason why this particular piece of furniture has earned its central place in the disciplinary imagination is plain. For it seems to cocoon the scholar in a sedentary confinement that insulates him or her almost completely from any kind of sensory contact with the surroundings. Being-in-the-armchair, if you will, is the precise inverse of being-in-the-world.

Here is where I differ from Radcliffe-Brown: I do not think we can do anthropology in armchairs. I can best explain why in terms of the difficulty that I, along with many colleagues (Sillitoe 2007: 150), routinely face in introducing what our subject is about, especially to novice students. Perhaps it is the study of human societies—not just of our own society, but of all societies, everywhere. But that only begs further questions. You can see and touch a fellow human being, but have you ever seen or touched a society? We may think we live in societies, but can anyone ever tell where their society ends and another begins? Granted that we are not sure what societies are, or even whether they exist at all, could we not simply say that anthropology is the study of *people*? There is much to be said for this, but it still does not help us to distinguish anthropology from all the other disciplines that claim to study people in one way or another, from history and psychology to the various branches of biology and biomedicine. What truly distinguishes anthropology, I believe, is that it is not a study *of* at all, but a study *with*. Anthropologists work and study *with* people. Immersed with them in an environment of joint activity, they learn to see things (or hear them, or touch them) in the ways their teachers and companions do. An education in anthropology, therefore, does more than furnish us with knowledge *about* the world—about people and their societies. It rather educates our *perception* of the world, and opens our eyes and minds to other possibilities of being. The questions we address are philosophical ones: of what it means to be a human being or a person, of moral conduct and the balance of freedom and constraint in people's relations with others, of trust and responsibility, of the exercise of power, of the connections between language and thought, between words and things, and between what people say and what they do, of perception and representation, of learning and memory, of life and death and the passage of time, and so on and so forth. Indeed the list is endless. But it is the fact that we address these questions in the world, and *not* from the armchair—that this world is not just what we think *about* but what we think *with*, and that in its thinking the mind wanders along pathways extending far beyond the envelope of the skin—that makes the enterprise anthropological and, by the same token, radically different from positivist science. We do our philosophy out of doors. And in this, the world and its inhabitants, human and non-human, are our teachers, mentors and interlocutors.

Anthropology as art and craft

In a recent, somewhat wistful essay, Maurice Bloch (2005) asks rhetorically 'Where did anthropology go?' Echoing a complaint that has rumbled on ever since the collapse of the nineteenth-century certainties of evolutionary progress, he worries that in the absence of any 'generalizing theoretical framework', anthropology is left 'without the only centre it could have: the study of human beings' (2005: 2, 9). He suggests a return to functionalism, understood in a broad sense as an understanding that is grounded in the circumstances of real human beings, in specific places, and embedded in the wider ecology of life. I am sympathetic, having myself put forward something similar under the rubric of the 'dwelling perspective' (Ingold 2000). As Bloch (2005: 16–17) says of his functionalism, this is not a theory so much as an attitude—let us say, a way of knowing rather than a framework for knowledge as such. Fundamentally, as a way of knowing it is also a way of being. The paradox of the armchair is that in order to *know* one can no longer *be* in the world of which one seeks knowledge. But anthropology's solution, to ground knowing in being, in the world rather than the armchair, means that any study *of* human beings must also be a study *with* them. Indeed, Bloch offers a fine example of how this might be done, recalling a discussion of a deeply philosophical nature with his hosts during fieldwork in a small Malagasy village. He describes the discussion as a seminar (Bloch 2005: 4). I am sure we can all recall similar conversations. They shape the way we think.

I referred above to the work of Hallowell—a profound contribution to the philosophy of the self, consciousness and perception. As we know,

however, this philosophy was shaped more than anything by endless conversations with his hosts, Ojibwa people of north-central Canada. One
thing he learned from them is particularly worthy of consideration here.
It concerns dreaming. The world of one's dreams, Hallowell's mentors
told him, is precisely the same as that of one's waking life. But in the
dream you perceive it with different eyes or through different senses, while
making different kinds of movements—perhaps those of another animal
such as an eagle or a bear—and possibly even in a different medium such
as in the air or the water rather than on land. When you wake, having
experienced an alternative way of being in that same world in which you
presently find yourself, you are wiser than you were before (Hallowell
1955: 178–81). To do anthropology, I venture, is to dream like an Ojibwa.
As in a dream, it is continually to *open up* the world, rather than to seek
closure. The endeavour is essentially comparative, but what it compares
are not bounded objects or entities but ways of being. It is the constant
awareness of alternative ways of being, and of the ever-present possibility of 'flipping' from one to another, that defines the anthropological
attitude. It lies in what I would call the 'sideways glance'. Wherever we
are, and whatever we may be doing, we are always aware that things might
be done differently. It is as though there were a stranger at our heels, who
turns out to be none other than ourselves. This sensibility to the strange
in the close-at-hand is, I believe, one that anthropology shares with art.
But by the same token, it is radically distinguished from that of normal
science, which defamiliarises the real by removing it altogether from the
domain of immediate human experience.

Turning from its underlying sensibilities to its working practices,
anthropology is perhaps more akin to craft than art.[3] For it is characteristic of craft that both the practitioner's knowledge *of* things, and what he
does *to* them, are grounded in intensive, respectful and intimate relations
with the tools and materials of his trade. Indeed, anthropologists have
long liked to see themselves as craftsmen among social scientists, priding
themselves on the quality of their handiwork by contrast to the mass-
produced goods of industrial data-processing turned out by sociologists
and others. Rarely, however, have they sought to spell out exactly what
craftsmanship entails. Rather ironically, introducing an edited volume
entitled *The Craft of Social Anthropology* published in 1967, Max
Gluckman explained that its purpose is to provide a guide to modern

---

[3] This is not the place for a discussion of the differentiation of art and craft, and I attach no
particular significance to it here.

fieldwork methods. The contributing authors, who broadly represented the so-called 'Manchester School' of social anthropology, had all tried, wrote Gluckman, 'to set techniques in the framework of theoretical problems, so that those who use the book may remind themselves of what they are aiming at when they collect their material' (Gluckman 1967: xi). The irony is that the language of data collection, hypothesis-testing and theory-building used throughout the book could hardly be further removed from the practice of craft, and in fact the term, so prominently displayed in the book's title, is never mentioned again. That anthropology is a craft seems to have been something that its contributors simply took for granted. A decade previously, however, C. Wright Mills had concluded his book *The Sociological Imagination* (1959) with an appendix that tackles the issue head-on. Apart from its presumption that all social scientists are men,[4] Mills's essay 'On intellectual craftsmanship' remains as relevant today as it was fifty years ago. Though addressed to social scientists in general rather than anthropologists in particular, it contains more words of wisdom than any number of theoretical treatises and methodological manuals.

This is how Mills begins:

> To the individual social scientist who feels himself a part of the classic tradition, social science is the practice of a craft. A man at work on problems of substance, he is among those who are quickly made impatient and weary by elaborate discussions of method-and-theory-in-general; so much of it interrupts his proper studies.   (Mills 1959: 215)

Thus the first thing about intellectual craft, for Mills, is that there is no division between method and theory. Against the idea that you start by setting a theoretical agenda, and then test it empirically by means of data collected in accordance with standard protocols, Mills declares: 'Let every man be his own methodologist; let every man be his own theorist; let theory and method again become part of the practice of craft' (1959: 246). The second thing about intellectual craft, then, is that there is no division, in practice, between work and life. It is a practice that involves the whole person, continually drawing on past experience as it is projected into the future. The intellectual craftsman, as Mills puts it, 'forms his own self as he works towards the perfection of his craft' (ibid.: 216). What he fashions, through his work, is a way of being. And thirdly, to assist him

---

[4] For the sake of consistency with citations from Mills, I shall continue in what follows to use the third person singular pronoun in its masculine form. Gender differences are irrelevant to my argument, however, and readers are welcome to substitute the feminine form as they wish.

in this project, he keeps a journal, which he periodically files, sorts and scrambles for new ideas. In it, he notes his experiences, his 'fringe-thoughts' that have come to him as by-products of everyday life, snatches of overheard conversations, and even dreams (ibid.: 216–17). It is from this heterogeneous reservoir of raw material that the intellectual craftsman shapes his work.

Mills's portrayal of craftsmanship certainly seems to fit, so far as anthropology is concerned. I am confident that most anthropologists would be happy to sign up to it, even if it goes against the grain of much of what has been published on the subject of theory and method. But what has become of ethnography? If theory and method are to come together again in craft, as Mills recommends, then should not every anthropologist be his or her own ethnographer, and vice versa? We can still recognise today the figure of the 'social theorist', sunk in his arm-chair or more likely peering from behind his computer screen, who pre-sumes to be qualified, by virtue of his standing as an intellectual, to pronounce upon the ways of a world with which he involves himself as little as possible, preferring to interrogate the works of others of his kind. At the other extreme is the lowly 'ethnographic researcher', tasked with undertaking structured and semi-structured interviews with a selected sample of informants and analysing their contents with an appropriate software package, who is convinced that the data he collects are ethno-graphic simply because they are qualitative. These figures are the fossils of an outmoded distinction between empirical data collection and abstract theoretical speculation, and I hope we can all agree that there is no room for either in anthropology. But what of the detailed descriptions of other people's lives, informed by prolonged fieldwork, that are characteristic of ethnography at its best? Should we not leave some space for them? Indeed we should. But something happens when we turn from the being *with* of anthropology to the ethnographic description *of.* And to explain what this is I must return to the notion of description itself.

Writing and correspondence

Earlier I likened the anthropological mode of descriptive integration to the integration of a landscape painting as it takes shape upon the artist's canvas. In painting, as also in drawing, observation and description go hand-in-hand. This is because both painting and drawing entail a direct coupling between the movement of the artist's visual perception, as it follows the shapes and contours of the land, and the gestural movement of the hand that holds the brush or pencil, as it leaves a trace upon a surface. Through the coupling of perception and action, the artist is drawn *in* to the world, even as he or she draws it *out* in the gestures of description and the traces they yield. As I have already mentioned, there is much in common between the practices of anthropology and art. Both are ways of knowing that proceed along the observational paths of being *with*, and both, in doing so, explore the unfamiliar in the close-at-hand. But by and large, ethnographers neither paint nor draw. 'What does the ethnographer do?'—Clifford Geertz once asked rhetorically—'he writes' (Geertz 1973: 19). Throughout the entire debate that has accompanied the so-called 'crisis of representation', the assumption has been that the graphic part of ethnography consists of writing and not drawing. Moreover it is writing understood not as a practice of inscription or line-making but as one of verbal composition, which could be done just as well on a keyboard as with a pencil or pen. Critically, the keyboard ruptures the direct link between perception, gesture and its trace that is prerequisite to observational description. It is for this reason that James Clifford, for example, can write that description involves 'a turning *away* from dialogue and observation towards a separate place of writing, a place for reflection, analysis and interpretation' (Clifford 1990: 52).[5]

There is nothing intrinsically wrong with this, but the separation deserves to be noted. Conventionally we associate ethnography with fieldwork and participant observation, and anthropology with the comparative analysis that follows after we have left the field behind. I want to suggest, to the contrary, that anthropology—as an inquisitive mode of inhabiting the world, of being *with*, characterised by the 'sideways glance' of the comparative attitude—is itself a practice of observation grounded in participatory dialogue. It may be mediated by such descriptive activities as painting and drawing, which can be coupled to observation. And of course it may be mediated by writing. But unlike painting and drawing, anthropological writing is *not* an art of description. We do not call it 'anthropography', and for good reason. It is rather a practice of *correspondence*. The anthropologist writes—as indeed he thinks and speaks—*to* himself, to others and to the world. His observations answer to his

---

[5] I think it could be argued that film and photography entail a comparable turning away, in so far as the mechanism of the camera breaks the flow of visuo-gestural activity that occurs in drawing and painting. Camera-work is thus more ethnographic than anthropological; painting and drawing more anthropological than ethnographic.

experience of habitation. This verbal correspondence lies at the heart of the anthropological dialogue. It can be carried out anywhere, regardless of whether we might imagine ourselves to be 'in the field' or out of it. Anthropologists, as I have insisted, do their thinking, talking and writing in and with the world. To do anthropology, you do not have to imagine the world as a field. 'The field' is rather a term by which the ethnographer retrospectively imagines a world from which he has *turned away* in order, quite specifically, that he might *describe it in writing*. His literary practice is not so much one of *non-descriptive correspondence* as one of *non-correspondent description*—that is, a description which (unlike painting or drawing) has broken away from observation. Thus if anyone retreats to the armchair, it is not the anthropologist but the ethnographer. As he shifts from inquiry to description he has of necessity to reposition himself from the field of action to the sidelines.

It has long been customary to divide the process of anthropological research into three successive phases: of observation, description and comparison. In practice, as Philippe Descola has pointed out, this three-phase model offers 'a purified definition of operations that are most often intertwined' (Descola 2005: 72). One cannot say where one ends and the next begins. An overall movement is nevertheless assumed from ethnographic particulars to anthropological generalities. It might seem from the foregoing that I have reversed this order, placing anthropology before ethnography rather than after it. But that is not really my intention. I do not believe that anthropology is any more *prior* to ethnography than the other way round. They are just different. It may be hard to carry on both at once, because of the different positionalities they entail, but most of us probably swing back and forth between them, like a pendulum, in the course of our working lives. My real purpose in challenging the idea of a one-way progression from ethnography to anthropology has not been to belittle ethnography, or to treat it as an afterthought, but rather to liberate it, above all from the tyranny of method. Nothing has been more damaging to ethnography than its representation under the guise of the 'ethnographic method'. Of course, ethnography has its methods, but it *is not* a method. It is not, in other words, a set of formal procedural means designed to satisfy the ends of anthropological inquiry. It is a practice in its own right—a practice of verbal description. The accounts it yields, of other people's lives, are finished pieces of work, not raw materials for further anthropological analysis. But if ethnography is not a means to the end of anthropology, then neither is anthropology the servant of ethnography. To repeat, anthropology is an inquiry into the conditions and possibilities of human life in the world; it is not—as so many scholars in fields of literary criticism would have it—the study of how to write ethnography, or of the reflexive problematics of the shift from observation to description.

This is a message that has critical implications for the way anthropology is taught. Too often, it seems to me, we disappoint our students' expectations. Rather than awakening their curiosity towards social life, or kindling in them an inquisitive mode of being, we force them into an endless reflection on disciplinary texts which are studied not for the light they throw upon the world but for what they reveal about the practices of anthropologists themselves and the doubts and dilemmas that surround their work. Students soon discover that having doubled up on itself, through its conflation with ethnography, anthropology has become an interrogation of its own ways of working.[6] As educators based in university departments, most anthropologists devote much of their lives to working with students. They probably spend considerably more time in the classroom than anywhere they might call the field. Some enjoy this more than others, but they do not, by and large, regard time in the classroom as an integral part of their *anthropological* practice. Students are told that anthropology is what we do with our colleagues, and with other people in other places, but not with them. Locked out of the power-house of anthropological knowledge construction, all they can do is peer through the windows that our texts and teachings offer them. It took the best part of a century, of course, for the people once known as 'natives', and latterly as 'informants', to be admitted to the big anthropology house as master-collaborators, that is as people we work *with*. It is now usual for their contributions to any anthropological study to be fulsomely acknowledged. Yet students remain excluded, and the inspiration and ideas that flow from our dialogue with them unrecognised. I believe this is a scandal, one of the malign consequences of the institutionalised

---

[6] The same doubling up is all too apparent, as well, in many fields of art, and the consequences of this involution are as damaging for art as they are for anthropology. An art that addresses nothing but its own practice will contribute little to human understanding. If the scope of collaboration between art and anthropology is marked out in terms of their mutual self-interrogation, then both will sink together. Much of the inherent potential of this collaboration is, I believe, being squandered on account of the confusion between anthropology and ethnography. Art and ethnography do not combine well. The former compromises ethnography's commitment to descriptive accuracy; the latter shies away from the immediacy and of art's observational engagement. Mixing art and ethnography is probably a recipe for bad art, and for bad ethnography. Combining art and anthropology, by contrast, could greatly enhance the power of both.

division between research and teaching that has so blighted the practice of scholarship. For indeed, the epistemology that constructs the student as the mere recipient of anthropological knowledge produced else-where—rather than as a participant in its ongoing creative crafting—is the very same as that which constructs the native as an informant. And it is no more defensible.

Anthropology is *not* ethnography. Ethnographers describe, principally in writing, how the people of some place and time perceive the world and how they act in it. In our dreams we might once have supposed that by adding up, comparing and contrasting the ways that people of all places and times perceive and act, we might be able to extract some common denominators—possible candidates for human universals. Any such universals, however, are abstractions of our own, and as Whitehead was the first to point out, it is a fallacy to imagine that they are concretely instantiated in the world as a substrate for human variation.[7] With its dreams of generalisation shattered, where should anthropology go? Should it continue to accumulate disparate but thematically oriented ethnographic case studies between the covers of edited volumes, in the hopes that some kinds of generalisation might still fall out? Should it abandon its project for the work of philosophers who have never mustered the energy or the conviction to leave their armchairs? Should it, on the other hand, join with the literary critics in their own, largely incomprehensible ruminations on the ethnographic project? Anthropology has tried all these things. Yet every direction leads off at a tangent from the world we inhabit. It is no wonder, then, that anthropologists are left feeling isolated and marginalised, and that they are routinely passed by in public discussions of the great questions of social life. I have argued for an anthropology that would return to these questions, not in the armchair but in the world. We can be our own philosophers, but we can do it better thanks to its embedding in our observational engagements with the world and in our collaborations and correspondences with its inhabitants. Let us call this philosophy of ours anthropology.

Note.   Many people have assisted me both in the preparation of this lecture and in subsequently revising it for publication. They include Maurice Bloch, Philippe Descola, Keith Hart, Heonik Kwon, Paul Sillitoe, James Urry and David Zeitlyn. I thank them all. The lecture was presented at the University of Edinburgh on 12

---

[7] This is the 'fallacy of misplaced concreteness', by which one comes 'to mistake a conceptual abstraction for an actual vital agent' (Whitehead 1938 [1926]: 66).

March 2007, and at the British Academy, London, on 14 March 2007. I would like to thank Janet Carsten and Joan Kenny for arranging the events in Edinburgh and London respectively, and Robin Jackson for his hospitality.

References

Bateson, G. (1973), *Steps to an Ecology of Mind* (London).

Bloch, M. (2005), *Essays on Cultural Transmission* (Oxford).

Boas, F. (1936), 'History and science in anthropology: a reply', *American Anthropologist*, 38: 137–41.

Bohm, D. (1980), *Wholeness and the Implicate Order* (London).

Clark, A. (1997), *Being There: Putting Brain, Body and the World Together Again* (Cambridge, MA).

Clifford, J. (1990), 'Notes on (field)notes', in R. Sanjek (ed.), *Fieldnotes: The Makings of Anthropology* (Ithaca, NY).

Collingwood, R. G. (1946), *The Idea of History* (Oxford).

Descola, P. (2005), 'On anthropological knowledge', *Social Anthropology*, 13(1): 65–73.

Durkheim, E. (1982), *The Rules of Sociological Method*, trans. W. D. Halls, ed. S. Lukes (London).

Evans-Pritchard, E. E. (1950), 'Social anthropology: past and present', *Man*, 198: 118–24.

Evans-Pritchard, E. E. (1951), *Social Anthropology* (London).

Evans-Pritchard, E. E. (1961), *Anthropology and History* (Manchester).

Geertz, C. (1973), *The Interpretation of Cultures* (New York).

Gluckman, M. (1967), 'Introduction', in A. L. Epstein (ed.), *The Craft of Social Anthropology* (London).

Hallowell, A. I. (1955), *Culture and Experience* (Philadelphia).

Ingold, T. (1986), *Evolution and Social Life* (Cambridge).

Ingold, T. (2000), *The Perception of the Environment: Essays on Livelihood, Dwelling and Skill* (London).

Kroeber, A. L. (1935), 'History and science in anthropology', *American Anthropologist*, 37(4): 539–69.

Kroeber, A. L. (1952), *The Nature of Culture* (Chicago).

Leach, E. R. (1961), *Rethinking Anthropology* (London).

Lévi-Strauss, C. (1953), *Race and History* (Paris).

Lévi-Strauss, C. (1968), *Structural Anthropology* (Harmondsworth).

Mills, C. W. (1959), *The Sociological Imagination* (New York).

Nadel, S. F. (1957), *The Theory of Social Structure* (London).

Radcliffe-Brown, A. R. (1951a), 'The comparative method in social anthropology', *Journal of the Royal Anthropological Institute*, 81: 15–22.

Radcliffe-Brown, A. R. (1951b), 'Review of E. E. Evans-Pritchard's *Social Anthropology*', *British Journal of Sociology*, 2: 364–6.

Radcliffe-Brown, A. R. (1952), *Structure and Function in Primitive Society* (London).

Radcliffe-Brown, A. R. (1953), 'Letter to Lévi-Strauss', in S. Tax (ed.), *An Appraisal of Anthropology Today* (Chicago).

Radcliffe-Brown, A. R. (1957), *A Natural Science of Society* (New York).

Sillitoe, P. (2007), 'Anthropologists only need apply: challenges of applied anthropology', *Journal of the Royal Anthropological Institute*, 13: 147–65.

Stanner, W. E. H. (1968), 'A. R. Radcliffe-Brown', in *International Encyclopaedia of the Social Sciences*, 13: 285–90 (New York).

Weiss, P. (1969), 'The living system: determinism stratified', in A. Koestler and J. R. Smythies (eds.), *Beyond Reductionism: New Perspectives in the Life Sciences* (London).

Whitehead, A. N. (1929), *Process and Reality: An Essay in Cosmology* (Cambridge).

Whitehead, A. N. (1938), *Science and the Modern World* (Harmondsworth).

Visions of European Unity since 1945

NOËL O'SULLIVAN

University of Hull

IN 1976, JEAN MONNET, a leading inspiration of the European Communities, concluded his *Memoirs* by expressing the hope that progress would continue towards a United States of Europe, which he described as 'only a stage on the way to the organized world of tomorrow'.[1] Although Monnet was ninety at the time, age had not dimmed the unfaltering confidence in the vision of European unity he shared with the Europhile leaders of his generation. In contrast, it is precisely their lack of this confidence which characterises the contemporary Europhile political élites, even though the French and Dutch rejection of the draft Constitutional Treaty in 2005 turned out to have been only a temporary setback for their members.

The full extent of this generational change is captured by a reminiscence at the end of Monnet's autobiography about a photograph he kept on his desk in Luxembourg. It was a photograph, he explained to visitors, of the *Kon-tiki*, a 'strange raft . . . whose adventure had thrilled the whole world, and which for me was the symbol of our own'. The young men who crewed the *Kon-tiki*, he wrote, 'chose their course and then they set out. They knew that they could not turn back. Whatever the difficulties, they had only one option—to go on . . . [F]or us too there is no going back.'[2] Needless to say, no member of the contemporary Europhile

Read at the Academy 17 May 2007.

[1] J. Monnet, *Memoirs* (New York, 1978), p. 524.

[2] Ibid.

generation would feel able to explain the nature of the European integration project by pointing to a photo of a strange craft like the *Kon-tiki*, and none would retain the sense of inevitability which Monnet took for granted. As Nicolas Sarkozy remarked not long after the French and Dutch rejection of the draft constitution, 'The forces driving the union's political movement have run out of steam.'[3]

This loss of confidence has not, however, been accompanied by a realisation by politicians of the need for the kind of intellectually substantial debate about the nature of the integration project which seemed unnecessary to Monnet's generation. In particular, no concern has been shown for the fate of what Elie Kedourie considered the greatest political achievement of the modern West.[4] This is a constitutional style of politics that limits the arbitrary power of governments by surrounding them with checks that ensure political accountability and promote the rule of law. The representative system of government associated with constitutionalism, Kedourie wrote in the last book he published, 'is one of a handful of original devices in the history of government to have been invented and perfected'.[5] Kedourie also believed, however, that constitutionalism is a precarious invention, since all governments have an interest in eroding checks and balances and evading political accountability. At the present day, he felt, the fragility of the constitutional tradition has been increased by the fact that all governments tend to reject the need for checks and balances because they claim to be pursuing more enlightened and democratic ideals than their opponents. Kedourie would therefore naturally have been suspicious of Europhiles who have relied on deliberate vagueness in order to avoid discussing the implications of European integration for constitutional government.

Despite misgivings of this kind, Kedourie might have sympathised with one aspect of the integration project. In Britain in particular, he feared that the constitutional tradition he admired had been greatly undermined since 1945 by an increasingly collectivist and populist style of government.[6] With this in mind, he might have welcomed the European Union as a counterbalance to the threat to the rule of law and individual

---

[3] N. Sarkozy, *Sunday Telegraph*, 8 Oct. 2006. See also his *Testimony* (Petersfield, 2006).

[4] See, for example, E. Kedourie, *Democracy and Arab Political Culture* (Washington, 1992), esp. pp. 2–5.

[5] Ibid., p. 4.

[6] See Kedourie's essays on 'Conservatism and the Conservative Party' and 'Lord Salisbury and Politics', in E. Kedourie, *The Crossman Confessions and Other Essays* (London and New York, 1984), pp. 37–46 and 47–68.

rights created at national level by what one of his contemporaries, Lord Hailsham, termed 'elective dictatorship'. Any sympathy Kedourie might have had for the integration project in this respect would have depended, however, on the commitment of the Europhile political élites to preserving at supranational level a constitutional tradition which has been weakened at the national one.

In the event, the draft Constitutional Treaty of 2005 showed little concern of this kind. Following the rejection of that treaty by French and Dutch voters, the draft constitution was replaced by the 'Reform Treaty' of Lisbon, which dropped the word 'constitution' but will, if ratified, implement much of the draft Constitutional Treaty by: conferring (from 1 January 2009) more power over foreign policy on unelected officials in Brussels; creating a new office of European president; reducing the size of the Commission by removing each member state's right to one commissioner; giving the force of law to the Charter of Fundamental Rights; removing fifty-five national vetoes; and eventually (between 2014 and 2017) relating voting weights more closely to population size.

Whether the Lisbon Reform Treaty amounts to the creation of a super-state of the kind the Constitutional Treaty was felt by many to aim at creating is arguable, since it is still possible to maintain that the EU remains 'a creature unlike any other'—neither, that is, a super-state, nor a federal union, nor an intergovernmental organisation, but an entity that is 'closest to the third, in that nation-states remain the main actors'.[7] Even if the continuing importance of nation-states is accepted, however, thoughtful commentators noted that the EU was already 'a polity in its own right' before the draft constitution was advanced.[8] Although it may still stop short of possessing full sovereignty, in other words, it participates in a shared, multi-level concept of sovereignty which is no longer the monopoly of nation-states.

What is clear, at least, is that the Reform Treaty has done little to define the nature of this sovereignty more precisely. Indeed, as one political analyst remarked, the worst consequence of the Reform Treaty for Britain and Europe alike is that it is likely to create increased legal uncertainty about the nature of the EU.[9] Britain's opt-out clauses, Bronwen Maddox rightly added, will not be exempt from this uncertainty since

---

[7] *The Economist: Special Report on the European Union*, 17 Mar. 2007, 16.
[8] H. Friese and Peter Wagner, 'Survey article: the nascent political philosophy of the European polity', *The Journal of Political Philosophy*, 10/3 (2002), 342.
[9] B. Maddox, *The Times*, 14 Dec. 2007, 13.

they will be tested in the European Court of Justice, without any guarantee that they will hold tight. It is, then, only after unpredictable legal contests that the implications of the Lisbon Amendment Treaty will be established.

This uncertain outcome did not, however, deter a leading member of the Europhile élites, Nicolas Sarkozy, the French President, from ignoring the demand of the British Prime Minister, Gordon Brown, that, following the incorporation into the Reform Treaty of the British opt-out clauses, the EU should concentrate on practical policies and abandon plans for further integration. Indeed, the day after the Treaty was signed, Sarkozy proposed the creation of a 'Reflection Group' which would deliberate on the next thirty years of European integration. After the rapid approval of this proposal by EU leaders, Sarkozy explained to French journalists that the aim of the Group was to come up with a new blueprint for the Union by 'defin[ing] a new European dream'.[10] Unfortunately, previous experience of a somewhat similar EU Reflection Group created several years earlier at the request of Romano Prodi did not suggest that much clarification of the integration project would be achieved, although it did indicate that the visionary element would continue to triumph over British pragmatism.

In the spring of 2002 Prodi, who was then President of the European Commission, inaugurated the kind of Reflection Group favoured by Sarkozy when he requested the *Institut für die Wissenschaften vom Menschen* in Vienna to set up one consisting of independent European intellectuals with the task of pondering on the broader spiritual and cultural aspects of European identity.[11] More precisely, Krzysztof Michalski, chairman of the Group from 2002–4, described its task as that of reflecting 'on those values particularly relevant to the continuing process of European unification' and 'advis[ing Prodi] on this field'.[12] After a series of public debates in several European capitals, the Group published the outcome of its deliberations under the general title *Conditions of European Solidarity*.[13] A summary of the conclusions published by four members of the Group emphasised two in particular.

[10] *Daily Telegraph*, 15 Dec. 2007, 8.
[11] The members of the Group were: Kurt Biedenkopf, Silvio Ferrari, Bronislaw Geremek, Árpád Göncz, John Gray, Will Hutton, Jutta Limbach, Krzysztof Michalski, Ioannis Petrou, Alberto Quadrio Curzio, Michel Rocard and Simone Veil.
[12] Michalski was Rector of the *Institut für die Wissenschaften vom Menschen.*
[13] These reflections were first published in German in the *Institut für die Wissenschaften vom Menschen's* journal *Transit — Europäische Revue*, nr. 26, 27 and 28 (Verlag Neue Kritik,

The first conclusion was that 'Europe is not a fact, but a task.'[14] This task, moreover, is an endless one, since 'There is no "finality" to the process of European integration.'[15] The Group stressed, however, that further economic and political integration is impossible without cultural integration. This, in turn, would depend in future on finding new sources of spiritual unity, since

> As the old forces of integration—the desire for peace, the existence of external threats, and the potential for economic growth—lose their effectiveness, the role of Europe's common culture—the spiritual factor of European integration—will inevitably grow in importance.[16]

Where then are the future sources of a common European culture to be found? To this, the Group replied that only an open-ended answer can be given since, as already observed, 'European culture, indeed Europe itself, is not a "fact": it is a task and a process.'[17] More precisely, this open-ended—or simply vague—characterisation of European culture was supported by the contention that definition of its content can be provided neither by philosophy nor by history but requires, rather, 'political decisions that attempt to demonstrate the significance of tradition in the face of future tasks that Europe's Union must address'.[18] This seemed to imply that, given sufficient political power and will, European culture could mean whatever the Europhile élites wanted it to mean.

This vagueness had the attraction for the Group members of making it possible to maintain that 'European culture *cannot* be defined *in opposition to a particular religion* (such as Islam).'[19] Whether Muslim fundamentalists would appreciate this as much as the Europhile élites is doubtful. Above all, however, it had the further attraction of providing the integration project with a potentially universal concept of European identity, since the fact that Europe is not itself a fact means that there cannot be any

---

Frankfurt a.M., 2003/2004). References in the text are to the first of the two English translation volumes, edited by Krzysztof Michalski and entitled *What Holds Europe Together?* (Budapest, 2006).

[14] 'What holds Europe together? Concluding remarks' by Kurt Biedenkopf, Bronislaw Geremek, Krzysztof Michalski and Michel Rocard, in Michalski (ed.), *What Holds Europe Together?*, p. 98.

[15] Ibid., p. 102.

[16] Ibid., p. 97.

[17] Ibid. Italics are in the original text.

[18] Ibid., p. 98.

[19] Ibid., p. 98. Italics are in the original text.

fixed, eternally defined, European boundaries, be they internal or external. Europe's boundaries ... must always be renegotiated. It is not geographical or national borders, then, that define the European cultural space—it is rather the latter which defines the European geographical space, a space that is in principle open.[20]

The first conclusion of the Reflection Group, then, appeared to be that European integration can mean in practice whatever the Europhile élites care to make it mean. The second conclusion, which served to enhance this vagueness, was that 'If the countries of Europe are to grow together into a viable political union, the people of Europe must be prepared for *European solidarity.*'[21] This solidarity, the Group maintained, entails readiness on the part of individuals voluntarily 'to open one's wallet and to commit one's life to others because they, too, are Europeans', and therefore cannot be imposed from above.[22] In this respect, needless to say, the Group was right. The trouble is, however, that solidarity of the intensely idealistic kind the Group's members envisaged is only ever to be achieved in a monastery, where wallets are non-existent and selfless commitment has religious underpinning: to apply it to European integration is merely to infuse politics with a quasi-religious rhetoric and an unattainable goal.[23]

There was little in the Reflection Group's deliberations about the nature of European integration, then, to provide a realistic answer to the question of what kind of Europe is to be created by the integration project, and even less which echoed Kedourie's hostility to arbitrary power and concern for constitutionalism. For this reason Kedourie would, or so I like to think, have looked favourably on an attempt to move beyond the highly restricted debate within the ranks of the Europhile political élites to the wider debate about the nature of European unity amongst

[20] 'What holds Europe together? Concluding remarks' by Biedenkopf, Geremek, Michalski and Rocard, p. 98.
[21] Ibid., p. 99.
[22] Ibid.
[23] For other contributions to the debate about the nature of the integration project during the years before the draft constitution and Reform Treaty, see for example: H. Friese and Peter Wagner, 'Survey article: the nascent political philosophy of the European polity', *The Journal of Political Philosophy*, 10/3 (2002), 342–64; Deirdre M. Curtin, *Postnational Democracy: The European Union in Search of a Political Philosophy* (The Hague, 1997); A. Weale and M. Nentwich (eds.), *Political Theory and the European Union: Legitimacy, Constitutional Choice and Citizenship* (London, 1998); Richard Bellamy and Dario Castiglione, 'Democracy, sovereignty and the constitution of the European Union: the republican alternative to liberalism', pp. 170–90, in Z. Bankowski and A. Scott (eds.), *The European Union and Its Order* (Oxford, 2000).

European intellectuals in the decades since 1945. Whether he would have been pleased by the outcome remains, of course, a matter for speculation. I should add that I will only be concerned with intellectually substantial contributions to this debate, so that brief ones, like Winston Churchill's call for the establishment of a United States of Europe in 1946, for example, will not be considered. Attention will mainly be restricted, moreover, to models of West European integration, with only passing reference to the discussion of pan-European integration which has occurred since the end of the Cold War.

With these limitations in mind, I want to turn now to the five main visions of European unity that have provided the framework for the post-war intellectual debate. The principal criticisms of the integration project by Eurosceptic contributors to the debate will then be examined. Finally, I will return to Kedourie's concern about the future of constitutional politics and consider from this point of view which vision, or visions, of European unity are especially relevant for the likely future course of the integration project.

The five main visions

1. The rational/bureaucratic vision

The first may be termed the rational/bureaucratic vision of European unity, of which Robert Schuman, Jean Monnet and Jacques Delors are the best known proponents. The most ambitious philosophical version of this vision, however, was developed by George Santayana in *Dominations and Powers*, which was published shortly after the Second World War.[24] In that book, Santayana argued that Europe's greatest need was for what he termed a 'liberal empire', characterised by a universal government which would be better suited to modern industrial societies than those of democratic nation-states. Since elements of this vision remain suggestive at the present day, it is worth asking what led Santayana to advocate a supranational liberal empire.

Santayana had particularly in mind a consideration which went far beyond the prevention of war and economic cooperation which preoccupied contemporaries like Monnet and Schuman. This was the belief that modern liberal democracy is doomed to self-destruction because it has no

---

[24] G. Santayana, *Dominations and Powers* (London, 1951).

conception of what he termed 'vital liberty'—of a rational good, that is, which takes into account the objective conditions of human existence. Instead, liberal democracy pursues only 'vacant liberty', which permits the pursuit of any ends, no matter how destructive of well-being they may be. More precisely, the liberal democratic ideal of 'vacant liberty' mistakenly attributes to the self a spiritual essence which can exist independently of matter. In addition, it rests on a mistaken belief in the power of the state to implement any ideals that liberal democratic politicians may adopt. To this may be added an equally mistaken tendency to assume that democratic self-government automatically means good government. Finally, modern liberal democracies entertain the absurd belief that the good society is one in which power will be replaced by the rule of reason.[25]

The aim of the liberal empire is to replace these self-destructive beliefs by a post-democratic system of rational government which will display three features. The first is the restriction of government to ensuring security, promoting prosperity and regulating economic activity. The inner spiritual world of moral and religious beliefs, in other words, will be free from government intervention. The second feature of the liberal empire, Santayana maintains, will be rule by an administrative élite, since parliaments cannot be trusted to govern in the rational way that vital liberty requires. Although administrative rule will necessarily be autocratic, Santayana adds, it will not be totalitarian since the administrative experts will be tolerant of every kind of spiritual diversity.[26] In particular, they will reject ideology of any kind, since this is incompatible with the impartiality they must display.[27] Finally, the choice of rulers for the liberal empire cannot be by democratic election, since that would merely perpetuate the various illusions just mentioned. Instead, the experts will be co-opted on a purely meritocratic basis from the members of each branch of the civil service, in much the same way that appointments and promotions are made in armies, banks, universities and church hierarchies.[28]

Ignoring other difficulties for the moment, what Santayana does not explain very convincingly is how the rule of administrative experts is to be legitimated for the demos of the liberal empire. He claims that all the political organs of the society will be accepted as representative provided

---

[25] I have given a fuller account of Santayana's critique of liberal democracy in N. O'Sullivan, *Santayana* (St Albans, 1992).
[26] Santayana, *Dominations and Powers*, p. 435.
[27] Ibid.
[28] Ibid., p. 382.

they reflect a consensus amongst the populace, rather in the way that Plato's philosopher rulers (whom Santayana himself does not mention) may claim to represent the citizens of their polis. The problem, however, is that a consensus may be extremely difficult to create in a modern liberal empire characterised by cultural diversity on a scale with which Plato did not have to cope. Santayana also claims that the political organs will be accepted as representative because citizens will appreciate the rationality of the policies they pursue. Unfortunately, the rationality of policies never guarantees consent to them since one of the most marked features of the human race ever since Adam and Eve has been an inability to agree on what is rational.

The echoes of Plato in Santayana's vision of a liberal empire may provoke the question of whether he intended it to be anything more than idealistic speculation. Santayana's answer is that there have been several occasions when something akin to the kind of liberal empire he envisaged has been created. In the ancient world, the Roman Empire is the out-standing example, from which Santayana drew the unsurprising lesson that a liberal empire can only be established by 'an exceptionally gifted and moralized community'.[29] So far as the modern world is concerned, Santayana concluded that neither Britain, nor the then USSR, nor the USA could provide the kind of rational leadership once offered by Rome in a form appropriate to earlier times. British imperial rule, for example, displayed too much high-handed contempt for subject peoples; in the Soviet case, the official communist ideology was in reality a formula for domination rather than for liberation; and in the American case, the USA tended to be too ready to identify its own commercial interests with the good of those over whom it exercised any influence. Santayana did not, in short, take seriously the possibility that any Continental European state could provide the kind of rational system of supranational rule he thought the post-1945 era required.

Even if the difficulty of identifying and legitimating a modern élite capable of creating a liberal empire is ignored, Santayana's version of the rational/bureaucratic model still presents two major problems. The first concerns his interpretation of modern European history as a history of 'vacant' freedom. The objection to this is that it risks caricaturing a long line of defenders of freedom during the past three centuries, from John Locke, through Constant and de Tocqueville to Michael Oakeshott, all of

---

[29] Ibid., p. 435.

whom were defending *civil* freedom, not vacant freedom. Civil freedom, it will be remembered, is freedom from arbitrary power. By its very nature, this kind of freedom is indeed 'vacant' in the sense that it does not imply a conception of the rational life of the kind Santayana wishes to defend. Yet civil freedom is nevertheless the condition for human dignity in the modern European world, and Santayana's failure to distinguish it from vacant freedom therefore leaves him open, as was just said, to the charge of misrepresenting the modern European constitutional tradition.

The second problem concerns Santayana's conception of 'vital' or rational freedom. For the sake of argument, let us grant that Santayana is right to hold that the Western world has naïvely believed for two centuries that democracy, science and prosperity would automatically bring individual happiness and social harmony. Let us also assume that we now know better and appreciate the need for something close to what Santayana terms 'vital' or rational freedom. The point is that it would be foolish to turn to governments of any kind, whether national or supranational, to create vital liberty for us, since to do so conflicts with the fundamental maxim of political prudence. This maxim was formulated by Hume with extraordinary clarity in a single sentence. Political writers, Hume wrote,

> have established it as a maxim that, in contriving any system of government, and fixing the several checks and controls of the constitution, every man ought to be supposed [to be] a *knave*, and to have no other end, in all his actions, than private interest.[30]

As Santayana's thought makes clear, then, the rational/bureaucratic vision is difficult to reconcile with constitutional government because it leaves the constitutional commitment entirely to the discretion of the administrative élite. To dream of rule by the wise and the good has always been tempting, but those who do so cannot complain if the outcome reveals their folly.

2. The organic vision

At the opposite extreme to the rational/bureaucratic vision is what may be termed the organic one. Although this is the least viable vision of

---

[30] D. Hume, 'Of the independency of Parliament', in *Essays Moral, Political and Literary* (London, 1963), p. 40. Italics in the original.

European unity, it is instructive to consider precisely why any attempt to implement this vision is bound to be disastrous.

The organic vision was originally inspired by a yearning for a return to the spiritual unity of the medieval era, understood as a time when Europe was identified with 'Christendom' and possessed a unity within which social and religious identity were fused and the principle of hierarchy was taken for granted at both human and cosmic levels. Whether the medieval world actually possessed an organic unity of this kind is irrelevant at present: all that matters is that during the Enlightenment an ideal conception of Christendom of this kind became the object of romantic nostalgia for thinkers disturbed by the rise of individualism, by the mediocrity they associated with the advent of mass society, and by what they considered to be the soul-destroying consequences of the new industrial division of labour. Echoes of this reactionary response to Western modernity, of which Novalis provides a striking early instance, have remained alive until the present day.[31]

If we jump now to the post-1945 decades, the main interest of latterday defenders of the organic vision lies in their attempts to rework it in secular terms. From this point of view, two particular reformulations of the organic vision merit consideration. One is by the Italian thinker, Julius Evola. Although Evola is associated with the extreme right of Italian politics, his thought illustrates the difficulties which any attempt to update the organic vision is bound to encounter. Evola's starting-point is a critique of the state-based form of nationalism which has dominated modern European history. To it he opposes what he considers to be a more genuine, European-wide form of suprastate nationalism. Defenders of the state-based form, he maintains, have a completely mistaken historical understanding of how European states actually acquired political unity. Far from being due to the rise of nationalism, Evola holds, state unification was largely the creation of dynastic considerations. Only when this has been fully appreciated will it be possible for Europeans to acknowledge that state-based nationalism is parasitic upon a deeper tradition of European unity that is at once spiritual and supranational. As soon as this realisation has finally dawned, Europeans will at last understand that nation, homeland and ethnic group

> subsist at an essentially naturalistic 'physical' level [and that] Europe (*Europa una*) should be something more than this. . . . The European Imperium will

[31] On Novalis, see B. Haywood, *Novalis: the Veil of Imagery: a Study of the Poetic Works of Friedrich von Hardenburg* ('s-Gravenhage, 1959).

> belong to a higher order than the parts which compose it, and to be European should be conceived as being something qualitatively different from being Italian, Prussian, Basque, Finnish, Scottish or Hungarian, something which appeals to a different aspect of our character.[32]

The 'higher order' European national identity which Evola defends in this passage is highly militant in that 'A European *nation* implies the levelling and cancelling of all "rival" nations in or beyond Europe.'[33] Within the European world, however, the organic nature of European nationalism is perfectly compatible with national cultural differences since it does not seek to destroy them but only to combine them in a higher unity.[34] The problem, however, lies in defining what the European spiritual essence into which the various existing nationalisms are to be combined actually is.

Evola fully acknowledges this problem: everyone, he notes, 'has their own idea about what European culture is . . .'.[35] This does not, however, create any uncertainty in his own mind about the 'true' nature of European spiritual identity. What is striking about his interpretation of it is that he rejects Christianity in favour of a Nietzschean reading of western history which characterises it in terms of what he calls 'the great European political Tradition', with Tradition always written with an upper case 'T'.[36] This Tradition was based on aristocratic warrior values and a hierarchically structured social order. In order to undo the damage done to it by democracy and recover lost spiritual values, Evola maintains, what is necessary is a radical programme of spiritual renewal. In what is, in effect, a right-wing version of Leninism, he wrote that this renewal requires that an aristocratic revolutionary élite should lead 'a revolt against the modern world in favour of what is nobler, higher, more truly *human*'.[37]

As Evola's version of the organic vision makes clear, it is impossible to identify a supranational European essence without introducing contestable moral commitments like his own Nietzschean ones. It has

---

[32] J. Evola, 'United Europe: the spiritual prerequisite', *Scorpion*, 9 (1986), 18–20; quoted in R. Griffin (ed.), *Fascism* (Oxford, 1995), p. 343.

[33] Ibid.

[34] On essentialism as applied to European identity, see for example G. Delanty, 'The limits and possibilities of a European identity: a critique of cultural essentialism', in *Philosophy and Social Criticism*, 21/4 (1995), 15–36.

[35] Evola, 'United Europe'; quoted in Griffin (ed.), *Fascism*, p. 344.

[36] Ibid., p. 318.

[37] Ibid., p. 344.

recently been argued, however, that this difficulty can be avoided by defining the European essence in a purely formal way which avoids any reference to substantive characteristics. This strategy has been adopted, in particular, by Rémi Brague, who has provided the second reformulation of the organic vision I want to consider. For Brague, the true European essence is an openness to otherness imparted by Rome, rather than by Greece and Christianity. More specifically, what Europe owes to its Roman heritage is not cultural creativity of any kind but the ability, rather, to absorb the cultural creativity of others in a dialectical spirit. Even if Brague's formal version of the essence of the European tradition is accepted, however, it dilutes the concept of a European cultural identity so much that, in the modern world at least, it no longer has sufficient political appeal to establish a supranational organic society. If Rome once managed to do that, it was because there was, within the empire, a profound fear of invasion by the barbarians and an imperial religion. Without those twin supports, the organic vision of European integration is no longer viable. Mention of the integrating effect of the barbarian enemy at the gate leads naturally, however, to the third vision of integration, for which the existence of an enemy is fundamental.

3. The 'conflictual' vision of European unity

The third vision of European unity is based on a possibility that Europhile thinkers have often been reluctant to consider. This is the possibility that any attempt to create a pan-European identity may be unable to avoid what Anthony Smith has called 'the logic of cultural exclusion'. By this Smith means the danger 'of an increasingly affluent, stable, conservative but undemocratic European federation, facing, and protecting itself from, the demands and needs of groupings of states in Africa, Asia and Latin America'. To some extent, Smith adds, this prospect 'is still mitigated by the remaining ex-colonial ties between certain European and certain African or Asian states', but if the European project achieves its political goals, it will 'also entail, not just economic exclusion, but also cultural differentiation and with it the possibility of cultural and racial exclusion'.[38]

Smith himself did not spell out the theoretical basis of the broader conception of political identity which underlies what may be termed the

[38] A. D. Smith, 'National identity and the idea of European unity', *International Affairs*, 68/1 (1992), 76.

'conflictual' vision. For that, it is necessary to turn to Carl Schmitt, who developed it in its most rigorous theoretical form. According to Schmitt, political unity does not rest on consensus, as progressive thinkers have maintained, but on conflict. More precisely, political unity can only ever be constituted by the relation between Friend and Foe.[39] Only the awareness of an enemy, in other words, creates maximum group solidarity. Applied to the current situation of the European Union, this means in particular that the disappearance of the Soviet Union as the significant European 'other' has made a European political identity of any kind unattainable until a new enemy is found. Reflecting on this theme, Ole Waever concluded a thoughtful essay on the European idea since 1945 by remarking that even though 'A very strong differentiation against an external other might not materialize . . . we can hardly expect not to see a certain increase in comparisons between Europe and, for instance, the Middle East.'[40]

From the standpoint of European integration, then, the spirit of liberal triumphalism in which the end of the Cold War was greeted was premature, since the unforeseen longer-term outcome may be a deepening crisis of European identity. As Mark Mazower observed, it is no longer clear, in particular, whether Europe is part of the 'West', or is a western outcrop of 'Eurasia', or both, or neither.[41] The response of the USA to its own version of the post Cold War identity crisis indicates the kind of danger that may result, which is that a neo-conservative 'war against terror' may be waged in which no enemy can be clearly identified. The attraction of this new style of 'war' is that the objective can be opportunistically defined to suit the government's electoral needs.

How much weight should be given to Schmitt's stress on the role of the Foe in political integration? This question can best be answered by considering the precise source of Schmitt's pessimism, which is his assumption that the only genuine form of political unity is the intense sense of solidarity that arises during war. To model political and social order on war, however, is an entirely arbitrary restriction of the concept of solidarity, since a less extreme kind is possible provided that we accept the complexity and messiness which peacetime brings with it.

---

[39] C. Schmitt, *The Concept of the Political* (New Brunswick, NJ, 1976).
[40] In K. Wilson and Jan van der Dussen (eds.), *The History of the Idea of Europe* (London, 1995), p. 209.
[41] M. Mazower, *Dark Continent: Europe's Twentieth Century* (London, 1998), pp. xiv–xv.

In one respect, however, the Schmittian conflictual vision is surely correct. This is that the end of the Cold War not only means that Europe has lost its 'significant other' but that it also confronts a radical change in its relation to the USA. More precisely, the end of the Cold War meant that Europe and the USA no longer automatically shared a common identity as fellow inhabitants of 'the West'. One result of this was spelt out clearly by Robert Kagan when he remarked that Europe must now accept the need to provide for its own defence, since it can no longer take for granted that it will be nursed through foreign crises by the American security umbrella, as it was for many decades after 1945.[42] Indeed, the possibility has now arisen that Europe and the USA might in future become bitter opponents, as US relations with France and Germany over the Iraq war of 2003 indicated.

Although the conflictual theory of political identity has been too closely based—at least in Schmitt's version of it—on wartime solidarity, then, it nevertheless provides a sobering reminder of realities which Europhile optimism may easily overlook.

4. The postmodern vision

Since the need to accommodate increasing cultural and social diversity is one of the principal challenges facing the European integration project, postmodern political theory is of especial relevance since its proponents have tended to celebrate diversity of every kind. In one form, this celebration of diversity is evident in the postmodern 'deconstruction' of what Lyotard termed the great 'metanarratives' of the western tradition. In another, it is also evident in the postmodern 'decentring' of the classical liberal-democratic image of the self, according to which each individual has a single core identity. According to the latter aspect of postmodern theory, every self is multiple, and the impression of unity is based on illusion. The work of Jacques Lacan embodies this conception of identity in a psychoanalytic form, that of Derrida in a philosophical one. What is mainly relevant in the present context, however, is not the subtleties of postmodern theories of identity but only the fact that they have promoted a positive response to what Ole Waever has described as 'the more general multiplication of identities' in Europe since the 1980s. These identities, Waever adds, are now seen as 'less fixed, less capable of being

---

[42] R. Kagan, *Paradise and Power: America and Europe in the New World Order* (London, 2003), p. 54.

reduced to a single dimension, or [to] one set of loyalty relationships'.[43] In this respect, the postmodern theory of the multiple self has served to reinforce the need for complex, multi-layered governance of a kind which will be considered below, in connection with contemporary visions of a republican Europe. What matters at present, however, is Waever's optimistic speculation that the new sense of multiple identities may prove particularly relevant in Eastern Europe, where it may help to check any revival of nationalism by strengthening a sense of multiple local, regional and supranational identities.[44]

There is, however, one great problem created by postmodern sympathy for multiple personal identities for which its more optimistic defenders have offered no satisfactory answer. This is that complex identities bring levels of personal stress that may be unacceptable to many Europeans. As Waever acknowledges, it may be excessively idealistic to assume that many individuals would welcome juggling increasingly complex national, European and global issues. Instead of promoting a deeper sense of European citizenship, he notes, the danger is that the burdens of a complicated personal identity may encourage the re-emergence of extremist ideologies, like neo-Nazism in Germany, which offer to remove the burden of complex identities by offering highly simplified ones that transfer political responsibility from the individual to a charismatic leader.[45]

5. The 'civil association' vision of European unity

The last vision of European unity I will consider is the civil vision. According to this vision, which was originally developed at national level by Hobbes and has been reformulated by a long line of thinkers down to the present, the key to political unity in highly diverse, modern social and cultural conditions is a formal or procedural concept of integration. More precisely, in the civil vision the source of civic integration is not identified with common cultural values, or a substantive ideal of community, or a shared ideology or religion, but with a body of rules recognised to possess sovereign authority.

For the European Union, an important attraction of this vision is that its formal nature means that it can accommodate cultural and social

---

[43] Ole Waever, in Wilson and van der Dussen (eds.), *The History of the Idea of Europe*, pp. 197–8.
[44] Ibid., p. 198.
[45] Ibid., pp. 207–8.

diversity. What divides Europhiles, however, is the fact that the basic requirements of the civil model can be interpreted in at least two different ways. One, which is the classical Hobbesian interpretation, approaches civil association 'from above', maintaining that the basic requirement is a single, centralised sovereign with absolute power to issue commands to its subjects. The other interpretation, which has been developed in the contemporary period by thinkers like Jürgen Habermas, rejects imposition from above in favour of a democratic approach which rests on a radically revised republican conception of sovereignty. Which of these two versions—the Hobbesian or the republican—is likely to prove the most viable for purposes of the integration project is perhaps the greatest question taxing Europhile theorists at the present time.

In order to make the civil model fit the European Union, which does not possess sovereignty of the classical Hobbesian kind, European officials have argued that civil association only requires cross-national acknowledgement of supranational rules and institutions as authoritative. It has been argued, in particular, that this rule-based version of the civil model corresponds closely to one of the most important features of the integration project, which is the development from the outset of a highly juridical style of politics. During the first eight years, for example, when only the Coal and Steel Community existed, the predecessor of the present European Court, the Court of Justice of the European Communities, 'handed down well over 100 binding decisions involving Community officials, member governments and business enterprises—large and small'. Never before, Stuart Scheingold has observed, had national governments 'undertaken and fulfilled such widespread "international" legal commitments'.[46]

The outcome of this development, which has been aptly termed 'governing with judges',[47] is described by its defenders as a novel kind of supranational constitutionalism completely unforeseen by early theorists of civil association like Hobbes. In this form of civil association, Alec Stone explains, 'The European Court of Justice, the constitutional court of the EC, has fashioned a kind of supra-national constitution [which] binds . . . governments and the parliaments they control. European politics is today, in part, constitutional politics.'[48] Two qualifications, however,

---

[46] S. A. Scheingold, *The Rule of Law in European Integration* (Westport, CT, 1976), p. vii.

[47] A. Stone, 'Governing with judges: the New Constitutionalism', in J. Hayward and E. Page (eds.), *Governing the New Europe* (Cambridge, 1995), p. 286. Italics in the original.

[48] Ibid., p. 286. Italics in the original.

must immediately be made about the nature and extent of this constitutional development. The first is that it is naturally somewhat precarious, since the judges have only limited power to take the initiative in situations in which powerful political and economic considerations conflict with their endeavours to secure the rule of law.[49] The second is that the kind of constitutionalism which has developed suits the Europhile political élites because it is perfectly compatible with administrative government. This, however, has left the new constitutionalism open to the charge of lacking democratic legitimation.

In response to this charge, the EU has argued that, appearances notwithstanding, the new supranational constitutionalism is in some sense democratic. To make this case was a central concern, for example, of the European Commission's 2001 *White Paper on European Governance*.[50] Although the extent to which the White Paper represented the Commission's view as a whole may be questioned, the contention it advanced at least had the merit of provoking reflection on the concept of 'governance' as a means of clarifying the nature of EU sovereignty. The juridical version of supranational civil association is democratic, the White Paper maintained, in the sense that it abandons the old Hobbesian concept of sovereignty in favour of a new, non-centralised and highly pluralist kind. In particular, the White Paper argued that this new kind is no longer 'top down' since it reflects the development 'from below' of multi-level, cross national forms of rule which it terms, in the title of the White Paper itself, 'governance'—a complex kind of rule, that is, in which individual member states share sovereignty instead of monopolising it as they used to do, in accordance with the old Hobbesian model.[51]

To what extent is the EU entitled to interpret the advent of governance as democratising the juridical model of civil association? The most telling objection to this claim is that governance has not altered the lack of political accountability of the EU ruling élite. On the contrary, it remains easy for the élite to evade parliamentary scrutiny by simply moving controversial issues into areas where no formal provisions for accountability exist.[52] Nevertheless, several distinguished Europhile

---

[49] See Scheingold, *The Rule of Law in European Integration*.

[50] European Commission, *European Governance: a White Paper*, COM (2001) 0428.

[51] Ibid., pp. 4 and 8.

[52] D. Wincott, 'Does the European Union pervert democracy? Questions of democracy in New Constitutionalist thought on the future of Europe', in Bankowski and Scott (eds.), *The European Union and its Order*, p. 123.

political theorists have defended the EU's claim to have democratised the old Hobbesian 'top down' model of civil association by pointing to the emergence of many new, complex kinds of multi-level and cross-national public realms that are encouraging widespread political participation amongst EU citizens. The result, they claim, is nothing less than an emergent form of European republicanism. In Britain, the most eloquent defender of a new European republicanism is Richard Bellamy, whose thought will be considered shortly.[53] Before doing so, however, it will be useful to consider the attempt made by Jürgen Habermas to construct a European version of republican theory, since he is the most influential representative of this school of thought.

The starting-point for Habermas's republican vision of European unity is his contention that no modern political unit can have a 'natural' or pre-political basis of the kind invoked by nationalist and democratic theorists during the eighteenth and nineteenth centuries. During that time, what was taken for granted was the existence of 'the people' as a coherent unit which comprises the nation, makes constitutions and tries to get its wishes expressed through political institutions of various kinds. Due to increasing social pluralism and the collapse of traditional ideas of social and political hierarchy, however, the old pre-political concept of the people is no longer relevant to modern politics. Now, every political identity, whether national or supranational, must be an artificial identity, in the sense that it must be consciously constructed through democratic participation in a public realm which permits universal and equal involvement in the formation of a rational political will grounded on universally valid ethical principles.

It is because Habermas believes that Europeans are now finally ready, after two traumatic centuries of internal and external conflict, to detach their political identity from the naturalistic, pre-political foundations formerly associated with it that he believes it can be given a universalist character. These principles, which Habermas deems to be implicit in non-instrumental forms of communication, are made explicit in constitutional democracies based on the rule of law. It is this belief in the radically artificial, or 'constructed', character of modern political identity which has inspired in particular Habermas's attempt to extend his ideal of

[53] R. Bellamy, 'Citizenship beyond the nation-state: the case of Europe', in N. O'Sullivan (ed.), *Political Theory in Transition* (London, 2000), p. 106.

constitutional patriotism from the domestic German context to the European one.[54]

Critics of Habermas have questioned in particular his conviction that political legitimacy requires a commitment to universal principles at both national and supranational level. Charles Turner, for example, has argued that Habermas's universalist sympathies were originally tailored specifically for a very special situation, viz. the situation in the post-1945 Federal Republic, when it was impossible to defend the 1949 Basic Law in terms which made any reference to Germany's past history of militant nationalism.[55] In this condition, Habermas regarded it as axiomatic that a German democrat required an essentially ahistorical political vocabulary completely purged of elements that contained even the slightest hint of Nazi exclusionism. The problem, however, is that Habermas's transference of his universalist sympathies from the German to the European context, in the form of what Habermas terms a 'European constitutional patriotism', exaggerates the extent to which traditional, pre-political elements have disappeared from other western polities. More generally, Anthony Smith, echoing Burke, has argued that in every state a sense of political solidarity continues to require a shared body of non-rational symbols, myths and rituals that cannot possibly be provided by the kind of rational discourse Habermas has in mind.[56] Without these, any political identity, whether national or supranational, will be too 'thin' and emotionally vacuous to provide a foundation for unity. In the case of European political identity, as Smith puts it, there is no European equivalent

> to Bastille or Armistice Day, no European ceremony for the fallen in battle, no European shrine of kings or saints. When it comes to the ritual and ceremony of collective identification there is no European equivalent of national or religious community. Any research into the question of forging, or even discovering, a possible European identity cannot afford to overlook these central issues.[57]

---

[54] See in particular: J. Habermas, 'The postnational constellation and the future of democracy', in *The Postnational Constellation* (Oxford, 2001); also his article, 'A constitution for Europe?' in *New Left Review*, 11 (Sept./Oct. 2001), 5–26. Also of interest is his earlier article, 'Citizenship and national identity: some reflections on the future of Europe', *Praxis International*, 12/1 (1992), 1–19.
[55] C. Turner, 'Jürgen Habermas: European or German?', *European Journal of Political Theory*, 3/3 (July 2004), 293–4.
[56] A. D. Smith, 'National identity and the idea of European unity', *International Affairs*, 68/1 (1992).
[57] Ibid., p. 73.

To this, Habermas's reply would be that Smith's position is too closely tied to the nineteenth-century development of the nation-state, with the result that he ignores the new forms of European social cohesion to which Habermas has drawn attention. In a recent work, *The Divided West* (2006), for example, Habermas has emphasised that any suggestion that his ideal of constitutional patriotism is merely an appeal to abstract principles is nothing more than 'a tendentious misrepresentation [by] opponents who would prefer something palpably national'. Every collective identity, he adds, 'even a postnational one, is much more concrete than the ensemble of moral, legal and political principles around which it crystallizes'.[58] Amongst the 'concrete' aspects Habermas includes welfare benefits, without which he concedes that constitutional patriotism would be too 'thin' an identity to evoke popular support. Since European member states operate wholly different welfare schemes, however, it is unrealistic to assume (quite apart from the sheer cost) that there could be a single model of economic and social unity acceptable to them all. More fundamental, however, is the criticism of Gadamer, for whom Habermas's conception of what is 'concrete' would still be far too abstract, even if substantive benefit were provided, since tradition alone can claim a genuinely concrete character.[59] In addition, Niklas Luhmann has pointed out that in the modern world there simply is no universally rational vantage point of the kind Habermas seeks, since 'The theorist of cognition himself becomes a rat in the labyrinth and must consider from which position he observes the other rats.'[60]

Most telling of all, perhaps, is the charge that Habermas greatly exaggerates the extent to which political conflict can be dealt with by democratic debate. Santayana, for example, incisively stated the sceptical point of view when he insisted, during Habermas's youth, that 'In a hearty and sound democracy all questions at issue must have been silently agreed upon and taken for granted when the democracy arose . . ..'[61] Above all, Santayana would have been especially puzzled by Habermas's conviction that universal democratic participation in an ideal speech situation would promote harmony. Even if the communicative transparency supposed to be produced by this produces perfect mutual understanding, such understanding may intensify mutual hatred—as it did between God and Satan

[58] J. Habermas, *The Divided West* (Cambridge, 2006), p. 53.
[59] H.-G. Gadamer, *Truth and Method* (London, 1988), esp. Second Part, Section 11.
[60] N. Luhmann, *Erkenntis als Konstruktion* (Bern, 1988), p. 24.
[61] G. Santayana, *Character and Opinion in the United States* (New York, 1956), pp. 127–8.

and still sometimes does between disillusioned lovers—rather than yield harmony.

In the face of these criticisms, supporters of Habermas's republican vision of European unity have defended his belief in the integrating power of the new kinds of public realm at every level of European life by reformulating his thought in less abstractly rationalist terms. In Britain, for example, Richard Bellamy has re-worked Habermas's republican conception of European political identity in the form of a universalist ideal of 'cosmopolitan communitarianism'.[62] Only this ideal, Bellamy maintains, can ground a political system suitable for a pluralist polity like the European one, in which 'European citizens belong to multiple *demoi* that reflect their varying communitarian attachments (some, but not all, of which either transcend or operate below the national community), whilst ensuring that the ways in which they deliberate meet cosmopolitan norms of fairness.'[63] It is vital, Bellamy adds, to recognise that this kind of political integration is not an autonomous process but one which extends into the sphere of society and culture, since its aim is nothing less than a transformation of the sense of European identity in a way which extends and deepens it. Echoing Habermas, he maintains that for this we need a new, more political conception of constitutionalism than classical liberal theory provides. This new constitutionalism will be 'of republican inspiration', linking the rule of law to the distribution of power in a way alien to liberal democratic theory.[64]

Although Bellamy's version of European republicanism echoes that of Habermas in some respects, it differs greatly in avoiding Habermas's quest for universal rational foundations. More modestly, Bellamy appeals instead to the Roman republican ideal of freedom from arbitrary domination developed in contemporary republican political theory.[65] Nevertheless, even Bellamy's subtle theorising cannot avoid a number of major difficulties which apply to every attempt to apply a republican version of civil association to the politics of the European Union—difficulties arising in each instance from the intensely idealistic nature of the republican project. One is that proponents of European republicanism

---

[62] Bellamy, 'Citizenship beyond the nation-state: the case of Europe', in O'Sullivan (ed.), *Political Theory in Transition*, p. 103.

[63] Ibid., p. 104

[64] Ibid.

[65] See P. Pettit, *Republicanism: A Theory of Freedom and Government* (Oxford, 1997), and Q. Skinner, 'The republican ideal of political liberty', in M. Rosen and J. Wolff (eds.), *Political Thought* (Oxford, 1999).

neglect the fact that the new multi-level, cross-national public realms which they welcome are often little more than interest groups of various kinds. Another is that even if the new public realms provide a more genuine sense of European citizenship than this allows, the sheer complexity of the politics they create may discourage rather than encourage active political participation.[66] More generally, the republican version of civil association, as Constant remarked long ago, assumes a popular desire for political participation of which there is little evidence at national level and still less at European level. Finally, European republicanism presents a major financial problem, insofar as its proponents usually acknowledge that it will only be viable if it incorporates a commitment to welfare provision. As Habermas expresses it, 'Democratic citizenship can only realize its integrative potential—that is, it can only found solidarity among strangers—if it proves itself as a mechanism that actually realizes the material conditions of preferred forms of life.'[67] For many of the poorer member states of the European Union, this must be a pipe dream, on any significant scale. Even for the more prosperous ones, the resources for welfare provision fall increasingly far short of expectations. Implementation of the social aspect of the republican vision is hardly helped, moreover, by the fact that British opposition has ensured that the EU, thus far at least, has no power to tax for that purpose.

Although powerful arguments have been made in favour of a republican interpretation of the 'civil' vision of European integration, then, they do not provide a convincing case for interpreting the outcome of the integration project, thus far at least, as a new, supranational republic. It will be useful, however, to balance the critique of Habermas by noticing two wholly tenable features of his 'civil' vision of European political identity. One is his recognition that European citizenship cannot be based upon a substantive ideal of community, whether cultural, religious or other, but must rest on a shared commitment to formal constitutional principles of the kind which only the civil vision provides. Only thus can the sheer diversity of European cultures and social orders be accommodated. The other tenable feature of Habermas's thought about a European civil identity is his recognition that it cannot be imposed from above, but must be spontaneously expressed through different national cultures and

[66] P. Magnette, 'European governance and civic participation: beyond elitist citizenship?', *Political Studies*, 51 (2003), 144–60, at p. 150.
[67] J. Habermas, 'The European nation-state: on the past and future of sovereignty and citizenship', *Public Culture*, 10/2 (1998), 409.

traditions.[68] What is problematic is not these two contentions but the elaborate rationalist underpinnings of Habermas's ideal of European constitutional patriotism.

Since the republican vision of civil association seems too idealistic to provide a plausible vision of the course of the integration project, it will be useful to consider briefly a more realistic version. The most instructive thinker in this case is Friedrich Hayek, whose political writings reveal an ambiguity at the heart of the alternative version of civil association which will, I want to suggest, be the principal reason why constitutionalism is unlikely to find a secure place in the future development of the integration project.

In an article written as the Second World War began, Hayek argued for an interstate federation on the ground that 'the abrogation of national sovereignties and the creation of an effective international order of law is a necessary complement [to] and the logical consummation of the liberal programme'.[69] In a later work, Hayek summarised the task of this liberal 'consummation' as that of 'limit[ing] the "popular will" without placing another "will" above it'.[70] Like Santayana's vision of a liberal empire, Hayek's vision identified the only political entity which could do this as a supranational civil association in which pluralism of every kind could prosper.[71] More precisely, Hayek described the federation as one which would simply provide 'a rational permanent framework within which individual initiative will have the largest possible scope'.[72] It would not, in other words, try to promote a common European cultural identity, or common European values of any kind. Neither would it promote democracy, whether in a republican or representative form. Its central commit-

---

[68] J. Habermas, 'Citizenship and national identity: some reflections on the future of Europe', *Praxis International*, 12/1 (1992), 1–19.

[69] F. Hayek, 'Economic conditions of inter-state federation', in *New Commonwealth Quarterly* (Sept. 1939), 146. I am indebted to Robert Bideleux for drawing my attention to this article.

[70] F. Hayek, *Law, Legislation and Liberty*, Vol. 1 (London, 1973), p. 6.

[71] For related theorising about supranational forms of civil association, see T. Nardin, *Law, Morality and the Relations of States* (Princeton, 1983). See also R. Bideleux, 'Civil association: The European Union as a supra-national liberal legal order', in M. Evans (ed.), *The Edinburgh Companion to Contemporary Liberalism* (Edinburgh, 2001), pp. 225–40; also 'What does it mean to be European? The problems of constructing a pan-European identity', in G. Timmins and M. Smith (eds.), *Uncertain Europe* (London, 2001), pp. 20–40; and 'The new politics of inclusion and exclusion: the limits and divisions of Europe', in A. Plesu and L. Boia (eds.), *Nation and National Ideology: Past, Present and Prospect* (Bucharest, 2002), pp. 28–40.

[72] Hayek, 'Economic conditions of inter-state federation', 141–3.

ment would instead be to the ideal of constitutional or limited government, since the citizens of the kind of federation he advocated 'will be
reluctant to submit to any interference in their daily lives when the government is composed of people of different nationalities and different
traditions'.

What must now be added is that this early exploration of the federal
ideal concealed an ambiguity in Hayek's conception of constitutionalism
which was referred to above but only became fully apparent in his later
work.[73] This is that what he valued about civil association was not so
much its intrinsic constitutional merits as its contribution (through the
free market) to the broader goal of human 'progress', conceived in part in
economic terms. Above all, what his vision always failed to provide was a
moral standpoint from which the intrinsic merits of constitutionalism
could be given priority over the functional ones. As a result, his version
of the civil vision, like that of the Europhile political élites, failed to provide any principled consideration for placing the rule of law above the
requirements of the market. More precisely, the problem created by this
ambiguous version of the civil ideal is that if economic growth falters and
rule by benign but arbitrary administrative power seems to offer more
effective means of restoring prosperity, there is no principled reason for
not succumbing to it. Although Hayek himself would have been appalled
by such an outcome, his constitutional philosophy provides no clear
means of resisting it. At the risk of banging the nail too hard, let me put
it yet another way: if an adverse economic situation occurred under pressure from globalisation, for example, Hayek's version of the civil vision
would provide no intellectual resources capable of underpinning the constitutional style of politics which Kedourie regarded as the distinctive
achievement of modern European politics. I have risked overemphasis
because the ambiguity in Hayek's conception of civil association is the
one which continues to lie at the heart of the integration project.

Sceptical responses to the unification project

Such, then, are the principal visions which have figured in the broader
intellectual debate about European unity since the Second World War.

---

[73] I have explored this ambiguity in detail in 'Visions of freedom: the response to totalitarianism', in J. Hayward, B. Barry, and A. Brown (eds.), *The British Study of Politics in the Twentieth
Century* (Oxford, 1999), pp. 72–9.

I will consider below what implications this analysis of them has for the future. Before doing that, however, I want to complete coverage of the post-war debate by considering very briefly the most pessimistic critics of the integration project. At the risk of failing to do anything like full justice to the critics, I shall concentrate in each case on highlighting the principal weaknesses of the position in question.

The most sceptical responses to the integration project come from three disparate schools of thought. One is Marxism.[74] The second consists of thinkers who emphasise the continuing tenacity of the hold of sovereign nation-states on European political experience. The third is a mixed group of thinkers who emphasise what may be called the dark side of the European integration project, both in relation to its past and its likely future.

1. Marxism

One of the most eloquent British exponents of Marxism, Alex Callinicos, formulated the Marxist critique of the integration project succinctly when he wrote that the emergence of a 'hybrid form of sovereignty' at EU level does not alter the underlying reality of intensifying capitalist development, facilitated by the removal of more and more restraints.[75] More generally, Callinicos contends, the EU and other leading international institutions—institutions, that is, such as the G-7, the IMF, the World Bank, the WTO and NATO—all 'operate in the interests of the United States and the other leading Western capitalist powers'.[76]

It is possible to offer a qualified defence of the integration project against this critique without any attempt to present the EU as an organisation free from serious blemishes. This cannot be done, however, simply by appealing, for example, to the EU human rights programme, the growth of regulative and juridical constraints on the market, or the social welfare dimension of EU aspirations, since all these aspects of the EU can readily be dismissed by Marxism as merely devices for making capitalist poison easier for the masses to swallow. The two great defects of Marxism lie elsewhere. One, as Elie Kedourie was fond of pointing out, is that the Marxist demonisation of capitalism relies ultimately on the

---

[74] Marxism is not synonymous with opposition to European integration, but in the present context attention will be confined to the Marxist critique of it.

[75] A. Callinicos, *Against the Third Way* (Cambridge, 2001), p. 138.

[76] Ibid., p. 99.

untenable assumption that capitalism is a zero sum game, in which the success of capitalists is always inevitably at someone else's expense. The problem for Marxism is that reality is more complex, since capitalist economic growth has benefited not only multinational capitalists but also large sections of the populations of the EU member states and is widely welcomed by them, so long at least as they continue to prosper.

Although Marxism may respond to this by dismissing the popularity of capitalism with the European masses as a form of 'false consciousness', this is merely to invoke a self-validating rhetorical device which insulates the Marxist from the need to confront facts which do not fit the dogmatic theory to which he subscribes. Nevertheless, there is an undeniable core of truth at the heart of Marxism, which is that capitalist production carries with it social and environmental costs that cannot be ignored. Dealing with those costs is, however, not helped by the second great weakness of Marxism, which is a dogmatically based appeal for revolution, despite the fact that this has only ever brought despotism to modern Europe.

2. The continuing primacy of the nation-state

In a polemical challenge to the orthodox Europhile interpretation of European history since 1945, according to which the predominant tendency is a movement away from the sovereignty of the nation-state towards European integration, Alan Milward has maintained that the basic reality of the post-war decades is the restoration of the nation-state to its central position in European political life. Nationally based experience, Milward maintains, has moulded European political life so profoundly that it is inconceivable that a supranational form of European unity can ever supplant it. To those who reply that there has surely been a significant surrender of national sovereignty since the Treaty of Rome, Milward's reply is that there has indeed been some surrender,[77] but that in a broader historical perspective this has been nothing more than a strategic device adopted for purely national ends.[78] The essence of post-1945 European history, in brief, is that nationally based democracy continues to be the primary reality of European political life.

It may immediately be conceded that Milward's interpretation of the integration project is quite plausible when restricted to its early stages,

---

[77] A. S. Milward, *The European Rescue of the Nation-State* (London, 1992), p. 4.
[78] Ibid., p. 45.

which can without much difficulty be interpreted in terms of the restoration of the nation-state.[79] By the 1980s, however, supranational European institutions had begun to take on a life of their own to such an extent that they could no longer be presented as an instrument of purely national purposes.[80] It does not follow from this, of course, that thereafter the nation-state ceased to be in many respects the basic unit of European life, but only that Milward's attempt to minimise the supranational dimension of the more recent stage of the integration project offers too much comfort to Eurosceptics.

3. The dark side of the integration project

The optimistic impression frequently created by Europhile publicists and politicians is that the post-1945 integration project is a continuation of the Enlightenment vision of a supranational legal order in which reason and morality replace national interest. This optimism has been severely bruised, however, by sceptics who have drawn attention to the less palatable origins of the integration project in fascist plans for European economic and political integration.[81] It would be a mistake, John Laughland has insisted, to dismiss the fascist vision as a militant one since in 1941 Hitler and Mussolini issued a joint communiqué which proclaimed that the fascist unification of Europe aimed at eliminating war from the European world.[82] It is true, of course, that this protestation of pacific intent must be taken with a pinch of salt, since Hitler and Mussolini naturally assumed that pacification would be presided over by fascist regimes. Scepticism of this kind is valuable, however, as an antidote to the naïve identification of the origins of the post-war integration project entirely with liberal and democratic values. Although this is a salutary historical reminder, it does not of course entail the absurd conclusion that the unification project is a fascist one.

There is, however, a second aspect of the post-1945 origins of the integration project which has provided ammunition for sceptics. This con-

---

[79] For an eloquent critique of Milward and a defence of the federalist case, see M. Burgess, *Federalism and European Union: The Building of Europe, 1950–2000* (London, 2000), pp. 56–76.
[80] R. Bideleux, '"Europeanisation" and the limits to democratisation in East-Central Europe', in G. Pridham and A. Ágh (eds.), *Prospects for Democratic Consolidation in East-Central Europe* (Manchester, 2001), p. 29.
[81] J. Laughland, *The Tainted Source: The Undemocratic Origins of the European Idea* (London, 1998), p. 12.
[82] Ibid., p. 19.

cerns the extent to which the European cooperation it required has depended on a widespread conspiracy of silence about the extent of European collusion with totalitarianism.[83] More specifically, Tony Judt has argued that the post-war ideal of European unity was from the beginning a fragile piece of myth-making which relied on minimising the post-war problems faced by defeated and occupied European states by attributing them entirely to German aggression in the first instance, and thereafter to Soviet aggression.[84] Only at a very late stage in post-Second World War history, Judt notes, did European countries finally begin to remove the veil of amnesia and face their past.[85] Only in the 1990s, for example, did the French ruling élite begin to confront the heritage of Vichy with any candour.[86] France was not alone in this amnesia: even in 1977, 'Not a single West German obituary made mention . . . of the fact that Hans-Martin Schleyer, chairman of the (West) German Confederation of Employers and victim of a terrorist attack, had made his fortune as the Nazi commander of a slave-labour factory in the eastern territories.'[87]

What Judt ignores, however, is the fact that there are two ways of interpreting the post-war story of Continental amnesia. Adenauer in West Germany, de Gaulle in France and de Gasperi in Italy all defended amnesia on the ground that it was the only way of consolidating support for post-war democratic regimes, as well as the only way of retaining a competent indigenous administrative class. Judt is right, nevertheless, to emphasise the danger created by official amnesia of oversimplifying post-war problems by attempting to explain them all as entirely the outcome of Nazi atrocities. He is no less right, moreover, to draw attention more recently to the problems presented by the reappearance of official amnesia in European states formerly occupied by the Soviet Union, insofar as they are tempted to attribute all their post-liberation problems to the part played in their history by the Soviet occupier.[88]

---

[83] See I. Deák, J. T. Gross, and T. Judt (eds.), *The Politics of Retribution in Europe* (Princeton, NJ, 2000). Judt is particularly concerned that non-German European nations were allowed by the Allies to pursue their own 'final solution' to the nationality problem by expelling their German minorities with little resistance.

[84] Ibid., p. 304.

[85] T. Judt, *The Times Literary Supplement*, 27 Feb. 1998.

[86] See A. Milward, *The Times Literary Supplement*, 14 Apr. 2000, 7.

[87] In R. Burns (ed.), *German Cultural Studies* (Oxford, 1995), p. 213.

[88] Ibid., p. 304.

What must now be added is that concern about the dark side of the integration project has not been confined to its past. In particular, misgivings about its future have been provoked by the indifference of the Europhile political élites to secularisation. Such misgivings are unsurprising when expressed by religious thinkers in countries like Italy and Central and Eastern Europe, where Catholicism remains widespread.[89] What is surprising, however, is a secular Nietzschean statement of pessimism which outdid Marxism in conjuring up the spectacle of a coming nihilism that will engulf not only the European Union but the whole globe. What is even more surprising is the fact that this occurred in England, where nihilism has always been in short supply.

In 1995, an eminent English academic, John Gray, ended an extended meditation on Heidegger by concluding that modern Western culture is now so totally pervaded by manipulative concerns that it must be completely abandoned.[90] A few years later, Gray attracted extensive publicity when he announced that the only hope lay in a spiritual revolution. The reasons for Gray's nihilistic view of the future included overpopulation, concern about the environment and misuse of diminishing resources, global warming, the spread of technologies of mass destruction, the growth of rogue or failed states, and the prospect of new epidemics.[91] Worst of all, Gray saw no realistic way of avoiding the coming doom: although he called for a spiritual revolution, he wrote that 'we can no more bring about [a spiritual and political] renewal by willing it than we can subject language to our purposes'.[92] It is possible, I think, to deal very shortly with this extreme pessimism, despite the immense learning with which it is defended. If it is well-founded, there are only two possible solutions: for the devout, there is prayer; for the rest of us, if we wish to remain cheerful, there is the chance to reread Rabelais (or Boccaccio, perhaps). There is not, I think, much else to be said.

What then is to be made of the sceptical contributions to the post-1945 debate about European integration, when they are taken as a whole? In each case, a genuine problem has been identified, but without yielding the conclusive case against the integration project which the critics set out

[89] On Italy, see for example the discussion of Augusto Del Noce's critique of secularisation by N. Bobbio, *Ideological Profile of Twentieth-Century Italy* (Princeton, NJ, 1990), pp. 165, 177–8, 200–1 (originally published in Italian in 1959). In the case of Central Europe, see for example the writings of V. Havel, *Living in Truth* (London, 1987).
[90] J. Gray, *Enlightenment's Wake* (London, 1995), p. 184.
[91] J. Gray, *Straw Dogs* (London, 2002).
[92] Gray, *Enlightenment's Wake*, p. 183.

to present. It is, nevertheless, particularly from those who recall the 'dark side' of the European past that two timely reminders may be derived about the limitations of the integration project. One is simply a reminder of the inescapable uncertainty of all political ventures to which Kedourie referred in his first book, when he alluded (with T. E. Lawrence especially in mind) to the constant possibility of the 'irruption into history of the uncontrollable force of a demonic will exerting itself to the limit of endurance'.[93] The other is that it would be foolish to think that the integration project somehow marked a completely new beginning, inspired by the dream that the dark past could in due course be replaced by a utopia of human rights, prosperity and (for example) carefully calibrated bananas. As the author of a thoughtful epilogue to a recent volume about *Darker Legacies of Law in Europe* (2003) observed, the fact that the Europhile political élites are now trying to salvage the draft European constitution does not mean that it is a good time to forget that 'The memory of a marriage goes back to courting, engagement and subsequent matrimonial life. But the identity of the couple who make up the marriage will also be determined by the previous pasts and memories of each of the partners.' Europe as we know it today, the author concluded, is not just a relatively recent product of the integration project, but is also 'the integration of European history', complete with its dark legacy.[94]

Conclusion

What emerges from the debate between defenders and critics of the various visions of European unity since 1945? Bearing in mind the constitutional perspective from which, as I suggested at the start, Elie Kedourie would have judged the integration project, four conclusions may be drawn. The first, unsurprisingly, is that not all the post-1945 visions of European unity are equally viable from the constitutional point of view. The least viable is the organic one, since the spiritual and cultural solidarity it demands points towards an authoritarian (or even totalitarian) form of rule at both national and supranational levels. The postmodern vision, by contrast, favours diversity and democracy, but leaves unclear whether the kind of democracy advocated is a constitutional one. The

---

[93] E. Kedourie, *England and the Middle East* (London, 1956), p. 88.
[94] J. J. Weiler, in C. Joerges and N. S. Ghaleigh (eds.), *Darker Legacies of Law in Europe* (Oxford, 2003), pp. 394–5.

third, 'conflictual', vision provides a salutary reminder of the role played by a political 'Other' as the source of European political identity but tends to subordinate constitutionalism to a 'decisionist' conception of politics which exaggerates the role of militant charismatic leadership in creating political integration. What remains are the rational/bureaucratic and the 'civil' visions which have shaped the integration project since the Second World War, and are likely to do so in future. Of these two visions, the former is in principle compatible with constitutionalism, but leaves the presence of a constitutional commitment entirely to the discretion of the administrative élite, which may decide that such a commitment impedes more effective ways of providing rational government. The civil vision, however, is fully compatible with constitutionalism.

The second conclusion concerns the limits set to the integration project by the 'Eurocentric' nature of the civil vision, which is only of intrinsic value to cultures in which individuality, freedom and opposition to arbitrary political power are deeply rooted. The main problem in this connection is presented by Islamic culture, and in particular by a Turkish application for EU membership. Whether the subordinate role of a 'preferential partnership' with Turkey envisaged by Nicolas Sarkozy, for example, would make the entry of Turkey into the EU compatible with the preservation of a coherent identity is arguable. More generally, a comment by the Swiss finance minister, Hans Rudolf Merz, after the negative French and Dutch referenda, provides a sceptical reminder of the danger of overstretch: 'European integration that goes beyond economy and security', the minister said, 'always stumbles at borders.'[95] As an English sceptic remarked in the same connection, it is worth recalling the lesson learned by both Napoleon and Hitler, which was that 'when European imperialists march to the east, they eventually lose in the west. The elastic is overstretched.'[96]

The third conclusion is that even if the Europhile political élites continue to interpret European integration in terms of civil association, defenders of the modern Western constitutional ideal should remain profoundly suspicious since the nature of the Europhile commitment to that ideal remains ambiguous. More precisely, the standpoint of the political élites has been shaped from the start of the integration project by a functional perspective of the kind that created the ambiguity already noticed

---

[95] Quoted by S. Jenkins, 'The peasants' revolt', *Sunday Times*, News Review Section, 5 June 2005, 1–2.
[96] Ibid.

in Hayek's writings. As in Hayek's case, what remains unclear is the extent to which a constitutional commitment is seen primarily in instrumental or non-instrumental terms. The potential dangers created by this ambiguity are intensified, in the case of the integration project, by the fact that potentially conflicting political, economic and moral objectives are pursued amongst which no clear priority has been settled. The economic objectives, for example, may conflict with the moral concern for human rights, and the political objectives may conflict with both the moral and the economic ones (since they may mean the growth of arbitrary power and bureaucratic inefficiency). The danger to the constitutional tradition which the ambiguous nature of the integration project presents is not merely a theoretical possibility. If it turns out, for example, that the élites have created excessive expectations about the ability of the integration project to shield their fellow citizens from globalised economic competition, it will be necessary to take very seriously Donald Rumsfeld's prediction of an intensified division between the 'old' and 'new' Europes. Reflecting on this disturbing possibility, a thoughtful British political analyst went a step further,[97] conjuring up the 'nightmare prospect' of a new iron curtain rising across Europe. To the west of this curtain would lie

> the old socialised economies of the original Common Market, stuck inside protectionist walls, and crippled by emigration, low birthrates and welfare burdens. These economies will be trapped by voters of the fearful right and the fearful left. Their borders will close and their politics become ever more introverted. To their east will be the 'new tigers' of the former Soviet bloc, untrammelled by social models, with open labour markets, natural resources and easy access to the Middle East and Asia. . . . They may be nasty, but they could be rich.[98]

In this situation, needless to say, the ideal of European integration would fall by the wayside of its own accord. But even if that danger did not materialise, the success or failure of the integration project would increasingly depend on the ability of the élites to reconcile European populations to significant falls in their prosperity and welfare, if not in their personal security as well. Whether any significant elements of the modern European constitutional tradition that Kedourie valued would survive the strains this would create is a matter for some doubt.

My final conclusion returns to the issue of legitimacy. None of the visions of European unity, it is clear, provides Europhile political élites

---

[97] Ibid.
[98] Ibid.

with a convincing means of dealing with the existence of a 'democratic deficit'.[99] Bluntly put, the fact that the legitimation of the integration project has thus far derived from treaties means that it seems impossible to ascribe anything more than a derivative legitimacy to EU institutions as they have so far evolved. As was seen, attempts have been made, especially by theorists of the republican ideal, to confer an independent claim to legitimacy on EU institutions through the concept of governance. Although these attempts were found to be unconvincing, other Europhile theorists have argued instead that the universal value of EU objectives such as the promotion of human rights makes any reference to a democratic deficit wholly inappropriate. A notable student of Eastern Europe politics has maintained, for example, that the promotion of human rights and civil association in that part of the world in particular is to be welcomed simply because it permits the protection of minorities by legal and constitutional safeguards that Eastern European states might otherwise fail to provide.[100] No matter how intrinsically valuable the objectives of Europhile élites may be, however, promoting them cannot remove the 'democratic deficit' simply because legitimacy does not derive from the ends or ideals an organisation pursues. It relates, rather, to its entitlement to pursue them at all. Once this issue is raised, no 'democratic' answer is available.

What qualifies this truth, however, is an important fact acknowledged even by a sceptic like Alan Milward, which is that 'national citizens have developed a strong secondary allegiance during the Community's existence'.[101] Reflection on the implications of this fact recalls what both Machiavelli and Burke knew well, which is that practice and prescription may in the course of time provide what ideal aspirations cannot. With this in mind I shall finish, in best English fashion, by giving an example from the world of cricket that provides food for thought about the future of legitimacy in the EU. The example is of how the committee of the MCC acquired its current authority to determine the rules of cricket.

The story is told by Michael Oakeshott, whom Elie Kedourie regarded as one of the two greatest modern philosophers of constitu-

---

[99] See R. Bellamy and D. Castiglione, 'Legitimizing the Euro-"Polity" and its "Régime": the normative turn in EU studies', *European Journal of Political Theory*, 2/1 (Jan. 2003), 7–34.

[100] Bideleux, '"Europeanisation" and the limits to democratisation in East-Central Europe', in Pridham and Ágh (eds.), *Prospects for Democratic Consolidation in East-Central Europe*, p. 26.

[101] Milward, *The European Rescue of the Nation-State*, p. 19.

tionalism, the other being Hegel. The Marylebone Cricket Club, Oakeshott relates, is a private club

> which, when it was founded in 1787, had little to distinguish it from many other such clubs. But in the course of about a century it came to be recognised as the custodian of the rules of cricket and the court of record (so to say) whose imprimatur is necessary for any change in those rules. This was an acquisition of authority, for the club never had any 'power' to enforce its decision. This authority was not acquired by succession to an office of authority previously held by some other occupant; office and occupant were coeval. Nor did it come by any act of authorisation. It was acquired merely by being acknowledged to have it. The earliest acknowledgement, it seems, was as a court of arbitration in respect of disputes on cricket matches; but gradually, in steps some of them distinct enough to be recorded, it acquired its present authority over the rules of the game. It retains this authority in the continuous recognition of those concerned that it has it; and this authority will lapse when it ceases to be recognised. It has nothing to do with the recognition of the desirability of the rules or with the constitution of the committee.[102]

Whether this story provides a close analogue to the possible future development of legitimacy in the case of the EU remains, of course, as yet unknown. Even if it does, however, the ambiguous interpretation of civil association by the Europhile political élites which would have made Kedourie pessimistic about the future of constitutionalism in the integration project is unlikely to disappear.

Note. I am indebted to Professor Jack Hayward for commenting on a draft of this lecture.

---

[102] M. Oakeshott, *On Human Conduct* (Oxford, 1975), p. 154, n. 1.

Byzantium and the Limits of Orthodoxy

AVERIL CAMERON
Fellow of the Academy

THE LIST OF RALEIGH LECTURES since the series began in 1919 includes many that have become classics, including Norman Baynes's 'Constantine the Great and the Christian Church' (1929) and more recently the lecture by Peter Brown on 'The Problems of Christianisation' (1992).[1] The only Raleigh lecture that has been on an unequivocally 'Byzantine' subject is that by Dimitri Obolensky on 'Italy, Mount Athos and Muscovy: the Three Worlds of Maximos the Greek' given in 1981. But perhaps it is no accident that if one takes the lectures by Norman Baynes and Peter Brown as at least touching on Byzantium, even if only concerned with its earliest history, all three have been on religious topics. The question is why this should be the case.

Certainly the Byzantines themselves had a high understanding of Orthodoxy. A fourteenth-century patriarch grandly stated that he had been given the 'care of all the world'.[2] They certainly give the impression of having what modern political theorists call a 'comprehensive doctrine', and they undoubtedly aspired to such an ideal.[3] In the sixth century the

---

Read at the Academy 26 April 2007.

[1] See Norman H. Baynes, *Constantine the Great and the Christian Church*, 2nd edn. (Oxford, 1972); Peter Brown, *Authority and the Sacred* (Cambridge, 1995), chap. 1.

[2] See D. Obolensky, 'Late Byzantine culture and the Slavs: a study in acculturation', in id., *The Byzantine Inheritance of Eastern Europe* (Aldershot, 1982), 17. 13.

[3] For the tension between modern liberal pluralist political theory and 'comprehensive doctrines' such as religious systems, see Raymond Plant, *Politics, Theology and History* (Cambridge, 2001); John Rawls, *Justice as Fairness: a Restatement* (Cambridge, MA, 2001).

Proceedings of the British Academy, **154**, 129–152. © The British Academy 2008.

poet Paul the Silentiary presented the emperor and the patriarch as the twin poles of the Byzantine state, in harmonious agreement.[4] But within only a few years of the composition of Paul's poem the emperor in question deposed the patriarch for not agreeing with him.[5] It was well known that emperors did their best to place in position patriarchs whose views suited their own, and Justinian acted in this way throughout his reign. In the ninth century a similarly disingenuous view of the complementary roles of the emperor and patriarch is ascribed to the patriarch Photius.[6] But Photius also had an agenda, and was himself at the centre of a famous schism; Byzantine authors, patriarchs and others who expounded these religious theories were often writing in order to justify a position, or to convey a lofty sense of order. They constructed Byzantium as a 'virtual reality', or an 'empire of the mind'.[7] Yet books published almost in successive years by two distinguished Byzantinists, Hélene Ahrweiler and Steven Runciman,[8] both point out how very often Byzantium fell short of this ideal, and on how many occasions the hoped-for internal order under God gave way to succession coups, the murder of actual and would-be emperors, and the deposition, exile and imprisonment of patriarchs. The Princes Islands were a favourite destination: the sixth-century patriarch Eutychius was kept there for a while, the future iconophile patriarch Methodius in the ninth century was imprisoned there, and also in the ninth century, the patriarchs Ignatius and Photius were both deposed and exiled, Ignatius with considerable suffering. It is time to ask how far the

---

[4] Paul the Silentiary, *Ekphrasis on S. Sophia*, ll. 921–66, 978–1029, ed. P. Friedländer, *Johannes von Gaza und Paulus Silentiarius: Kunstbeschreibungen justinianischer Zeit* (Leipzig and Berlin, 1912); the poem was recited in the Epiphany season of AD 563 to celebrate the restoration of the church, partly in the imperial palace and partly in the patriarchal palace adjoining the church, and the emperor and the patriarch are each separately praised: see Mary Whitby, 'The occasion of Paul the Silentiary's *Ekphrasis* of S. Sophia', *Classical Quarterly*, 35 (1985), 215–28, at 217–18.

[5] Evagrius, *Ecclesiastical History*, IV. 38; Eustratius, *V. Eutych.* 1015–1146, ed. C. Laga, CCSG 25 (Turnhout, 1992). Eutychius was deposed in AD 565, and five years later Justinian's successor Justin II also deposed Anastasius, the patriarch of Antioch (Evagrius, V. 5); both were reinstated later under different emperors.

[6] Preface to the *Epanagoge* (titles II and III), J. and P. Zepos (eds.), *Ius Graecoromanum*, 8 vols. (Athens, 1931), 2. 229–368, 410–27; for the complex relationship between emperor and patriarch, and the larger claims made for the latter in the Palaeologan period, see E. Patlagean, 'Théologie politique de Byzance. L'empereur, le Christ, le patriarche', in G. Firolamo (ed.), *Teologie politiche: Modelli a confronto* (Brescia, 2005), pp. 149–61, especially pp. 158–61.

[7] Jonathan Shepard, 'The Byzantine commonwealth 1000–1550', in M. Angold (ed.), *Cambridge History of Christianity* V (Cambridge, 2006), pp. 3–52, at p. 45.

[8] H. Ahrweiler, *L'Idéologie politique de l'empire byzantin* (Paris, 1975); Steven Runciman, *The Byzantine Theocracy* (Cambridge, 1977), given as a series of lectures on church and state in Byzantium at the Weil Institute in Cincinnati in 1973.

common equation of Byzantium with Orthodoxy is justified, and what the Byzantine notion of 'Orthodoxy' amounted to.

We can see the Byzantine habit of self-conscious theorising about Orthodoxy again in the twelfth century when the commentator Theodore Balsamon and others debate in detail the respective positions and privileges of the patriarch and the emperor.[9] Two centuries earlier the patriarch Nicholas Mystikos justified as an imitation of divine mercy in action the very Byzantine notion of *oikonomia* ('economy', or as his translators have it, 'dispensation'), namely the flexibility to temper strict correctness with what we might now see rather as creative interpretation.[10] By this means it was possible to maintain the theory that God was directing the Byzantine world order, even if the Byzantines themselves sometimes bent the rules. But again, the words of the patriarch, which are apparently about the religious and political order, are in fact highly partisan; they are part of a passionate argument directed at the wrong use of such dispensation by the Pope in the intense battle over whether or not the Emperor Leo VI was allowed to marry for a fourth time. Nicholas Mystikos himself had become patriarch with the Emperor Leo's blessing. He had himself been willing to use this 'dispensation' to justify baptising the child of this contested fourth marriage (no less than the future Emperor Constantine VII Porphyrogenitus); but there he drew the line. He barred the door of St Sophia to the emperor at Christmas and was forced to abdicate as a result.[11]

Nicholas's letter was written after these events and is full of his indignation on hearing that Rome had been willing to give the emperor a let-out.[12] Nicholas was reinstated after the emperor's death and even became regent for the young Constantine VII, only to be ousted again by the very Zoe whose marriage to the emperor Leo VI he had violently opposed. Yet despite such a series of events (which was by no means uncommon in the history of Byzantium), both Runciman and Ahrweiler were willing to agree that Byzantium was in fact governed by a strong sense of order and

---

[9] G. Dagron, *Emperor and Priest: the Imperial Office in Byzantium*, Eng. trans., Past and Present Publications (Cambridge, 2003), pp. 256–64.

[10] Ahrweiler, *L'Idéologie politique*, p. 146; cf. *Ep.* 32, ed. R. J. H. Jenkins and L. G. Westerink, *Nicholas I, Patriarch of Constantinople: Letters*, CFHB 6 (Washington, DC, 1973), pp. 215–37, at p. 236 (AD 912). On 'economy' see G. Dagron, 'La règle et l'exception: analyse de la notion d'économie', in D. Simon (ed.), *Religiöse Devianz: Untersuchungen zu sozialen, rechtlichen und theologischen Reaktionen auf religiöse Abweichung im westlichen und östlichen Mittelalter* (Frankfurt am Main, 1990), pp. 1–18.

[11] Runciman, *The Byzantine Theocracy*, p. 101.

[12] *Ep.* 32, p. 234.

divine guidance.[13] One might more reasonably say that in writing Byzantine history there is a particularly acute problem in reconciling the 'is' and the 'ought' in the written sources, that is, there is such a wealth of normative and 'official' discourse that historians should immediately assume a gap between that and what actually happened. Orthodoxy, in other words, might be used to justify dubious actions, but did not necessarily govern what actually happened in practice. Members of the secular and ecclesiastical elite such as the patriarch Nicholas Mystikos may have found ways of explaining away the discrepancy, but we should not be fooled in the same way. We should not take Byzantine Orthodoxy at face value.

The real theme of this lecture is Byzantine exceptionalism. For a variety of reasons having to do both with its historic reception and its relative inaccessibility, Byzantium is not an easy subject,[14] and in terms of its historiography Byzantine Orthodoxy has proved particularly awkward, at least for those outside the Orthodox tradition.[15] On the one hand the available material for Byzantium, art historical and textual, is heavily skewed towards religious history, and thus risks giving a false impression. On the other, from the viewpoint of western liberal pluralism, as from that of the frequent unfavourable comparisons made of Byzantium with western Europe, Byzantine Orthodoxy even now often gives the impres-

---

[13] Ahrweiler, *L'Idéologie politique*, pp. 146 f.; Runciman, *The Byzantine Theocracy*, pp. 161–2. Both emphasise the Platonising roots of the bland Eusebian political theory which continued to be voiced throughout Byzantine history.

[14] For this see Averil Cameron, *The Byzantines* (Oxford, 2006), pp. viii–xi.

[15] It is noteworthy that most historians use terms such as 'the church', Christianity, or 'Orthodoxy' rather than 'religion' to indicate their subject matter: for instance A. Ducellier (ed.), *Byzance et le monde orthodoxe* (Paris, 1986), a book which covers many areas of Byzantine life, but which uses Orthodoxy as a very strong framing device; Michael Angold, *Byzantium. The Bridge from Antiquity to the Middle Ages* (London, 2001), chap. 7, pp. 122–45, 'The triumph of Orthodoxy'; G. Dagron, 'L'iconoclasme et l'établissement de l'Orthodoxie (726–847)', in G. Dagron, P. Riché and A. Vauchez (eds.), *Evêques, moines et empereurs (610–1054)*, J.-M. Mayeur, *et al.* (eds.), *Histoire du christianisme des origines à nos jours* IV (Paris, 1993), pp. 93–165; D. M. Nicol, *Church and Society in the Last Centuries of the Byzantine Empire 1261–1453* (Cambridge, 1979); Joan Hussey, *The Orthodox Church in the Byzantine Empire*, Oxford History of the Christian Church (Oxford, 1986); Rosemary Morris (ed.), *Church and People in Byzantium* (Birmingham, Society for the Promotion of Byzantine Studies, 1990); A. Ducellier, *L'Église byzantine. Entre pouvoir et esprit (313–1204)*, Bibliothèque de l'Histoire du Christianisme (Paris, 1990); Michael Angold, *Church and Society in Byzantium under the Comneni, 1081–1261* (Cambridge, 1995); id. (ed.), *Eastern Christianity*, Cambridge History of Christianity, 5 (Cambridge, 2006); Derek Krueger (ed.), *Byzantine Christianity*, People's History of Christianity, 3 (Minneapolis, 2006).

sion of being a not wholly welcome comprehensive system with little room for individual choice.

The use of the term 'Orthodoxy' in my title is deliberate. In today's world Orthodoxy is again raising its head, and in its modern sense it is often consciously or unconsciously elided with 'Byzantine Orthodoxy' or with the idea of the Byzantine 'inheritance' or 'legacy'. There are an estimated three million Orthodox in the world today according to the official website of the ecumenical patriarchate, and while this may be an exaggeration other common estimates put the figure at between 220 and 300 million. At least thirteen countries have majority Orthodox populations and many others have large Orthodox minorities. The timeliness of my topic is clear if we reflect on the degree to which as a result of the changes since 1991 Byzantine Orthodoxy is being drawn into sometimes highly contentious agendas about contemporary national identity.

Orthodoxy has also been given a place since 1991 in the clash of civilisations rhetoric, notably in the 1996 book of that title by Samuel Huntington.[16] Here the term is used (very questionably) to denote a whole 'civilisation', distinct both from western Christendom and from the Islamic world. There are eight entries for Byzantium in the index of Huntington's book, and the references are always to distinguish Byzantium from the west and to align it with the east, or with an essentialist Orthodox civilisation. He writes of 'the great historical line' dividing east and west, and provides a map with a heavy line drawn on it, marking 'the end of Europe'. In the Huntington rhetoric there is no space for the actual diversity of Byzantium, the mixed ethnic range in the population at different times, the shifting borders or any questioning of the role of religion as a defining characteristic of a 'civilisation' as a whole. Such views raise questions as to how Byzantium fits into the related theme of the Crusades, where its place is uneasily ambiguous; but most importantly, the idea of an 'Orthodox civilisation' depends on a highly contestable essentialism, applied by extension also to Byzantium, but which, for example, ignores the severe problems of Orthodox ecclesiology which existed in Byzantine times as much as today.[17] 'Orthodoxy' is also

---

[16] Samuel P. Huntington, *The Clash of Civilizations and the Remaking of World Order* (New York, 1996).

[17] Both Macedonia and Montenegro have local Orthodox churches whose legitimacy is keenly disputed; Byzantium allowed local ecclesiastical autonomy at an early date in Bulgaria (though for the complexities see C. Hannick, 'Les nouvelles chrétientés du monde byzantin: Russes, Bulgares et Serbes', in Dagron, Riché and Vauchez (eds.), *Evêques, moines et empereurs*, pp. 909–39, at pp. 921–37).

having a revival as a theme in current scholarship on Byzantium. Thus a book by Mark Whittow on the history of Byzantium from the seventh to the tenth century is called *The Making of Orthodox Byzantium*;[18] a recent collection of essays is entitled *Byzantine Orthodoxies*;[19] one of the eight major themes at the 2006 International Byzantine Congress in London was Orthodoxy, and one of the most interesting plenary papers, given under the theme of 'Empire', memorably concluded that Byzantium's 'soft power' rested on the force of its religion.[20] The Orthodoxy of Byzantium was a central theme of Dimitri Obolensky's classic book, *The Byzantine Commonwealth*,[21] which argued for the use of Orthodoxy by Byzantium as a means of developing wider spheres of influence in neighbouring states. While there may have been some questioning of specific parts of the argument, the book's central theme of medieval Byzantium as what Jonathan Shepard now calls a 'force-field' remains potent and is still very much bound up with its Orthodoxy.[22] In his Congress paper Shepard cautiously concludes that 'commonwealth' is a justifiable term, basing himself on the idea of 'acquisitional societies' and 'superordinate centres'. After positing three circles of influence—'the Byzantine commonwealth', the Christian and Islamic Orient, and Latin Christendom—in which Byzantium exerted a 'force-field', he concludes that Byzantium should be seen 'less as a state than as a politico-cultural sphere', with its presence in the three circles having a 'protean quality'. He returns to the idea of a Byzantine 'commonwealth', arguing that its strength came not least from the fact that the message was 'multi-channelled', Byzantium

[18] Mark Whittow, *The Making of Orthodox Byzantium, 660–1025* (London, 1996).

[19] Andrew Louth and Augustine Casiday, eds., *Byzantine Orthodoxies* (Aldershot, 2006).

[20] Jonathan Shepard, 'Byzantium's overlapping circles', in Elizabeth Jeffreys (ed.), *Proceedings of the 21st International Congress of Byzantine Studies, London, 21–26 August, 2006* (Aldershot, 2006), I, *Plenary Papers*, 15–55; for the idea of 'soft power' (culture, religion, values, in contrast with the use of force or economic pressure) see Joseph S. Nye Jr., *Soft Power. The Means to Success in World Politics* (New York, 2004).

[21] Dimitri Obolensky, *The Byzantine Commonwealth: Eastern Europe 500 to 1453* (Oxford, 1971); cf. also Garth Fowden, *Empire to Commonwealth: Consequences of Monotheism in Late Antiquity* (Princeton, 1993).

[22] See Shepard,'The Byzantine commonwealth, 1000–1550', pp. 49–52. For some reservations about Byzantine 'mission' see the contributions by S. Ivanov and V. Vavrinek, in Jeffreys (ed.), *21st International Congress of Byzantine Studies*, II, *Abstract of Panel Papers*, pp. 32–3, 34–5, with C. Raffensperger, 'Revisiting the idea of the Byzantine Commonwealth', *Byzantinische Forschungen*, 28 (2004), pp. 159–74; on the anachronism of the term 'commonwealth': E. Patlagean, *Un Moyen Âge grec. Byzance, IXe–XVe siècle* (Paris, 2007), p. 387. The title of the paper by S. Averintsev, 'Some constant characteristics of Byzantine Orthodoxy', in Louth and Casiday (eds.), *Byzantine Orthodoxies*, pp. 215–28, speaks for itself in terms of essentialist approaches.

offering not just one but a broad spectrum of models.[23] All the same, he tellingly echoes Obolensky's view that Byzantium's soft power derived from 'its credible show of majesty and piety'. The language of circles and 'spheres of influence' is in fact the language of Huntington; so is Shepard's language of 'order'. It surely cannot be an accident that Shepard also cites the book by Mary Helms from which Huntington derived his model of centres and circles.[24]

What strategies can historians adopt in order to deal with this problem? First of all, I want to argue that Byzantine Orthodoxy was not at all something fixed and easily identifiable. It is far from being agreed, for instance, when Byzantine Orthodoxy can be said to have been fully established. Given the fact that, unlike the western medieval kingdoms, the Byzantine state grew directly out of the Roman empire, even to the extent that the Byzantines considered themselves to be 'Romans', this is connected with the perennial question of when 'Byzantium' can be seen as being established. If 'Byzantium' begins with Constantine's dedication of the city of Constantinople in AD 330, a settled 'Orthodoxy' was still a long way in the future; even if a later date is chosen for the start of the Byzantine empire, say the seventh century, it remains impossible to separate Byzantine religion from the religious struggles of the earlier period.[25] A common answer to the question as to when Orthodoxy was established in relation to the Byzantine period proper follows the propaganda of the Byzantines themselves and makes the key period the ending of the Iconoclastic controversy in the ninth century.[26] But important as this was, the 'event' itself was carefully stage-managed;[27] nor, contrary to the official propaganda of the time, did it mean the end of challenges and contests. I will return to this point below.

[23] Shepard, 'Byzantium's overlapping circles', pp. 27, 53–5.

[24] Shepard, 'The Byzantine commonwealth, 1000–1550', p. 12.

[25] For this see Averil Cameron, 'Enforcing Orthodoxy in Byzantium', in Kate Cooper and Jeremy Gregory (eds.), *Discipline and Diversity*, Studies in Church History, 43 (Woodbridge, 2007), pp. 1–24.

[26] Cf. Dagron, 'L'iconoclasme et l'établissement de l'Orthodoxie (726–847)'. That is certainly the view enshrined in the document known as the Synodikon of Orthodoxy (J. Gouillard (ed.), 'Le Synodikon d'orthodoxie', *Travaux et Mémoires*, 2 (1967), 1–313), produced at the time, and in the fifteenth-century 'Triumph of Orthodoxy' icon in the British Museum (on which see D. Kotoula, 'The British Museum Triumph of Orthodoxy icon', in Louth and Casiday (eds.), pp. 121–8).

[27] P. Karlin-Hayter, 'Methodios and his synod', in Louth and Casiday (eds.), *Byzantine Orthodoxies*, pp. 55–74.

We also have to be careful not to simplify Byzantium's religious message to other peoples. To take only one example, even at the height of their medieval state, the Serbs, seen now as quintessentially Orthodox, had a far from straightforward relationship with Byzantine Orthodoxy. Their rulers may have married Byzantine wives, but they were also liable to put them aside in favour of Catholic ones; they were courted by the pope and themselves gave Rome grounds to hope for success. Nor were the Serbs the only people whose rulers were presented with a choice between Rome and Byzantium; some, like Hungary, eventually opted for Rome.[28] In medieval Serbia, religious affiliations were in practice divided, with Catholic dioceses on the Adriatic coast and Orthodox ones further inland, and Stephen the First-Crowned, brother of the famous S. Sava, the co-founder with their father Stefan Nemanja of the Hilandar monastery on Mt Athos, actually received his crown from the pope.[29] We can hardly hope to recapture real religious inclination in such matters, but one can see clearly enough that it was not obvious that Orthodoxy was universal or that it would prevail.

Emphasis on the Orthodoxy of Byzantium is traditional in the subject, and its revival as a topic (if that is not too strong a term) is not surprising. But a different and major strand in recent scholarship on earlier periods of Christianity (admitted in the title of Louth and Casiday's book, *Byzantine Orthodoxies*, even if not fully expressed in it), has been to question essentialist views of religion, 'Orthodoxy' and the like from a constructivist position. A mass of recent scholarship on the early Christian and late antique periods has shown the extent to which Christian orthodoxy was in fact constructed by the labelling and identification of heterodoxy. Its definition was fought over, using a range of tactics from polemic against other groups to exhortations addressed to Christians to separate themselves from heretics.[30] Just as in the related

---

[28] In sharp contrast to the unquestioning emphasis on the Orthodoxy of medieval Serbia in Ducellier, *Byzance et le monde orthodoxe*, especially chap. 8, see E. Patlagean, 'Les états d'Europe centrale et Byzance, ou l'oscillation des confins', *Revue historique*, 302. 4 (2000), 827–68; also ead., *Un Moyen Âge grec*, p. 69.

[29] The tensions between the Catholic dioceses on the Adriatic littoral and the more central Orthodox areas, as well as the pressures exerted by neighbouring Catholic powers, are well brought out by L. Maksimović, 'La Serbie et les contrées voisines avant et après la IVe croisade', in Angeliki E. Laiou (ed.), *Urbs Capta. The Fourth Crusade and its Consequences*, Réalités byzantines, 10 (Paris, 2005), pp. 269–82.

[30] See Cameron, 'Enforcing Orthodoxy in Byzantium', pp. 6–7; for the industry that went into producing handbooks against all kinds of heresy see Averil Cameron, 'How to read heresiology', *Journal of Medieval and Early Modern Studies*, 33/3 (2003), 471–92.

debates on Hellenism and Romanisation, the categories 'Greek' and 'Roman' are nowadays seen as constructed, rather than as absolutes, so the term 'Orthodox' was not a given, but a focus of contestation.[31] It is time for the same 'hermeneutic of suspicion' to be applied to the later Byzantine source material as well. There is a gap to be addressed not only between the 'is' and the 'ought' within Byzantine society itself, that is, between the normative texts and the rest,[32] but also within our own historical methodology.

Titles containing the words 'limits of' have been used before. The subtitle of Arnaldo Momigliano's *Alien Wisdom*, published in 1975, was *The Limits of Hellenization*.[33] Benjamin Isaac's book on the Roman army in the east was called *The Limits of Empire*. Closer to today's subject, Steven Runciman gave one of the chapters in his *Byzantine Theocracy* the title 'The limits of imperial control'.[34] Such titles usually convey the wish to overturn, or at least to question, a familiar view, and my title is no exception. I wish to move the study of Byzantium away from Orthodoxy as a given into consideration of the sociology of Byzantine 'religion'; away from western secularist and pluralist agendas and assumptions based on ideas about the desirability of a separation of church and state; and from a focus on Orthodox faith and spirituality, and 'the Orthodox legacy', to some simpler but perhaps more basic questions about the place of religion in the working of Byzantine society, questions which might rescue Byzantium from its constant relegation to the 'eastern' and 'non-Enlightenment' sphere of autocracy and religious conservatism.[35]

---

[31] For the debates on 'Romanisation', especially vigorous among archaeologists; see for example (from a large literature) D. Mattingly, 'Vulgar and weak "Romanization", or time for a paradigm shift?', *Journal of Roman Archaeology*, 15 (2002), 536–40; G. A. Cecconi, 'Romanizzazione, diversità culturale, politicamente corretto', *Mélanges de l'École française de Rome, antiquité*, 118.1 (2006), 81–94.

[32] For similar methodological issues in a different culture see Sarah Foot, *Monastic Life in Anglo-Saxon England, c.600–900* (Cambridge, 2006).

[33] Arnaldo Momigliano, *Alien Wisdom: the Limits of Hellenization* (Cambridge, 1975), rev. Italian edn., *Saggezza straniera. L'Ellenismo e le altre culture* (Torino, 1980); cf. also J.-C. Cheynet, 'Les limites de pouvoir à Byzance: une forme de tolérance?', in K. Nikolaou (ed.), *Toleration and Repression in the Middle Ages* (Athens, 2002), pp. 15–28.

[34] Cf. B. Isaac, *The Limits of Empire. The Roman Army in the East*, rev. edn. (Oxford, 1992); see also William E. Klingshirn and Mark Vessey (eds.), *The Limits of Christianization. Essays on Late Antique Thought and Culture in Honor of R. A. Markus* (Ann Arbor, 1999).

[35] On the alleged 'Caesaropapism' of Byzantium see in particular Dagron, *Emperor and Priest*, pp. 282–312.

The latter assumption about Byzantium is still very much alive. I was startled a while ago to be sent copies of *Awake* and *The Watchtower*, both carrying articles about Byzantium; it was taken as read that the Byzantine church was subordinated to political ends, and this was held up as 'an unholy mix' . . . and no part of 'true religion'.[36] We clearly need to start from the beginning. I wish to begin here, therefore, by arguing rather simply against the view that 'Orthodoxy' is the 'best frame of reference' within which to study and write the history of Byzantium culture.[37]

* * *

How religious was Byzantium? Was Orthodoxy really as dominant as it seems? One question faced by modern sociologists of religion is how to measure the depth of religion in a given society, an endeavour which is difficult even in contemporary circumstances, and even more so when dealing with medieval source material which is itself highly ideological.[38] Phenomenological approaches to the sociology of religion, followed by many historians of Byzantium, stress the element of religious experience, and the sense of the sacred or the holy,[39] and certainly Byzantine art and Byzantine spirituality offer much material for this. To all appearances Byzantium certainly had most of the trappings associated with modern Orthodox societies if not more: its ruler played a quasi-sacral role[40] and intervened in ecclesiastical affairs (a striking example was Manuel I Komnenos's *Novel* or 'Conciliar Edict' of 1166, by which the emperor unashamedly imposed his own views against ecclesiastical opposition);[41] the great religious controversies (Christology, iconoclasm, union with Rome, hesychasm) were at once political and ecclesiastical; public cere-mony was intertwined with religious processions and liturgies; the num-

---

[36] *Awake*, 8 Oct. 2001, 12–15; *The Watchtower*, 15 Feb. 2002, 8–12, citing Norman Davies, *Europe: a History* (Oxford, 1997), p. 246, 'The Empire defended the Orthodox Church, and the Church praised the Empire. This "Caesaropapism" had no equal in the West, where secular rule and papal authority had never been joined.'

[37] As argued by Paul Magdalino, unpub. plenary paper given at the 21st International Byzantine Congress, 2006.

[38] For the perils inherent in hagiographic sources see P. Odorico and P. Agapitos (eds.), *Les vies des saints à Byzance: genre littéraire ou biographie historique?* (Paris, 2004).

[39] Lawrence A. Young, 'Phenomenological images of religion and rational choice theory', in Lawrence. A. Young (ed.), *Rational Choice Theory and Religion: Summary and Assessment* (New York, 1997), pp. 133–46.

[40] For this see Dagron, *Emperor and Priest*.

[41] Magdalino, *The Empire of Manuel I Komnenos*, pp. 287–8.

ber of clergy, church buildings and monasteries was extremely large, and accounted for a major part of Byzantine economic activity;[42] church law, in the shape of the canons,[43] applied equally with public law; and the art of Byzantium was dominated by religious production and religious patronage, exemplified by icons, church architecture, decoration and equipment, such as gospel books.[44] For all these reasons western critics from the sixteenth century to modern times have depicted Byzantium as a society in which there was no separation between church and state, and no civil society, thereby denigrating it by an unfavourable comparison with the Protestant, Catholic or enlightened west.[45]

Among modern sociological theories of religion, a dominant view holds that secularisation goes hand in hand with modernity, and tends to regard pre-modern societies as highly religious more or less by definition, without questioning what that embeddedness actually meant in practice. A similar assumption is also made by advocates of the competing rational-choice theory of religion, who emphasise faith and individual choice in modern religion and see medieval societies not as an 'age of faith' but as a time when religion was a simply part of the fabric of life.[46] In each case pre-modern religion suffers as a topic in its own right.

---

[42] There is no dedicated chapter on the economics of Orthodoxy in the 3-vol. *Economic History of Byzantium*, ed. Angeliki E. Laiou (Washington, DC, 2002), but see E. Papagianni, 'Legal institutions and practice in matters of ecclesiastical property', ibid., 3. 1059–69 with bibliography; Papagianni demonstrates very clearly how often the economic and financial interests of the state and the church were at odds and how often emperors were unsuccessful in their attempts at control. A useful outline of the property and financial issues relating to Byzantine monasteries and of the organisation and emoluments of the clergy, can be found in B. Caseau-Chevalier, *Byzance: économie et sociéte. Du milieu du VIIIᵉ siècle à 1204* (Paris, 2007), pp. 195–260.

[43] For a good introduction to the issues see Ruth Macrides, 'Nomos and kanon on paper and in court', in Rosemary Morris (ed.), *Church and People in Byzantium* (Birmingham, 1990), pp. 61–86, and see her papers in Macrides, *Kinship and Justice in Byzantium, 11–15th centuries*, Variorum Collected Studies Series, 642 (Aldershot, 1999).

[44] Paul Magdalino, *L'Orthodoxie des astrologues: La science entre le dogme et la divination à Byzance (VIIᵉ–XIVᵉ siècle)*, Réalités byzantines, 12 (Paris, 2006), p. 12, argues that the interpenetration of religion and culture at some periods of Byzantium was conspicuously greater than anything in the west or the Islamic world; on the other hand the book argues for the continuing importance of astrology in Byzantium, and the attachment of emperors to horoscopes even in late Byzantium; Manuel I even wrote a treatise defending astrology (ibid., pp. 114–22).

[45] For discussion see Dagron, *Emperor and Priest*, pp. 282–312; for the modern secularisation thesis, according to which secularisation is assumed to go hand in hand with modernism and rationalism: e.g. Bryan Wilson, *Religion in a Secular Society: a Sociological Comment* (London, 1966); for discussion and criticism see S. Bruce (ed.), *Religion and Modernization: Sociologists and Historians Debate the Secularization Thesis* (Oxford, 1992).

[46] So I. R. Iannacone, 'Rational choice: framework for the scientific study of religion', in Young (ed.), *Rational Choice Theory*, pp. 25–45.

Given what seems to be a lack of critical overall analysis, it is simply too dangerous for historians to be taken in too easily by Byzantine appearances of Orthodoxy; the interpretation of Byzantium suffers, in fact, from an overdose of the wrong sort of religion. The danger inherent in the acceptance of Orthodoxy as the obvious framework of analysis is that it risks obscuring the actual complexities, and while the place of secular as well as religious elements in late antique and Byzantine culture is beginning to receive more attention,[47] using the framework of 'Orthodoxy' brings with it the clear risk of conflating the religion and the society.

Orthodoxy in Byzantium is and was hard to define, and for that very reason it was at all times contested and fought over. Yet even a scholar like Paul Magdalino writes, in the context of a highly original argument about the lively continuation of astrology, of 'the Orthodoxy' of different Byzantine periods, thus raising the question of what this objectified 'Orthodoxy' might have been.[48] Like any process of religious ethnography, describing or writing a history of Byzantine Orthodoxy also risks importing the assumptions of the individual investigator—especially if those who write on it do so from within the Orthodox tradition. Finally, and of course very importantly, many Byzantines were not in fact Orthodox.

The word 'orthodoxy' seems simple enough: it means in Greek 'right opinion'.[49] In the fifth century AD a north Syrian bishop could compose in Greek a dialogue between an imaginary 'orthodox' and a spokesman

---

[47] For Byzantine art see Eunice Dauterman Maguire and Henry Maguire, *Other Icons: Art and Power in Byzantine Secular Culture* (Princeton, 2007); Henry Maguire, *Earth and Ocean: The Terrestrial World in Early Byzantine Art* (University Park, Pa., 1987); the spectacular mosaic floors known from Jordan in the sixth to eighth centuries continued to display a lively knowledge of the themes of Greek mythology and poetry, for which see M. Piccirillo, *The Mosaics of Jordan* (Amman, 1993). Other attempts to get round the problem have focused on 'daily life'; for the secular in relation to late antiquity see D. M. Gwynn and S. Bangert (eds.), *Religious Diversity in Late Antiquity*, Late Antique Archaeology 6 (Leiden, forthcoming); E. Rebillard and C. Sotinel (eds.), *Frontières du profane* IV: *Les activités économiques: une sphère profane par excellence?*, *Antiquité tardive*, 14 (2006), 15–116.

[48] Magdalino, *L'Orthodoxie des astrologues*, e.g. p. 132. It is very hard to avoid such language: see e.g. Dagron, 'Le temps des changements', p. 318, 'the Church' called to order those who defended classical tradition; Magdalino, op. cit., p. 40, George of Pisidia (7c) as representative of 'the official thought of the Church', p. 135, opposition to Manuel I's treatise on astrology as 'la réaction orthodoxe'.

[49] But for the complex steps by which 'orthodoxy' came to be defined and legally enforced and heterodoxy punished see Caroline Humfress, *Orthodoxy and the Courts in Late Antiquity* (Oxford, 2007), especially pp. 217–42.

for heterodoxy;[50] and this is far from being the only such set-piece text.[51] In one of the recently much-studied highly stylised Greek apologetic disputations designed to demonstrate the superiority of Christianity over Judaism we also find a so-called 'orthodox' interlocutor, identified as an abbot; yet just how contrived such a character is can be seen from the fact that such dialogues usually end with the discomfiture, defeat and conversion of his opponents, the Jews.[52] Other sets of questions and answers in both Greek and Syriac put together in the early Byzantine period vividly demonstrate the anxiety felt on all sides as to what was or what was not orthodox.[53]

Indeed it will rightly be objected that religion, Christianity or other, is not just about doctrine. 'Lived Orthodoxy',[54] spirituality, liturgy and lay piety are just some of the elements that went up to make Byzantine Orthodoxy.[55] In theoretical terms religion has been seen variously as: a system of belief, whether or not including an actual reference to God or a divine entity; a way of ordering meaning; a system of symbols; or a bundle of practices.[56] In one discussion, no less than eight dimensions have been identified in a religion,[57] all of which certainly applied in one form or another in Byzantium. Spirituality and prayer were central characteristics of Byzantine religion, and while this paper concentrates on doctrinal, political and structural matters, Andrew Louth has memorably emphasised the importance of liturgical life, religious sensibility and

---

[50] Theodoret, *Eranistes*, ed. G. H. Ettlinger (Oxford, 1975); *Eranistes*, the name given to the interlocutor, seems to mean a 'collector' of divergent views (Ettlinger, p. 5, n. 2).

[51] Cf. A. Alexakis, 'The dialogue of the monk and recluse Moschos concerning the holy icons, an early iconophile text', *Dumbarton Oaks Papers*, 52 (1998), 187–224, also dated by its editor to the fifth century, though see 209–10.

[52] See I. Aulisa and C. Schiavo, *Dialogo di Papisco d Filone giudei con un monaco* (Bari, 2005).

[53] See e.g. Y. Papadoyannakis, 'Defining orthodoxy in Pseudo-Justin's *Quaestiones et responsiones ad Orthodoxos*', in Eduard Iricinschi and Holger Zellentin (eds.), *Heresy and Identity in Late Antiquity* (Tübingen, 2008), pp. 115–27.

[54] For this term in relation to the historiography of medieval and later Russian Orthodoxy see Stella Rock, 'Russian piety and Orthodox culture 1380–1589', in Angold (ed.), *Eastern Christianity*, pp. 253–75, at p. 255.

[55] For lay piety in Byzantium see Sharon E. J. Gerstel, 'The layperson in church', in Krueger (ed.), *Byzantine Christianity*, pp. 103–23 and Alice-Mary Talbot, 'The devotional life of laywomen', ibid., pp. 201–20; Sharon E. J. Gerstel and Alice-Mary Talbot, 'The culture of lay piety in medieval Byzantium 1054–1453', in Angold (ed.), *Eastern Christianity*, pp. 79–100.

[56] Defining religion: Alan Aldridge, *Religion in the Contemporary World: a Sociological Introduction* (Oxford, 2000), pp. 22–32.

[57] On definitions, see also F. Bowie, *The Anthropology of Religion, an Introduction* (Oxford, 2000, 2006), pp. 18–22, cf. N. Smart, *Dimensions of the Sacred: an Anatomy of the World's Beliefs* (London, 1996).

prayer, and described, from an Orthodox viewpoint, the great councils as 'simply [seeking] to preserve the integrity of such prayer and worship by ruling out misunderstanding'.[58] Religious behaviour, as opposed to doctrine, was also certainly important: some disputed issues in Byzantine religion, as in the hate literature directed against the Latins, were not about belief at all but about matters such as the use of unleavened or leavened bread, or the wearing or non-wearing of beards.[59]

The nature of the available source material is a major problem. A case has been made recently for an Orthodox 'mentality' or *habitus* as the binding factor in the eighteenth-century Balkans.[60] Such a view is perhaps somewhat idealistic. But quite apart from the danger of projecting later conditions back into earlier periods, it is a methodological problem for historians that while Byzantine history is rich in written sources it does not in general have the more personal materials on which this kind of case could rest.

* * *

What Byzantium did have was a coercive and interventionist state. As part of its religious development Byzantium inherited from early Christianity an intense focus on doctrinal formulations ('right belief'),

---

[58] Andrew Louth, *St John Damascene: Tradition and Originality in Byzantine Theology* (Oxford, 2002), p. 156. This book presents an original and sympathetic analysis of the theological writings of John of Damascus (eighth century) as a summing up and handing on of Orthodox tradition.

[59] For the themes in this anti-Latin literature see Tia M. Kolbaba, *The Byzantine Lists: Errors of the Latins* (Urbana, IL, 2000); ead., 'Byzantine perceptions of Latin "religious errors": themes and changes from 850 to 1350', in Angeliki E. Laiou and R. P. Mottahadeh (eds.), *The Crusades from the Perspective of Byzantium and the Muslim World* (Washington, DC, 2001), pp. 117–43; ead., 'The Orthodoxy of the Latins in the twelfth century', in Louth and Casiday (eds.), *Byzantine Orthodoxies*, pp. 199–214.

[60] Paschalis M. Kitromilides, '"Balkan mentality": history, legend, imagination', *Nations and Nationalism*, 2 (1996), 163–91; id., 'Orthodox culture and collective identity in the Ottoman Balkans during the eighteenth century', in Kate Fleet (ed.), *The Ottoman Empire in the Eighteenth Century, Oriente Moderno*, NS 18.1 (1999), 131–45.

[61] See Peter Brown, 'Christianization and religious conflict', in Averil Cameron and Peter Garnsey (eds.), *The Late Empire, AD 337–425*, Cambridge Ancient History XIII (Cambridge, 1998), pp. 632–64, esp. pp. 647–50; Michael Gaddis, *There Is No Crime For Those Who Have Christ: Religious Violence in the Christian Roman Empire* (Berkeley, 2005); Michael Whitby, 'Factions, bishops, violence and urban decline', in Jens-Uwe Krause and Christian Witschel (eds.), *Die Stadt in der Spätantike—Niedergang oder Wandel?*, *Historia* Einzelschrift, 190 (Stuttgart, 2006), pp. 441–62; for the symbolic violence of the attempt to impose doctrinal orthodoxy see Averil Cameron, 'The violence of orthodoxy', in Iricinschi and Zellentin (eds.), *Heresy and Identity in Late Antiquity*, pp. 102–14.

which could at times even give rise to actual violence.[61] The height of this violence, sometimes led by bishops or monks, was reached in the early Byzantine period, but it is a mistake to think that the matter was somehow settled, either with the ending of the iconoclast episode in the ninth century or at any other time. It may also have suited ecclesiastical commentators to claim to leave physical punishments to the state,[62] but suffering imposed by the state in the name of religion sometimes reached considerable lengths. A quite enormous amount of effort also had to be put at all periods into 'selling' and enforcing the Orthodoxy of the day, and recent scholarship has revealed in dramatic relief just how far this might go at times of specially intense effort, as during the Monothelete and iconoclastic controversies of the seventh to ninth centuries.[63] Byzantine 'Orthodoxy' was in fact characterised, as I have suggested, not only by personal struggles between emperors, patriarchs and others, but also by a sustained propagandistic output of heresiological and apologetic writing, by the blatant manipulation or even forgery and falsification of texts (the 'hard sell'), and by continual battles between individuals and party groups, for instance in local synods; the subject at stake was the very definition and control of what was to count as Orthodox. The 'lists' of names so characteristic of coercive systems were produced in plenty in Byzantium.[64] Tellingly, even if the conclusion to Runciman's *The Byzantine Theocracy* stressed the apparently unchanging influence of the hopeful, even complacent, Christian political theory first enunciated by Eusebius of Caesarea in the fourth century, it is these struggles, and the instability which they represent, which are in fact the central subject of the book.

Against this evidence an attempt has been made recently by some historians to argue for actual toleration, both in late antiquity and Byzantium. But in fact the principle of coercion started early and was

[62] So Theodore Balsamon in the late twelfth century: see Macrides, 'Nomos and kanon', 84; see also E. Patlagean, 'Byzance et le blason pénal du corps', in *Du châtiment dans la cité: Supplices corporels et peine de mort dans le monde antique*, Table ronde organisé par l'École française de Rome avec le concours du Centre national de la recherche scientifique, Rome, 9–11 novembre 1982 (Paris, 1984), pp. 405–26.

[63] For an introduction to the issues and an indication of the intensity of effort, see Maijastina Kahlos, *Debate and Dialogue: Christian and Pagan Cultures c.360–430* (Aldershot, 2007); Richard Lim, 'Christian triumph and controversy', in G. W. Bowersock, Peter Brown, and Oleg Grabar (eds.), *Late Antiquity: a Guide to the Post-Classical World* (Cambridge, MA, 1999), pp. 196–217; Averil Cameron, 'Texts as weapons. Polemic in the Byzantine dark ages', in Alan K. Bowman and Greg Woolf (eds.), *Literacy and Power in the Ancient World* (Cambridge, 1984), pp. 198–215, at pp. 208–10; S. Wessel, 'Literary forgery and the Monothelete controversy: some scrupulous uses of deception', *Greek, Roman and Byzantine Studies*, 42 (2001), 201–20.

[64] See Cameron, 'How to read heresiology'; Adam Michnik, 'The ultras of moral revolution', *Daedalus* (winter, 2007), 67–83, at 69.

inherited without question by Byzantium. As I have argued elsewhere, various forms of direct and indirect enforcement were practised throughout the Byzantine period, including anathematisation, deposition, expunging of names from the records, burning of heretical books.[65] In legal terms, a pattern was set by the pagan Emperor Diocletian's legislation against the Manichaeans, and the same approach was already evident in the way that Constantine dealt with allegedly deviant Christians; it acquired the full weight of the law through the legislation of Theodosius I at the end of the fourth century and Justinian in the sixth, when not only paganism but also Christian heterodoxy became theoretically illegal.[66] This was taken to its limits by Justinian before the Second Council of Constantinople in 553, when dissenting bishops were summoned to Constantinople and harangued, with large-scale depositions following.[67] Like many other rulers in their attempts to deal with recalcitrant problems, Justinian alternated between persuasion and force, sometimes employing both simultaneously. But there were also passionate divisions at many other points in Byzantine history, not least for instance when after his carefully stage-managed return to Constantinople in 1261 Michael VIII Palaiologos was willing to contemplate union with Rome. A bitter divide had already arisen over Michael's blinding of the heir to the throne, John IV Laskaris, and the same patriarch who had crowned him excommunicated him and was himself deposed in turn.

As part of this process, Orthodoxy whenever or however defined was also put constantly on display; in the liturgy, in art, in official documents, in writing. It was constantly necessary to repeat, to demonstrate and to reinforce, simply because nothing could be taken for granted. A good example is the official and visible process for the reception back into the community of recanting heretics. We see this happening during the ebb and flow of the iconoclastic controversy and examples survive from

[65] Cameron, 'The enforcement of Orthodoxy in Byzantium'; for the burning of mathematical books by local bishops see also CJ I.4.10.

[66] For the precedent set by Diocletian's edict and the legal framework for imposing Christian Orthodoxy see Cameron, 'Enforcing Orthodoxy in Byzantium', pp. 2–3; cf. K. L. Noethlichs, *Die Gesetzgeberischen Massnahmen der christlicher Kaiser des vierten Jahrhunderts gegen Häretiker, Heiden und Juden* (Cologne, 1971); C. Humfress, 'Roman law, forensic argument and the formation of Christian orthodoxy (III–VI centuries)', in S. Elm, E. Rebillard, A. Romano (eds.), *Orthodoxie, christianisme, histoire* (Paris, 2000), pp. 125–47; ead., *Orthodoxy and the Courts*, pp. 243–68.

[67] For the background see now Celia Chazelle and Catherine Cubitt (eds.), *The Crisis of the Oikoumene. The Three Chapters and the Failed Quest for Unity in the Sixth-Century Mediterranean* (Turnhout, 2007).

widely differing periods in Byzantine history; it was always regarded as essential that this should be a public event, with the formal signing of documents; private repentance was not enough.[68] Not surprisingly, some, perhaps even many, were prepared to toe the line: as the religious kaleidoscope changed, bishops were required at times to recant formally, and our sources permit us to see some of their changing allegiances in the eighth and ninth centuries as the balance shifted from one side to the other during the iconoclast controversy.[69] When icons were restored there was a clean-out of existing personnel. Methodius was enthroned as patriarch while his iconoclast predecessor was still in place; he justified his authority by terming himself an apostle, and some two or three thousand on one estimate, or possibly even more, iconoclasts were removed and replacements quickly found and ordained.[70] Characteristically—and this should act as a caution—the historical sources for this crucial episode are, to quote Patricia Karlin-Hayter, not only 'biased, cryptic and incoherent', but also 'evasive': 'where there is an awkward question they evade it'.[71] Yet if the reality has been distorted in the telling, the intention was clear enough.

These efforts at control were it would seem less successful than might appear. Historians often say that the Byzantine state aspired to define and control Orthodoxy. But the 'state', the central platform of Byzantine specificity according to many historians,[72] is not easy to define. At most periods of Byzantine history it might seem obvious that a complex bureaucracy administered law, taxation and governance, not to mention the army. However, even this impression may mislead. In a recent book Evelyne Patlagean argues for a strong 'public' realm even in late Byzantium, defining this as consisting of three elements: the imperial

---

[68] See e.g. P. Eleuteri and A. Rigo, *Eretici, dissidenti, musulmani e ebrei a Bisanzio: una racolta eresiologica del XII secolo* (Venice, 1993); abjuration formulae for Muslim converts: PG 140.124–36.

[69] Karlin-Hayter, 'Methodios and his synod', 56–8; nor were the monks of this period by any means as clearly opposed to the iconoclasts as was later claimed: see M.-F. Auzépy, 'Les monastères', in B. Geyer and J. Lefort (eds.), *La Bithynie au Moyen Âge, Réalités byzantines*, 9 (Paris, 2003), pp. 431–58, at pp. 436–9.

[70] Ibid., pp. 63, 73.

[71] Ibid., p. 65.

[72] For discussion of 'Byzantine specificity' in relation to the economic history of Byzantium see Angeliki E. Laiou, 'Methodological questions regarding the economic history of Byzantium', *Recueil des travaux de l'Institut d'études byzantines*, 29 (2001/2), 9–22, at 16–17, 20; central role of the state: N. Oikonomides, 'The role of the Byzantine state in the economy', in Angeliki E. Laiou (ed.), *Economic History of Byzantium* (Washington, DC, 2002), 3. 973–1058.

power, the church and the *demosion* or fiscal apparatus.[73] But even if one accepts this general proposition, it seems to me that the argument (which admittedly has other objectives) works only if it passes over the constant and plentiful evidence of contest and struggle between emperors, would-be emperors and leading churchmen. 'The imperial power' and 'the church' are abstract concepts, whereas emperors and patriarchs in Byzantine history were all too human. Both emperors and patriarchs aimed at achieving control, but very often the effectiveness of this control was in fact extremely limited.

* * *

It is probably correct to say that Byzantium was trying to be an autocracy. Certainly some former Soviet Byzantinists, including Alexander Kazhdan, have seen it in that light,[74] and the Byzantine legacy features repeatedly in the historiography of Russia as an explanation for the latter's political conservatism and absolutism.[75] A mass of canon law in Byzantium aimed at regulating daily and personal life, and coexisted with imperial lawcodes, still based heavily on Roman imperial law. Here again, late antique historiography[76] can help the historian of Byzantium to see that repeated and elaborate laws do not in themselves prove that society actually ran according to their prescriptions. This mass of legislation required complex interpretation and commentary, and frequent excep-

---

[73] Patlagean, *Un Moyen Âge grec.*

[74] See Alexander Kazhdan and Giles Constable, *People and Power in Byzantium: an Introduction to Modern Byzantine Studies* (Washington, DC, 1982), p. 34: 'the average Byzantine . . . felt alone and solitary in a dangerous world, naked before an incomprehensible, metaphysical authority'; Aaron Gurevich, 'Why I am not a Byzantinist', *Dumbarton Oaks Papers*, 46 (1992), 89–96, for example at 93: 'The closer I studied Byzantine history, the more I came to suspect that I was studying something already familiar to me: that in another place and at another time, with different names and in a different language, this was the same history that had been endured and was still being endured in my own country', and 95: 'can one imagine a Magna Carta in Byzantium or in Rus? Is it conceivable that a Byzantine emperor or a Russian tsar could view himself, or might be viewed by others, as *primus inter pares*?'

[75] See e.g. Richard Pipes, *Russian Conservatism and its Critics: a Study in Political Culture* (New Haven, CT, 2005), with examples of Russian appeals to the Byzantine tradition, including Byzantine Orthodoxy, though with a limited understanding of the actual issues surrounding Byzantium.

[76] See e.g. Jill Harries and Ian Wood (eds.), *The Theodosian Code: Studies in the Imperial Law of Late Antiquity* (London, 1993); Jill Harries, *Law and Empire in Late Antiquity* (Cambridge, 1999), esp. at pp. 77–98, 'the efficacy of law'.

tions in the name of 'economy' or 'flexibility'. In the provinces the inter-action of religious and secular law was complex and personal issues equally so. The task of judges was difficult and, surprisingly perhaps, legal knowledge was not necessarily considered to be the only basis for a good judgement.[77] We are fortunate to have detailed material about actual cases from Constantinople and the provinces, and this gives an impression very far from that of a successful autocracy at work. In the Soviet system in Russia, so-called 'informal' mechanisms, local variety, flexibility, and ways round the system worked alongside state control,[78] and I would suggest that the same can be seen at many levels in Byzantium when ecclesiastical or legal rules clashed with other interests, as for instance over ordination at ages younger than the age prescribed. The Byzantine bureaucracy depended on a delicate balance of imperial control, personal interest and connections and payment for offices and titles,[79] and the working of ecclesiastical law and the ecclesiastical hierarchy is not likely to have been very different.

This complex interplay of interests is especially obvious in the deal-ings in matters of imperial marriage and family negotiations on the part of emperors of the eleventh century and later, who were themselves mem-bers of a family-based aristocracy and shared its objectives in wishing to evade and manipulate the legal restrictions on marriage on which they nevertheless publicly insisted.[80] It would be simplistic to interpret the imperial and ecclesiastical legislation which sought to prohibit marriage to the sixth or even seventh degree of relationship either as totally effective or merely as a product of Orthodoxy. Indeed, as has been pointed out, this issue became one of the main fields in which the famous

---

[77] See Leonora Neville, *Authority in Byzantine Provincial Society, 950–1100* (Cambridge, 2004); Cameron, *The Byzantines*, pp. 92–4; I. Ševčenko, 'Was there totalitarianism in Byzantium? Constantinople's control over its Asiatic hinterland in the early ninth century', in Cyril Mango and Gilbert Dagron (eds.), *Constantinople and its Hinterland* (Aldershot, 1995), pp. 91–105.

[78] See for this debate in relation to the Soviet Union and post-Soviet Russia, e.g. Alena V. Ledeneva, *How Russia Really Works: the Informal Practices That Shaped Post-Soviet Politics and Business* (Ithaca, NY, 2006).

[79] See for instance N. Oikonomides, 'The role of the Byzantine state in the economy', in Angeliki Laiou (ed.), 2002, *The Economic History of Byzantium*, 3 (Washington, DC, 2002), pp. 973–1058.

[80] The restrictions on marriage culminated with the *Tomos* of Sisinnios (AD 997); see Angeliki E. Laiou, *Mariage, amour et parenté à Byzance aux XIe–XIIIe siècles*, Travaux et Mémoires du Centre de recherche d'histoire et civilisation de Byzance. Monographies, 7 (Paris, 1992); Patlagean, *Un Moyen Âge grec*, pp. 84–92; for the complexities and ambiguities surrounding such prohibitions in the fourth century AD, and for the difficulties and the opportunities for control involved in their application (which affected the west as well as the east) see J. Goody, *The Development of the Family and Marriage in Europe* (Cambridge, 1983), pp. 83–156.

Byzantine 'economy' had to be invoked.[81] Another example of the complex and shifting interplay between the religious and the secular is provided by the intermingling within individual families in the same period of holders of secular official posts and ecclesiastics; the same family often produced both, and the membership of synods of the twelfth century was drawn from the imperial family and secular officials as well as ecclesiastics. Magdalino, who is in this also followed by Angold, refers to this composite secular and ecclesiastical class as 'the Guardians of Orthodoxy'.[82] Taking up the same idea, Angold qualifies the term by saying that Orthodoxy here must be understood in the 'political', as opposed to 'ritual' sense, according to the dual formula proposed by Hans-Georg Beck in 1978.[83] But this is not very helpful in that it still rests on a basically secularist or reductionist view of Byzantine Orthodoxy as politically driven or state-controlled. It fails to do justice to the reality of Byzantine Orthodoxy as a shifting and complex mass of competing drives, motivations and interests. In the same contribution Angold admits that this hoped-for alliance did not in fact deliver social cohesion in the crucial period before the Fourth Crusade, not least because there was no clear succession procedure for emperors and because the vital relation between emperor and patriarch depended heavily on these family relationships and the individuals concerned.[84] The only possibility for regime change in such circumstances, as he points out, was to resort to a coup, when the very parties who were supposed to present a united front (and in so doing to ensure the smooth functioning of the system) might be on opposite sides.

A case can be made on many other fronts for the actual lack of a settled Orthodox framework in Byzantium, not least in the case of Byzantine monasteries and monasticism, so much a feature of Byzantine life and society, yet so individual and differentiated in character and practice. In fact monks and ascetics were often sources of tension and in some

---

[81] See Dagron, 'Le temps des changements (fin X^e–milieu XIe siècle)', in Dagron *et al.* (eds.), *Evêques, moines et empereurs*, pp. 297–337, at pp. 310–15.

[82] Paul Magdalino, *The Empire of Manuel I Komnenos, 1143–1180* (Cambridge, 1993), pp. 316–412, cf. id., *L'Orthodoxie des astrologues*, p. 12; Dagron, 'Le temps des changements', p. 317 on the idea of the 'religion des philosophes', a term taken from J. Gouillard, 'La religion des philosophes', *Travaux et Mémoires*, 6 (1976), pp. 305–24 ; Michael Angold, 'Byzantine politics vis-à-vis the Fourth Crusade', in Laiou (ed.), *Urbs Capta*, pp. 55–68, at p. 56.

[83] Hans-Georg Beck, *Das byzantinische Jahrtausend* (Munich, 1978), pp. 87–108.

[84] Angold, 'Byzantine politics', especially pp. 57–67, cf. p. 57 'imperial authority was brittle and vulnerable'; see also Magdalino, *L'Orthodoxie des astrologues*, p. 70.

periods attracted sharp criticism.[85] We have seen that monks were as likely to follow changing religious trends as others. Byzantine monasteries fulfilled a variety of important functions, but many of them had little to do with 'religion' as such.

* * *

Finally, as has been increasingly emphasised in recent scholarship, just as it was not uniformly Greek, Byzantium was very far from being uniformly Orthodox. As a friend and colleague once remarked, the Byzantine empire was 'like a concertina'—its boundaries (insofar as they existed) went in and out all the time.[86] Even within those boundaries, populations were moved about, sometimes on religious grounds;[87] some of this would certainly fall within the much-studied modern phenomenon of forced migration. Slaves and prisoners were also a substantial element in the population at different times.[88] Byzantium was certainly diverse, even

[85] See Michael Angold, 'Monastic satire and the Evergetine monastic tradition in the twelfth century', in Margaret Mullett and Anthony Kirby (eds.), *The Theotokos Evergetis and Eleventh-Century Monasticism* (Belfast, 1994), pp. 86–102.

[86] Frontiers and boundaries are not concepts that can be readily applied to the Byzantine empire, whose inhabitants in any case claimed universal rule: G. Dagron, 'Byzance et la frontière: idéologie et réalité', in O. Merisalo (ed.), with the collaboration of P. Pahta, *Frontiers: Proceedings of the Third European Congress of Medieval Studies (Jyväskyluä, 10–14 June, 2003)* (Louvain-la Neuve, 2006), pp. 303–18; J. Shepard, 'Emperors and expansionism: from Rome to Middle Byzantium', in David Abulafia and Nora Berend (eds.), *Medieval Frontiers: Concepts and Practices* (Aldershot, 2002), pp. 55–82.

[87] C. Morrisson, 'Peuplement, economie et société de l'Orient byzantin', in C. Morrisson (ed.), *Le monde byzantin I: L'Empire romain d'Orient (330–641)* (Paris, 2004), pp. 193–220, at pp. 198–9; the spread of languages: B. Flusin, 'La culture écrite', ibid., pp. 255–76, at pp. 259–60; G. Dagron, 'Formes et fonctions du pluralisme linguistique à Byzance (IX<e>–XII<e> siècle)', *Travaux et Mémoires*, 12 (1994), 219–40; minorities, including Jews: G. Dagron, 'L'Église et l'État (milieu IX<e>–fin X<e> siècle', in Dagron *et al.* (eds.), *Evêques, moines et empereurs*, pp. 167–240, at pp. 226–34, with Dagron, 'Le temps des changements', ibid., pp. 333–7; P. Charanis, 'Ethnic changes in the Byzantine empire in the 7th century', *Dumbarton Oaks Papers*, 13 (1959), 25–44; G. Dagron, 'Minorités ethniques et religieuses dans l'orient byzantin à la fin du X<e> et au XI<e> siècle: l'immigration syrienne', *Travaux et Mémoires*, 6 (1972), 177–216; V. Tapkova-Zaïmova, 'Migrations frontalières en Bulgarie médiévale', in M. Balard and A. Ducellier (eds.), *Migrations et Diasporas Méditerranéennes (X<e>–XVI<e> siècles)* (Paris, 2002), pp. 125–31; H. Ahrweiler and Angeliki E. Laiou (eds.), *Studies on the Internal Diaspora of the Byzantine Empire* (Washington, DC, 1998).

[88] Michael McCormick, *The Origins of the European Economy: Communications and Commerce AD 300–900* (Cambridge, 2001), esp. pp. 733–77 (particularly pp. 744–5, 760, 773); id., 'The imperial edge. Italo-Byzantine identity, movement and integration, AD 650–950', in Ahrweiler and Laiou (eds.), *Studies in the Internal Dispora*, pp. 17–52, at pp. 34–36; Stephen W. Reinert,

if not exactly multicultural. The patriarch Nicholas Mystikos mentioned earlier wrote to the Caliph al-Muqtadir in AD 922, addressing him as the ruler of the Saracens 'chosen by God', and reassuring him that Muslims in Constantinople had been free to repair the mosque in the city and that there had been no attempts at enforced conversion; it had always been the policy of Roman emperors, he says, to treat prisoners well and especially to guarantee their religious freedom.[89] Again surely a disingenuous argument, but one that shows that there was a Muslim presence, like the Jewish one, in Constantinople itself.[90] Byzantine interests in the Balkans meant dealing with Slav populations not yet Christianised, and when the Byzantines recovered Bulgaria in the early eleventh century their new ecclesiastical organisation was faced with the task of integrating Greek and Slav elements. When Byzantine fortunes improved in Anatolia in the tenth century both Muslim and heterodox populations were brought within the empire's sphere.[91] Non-Chalcedonian Armenians were to be found all over the empire and in the army.[92] The use of foreign mercenaries in the armies was another source of diversity. Equally, many Byzantine Christians found themselves living under Arab or Turkish rule, and this posed difficult problems for the canonists.[93] The continued production of anti-heresy manuals, disputations designed to show the superiority of orthodoxy over Jews and Muslims, and anti-Latin texts demonstrates that Orthodoxy still had to be renewed and defended, if anything even more vigorously.[94] Many Latins were living in Byzantine territory both before and, of course, after 1204, when its population and religious composition

---

'The Muslim presence in Constantinople, 9th–15th centuries: some preliminary observations', ibid., pp. 125–50, at pp. 126–30.

[89] Nicholas Mystikos, *Ep.* 102, ed. Jenkins and Westerink, pp. 373–83.

[90] The mosque was later closed, then restored, and a second one built: Reinert, art. cit., 138–43; after destruction by the Crusaders in 1204, a further mosque was built after 1261: A.-M. Talbot, 'The restoration of Constantinople under Michael VIII', *Dumbarton Oaks Papers*, 47 (1993), 252–3.

[91] M. Tahar Mansouri, 'Déplacement forcé et déportation de populations sur les frontières orientales entre Byzance et l'Islam (VIIᵉ–Xᵉ siècles)', in Balard and Ducellier (eds.), *Migrations et Diasporas*, pp. 107–14.

[92] See G. Dédéyan, 'Reconquête territoriale et immigration arménienne dans l'aire cilicienne sous les empereurs macédoniens (de 867 à 1028)', ibid., pp. 11–32; S. Peter Cowe, 'The Armenians in the era of the Crusades 1050–1350', in Angold (ed.), *Eastern Christianities*, pp. 404–29; for Byzantine attempts to suppress the Armenian church structure in the eleventh century, see 406–7; also N. Garsoian, 'The problem of Armenian integration in to the Byzantine empire', in Ahrweiler and Laiou (eds.), *Studies on the Internal Diaspora*, pp. 53–124.

[93] See Dagron, *Emperor and Priest*, p. 257.

[94] See Cameron, 'Enforcing Orthodoxy in Byzantium', at p. 18.

became much more mixed and more complex;[95] as a result simple definitions of Byzantine identity become less and less adequate, as has become sharply evident in the methodological dilemmas facing the Prosopography of the Byzantine World project[96] as it moves into the post-1204 period.

Under the severe external and internal pressures experienced in late Byzantium the divisions within Byzantine Orthodoxy became even sharper.[97] As their numbers and their lands contracted, and their populations became more diverse, the Byzantines had to contend with missions from the Catholic west and with a growing awareness of Latin writers including Augustine and Aquinas. Fierce arguments as to the rival merits of Plato and Aristotle formed a backdrop to periods of civil war and vassalage to the Ottomans. In the fourteenth century Byzantium was deeply split over hesychasm, finally declared official and its opponents excommunicated after a series of church councils in 1351. The victorious hesychasts then wrote the story for posterity just as the iconophiles had done in the ninth century.[98] Soon after, the higher echelons at least were split again over Union with Rome, and John VIII and an entourage of hundreds, including Gemistos Plethon, whose lectures in Florence made a great stir, George Scholarios and the future Cardinal Bessarion, spent many months in Italy at the Council of Ferrara/Florence in 1438–9. Among the Orthodox delegation the fall-out after the Council was considerable: Scholarios and Mark Eugenikos became passionate anti-unionists, while Plethon's last work, the *Book of the Laws*, was to be burned by Scholarios after the latter had been appointed patriarch by Mehmet II; Bessarion left Orthodoxy for the Roman church, and Isidore of Kiev followed the same route.[99]

* * *

[95] J.-C. Cheynet, 'L'implantation des Latins en Asie Mineure avant la Première Croisade', in Balard and Ducellier (eds.), *Migrations et Diasporas*, pp. 115–24; after 1204, see the discussion by David Jacoby, 'The economy of Latin Constantinople, 1204–61', in Laiou (ed.), *Urbs Capta*, pp. 195–214.

[96] <http://www.pbw.kcl.ac.uk>.

[97] Magdalino, *L'Orthodoxie des astrologues*, p. 140.

[98] So Dirk Krausmueller, 'The rise of hesychasm', in Angold (ed.), *Eastern Christianity*, pp. 101–26, at p. 102.

[99] Michael Angold, 'Byzantium and the west, 1204–1453', in Angold (ed.), *Eastern Christianity*, pp. 53–78, at pp. 73–8.

The ideal of Orthodoxy as a comprehensive doctrine undeniably provided Byzantium as a society with an abiding ideology which contributed to its longevity. Yet no society—let alone a whole civilisation—can be reduced to its religion. Nor should the self-interested assertions of contemporaries be allowed to mislead. I have argued that there are distinct dangers for the historian in the tempting and familiar strategy of approaching Byzantium through its Orthodoxy. For the Byzantines, the idea of 'Orthodoxy' was a highly useful watchword and rallying point, but it was also a field of contestation. Nor is it the only framework through which Byzantine society can be understood.

I would argue in conclusion for the need to normalise Byzantium, to remove it, in historiographical terms, from its habitual exceptionalism. At the same time, given our contemporary concerns about pluralism and religious systems, about religion and democracy, and about political theory, it seems exactly the right moment to return to the subject of the political theory and religion of Byzantium.

Hamlet's Two Fathers

DAVID BEVINGTON

University of Chicago

MY PURPOSE HERE is to revisit the psychoanalytical explanation proposed by Sigmund Freud, and elaborated by Freud's disciple, Ernest Jones, in his *Hamlet and Oedipus*, for Hamlet's famous delay in revenging the death of his royal father by killing Claudius. That thesis, briefly, is that Hamlet is in the grip of an oedipal crisis as a result of the emotional shock he has suffered from the sudden death of his father and his mother's hasty marriage to Hamlet's uncle, Claudius. In ways that Hamlet cannot himself perceive, because the hidden truth about himself is too terrible to acknowledge consciously, Hamlet yearns to possess his own mother and is jealous of his uncle-rival. But how can he punish Claudius for the thing that he, Hamlet, secretly and unconsciously desires for himself? The result is a paralysis of the will. Hamlet is capable enough of forthright action on other fronts, and indeed slays or is responsible for the deaths of a number of people in the play, notably Polonius, Rosencrantz, Guildenstern, and Laertes, and can be said to contribute at least partly to the deaths of Ophelia and Gertrude. Only the prospect of slaying Claudius prompts him to stall and to berate himself as a 'rogue and peasant slave', 'an ass', 'a coward', who, though

> Prompted to my revenge by heaven and hell,
> Must like a whore unpack my heart with words

Read at the Academy 23 April 2007.

Proceedings of the British Academy, **154**, 153–175. © The British Academy 2008.

> And fall a-cursing, like a very drab,
> A scullion!   (2.2.585–8)[1]

We have Hamlet's own words for an admitted failure to act as circumstances require. This view of the play was much popularised by Laurence Olivier's 1948 film, which begins with the camera panning past the window of Gertrude's bedchamber while a sepulchral voice, that of Olivier himself, informs us that 'This is a story about a man who could not make up his mind.'[2]

I hope to argue that, whereas the Freud–Jones thesis is deeply flawed in its analytical explanation of the cause of delay, the oedipal and pre-

---

[1] Quotations in this essay are from David Bevington (ed.), *The Complete Works of Shakespeare* (New York, 2003, 2008).

[2] Ernest Jones, *Hamlet and Oedipus: A Classic Study in the Psychoanalysis of Literature* (first pub. 1949; Garden City, New York, 1954), chap. III, 'The Psycho-Analytical Solution', pp. 51–79. Jones expands on a hypothesis suggested by Freud in a footnote to his '*Die Traumdeuting*' (*The Interpretation of Dreams*), published in November 1899 but dated 1900, S. 183. See Peter Gay, *The Freud Reader* (New York, 1989), pp. 129–72, and Peter Gay, *Freud: A Life for Our Time* (New York, 1988), pp. 104–17. Freud read the manuscript of Jones's essay when the two were together at Clark University, Worcester, Massachusetts, in 1909; see Nathan G. Hale, Jr., *Freud and the Americans: The Beginnings of Psychoanalysis in the United States, 1876–1917* (New York and Oxford, 1995), p. 204. See also Gilbert Murray's classic essay on 'Hamlet and Orestes' in *The Classical Traditions in Poetry* (Cambridge, MA, 1927); Frederic Wertham, 'The Matricidal Impulse: Critique of Freud's Interpretation of *Hamlet*', *Journal of Criminal Psychopathology*, 2 (1941), 455; and Leonard Shengold, *'The Boy Will Come to Nothing!' Freud's Ego Ideal and Freud as Ego Ideal* (New Haven, 1993), p. 32, on Freud's view of 'the displacement from father-murder to brother-murder' in *Hamlet*. Shengold, p. 33, n. 7, calls attention to the Scylla and Charybdis episode in James Joyce's *Ulysses* in which Stephen Daedalus sees *Hamlet* as representing Shakespeare's reaction to having been cuckolded by his brothers Edmund and Richard, with both King Hamlet and young Hamlet as Shakespeare's own composite self-portrait. Cf. Joyce's portrayal of himself as both Bloom and Stephen in *Ulysses*. Peter Gay, 'Freud and the Man from Stratford', *Reading Freud* (New Haven, 1990), pp. 5–53, has some astute things to say about what Shakespeare, and *Hamlet* particularly, meant to Freud, in the English original as well as in Schlegel's German translation. Freud's interest in the authorship question in his late years was stimulated by his admiration for J. Thomas Looney's *Shakespeare Identified* (London, 1920–1; rpt. Port Washington, NY, 1975), a work that in Freud's view seemed to bring to light heretofore unperceived truths about Shakespeare much as Freud saw himself as the discoverer of the psychic unconscious. Looney's chapters on *Hamlet* struck Freud as rich in psychological penetration and authorial self-delineation. On Olivier's 1948 film, see Norman Holland, *Psychoanalysis and Shakespeare* (New York, 1964, 1966), p. 166 and Olivier's Foreword to his '*Hamlet': The Film and the Play*, ed. Alan Dent (London, 1948). Jaques Lacan's analysis differs from that of Freud and Jones, but still the argument is posited on the assumption that Hamlet cannot, for psychological reasons, raise his arm against Claudius; see 'Desire and the interpretation of desire in *Hamlet*', translated by James Hulbert, with French text edited by Jacques-Alain Miller from transcripts of Lacan's seminar, in Shoshana Felman (ed.), *Literature and Psychoanalysis, The Question of Reading: Otherwise*, Yale French Studies, 55–6 (1977), 11–52.

oedipal nature of Hamlet's dilemma is indeed a key to understanding. A psychological reading can validate the larger claim of Freudian analysis, that the play of *Hamlet* offers a subtext for which a psychological reading offers a text, bringing to the surface the dilemmas and challenges of emotional conflict that are latent in the original but not immediately apparent for lack of an analytical vocabulary and method, and because the nature of the dilemma is concealed from the protagonist himself. Janet Adelman's essay on '*Hamlet* and the Confrontation with the Maternal Body', to which this present essay is particularly indebted, offers a powerful model of just such an investigation; other critics who seem to me especially useful include Avi Erlich, K. R. Eissler, Norman Holland, C. L. Barber and Richard Wheeler, René Girard, and Joel Fineman.[3] The failure of the Freud–Jones analysis to come up with a satisfying explanation for Hamlet's delay should not turn us away from other attempts to make use of the same method.

The Freud–Jones analysis runs into several problems. For one thing, people do often punish other people for desires they cannot admit in themselves. And in fact Hamlet does attempt to kill Claudius. When Hamlet kills Polonius hidden behind the 'arras' or tapestry hangings in the Queen's private chambers, he does so with every good reason to think that he is killing his uncle. (Perhaps not seeing his victim on this occasion helps.) Hamlet has just passed up an opportunity to kill Claudius at prayer, unguarded and presumably unarmed. Ostensibly, at least, this delay on Hamlet's part is motivated not by scruples of conscience or morality.[4] Hamlet says nothing about how unfair or ungentlemanly it

---

[3] Janet Adelman, 'Man and wife in one flesh: *Hamlet* and the confrontation with the maternal body', *Suffocating Mothers: Fantasies of Maternal Origin in Shakespeare's Plays, 'Hamlet' to 'The Tempest'* (New York and London, 1992); Avi Erlich, 'Psychoanalysis as a critical method for *Hamlet*' and 'Freud's Misleading Hunch about *Hamlet*', *Hamlet's Absent Father* (Princeton, 1977), pp. 3–18 and 19–42; K. R. Eissler, *Discourse on Hamlet and 'Hamlet'* (New York, 1971), pp. 7 ff.; Norman Holland, *Psychoanalysis and Shakespeare*; C. L. Barber and Richard P. Wheeler, *The Whole Journey: Shakespeare's Power of Development* (Berkeley, 1986); Richard P. Wheeler, *Shakespeare's Development and the Problem Comedies: Turn and Counter-Turn* (Berkeley, 1981), pp. 161, 190–200; René Girard, 'Hamlet's dull revenge', *Literary Theory/Renaissance Texts*, ed. Patricia Parker and David Quint (Baltimore, 1986), pp. 280–302; and Joel Fineman, 'Fratricide and cuckoldry: Shakespeare's doubles', in Murray M. Schwartz and Coppélia Kahn (eds.), *Representing Shakespeare* (Baltimore, 1980). See also below, n. 4.

[4] An ambivalent reading is of course possible, and is argued for by Girard, 'Hamlet's Dull Revenge', p. 297: 'When Hamlet does not seize the opportunity to kill Claudius during his prayer, it could be a failure of the will or a supreme calculation; it could be instinctive humaneness or a refinement of cruelty.' My point is that the text is far more plain on the side of a calculated desire for a punitive revenge.

would be for him to attack a defenceless opponent, no matter how loath-some; to the contrary, he insists to himself (and to us as audience) that he spares Claudius's life at this moment because he does not wish to send Claudius's soul to heaven. To do so, he says, would be 'hire and salary, not revenge' (3.3.79). Claudius took Hamlet's father 'grossly, full of bread, | With all his crimes broad blown, as flush as May' (80–1). This confirms what the Ghost has told Hamlet about his fate in the afterlife: that he is

> Doomed for a certain term to walk the night,
> And for the day confined to fast in fires,
> Till the foul crimes done in my days of nature
> Are burnt and purged away.   (1.5.11–14)

Having died 'Unhouseled, disappointed, unaneled' (78)—that is, not hav-ing received the sacrament of Extreme Unction and with it the remission for the ordinary but 'deadly' sins of pride, covetousness, gluttony, etc., to which all mortals are prone in their daily lives—Hamlet senior must now, for a time, inhabit a realm of 'sulfurous and tormenting flames' (3). Hamlet worries that if he were to kill Claudius now he would send his soul to heaven and his revenge would have failed dismally. The audience or reader knows that Claudius's prayer is not working, and that his soul is in torment, so that Hamlet is misled by the outward appearance of pious devotion, but that does not gainsay the logic of Hamlet's determination to seek a suitable revenge. He will instead kill Claudius

> When he is drunk asleep, or in his rage,
> Or in th'incestuous pleasure of his bed,
> At gaming, a-swearing, or about some act
> That has no relish of salvation in't—
> Then trip him, so that his heels may kick at heaven,
> And that his soul may be as damned and black
> As hell, whereto he goes.   (3.3.89–95)

Nor need Hamlet wait long. Summoned to his mother's chambers, he goes there at once, hears a man's voice behind the arras, and stabs him. Who else but Claudius would be in the Queen's private chambers? Hamlet strikes the wrong man, but it is not for lack of resolute action intended against Claudius.

I will come back to the issue of delay and to the complex matter of sorting Hamlet's decision-maker's process of when he should act and when he should pause, only noting here that the issue is inherently puz-zling and does not depend on an emotional incapacity to make a decisive move.[5] To be sure, Hamlet flails himself for procrastination, so that we cannot dismiss this problem, but we should remember that the thesis of morbid or excessive delay on Hamlet's part is an early Romantic notion, having been put forward even before Goethe and then in England by Coleridge, and that it says at least as much about the Romantic age and about those writers as it does about Shakespeare's play.[6] Coleridge especially was victimised by his own drug addiction and melancholic indolence; he is talking partly about himself when he speaks of Hamlet as one who suffers from 'an overbalance in the contemplative faculty' and who

[5] Maynard Mack observantly points to 'the play's emphasis on human weakness, the instability of human purpose, the subjection of humanity to fortune—all that we might call the aspect of failure in man'. Given these intractable problems surrounding the nature of action in an imperfect world, 'The ghost's injunction to act becomes so inextricably bound up for Hamlet with the character of the world in which the action must be taken—its mysteriousness, its baffling appearances, its deep consciousness of infection, frailty, and loss—that he cannot come to terms with either without coming to terms with both' ('The world of *Hamlet*', *The Yale Review*, 41, 1952, 502–23). Meredith Skura similarly argues of Hamlet's world that 'it is no wonder he is sick of action, sick of sexuality, sick of everything that means becoming an adult in such a world ... there are impurities enough in what we see of the world and of Hamlet's current motives without having to invoke unconscious motives from a past world' (*The Literary Uses of the Psychoanalytic Process* (New Haven, 1981), pp. 42–3). The idea goes back at least to Friedrich Nietzsche's *The Birth of Tragedy*: 'Not reflection, no—true knowledge, an insight into the horrible truth, outweighs any motive for action, both in Hamlet and in the Dionysian man' (originally pub. in 1872; in *Basic Writings of Nietzsche*, ed. and trans. Walter Kaufmann (New York, 1968), pp. 59–60). The matter is ably discussed by John Russell in his *Hamlet and Narcissus* (Newark, London and Toronto, 1995), pp. 39–41. Roy Walker, *The Time is Out of Joint: A Study of 'Hamlet'* (London, 1948), similarly argues that 'great evils threaten the little world of Elsinore', in which context we are to understand that Hamlet 'did *not delay*' (pp. 8, 152).

[6] Goethe says of Hamlet: 'A beautiful, pure, and most moral nature, without the strength of nerve which makes the hero, sinks beneath a burden which it can neither bear nor throw off; every duty is holy to him—this is too hard' (*Wilhelm Meister's Apprenticeship*, 1778, translated by Thomas Carlyle, quoted in Claude C. H. Williamson, compiler, *Readings on the Character of Hamlet, 1661–1947* (London, 1950), p. 24. See also A. C. Bradley in *Shakespearean Tragedy* (London, 1904, 2nd edn., 1924), p. 109). On the history of the 'delay' thesis even before Goethe, see Brian Vickers, 'The emergence of character criticism, 1774–1800', *Shakespeare Survey 34* (1981): 11–21, and Vickers, *Returning to Shakespeare* (London, 1989), pp. 197–211. Coleridge, like Goethe and Schlegel, regards Hamlet as 'thought-sick', being possessed of 'an overbalance of the contemplative faculty' carried to 'morbid excess' and 'a great, an almost enormous, intellectual activity, and a proportionate aversion to real action consequent upon it' (*Notes and Lectures upon Shakespeare*, 1808, quoted in Williamson, *Readings*, pp. 31–2; see also Bradley, *Shakespearean Tragedy*, p. 103). Cf. A. W. Schlegel, *Dramatic Art and Literature*, 1810: with Hamlet 'the poet loses himself in labyrinths of thought, in which neither end for beginning is discoverable' (quoted in Williamson, *Readings*, pp. 38–9). See also Morris Weitz, *Hamlet and the Philosophy of Literary Criticism* (Chicago, 1964), pp. 4–5. Weitz's own view is that 'Shakespeare contrasts in *Hamlet* a grief that seeks consolation with a grief that remains inconsolable and thereby results either in dullness and loss of memory (the sin of sloth) or in hasty anger and rashness (the sin of ire)', p. 84.

'vacillates from sensibility and procrastinates from thought, and loses the power of action in the energy of resolve'. Coleridge sees this aspect of Hamlet in himself; we all tend to do the same, since Hamlet is so compellingly drawn and so adept at universalising his philosophical ideas. At the same time, Coleridge downplays aspects of Hamlet's character that do not suit Coleridge's own temperament.

The characters in Shakespeare's play also read Hamlet through their own eyes. To Polonius, the diagnosis of Hamlet's affliction is easy: he suffers from the same sort of love melancholy that Polonius himself knew as a callow youth. 'And truly in my youth I suffered much extremity for love, very near this', he assures us (2.2.189–91). Polonius is utterly confident of his own diagnostic skills: 'If circumstances lead me, I will find | Where truth is hid, though it were hid indeed | Within the center', he promises Claudius (157–9). Ophelia obediently shares her father's view, all the more so since it casts her in the role of the desired yet unattainable young beauty of the Petrarchan sonnet tradition, for lack of whom Hamlet has fallen into his malaise:

> I, of ladies most deject and wretched,
> That sucked the honey of his music vows,
> Now see that noble and most sovereign reason
> Like sweet bells jangled out of tune and harsh,
> That unmatched form and feature of blown youth
> Blasted with ecstasy.   (3.1.158–63)

To Rosencrantz and Guildenstern, Hamlet is suffering from frustrated political ambition. How could they think otherwise? Gertrude knows only too well what the problem is from her perspective: 'I doubt it is no other but the main', she says to her new husband, 'His father's death, and our o'erhasty marriage' (2.2.56–7). She is of course partly right; so are they all.

Claudius probably is closest to the truth, since he alone knows what it is that he has done and why Hamlet is intent on revenge; Claudius alone perceives that Hamlet is not mad. That they are all partly right and yet misled by partiality should warn us that analysis of Hamlet's character is apt to be an unwitting exercise in self-revelation. Hamlet himself is contemptuous of simplistic attempts at diagnosis. 'Why, look you now', he expostulates to Rosencrantz and Guildenstern, 'how unworthy a thing you make of me! You would play upon me, you would seem to know my stops, you would pluck out the heart of my mystery' (3.2.363–5). If they cannot even play upon the recorder that he has just handed them, how can they hope to sound Hamlet 'from my lowest note to the top of my compass'? "Sblood', he exclaims, 'do you think I am easier to be played on than a pipe?' (365–9). Part of Hamlet's appeal, indeed, is that he cherishes a view that humans are infinitely complex and unique. We all share that sense that no one really understands us. Hamlet is our model.

Given these formidable difficulties of wondering what motivates Hamlet, my suggestion is that we search in the area of psychological fantasy—not just Hamlet's fantasy, but also that of the play and of the playwright. Shakespeare has reconfigured the story he found in his chief sources, the *Historica Danica* of Saxo Grammaticus (1180–1208) and the French redaction by François de Belleforest (*Histoires Tragiques*, 1576) to a remarkable degree, and nowhere more so than in the portrayal of Hamlet in relation to his father and his uncle: the two sexual partners of Hamlet's mother, Gertrude. Shakespeare supplies his protagonist with the image of two fathers, one a true father and the other a stepfather, one revered and virtually disembodied, the other opportunistic and incestuously carnal. To view these two men, one now dead and the other all too manifest in 'this too too solid [or sullied, or sallied] flesh' (1.2.129), as antithetical projections of Hamlet's imaginings about male parentage is to explore Hamlet's reasons not for delaying, but for deciding how he should go about fulfilling his father's command in a world where action is so deeply problematic—a world that, in his view, is 'an unweeded garden | That grows to seed'; 'Things rank and gross in nature | Possess it merely' (135–7).[7] That perception, once Hamlet has sorted out carefully

---

[7] On the *Historica Danica*, see William F. Hansen, *Saxo Grammaticus and the Life of Hamlet* (Lincoln, NE, 1983), esp. pp. 66–91. Avi Erlich contrasts King Hamlet and Claudius, and disagrees with Ernest Jones as I do, but still holds to the proposition that Hamlet delays indecisively. Erlich's hypothesis is that Hamlet identifies strongly with his father, as most men do; in this case he 'wants his father back more than he wants to have been the one who killed him', and is 'unable to acknowledge this because it means accepting that his father was finally weak and victimized. On the conscious level, Hamlet must pretend that his father was strong and good, a "radiant angel", but on the unconscious level he has incorporated an image of a weak father who "steals away". This results in ambivalence, indecision, and a secret wish that his father kill Claudius himself and thereby give his son a clear model of purposeful action in the world' (*Hamlet's Absent Father*, p. 23). Hamlet 'fantasizes a primal-scene castration of his father'; he also 'fantasizes his own castration, or, at least fears his failing to remain erect' (p. 64). Eissler's view is that though Hamlet is held back for a long time 'by inner forces of whose nature he [i]s ignorant', he eventually, 'through his maturation', becomes 'capable of performing the deed' (*Discourse on Hamlet and 'Hamlet'*, pp. 148; see also pp. 122 and 379). See also Theodore Lidz, who notes, as have other psychoanalysts, that 'in *Hamlet* the father figure is split into an idealized King Hamlet, whom Hamlet can love, and a bad Claudius, whom Hamlet can hate and find disgusting because of his sexuality'. But Lidz too clings to the traditional explanation of Hamlet's purported delay by positing that 'Hamlet may have had difficulty in disposing of the father figure he needs as a barrier between his mother and his recrudescent oedipal fantasies'. Lidz's explanation

who is innocent and who is guilty, constitutes a call to action, not to emotional paralysis. And act he does, taking great care to distinguish how to proceed against a less guilty mother on the one hand and a confirmedly evil uncle on the other.

Janet Adelman, in a brilliant essay, also portrays Hamlet as choosing between two fathers. She sees this phenomenon in *Hamlet* as going beyond Shakespeare's earlier studies of the relations between a son and two father figures (especially in the *Henry IV* plays and *Julius Caesar*) by the introduction of the mother. Gertrude, by being a sexual partner first for Hamlet's biological father and then for his hated uncle, 'threatens to annihilate the distinction between the fathers and hence problematizes the son's paternal identification'. Moreover, because Gertrude and Ophelia now replace the nurturing young heroines of Shakespeare's romantic comedies of the 1590s, 'the play conflates the beloved with the betraying mother, undoing the strategies that had enabled marriage in the comedies'. Adelman argues further that the structure of *Hamlet* 'is marked by the struggle to escape from this condition, to free the masculine identity of both father and son from its origin in the contaminated maternal body'. I agree wholeheartedly with Adelman's analysis of how the father is split in two, just as the image of the mother is also bifurcated into the

---

for the delay is that Hamlet has suffered two serious traumas, Ophelia's rejection of him and his father's revelations of the murder, as a consequence of which 'Hamlet's world falls apart', causing him to decline into something pathologically close to real madness. The pretence of madness is a mechanism 'to retain a modicum of self-control' (*Hamlet's Enemy: Madness and Myth in 'Hamlet'* (New York, 1975), pp. 54–9, 111). John Dover Wilson, while insisting that 'It is entirely misleading to attempt to describe Hamlet's state of mind in terms of modern psychology at all', nonetheless opts for the common view that 'In *Hamlet* Shakespeare set out to create a hero labouring under mental infirmity' (*What Happens in 'Hamlet'* (New York, Cambridge, 1935, 2nd edn., 1937), p. 218). Wilson sees the procrastination as especially predominant in the last two and a half acts (pp. 202–3). Meredith Anne Skura, *The Literary Use of the Psychoanalytic Process* (New Haven, CT, 1981), has some fine perceptions on the oedipal world in which Hamlet finds himself; she argues well that Hamlet is 'sensitive but not neurotic' in his response to the dismaying events surrounding him, all of which provide an 'objective correlative for his behavior in a world fallen in his idealistic eyes' (pp. 41–3). See also pp. 46–53, 97–9, and 233–7.

For an astute summary of these and other positions on the question of Hamlet's purported delay, and on the potential of psychoanalysis for literary interpretation, see Holland, *Psychoanalysis and Literature*, pp. 173–206, and Russell, *Hamlet and Narcissus*, pp. 13–38 and 183–204. Russell's particular emphasis is on Hamlet's resolution of his predicament by 'his surrender to one of the deepest and most powerful of narcissistic fantasies, the fantasy of death' (p. 38).

familiar Freudian opposites of 'virgin and whore, closed or open, wholly pure or wholly corrupt'.[8]

I do wish to resist, however, Adelman's critical endeavour to collapse the two fathers into each other. The claim that Hamlet senior's 'foul crimes done in [his] days of nature' suggest a common sinfulness linking the two brothers is, I think, a misreading of late medieval Catholic theology. Hamlet senior is in Purgatory because he was 'unhousled' and 'unaneled' at the moment of his death, not having received Extreme Unction (1.5.78); his 'crimes' were those to which, in the traditional Christian view, any human being is prone in the course of daily existence. When Hamlet later describes how Claudius 'took my father grossly, full of bread, | With all his crimes broad blown, as flush as May' (3.3.80–1), he invokes a proverbial truth about the inherent sinfulness to be found even in the best of men. We learn nothing else of a supposed criminality in Hamlet senior. Surely it is an oversimplification to claim, as does René Girard, that 'the old Hamlet, the murdered king, was a murderer himself'.[9] Presumably Girard has in mind the old Hamlet who, 'in an angry parle . . . smote the sledded Polacks on the ice' and, having been 'Dared to the combat', vanquished old Fortinbras in a contest for their two kingdoms (1.2.66–88). But to label these deeds as murder is to overlook the context in which they are presented by Horatio as the mighty achievements of a chivalric warrior, a demigod among men. I will argue that the images of the two fathers remain sharply delineated in Hamlet's consciousness from first to last, and that the contrast has objective support

---

[8] Adelman, *Suffocating Mothers*, pp. 14–19. Peter Erickson, *Patriarchal Structures in Shakespeare's Drama* (Berkeley, 1985), astutely argues that when Hamlet's actual mother fails him through her inconstancy to the memory of her dead husband, the son 'finds an image of his "true mother" in the speech he selects for the player's recitation'. Hecuba mourns for Priam with so great a sorrow that it induces 'a sympathetic response in the cosmos, the gods themselves holding up the mirror to her maternal nature' (p. 74).

[9] Girard, 'Hamlet's dull revenge'*,* p. 283. Margaret Ferguson is similarly too ready to argue that old Hamlet's references to the 'blossoms of my sin' and the 'imperfections on my head' are evidence of a guilt more or less equating him as a sinner with Claudius ('*Hamlet*: letters and spirits', *Shakespeare and the Question of Theory*, ed. Patricia Parker and Geoffrey Hartman (New York and London, 1985), pp. 292–309, esp. p. 297). Much more convincing, to me, is the argument of Barber and Wheeler, *The Whole Journey*, pp. 249 ff., that the Ghost is for Hamlet an image of the 'heroic male identity' that Hamlet longs to find in himself. The Ghost is 'a fully heroic embodiment of legitimate paternity', whose appearance invites Hamlet 'to undertake again the process of becoming a man' (p. 253). On the other hand, I cannot go along with Barber and Wheeler in their insistence of a parricidal wish in Hamlet directed against his father (see p. 266). Such an unconscious wish, posited by Freudian criticism, would seem to be rendered moot by the death of old Hamlet. Hamlet is saved from any such unconscious prompting by the fact that his father has been unjustly murdered.

elsewhere in the text, even if Hamlet is admittedly inclined to idealise his dead father. Of course Hamlet sees much of himself in both fathers; he too is a sinner, being human, and freely acknowledges to Ophelia that 'we are arrant knaves all' (3.1.130). 'Use every man after his desert', he lectures Polonius, 'and who shall scape whipping?' (2.2.529–30). To acknowledge that the human spirit is caught up in an eternal battle between good and evil is not, however, to minimise the difference between good and evil. Hamlet's problem is not to overcome any emotional paralysis of the will in confronting the image of two fathers, but instead to figure out what to do in order to avenge his father's death on Claudius, and at the same time recover his mother from her deeply offensive and (in Hamlet's view) self-destructive behaviour. The task is not easy.

Hamlet's dead father is imagined by the mourning son to be a perfect model of wisdom, restraint, and compassionate caring for his spouse. Claudius, conversely, is a sexual monster and a murderer. The contrast is extraordinarily polarised in Hamlet's imagination: it is to juxtapose 'Hyperion to a satyr' (1.2.140), that is, the god of the sun as contrasted with the spiteful and lecherous half-goat, half-human creature of classical mythology.[10] This polarisation would seem to offer material for reflecting on a radically divergent view of fathers, not just in Hamlet's view but in the dramatist's imagination as well. Nothing in Shakespeare's sources for this play could have pointed him in this direction.

'Look upon this picture, and on this', Hamlet instructs his mother in the so-called 'closet' scene as he shows her two likenesses, of Hamlet senior and of Claudius—perhaps contained as miniature paintings in two lockets, one of his father worn around his neck by Hamlet, the other of Claudius now worn by his new bride. The pictures are 'The counterfeit presentment of two brothers'.

> See what a grace was seated on this brow:
> Hyperion's curls, the front of Jove himself,
> An eye like Mars to threaten and command,

---

[10] Adelman, *Suffocating Mothers*, p. 19: 'The identification of Old Hamlet with Hyperion makes him benignly and divinely distant, separate from ordinary genital sexuality and yet immensely potent, his sexual power analogous to God's power to impregnate the Virgin Mother (often imagined as Spirit descending on the sun's rays) and to such Renaissance mythologising of this theme as the operation of the sun on Chrysogonee's moist body (*The Faerie Queene*, 3.6.67). Ordinary genital sexuality then becomes the province of Claudius the satyr: below the human, immersed in the body, he becomes everything Hyperion/Old Hamlet is not, and the agent of all ill.'

A station like the herald Mercury
New-lighted on a heaven-kissing hill—
A combination and a form indeed
Where every god did seem to set his seal
To give the world assurance of a man.
This was your husband. Look you now what follows:
Here is your husband, like a mildewed ear,
Blasting his wholesome brother. Have you eyes?
Could on this fair mountain leave to feed
And batten on this moor?   (3.4.54–68)

What was Hamlet senior really like? When he is given a chance to speak in his own person (unless one posits the untenable position that he is merely a phantom in Hamlet's imagination), we learn several things. Hamlet senior speaks throughout with the sensibility of a spirit moved by human feelings of revenge, disappointment, and regret; he is integrally the spirit of the man who has died. He was, and still is, infuriated at his brother's murderous perfidy, and is deeply unhappy about the falling off of his 'most seeming-virtuous queen' from himself to 'a wretch whose natural gifts were poor | To those of mine' (1.5.47–53). As his son Hamlet will do throughout the play, Hamlet senior posits an impassable gulf between a virtue that cannot be moved and a lustfulness that will 'prey on garbage', even when offered the opportunity to be linked 'to a radiant angel'. Father and son thus denounce Gertrude as having entered into a sexual partnership with an 'incestuous' and 'adulterate beast' who has won her to his 'shameful lust' (42–6).

The words 'incest' and 'incestuous' resonate throughout the play, in the speeches of both Hamlet and his dead father. Even before Hamlet encounters his father's ghost on the battlements, he grieves in soliloquy that his mother has employed such 'wicked speed, to post | With such dexterity to incestuous sheets' (1.156–7). The Ghost bids Hamlet not to 'Let the royal bed of Denmark be | A couch for luxury and damnèd incest' (1.5.84). Hamlet resolves, as we have seen, to kill Claudius not at prayer but when he is drunk or asleep or, most of all, when he is 'in th' incestuous pleasure of his bed' (3.3.89–90). And when Hamlet finally achieves the fervently desired goal of killing his uncle-stepfather, he underscores the crime of incest as an ultimate justification of the homicide: 'Here, thou incestuous, murderous, damnèd Dane, | Drink off this potion. Is thy union here? | Follow my mother' (5.2.327–9). With his grim pun on 'union' as referring both to the pearl that Claudius has thrown into the poisoned drinking cup (270) and to the sexual and marital union of Claudius and Gertrude,[11] Hamlet wryly consigns Claudius to an eternity of incestuous embrace. 'Follow my mother.'

Today we are apt to regard marriage with a deceased brother's wife as outside the proscription against incest, but clearly this has not always been the case; witness the prolonged and at times hysterical debate in the British Parliament during the late nineteenth century against marriage with a deceased wife's sister—a phenomenon that Gilbert and Sullivan's *Iolanthe* could refer to as 'that annual blister'. Henry VIII, famously, had married his deceased brother's wife—unless, of course, one considers that previous marriage of Katharine of Aragon to Arthur as invalid. In *Hamlet*, the words 'incest' and 'incestuous' appear with a frequency that is highly marked in the Shakespeare canon: they appear five times, as also in *Pericles* (where incest figures in the plot), and otherwise only three scattered metaphorical instances in *Measure for Measure* (3.1.141)*, King Lear* (3.2.55), and *The Rape of Lucrece* (921). The unusual emphasis in *Hamlet* underscores a point: father and son are as one in denouncing Gertrude's marriage as a morally offensive act. Perhaps we should say that the 'father' here is as the son identifies with and idealises him; the Ghost does appear to be real in his appearing to Horatio and the men on watch, but the character as Shakespeare presents him blends so imperceptibly into the King Hamlet of young Hamlet's memory that we have trouble distinguishing what is fact from what is filial idealisation.[12]

Certainly King Hamlet is a figure of the past, identified throughout with a kingdom of Denmark that no longer exists under Claudius. King

---

[11] See Harry Levin, *The Question of Hamlet* (Oxford, 1959), p. 98.

[12] When the Ghost accuses Claudius of being not only an 'incestuous' but also an 'adulterate beast' (1.5.43), a possible inference is that the Ghost suspects Claudius and Gertrude of having been lovers before the murder took place. Bertram Joseph's attempt to explain away the word 'adulterate' as applying to sin generally in late medieval and Renaissance texts (*Conscience and the King: a Study of Hamlet* (London, 1953), pp. 17–18) has won some adherents, including Rebecca Smith, 'A Heart Cleft in Twain: the Dilemma of Shakespeare's Gertrude', in Carolyn Ruth Swift Lenz, Gayle Greene, and Carol Thomas Neely (eds.), *The Woman's Part: Feminist Criticism of Shakespeare* (Urbana, 1980), pp. 194–210, but has also been cogently refuted by Adelman (*Suffocating Mothers*, pp. 15 and 38, n. 7). More simply, the Ghost may regard Gertrude's hasty desertion of him as 'adulterous' in the sense of being flagrantly disloyal to his memory and to their marriage bed. The marriage, in the Ghost's view, should have lasted eternally or at least more than 'a month'. The word 'adulterate' and its various cognates do not appear elsewhere in *Hamlet*, unlike 'incest' and 'incestuous', which are repeatedly applied to Claudius. Wilson, *What Happens in 'Hamlet'*, pp. 292 ff., points out that in Belleforest's version of the story, Hamlet's father declares of the murderer 'that before he had any violent or bloody hands, or once committed parricide upon his brother, he had incestuously abused his wife'. Wilson is convinced of Gertrude's infidelity before her husband's death, but Shakespeare's text leaves that possibility very much in doubt and, in my mind, quite improbable.

Hamlet, the embodiment of ancient chivalry, 'smote the sledded Polacks on the ice' and slew Fortinbras of Norway in an armed combat in which the two contestants wagered their whole kingdoms on the outcome (1.1.67–99). We can scarcely imagine Claudius accepting such a challenge, and indeed today we can perhaps admire his choice of astute diplomacy over military intervention. Claudius disarms the threat of an invasion by young Fortinbras with a negotiated deal that saves face and leaves everyone happy except Poland, whom young Fortinbras is now licensed to invade instead of Denmark. King Hamlet may seem today to be something of a cowboy, to use the phrase picked out these days for President Bush, but in Horatio's view and that of Denmark generally he is remembered and mourned as 'our valiant Hamlet' (88). The point here is that King Hamlet is remembered and idealised as a heroic figure, brave, resolute, incorruptible.

Another important memory of the dead King Hamlet is that he was protective of his wife, even while privately aware of what the play poses as her weaknesses as a woman and hence her need for his firm male guidance and his gentle forbearance. Again, the attributes can be identified both in Hamlet's idealisations of a dead father and in verifiable spoken testimony. Hamlet remembers a father who was 'so loving to my mother | That he might not beteem the winds of heaven | Visit her face too roughly' (1.2.140–2). This is no doubt as a son should remember his father, but the Ghost too remembers his marriage to Gertrude as one of exalted and mutual respect: his love for Gertrude, he tells his son, 'was of that dignity | That it went hand in hand even with the vow | I made to her in marriage' (1.5.49–51). The play called 'The Murder of Gonzago', which the travelling players put on before Claudius and Gertrude and all the court, offers further suggestions as to the kind of husband we are to perceive in the dead King Hamlet, granted of course that this evidence is by way of an indirect analogy in a play put on at Hamlet's specific request. Since Hamlet has also asked the First Player if he and his company could, 'for a need, study a speech of some dozen or sixteen lines which I would set down and insert in't' (2.2.540–3), we may find ourselves wondering if the play-within-the-play's pointed observations on fatherly wisdom and motherly lack of self-knowledge are embodied in Hamlet's additions.[13] Certain it is that the play-within-the-play, though designed in the final instance to 'catch the conscience of the King' (2.2.606), devotes

---

[13] See Adelman, *Suffocating Mothers*, p. 25.

a great deal of its emotional intensity to the portrait of a royal marriage and to the moral failures of the wife. The Player King, knowing that he will die soon, offers his wife the comfort of looking forward to another marriage. When the Player Queen protests that she could never do such a thing, and that re-marriage would be tantamount to murdering her first husband ('A second time I kill my husband dead | When second husband kisses me in bed', 3.2.182–3), her wisely compassionate husband offers her forbearance for the yielding to circumstance that he knows will be her destiny. 'Our wills and fates do so contrary run | That our devices still are overthrown', he concludes (209–10), in a typically sententious observation to which his age and male authority give him special access. As Hamlet remembers and idealises his parents in their marriage, his father was nearly godlike in his capacity for the compassionate understanding of human weakness, even in his wife.

The Player King in 'The Murder of Gonzago' is, like Hamlet's own father, old and near death. His prediction of his own imminent demise is unconsciously and ironically proleptic of the murder; it also speaks to the sense in which King Hamlet was old. Hamlet remembers that 'His beard was grizzled', and Horatio confirms this feature from his own observation of the Ghost: 'It was, as I have seen it in his life, | A sable silvered' (1.2.245–7). The Player King lays stress on the fact that 'My operant powers their functions leave to do' (3.2.172). A feature of this remembering on Hamlet's part is that it imagines a father who is old enough to be thought of no longer as a sexual partner for Hamlet's mother. Even when Hamlet recalls how Gertrude 'would hang on him [old Hamlet] | As if increase of appetite had grown | By what it fed on' (1.2.143–5), the image is notably decorous and even chaste when we contrast it with Hamlet's imaginings of Claudius as the grotesque and satyr-like possessor of Gertrude's body. Kenneth Branagh's four-hour film of *Hamlet* offers a persuasive glimpse of old Hamlet's fatherly aging: in a flashback, we are shown Gertrude and a trimly athletic Claudius enjoying a game of shuffleboard, visibly comfortable in each other's company, while a rose-cheeked and roly-poly older King Hamlet sits to one side, beaming genially and unjealously on the companionable activity of his wife and brother.

The relationship of Hamlet's parents is thus remembered and expurgated in Shakespeare's play in the chaste vein of Joachim and Anna, for example, the legendary parents of Mary. In this account, Joachim was regularly thought of as long past childbearing, so that the birth of Mary could be understood as miraculous and essentially parthenogenetic.[14] And of course the same is true of legends about Mary and her husband Joseph. In the medieval cycle plays, Joseph is the comic *vieux jaloux* no longer capable himself of siring a son and disturbed by his wife's pregnancy until he is visited by the Angel with the good news of the Incarnation.[15] The comparable de-sexualising of old Hamlet offers a significant psychological defence for the son, enabling him to identify with the imagined saint-like father as a means of warding off those aspects of Claudius that Hamlet wishes to deny in himself. Not coincidentally, perhaps, Hamlet thinks of Polonius as very old; he is, after all, the father of the young woman with whom Hamlet has been emotionally engaged. Polonius calls to Hamlet's mind the 'satirical rogue' who says 'that old men have gray beards, that their faces are wrinkled, their eyes purging thick amber and plum-tree gum, and that they have a plentiful lack of wit, together with the most weak hams' (2.2.197–201). Old age can be daunting, even disgusting, but in the case of King Hamlet it also insures against potency.

Hamlet is no less aware of, and concerned about, his mother's continued sexual activity at a time of life when, in the son's anxious view, erotic desire should no longer be operant. 'At your age | The heyday in the blood is tame, it's humble, | And waits upon the judgment', he lectures her (3.4.69–71). Gertrude may be all of fifty; we do not know. In Zeffirelli's film of *Hamlet*, Glenn Close portrays her as a vibrantly sexual woman, erotically attracted to Alan Bates, appropriately enough for modern audiences in which the expectation is of continued sexual activity well past menopause. Hamlet is strongly of the opposite view. 'O shame, where is thy blush?' he hurls at Gertrude.

> Rebellious hell,
> If thou canst mutine in a matron's bones,
> To flaming youth let virtue be as wax
> And melt in her own fire. Proclaim no shame
> When the compulsive ardor gives the charge,
> Since frost itself as actively doth burn,
> And reason panders will.   (3.4.82–9)

In Hamlet's opinion, a woman like Gertrude, in her middle years, should understand that sexuality is no longer appropriate when one is past childbearing, and indeed is indecent. It offers a horrendous model to younger

---

[14] See for example the play of 'Joachim and Anna' in the N-Town cycle.
[15] See 'Joseph's Trouble about Mary' in the York cycle, or 'Joseph's Doubt' in the N-Town cycle.

women; if desire can 'mutine in a matron's bones', then, *a fortiori,* young women cannot be expected to offer any defence against lustful desire. The deep puritanical mistrust of carnality that Hamlet imagines himself to share with his father is immeasurably reinforced by the prospect of a mother who, Hamlet may well suppose, is newly sexually active with her new partner in a way that she was not in her own lawful wedlock of many years. (Perhaps we should recollect at this point that Anne Hathaway was eight years older than Shakespeare when they conceived a child in 1582, that their marriage was hastily arranged because of the pregnancy, that he lived apart from his wife and family for most of his adult life, and that he and Anne had no more children after the birth of their twins in 1585.)

Boys and young men are generally uncomfortable thinking about their parents as sexual partners, as Freud observes; the same can certainly be true of young women, but Freud is interested in the young male, and so, in *Hamlet,* is Shakespeare.[16] If this is generally true, how much more so is it true in Hamlet's feelings about the incestuous coupling of a murderous uncle and stepfather with Hamlet's mother! In every way, Claudius is depicted as the monstrous opposite of King Hamlet. It is as though Shakespeare creates two images of the father for Hamlet, two divided sensibilities of the same awesome and frightening figure, of whom one is safely dead and therefore idealised and desexualised to keep him from becoming a rival for the mother, while the other continues to possess the mother as a hated rival. Shakespeare transforms the raw material of his source story into a fable of divided and ambiguous feelings about the father. Hamlet's loathing of his own sexuality intensifies his hatred for the uncle and stepfather who embodies the promptings that Hamlet longs to disown and suppress in himself.

'Look here upon this picture, and on this.' To turn from King Hamlet to Claudius, as Gertrude has done, and as Hamlet now bids her direct her gaze from one portrait to the other, is to turn from a loving and almost saintlike older husband to one who, in Hamlet's imagination, is the incarnation of lust. Having averted his gaze from any suggestion of sexual activity on the part of his true father, Hamlet now positively wallows in the images of animalistic coupling between Claudius and Gertrude. 'Nay', he upbraids her, 'but to live | In the rank sweat of an enseamèd bed, | Stewed in corruption, honeying and making love | Over the nasty sty!' (3.4.93–6). 'Enseamèd' here means saturated in the grease and filth of

[16] See Lidz, *Hamlet's Enemy,* pp. 10–12.

passionate lovemaking. To be 'stewed' in corruption is to be soaked and bathed in it, with the suggestion of a 'stew' or brothel, and perhaps too with the suggestion of soaking in a hot tub as a treatment for venereal disease. Part of what is so distressing about this image in Hamlet's mind is that he is now picturing his mother as co-partner in a grotesque coupling that is both lubricated and cemented by the mingling sweat of their two bodies.[17]

Even when Hamlet exhorts his mother to stay out of Claudius's bed, he does so in negative terms that again conjure up the sexual act in all its primal vigour and horror. When Gertrude asks what she should do now, Hamlet replies,

> Not this by no means that I bid you do:
> Let the bloat king tempt you again to bed,
> Pinch wanton on your cheek, call you his mouse,
> And let him, for a pair of reechy kisses,
> Or paddling in your neck with his damned fingers,
> Make you to ravel all this matter out
> That I essentially am not in madness
> But mad in craft.   (3.4.188–95)

Hamlet need not have dwelt on this sexual foreplay in order to beg her to keep his secret. Hamlet is obsessed with the forbidden image of his mother as a sexual object being avidly groped at the neck and breasts by her sexual partner. The sexuality that Hamlet loathes in himself is scapegoated onto the hated uncle, the false father who has supplanted Hamlet's blood father by killing that good angel and taking his place as the seducer. Whether Hamlet unconsciously desires his mother is not clearly enunciated in the text; perhaps we catch a hint of this, as Janet Adelman has suggested to me, in Hamlet's description to Horatio of how Claudius has 'killed my king and whored my mother, | Popped in between th'election and my hopes' (5.2.64–5), where 'popped in' has possibly migrated from the political to the material domain.[18] The standard Freudian oedipal explanation, of course, is that Hamlet's disgust is a recoil from his own forbidden and unconscious desire. Whether or not that is a plausible

---

[17] For Linda Bamber, *Comic Women, Tragic Men* (Stanford, 1982), pp. 71 ff., *Hamlet* is, of all Shakespeare's tragedies, 'the one in which the sex nausea is most pervasive'. She analyses 3.4 as the scene in which Hamlet's loathing 'comes to its climax'. Robert Ornstein, *The Moral Vision of Jacobean Drama* (Madison, 1960), sees this revulsion in *Hamlet* as integrally related to the pathology of the age (p. 17).

[18] Janet Adelman, in private conversation. I am greatly indebted to her for a careful reading and much assistance in this project, in addition to what she has written so cogently on the subject.

explanation, the fact that any such erotic desire for the mother is so concealed or simply absent in the text of *Hamlet* is interesting in itself;
Shakespeare does not take his exploration of Hamlet's character in that
direction. Instead, he focuses on the monstrosity of Claudius's pawing
over his wife's body. Claudius becomes in this scapegoating imagery a
'paddock' or toad, a 'bat', a 'gib' or tomcat (197), a loathsome animal
who is all the more to be expunged and repudiated because he embodies
the lust that Hamlet hates in himself.

What is Hamlet then to do? The Freud–Jones hypothesis of emotional
fibrillation leading to a paralysis of the will is plausible enough in the
abstract, but, as I've already suggested, runs into difficulty in the play
when Hamlet does indeed make a concerted attempt to kill Claudius,
managing instead to kill Polonius. The consequence of that act prompts
Hamlet to reflect on the very nature of forthright action. His attempt to
fulfil his father's behest has led to the death of a foolish but innocent man,
innocent at least to the extent of not deserving to die thus. 'For this same
lord, | I do repent', Hamlet tells his mother, and then goes on to explain
what he thinks the event must mean: 'heaven hath pleased it so | To pun-
ish me with this, and this with me, | That I must be their scourge and
minister' (3.4.179–82). Even if Polonius is, in Hamlet's view, guilty of
snooping, Hamlet sees that he too has erred rashly and will have to suffer
the consequences. As Fredson Bowers has acutely shown, this analysis
proves to be prophetic, for the rest of the play devolves by intricate logical steps from this pivotal event.[19] Ophelia goes mad. Laertes returns
from Paris, furiously intent on revenge against the slayer of his father, and
enters into a conspiracy in which the underhanded method of a secret
poison is to be used to murder Hamlet. Laertes becomes an instructive
example, for Hamlet and for us, of the often unintended consequences of
rash and precipitate action: he is right in identifying Hamlet as the slayer
of Polonius, but fatally misled in not understanding Claudius's greater
villainy as the cause behind it all. And so Laertes goes to his death
begging forgiveness from Hamlet.

Hamlet well perceives that rashness has its honourable place in human
action. 'Rashly', he says to Horatio in recounting his adventures at sea,

> And praised be rashness for it—let us know
> Our indiscretion sometimes serves us well
> When our deep plots do pall, and that should learn us

---

[19] Fredson T. Bowers, 'Hamlet as Minister and Scourge', *PMLA*, 70 (1955), 740–9.

> There's a divinity that shapes our ends,
> Rough-hew them how we will. (5.2.6–11)

This passage, that so inspired Melville in writing the mat-weaving episode in *Moby Dick* (chap. 47), helps explain a number of Hamlet's finer improvisations during his absence from Denmark: his discovery of the packet of materials being conveyed by Rosencrantz and Guildenstern to England bidding the English king to execute Hamlet, Hamlet's substitution of their names for his own, and so on. (Michael Almeyereda's 2000 film *Hamlet* presents us with a brilliant updating of this episode: on an overnight flight to England, Hamlet finds the incriminating death sentence in the laptop of his travelling companions and simply back-spaces the computer message in order to change the names.) At the same time, Hamlet wishes to understand the essential role of rashness in the larger providential context of a 'divinity that shapes our ends'.[20] In the case of the substituted message to the King of England, 'even in that was heaven ordinant' (48) by seeing to it that Hamlet had his father's signet in his purse so that he was able to seal the packet with a royal impression and thereby make the delusion entirely successful. Rashness thus has a purpose, but one that must be seen as sublimated to a greater plan—a plan that will find a way to bring about the play's resolution by means of an event like the killing of Polonius that was, in its own terms, a miscalculation.

Increasingly, as the play draws toward its close, Hamlet comes to terms with his psychological dilemma about two contrasting father figures by appealing to divine will, to a heavenly father, about whose oneness and perfection there can be no doubt. The image of old Hamlet as idealised father is subsumed into this heavenly father, although in a curious way, since Hamlet now senses that carrying out the literal instruction of his fleshly father must yield to the promptings of a 'divinity that shapes our ends' and that will somehow provide an opportunity for revenge more rich and appropriate that Hamlet could himself devise. Even in these things is heaven 'ordinant' (5.2.48). Hamlet's dead father is scarcely mentioned in the last scenes of the play; providence takes his place in *Hamlet*.[21]

---

[20] William Beatty Warner, *Chance and the Text of Experience: Freud, Nietzsche, and Shakespeare's 'Hamlet'* (Ithaca, 1986), argues throughout against the long history of criticism of *Hamlet* that has 'minimized the import of what we have found so much of in the drama, the virulent force of chance and the constitutive role of language' (p. 164). Wilson (*What Happens in 'Hamlet'*, p. 141) observes that 'The idea of having a play was a sudden inspiration on Hamlet's part; as ever, when he acts, he acts on impulse.'

[21] This point was made to me in private conversation by Janet Adelman.

How then is an individual to steer his or her way between rash or forthright action and a passive acquiescence to the will of providence? Hamlet greatly admires Fortinbras's self-confident ability to get on with what he determines to do, even while savouring the irony that Fortinbras's marching against Poland will lead to

> The imminent death of twenty thousand men
> That for a fantasy and trick of fame
> Go to their graves like beds, fight for a plot
> Whereon the numbers cannot try the cause,
> Which is not tomb enough and continent
> To hide the slain.   (4.4.61–6)

All this brave achievement is 'Even for an eggshell' (54). Hamlet's wise perception of what is so ultimately ironic and even absurd about such forthright action helps us to understand too that the active choice is not unequivocally the right choice in a given situation. The essential rightness of that perception is another reason for mistrusting an analysis of the play that ascribes Hamlet's inactivity (and his own impatience with his delay) to psychological vacillation.

The play's ending is a riddle in these terms. Hamlet discovers, after having flailed himself ceaselessly for inactivity, that his best clue is to await the call of providence—a providence that will surely not fail the individual who is properly attuned to its benign larger intent. 'There is special providence in the fall of a sparrow', Hamlet tells Horatio. 'If it be now, 'tis not to come; if it be not to come, it will be now; if it be not now, yet it will come. The readiness is all' (5.2.217–20). The riddle is that this resolution seems wholly out of harmony with the ethic of revenge, which, as embodied in unadulterated form in Shakespeare's source, sees nothing problematic with boldly resolute action.[22] Indeed, Saxo Grammaticus's saga valorises such action in an ending that is purely and simply one of satisfying the hero's need and desire to avenge the death of a father. Shakespeare's play chooses a path that provides a far more aesthetically satisfying picture. If Hamlet were to kill Claudius in cold blood, at prayer or otherwise, what would we think of him? Vengeance, when successfully carried out, has a chilling effect, as in Thomas Kyd's *The Spanish Tragedy*, for example, or Thomas Middleton's *The Revenger's Tragedy*. *Hamlet* is unique among Elizabethan revenge plays, and it is so precisely because the protagonist finally offers himself as a passive instrument of

---

[22] Levin, *The Question of Hamlet*, pp. 23–4.

providence rather than as the avenger. Providence sees to it that Hamlet is not disappointed: he kills Claudius not in cold blood but as a justifiable response to a threat on his own life, and he achieves the surcease of death for which he has so fervently longed. At least this is Hamlet's interpretation of his own story. Horatio has quite a different and more stoic reading

> Of accidental judgments, casual slaughters,
> Of deaths put on by cunning and forced cause,
> And, in this upshot, purposes mistook
> Fall'n on the inventors' heads.   (5.2.383–6)[23]

We hear these divergent interpretations arguing with one another as the play ends, just as Hamlet and Horatio have shared a loving friendship in which they have disagreed about many things.

King Hamlet, in commanding Hamlet to kill Claudius, is careful to specify that Hamlet is not to harm Gertrude. 'Leave her to heaven', he exhorts Hamlet, 'And to those thorns that in her bosom lodge, | To prick and sting her' (1.5.87–9). Does Hamlet proceed accordingly with his mother? He speaks to her so sharply in the closet scene, even brutally, that she fears at first for her life, and the Ghost of the father is prompted to intervene as well; he feels the need to 'whet' Hamlet's 'almost blunted purpose', and urges that the son 'step between her [Gertrude] and her fighting soul' (3.4.115–17). Yet Hamlet has promised himself (and us) that he will never allow 'The soul of Nero' to 'enter this firm bosom'; he will 'speak daggers to her, but use none' (3.2.393–5). This uncertainty about Hamlet's intent is instructive. It offers us two radically different and yet complementary readings of the closet scene. In one, Hamlet is the caring son and moralist who is seriously worried that his mother is heading straight for hell; hence his preaching to her, 'Confess yourself to heaven, | Repent what's past, avoid what is to come' (3.4.156–7). Arguably, he succeeds in his attempt to coach her in how to overcome the deleterious and pernicious effects of surrendering to 'custom' and 'habit' (168–9).[24] The other Hamlet is the angry and fearful child caught in an

---

[23] Eissler sees Horatio as a superego figure in the play (*Discourse on Hamlet and 'Hamlet'*, p. 382). He also proposes that Yorick 'is a thinly disguised father image', 'the only person in the entire play of whom Hamlet speaks with unreserved tenderness' (pp. 84–5). In this he agrees with Norman Symons, 'The graveyard scene in *Hamlet*', *International Journal of Psycho-Analysis*, 9, 96–119, at 101.

[24] See Warner, *Chance and the Text of Experience,* pp. 255–6. The unauthorised 1603 quarto of *Hamlet* offers a strong case for the Queen's coming around to Hamlet's side, at least in that version of the play. After the Ghost has left them together in her chambers (3.4), the Queen says in Q1: 'But as I have a soul, I swear by heaven | I never knew of this most horrible murder.' And then, when Hamlet has bid her 'assist me in revenge, | And in his death your infamy shall die',

oedipal crisis of epic proportions who calls out for his mother to abandon her incestuous and erotic attachment to the father in favour of reclaiming her needful child.[25] Joseph Papp's production of the play at New York's Public Theatre in 1968 astutely captured the spirit of this interpretation by starting the play with a manacled Hamlet in a coffin-like cradle at the foot of Claudius's and Gertrude's bed. The exhilarating ambiguity of this dual interpretation of Hamlet and his mother is of a piece with the play's similarly bifurcated and anxious approach to the dual image of the father as saint and as lecher. Part of Shakespeare's magic is to capture such ambiguity in dramatic form, where the very genre of theatre thrives on the clash of rival ideologies.

In the psychological terms of Hamlet's emotional crisis, the play's ending offers something far more substantial than confirmation of a purported oedipal anxiety about killing a father for the crime of desire that the son unconsciously harbours in his own psyche. Hamlet does kill Claudius, and is evidently reconciled to his mother; he and Gertrude appear to forgive each other (though the point is disputed in scholarly analyses of the play) and die reunited in an implicit repudiation of Claudius and all that he stands for.[26] The son has incorporated aspects of

---

the Queen replies: 'Hamlet, I vow by that majesty | That knows our thoughts and looks into our hearts, | I will conceal, consent, and do my best, | What stratagem soe'er thou shalt devise' (sig. G3–3v). Whatever the status of this problematic text, it seems to provide evidence that in some performances of a play called *Hamlet*, prior to 1603, the Queen declared her allegiance to her son. When the King enters a few moments later, her statement in Q1 that she has found Hamlet 'as raging as the sea' would appear to be a fabrication intended to protect her son from Claudius's prying investigation.

[25] Eissler diagnoses Hamlet as one whose misogyny is paradoxically heightened by his own powerful attachment to his mother: 'the hasty marriage of his mother had aroused a conflict with regard to his general relationship to women' (*Discourse on Hamlet and 'Hamlet'*, p. 420). 'His mother's behavior . . . is the primary root of Hamlet's distrust of emotionality, which is then extended from there to his own emotions' (p. 110). Wertham posits an 'Orestes complex' to illuminate the way in which 'Hamlet was more preoccupied with his mother's adultery than with his father's murder and that her infidelity turned his excessive attachment to the mother into bitter hostility' (Lidz, *Hamlet's Enemy*, p. 10, paraphrasing Wertham, 'The Matricidal Impulse').

[26] Cf. Thomas M. Kettle, 'A new way of misunderstanding *Hamlet*' (1905), in *The Day's Burden* (New York, 1918): 'The problem is set wholly from the outside. It is not a product of Hamlet's superculture, but of the sin of his uncle and the lesser sin of his mother . . . the play ends, thanks to Hamlet's course of action, in absolutely the best way in which it could end' (quoted in Claire Sacks and Edgar Whan (eds.), *'Hamlet': Enter Critic* (New York, 1960), pp. 140–1). Adelman (*Suffocating Mothers*, p. 34) is more sceptical: 'In the end we do not know whether or not Gertrude herself has been morally reclaimed', though Adelman does allow that 'Hamlet at least believes that she has returned to him as the mother he can call "good lady" (3.4.182)'. See above, n. 24 on the testimonial of Q1, where the Queen unambiguously aligns herself with her son. Adelman also takes the view that Hamlet 'shows very few signs of interest in his mother as a real

the idealised father, having completed the act of revenge not on murderous terms but at the promptings of a higher providential destiny. He has
scapegoated his own worst sexual self onto the hated figure of Claudius,
who dies unbewept and forgotten. Hamlet has partly come to terms with
his own sexuality by acknowledging his guilt and by etherialising sexual
desire into a moral insistence on chaste behaviour and penitent acknowledgement of weakness both in himself and in his mother. To be sure, the
price for this mood of calm and self-possession is high, as Adelman
points out: 'the parents lost to him at the beginning of the play can be
restored only insofar as they are entirely separated from their sexual bodies'. This is 'a pyrrhic solution' that 'does not bode well for Shakespeare's
representation of sexual union' in his subsequent tragedies (Adelman,
p. 35). Hamlet's own desire for sexual coupling with Ophelia is a necessary casualty of his family crisis, and he dies, so that his story is truly
tragic and even heroic; but it is also one in which Hamlet has found a
dearly bought resolution. Perhaps he is able now at last to affirm what he
said earlier to the ghost of his dead father: 'Rest, rest, perturbèd spirit!'
(1.5.192).

---

person who might be won to repentance' (p. 257, n. 43); and Bamber, *Comic Women*, p. 71, insists
that 'there is no reconciliation with women at the end of the play, as there is in the other
tragedies'. This seems to me unnecessarily severe. Of course Gertrude is a fantasy-object to
Hamlet in this scene, but she is also his mother, and his distress at her behaviour arises in good
part at least out of a deep caring for her. He wishes to protect her from herself as Hamlet's father
had done during his lifetime. At the same time, one should not oversimplify Hamlet's longing
to reform his mother as high-minded and selfless, as Bradley argues in *Shakespearean Tragedy*
(p. 115) and Roland Mushat Frye in *The Renaissance Hamlet* (Princeton, 1984), pp. 152 and
162. Hamlet's motives are at once deeply self-centred and well intended.

Celtic Origins, the Western and the Eastern Celts

WOLFGANG MEID
University of Innsbruck

IT IS A GREAT HONOUR for me to be invited to give the renowned Sir John Rhŷs Memorial Lecture. But it also fills me with a certain amount of anxiety that I may not be quite up to this task, and disappoint my audience. The announced title of my lecture, 'Celtic Origins, the Western and the Eastern Celts', may have led you to suppose that what I am going to present will be, in a balanced way, a general survey of the Celtic question. However, the main focus of my paper will be on the less known eastern Celts on whom I recently did some research. But in order to achieve some balance, these remarks must be placed in a more general framework in which the controversial Celtic question itself must be addressed, and the question of Celtic origins plus the movements and distribution of Celtic-speaking groups brought into perspective, together with the linguistic and cultural aspects attached to them. This seems an impossible task to cover in one hour, and instead of showering linguistic and archaeological data upon you, I will just state my opinions on some of the more controversial matters.

Some preliminaries

I am by profession an historical linguist—not so much the sound-shifting type, but rather a philologist interested in the traditions of or about the

Read at the Academy 6 March 2007.

Proceedings of the British Academy, **154**, 177–199. © The British Academy 2008.

various peoples who speak, or once spoke, an Indo-European language. Therefore my approach will be tainted by that. I am not an archaeologist preoccupied with material culture and its remains, and so I am not an expert in this field. But I understand that a number of archaeologists, especially in Britain, have problems with the notion 'Celtic', some of them suspecting even that this is a fictitious concept with a fictitious reality behind it, whereas, on the contrary, many Continental archaeologists are quite carefree in their use of this term as a cultural label. But 'Celtic' is not primarily a cultural label; rather it is, when it first emerges, an ethnic label, referring to the *Keltoí* or *Kéltai,*[1] *Celtae,* an ethnic group in Western Europe to which—and this is the important point—a distinct language can be attributed. This language—or rather, group of closely related dialects—can be therefore called 'Celtic'.

So far, so good. But here Comparative Linguistics stepped in and was able to show that this Continental Celtic language group attested by inscriptions from France, Switzerland, northern Italy and Spain, as well as by onomastic evidence from a much wider area, had close relations in Britain and Ireland, and that this ensemble constituted a distinct subgroup within the Indo-European family of languages. And now scientific terminology comes in: onto this whole Indo-European sub-group, by extension, and in view of the mutual linguistic relationship of its dialects, the label 'Celtic' was attached, although the ethnic term 'Celts' did perhaps not apply to the speakers of these so-called 'Celtic' dialects in Britain and in Ireland, who preferred to call themselves *Brittones, Scotti* or just by any other tribal names.[2]

But the non-attestation of this ethnic term for the people of Britain and Ireland does not mean that there was no awareness of this notion. We know—Caesar refers to this[3]—that detachments of Continental Celtic tribes crossed over the Channel in recent prehistoric times to settle in southern Britain, retaining for the most part their original names,[4] and though Caesar here gives their origin *ex Belgio,* at least some of them

---

[1] The form Κελτοί is found with Herodotos and other Greek writers. Strabo says this name cited by him in the variant form Κέλται is the older one; he himself refers to the Celts constantly as Γαλάται.

[2] A similar situation, by the way, is found in the Germanic area; *Germani,* the name of a rather obscure tribe, being extended to the whole or the greater part of the Germanic-speaking ethnos which conceived itself rather as tribal entities, *Saxones, Francones* etc.

[3] *Bellum Gallicum* 5. 12, 1–2.

[4] In fact, tribal names such as *Atrebates* and *Parisii* occur on both sides; *Catuvellauni* (in South Britain; their king *Cassivellaunus,* Caesar) and *Catalauni* (in the Marne region: Châlons) may also be compared.

must have come from the area where the inhabitants—again according to Caesar[5]—called themselves *Celtae*.[6] It is almost certain that these emigrants took this name over with them, and if not used any further must have at least remembered it. The Bretons in Bretagne may serve here as a parallel: they are by origin *Brittones* from Britain who have held on to their name in their new surroundings.

Therefore one should not deny outright the people of southern Britain their Celticity solely on the basis of the non-attestation of this term which may be simply due to the scarceness of the sources. Negative evidence cannot constitute positive proof.[7]

Language is a means of communication, essential to people living together, and these people have a way of life which one may call their 'culture'. But with Celtic allegedly being a fictitious term, archaeologists have difficulty in applying this epithet to the material remains they excavate, holding that they cannot find sufficient proof that these remains constitute evidence of 'Celtic' culture in these isles. This may be so for the material remains which cannot speak out sufficiently for themselves, or for the people who left them. The fact that people live together in rather small communities makes their culture variable on a small scale. There is no such thing as a uniform Celtic culture, just as there is, and was, no such thing as a uniform Celtic language, not even in prehistoric times—notions like Proto-Celtic, 'Urkeltisch', or Common Celtic are notional abstracts which do not stand for a uniform language but mean that this language, in spite of variations on a lower level, is characterised by a set of common features which distinguishes it from other languages of Indo-European descent. The emergence of linguistic Celticity is a gradual process spanning many centuries. In this process the original feeling of linguistic identity may be transformed and eventually lost, and Celtic consciousness reintroduced by other means.

Celtic perhaps branched off from the Indo-European mainstream in the second millennium BC. It has certain features in common with eastern Indo-European languages,[8] a fact which tends to show that the ancestors of the Celts came from eastern parts of Europe, settling then in central

---

[5] *Bellum Gallicum* 1. 1, 1.

[6] This narrow relation of Britain with *Gallia omnis* is evident from a number of passing remarks throughout the whole of Caesar's *Commentarii*.

[7] The other general term for the Celts, Γαλάται, or other names built on the basis of the pan-Celtic root *gal-*, valour'—the British ethnicon *Galatini*, the Irish tribal name (in Leinster) *Galeóin*—also seem to have been known in Britain and Ireland.

[8] See K. H. Schmidt, *Celtic: a Western Indo-European Language?* (Innsbruck, 1996).

and western Europe where, in the late second and in the early first millennium BC, their ethnogenesis, or rather ethnic consolidation, seems to have taken place. They had perhaps some share in the Urnfield and Hillfort culture of the second millennium BC, and a larger share in the following Hallstatt culture (roughly 800–400 BC), especially in its western part, but definitely Celtic in character is the so-called Latène civilisation (from 400 BC onwards).

Celtic origins

This said I wish to return for a moment to the question of Celtic origins. I said that the Celts, or rather their linguistic ancestors, came originally from the east. There is an alternative theory, fashionable at the moment but nevertheless erroneous in my view, that the Celtic languages came into being and developed as the language of the megalithic population of the Atlantic fringe. Professor Barry Cunliffe poses a question which he is inclined to answer in the affirmative: 'Could it be that, far from being a language introduced by invaders or migrants moving in from central Europe, it was the language of the indigenous Atlantic communities which had developed over the long period of interaction beginning in the fifth millennium BC?'[9]

The answer to this is a blunt 'No', as a positive response would ignore the Indo-European origins and connections of Celtic. It is only true insofar as the very late forms of Celtic developed in the British Isles, but Celtic speech itself was introduced from outside, and that means by a sufficient number of immigrant speakers—sufficient to cause the non-Indo-European language of the original population to disappear. You can't quite do without migrations. Likewise, English was brought onto this island, and the inmates of the three boats of Hengist and Horsa evidently would not have been sufficient to force their language onto the British-speaking populations.

The eastern origin and westward drift of Celtic, and the staged development of Celtic itself may be illustrated by two models taken from a recent publication by Patrizia de Bernardo Stempel (Figs. 1 and 2).[10]

---

[9] B. Cunliffe, *The Celts: a Very Short Introduction* (Oxford, 2003), p. 26.
[10] P. de Bernardo Stempel, 'Language and the historiography of Celtic-speaking peoples', pp. 45 f., figs. 15 and 16.

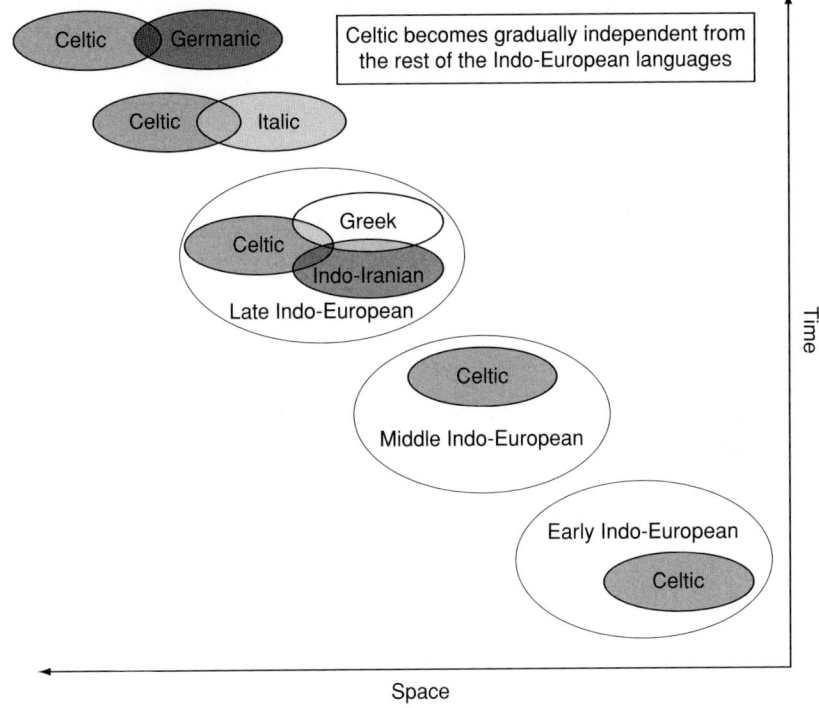

Figure 1. The westward drift of Celtic (from P. de Bernardo Stempel, 'Language and the historiography of Celtic-speaking peoples', fig. 16).

Of course in the early stages of the drift model the designation 'Celtic' must not be taken literally. By 'Celtic' is meant dialect features (isoglosses) which contribute to the gradual making of Celtic as we later find it. I cannot comment here on the stage model, which is a matter for future discussions, nor can I say that I agree with every detail, but the notion of a staged development, evidenced by preserved features of these stages in the linguistic record, seems correct.

By the time of the Latène civilisation the Celtic territory was already more widespread than the extent of the Latène civilisation, so Celtic culture and Latène are not synonymous concepts. Earlier movements of Celtic speakers, into northern Italy, the Iberian Peninsula and Ireland, brought still archaic forms of Celtic speech and forms of Hallstatt culture to these parts. Latène forms were introduced only later, secondarily.

The Latène territory of Celtic, that is Gaul in its widest sense, and by extension Britain, is linguistically *p*-Celtic, by which is meant that it shows the innovation by which the Indo-European labiovelar, $*k^w$, was

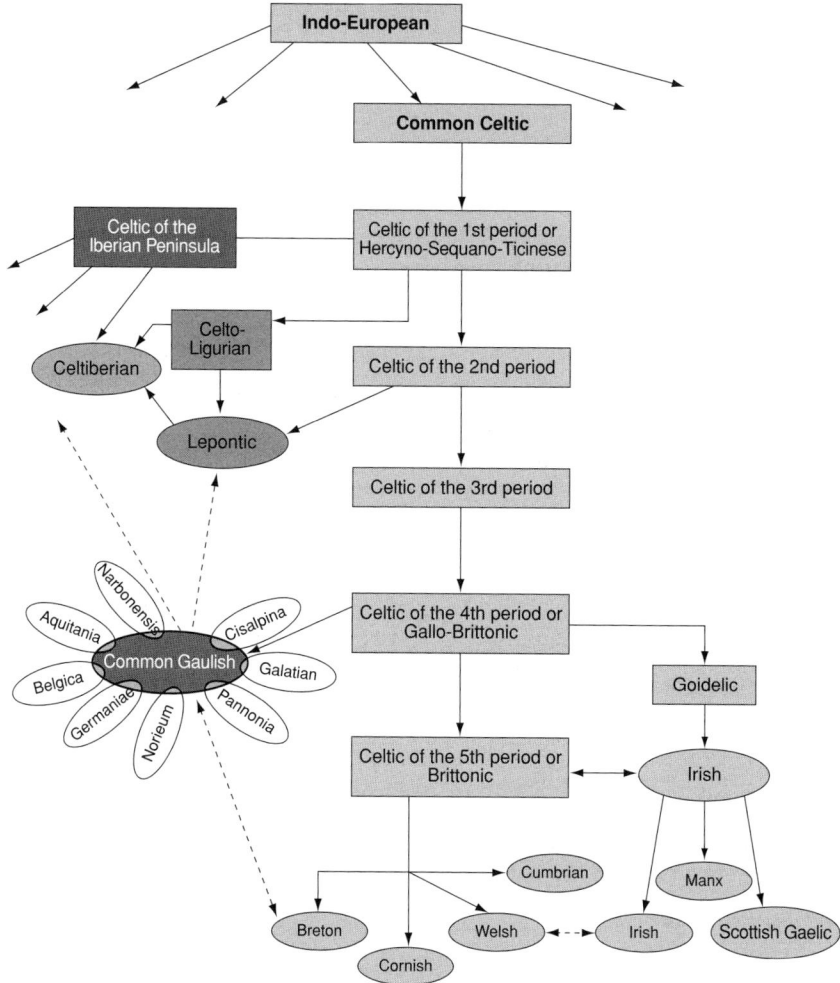

Figure 2. A gradual-development model of Celtic (from P. de Bernardo Stempel, 'Language and the historiography of Celtic-speaking peoples', fig. 15).

transformed to *p*, whereas in the archaic Celtic periphery $*k^w$ was retained. Even in Gaul there are isolated instances of retained $*k^w$, such as in *Sēquana*, the river Seine, and in the month-name EQVOS in the Coligny calendar, as against normal Gaulish-Britisch **epos* in the name of the horse-goddess *Epona*.

The older, Indo-European **p* had already been lost earlier (*atir* in Gaulish, *athir* in Irish, as against Latin *pater*). This loss of **p* is Common

Celtic, one of the oldest features which distinguish Celtic from other Indo-European languages (in Germanic *p became f: *father*).

Curiously enough the voiced labiovelar, *g^w, became b everywhere (Indo-European *$g^w\bar{o}us$ > Ir. *bó*, Celtiberian *bou-stom* 'cattle stand'). Hence, this shift is also very early, in fact common Celtic, whereas *k^w > p is later and regionally restricted, a dialect feature.

So there is a gradual development of and within Celtic, a variety in space and time, but there is also continuity in identity. If we apply this to the cultural level, there is bound to be diversity in time and space also, because there cannot be cultural uniformity over so vast a territory and stretch of time, with so many populations of ever varying Celtic speech. But there can be, and must have been, common traits, perceived similarities. It is by and large not the archaeological record which reveals these common cultural features but rather the combined linguistic, literary and oral traditions supplemented, where the former are missing or scarce, as on the Continent, by historical testimony. There are if not identical at least similar systems or patterns of human behaviour, of social structures and government which pervade the Celtic world. Raimund Karl has made a notable effort to describe and explain them in his recent book on ancient Celtic social structures.[11] To mention just a few at random: the commitment to 'heroic' values and war-like behaviour; heads as trophies; social status—an inequality implying a different honour-price according to rank; various forms of legal marriage or sexual union; rules of inheritance; the joint family as owner of landed property, as in the Early Irish system, where the joint family (four generations) is the owner of landed property; the system of fosterage, meaning the education of children outside their own families; legal contracts, surety, hostages; etc.

Many of these concepts, or practices, are found in other societies too, and therefore by themselves would not seem to be indicators of any specific Celtic culture. Indeed the concept of the territorial unit and its population, the *$*teut\bar{a}$, or of the unit of common genetic descent, *$*gentis$, *$*g\text{n}tis$ or the like, occurs all over Europe, and is an Indo-European heritage. But the occurrence of such concepts, if bound together with a definite linguistic terminus (a specific word) and co-occurring with other concepts and related termini, such as the co-occurrence of *$*teut\bar{a}$ and *$*r\bar{e}ks$ (Irish *túath, rí* with equivalents in all Celtic languages) is proof of a certain social structure within the Celtic realm. It may not have been

[11] R. Karl, *Altkeltische Sozialstrukturen* (Budapest, 2006).

present at every place (the Celtic *rīks* may have been deposed and king-ship abolished), but it is there as an ideal, as the many personal names in *-rix* show. It is set off from the Germanic world where **teutā* and **teutonos* (later **kuningas*) is the formal expression of the equivalent constellation; but Celtic **rīg-* had already made its impact, as the term **rīkja-* (German *Reich* and cognates) from Celtic **rīgiom* and the adjective **rīkja-* 'rich' (< **'kingly'*) show. Add to this the institution of the **ambaktos* (also borrowed into Germanic).[12] Where this word as such does not occur, as in Hispanic Celtic, it is at least present as a personal name, *Ambatus*, which in this form is typical for Hispania.

As regards the reconstruction of Indo-European lexemes, a generally agreed principle is that if a word occurs in three individual Indo-European languages (or language groups) it may be safely posited for the protolanguage. (Indeed, I should say, even two occurrences in widely separate languages may be sufficient.) Applying this principle to the ancient Celtic dialects, when three go together—e.g. Irish, Welsh and Gaulish, or Celtiberian—a certain cultural terminus, and the concept behind it, may be posited for Common Celtic, even if it is not attested in all of the Celtic dialects, particularly in the Continental Celtic ones which are notoriously of fragmentary attestation. Thus, the concept and institution of the *druid*, under this term (with its archaic word-formation: **dru-wid-s*) which is attested from Gaul, Britain and Ireland, but not from Spain, must nevertheless be presupposed for Common Celtic; **dru-wid-s* means 'who has the wisdom of the oak', the oak being the world-tree, symbol of the universe. Equally of pan-Celtic currency are the **wātis*, the **bardos*, the **ambaktos* and other representatives of the social system, for instance the *vassus*. The etymological background of the **wātis* is present in Italic (Latin *vātēs*) and Germanic (in the name of *Wōdan* and related vocabulary)[13] and thus transcends Celtic, therefore by implication is a pre-Celtic inheritance. The word **bardos* is based on an already Indo-European collocation 'putting praise (upon someone)', *$*g^w r(ə)$- $d^h\bar{e}$-*, as evidenced by Vedic Indic *gíras dhā-*.[14] In this way linguistic evidence may supplement, or act as substitute for, archaeological evidence where this is missing, or cannot speak out clearly enough for itself. You would not know about a druid or many other things from the archaeological record; the real proof

---

[12] Old High German *ambaht* 'officer', *ambahti* 'office' (Modern German *Amt*) and cognates.

[13] W. Meid, *Aspekte der germanischen und keltischen Religion im Zeugnis der Sprache* (Innsbruck, 1991), pp. 25–7, with n. 24.

[14] For references, see W. Meid, *Keltische Personennamen in Pannonien* (Budapest, 2005), p. 220.

of cultural concepts lies in the combined linguistic and philological record.

Some other examples of cultural notions include the following. 'Peace' is conceived as friendship, as a state of mutual love: *karantiom. This Celtic term replaced an Indo-European one based on the root *prī- 'to love', in Germanic *friþu- (German Friede). The opposite of peace is enmity. The enemy (Latin inimicus) in Old Irish is námae going back to *nāmant- which is quasi 'non amans'. This is an archaic, isolated word, but it is attested in Gaulish personal names, such as Namanto-bogius 'who "breaks" the enemy', or Ad-namatus 'facing the enemy', frequent in Pannonia.[15] So the opposed notions of friend–foe underlie those of peace and war, a semantically structured opposition.

To remain in the realm of war, the war-god is of course a very prominent figure in the Celtic pantheon, but we do not know the real name of this Celtic 'Mars'. According to Hispanic testimony,[16] he may have been called Neitos (Nētus, Nētō), related to Irish niath 'hero', but this is not sufficient evidence to award this name Common Celtic currency. 'Mars' occurs under many names or epithets, in Noricum as Latobius 'he who smites in fury'.[17] The many epithets, together with iconographic evidence, testify to his existence. There is also a war-goddess, or demon, Bodb in Irish, who may appear also in the shape of a crow (the bird that feeds on the carcasses of men fallen in battle). There is no direct cognate in Gaulish (apart from the lexical element occurring in names), but on Gaulish coins a crow is often depicted flying over the head of a mounted warrior riding into battle. This gives the concept 'Bodb' = war demon universal Celtic currency. One may note in this context that the Hispanic Celts thought it honourable for the fallen warrior to be defleshed by birds of prey because they were supposed to carry his soul to heaven.[18]

Speaking of Gods there is a great variation of names or epithets. The only pan-Celtic god known by name is Lugus, attested by corresponding

---

[15] Ibid., pp. 135, 160; also W. Meid, 'Freundschaft und Liebe in keltischen Sprachen', in L. Sawicki and D. Shalev (eds.), Donum grammaticum. Studies in Latin and Celtic Linguistics in Honour of Hannah Rosén (Leuven, 2002), p. 261.

[16] Macrobius, Saturnalia, 1.19.5, and inscriptions; see W. Meid, Die erste Botorrita-Inschrift. Interpretation eines keltiberischen Sprachdenkmals (Innsbruck, 1993), p. 100, for further references.

[17] W. Meid, 'Mars Latobius', in M. Ofitsch and Chr. Zinko (eds.), Studia Onomastica et Indogermanica. Festschrift für Fritz Lochner von Hüttenbach zum 65. Geburtstag (Graz, 1995).

[18] According to two ancient testimonies, Silius Italicus, 3.341–3 and Aelianus, de natura animal- ium, 10.22; see J. M. Blázquez Martinez, Religiones primitivas de Hispania, I (Rome, 1962), pp. 12 f.

forms from Gaul, Spain, Ireland and Wales, and in addition by quite a number of place-names of the type *Lugu-dunum*. His Roman cover-name seems to have been *Mercurius*, according to Caesar the god most venerated in Gaul. Lugus has affinities to the Germanic *Wōdan* who is also equated with Mercurius (*Mercurii dies = Wednesday, Odinsdag*). The Irish *Lug* is *il-dánach* 'many-gifted', and there is a curious dedication by a guild of cobblers, *collegium sutorum*, from Spain, not simply to Lugus, but to a plurality of *Lugoves*.[19] This multipersonal Lugus, like Mercurius, apart from other functions, must have also been a god of roads and travellers. Travellers wear out shoes, and are in need of either new ones or repairs, from which cobblers benefit. This explains the connection.

I think there is a lot to be said in favour of recurrent traits of Celtic culture. In order to find them and put them on a secure basis, an interdisciplinary approach seems to promise better results than one following only one particular line, because there is always the chance that we may discover structural patterns. So we had better forget such preposterous notions that there were no Celts, and consequently there was no such thing as Celtic culture. If it cannot be recognised in material culture, it is abundantly present in the linguistic and philological record, clear to see for everyone who cares to look.

But it must also be stressed that everywhere, in the course of their expansion, the Celts came in contact with other populations, partly of the same Indo-European origin (previous layers of settlement) and partly of non-Indo-European descent (Aquitanians, Iberians, Etruscans, Pannonians, etc.), and this gave rise to processes of cultural as well as ethnic assimilation and admixture. Even where Celtic communities maintained their identity they were no pure-bred societies, hence Celtic culture is of the same, hybrid character.

Eastward movements

But I feel I have already dwelt too long on these preliminaries. I said before that the Celts originally came from the East. But there is also a secondary movement back eastwards. You are perhaps familiar with the account, by Livius, of the legendary exodus of a mass of people from Gaul, partly into Italy, partly into the regions of the Hercynian forest

---

[19] *CIL*, II. 2818.

(*Hercynia silva*), the huge expanse covering central and east-central Europe.[20] There are movements, from at least the fourth century BC onwards, to the eastern Alpine regions, to Noricum, and along the Danube into Bohemia, Pannonia and further. They even made excursions into Greece (pillaging Delphi in 279), and some crossed over to Asia Minor and settled there (the redoubtable *Galátai*).[21]

Maybe some of these emigrants came from eastern France or southern Germany where the transition of the Hallstatt to the subsequent La Tène civilisation seems to have caused unrest, the Late Hallstatt centres being partly destroyed or abandoned, and the area apparently depopulated, as the scarcity of find materials tends to show.

Be that as it may, there is, more or less at the same time, settlement of Celtic tribes in Noricum and Pannonia. In Noricum they established a sort of confederate kingship (*regnum Noricum*) which came to be on good terms with the Romans who, however, took it over completely in AD 14, apparently without great difficulty. Before that the *Boii*, who had aggressively impinged on Dacian territory, were defeated and decimated by the Dacian king Burebista, and lost much of their power and significance. A strong Celtic settlement was near Aquincum (present-day Budapest), under the tribal name *Aravisci* or *Eravisci*, and other settlements were further inland, one near present-day Zagreb. But to the south, in the area of the *Dravus* and *Savus* river systems, was Pannonian territory, inhabited by very warlike tribes with near connections in Dalmatia; they also spoke an Indo-European language, which was different from Celtic (Fig. 3). Up to the middle of the last century this language was considered to be Illyrian, but the concept of Illyrian had been driven to extremes by then, and broke apart.[22] Illyrian properly speaking must be assumed to be restricted to the original Illyricum—present day Albania and the Kosovo region—but Pannonian is a near relation. The Pannonian language and the population speaking it originally extended much further north; the immigrating Celts overlaid it, not without conflicts, but later some form of coexistence and assimilation arose. Neither the Pannonians nor the Celts have left us with linguistic documentation in form of texts, the only

---

[20] Livius, *Ab urbe condita*, 5. 34–5; also Iustinus, *Epitoma* (excerpts from the lost *Universal History* of Pompeius Trogus), 24.4.1–4, who gives their numbers as 300,000.

[21] The evidence for these movements and settlements is well-known; for the most recent collections of the onomastic evidence see the publications by Sims-Williams (2006) and Raybould and Sims-Williams (2007).

[22] As to the Illyrian problem see Meid, *Keltische Personennamen*, pp. 10 f. with nn. 3, 4, 5, and p. 22, n. 14 with discussion and further references.

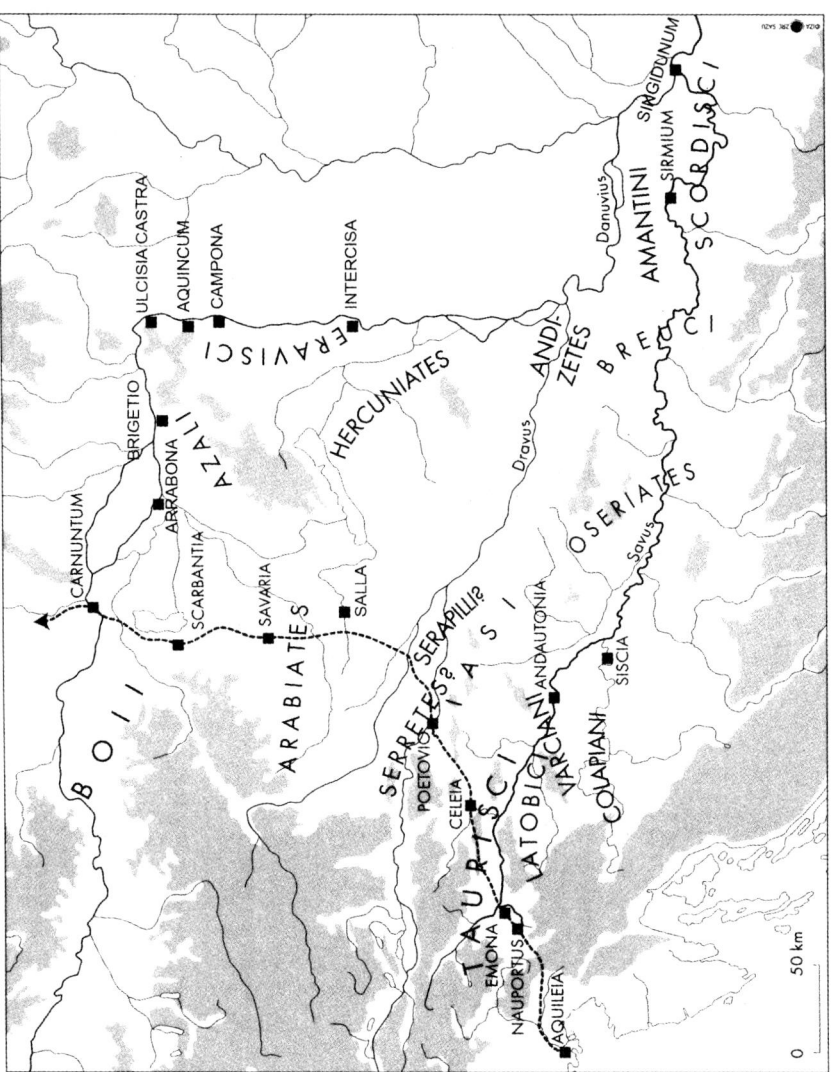

Figure 3. Tribal territories and places in Pannonia (from W. Meid, *Keltische Personennamen in Pannonien*, p. 346). Celtic tribes are the *Boii*, the *Eravisci*, the *Hercuniates*, the *Taurisci*, the *Latobici*, possibly the *Varciani*; the *Scordisci* are also Celtic by origin, but with strong Pannonian and Illyrian admixture. The other tribes on the map are presumably

linguistic evidence being personal, tribal and local names. It must be said that the local names in the Celtic settlement area are mostly Pannonian in origin, which shows that the Pannonians were the earlier population; *Aquincum, Arrabona, Campona, Ulcisia castra, Scarbantia* are such non-Celtic names. The name *Pannonia* itself is derived from an Indo-European root **pan-* denoting swampy territory,[23] which is characteristic for the Dravus/Savus region, and must have originally referred to that region, but was later extended to cover the whole Roman province. On account of its preserved Indo-European **p* this name *Pannonia* cannot be Celtic, the Celtic equivalent being attested in Gaulish as *anam*, glossed 'paludem' ('swamp').[24]

Personal names

Celtic or Pannonian personal names are attested mostly from funerary inscriptions of the Roman period, the Romans having added Pannonia to their empire in the late first century BC and second centuries AD. There are about 500 Celtic names or name families attested, perhaps more, but some of the names cannot be safely attributed.

Some remarks on a typology of these names

Personal names may be compounded, frequently with *-rix* or *-marus* ('great') as second parts elements, and then have an aristocratic or heroic connotation:

Bitu-rix	'king of the world'
Dago-rix	'king of good men' (or 'good king')
Nerto-marus	'great in strength' (Welsh *nerthfawr*)
Ressi-marus	'great in attack'
Brogi-marus	'great in land'.

Some of these occur quite frequently, as also, for example, does the prefix compound *Ad-namatus* 'facing the enemy' (Figs. 4 and 5).

---

[23] *IEW*, 807 f.

[24] In a fifth-century glossary of late Gaulish words or names, called 'Endlicher's Glossary'.

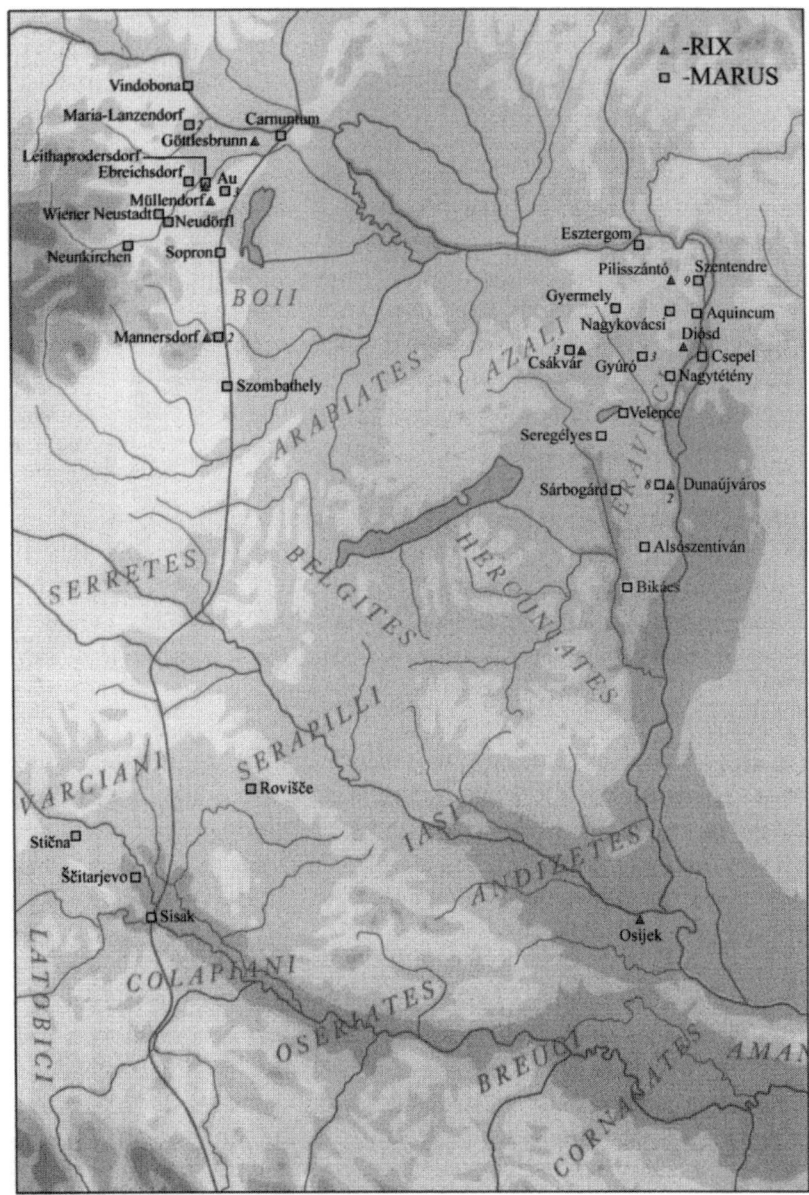

Figure 4. Distribution of Celtic compound names in *-rix* and *-marus* (from W. Meid, *Keltische Personennamen in Pannonien*, p. 347).

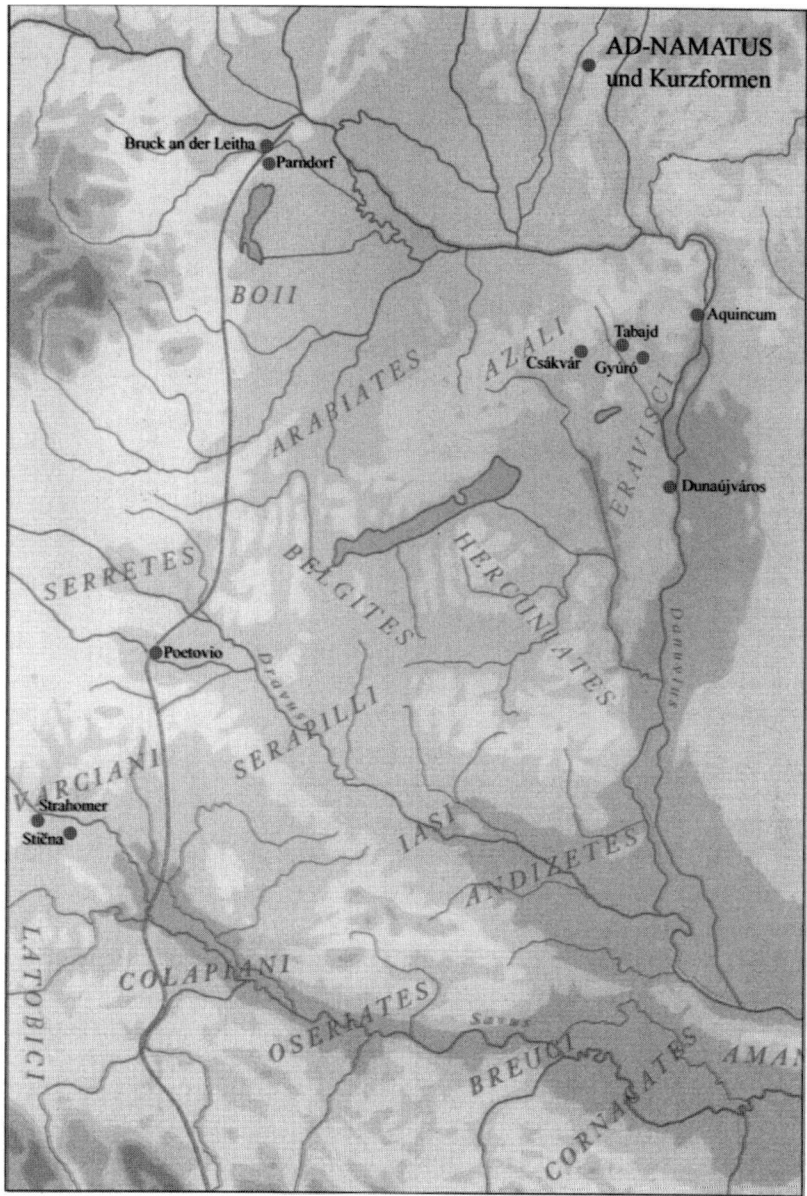

Figure 5. Distribution of *Ad-namatus* and shortened forms (from W. Meid, *Keltische Personennamen in Pannonien*, p. 348).

Other names are built on one stem only like

Cano	'singer'
Catus	'fighter'
Boudio	'victor'
Vindo	'fair one'
Suadra	'sweet one'.

Some may be shortened from compound names—e.g. *Catus* from *Catu-marus*

It is noteworthy that compound names are much more frequent in the Celtic inventory than among Pannonian names where they are rare.

Co-occurrence of Celtic personal names with other cultural markers

In the regions where we find a greater concentration of Celtic names we also find burial mounds, chariot graves or ornamented grave stones depicting the passage of the dead person to the other world on a chariot or wagon whereas in the Pannonian regions these features are notably absent. This co-occurrence of Celtic personal names with other distinct cultural markers reveals a complex cultural identity of the population involved.[25]

Sociological significance of the funeral inscriptions

It is interesting to study the sociological significance of these funeral inscriptions as regards the coexistence of the original Pannonian and Celtic elements, where we can find evidence of either ethnic cohesion or assimilation of the groups involved. There is, on the one hand, a strong tendency of the ethnic groups to keep apart, that is of cohesion within the ethnic group, and yet on the other hand a tendency towards social contacts, of breaking the barriers, shown by intermarriage between members of the different ethnic groups.

As was usual in these inscriptions, the dead person's name is given with his or her father's name (the patronym), and the names of other family members are often mentioned which allows one to recognise certain social structures.

One family may exhibit either exclusively or preponderantly Celtic names or, on the contrary, Pannonian names. This shows that such fami-

---

[25] Meid, *Keltische Personennamen*, pp. 45 ff.

lies held on to ethnically based name traditions, and so suggests a certain ethnic background. But we also can find a mixture of Celtic and Pannonian names in one family which tends to show that the ethnic boundaries were already loosened. There is also a strong influence of Roman or Italic name traditions. From the Roman point of view the Pannonian population, at least its lower classes, were peregrines, but the privileged ranks were awarded Roman citizenship and therefore had to adopt the Roman name system, but could in this case retain their original name as cognomen.

I shall give now a few examples of possible constellations:[26]

1   Several good Celtic names in one and the same family, signifying adherence to Celtic name tradition:

Atpomarus, Brogimarus brothers; father *Ilo*; *CIL*, III. 4580, Maria Lanzendorf.

Belatomarus and several other mostly Celtic names in the family: *Verclovus, Veico, Cobua, Cocate, Sura, Vindaina*; Hild, 399.2, Neudörfl.

Deiva, father with incompletely transmitted name in *-rix*, grandfather and grandson *Blatumarus*; *RIU*, 1160, Intercisa.

Vindo Saturnini f. and *Ammuta Mogetionis f.*, married couple with son-in-law *M. Ulpius Brogimarus*; *RIU*, 1482, Sárbogárd. Noteworthy here is that *Saturninus* with a Roman name has given his son a Celtic name; the Roman citizen *M. Ulpius* has preserved his Celtic name as cognomen.

Dallo with daughter *Brogimara* and son-in-law *Magio*; their daughter *Iantuna*; *CIL*, III. 3594, Aquincum.

T. Flavius Cobromarus and *Tincomara*, brother and sister; mother *Summa Calitigis f.* with Celtic patronym; Hild, 249, Au.

C. Iulius Macimarus and son *C. Iulius Comatumarus*, in the context of a Celtic family; other names *Magio, Ressona, Namuso*; *CIL*, III. 3377, Gyúró.

Ressimarus, son has Roman name *Urbanus*, but is married to *Ressilla Adnamati f.*; their son *Iantumarus*; *CIL*, III. 5290, Poetovio region.

2   Marriage between persons with Celtic names: partner chosen from the same ethnic-social milieu:

Nertomarus and *Retdimara Atalonis f.*; their son *Sacro*; *RIU*, 918, Szentendre.

Nertomarus and *Toutomara*, stone in Museum Mannersdorf.

Magimarus and *Adnama Asionis f.*; *CIL*, III. 10352, Csákvár.

Comato and *Comatuia*; son *Senio*; *RIU*, 1256, Intercisa.

3   The male partner has a Roman first name, but is of Celtic lineage, as his patronym indicates; the female partner has a Celtic name:

See sub 1. already *Urbanus Ressimari f.*, married to *Ressilla Adnamati f.*

Tertio Noibionis f., wife *Satimara Atresi f.*; *RIU*, 925, Szentendre.

---

[26] Ibid., pp. 311–15 with further examples and references.

Quartus Adnamati f., wife *Catulla Coi f.*; *CIL*, III. 10895, boundary region of
   Noricum and Pannonia.

4 Marriage between persons with non-Celtic Pannonian names;
examples from the region of Emona (Ljubljana):

Enignus Plunconis f. and *Enna Oppalionis f.*; *CIL*, III. 3793, Ig.
Voltrex Buctoris f. and *Eninna*; *CIL*, III. 2323, Ig.

5 Intermarriage between persons of different name traditions,
indicating ethnically mixed relationships. There are two possibilities:

(*a*) The male partner has a Celtic name, the female partner a Pannonian
name:

Comatumarus Saconis f. and *Blastaiu Batei f.*; *RIU*, 895, Szentendre.
Segillus Iliati f. and *Abua Tapponis f.*; *CIL*, III. 11302, Fischau.
Lucco Treni f. (man from Britain) married to *Tutula Breuci f.* from the Pannonian
   tribe of the Azali, *CIL*, XVI. 49 (military diploma).

(*b*) The male partner has a Pannonian name, the female partner a Celtic
name:

Mesio and *Comatumara Vani f.*; *RIU*, 899, Szentendre.
Deuso Agisi f. and *Adbugiouna Atnamati f.*; *CIL*, III. 10883, Poetovio.

The cases where the Celtic name tradition continues in one and the
same family are so frequent that they need not be demonstrated with further examples. Interesting, however, are breaks within this tradition.
These may be due to the influence of the Roman system of name-giving,
but there are also changes from Celtic to Pannonian and vice versa. One
would expect that in the course of Romanisation fathers with a Celtic
name might give their sons Roman names. This happens indeed, but
equally frequently fathers with a Roman name have children with Celtic
names. This speaks in favour of a certain persistence of the Celtic name
tradition, and has perhaps to do with a family tradition in a wider sense,
perhaps also the influence of the mother's side (the mother is often not
mentioned).

6 Examples for the change of the naming mode within the lineage.
There we find four variants:

(*a*) Father with Celtic, son/daughter with Roman name:

Ressimarus, son *Urbanus*; *CIL*, III. 5290.
Matumarus, son *M. Cocceius Florus*;[27] *CIL*, III. 3546.

---

[27] *Cocceius*, though Celtic in origin, is here the emperor Nerva's gentilicium.

Miletumarus, son *Quartio*; *CIL*, III. 3405/06.
Adnamo, son *Absucus* (but the latter's sons have Celtic names: *Nertomarus, Locco, Atedunus*); *RIU*, 1146.
Mogetius, son *Primus*, daughter *Gemella*; Hild, 421.
Diassumarus, son *Danuvius*, grandson *Maturus*; *RIU*, 1221.

(*b*) Father with Roman, son/daughter with Celtic name:

Bassus, son *Alorix*; *AE*, 1969/70, 493.
Florus, son *Dullibogius*; *RIU*, 1547.
Optatus, son *Togivepus*; *ILJ*, 304.
Aurelius Respectus, son *Troucetimarus*; *RIU*, 724.
Quintaius, daughter *Comatimara*; *CIL*, III. 3621.
Quintio, daughter *Oxidubna*; *CIL*, III. 3546.
Lucius Bonati f. and *Iulia Prisca*, daughter *Bussugnata*; *CIL*, III. 3930.
Saturninus, son *Vindo*; *RIU*, 1482.
Ianuarius, daughter *Otiouna* (same name as mother); *RIU*, 1251.

(*c*) Father with Pannonian, son/daughter with Celtic name:

Veladetus, son *Rituris*; *RIU*, 1364
Scupus (Pannon.?), daughter *Vercombera*; *RIU*, 1364
Battus, daughter *Verbugia*; *CIL*, III. 10944
Gripo, daughter *Uxela*; *CIL*, III. 13406
Bucco, daughter *Bietumara*; *RIU*, 1235
Trippo, son *Annamatus*; *CIL*, III. 3372

(*d*) Father with Celtic, son with Pannonian name:

Annamatus, son *Prenses*; *CIL*, III. 3374
Vercombogio, son *Teutio*; *RIU*, 838
Nertomarus, son *Cusa*; *RIU*, 1219

One can see from these constellations that the Celtic name system, with its typical formations and semantically meaningful names, continued from pre-Roman times, was—on the whole—well preserved at the beginning of Roman rule and persisted for some generations. This tradition was loosened to some extent, but was not abandoned.

There are further arguments in favour of this. One is the popularity of certain names, shown by their frequency. Another is that certain names or name elements reoccur in one and the same family; for example, the grandfather's name reoccurs as the name of the grandson, following an old inherited tradition according to which the grandson reincorporates the soul of the dead grandfather.

There is another important point, which touches the language question. It is clear that the Celtic personal names in Pannonia, indeed the whole naming system, derive from a fully living and functioning language, in this case a language of Gaulish type. But we do not know for certain if this language was still universally spoken in the second century AD. Naming traditions may continue for some time even after the language from which they are derived has been abandoned. This results—to use German terminology—in 'Namenlandschaften' (onomastic territories) which continue earlier 'Sprachlandschaften' (linguistic territories).[28] But there is one clue. In our record there are many persons who had reached a very advanced age, not merely octogenarians but also persons who had attained 100 years of age. Since as a rule the patronym is also given, the time when this Celtic father gave his son a Celtic name or was himself named by his father may date back before the Roman occupation, or at least into its earliest phase when there could not have been any question of Latin disposing of the native Celtic idiom. These very old people could hardly have forgotten their native language during their lifetime. This supports the assumption that in this society Gaulish was still a living language, a means of communication between its members in places where Latin was not obligatory. The same probably held true for the Pannonian language, and considering the coexistence of the two ethnic groups parts of the population must have been bilingual. Pannonia must have been a polyglot region—Latin, Greek, and Oriental languages were also present, as also to some extent were Germanic dialects, given the foreign elements in the military and commercial orders.

Therefore we can assume that Celtic—in the form of Gaulish—was still a spoken language in the first and in the greater part of the second century AD. How long it stayed alive we cannot tell because the massive invasions by Germanic, Sarmatian and Hunnic tribes from the third century onwards did away with the older social structures. But in the first two centuries these structures seem to have still been intact. Another argument in favour is the relative frequency of Celtic personal names in Noricum and Pannonia attested in Latin inscriptions compared with the western Gaulish provinces.[29] The western Gaulish territory is about four

---

[28] For the terminology and model investigations see J. Untermann, 'Namenlandschaften im alten Oberitalien' and, for the Balkans, various articles by R. Katičić quoted in Meid, *Keltische Personennamen*, p. 11, n. 4.

[29] P. Sims-Williams has worked out, on the basis of Latin inscriptions, statistics on the relative frequency of Celtic compound names in the different Roman provinces, by which Noricum and Pannonia come out on top: see his article 'The five languages of Wales in the pre-Norman inscriptions', *Cambrian Medieval Celtic Studies*, 44 (Winter, 2002), pp. 10–14, and Meid, *Keltische Personennamen*, pp. 326 f.

times as large as Pannonia and Noricum taken together, yet has about the same relative percentage of Celtic personal names.

In Gaul, which came under Roman rule earlier under Caesar and Augustus, Gaulish survived at least into the third century AD, in remote places still later. Therefore it is likely that in Noricum and Pannonia which came under Roman rule about half a century later the native Celtic idiom survived into the second century, and could have survived longer if the conditions had not become so unfavourable. In Galatia, to where some of the Danubian Celts emigrated and established themselves, according to one testimony, but which perhaps is open to doubt, the native language survived into the fourth century.

For Pannonia there is some archaeological support. Recent large-scale excavations have shown that distinct Celtic features were preserved into the second century AD. From this it may be assumed that there were still groups which preserved their Celtic identity. Cultural features alone cannot tell us anything about the language of the people involved, but if these groups were indeed Celts and felt their identity therein, then these people will—in all probability—also have held on to their native language. Linguistic and archaeological data thus support each other.

Conclusions

To sum up, though we do not have linguistic testimony for either Pannonian or Celtic in the form of texts, the regular formation and semantic transparency of the Celtic personal names, especially the compound ones, as well as the lack of unmeaningful or nonsensical compounding, suggest that we have to deal with a living language. This is also supported by the fact that many name bearers died very old, came from a still intact Celtic milieu, and were probably still Celtic-speaking.

Though subsequently there is a strong Roman influence—the basic language of the epitaphs is Latin of course—this Latin is quite often faulty suggesting that the mastery of Latin in the native population was not at a high level. The stones themselves show native symbols and motifs—women, for example, are depicted in their native costumes.

We conclude then that in the Celtic tribal territories Celtic, meaning a variety of Gaulish, was still the spoken vernacular. The same holds true for Pannonian, in the southern territories inhabited by Pannonian tribes. In regions with a mixed population probably both languages were spoken and understood. Historically, the Pannonian-speaking population was the older one, and the Celts had superseded it.

The Romans respected the native societies, their customs and cults, and conceded them partial self-administration. As regards the co-existence and cultural assimilation of the originally different ethnic groups, a telling example seems to be furnished by the veneration of the Eraviscan tribal god. And I wish to conclude with this final comment. This tribal god continued to be worshipped under Roman cover as *Jupiter Teutanus* who had his yearly cult feast on 11 June, near midsummer-time.[30] The name of *Teutanus* is interesting because it exhibits non-Celtic, rather Pannonian linguistic features;[31] the Celtic equivalent would have been *Toutonus* or *Toutatis*, as attested several times. It is actually the cult of the pre-Celtic substratum population which survives here, taken over by the Celts and continued by the Roman authorities. The same holds true for *Noreia*, the tutelary goddess of Noricum who also has a non-Celtic name.

These instances show that we need to approach the concept of Celtic culture with the necessary circumspection as something subject to ever changing conditions and circumstances.

References

Abbreviations

AE   *L'Année épigraphique*
CIL   *Corpus Inscriptionum Latinarum*
Hild   F. Hild, *Supplementum epigraphicum zu CIL III. Das pannonische Niederösterreich, Burgenland und Wien 1902–1968*. Diss. Wien 1968.
IEW   J. Pokorny, *Indogermanisches etymologisches Wörterbuch*, Bern/München 1959.
ILJ   *Inscriptiones Latinae qui in Iugoslavia . . . repertae et editae sunt. Situla* 5. 19. 25. Ljubljana 1963. 1978. 1986.
RIU   *Die römischen Inschriften Ungarns*. Vols. 1–6. Budapest 1972–2001.

[30] Meid, *Keltische Personennamen*, pp. 57 f. with n. 80 (with further references).
[31] It is reminiscent of the name of the Illyrian queen *Teutana* which may just have been her regal title, Illyrian being linguistically a close relation of Pannonian. For further discussion see ibid., pp. 59–62.

Other

Blázquez Martinez, J. M. (1962), *Religiones primitivas de Hispania*, I (Rome).

Cunliffe, B. (2003), *The Celts. A Very Short Introduction* (Oxford).

de Bernardo Stempel, P. (2006), 'Language and the historiography of Celtic-speaking peoples', in S. Rieckhoff (ed.), *Celtes et Gaulois, l'archéologie face à l'histoire, I: Celtes et Gaulois dans l'histoire, l'historiographie et l'idéologie moderne* (Glux-en-Glenne), pp. 33–56.

Karl, R. (2006), *Altkeltische Sozialstrukturen* (Budapest).

Meid, W. (1991), *Aspekte der germanischen und keltischen Religion im Zeugnis der Sprache* (Innsbruck).

Meid, W. (1993), *Die erste Botorrita-Inschrift. Interpretation eines keltiberischen Sprachdenkmals* (Innsbruck).

Meid, W. (1995), 'Mars Latobius', in M. Ofitsch and Chr. Zinko (eds.), *Studia Onomastica et Indogermanica. Festschrift für Fritz Lochner von Hüttenbach zum 65. Geburtstag* (Graz), pp. 125–7.

Meid, W. (2002), 'Freundschaft und Liebe in keltischen Sprachen', in L. Sawicki and D. Shalev (eds.), *Donum grammaticum. Studies in Latin and Celtic Linguistics in Honour of Hannah Rosén* (Leuven), pp. 255–63.

Meid, W. (2005), *Keltische Personennamen in Pannonien* (Budapest).

Raybould, M. E. and Sims-Williams, P. (2007), *A Corpus of Latin Inscriptions of the Roman Empire containing Celtic Personal Names* (Aberystwyth).

Raybould, M. E. and Sims-Williams, P. (2007), *The Geography of Celtic Personal Names in the Latin Inscriptions of the Roman Empire* (Aberystwyth).

Schmidt, K. H. (1996), *Celtic: A Western Indo-European Language?* (Innsbruck).

Sims-Williams, P. (2002), 'The five languages of Wales in the pre-Norman inscriptions', *Cambrian Medieval Celtic Studies*, 44 (Winter), 1–36.

Sims-Williams, P. (2006), *Ancient Celtic Place-Names in Europe and Asia Minor*, Publications of the Philological Society, 39 (Oxford).

Untermann, J. (1959–61), 'Namenlandschaften im alten Oberitalien', *Beiträge zur Namenforschung*, 10 (1959), 74–108, 121–59; 11 (1960), 273–318; 12 (1961), 1–30.

Artists and Craftsmen in the Late Bronze Age of China (Eighth to Third Centuries BC): Art in Transition

ALAIN THOTE

École Pratique des Hautes Études, Paris

WE POSSESS VERY LITTLE INFORMATION on the artists and craftsmen of early China. In spite of the large number of written sources transmitted by the literati tradition and their wide scope, no early text provides any clues, even indirectly, concerning the status of these individuals in society or the environment in which they worked. The only information available to us regarding the people involved in artistic production of the Late Bronze Age derives from the artworks themselves. Lasting from the eighth to the third centuries BC, the period I shall consider covers more than five centuries. Naturally, one may expect that important changes occurred in the arts over such a long period. Indeed, particularly dramatic changes in the arts took place around the turn of the fourth century BC, following the evolution of societies in the eastern part of present-day China.[1] The nature of artistic creation was deeply affected, and this in turn had lasting effects on the people involved in the creation process. To some extent, therefore, the study of artistic change should help us understand the way in which artists and craftsmen worked in ancient China, and this is the basis on which I shall approach the topic. To start out, I am using the words 'artist' and 'craftsman' (or 'artisan') in an undifferentiated way,

---

Read at the Academy 31 May 2007.
[1] See Gernet (1990); Loewe and Shaughnessy (1999).

Proceedings of the British Academy, **154**, 201–241. © The British Academy 2008.

but later on it will be necessary to consider closely the question of how to refer to the producers of art in early China. I should also note at the outset that most of my examples will be drawn from just two major categories of artistic production, lacquer and bronze. In a more extensive treatment of the topic, however, other media could also be cited in support of the argument I have to offer.

The use of lacquer, a secretion from a tree that grows only in the Far East, appeared in the Neolithic period in south-eastern China around 5000 BC.[2] In contrast, the first Chinese bronzes were cast a long time after, in the early second millennium BC.[3] Although bronze and lacquer were different media and each had specific properties, both played a major role in the development of the arts in ancient China. More precisely, in the Eastern Zhou period (771–256 BC) their respective style systems interacted on several levels. Today, I am going to focus on these interactions with a view to understanding better the role of artists and craftsmen in the art history of this period. Let me begin with a quick overview of the artistic evolution between the late Western Zhou period (*c*.850–771 BC) and the dawn of the empire, as seen from three artefacts that incorporate human representations. The bronze cylinder box and the water container in Figure 1 come from the cemetery of the Jin princes in Shanxi province and can both be dated to about the ninth century BC.[4] Respectively four and two naked men bear what look like heavy containers. Although they are of small size and their traits are not very detailed, we can guess that the effort exerted to lift the containers is considerable. Undoubtedly, their humiliating positions indicate that these men were deprived of their identity. One may suspect they were captured enemies, bound and submissive prisoners.[5] In fact, in Central China very few human beings were shown in the arts of the Western Zhou (*c*.1050–771 BC) period, in particular on

[2] For a general presentation of lacquer techniques, see Garner (1979) and Ma Wenkuan (1981). On lacquers of the Warring States period, see Hong Kong (1994) and Tôkyô Kokuritsu Hakubutsukan (1998).

[3] See Bagley (1987). On later developments of Chinese bronzes, see Rawson (1990).

[4] The pourer (*c*.800 BC) comes from Tomb 31 at Tianma-Qucun Beizhao in Shanxi province (*Wenwu* (1994), 8: 22–33, 68; see front cover and 25, fig. 4.4), and the box (late ninth century BC) from Tomb 63 (*Wenwu* (1994), 8: 4–21; see 14, fig. 24.4). Several other bronze vessels or containers from the Late Western Zhou period (*c*.850–770 BC) also rest on feet in the shape of naked prisoners. Door guardians whose right or left leg have been cut following a punishment are found on some bronze vessels (*Kaogu yu wenwu* (1981), 4, 31, fig. 3.1, 3.6).

[5] Another small sculpture of a kneeling man with his hands bound behind his back has a short inscription recording that a Jin prince engaged in a battle against the Huaiyi, a population living in south-eastern China, and captured their king. See Su Fangshu and Li Ling (2002).

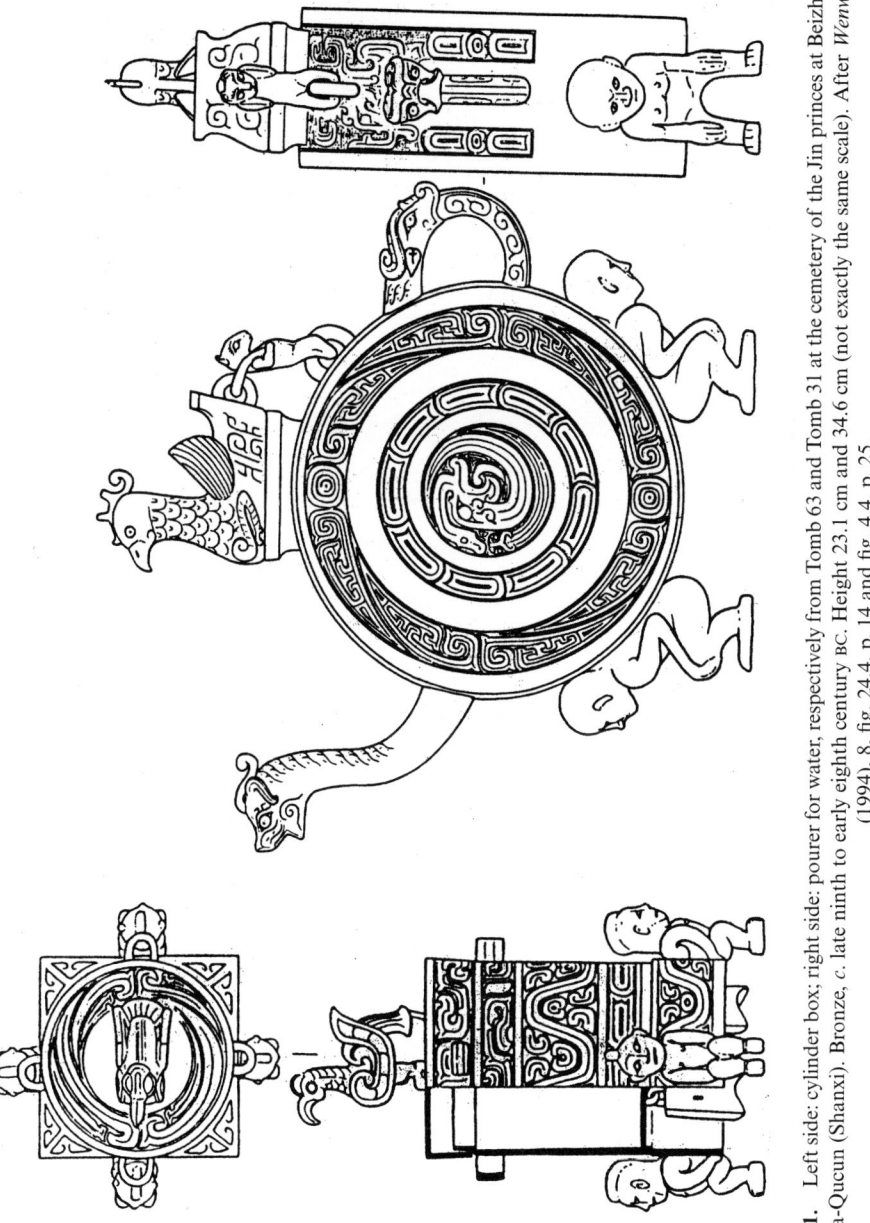

Figure 1. Left side: cylinder box; right side: pourer for water, respectively from Tomb 63 and Tomb 31 at the cemetery of the Jin princes at Beizhao Tianma-Qucun (Shanxi). Bronze, c. late ninth to early eighth century BC. Height 23.1 cm and 34.6 cm (not exactly the same scale). After *Wenwu* (1994), 8, fig. 24.4, p. 14 and fig. 4.4, p. 25.

bronzes.[6] Furthermore, the only humans to be represented at that time are kneeling, naked, and even physically handicapped. It seems that for religious reasons artists avoided representing men. And there are almost no examples of female images at this early time.

Four centuries or so later than those bronzes, the object in Figure 2 represents a guard from a palace wearing a long robe and bearing a sword. Both indicate his rank in a noble house. This is not an autonomous sculpture, but part of a chime stand found in the tomb of the marquis Yi of Zeng who died around 433 BC.[7] In contrast to the former human rep-

Figure 2. Guardian, detail from the bell stand discovered in Tomb 1 at Suixian Leigudun, Hubei province (tomb of Zeng Hou Yi). Bronze covered with lacquer, mid fifth century BC (date of burial *c.*433 BC). Height 116 cm (with the stand). After *Zeng Hou Yi mu* (1989), fig. 39.3, p. 79.

[6] Small carved jades from the Shang and Western Zhou periods show men or women in various attitudes. It seems that at certain periods such themes were sources of inspiration.
[7] *Zeng Hou Yi mu* (1989), pp. 77–84.

resentation, here the artist has emphasised the soldier's beauty. Lacquer was coated on the dress of the soldier to make him look even more vivid.

At the dawn of the empire, the evolution towards a full representation of man as an individual had been fully achieved. An entire army of life-sized warriors, officers and generals of all grades, amounting to more than six thousand men, was interred close to the tomb of the First Emperor (Fig. 3).[8] Each of these soldiers had been shaped with individual characteristics, instead of stereotyped features.[9] This major artistic change, in which the human figure evolved from generalised figures subjected to humiliating positions to figures possessing specific and detailed features, mirrored a comparable social and religious evolution that occurred step by step, culminating with a decisive shift around 200 BC.[10] The three human representations we just saw epitomise three stages in a development toward a concept of autonomous sculpture. At the end of the evolution, one sees a keen interest on the part of the artists for human shapes, which did not exist earlier.

Until the turn of the fourth century BC, the arts in China were mainly of a religious nature, and dominated by bronze production. The vessel in Figure 4 belongs to a set of seven ritual vessels of the same shape and decoration.[11] Only their size indicates a slight difference, with height varying between 61 and 68 centimetres. Each of them weighs more than 200 pounds (91 kilograms). This series of tripods was cast for a member of the royal family of Chu who acted as prime minister of the kingdom between 558 and his death in 552 BC. They all come from the Chu royal

[8] For the content of the first pit (of a total of four), see *Qin Shihuang ling bing ma yongkeng yi hao keng fajue baogao 1974–1984*. The figure of six thousand is an estimate, since only a part of the pit has been excavated to date.

[9] Ledderose (2000), pp. 70–3, demonstrates that the use of modules for thumbs, hands, heads, details of the faces, bodies, etc., allowed the warriors' makers to produce an enormous quantity of diverse figures.

[10] The first portraits painted on silk appear during the third century BC. Two of them were used in a funerary context at Changsha, in the Chu kingdom. Until now, due to poor conditions of preservation, they are the only testimony of a probably much larger phenomenon, but we are aware of other portraits that have already decayed. These are authentic artworks, and even if we know neither the name of the persons represented nor the names of the painters, each of these portraits is evidence of a specific relationship between two persons, the painter and the person who was represented (or possibly the family of the deceased). They respectively come from Tomb 365 (formerly Tomb 1 at Changsha Zidanku) and from a tomb at Changsha Chenjiadashan. See *Changsha Chu mu* (2000), vol. 1, p. 428, and fig. 340, p. 433; vol. 2: colour plate 48; *Hunan Sheng Bowuguan* (1983), figs. 52 and 53.

[11] *Xichuan Xiasi Chunqiu Chu mu* (1991), pp. 114–25. Two more *shengding* come from Tomb 1 in which the spouse of the owner of Tomb 2 was buried (*Xichuan Xiasi Chunqiu Chu mu* (1991), pp. 54, 59–62.

Figure 3.   Kneeling archer from Pit no. 1 at Lintong (Shaanxi). Earthenware, *c.*220–210 BC.
Museum of the Terra-cotta Army for the First Emperor of Qin, Qin Shuihuangdi (r. 221–210 BC).
Height 118 cm. After *Chine. La gloire des empereurs* (2000), p. 230.

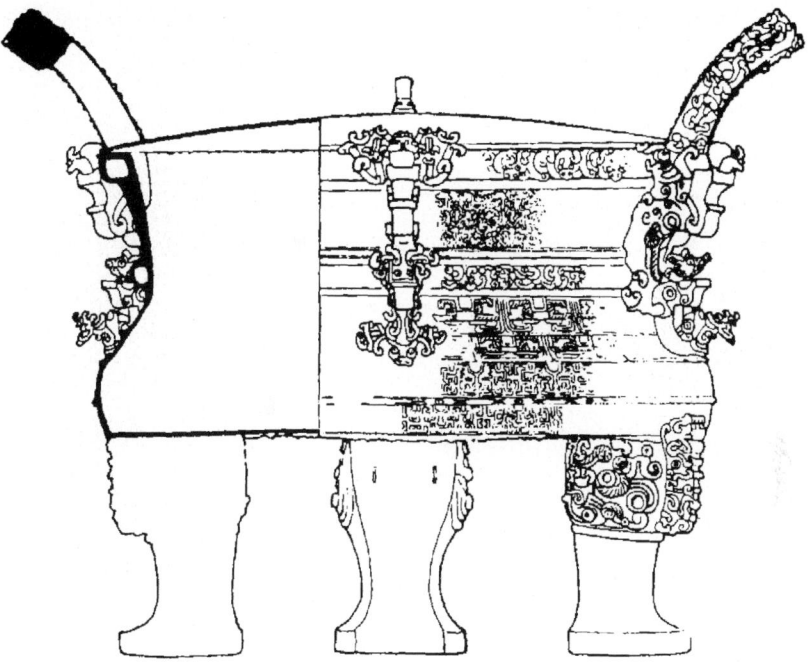

Figure 4.   *Shengding* vessel, from Xichuan Xiasi Tomb 2 (Henan). Bronze, *c.* mid sixth century BC. Height 66 cm. After *Xichuan Xiasi Chunqiu Chu mu* (1991), fig. 93, p. 115.

foundries, as evidenced by the excellent quality of the cast and the identity of the patron himself. At that time, the best craftsmen worked for the king's workshops, and such vessels were made to enhance the power of their owner. The shape itself is typical of the official art of the Chu kingdom, with a constricted belly, and appendages in the shape of living dragons, even if the rendering of these animals is rather abstract. The ritual function of these tripods is expressed in their dedicatory inscriptions of more than ninety characters each, cast on the inner wall of the vessels (Fig. 5). The so-called 'bird-script' used for the calligraphy, with its handsome characters, is a testimony to the perfect mastery of writing by the administrators responsible for the foundries of the Chu kingdom. In the inscription, the owner explains that he has made these vessels to perform sacrifices to his ancestors, and in particular to his deceased father, in order to show his filial piety. He praises the virtues of his way of governing his people, and declares that he displays righteous conduct. At the end of the inscription, he expresses the wish that his sons and grandsons will

Figure 5. Rubbing of the inscription on the bronze tripod reproduced in Fig. 4. After *Xichuan Xiasi Chunqiu Chu mu* (1991), fig. 95, p. 117.

in turn perform the sacrifices that he himself will deserve after his death. Only a wealthy and powerful state could possess foundries able to produce such vessels, since they required very large quantities of raw materials, craftsmen who had mastered sophisticated techniques, and a complex organisation of the manufacturing process, with many subdivisions. These workshops employed several hundred specialised workers, skilled craftsmen, designers, and administrators responsible for the production, organised together in a very hierarchical system. It seems likely that the workshops were organised on a model close to the foundries of Houma in the north. Technique, design and factory organisation interacted in the production of bronzes, which appears to be the result of a collective effort coordinating the interventions of each person at a particular moment of the process.[12]

Until the fifth century BC, ritual bronzes were the dominant mode of expression in visual and material culture, and as such they exerted considerable influence on all other areas of artistic production. For example, the main motifs on the lacquer coffin of the early seventh century BC reproduced in Figure 6(a) belong to the same repertoire of motifs as contemporary bronze vessels, such as those seen in Figure 6(b). The artists responsible for the decoration of the coffin painstakingly used their brush to copy the same motifs without taking advantage of the fluid nature of the lacquer. This coffin, made for the wife of a ruler of a small principality in Central China, is one among several other comparable examples that are provided by the archaeological records.[13] Until the fifth century BC,

---

[12] Bagley (1993) and Bagley (1995).

[13] The following examples of lacquer decoration inspired by bronze decoration are taken from different sites dated between the eighth and the fifth centuries BC, distributed over a broad area of northern China, from Shandong to Gansu. Due to bad conditions of preservation, few lacquer wares have been excavated in the Central Plain and its periphery. However, the dating and location of the sites mentioned hereafter tend to support the argument in favour of a situation shared by the artistic production of the main principalities. The sites are listed according to their location, starting from the east. In the Shandong peninsula, mid-sixth-century tombs M 4 and M 6 at Haiyang Zuiziqian contained lacquer furniture and several fragments of objects with dragon motifs and geometric decoration (*Haiyang Zuiziqian* (2002), colour plate 17.1 and 23.1, 23.2). A fifth-century tomb at Linzi Langjiazhuang, Shandong province has provided lacquer trays and *dou* high footed cups with black on red or red on black lacquer decoration closely linked to bronze decoration (*Kaogu xuebao* (1977), 1, fig. 13, p. 82, fig. 28, p. 101, plate 16). By contrast, the fragment of a plate from the same tomb shows a new kind of decoration using lacquer as a painting medium (reproduced in *Kaogu xuebao* (1977), 1, fig. 14, p. 82). In Central China, a seventh- to sixth-century BC tomb at Luoyang Zhongzhoulu, in Henan (M 2415), contained the remains of the cover of a bamboo casket with a decoration that is reminiscent of bronze surface decoration (*Luoyang Zhongzhou lu* (1959), fig. 100, p. 128). In the most western

Figure 6. Comparison of motifs from a lacquer coffin (*a*) and rubbings of bronze motifs of vessels (*b*) from the tomb of Huang Meng Ji, wife of a prince of Huang. Site of Guangshan Baoxiangsi (Henan), *c*.700 BC. After *Kaogu* (1984), 4, fig. 6, p. 307 and fig. 22.1–3, p. 321.

part of the Zhou cultural sphere are located two main cemeteries of the Qin rulers. Although both had been severely plundered, they still contained lacquer objects or fragments of the highest interest. Tomb 2 at Lixian Dabaozishan in Gansu, presumably the tomb of Duke Wen of Qin who died in 716 BC contained a lacquer chest with dragon motifs in black against a red background inspired by bronze decoration, though less regular in their rendering (Zhu Zhongxi (2004), fig., p. 15). Two centuries later, the burial furniture of the tomb of Duke Jing of Qin (r. 576–537 BC) at Fengxiang comprised several lacquer vessels and objects decorated in the same style as the textured decoration so common on sixth-century ritual bronzes. See *Zhongguo qiqi quanji* (1997), figs. 32 and 33 (*gui* vessels), 35 (small plate), 38 (spatula), 43, 49–51 (fragments from several different objects).

most of the lacquer artefacts that are part of the burial furniture in tombs of the elites similarly show examples of decoration modelled on the bronze repertory. To this general domination of bronze decoration we find some exceptions. However, these can be explained as the result of the development of contacts and exchanges inside the Zhou cultural sphere and on its periphery. For example, from the tomb of a Duke of Qin, who died in the late sixth century BC in Shaanxi, comes an ornament carved in wood and lacquered (Fig. 7). Although the animal represented, a running boar, has all the characteristics of the animal style of the steppes, this object was clearly produced in a Chinese workshop.[14] In fact, the long domination of bronze decoration over the arts was already weakening by the sixth century BC for several reasons. The contacts with non-Chinese populations living in the peripheral areas of the Chinese principalities are one such reason, and their effects may be seen also in the introduction of copper inlay decoration. It was models foreign to Chinese traditions that inspired the contrast of colours brought by the inlays.[15]

In the sixth and fifth centuries BC, bronze art experienced an extraordinary renewal that allowed it to keep its dominant role among the arts, even if a progressive decline of its influence was to be felt. The tomb of the Marquis Yi of Zeng, which I have already mentioned, dates to the late fifth century BC, when the influence of bronze art was challenged by new artistic interests. The furniture of the tomb reflects this turning point in the arts, between tradition and innovation. In continuity with the tradition, bronze ritual vessels and musical instruments for religious ceremonies constitute the main part of its furniture. A set of sixty-five bells on a stand used to accompany the rituals is a true masterpiece of the funerary and religious art of the mid-fifth century BC.[16] This set is, however, one of the last to possess musical properties. In fact, shortly after the bells were made, the technique was lost, and most of the bells cast in the fourth century BC could no longer produce harmonious tones. This can be taken

---

[14] Thote (2006).

[15] Jacobson (1988) appropriately discusses the artistic interchange between early China and the nomad world of eastern Eurasia, showing how metal inlay reappeared in Chinese bronze casting during the sixth century BC (see pp. 203–8). The first use of appliqué-like inlays of copper can be dated to about the mid-sixth century BC, as exemplified by an oval shaped bronze box, two water containers from Tomb 2 and two wine jars from Tomb 3 at Xichuan Xiasi, Henan province, in a Chu cemetery. See respectively *Xichuan Xiasi Chunqiu Chu mu* (1991), fig. 115, p. 138, fig. 106, p. 130, and fig. 168, p. 227; and Thote (2000), pp. 145–9.

[16] *Zeng Hou Yi mu* (1989), pp. 76–134; Falkenhausen (1993); Bagley (2005).

Figure 7. Fragment of a lacquer decoration on wood, from the tomb of the Duke Jing of Qin (r. 576–537 BC), at Fengxiang Nanzhihui (Shaanxi), c. mid sixth century BC. Dimensions unknown. Drawing by the author from *Zhongguo qiqi quanji* (1997), fig. 46.

as a sign of the quick decline that the bronze workshops specialising in this particular kind of production underwent after 400 BC.

The burial items from the tomb reflect the taste of the Chu court, and include several artefacts made in the royal workshops, such as a pair of basins to cool or warm wine (Fig. 8). The surface decoration of the bronze, which is composed of small curls, commas in light relief, was invented around the mid-sixth century BC and remained in vogue for more than two centuries without change.[17] On the other hand, the square shape of the basin and its cubic appendages are clearly inspired by wood carving, one of the sources from which bronze craftsmen took inspiration in the Chu kingdom.

Two pairs of lidded cups were found in the eastern compartment of the tomb, placed close to the owner (Fig. 9).[18] Given the fact that they were not included among the ritual items, they must have been made for the marquis's personal use. Yet, except for the heavy square handles, they are shaped like ritual bronze cups (Fig. 10). Moreover, one part of the decoration on the lacquer cup is modeled on the repetition of the tiny motifs so common on the bronzes. Furthermore, the decoration is framed by bands of motifs commonly used in copper inlay decoration, and the registers on the cup match well the traditional repetitive and geometric patterns of the bronzes (Fig. 11). Finally, the heavy appendages composing the handles also remind us of the dragons from the basin, even though they are rendered in a manner difficult to decipher appropriately. Only the bulging red eyes can guide us in our efforts to see the motifs as dragons.

Another exceptional bronze is a drum stand, also from the tomb of the marquis (Fig. 12).[19] It is composed of eight elements assembled with tenon and mortise—as with more ordinary wooden examples. The drum

---

[17] Jessica Rawson (1987), pp. 49–52, has articulated very precisely the defining features of southern bronze decoration.

[18] The marquis Yi of Zeng was buried in the eastern compartment of the tomb, while the ritual furniture comprising a complete set of bronze vessels and musical instruments was deposited in the central compartment. The four lidded cups are stylistically very close. See *Zeng Hou Yi mu* (1989), pp. 368–9.

[19] This bronze sculpture is often described as the representation of an auspicious crane, due to the combination of the deer antlers with the bird. Later sources would see a symbol of longevity related to immortals in this sculpture (*Zeng Hou Yi mu* (1989), p. 250). However, the cult of immortals was still unknown in the late fifth century BC, making such an interpretation ill-founded.

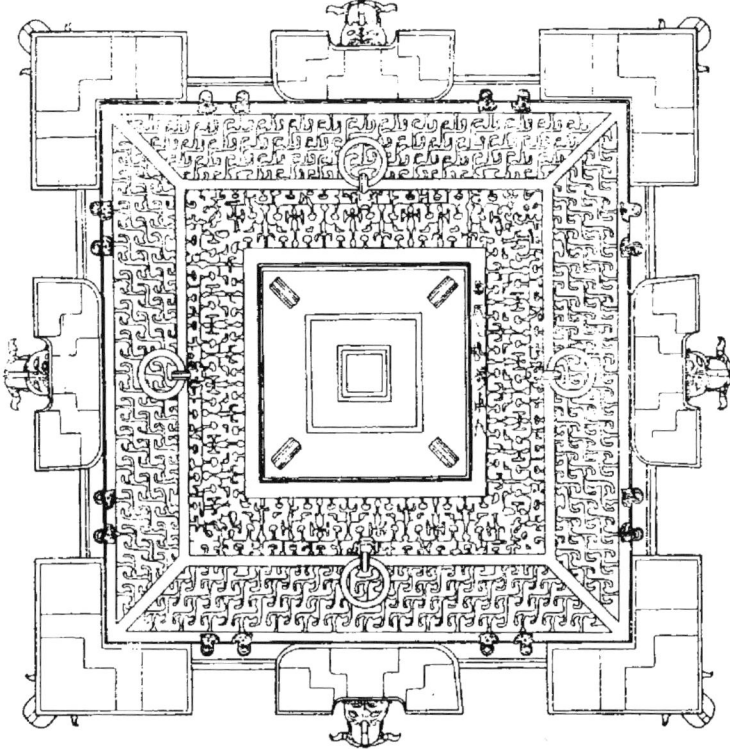

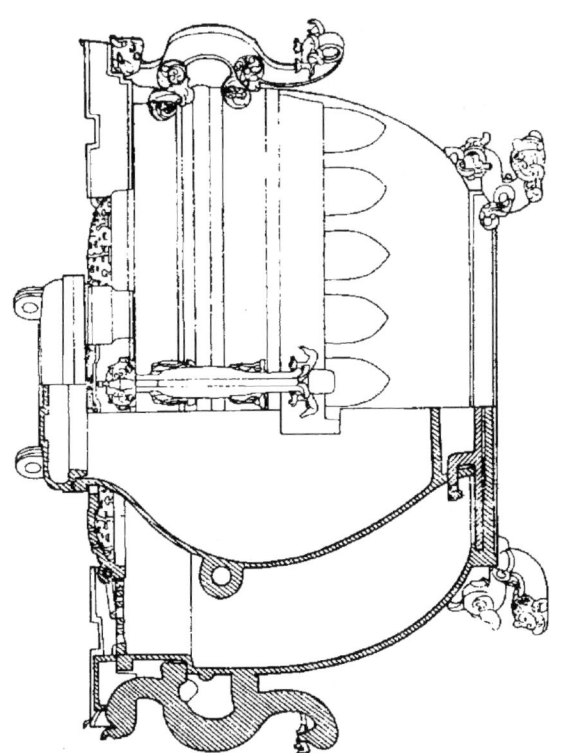

Figure 8. Square basin to cool or warm wine contained in a *fou* vessel, from Tomb 1 at Suixian Leigudun (Hubei) (tomb of Zeng Hou Yi). Bronze, mid fifth century BC (date of burial *c*.433 BC). Height 63.2 cm (basin), 51.8 cm (*fou*). After *Zeng Hou Yi mu* (1989), fig. 122, p. 224 and fig. 88.4, p. 185 (rubbing of the lid from the *fou*).

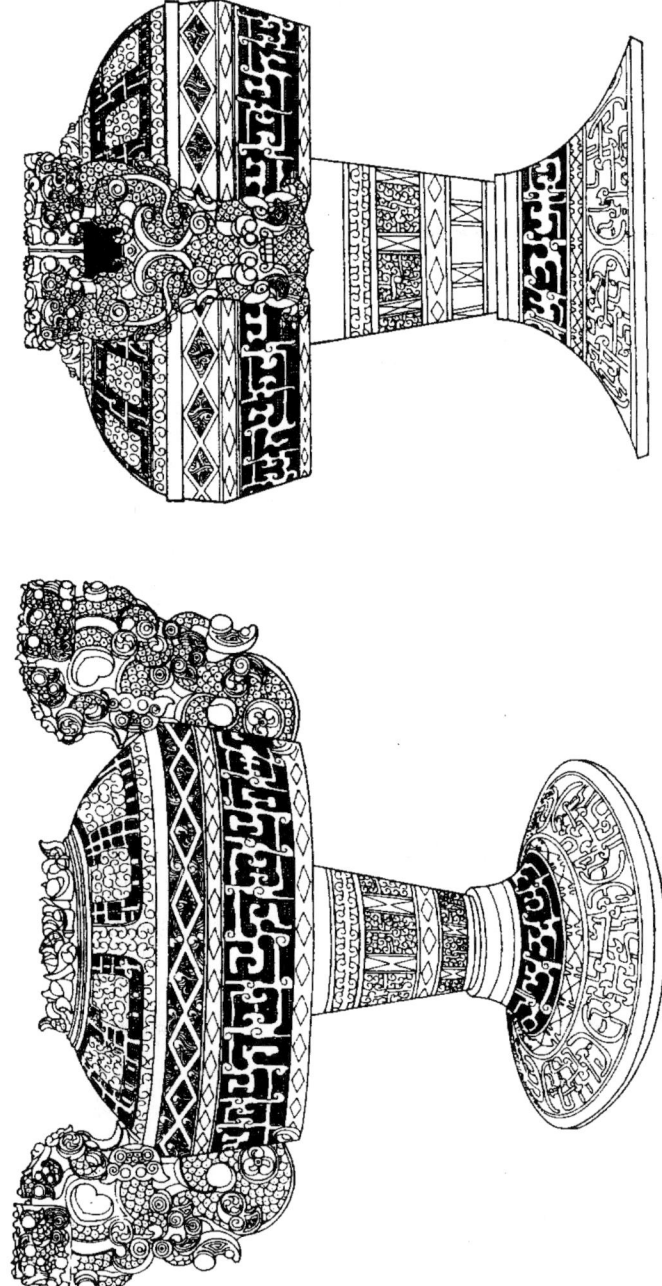

Figure 9. Cup, lacquered wood, from Tomb 1 at Suixian Leigudun, Hubei province (tomb of Zeng Hou Yi), mid fifth century BC (date of burial *c.*433 BC). Height 24.3 cm. After *Zhanguo Zeng Hou Yi mu* (1984), p. 2–3.

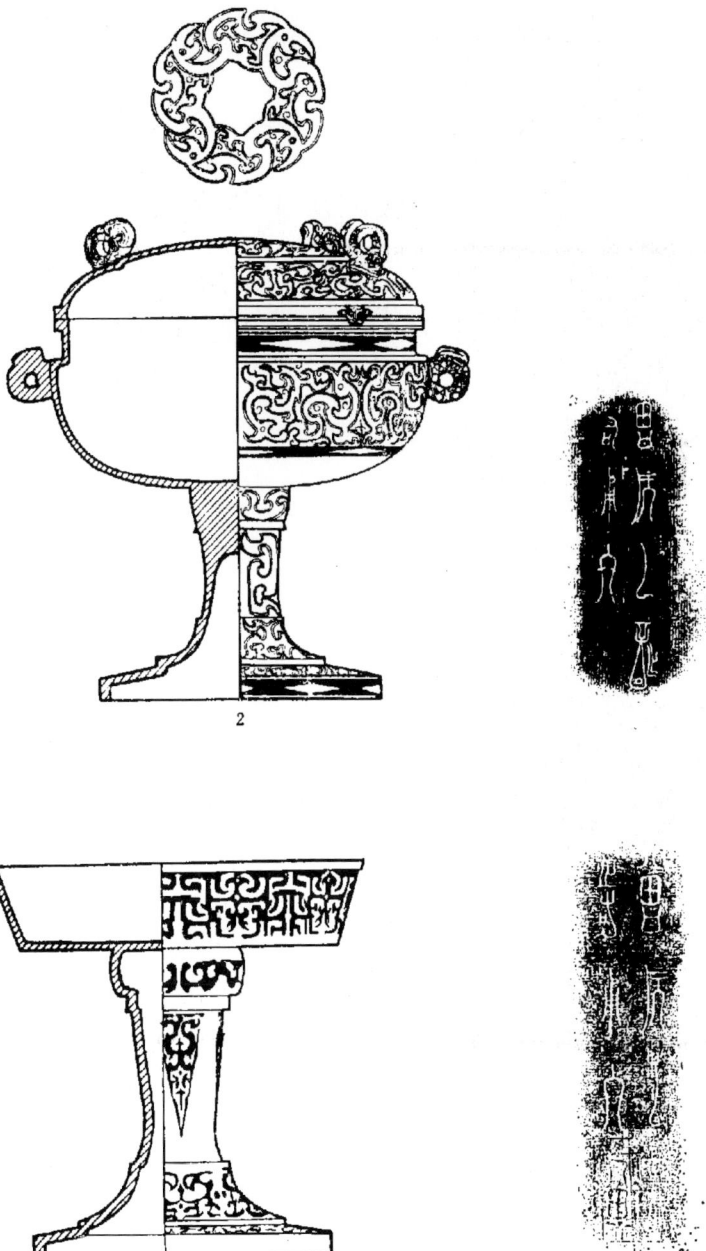

Figure 10.   Two cups from the ritual set found in the central compartment of Tomb 1 at Suixian Leigudun, Hubei province (tomb of Zeng Hou Yi). Bronze inlaid with turquoise, mid fifth century BC (date of burial *c*.433 BC). Height 21.6 cm (top, from a pair) and 26.4 (below). After *Zeng Hou Yi mu* (1989), fig. 111, p. 212 and fig. 112.2, fig. 112.3 (rubbings of the inscriptions).

(a)

(b)

Figure 11. Inlay decoration (*a*) and surface bronze motifs (*b*) of ritual vessels from Tomb 1 at Suixian Leigudun (Hubei) (tomb of Zeng Hou Yi), mid fifth century BC (date of burial c.433 BC). After *Zeng Hou Yi mu* (1989), fig. 89.2, p. 187 (*a*) and fig. 83.4, p. 180 (*b*).

made with wood and leather had already begun to decay when it was discovered. It was suspended by rings at the two points of the antlers and at the beak of the bird. Although the shape of this object has so far proved unique, drum stands made of various zoomorphic elements combined together were often deposited in Chu tombs.[20] Not only were they functional, but they probably also possessed a symbolic meaning.

[20] On its function, see Thote (1987), *The Golden Age of Archaeology* (1999), pp. 296–8, *Music in the Age of Confucius* (2000), pp. 136–7. Several other drum-stands have been discovered in tombs of the Chu kingdom. In most of the cases, the stand is an animal (a reclining deer, for example), or a combination of animals (long-necked bird and tigers). See Gao Zhixi (2000), pp. 323–7.

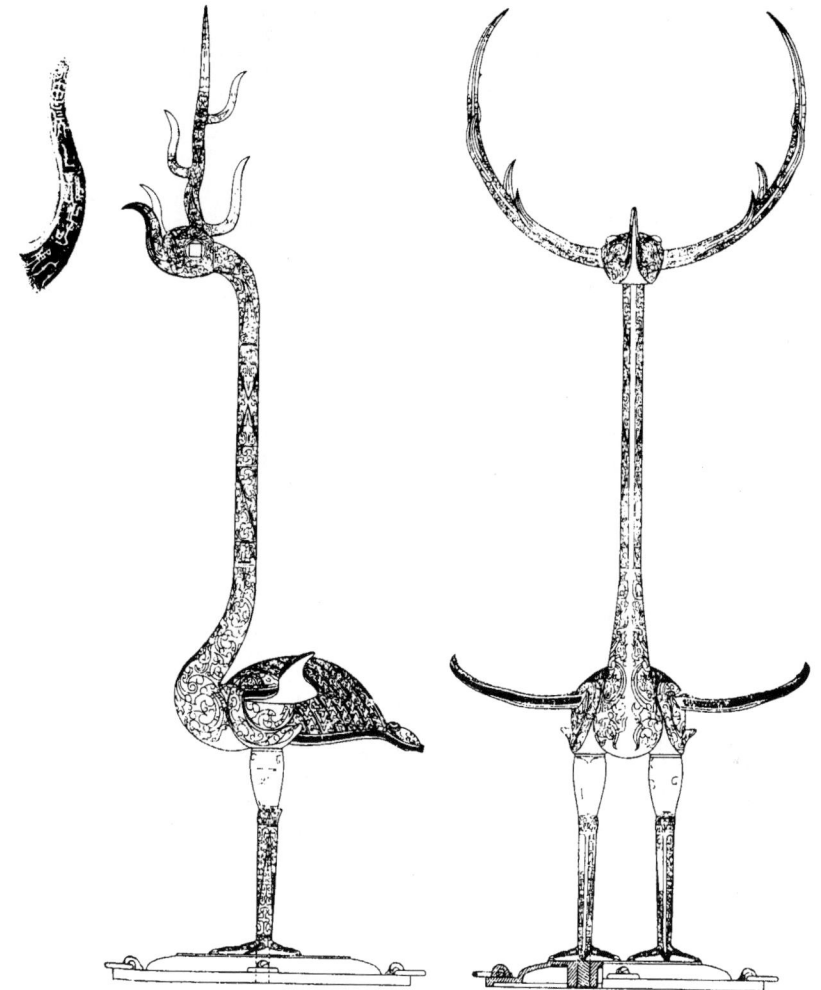

Figure 12.   Drum stand, bronze, from Tomb 1 at Suixian Leigudun (Hubei) (tomb of Zeng Hou Yi), mid fifth century BC (date of burial *c*.433 BC). Height 143.5 cm. After *Zeng Hou Yi mu* (1989), fig. 147, p. 251.

All of the objects just reviewed, all from the tomb of the Marquis Yi of Zeng, exemplify the complex relationship, with mutual borrowings, that had been established between the two very different modes of artistic expression in bronze and lacquer by the fifth century BC. In itself, the existence of a relationship is not surprising, given that at any time we may find several correspondences in various arts that can define an overall style. However, the particular interest of the examples I have given is that at this time, and even as late as the fourth century BC, borrowings were more likely to go from bronze to lacquer than the other way.

Yet another example from the tomb of the marquis is even more striking. The two encased coffins in which the deceased was buried show contrasting modes of decoration. On the walls of the smallest coffin the complex iconographic program is for the most part independent of bronze decoration. The paintings reproduced in Figure 13 show that lacquer craftsmen had at that time begun to exploit lacquer as an independent medium. When looking at the larger coffin, however, it appears that bronze decoration still exerted a strong influence on lacquer painting (Fig. 14). Its main motifs are careful copies of interlace decoration from bronze vessels and objects of the eighth or seventh century BC that were no longer in use in the fifth century BC.[21] How can we explain such a phenomenon? It seems to me that as long as the traditional religion based on the cult of the ancestors and the use of ritual vessels was influential in the life of the elites, artists and craftsmen had few choices in their work, at least for religious art. Their creativity and their sources of inspiration were monopolised by the needs of the ancestral cult. Their artistic models, limited in number, guided their work in a certain direction. One may suppose that the lacquer workshops were located close to the bronze

Figure 13. Lacquer decoration on one side of the coffin containing the remains of the marquis Yi of Zeng, from Tomb 1 at Suixian Leigudun (Hubei), mid fifth century BC (date of burial c.433 BC). Height 132 cm, Length 250 cm. After *Zeng Hou Yi mu* (1989), fig. 22, p. 39.

[21] Thote (1991).

Figure 14. Lacquer decoration on the large coffin of the marquis Yi of Zeng, from Tomb 1 at Suixian Leigudun (Hubei), mid fifth century BC (date of burial *c*.433 BC). Height 2.19 cm, Length 320 cm. After *Zeng Hou Yi mu* (1989), fig. 15, p. 25.

workshops and that both were placed under the authority of the royal administration. Consequently, their production was intimately linked. This implies also that their organisation may have been very similar, with a strong hierarchy of specialised craftsmen and artists.[22]

However, in ancient China it is difficult to make a clear distinction between the respective functions of 'artists' and 'craftsmen'.[23] Even the finest bronzes come in pairs, such as the *fanghu* vessel from the sixth century BC in Figure 15. These two *fanghu* are almost identical to a number of vessels, also grouped in pairs, found in different tombs.[24] Although found in distant sites, they probably were all cast in the royal manufactories of Chu, following very close models.[25] Most of the bronzes were made in series and, despite their excellent craftsmanship and distinctive beauty, they had numerous duplicates. Therefore, the concept of uniqueness does not fit well with regard to the bronzes of the early part of the Eastern Zhou period, and under these conditions, it is difficult to distinguish clearly between artist and craftsman roles. The producers worked together in large workshops, in which each person was responsible for a precise task.[26] It is unlikely that anyone had the status of an individual artist, not even the designers who imagined the most outstanding pieces. Their creative work depended strongly on execution that involved numerous skilled craftsmen.

Compared with bronze workshops, lacquer workshops were smaller and could be run on a family scale, although they probably were not independent. One cannot conceive of the existence in these early times of a market. The basic organisation of the workshop was probably similar to that of bronze workshops. Whether in bronze or in lacquer, this art remained anonymous. We do not know a single artist's or artisan's name

[22] Like the organisation described by Bagley (1993, 1995).

[23] Apparently, in ancient Greece and later in the West there was no verbal distinction between craft and art. However, sculpture and painting in ancient Greece can qualify as art. See Robertson (1991), pp. 2–3.

[24] Compare the pair of *fanghu* found in Tomb 1 at Xichuan Xiasi, in western Henan (*Xichuan Xiasi Chunqiu Chu mu* (1991), figs. 63–4, pp. 73–4), with a pair of *fanghu* from Xinzheng Lijialou, in central Henan (*Zhongguo qingtongqi quanji. Dong Zhou 1* (1998), no. 23), mid sixth century BC, and with the slightly later pair from the tomb of the Marquis Shen of Cai in Shouxian, Anhui province (*Shouxian Cai Hou mu chutu yiwu* (1956), pls. 7 and 8), late sixth century BC.

[25] So (1983).

[26] On labour division in bronze workshops, see Bagley (1993).

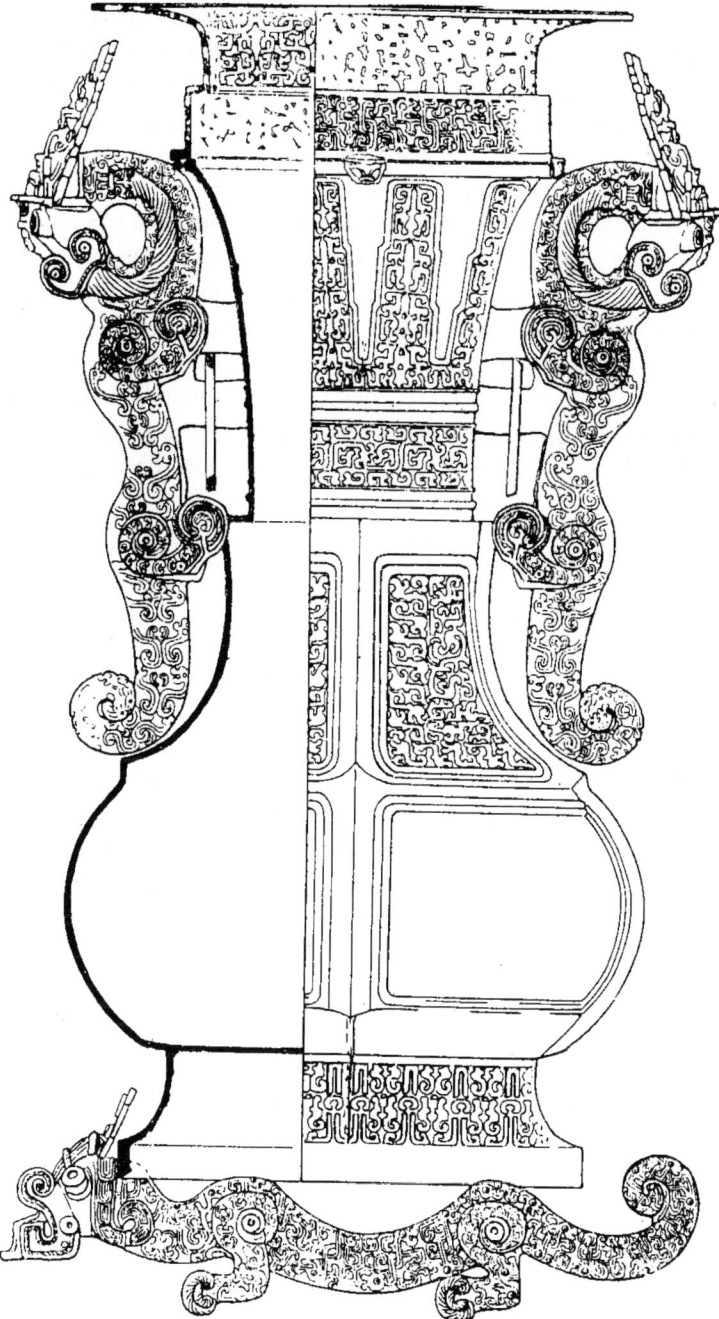

Figure 15. *Fanghu* vessel from a pair, from Tomb 1 at Xichuan Xiasi (Henan). Bronze, *c.*mid sixth century BC. Height 79 cm. After *Xichuan Xiasi Chunqiu Chu mu* (1991), figs. 63–4, pp. 73–4.

before the fourth century BC.[27] None of the objects I have shown has a signature. No textual sources from the Eastern Zhou period have supplied a name.

The only names that we find in inscriptions on bronzes are those of the patrons for whom the bronzes were cast (Fig. 5). In the case of Marquis Yi of Zeng, more than two hundred bronze inscriptions give his name (for example, on the bronzes reproduced in Figures 8, 10, 12, 18).[28] Most of them were cast with the objects, though some were engraved with a needle.[29] We know the name of the marquis; we have, however, absolutely no idea of the names of any of the individuals who produced these extraordinary works of art. Who indeed were the men who created these masterpieces? Chinese antiquity in no way can be compared with Greece and its numerous artists, such as Phidias or Euphronios, whose names are known from their signatures or from specific mentions in textual sources. The masterpieces of famous sculptors were copied again and again in such a way that it is still possible to reconstitute the individual style of an artist such as Praxiteles.[30] Although we refer to these men as artists, Greek potters and painters were both considered artisans. They were placed in a hierarchical position, the owner of the workshop being

---

[27] For an investigation into the bronze craftsmanship of Qin centered on the officers in charge of the workshops, see Sumiya Sadatoshi (1982). In fact, it is only in the first century BC that the name of the caster who organized the casting of a bronze appeared inscribed on a vessel for the first time. The name 'Chengdu' appears in several inscriptions found on excavated lacquers of the Warring States period (Shen Zhongchang and Huangjiaxiang 1987), and of the Han period (Pirazzoli-t'Serstevens 1990).

[28] An exact count is still difficult to establish in spite of the numbers provided in the report. However, the total number of inscriptions mentioning the name of the tomb's owner is very high. According to the archaeologists, eighty-seven ritual bronzes (eighty-nine by my count) of a total of one hundred and seventeen have inscriptions. To these bronzes, including vessels and accessories of all kinds, weapons (38 dagger-axes *ge*, 2 halberds *ji*), bells (45), and various other items such as the drum-stand in Fig. 12 must be added. In many cases, a vessel has two inscriptions, one on its wall and one on its lid. See *Zeng Hou Yi mu* (1989), pp. 186–250 *passim* (vessels, accessories, sculpture), pp. 261–3, 284–6 (weapons), pp. 533–48 (bells).

[29] With the exception of a *zun* and a basin, all the bronze vessels were cast for the marquis. In fact, when the *zun* and the basin became the property of the marquis, an earlier inscription was partly erased to change the name of the owner. There is a high probability that these two bronzes were cast in the late sixth century or early fifth century BC. See *Zeng Hou Yi mu* (1989), pp. 228–32, 234. The style of their decoration, probably cast using the lost wax technique, is close to the style of a bronze altar found in Tomb 2 at Xichuan Xiasi, dating to about the mid sixth century BC (*Xichuan Xiasi Chunqiu Chu mu* (1991), pp. 126, 128). Many weapons belonging to two other marquises of Zeng were deposited in the tomb of Zeng Hou Yi.

[30] Robin Osborne (1998), pp. 225–35, claims that with Praxiteles the artist's life and his work became conjoined, following a development that lead to the 'invention of the artist' in mid fourth-century BC Greece.

considered as above the painters.[31] Rather often, it happened that both wrote or inscribed their names on their works. These signatures allowed the customers to identify them, a requirement in a context of sharp competition between workshops and also between potters and between painters.[32]

In ancient China, there was no room for individuals involved in the production process to be acknowledged as artists. Only the artefacts supply information on the producers of the early period. Even then, it is still impossible to identify the personality of any of them through their creations.[33] Today, in the best cases, we can only determine regional or local characteristics of bronze, lacquer or jade production. The human figure was central in the art of ancient Greece: historical figures, heroes and social images of people, as well as representations of gods who looked like men and women (Fig. 16). In the case of China, there is nothing comparable. Images of humans were not highlighted until the fifth century BC, and the images provided by the first pictorial bronzes do not show any individual to whom we could put a name (Fig. 17). No names were attached to the hieratic guardians in ceremonial robes carrying a sword shown in Figure 2. In fact, these remain anonymous figures created by men who remain anonymous to us. Probably, the names of some producers were known in a rather limited circle. However, the conditions in which artworks were produced did not allow them to work independently and be recognised as individuals. Lacquer, jade and bronze workshops were attached to the palaces of the main elite families. They needed numerous skilled and specialised workers organised in a strict hierarchy, and they required very costly raw materials that only well-organised networks could supply. In addition to these specific conditions of artistic production, the fundamentally religious nature of this production suggests that the mention of artists' names had to be avoided.

---

[31] As revealed by several features, in particular their signatures, although the potters' names were presumably written by the painters. Some potters were simultaneously painters. Also, in place of the potters, the workshop's owners may have had their names written on the products created under their direction. See Hemelrijk (1991). It seems that painters' personal pride waned by the early fifth century BC (Williams (1991), p. 117).

[32] Hemelrijk (1991), p. 256 mentions that the confusing associations between painters and potters were the rule rather than the exception in the late sixth-century BC Attic workshops.

[33] By contrast, in Greek vases, even though numerous pottery painters are nameless, their styles and themes tell us something of their artistic personality. It is possible to distinguish the work of individual painters, to identify the workshops, and to trace the connections between vase painters. Simultaneously, the images they created introduce us into the distinctive culture, society and ideas of the places where the pots were produced.

Figure 16. Attic red-figure cup. Theseus, Athena and Amphitrit, signed by Euphronios, potter, and attributed to Onesimos, painter. Earthenware, *c*.500–490 BC, Diam. 39.9 cm. After *Chefs-d'oeuvre de la céramique grecque dans les collections du Louvre* (1994), no. 50, p. 111.

Figure 17. Decor of a pictorial bronze with a hunting scene on a chariot, rubbing. Fifth century BC. After Chen Fangmei (1989), fig. 77.

Around 450 BC, a century after the casting of the tripods from Xiasi, the Marquis Yi of Zeng had a series of nine *ding* vessels of the same kind cast for himself. Though smaller—they are about 45 centimeters in diameter—they still express the power of a wealthy vassal of the Chu king (Fig. 18).[34] The inscription found on each is much shorter, saying that the vessels were cast for Zeng Hou Yi for his eternal use. The decoration is less creative than on the earlier *shengding*. And this general tendency is to be felt not only in the ritual bronzes of the Chu kingdom, but also in all the principalities that composed China in the last two centuries of the Eastern Zhou period. Tianxingguan tomb 2 near Jiangling, dated to around 350–330 BC, contained *shengding* of much lower quality, and without any inscriptions (Fig. 19).[35] In fact, after a flourishing development of the bronze workshops in the sixth and fifth centuries BC, the production of the ritual vessels that had been so essential for the ancestral cult decreased substantially. In particular, the sets made for the tombs were either cast without any care or were replaced by earthenware models of vessels.[36]

The potters were trained to imitate the shape and decoration of the bronzes. Even wealthy tomb owners would accept such substitutes instead

---

[34] *Zeng Hou Yi mu* (1989), vol. 1, pp. 192–6; vol. 2, colour plate 7.2; plate 51.

[35] *Jingzhou Tianxingguan er hao Chu mu* (2003), pp. 42–51; colour plates 10, 11; and plates 6–11. Although the examples used in my argument (Figs. 4, 18, 19) all come from the Chu kingdom and its periphery, examples taken from central or northern China would lead to the same conclusions. Compare the ritual vessels from Houma cast when the quality of the workshops was at its best with the ritual vessels of king Cuo of Zhongshan (*Taiyuan Jinguo Zhao qin mu* (1996); *Cuo mu—Zhanguo Zhongshan guo guowang zhi mu* (1996)).

[36] On the development of *mingqi* vessels of ceramics or metal, by definition of low quality, see Falkenhausen (2006), pp. 302–6.

Alain Thote

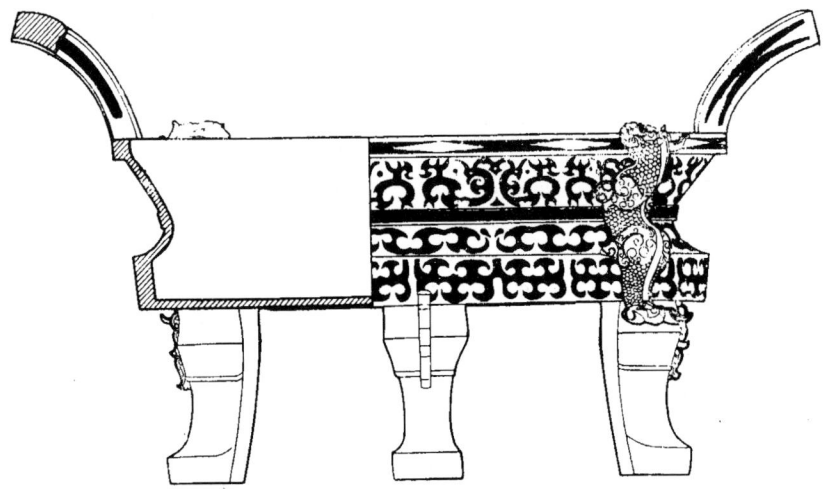

Figure 18. *Shengding* tripod, from Tomb 1 at Suixian Leigudun (Hubei). Bronze, mid fifth century BC (date of burial *c*.433 BC). Height 35.2 cm. After *Zeng Hou Yi mu* (1989), fig. 96, p. 194.

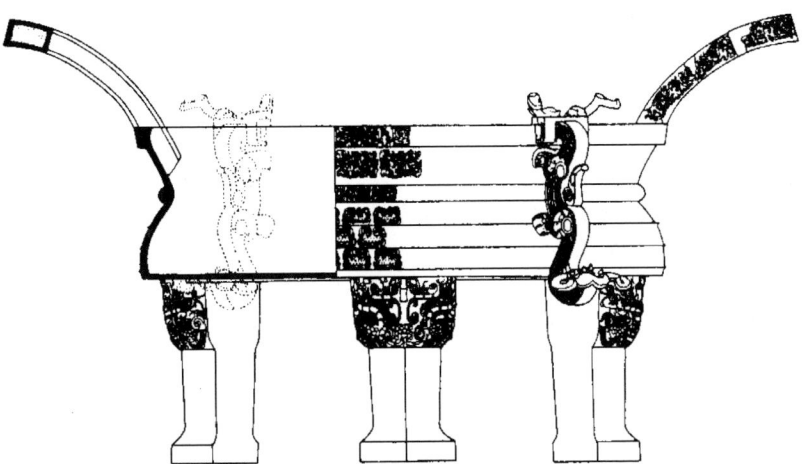

Figure 19. *Shengding* tripod, from Tomb 2 at Jingzhou Tianxingguan (Hubei). Bronze, *c*.330 BC. Height 42 cm. After *Jingzhou Tianxingguan er hao Chu mu* (2003), fig. 26, p. 44.

of real bronze vessels. Also, defective bronzes with holes in their sides were put into tombs. In several cases, their surface was not smoothed, nor had the earth remaining from the mould section been wiped away. This major shift in the quality of burial ritual vessels may have provoked a substantial change in the scale and organisation of bronze production.

Indeed, at the same moment, some bronze workshops specialised in the production of luxurious objects for daily life, such as tables, belt hooks, lamps, food containers, and dishes (Fig. 20).

What happened between the fifth and the fourth centuries? In less than a century, the nature of artistic production changed all at once. After having been mainly limited to religious expression, art turned to categories in which new forms of sensibility could be expressed. These dramatic changes make the fourth century BC a key period in the development of the arts of ancient China. In fact, in terms of creativity, from that period on lacquers tended to play an influential role comparable to the role bronzes had played in earlier times, when they were the main source of inspiration for artists.[37]

Earlier craftsmen had not been unaware of the potential qualities of lacquer. However, once they understood these properties more fully, then the relationship between bronze art and lacquer craftsmanship tended to reverse, and this change can be taken as a sign of a major break in the artistic evolution of pre-imperial China. The lacquer box in Figure 21 comes from a tomb that can be dated to 316 BC.[38] In several regards, this object is a landmark in the development of the arts. On the side of the cover, a register is painted with scenes representing an embassy sent from one state to another (total length of the register: 87.4 cm, height 5.2 cm). It comprises five scenes (Fig. 22):

(1) the chariot of the ambassador being driven in the countryside;
(2) servants announcing his arrival and a man kneeling on the soil to greet the ambassador;
(3) the host coming to greet the ambassador;
(4) the encounter of the ambassador and the host while a chariot is waiting; and

---

[37] Although I assume that lacquer shapes and decoration tended to influence the production of bronze vessels in the fourth and third centuries BC, and more broadly played a significant role in the development of the arts, I agree that other sources such as textile designs and embroidery became influential around the same time, as Roderick Whitfield reminded me (on the influence of textile designs, see Mackenzie (1999)). However, these other sources were by far of secondary importance in the process. What is fundamental in this evolution is that bronze vocabulary and designs were no more the dominant expression in the arts once secular concerns replaced the earlier preoccupation with ritual functions (Lawton (1982), pp. 20–3, 181–90). Conversely, the renewal of bronze designs that occurred in the fourth century BC came from several sources, among which lacquer was the most important.

[38] *Baoshan Chu mu* (1991). On Chu lacquer, see Hou Dejun (1995), pp. 194–250.

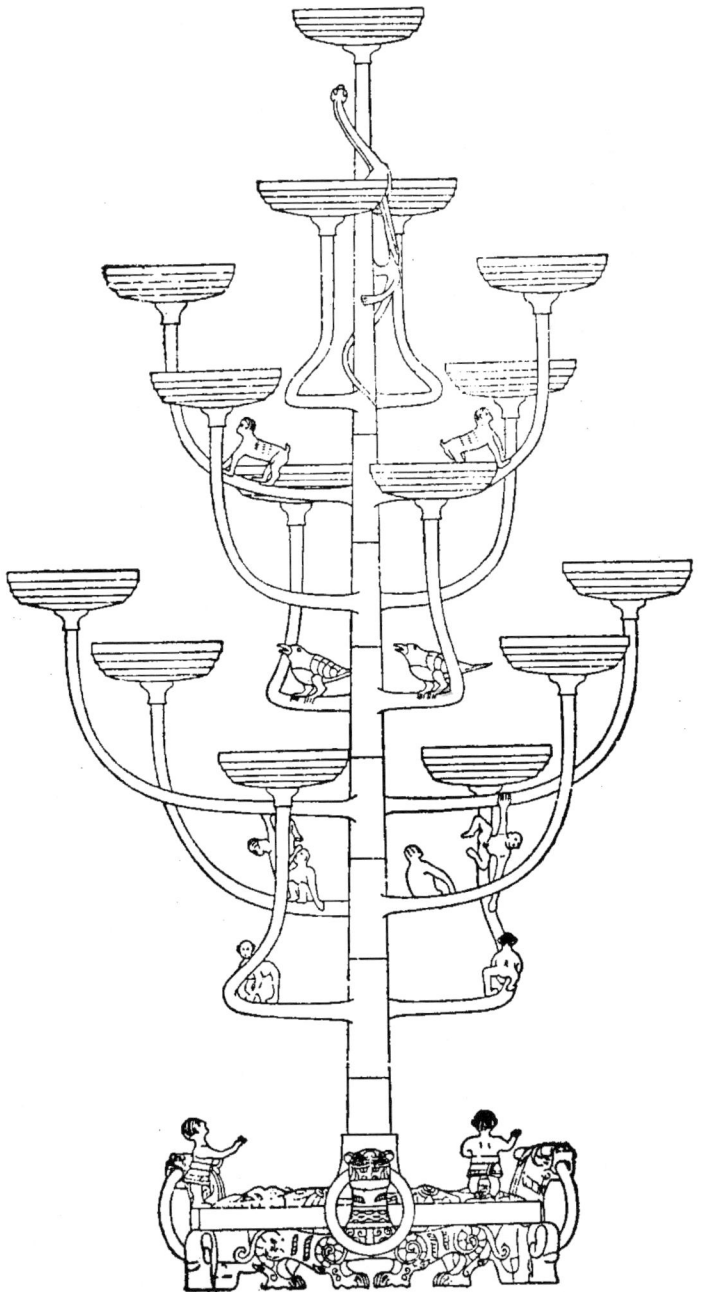

Figure 20.   Lamp, from the tomb of King Cuo of Zhongshan at Pingshan (Hebei). Bronze, late fourth century BC. After *Cuo mu—Zhanguo Zhongshan guo guowang zhi mu* (1996), fig. 48A, p. 134.

Figure 21. Box *lian*, from Jingmen Baoshan Tomb No. 2 (Hubei). Dry lacquer technique, *c.* late fourth century BC (date of burial: 316 BC). After *Wenwu* (1988), 5: colour plate 1.2.

(5) the countryside symbolised by wild boars running between two willows (this scene framed by trees marks the beginning and the end of the series).

The event must have been important since all the stages are illustrated, from departure to arrival. It probably had a historical value, or at least was inspired by a story, now lost. The artist has introduced two dimensions in his painting: the immaterial notion of time and the physical sense of space.[39] On the one hand, the painting comprises four successive moments that are each framed by trees, like the scroll paintings of later centuries. On the other hand, the artist has tried to use three-dimensional space and a natural setting. An allusion to nature is given by the willows that are among the first trees to be represented in ancient China. Flying birds—presumably wild geese flying in couples—suggest the sky while the wind seems to blow through the branches and leaves. Space is also suggested in the representation of the chariots, with the three superimposed horses, and the three men in the box of the chariot, one in front, one behind, and the third seen from the back. Along the road there are

[39] Wu Hung (1999), pp 705–6; Thote (1999), pp. 206–10.

Alain Thote

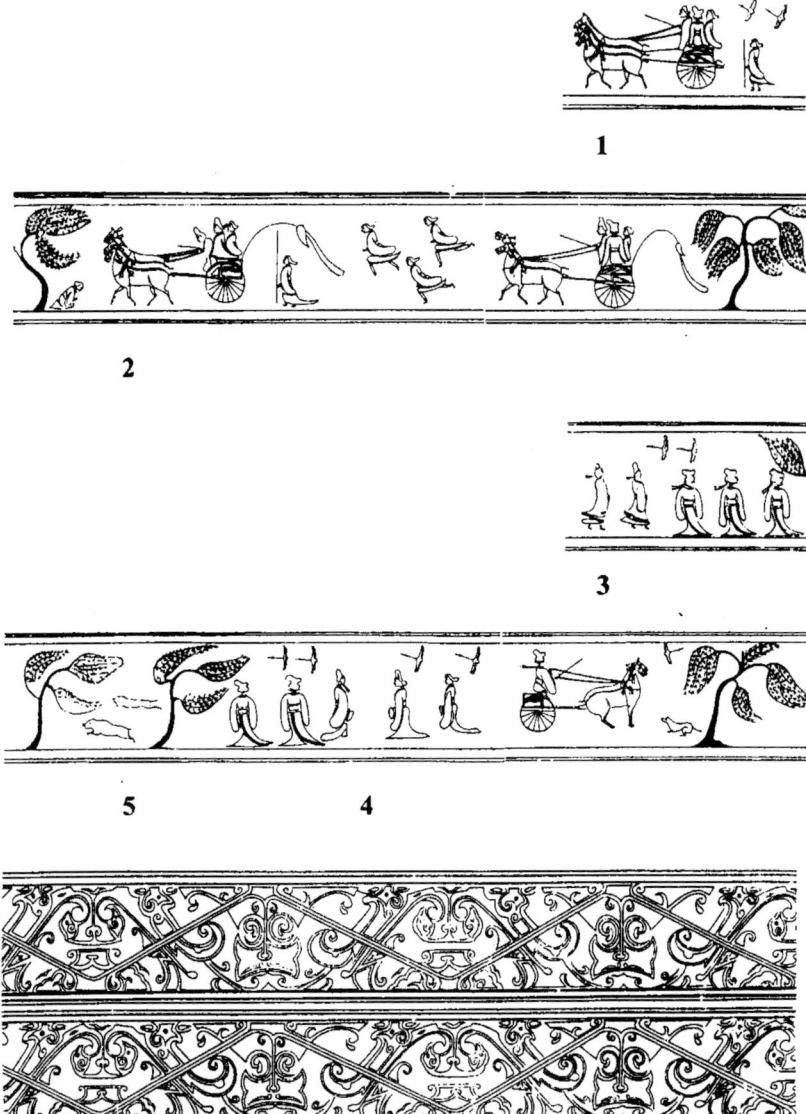

1

2

3

5   4

Figure 22. Detail of the designs on the lacquer box from Jingmen Baoshan Tomb No. 2 (Hubei). After *Baoshan Chu mu* (1991), p. 144–5, figs. 89 (B).

several people who also are seen from the back. Compared with earlier pictorial bronzes (Fig. 17), many innovations can be seen here. The box belongs to the luxury items of its time, and the most advanced techniques contributed to the manufacture of this object. The core of dry lacquer is one among very few examples found in Chu tombs. To achieve the painting, it was necessary to produce different colours with natural pigments mixed with oil, or in a few cases with raw lacquer. At least seven colours were used, which is nearly the widest range found on any lacquerware from that time. The background is in black, and most of the painting was done without using line drawing.

By the mid-fourth century BC, at the same time as painting was invented, wood carving began to reveal a sensibility previously unknown. On the small screen in Figure 23 a large number of different animals, more than fifty, has been represented together: snakes, frogs, deer and birds. This is an allegory of life and death seen through the dangers of life. Several creatures, either prey or predators, are assembled on the screen, and all the combinations show different moments of the fights in which the animals are engaged. Some of the snakes are ready to swallow up frogs or bite deer, while others have already been seized by birds. On the base, interwoven snakes make a compact composition. A closer look shows that these snakes are covering the body of supine birds that they have probably just killed. By fixing all these dramatic moments where life and death are in balance, the artist wanted to create emotion in the viewers. Animals in combat had appeared in Chinese art earlier. However, on such a screen the psychological relationship between artist and viewers is much stronger than before.

It seems that the artists had realised for the first time that they possessed the power to create all kinds of emotion through their works, such as fear and joy. For example, the lamp in Figure 20 shows monkeys playing in a tree while a child is throwing something up to them.[40]

At the same time, the lacquer designers explored new avenues in the decors they created. In particular, they invented geometric compositions based on contrasting effects of colours in such a way that it is sometimes difficult, if not impossible, to distinguish basic motifs from the

---

[40] Bagley (2006) has shown that the imaginary animals of the fifth century BC and later, testify to a fundamental change of character from their predecessors. He argues that an influence from the steppes and the Near East provoked this change, in which the animals take on a more familiar appearance.

Figure 23.   Screen, from Jiangling Wangshan Tomb 1 (Hubei). Painted lacquer on wood, c. 330–320 BC. Height 15 cm, Length 51.8 cm. After *Jiangling Wangshan Shazhong Chu mu* (1996), fig. 66.

background.[41] The lacquer decoration became extremely inventive, and it seems that this inventiveness can be seen as the very beginning of a trend toward pure ornamentation.

Several categories of objects exhibit evidence of the development of a taste for decorative arts. These new lacquer décors prompted the bronze artists to invent techniques that would render the fluidity of the brush on the surface decoration of the bronzes, as well as the contrasts of colours of the lacquer decoration (Fig. 24).[42] From then on, lacquer art would provide the visual cues for the bronze decoration, and also in some cases for shapes. In fact, in the fourth century BC the lacquer craftsmen not only found new methods to produce several different colours, but they also adopted techniques that allowed wood to be bent into cylindrical forms made with thin walls, and invented dry lacquer, using cloth to replace wood for the core of the containers.[43] The numerous properties of lacquers, and specifically the fluidity of designs made with the brush, prompted bronze artisans to imitate the new styles with the help of novel inlay techniques that could introduce contrasts of colours and likewise give the illusion of brushstrokes. To imitate lacquer painting, bronze craftsmen had to solve several technical problems: how to adapt the designs to a round surface; how to create contrasting colours; how to give a natural fluidity to the shapes of the inlays; and, finally, how to produce a smooth surface. Therefore, they invented specific inlay techniques based on copper, silver or gold wires, to which semi-precious stones could be added. Strikingly, even if one can define the style of the lacquers and the bronzes, no two pieces are exactly alike. The inventiveness shown by these designs is in startling contrast to the standardised bronze production for the ritual vessels of the same period. Indeed the taste for ornament that developed during the fourth and third centuries BC initiated a flourishing development of styles and techniques.

It seems, too, that lacquer and bronze workshops from the late Warring States period on did not function in the same way as in earlier times. All the connections between bronzes and lacquer wares point to a complete renewal of the sources of inspiration for bronze decoration.

---

[41] Some of these designs can be labelled as 'optical games' or 'optical effects' (Thote (1996), pp. 159 and 161). On the relationship between figure and ground, see Lawton (1982), p. 20, Thote (2006), pp. 353–6.

[42] On inlay decoration of the late Eastern Zhou period, see So (1980, 1995).

[43] Garner (1979), pp. 34–8, Hou Dejun (1995), pp. 219–26. In fact, at least two different traditions of lacquer craftsmanship in the Warring States period can be identified, located in Qin and Chu respectively (Thote 2006).

Figure 24. *Zun* vessel, from Jiangling Wangshan Tomb 2 (Hubei). Bronze with inlaid patterns inspired by lacquer decoration, *c.*330–320 BC. Height 17.1 cm, Diam. 24.7 cm. After *Jiangling Wangshan Shazhong Chu mu* (1996), fig. 91, p. 135.

Once the bronze workshops were no longer mainly confined by the casting of ritual vessels and related objects, artists became free to look for new sources of inspiration. They emulated several different artistic traditions that probably expressed a greater freedom since they were associated with the secular arts. At the very least, the extremely great variety of the arts during the fourth and third centuries BC seems to indicate that artists benefited from an environment that was very different from standardised workshops of earlier periods such as those at Houma, opening new avenues for exploration. One sign of a significant departure from the tradition can be found in the appearance of artisans' names on objects in the late fourth or early third century BC.[44] These names were not added in order to vaunt the work of the craftsmen, as in the case of a signature. On the contrary, they were meant to make the artisans responsible for their work, sometimes at the cost of their lives. This was a mechanism imposed by their superiors to control the quality of craftsmanship. In the same spirit, bamboo slips from a tomb which is dated to 217 BC reproduce the texts of laws that regulated craftsmen's work in the Qin kingdom.[45] It seems to me that this system of control by which individual names were provided on manufactured objects may have been created precisely because artists and craftsmen had already begun to enjoy a relative freedom in their work or in the trade of their products.[46] Moreover, such inscriptions testify to a significant departure from the former conditions of manufactured work. Probably, artists began to be involved in the creation of the designs, while craftsmen had to adapt these designs to a large number of shapes, and to make use of all kinds of techniques. The fourth century BC, then, appears to be the stage in Chinese art history when

[44] Shen Zhongchang and Huangjiaxiang (1987). The phenomenon increased during the Western Han period and culminated at the end of the first century BC, as indicated by several objects found at Lolang in Korea, and in several other places. One ear cup dated to AD 4, found in Lelang in North Korea and now in the British Museum, bears an inscription recording the date, the location of the workshop, the techniques used, the name of each artisan according to his specialty, and the name of the administrators of the workshop. For lacquer wares with marks of the Han period, see Umehara Sueji (1943), Yu and Li (1975), Pirazzoli-t'Serstevens (1990), pp. 525–7. On the history of the Qin and Han workshops in Shu commandery, see Barbieri-Low (2001).

[45] Yunmeng Shuihudi Qin mu Bianxiezu (1981); Shuihudi Qin Mu Zhujian Zhengli Xiaozu (2001); Hülseve (1985).

[46] During the Qin period, in addition to the governmental factories private workshops also existed. The state factories of the Guanghan and Shu commanderies originally were private workshops during the Qin period. They became state owned around 140 BC. They produced lacquers, and bronze elements with gold and silver inlays for lacquers, mirrors, containers. See Pirazzoli-t'Serstevens (1990).

artists began to depart from craftsmen, gaining a status that allowed them to create with a certain degree of freedom.

Note. I wish to express my gratitude to the British Academy, and in particular to Professor Dame Jessica Rawson, for inviting me to give this lecture. Helpful comments have been made by the audience, as well as on two earlier occasions by several scholars at Princeton University and Columbia University where I presented different versions of this lecture. My paper also benefited from discussions with Robert Bagley and Jonathan Hay. To them all, I express my thanks.

References

Bagley, R. (1987), *Shang Ritual Bronzes in the Arthur M. Sackler Collections*, Ancient Chinese Bronzes from the Arthur M. Sackler Collections, vol. 1 (Cambridge, MA).

Bagley, R. (1993), 'Replication techniques in Eastern Zhou bronze casting', in Steven Lubar and W. David Kingery (eds.), *History from Things: Essays on Material Culture* (Washington and London), pp. 234–41.

Bagley, R. (1995), 'What the bronzes from Hunyuan tell us about the foundry at Houma', *Orientations*, 26, Jan.: 46–54.

Bagley, R. (2005), 'The prehistory of Chinese music theory' [Elsley Zeitlyn Lecture on Chinese Archaeology and Culture], *Proceedings of the British Academy*, 131 [2004]: 41–90.

Bagley, R. (2006), 'Ornament, representation, and imaginary animals in bronze age China', *Arts Asiatiques* [*L'autre en regard. Volume en hommage à Madame Michèle Pirazzoli-t'Serstevens*], 61: 17–29.

Baoshan Chu mu (1991), ed. Hubei ei Sheng Jing Sha Tielu Kaogudui (Beijing).

Barbieri-Low, A. J. (2001), *The Organization of Imperial Workshops During the Han Dynasty* (Ph.D. dissertation, Princeton University).

Changsha Chu mu (2000), 2 vols., ed. Changsha Bowuguan (Beijing).

Chefs-d'oeuvre de la céramique grecque dans les collections du Louvre (1994), ed. M. Denoyelle (Paris).

Chen Fangmei (1989), *Shang Zhou qingtong jiuqi tezhan tulu* (Taipei).

Chine. La gloire des empereurs (2000), ed. Petit Palais (Paris).

Cuo mu— Zhanguo Zhongshan guo guowang zhi mu (1996), ed. Hebei Sheng Wenwu Yanjiusuo (Beijing).

Falkenhausen, L. von (1993), *Suspended Music. Chime-bells in the Culture of Bronze Age China* (Berkeley, Los Angeles and Oxford).

Falkenhausen, L. von (2006), *Chinese Society in the Age of Confucius (1000–250 BC). The Archaeological Evidence* (Los Angeles).

Gao Zhixi (2000), *Chu wenwu tulu* (Wuhan).

Garner, Sir H. (1979), *Chinese Lacquer* (London and Boston).

Gernet, J. (1990), *Le monde chinois* (Paris).

Haiyang Zuiziqian (2002), eds. Yantai Shi Bowuguan, Haiyang Shi Bowuguan (Jinan).

Hemelrijk J. M. (1991), 'A closer look at the potter', in Tom Rasmussen and Nigel Spivey (eds.), *Looking at Greek Vases* (Cambridge), pp. 233–56.

Hong Kong (1994), *Lacquerware from the Warring States to the Han Periods excavated in Hubei Province* (Hong Kong).

Hou Dejun (1995), *Chu guo de kuangye, xiuqi he boli zhizao* (Wuhan).

Hülseve, A. F. P. (1985), *Remnants of Ch'in Law: An Annotated Translation of the Ch'in Legal and Administrative Rules of the 3rd Century BC Discovered in Yün-meng Prefecture, Hu-pei Province in 1975* (Leiden).

Hunan Shen Bowuguan (1983), ed. Gao Zhixi (Beijing).

Jacobson, E. (1988), 'Beyond the frontier: a reconsideration of cultural interchange between China and the early nomads', *Early China*, 13: 201–40.

Jiangling Wangshan Shazhong Chu mu (1996), ed. Hubei Sheng Wenwu Kaogu Yanjiusuo (Beijing).

Jin Hou mudi chutu qingtongqi guoji xueshu yantaohui lunwenji (2002), ed. Shanghai Bowuguan (Shanghai).

Jingzhou Tianxingguan er hao Chu mu (2003), ed. Hubei Sheng Jingzhou Bowuguan (Beijing).

Lawton, T. (1982), *Chinese Art of the Warring States Period: Change and Continuity, 480–222 BC* (Washington, DC).

Ledderose, Lothar (2000), *Ten Thousands Things. Module and Mass Production in Chinese Art* (The A. W. Mellon Lectures in the Fine Arts, 1998. Bollingen Series XXXV. 46, Princeton) (Princeton).

Loewe, M. and Shaughnessy, E. L. (eds.) (1999), *The Cambridge History of Ancient China* (Cambridge).

Luoyang Zhongzhou lu (1959), ed. Zhongguo Kexueyuan Kaogu Yanjiusuo (Beijing).

Mackenzie, C. (1999), 'The influence of textile designs on bronze, lacquer and ceramic decorative styles during the Warring States Period', *Orientations*, September: 82–91. [Repr. (2001), *Chinese Bronzes: Selected Articles from Orientations 1983–2000* (Hong Kong), pp. 337–46].

Ma Wenkuan (1981), 'Lüe tan Zhanguo shiqi de qiqi', *Zhongguo lishi bowuguan guankan*, 3: 109–14.

Music in the Age of Confucius (2000), ed. Jenny F. So (Washington).

Osborne, R. (1998), *Archaic and Classical Greek Art* (Oxford).

Pirazzoli-t'Serstevens, M. (1990), 'Ateliers, patronage et collections princières en Chine à l'époque Han', *Comptes rendus de l'Académie des Inscriptions et Belles-Lettres des séances de l'année 1990, avril-juin*: 521–35.

Qin Shihuang ling bing ma yongkeng yi hao keng fajue baogao 1974–1984 (1988), 2 vols., ed. Shaanxi Sheng Kaogu Yanjiusuo and Shihuangling Qing Yongkeng Kaogu Fajuedui (Beijing).

Rawson, J. (1987), *Chinese Bronze: Art and Ritual* (London).

Rawson, J. (1990), *Western Zhou Ritual Bronzes from the Arthur M. Sackler Collections*, Ancient Chinese Bronzes from the Arthur M. Sackler Collections, vol. 1 (Cambridge, MA).

Robertson, M. (1991), 'Adopting an approach, I', in Tom Rasmussen and Nigel Spivey (eds.), *Looking at Greek Vases* (Cambridge), pp. 1–12.

Shen Zhongchang and Huangjiaxiang (1987), 'Cong chutu de Zhanguo qiqi wenzi kan "Chengdu" de deming', in Xu Zhongshu (ed.), *Ba Shu kaogu lunwenji* (Beijing), pp. 186–90.

Shouxian Cai Hou mu chutu yiwu (1956), ed. Anhui Sheng Wenwu Guanli Weiyuanhui and Anhui Sheng Bowuguan (Beijing).

Shuihudi Qin Mu Zhujian Zhengli Xiaozu (2001), *Shuihudi Qin mu zhujian* (Beijing).

So, J. (1980), 'The inlaid bronzes of the Warring States Period', in Wen Fong (ed.), *The Great Bronze Age of China* (New York), pp. 305–20.

So, J. (1983), '*Hu* vessels from Xinzheng: toward a definition of Chu style', in George Kuwayama (ed.), *The Great Bronze Age of China: A Symposium* (Los Angeles), pp. 64–71.

So, J. (1995), *Eastern Zhou Ritual Bronzes from the Arthur M. Sackler Collections*, Ancient Chinese Bronzes from the Arthur M. Sackler Collections, vol. 3 (New York, The Arthur M. Sackler Foundation (in association with the Arthur M. Sackler Gallery, Smithsonian Institution).

Su Fangshu and Li Ling (2002), 'Jieshao yi jian "Jin Hou tongren"', in Shanghai Bowuguan (ed.), *Jin Hou mudi chutu qingtongqi guoji xueshu yantaohui lunwenji* (2002), pp. 411–20.

Sumiya Sadatoshi (1982), 'Shin ni okeru seidô kôgyô no ikkosatsu: kokan o chûshin ni', *Sundai shigaku*, 55: 52–85.

Taerpo Qin mu (1998), ed. Xianyang Shi Wenwu Kaogu Yanjiusuo (Xi'an).

Taiyuan Jinguo Zhao qin mu (1996), ed. Shanxi Sheng Kaoguyanjiusuo and Taiyuan shi Wenwuguanli Weiyuanhui (Beijing).

The Golden Age of Archaeology: Celebrated Discoveries from the Peoples's Republic of China (1999), ed. Yang Xiaoneng (Washington).

Thote, A. (1987), 'Une sculpture chinoise en bronze du Ve siècle avant notre ère: essai d'interprétation', *Arts Asiatiques*, 42: 45–58.

Thote, A. (1991), 'The double coffin of Leigudun tomb no. 1: iconographic sources and related problems', in Th. Lawton (ed.), *New Perspectives on Chu Culture during the Eastern Zhou Period* (Washington, DC), pp. 23–46.

Thote, A. (1996), 'I Zhou orientali', in M. Pirazzoli-t'Serstevens (ed.), *Storia Universale dell'Arte: La Cina* (Turin), pp. 95–165.

Thote, A. (1999), 'De quelques conventions picturales: le char et ses représentations aux Ve–IVe siècles avant notre ère', *Études chinoises*, 18: 179–220.

Thote, A. (2000), 'L'archéologie de Qin et de Chu à l'époque des Printemps et Automnes (770–481 avant notre ère)', in *Chine, la gloire des empereurs* (Paris), pp. 124–58, 178.

Thote, A. (2006), 'Lacquer craftsmanship in the Qin and Chu kingdoms: two contrasting traditions (late 4th to late 3rd century BC)', *The Journal of East Asian Archaeology*, 5, 1–4 [2003]: 336–74.

Tôkyô Kokuritsu Hakubutsukan (1998), *Urushi de kakerareta shimpi no sekai— Chûgoku kôdai shikki ten* (Tokyo).

Umehara Sueji (1943), *Shina Kandai kinen mei shikki zusetsu* (Kyôto).

Williams D. (1991), 'Vase painting in fifth-century Athens', in Tom Rasmussen and Nigel Spivey (eds.), *Looking at Greek Vases* (Cambridge), pp. 103–18.

Wu Hung (1999), 'The art and architecture of the Warring States Period', in Loewe, M. and Shaughnessy, E. L. (eds.), *The Cambridge History of Ancient China* (Cambridge), pp. 651–744.

Xichuan Xiasi Chunqiu Chu mu (1991), ed. Henan sheng wenwu yanjiusuo, Henan sheng Danjiang kuqu kaogufajuedui, Xichuan xian bowuguan (Beijing).

Yu Weichao and Li Jiahao (1975), 'Mawangdui yi hao mu chutu qiqi zhidi zhu wenti—cong Chengdu Shi Fu zuofang dao Shu Jun gongguan zuofang de lishi bianhua', *Kaogu*, 1975, 6: 344–8.

Yunmeng Shuihudi Qin mu Bianxiezu (1981), *Yunmeng Shuihudi Qin mu* (Beijing).

Zeng Hou Yi mu (1989), 2 vols., ed. Hubei Sheng Bowuguan (Beijing).

Zhanguo Zeng Hou Yi mu chuta wenwu tu'an xuan (1984), ed. Hubei Bowuguan and Beijing gongyi meishu yanjiusuo (no location).

Zhongguo qingtongqi quanji. Dong Zhou 1 (1998) (Beijing).

Zhongguo qiqi quanji. Chunqiu Zhanguo (1997), ed. Jia E (Beijing).

Zhu Zhongxi (2004) (ed.), *Qin Xichui ling qu* (Beijing).

Seventeenth-Century Draining of the Fens and the Impact on Navigation

MICHAEL CHISHOLM
Fellow of the Academy

THE BODY KNOWN AS the Conservators of the River Cam was established by Act of Parliament in 1702 as a navigation authority, its jurisdiction running from Clayhithe to Cambridge (Fig. 1). To celebrate the tercentenary, I set out to write a history of the three hundred years' existence of the Conservators, and quickly encountered two unexpected problems (Chisholm 2003).

Minutes of the Conservators' meetings, held at the Cambridge Record Office and dating back to 1707, were examined for evidence about improvements to the river, specifically the building of locks. As recorded, four structures existed in 1709, possibly in 1708, but they were identified as sluices. According to the *Oxford English Dictionary*, a sluice is not a structure through which vessels may pass; all the definitions exclude that possibility. Nevertheless, in 1750 the four sluices on the Cam were described in the Conservators' minutes in a manner that leaves no doubt that they were pound locks. They had upper and lower doors and they had slackers, the latter being the small guillotine gate in the vee doors of a lock that allow the pen to be filled or emptied.

That the locks on the Cam were being described as sluices prompted the following question: In the seventeenth century, what was the Fenland meaning of the word 'sluice'? Once that question had been posed, it became necessary to examine the literature on the draining of the Fens, particularly from 1649, when Parliament paved the way for the scheme undertaken by Cornelius Vermuyden for the Adventurers, led by the fifth

Read at the Academy 6 February 2008.

Proceedings of the British Academy **154**, 243–272. © The British Academy 2008.

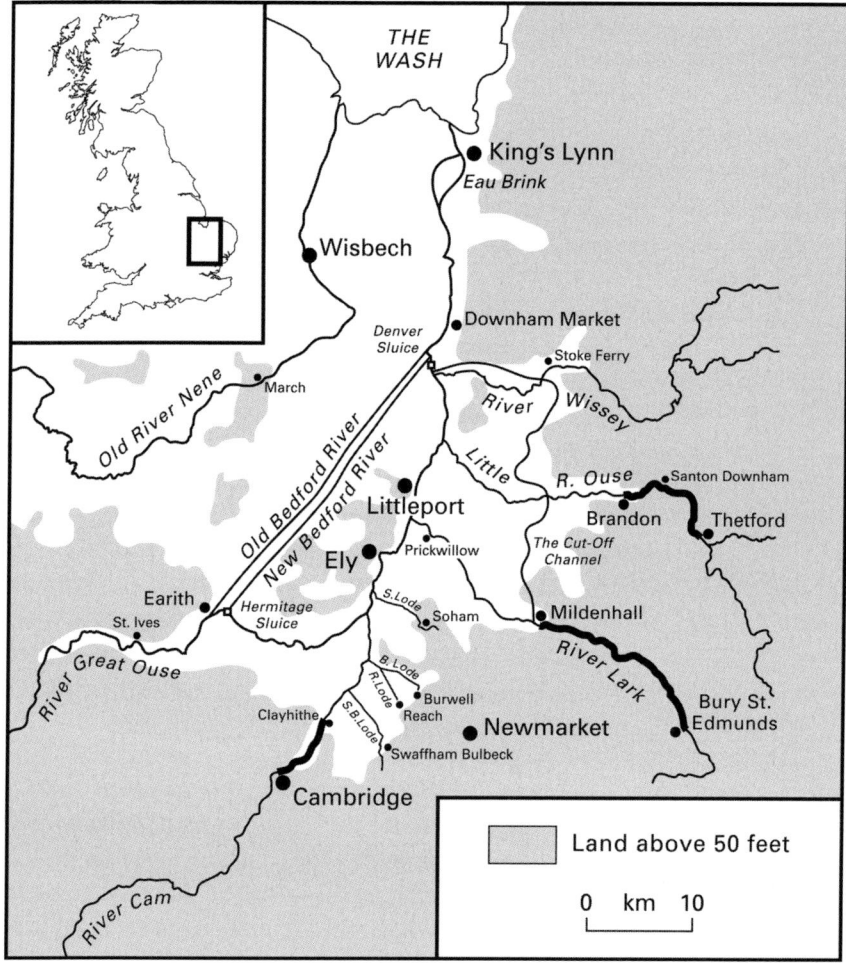

Figure 1. The modern drainage system of the Fens. The thickened sections of the Cam, Lark
and Little Ouse delineate the original statutory navigations—see text.

Earl of Bedford, acting as the body that came to be known as the
Corporation of the Bedford Level. Drainage in general was one of the
leading economic projects of the period (Willmoth 1993: 89), and the
Fens was the single largest of those enterprises. It was strategically significant in the context of rivalry with European countries, particularly the
Dutch (three wars), with the consequential need to maximise domestic
self-sufficiency, and also to equip merchant ships and the men of war.

Perusal of the literature about this enterprise revealed the widespread
opinion that the drainers were not interested in navigation and made no

explicit provision for river commerce; indeed, the general view seems to have been that river trade was seriously impaired. However, this presentation of history could not be reconciled with the fact that the Cam Conservancy was established as a commercial enterprise, reliant upon tolls to fund its capital and recurrent expenditure, and that in 1710 the Conservators had begun to repay the capital invested by the University of Cambridge and by the Town. Furthermore, the 1702 Act specified the maximum tolls that could be levied on named commodities, four of which are particularly relevant in the present context. Coal (specifically, sea coal) and wine could only reach Cambridge from King's Lynn (henceforth, Lynn), the coal originating in north-east England for coastwise shipment to Lynn, and the wine coming from mainland Europe. In addition, salt and salt fish imply access to coastal production sites below Denver Sluice and/or goods shipped into Lynn and thence upriver to Cambridge. Because the Cam Conservancy was doing well early in the eighteenth century, it was clear that trade along the Ouse to Lynn and the Wash must have been reasonably good. Consequently, it seemed evident that there must be something wrong with the widespread view that draining the Fens had been seriously prejudicial to river commerce.

Since the paper on the Cam was published, two further papers show beyond doubt that navigation was not impaired, and that, if anything, it was improved by the drainage enterprise (Chisholm 2006, 2007). Exploring the literature has shown that there are two distinct and essentially contradictory strands of scholarship, with surprisingly little intercommunication: one strand portrays the drainage works as having been seriously prejudicial to navigation; the other indicates that trade continued and even flourished. The Appendix provides chronological tabulations of literature reflecting these two conflicting interpretations of the impact of the drainage works.

The present paper focuses upon the Ouse above Denver Sluice and the three main tributaries—the Little Ouse, Lark and Cam—since it is this section of the Fenland waterways, and the outfall below Denver, about which representations were made that navigation had been prejudiced by the works undertaken by Vermuyden (see Fig. 1). The key evidence will be summarised showing that the drainage works were not the disaster for river traffic that is often represented. This fundamental finding raises a number of questions that can be identified but for which there are inadequate answers at the present time. But first, it is necessary to describe very briefly the nature of the scheme to drain the meres and marshes of the extensive lowland basin that debouches into the Wash.

Vermuyden's drainage works, post 1649

The first comprehensive attempt to drain the Fens began in the 1630s, for the purpose of creating 'summer ground', i.e., summer grazing. However, this project suffered from deficiencies of concept and in any case was sorely neglected during the Civil War. A new start was made with an Act of Parliament in 1649 during the Republic, confirmed after the Restoration by another Act in 1663. Vermuyden's scheme was adopted by the Corporation and he was put in charge. The Fens occupy a low-lying basin across which several rivers flow from the surrounding uplands. These rivers regularly inundated the swampy lands and it was necessary to ensure that the upland waters could be carried across the Fens to the sea without spilling over the banks. To this end, the 100-foot cut, otherwise known as the New Bedford River, was dug from near Earith to Denver, shortening the Ouse and therefore increasing its velocity. This channel was built parallel to the existing 30-foot cut, the Old Bedford River (1631), with the intervening space—the Hundred-Foot Washes—providing temporary storage for flood waters. Embankments were built along the new watercourse and elsewhere the river banks were raised and strengthened. Excess water on the land was allowed to drain through culverts into the main channels, the culverts being equipped to prevent the river flooding onto the reclaimed land at times of high water.

To divert the Ouse near Earith, Vermuyden built Hermitage Sluice, and another sluice was built at Denver, then known as Salter's Lode, in order to prevent the tides running up the Ouse from Denver to Hermitage. Because of the diversion at Hermitage Sluice and the removal of the tides, the character of the Ouse between Denver and Hermitage changed dramatically. On the other hand, the New Bedford River was tidal, as also some of the Ouse above Earith.

These are the main features of the engineering works undertaken by Vermuyden. In addition, he wanted to shorten the course of the Ouse below Denver in order to increase the discharge of land waters in the outfall, a scheme that was not implemented until early in the nineteenth century (the Eau Brink). He also wanted to divert the rivers that flow into the Fens around the eastern edge, such as the Little Ouse, by means of a channel that would carry their waters to the outfall at Denver. Thereby, the problem of flooding would have been reduced but this major part of the scheme was not undertaken until after the Second World War, in the form that is known as the Cut-Off Channel.

The reward for success was to be the acquisition of 95,000 acres by the Adventurers to recompense them for their investments, this being almost one-third of the total area to be drained—somewhat over 300,000 acres (470 square miles). To maintain the drainage works, taxes were to be levied on the improved lands, which were intended to include 'winter ground', or arable land, in addition to summer grazing. Corn and other foodstuffs were to be grown, as well as hemp (for sails, ropes and twine) and flax for linseed oil.

Objections to the scheme

It is well known that those Fenmen who would lose their traditional livelihoods, such as fishing, fowling and harvesting reeds, fiercely resisted the whole scheme, and continued to harry the drainers after the works were completed. Likewise, navigation interests were hostile to the enterprise before it was started, and persisted with those objections for nearly fifty years after the 1649 Act and the successful completion of the drainage works in 1653.

Badeslade (1766) provides a large amount of documentation on the prejudicial effects for navigation that were anticipated and which, he claims, actually occurred; this is in fact the major source for the belief that river commerce was impaired. Lynn led the way, with numerous petitions for Denver Sluice and other works to be dismantled, culminating in the unsuccessful submission of a Bill to Parliament for this purpose in 1696. Lynn's supporters claimed that the outfall below Denver had become shallower and less navigable, and that the non-tidal Ouse and its tributaries above the Sluice were less good for the passage of vessels because of the loss of the tides, silting and water levels being kept low for the benefit of land drainage. However, the objectors in Cambridge, Bury St Edmunds, Thetford and elsewhere were not supported by the Dean and Prebendary of Ely Cathedral, and support for the retention of the New Bedford River was forthcoming from St Ives. In fact, with the benefit of the tidal New Bedford River, circumstances for river traffic were much improved along the Ouse above Hermitage Sluice all the way to Bedford (Chisholm 2007; Summers 1973; Wood 1992, 1998).

The basis for Lynn's objections in 1696 lay in the belief that Denver Sluice had so altered the tidal regime of the outfall that it was silting up, that there were delays at the Sluice and that navigation had been impaired on the Ouse and its tributaries above Denver. However, at no point did Lynn allege that the Sluice had been built without a lock, although the Bill did claim that there were 'long and frequent stops and delays to barges, boats, and vessels in the passage through the same' (Badeslade 1766: 64).

Misunderstood sluices

Given the persistence of Lynn and other objectors, it has been supposed that no lock was provided and that the stops and delays at Denver arose in the following manner. The Sluice was equipped with doors that would swing open when the river stood higher than the tidal outfall and close when the tide rose above river level. With this regime, it would be possible for boats to pass at limited times during the tidal cycle, when the gates were open and the rush of water sufficiently moderate to be manageable by vessels. This appears to be the mode of operation at Denver envisaged by one well-known author: 'Navigation was seriously impeded and confined to certain times of the tide. Passage through the sluice was fraught with danger, and became notorious among watermen. When the doors were opened the resulting torrents of water capsised boats. Several were sunk and their cargoes lost' (Summers 1973: 81). In addition, when floods came down the New Bedford River, it is thought that the doors of Denver Sluice were forced to remain closed for long periods. Altogether, it was possible to perceive the Sluice and the associated works as creating a direct impediment to navigation, though not an absolute barrier, and many scholars in addition to Summers have described Denver Sluice as an 'obstacle' (e.g., Darby 1956: 98–9; 1983: 120; see also Chisholm 2003, 2006 and 2007).

The belief that the sluices at Denver and Hermitage were obstacles for river traffic in the seventeenth century has recently been articulated in a collection of essays published to honour Peter Mathias, an eminent economic historian (Bruland and O'Brien 1998). It is said that Denver Sluice was:

> . . . built with little consideration for navigation with a non-navigable sluice-gate which was destroyed by heavy flooding in 1713. When it was rebuilt between 1748–51, the traffic on the river had increased to such an extent, and merchant capital had begun to play so significant a role in the finance of local schemes, that local landowners under the umbrella of the Bedford Level Corporation ensured that the sluice be built with a navigable lock specifically to serve the needs of navigation. Improvement of the network continued through

to the 1760s, by which date a further five tributaries, the Ivel, the Stoke [Wissey], the Lark, Cam and Little Ouse were made navigable to King's Lynn. (Wood 1998: 201)

Denver Sluice was indeed partially destroyed in 1713 and then rebuilt in 1748–51, but the temporary reintroduction of the tides on the Ouse did not prove to be much of an improvement for shipping, as had been hoped by many. A likely source for the belief that Denver Sluice did not incorporate a lock when it was first completed in 1652 is the assessment made in 1745 by Labelye. This was prepared when he probably entertained the hope that he would be commissioned to rebuild the Sluice, in which regard he was disappointed. Labelye asserted that the original structure made no provision for navigation, an assertion that was accepted by Harris in his 1953 study of Vermuyden (see also Chisholm 2006: 743). In the same year that Harris' study appeared, Skempton published his study of the engineers of English river navigations, in which he dismissed Vermuyden as 'not concerned with river navigation' (Skempton 1953: Table IV).

Wood is in honourable but mistaken company in believing that Denver had no lock when it was first built. She is also mistaken with respect to the tributary rivers that she mentions as being improved after 1751. The Ivel joins the Ouse above Hermitage Sluice, and therefore was not directly affected by Denver; the Navigation Act was obtained in 1757 and was a logical continuation of improvements to the upper Ouse that had been initiated in the early seventeenth century. On the other hand, Navigation Acts had been passed for three other tributary rivers before the partial collapse of Denver in 1713 and long before it was rebuilt in 1748–51—the Little Ouse in 1670, the Lark in 1698 and the Cam in 1702. For these three rivers, the statutory navigations applied only to the upper reaches, outside the main extent of the Fens (see Fig. 1). As for the Stoke or Wissey, there has been no Navigation Act, such improvements as there were for vessels being occasioned by works intended to improve drainage. The fact that three statutory navigations were established in the half century after Denver Sluice was completed in 1652 shows, beyond all reasonable doubt, that the condition of the rivers below the jurisdiction of the navigation authorities was fully acceptable for vessels, and that the same was true of the Ouse to Denver and Lynn.

That Denver Sluice did have a lock from 1652

Some general considerations

The root of the uncertainty about Denver Sluice lies in the destruction of the early Corporation records in the Fire of London in 1666. Although contemporary copies of many documents had been taken and escaped destruction because they were housed in Ely, the original drawings and specifications for the Sluice were, apparently, not copied and were lost in the fire. In addition, as already noted, the *Oxford English Dictionary* defines the word 'sluice' in a manner that precludes the passage of boats. However, Vermuyden was Dutch, and the technology employed for the drainage works was that of his countrymen, who were the European leaders in hydrological matters. The Dutch have a word 'sluis' with the same Latin root, 'excludere', as the English 'sluice'. In the Low Countries, a sluis has two meanings: it is the primary word for a lock; and it is also used for water control structures, which may or may not incorporate a lock (Chisholm 2003: 197). Versions of the same word for a lock are found in several European languages, including German, Norwegian and French. The English meaning, as recorded by the *Oxford English Dictionary*, is out of step with the usage employed by our near Continental neighbours.[1]

Consequently, the expectation is that sluices built across navigable rivers in the Fens incorporated locks to allow vessels to pass, Denver Sluice included. There is another cogent reason for assuming that this was the case. The 1649 Act was passed during the Republic headed by Oliver Cromwell and was then confirmed after the Restoration by another Act in 1663. Both Acts explicitly required that navigation must not be prejudiced. Consequently, had Denver Sluice been built without a lock, the objectors would have had a strong case in law for it to be prohibited before construction, or pulled down once built. So far as is known, no such lawsuit was ever initiated.

Unfortunately, matters were not as clear as one might expect. The 1663 Act specified that navigation should not be prejudiced, the test being that the state of navigations should be as in 1637, when Charles I granted a charter for the initial attempt to drain the Fens, with the implication that the rivers should remain tidal and that no locks be built. Therefore,

---

[1] The editor of the *OED* has been supplied with relevant material and will reconsider the definition of 'sluice' when the word is reached in the ongoing revision process.

attempts to have Denver Sluice removed were attempts to keep the navigation as it had been prior to 1652. Viewed in this light, the fact of the objections proves that there was opposition to *changing* the conditions for river traffic but this does not necessarily mean that the conditions had *deteriorated*. This distinction has not hitherto been apparent in the literature about the draining of the Fens, with the result that the objections have been too readily accepted as evidence that matters really did get worse.

On a tidal river, the flood tide provides much energy to carry vessels inland against the flow of the river, and the ebb reinforces the river's contribution. Supplementary power was provided by sails when the wind was right, with additional options being the use of poles and hauling, or haling, by men or horses. However, the times available for moving up and down river efficiently were dictated by the daily and monthly tidal rhythms. When the Ouse became non-tidal above Denver Sluice, conditions changed dramatically. It was not possible to rely upon the wind, because the wind itself is variable and the rivers are sinuous, and poling was an arduous occupation. Craft had to be hauled, either by horses or men — generally horses — instead of relying on the help of the tides. In effect, there had to be a revolution in the manner by which craft navigated. So far as is known, nobody has examined this reorganisation of the river traffic in any detail but it is easy to see that there would have been both winners and losers. It may be that some objections to the drainage scheme were motivated by the fear of losing livelihoods on the river as a result of the change to non-tidal conditions, or the realisation that this was actually happening. This is an aspect of the drainage enterprise that awaits exploration.

Apart from the legal requirement of no detriment to navigation, there is another basic reason why locks would have been necessary on the navigable rivers. The whole purpose of the project was to increase the commercial output of the Fens, which necessarily meant that landowners would need to obtain requirements such as bricks and coal, and simultaneously to market their products. Without good transport, profits could not be envisaged, and without profits there would be no possibility of recovering the sums invested and ensuring a tax revenue stream to maintain the fixed assets. From the available accounts (e.g., Darby 1936: 273), it is clear that numerous bridges and roads were built but it is difficult to imagine that horse-drawn wagons using circuitous routes over soft terrain could have sufficed for long distance traffic with heavy loads. The waterways were the obvious means for the movement of bulky goods such as corn, much of which found its way to Lynn for coastwise shipment to the north-east of England. Consequently, it is inconceivable that the Corporation was indifferent to navigation, and one must expect that provision was made. Whether that provision was adequate then becomes the issue to consider. This issue needs to be examined alongside the adequacy or otherwise of the land drainage, because it is well known that the Corporation faced crises as the peat shrank, that there was a chronic shortage of funds, and that it was impossible to attend to everything that needed to be done.

Specific evidence

Thus far, the emphasis has been placed upon the word 'sluice'. However, in the mid-seventeenth century the more common word for a lock was 'sasse', a word of obscure origin but unequivocal meaning. In many contexts, the two words were used interchangeably, almost certainly for the following reason. Because a lock allows vessels to move from higher to lower water, and vice versa, there must be a weir beside the lock to maintain the river's water level above the lock, and it may be necessary to have sluice gates to manage the flow of water over the weir. In all essential respects, a sasse was identical to a sluice constructed with a lock.

Denver Sluice was described as a sasse very soon after it had been constructed, the earliest such reference identified by the present author being contained in a study of the Fenland riots. Attempts were made in 1653 to demolish by force the 'double sasse' at Salter's Lode and the Corporation's Accounts Books record payment: 'For the foot guard that defended the great Dam and Sasse over the Ouse' (Lindley 1982: 183). About five years after this episode, Jonas Moore published his map of the entire Fens, at a scale of two inches to the mile. This map identifies fourteen structures on rivers and major lodes, using variants of the single chevron (<) later used by the Ordnance Survey for locks, the variants being a single pair of chevrons or two pairs. Of these fourteen structures, seven are labelled as being sasses. In other words, Moore records fourteen locks on the Fenland river system. The word sluice does not appear. Denver, described as Denver Dam, is portrayed as a complex structure of five channels, one of which has the symbol << and another << <<, leaving no doubt that there was at least one lock for vessels. The third contemporary document to note is Dugdale's major study, first published in 1662, only ten years after Denver had been completed. He refers to the sasse at Salter's Lode 'set up of late years' and then subsequently mentions: 'Two great sasses at Salters Lode, for the passage of boats and other great vessels' (Dugdale 1772: 177 and 415).

There can be no doubt that Denver Sluice did incorporate a lock for the benefit of navigation, a fact that explains why Lynn's petition to Parliament in 1696 did not allege the absence of such a facility (Badeslade 1766: 63–4). The basis for Lynn's complaint was threefold: the loss of the tides above Denver; silting, above and below the Sluice; and that there were stops and delays for vessels passing through it. Badeslade was a fierce critic of Vermuyden's scheme, adopting the same stance as Lynn, and he actually acknowledges that there was a sasse across the Ouse at Denver from the time the structure was first completed (Badeslade 1766: 43 and 55).

Lynn's application to Parliament elicited two public rejoinders from the Corporation, documents that appear to have been completely ignored in the literature.[2] One of these documents has the brief title 'The case of the Corporation of the Great Level of the Fens' and refers to the sluices at Hermitage and Denver, both being described as 'a navigable sasse or sluce'. It appears that this document was issued in an attempt to prevent the Bill being submitted because the second one uses the same short title supplemented by the phrase 'Bill depending in Parliament' and is a significantly fuller text. This second document refers to the sluice at Denver Dam, clearly meaning the lock or sasse mentioned in the first one, and reads in part as follows:

> I. The navigation in the New Cut River to St Ives, Huntingdon, and St Neots, is much quicker than before; by which means, the counties of Huntingdon, Bedford, Buckingham, and part of Northamptonshire, are far better accommodated than formerly.

> II. As to the navigation of the river Great Owse, above the said sluice, there are fresh doors at the sluice, by which all the waters upwards, are (when low) held up, whereby the navigation is maintained at all times of the year; which before, was by the lowness of the water, perfectly obstructed for some months in dry seasons, so that by means of those fresh doors, the navigation to Cambridge, Norfolk and Suffolk, through the Level, is much more certain than formerly, which does more than compensate the not flowing of tides in those rivers: and if boats, or vessels, be at any time stopp'd by the sluce, 'tis for want of observing the times of the tides, which being observ'd, the navigation is free and open.

---

[2] They were drawn to the attention of the author by Paul Richards (Cambridge RO R79/104 (R. Ouse)).

The Corporation's first document points out that: 'No decree against them by Lynn, or any others, was ever obtained.' The Bill before Parliament in 1696 did not proceed to enactment.

It will be recalled that Skempton, writing in 1953, dismissed Vermuyden as not being interested in navigation. By 2002, he had revised his opinion. Among other things, he accepted that Denver did incorporate a sasse and that water levels were maintained up the river to Ely and beyond, adding that the sasse or lock was 24 feet wide (Skempton *et al.* 2002: 739–47).

The starting point for further enquiry is provided by the indisputable facts that the drainers did make provision for navigation and that Denver Sluice did incorporate a lock from the beginning. Recent work shows that the highly negative view portrayed in much of the literature is fundamentally wrong. On the other hand, is it appropriate to accept the Corporation's own assessment, or does this err in the opposite direction? It is to this question that we now turn.

Further considerations

The Ouse above Hermitage Sluice

Little will be said at this juncture about the first claim made by the Corporation because the upper part of the Ouse river system has been thoroughly studied and there can be no doubt that the tidal New Bedford River was a considerable benefit for trade above Hermitage Sluice (Summers 1973; Wood 1992, 1998). For example, Summers (1973: 70) notes that the New Bedford River resulted in freight costs between Lynn and St Neots falling by almost 40 per cent, a finding that is consistent with other evidence and confirms the Corporation's claim.

Dry season low water

The Corporation's claim that, before Denver Sluice was constructed, navigation could be seriously impaired on account of low water is fully substantiated by independent evidence dating from 1605 in the case of the Ouse at Ely. In July of that year, the depth of water at Ely was only 14 inches, and no more than 18 inches or 2 feet a little downstream at some 'Hards' (Dugdale 1772: 380–1). Some years later, in 1618, the Cam was reported to be navigable without difficulty to Clayhithe but that, beyond this point, the river posed considerable problems, problems that would have been exacerbated at times of low flow (Atkins 1618: 93–4).

The Hards identified by Dugdale can be located with some precision as being very near the Old Plough, midway between Ely and Prickwillow. The Old Plough stands on a small island of Kimmeridge Clay, at the point where the river, formerly flowing northward from Stuntney, turned east to Prickwillow (Fig. 2). In the twelfth century, the Ouse was diverted to run past Ely and thence by the Old Plough to Prickwillow. The Hards were located where this twelfth-century diversion cut through the edge of the Kimmeridge Clay upon which the Old Plough stands. Badeslade (1766: Abstract, p. i) refers to keels with 40 tons sailing 36 miles from Lynn, and the Hards are almost exactly at this distance along the former channel of the Ouse from the Old Bar Beacon, which marked the entrance to Lynn Haven (Chisholm 2007: 180).

Although the size of vessel given by Badeslade should be accepted with caution, there is incontrovertible evidence that transhipment occurred in the river by the Old Plough. In 1830, the Ouse was diverted again, to run direct from Ely to Littleport, and the channel passing the Old Plough became farmland. At times when the land has been ploughed, a scattering of coal can be gleaned along about 250 metres of the pre-1830 channel near the Old Plough, but not beyond these limits, this scattering being consistent with spillages as coal was unloaded from larger vessels into smaller craft (Chisholm 2008). The fact of transhipment at this point confirms the existence of the Hards, which would have been obstacles at times of low flow. Although we do not have independent evidence to date these spillages, it is reasonable to suppose that they occurred prior to the Fens being drained. Transhipment on account of the Hards implies that there would indeed have been problems for navigation at times of low water.

Navigation Acts

Badeslade states that, with sluices located at Hermitage and Denver, the level of the Ouse was lowered so much that navigation to Cambridge would have been impossible if locks had not been constructed on the Cam. It is indeed reasonable to think that diverting the Ouse down the New Bedford River would have the effect of reducing water levels, a view that the present author accepted (Chisholm 2003: 184). Closer examination reveals that this simple view is wrong.

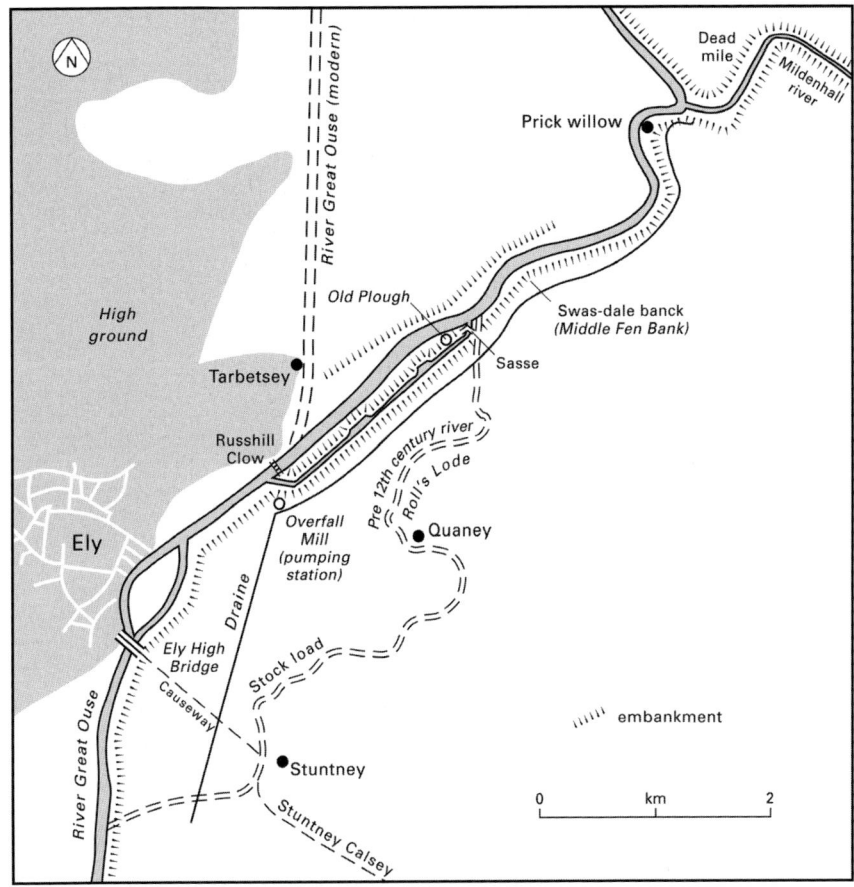

Figure 2. The lock that it was intended should be built on the former course of the Ouse near Ely. Re-drawn from Moore *c*.1658, with some additions shown in italic. Reproduced from the *Proceedings of the Cambridge Antiquarian Society* (2007, 96: 181).

The geography of the three privately sponsored statutory navigations on rivers tributary to the Ouse between Denver and Hermitage has already been noted; the navigations applied only to the upland reaches, where navigation had always been more difficult than in the Fens. The timing of the Acts is also noteworthy. Although an Act was obtained in 1670 for the Little Ouse, it was another three decades before legislation reached the statute book for the Lark and the Cam, a fact that indicates very clearly that there could not have been a serious general deterioration of the rivers for commercial traffic.

The Little Ouse is particularly instructive. Roger North, who attended school in Thetford 1663–5, records that the river was navigable to the town, which was the traditional head of navigation (Jessop 1972: 11). A few years later, in 1668, a major sandstorm blocked the river for three miles about Santon Downham, reducing the freight that could be carried by vessels from around ten tons to two (Wright 1668: 724). This catastrophic event was the culmination of nearly a century's advance of mobile sands following a blowout at Lakenheath Warren. It is a curious fact that, although the mobile sands of the Breckland and the 1668 event are well known in the literature on the landscape of Suffolk and on farming the sandy soils, the impact upon the Little Ouse has been virtually completely ignored by scholars concerned with draining the Fens and river navigation. Furthermore, the 1670 Act also provided for the river Waveney, which flows from near the headwaters of the Little Ouse eastward to the North Sea. This river was completely unaffected by Vermuyden's works.

On this evidence, and the details recorded for the Lark and Cam (Chisholm 2007), it is evident that the Navigation Acts should be viewed: first, as part of the commercially driven movement to improve river navigations; and second, in the case of the Little Ouse, as the response to a localised and highly unusual problem. It is a mistake to view these Acts as being occasioned by the draining of the Fens, and therefore a mistake to treat them as evidence that navigation conditions had deteriorated.

Evidence regarding freight traffic

So far as is known, there are no records for the total volume or value of river traffic in the seventeenth century, with the consequence that it is necessary to piece together disparate sources of information. The best information pertains to the Cam and it happens that this is the most useful tributary of the Ouse to consider because it joins that river the furthest upstream between Denver and Hermitage.

A remarkable time series for coal prices in Cambridge was compiled in the nineteenth century by Thorold Rogers (1887) and is reproduced by Nef (1932: 405). Rogers used the records of King's College to obtain the retail price paid for coal each year for a period extending from the late sixteenth century into the eighteenth. Fig. 3 shows the Cambridge series for the entire seventeenth century and also the less complete information for Westminster School in London. To provide a basis for comparison, prices at Newcastle upon Tyne are also shown, these prices being the prices to

shipmasters, equivalent to wholesale prices. The coal was shipped coastwise to Lynn and then up the rivers to Cambridge. It is clear that the Civil
War seriously disrupted the coal trade to Cambridge, as shown by the
very sharp rise in price. However, prices then returned to the level that
preceded the turmoil, and there is nothing in the series to suggest that the
trade was significantly hampered by the construction of Denver Sluice in
1652.

Another piece of the jigsaw is provided by Stourbridge Fair, held on
what is now known as Stourbridge Common, adjacent to the Cam just
downstream of Cambridge. This fair was established in 1211 but had
become a pale shadow of its former glory by the nineteenth century. The
copious literature about the fair shows that, although it suffered long
term decline, there was no evident reduction in the scale and compass of
the event as a consequence of the completion of Denver Sluice in 1652.
That the river continued to play a vital role is clear from a visitor's
account in 1681, he noting the river as being 'thick set with boats for a

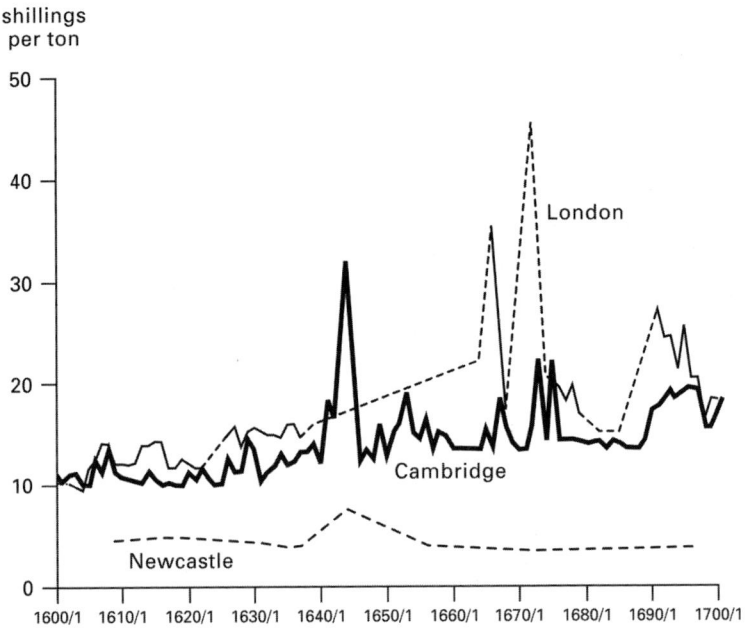

Figure 3. The annual price of coal in Cambridge throughout the seventeenth century. Reproduced
from the *Journal of Historical Geography* (2006, 32: 739). Prices at Newcastle approximate
to wholesale prices, being prices paid by shipmasters. Sources: Mitchell 1988; Nef 1932.

mile in length with all sorts of provisions' and that there were 'vast heaps of coal' on the bank (Baskerville 1681: 273). Despite the fears that had been expressed about the impact draining the Fens would have upon navigation generally, and on the Cam in particular, and despite the protests that continued until the end of the century, the literature about the fair is notably silent about any actual impact, adverse or positive (Chisholm 2007). This total silence has to imply that river commerce carried on much as it had before the Fens were drained and, therefore, that the drainage works were of little moment in considering the fortunes of the fair.

The third piece of evidence to mention in the present context relates to a navigable waterway that joins the Cam between Cambridge and the Ouse. Commercial End is located near Swaffham Bulbeck, and formerly had direct access to the Lode that joins the Cam. The Merchants House at Commercial End is a fine dwelling dating from the late seventeenth century and noted in Pevsner's *Buildings of England*, standing adjacent to a basin and quayside and to former warehouses. The present-day building incorporates a significant external wall from a pre-existing one, and it is known that the mercantile concern had been in business for upwards of two centuries at the time it was auctioned in 1824 (Chisholm 2007). There is no doubt that a thriving business was in existence in the early part of the seventeenth century, and that it continued to prosper after Denver Sluice had been built.

The three pieces of information that have been cited above are the most striking in a considerable corpus recently collated (Chisholm 2007). The evidence is consistent, that trade over the river system above Denver Sluice continued and flourished after the Fens had been drained, confirming the claim made by the Corporation in 1696.

Why did objections to the drainage scheme persist after 1652?

The initial problem, the meaning of the word 'sluice' in the Fenland context, has been solved, that sluices on navigable waterways did incorporate locks. It is also absolutely clear that the Ouse between Denver and Hermitage, and the tributaries, continued to be important navigations. Therefore, why did objections from Lynn and elsewhere continue to be made, claiming that navigation had been sufficiently seriously prejudiced that the sluices at Denver and Hermitage should be pulled down and the

New Bedford River abandoned? In addition, why have so many scholars accepted the allegations that the drainage scheme was so detrimental to trade interests, ignoring accessible evidence that proves the contrary? Having solved the initial problem, there is now a substantial body of further matters to be probed in order to arrive at a balanced view about the relationship between drainage and navigation in the Fens during the seventeenth century.

To understand why objections on navigation grounds continued so persistently after the drainage scheme had been declared a success in 1653, it appears to be necessary to consider a complex set of interlocking factors. On the basis of existing knowledge, the main headings that seem to be relevant can be set out, with, in some cases, limited information by way of amplification. In other words, it is possible to suggest lines of enquiry, or even hypotheses, that warrant further examination.

Theoretical approaches to drainage and navigation

Vermuyden's approach has already been briefly described but not the fact that there was a contemporary alternative view associated with Westerdyke (see Chisholm 2006), to which Badeslade (1766) was an explicit adherent; he gives a very clear statement of the fundamental premiss in the abstract that introduces his book. Badeslade is categorical that rivers are kept clear of silt and maintained in a navigable state by the action of the tides. From this fundamental proposition it follows that a sluice, such as the one at Denver, would necessarily have a seriously adverse impact on the tideless river navigation. Consequently, in order to maintain the navigability of the rivers while also enabling the land to be drained, the fundamental strategy would have to be the construction of strong and high embankments adequate to hold flood waters crossing the Fens; and no sluices should be built across the rivers to block the tides.

From a modern viewpoint, it is not easy to accept Badeslade's fundamental postulate and the strategy that logically follows. But we need to remember that hydrological science was in its infancy in the seventeenth century, that the ideas associated with Westerdyke had had their supporters from the mid-sixteenth century or earlier, and that this support continued well into the eighteenth century (e.g., Elstobb 1779). Echoes of the debate have been audible in more recent times (Miller and Skertchly 1878: 182 ff.; Bevis 2003: 14), testifying to the longevity of ideas that the general consensus now regards as incorrect.

To understand what was happening in the seventeenth century, this polarisation of opinion must provide an important starting point. Equally important, the views of Westerdyke and Badeslade apparently received clear support from what actually happened after Denver Sluice had been completed in 1652 and the scheme as a whole declared successful the following year. Very quickly, lands that had been drained became swampy and waterlogged, with the visible fact that gravity drains could no longer cope because rivers were standing higher in relation to the land than previously was the case. This visible evidence, it was thought by many, could have only one cause—the river beds must be rising because the channels were silting. Thereby, so it seemed, there was clear evidence that Denver Sluice in particular was seriously prejudicial to navigation on the non-tidal Ouse and its tributaries.

As we now know, the land surface was becoming lower on account of the peat shrinking, first by compaction when the excess water was removed, and then by aerobic destruction of the organic matter. It took some time before there was general acceptance that the problem of waterlogged land arose from the shrinkage of the peat, not from the silting of river channels (Skertchly 1877: 51), and that the solution lay in pumping water over the embankments into the rivers. Meantime, those who adhered to Westerdyke's approach had evidence that appeared to support their argument that Denver Sluice should be removed.

Personal and corporate interests

Some of the testimony regarding the adverse impact on navigation arising from draining the Fens is unreliable. Badeslade had a polemical interest in arguing the case that Vermuyden had chosen the wrong way to proceed, his book appearing at a time of intense debate regarding the wisdom of rebuilding Denver Sluice after its partial destruction in 1713. One of the less credible claims that he makes is the following. Along the course of the Ouse above the confluence with the Cam and up to Hermitage, he states that, whereas 'boats and barges' had previously plied, 'grass and fodder is now mown' because the water level had fallen by at least five feet on account of Hermitage Sluice diverting the Ouse (Badeslade 1766: 62). Such a drop would have been impossible, given that the river immediately downstream, in 1608, did not exceed four feet in depth for much of the way to Ely (Chisholm 2007).

When Charles Labelye prepared his 1745 assessment of the situation in the Fens, he asserted that no lock had been provided in the original

Denver Sluice. He was a respected engineer with a pioneering mathematical approach, whose main project had been the difficult task of building Westminster Bridge across the river Thames, a successful ten-year project that commenced in 1738. Labelye had come to England in the 1720s from Switzerland, knowing no English but quickly mastering the language. Furthermore, he had very little personal knowledge of the Fens, having travelled there only once, briefly, prior to the short visit that provided the basis for his 1745 report (Skempton *et al.* 2002: 389–92). The fact that he was wrong in stating that the original sluice at Denver had no lock implies either that he was genuinely mistaken, or that he sought to portray the original structure in as bad a light as possible, in the hope of winning the rebuilding contract. However the mistake was made, his national standing lent credence to the error.

With these two examples in mind, one has to wonder about some of the other testimony contributing to the view that river traffic was impaired by draining the Fens. For example, a Mr John Attleson claimed that, prior to the construction of Denver Sluice, 'large barges and vessels' with some 35–40 tons could regularly and easily reach Cambridge, whereas only 11–13 tons could be carried thereafter (Badeslade 1766: 61–2). The evidence compiled by Chisholm (2007) shows, beyond reasonable doubt, that both parts of this claim are wrong. According to Badeslade, Mr Attleson was about 80 years old and had known the rivers for upwards of sixty years. Seven other witnesses are named who supported Mr Attleson's testimony, but their claims are contradicted by other evidence that appears to be considerably more reliable. So who were they all, what were their interests in the river and, possibly, what obligations did they owe and to whom?

On the evidence that has recently been marshalled, it is clear that many of the claims regarding the good state of the river navigations before 1652 do not stand up to scrutiny, and that the same is true of testimony about the adverse effects of the drainage works (Chisholm 2007). In this context, the following observation by Summers is particularly interesting. Impressed by the volume and persistence of the testimony that navigation had been prejudiced, she says: 'It is surprising that the Bedford Level Corporation was able to induce witnesses to testify that the river [Ouse] was in a reasonable condition' (Summers 1973: 82). The implication is clear, that no inducements were offered by the complainants, which seems improbable. It appears that the credentials and reliability of *all* witnesses and protagonists, on both sides of the argument, need to be examined with considerable care, something that has not been essayed.

Possible explanations for the protests

If we now return to the contrast between the impact of the New Bedford River and of Denver Sluice on their respective parts of the Fenland waterways we can discern a possible explanation for the protests that emanated from places such as Thetford and Cambridge. In 1696, the Corporation of the Great Level correctly claimed that navigation along the New Bedford River had yielded substantial benefits for destinations above Hermitage Sluice. The language they used for the Ouse and tributaries above Denver was more circumspect, that the greater reliability of water in the rivers 'does more than compensate for the not flowing of the tides'. Both of these assessments have been confirmed, with the implication that there was a change in the *relative* trade advantages of the two areas identified, to the benefit of the areas accessible to the Ouse above Hermitage Sluice. Therefore, it may be that the objections from places above Denver Sluice that have been so prominent in the literature arose from the perceived loss of competitive advantage. To regain the relative advantage that existed before the drainage works were undertaken would necessarily mean the removal of the sluices at Denver and Hermitage, and the abandonment of the New Bedford River. However, the case could not reasonably be presented in these terms, and therefore there would have been the need to marshall evidence that conditions had become worse than hitherto for those areas affected by the removal of the tides (Chisholm 2007). This possibility must be viewed as an hypothesis that is worthy of exploration to help us understand what was going on inland, though it is not clear that it offers any explanation for the attitude of Lynn.

This leads to the further general thought. To what extent may the protests about impaired navigation have been motivated by quite other goals that could not be stated publicly? Is it the case that navigation issues were used by local or national interests as the issue that could be pursued, when the real goals could not? It seems that there is now enough doubt about the reliability of the testimony concerning the adverse effects of draining that the motives of the individuals and bodies concerned need to be examined very carefully, if there are extant sources suitable for the purpose.

Practical considerations

Draining the Fens raised a substantial number of practical problems that
need to be examined anew given that provision was in fact made for navigation, and that river commerce over the Ouse above Denver and on the
tributary rivers did flourish. Of these issues, the over-riding matter is that
of finance.

Finances and competing claims

By tradition, the rivers had always been open and free for navigation and
this situation continued after 1649, there being no charges for passing
through locks or tolls on freight, other than on the statutory navigations.
The cost of providing for navigation therefore fell upon landowners, in
the form of taxes levied by the Corporation. This being the case, it is easy
to conclude that any perceived deficiencies in the provision for river traffic must have been because navigation needs were given a lower priority
than the needs for land drainage. This attitude is succinctly stated as follows: 'Where the administration of Navigation was concerned an examination of the Corporation's attitude reveals its apparent determination to
fulfil its legal obligations within limits rigidly defined by the requirements
of drainage' (Summers 1973: 78).

On the other hand, the pressure for Denver Sluice to be removed arose
from landed interests as well as from those whose basic complaint was
about navigation, with the result that, at the end of the seventeenth century: 'The navigation party gained the support of the whole of Norfolk
Marshland and many South Level landowners, who were concerned
about the continuing floods and looking for a scapegoat. Pastures, they
pointed out, were completely drowned, and roads impassable' (Summers
1973: 83).

The fact that there were considerable landowner interests arguing for
the removal of key parts of Vermuyden's drainage works shows that dissatisfaction was not confined to those with a direct interest in navigation
and suggests that the Corporation was faced with seemingly insoluble
problems. What is required is a careful re-examination of the documents
used by Summers, and numerous other scholars, with the following questions in mind. Given the scale and nature of the competing claims, and
given that river commerce did flourish, does it really appear that there was
a consistent policy of placing a lower priority on navigation matters than
on those affecting drainage? To what extent did complaints about naviga-

tion refer to the main waterways or to the minor drains, where sluices may indeed have been barriers for boats? In other words, to what extent may one accept the judgement of Summers that is reported above?

Management of water levels

It is widely believed that the drainage works resulted in lower water levels in the rivers than had been the case previously. Diverting the Ouse down the New Bedford River reduced the flow in the Ouse below Hermitage Sluice which, considered on its own, should result in lower water levels in the main river and its tributaries. In addition, on the assumption that drainage interests were paramount, water levels would be kept as low as possible in order to maximise drainage and the capacity for storing flood waters (Summers 1973: 20). The overall effect was held to be that waters were often too shallow for the passage of boats, with serious adverse effects on trade. This assessment is consistent with the view that the 'ruthless drainage interest' had 'little thought or sympathy to spare for the comparatively less pressing problems of navigation' (Summers 1973: 15), a view apparently supported by the phraseology of Darby's last book on the Fens (Darby 1983: 99–102).

However, in his 1936 contribution to the *Victoria County History*, Darby himself offers a radically different interpretation of the way in which water levels were managed: 'Every care was taken to provide an adequate water-level for navigation in the Ouse, the Cam, and the Nene.' He continues with the following observations: 'The large and powerful navigation interests involved in the Fens always insisted on the maintenance of adequate levels of water in the arterial drains for the uninterrupted passage of boats and barges. When the ideal of every fenland engineer was to keep the level of water in the internal drains low enough to contain a sudden flood at any time, this compulsory height of water became a severe, and rather unnecessary, handicap' (Darby 1936: 273 and 277).

Two diary records, which appear to have been overlooked in the context of navigation, confirm that the internal drains were indeed used for transport. In 1670, John Evelyn stayed at Burrow-Green (now Burrough Green), south of Newmarket, and in a day excursion on horseback visited some meres in the Fens that were in the process of being drained by 'engines'. The water was being discharged into 'two rivers, or graffs, cut by hand, and capable of carrying considerable barges' (Bray 1850: 49). Some fifty years later, Daniel Defoe travelled from Lynn to Downham

Market, whence his party: 'Pass'd the fenn country to Wisbich, but saw nothing that way to tempt our curiosity but deep roads, innumerable dreyns and dykes of water, all navigable . . .' (Cole and Browning 1962: 74). The navigable drains and dykes must have had trade connections to the arterial river system by one means or another.

Darby's 1936 assessment of the main rivers is supported by the plentiful evidence that river traffic did in fact continue and prosper, as has been summarised above and in recent publications. In addition, there is incontrovertible evidence that Vermuyden recognised the problems posed for navigation by the removal of the tides and the shallowness of the Ouse in, and downstream of, Ely, and that there were proposals for rectifying the matter. Unfortunately, it is not known for certain how much was actually done. In March 1652, he reported in person to the Lords Commissioners of Adjudication, meeting in Ely, that he had made a gage (a clow or weir?) to hold up the Ouse at Rasshell Hill (now Roswell Pits), and had dug a 'little cut' about one mile long, the effect being to narrow the river and to maintain a greater depth (Wells 1830, vol. 1: 273–4; see also Chisholm 2008). This project has been overlooked in the literature. Making his 1652 report, Vermuyden was reporting on his future plans for the Middle Level, but he couched his comments about works near Ely in the past tense, implying that they had already been implemented. Whether these works had actually been carried out is uncertain and, within six years, it is clear that plans had changed; it was clearly intended to build a lock near the Old Plough, at the downstream end of what may have been the 'little cut' (Fig. 2), but there is no known direct evidence that such a lock was ever constructed (Chisholm 2007: 181).

The inference is that, with experience in its management, Denver Sluice could be operated in a manner that enabled an adequate depth of water to be maintained most of the time, as claimed by the Corporation in 1696, rendering a lock unnecessary (Chisholm 2007 and 2008). This implies that, after the drainage works had been completed, the normal minimum depth of water in Ely and immediately downstream was somewhat more than the 3.5 feet required by the standard lighter with a full load.

Although it is reasonable to conclude that navigation became more reliable after 1652 than was previously the case, low water remained a problem until the early nineteenth century or even later. This is shown by the following observation in a work on the agriculture of Cambridgeshire: 'freights vary in proportion to the supply of water, increasing as the water decreases' (Gooch 1811: 28).

Size and nature of vessels

It is commonly believed that the effect of draining the Fens was to reduce the size of vessel that could ply the Ouse to Ely and higher upriver (for example, Wilson 1972), but Summers, assuming that the depth of water was reduced, offers a more complicated interpretation of what happened: 'The Navigation users evolved two methods of coping with the situation. One expedient involved the use of smaller boats carrying less goods; the other was the use of large boats towed by more horses to drag the boats along the river bed, entailing the employment of an increasing number of men and boys to look after the horses. Neither method of navigation did anything to lower or even stabilise freight charges . . .' (Summers 1973: 82). No references are given for either statement. I have not encountered any other author who proposes that larger vessels were routinely dragged along the river bed. As for the alternative, that vessels became smaller, it is generally accepted that, after the drainage works had been completed, the standard freight vessel on the Ouse system was the lighter, capable of carrying about 25 tons of freight, and that these were operated as 'gangs' or 'strings' of five or even more vessels. These craft were able to penetrate well inland of Ely, whereas the previous limit above the Hards had been about 13 tons of cargo (Chisholm 2007). Consequently, it appears that vessels reaching Ely and higher upstream were bigger after 1652 than before.

Conclusion

The fact that there are such divergent views in the literature regarding the management of water depths, and the size of craft that could negotiate the Ouse above Denver and the main tributaries, shows very clearly that the source materials need to be examined afresh. Although a start has been made on this task, there is much to be done. For this work to be fruitful, the available sources need to be approached on the basis of questions to be examined, of ideas to be tested, and hence to be verified, refuted or modified. Too often in the past, the approach has been based upon a false certainty, that the drainage works were prejudicial to river commerce.

We now know that the sluices which were built across navigable waterways must be understood in the terms used by the Dutch, as water control structures incorporating pound locks. We also know that there is good evidence for river trade having continued and flourished over the Ouse from Lynn to the heads of navigation on the tributary rivers and lodes. These two facts provide the basis for re-evaluating the impact that draining the Fens had upon navigation, the opportunity to arrive at a balanced view regarding the problems that undoubtedly there were, and hence the extent to which the Corporation did or did not make adequate provision for navigation. Enquiries along these lines need to take account of two things. What were the circumstances before 1652 and how do they compare with the situation afterwards? And, given the pressures on the Corporation, to what extent were navigation interests treated as being of lesser importance than land drainage? One has to remember that the Corporation had a legal obligation to maintain the navigability of the rivers, and that there was a powerful commercial reason for this being done.

There are numerous sub-headings to these broad questions, of which but a few will be mentioned. There are two inter-related issues of critical importance: how were water levels managed, and by what means; and how did the size and nature of vessels evolve, and the manner in which they were managed, to compensate for the loss of the tides? It is virtually certain that, contrary to popular belief, sea-going craft did not navigate above Lynn in the years prior to 1652, and that craft plying the waterways to Ely and higher upriver were actually larger after Denver Sluice was built than hitherto—carrying 25 tons instead of some 13. There is also reason for believing that water depths at or above 3.5 feet became more reliable than hitherto. A river section of particular interest in this context is the Ouse below Ely, where it appears that some major engineering may have been undertaken but that no lock was constructed. The manner in which Denver Sluice was managed is also crucially important.

The situation in the outfall below Denver deserves particular scrutiny. Many authors have accepted the allegation that the Sluice caused the channel to silt up and to become much less suitable for navigation. However, the outfall was and remains a highly dynamic river system, with constant changes going on as sandbanks shift and the channels move, and careful examination of the evidence for the eighteenth century shows that there was in fact no long term deterioration, despite the protestations of Lynn (Barney 1997). It seems probable that the same was true in the seventeenth century. If that is indeed the case, then one is driven to ask what was going on in Lynn, and why did they interpret changes in the channel as proving the detrimental impact on navigation of Denver Sluice, and the drainage scheme in general? How much credence is to be attached to evidence and affidavits which show worsening conditions, and is there other evidence that has been overlooked?

There are other issues that deserve to be examined in more detail than has been the case to date, such as the scale of the damage to embankments used by horse teams hauling, or haling, the boats (plus the use of the same banks for droving livestock), and the impact of the belated imposition of tolls for such use.

Enough has been said to show that the history of the draining of the Fens needs to be revisited, in order to establish the true relationship between drainage and navigation interests. With some basic misconceptions having been removed, the way is open for dispassionate work to be done, not just on the Corporation's documents but also using other available seventeenth-century sources of information.

Note.   The present paper draws upon the work embodied in the papers of mine that are included in the Appendix, Part B. In preparing those papers, I have had the privilege to receive much help from numerous people and organisations, and their contributions are gratefully recorded in those papers. Without their help, it would not have been possible to make anything like the progress that has been made.

The illustrations have all been drawn by Ian Agnew, Department of Geography, University of Cambridge. Figure 2 is reproduced from my 2007 paper in the *Proceedings of the Cambridge Antiquarian Society*, and Figure 3 from my 2006 paper in the *Journal of Historical Geography*.

References

Note that the Appendix provides chronological tabulations of literature that can be classified into two schools of thought, that the drainage works were inimical to navigation, and that they were not. Literature cited in the text and contained in the Appendix is not included in the list of references below.

Atkins, R. (1618), 'Mr Atkyns's report'. Reproduced in S. Wells, *The History of the Draining of the Great Level of the Fens called the Bedford Level*, vol. 2, Appendix 11 (London), pp. 71–97.

Baskerville, T. (1681), 'Thomas Baskerville's journeys in England', Historical Manuscripts Commission, *Duke of Portland's MSS*, vol. 2, 1893 (London), pp. 263–74.

Bevis, T. (2003), *Prisoners of the Fens* (March).

Bray, W. (ed.) (1850), *Diary and Correspondence of John Evelyn FRS*, vol. 2 (London).

Bruland, K. and O'Brien, P. (eds.) (1998), *From Family Firms to Corporate Capitalism. Essays in Business and Industrial History in Honour of Peter Mathias* (Oxford).

Cole, G. D. H. and Browning, D. C. (eds.) (1962), *A Tour through the Whole Island of Great Britain* (London).

Darby, H. C. (1936), 'The Middle Level of the Fens and its reclamation', written in collaboration with Phyllis M. Ramsden, in the *Victoria History of the Counties of England. Huntingdon*, vol. 3 (London), 249–306.

Dugdale, W. (1772), *The History of Imbanking and Draining of Divers Fens and Marshes both in Foreign Parts and in this Kingdom* (London), first pub. 1662.

Gooch, W. (1811), *General View of the Agriculture of the County of Cambridge* (Cambridge).

Jessop, A. (ed.) (1972), *The Lives of the Norths*, vol. 3 (n.p.).

Lindley, K. (1982), *Fenland Riots and the English Revolution* (London).

Miller, S. H. and Skertchly, S. B. J. (1878), *The Fenland, Past and Present* (Wisbech).

Mitchell, B. R. (1988), *British Historical Statistics* (Cambridge).

Moore, J. (*c.*1658), 'A mapp of the Great Level of the Fens', at a scale of two inches to the mile. Repr. 1684.

Nef, J. U. (1932), *The Rise of the British Coal Industry*, vol. 2 (London).

Rogers, J. E. T. (1887), *A History of Agriculture and Prices in England*, vol. 5 (Oxford).

Skertchly, S. B. J. (1877), *The Geology of the Fenland. Memoirs of the Geological Survey. England and Wales* (London).

Wells, S. (1830), *The History of the Draining of the Great Levell of the Fens, called the Bedford Levell*, 2 vols. (London).

Willmoth, F. (1993), *Sir Jonas Moore. Practical Mathematics and Restoration Science* (Woodbridge).

Wright, T. (1668), 'A curious and exact relation of a sand-floud, which hath lately overwhelmed a great tract of land in the county of Suffolk', *Philosophical Transactions of the Royal Society of London*, 3: 722–5.

Appendix

As indicated in the introduction to this paper, there are two strands of thought in the literature regarding the impact of the drainage works upon navigation over the Ouse and its tributaries above Denver Sluice. The ascendant strand holds that the drainage works were inimical to navigation, in contrast to the view expressed by others that river trade flourished. This Appendix provides a non-exhaustive list of the literature in two parts, reflecting the two contrasting positions.

The year 1745 has been selected as the starting point, this being the year in which Labelye (p. 20) asserted of Denver Sluice, before it had partially collapsed in 1713, that: 'So little regard was had to the inland navigation, that no lock was provided, nor any contrivance to let the boats pass when the gates were shut.' With the advantage of present day hindsight, it appears that this statement may have been the primary source of the common belief that the sluice had no lock when it was originally built.

The classification of literature into the two schools of thought identified below involves a degree of judgement and is necessarily imperfect. For example, Darby's 1936 essay in the *VCH* expressly notes the efforts made by the Corporation to maintain water levels for navigation, and that sluices were constructed that permitted the passage of boats. However, his later publications omit this material, but do retain the observation that, when Denver Sluice was partially destroyed, 'the obstruction to navigation was thus demolished' (Darby 1936: 280).

The two lists include literature that is not cited in the body of the paper.

A. That drainage was inimical to navigation

Many of the texts listed below state that Denver Sluice was an obstruction and/or that no lock facilities were provided when it was first constructed but this is not the sole criterion for inclusion.

1745   Labelye, C., *The Result of a View of the Great Level of the Fens* (London).

1745   Elstobb, W., *The Pernicious Consequences of Replacing Denver-Dam and Sluices* (Cambridge).

1766   Badeslade, T., *The History of the Ancient and Present State of the Navigation of the Port of King's Lynn, and of Cambridge* (London), first pub. 1725.

1778   Bentham, J., *The Claim of Taxing the Navigations and Free Lands for the Drainage and Preservation of the Fens* (London).

1779   Elstobb, W., *Report on the State of the Navigation between Clay Hithe and Denver Sluice* (Cambridge).

1793   Elstobb, W., *An Historical Account of the Great Level of the Fens Called Bedford Level, and other Fens, Marshes and Low-Lands in the Kingdom, and other Places* (London).

1894   Sweeting, W. D., 'Opposition to the drainage schemes', *Fenland Notes and Queries*, 2: 219–21.

1906   Gaches, L., 'Drainage of the Great Level', *Fenland Notes and Queries*, 6: 262–8 and 353–62.

1914   Cox, J. C., *Cambridgeshire* (London).

1953   Harris, L. E., *Vermuyden and the Fens. A study of Sir Cornelius Vermuyden and the Great Level* (London).

1953   Skempton, A. W., 'The engineers of the English river navigations, 1620–1760', *Transactions of the Newcomen Society*, 29: 25–54.

1956   Darby, H. C., *The Draining of the Fens* (Cambridge), first pub. 1940.

1967   Hills, R. L., *Machines Mills and Uncountable Necessities. A Short History of the Drainage of the Fens* (Norwich).

1972   Wilson, J. K., *Fenland Barge Traffic* (Kettering).

1973   Summers, D., *The Great Ouse. The History of a River Navigation* (Newton Abbot).

1976   Summers, D., *The Great Level. A History of Drainage and Land Reclamation in the Fens* (Newton Abbot).

1977   Boyes, J. and Russell, J., *The Canals of Eastern England* (Newton Abbot). (Specifically chap. 7, p. 326, fn. 89.)

1983   Beckett, J., *The Urgent Hour. The Drainage of the Burnt Fen District in the South Level of the Fens 1760–1981* (Ely), first pub. 1974.

1983   Darby, H. C., *The Changing Fenland* (Cambridge).

1985   Dymond, D., *The Norfolk Landscape* (London).

1992   Wood, F. J., *Inland Transport and Distribution in the Hinterland of King's Lynn 1760–1840* (Unpub. Ph.D. thesis, University of Cambridge).

1993   Paget-Tomlinson, E., *The Illustrated History of Canal and River Navigations* (Sheffield).

1998   Wood, F., 'Fuelling the local economy: the Fenland coal trade, 1760–1850', in K. Bruland and P. O'Brien (eds.), *From Family Firms to Corporate Capitalism. Essays in Business and Industrial History in honour of Peter Mathias* (Oxford), pp. 199–215.

2003   Gerrard, V., *The Story of the Fens* (London).

2003   Hills, R. L., *The Drainage of the Fens* (Ashbourne).

B. That drainage was not inimical to navigation

1751   Kinderley, N., *The Ancient and Present State of Navigation of the Towns of Lynn, Wisbech, Spalding and Boston* (London).

1753   Carter, E., *The History of the County of Cambridge* (Cambridge).

1773   Caraccioli, C., *An Historical Account of Sturbridge, Bury and the Most Famous Fairs in Europe and America* (Cambridge).

1830   Telford, T., 'Navigation inland', *The Edinburgh Encyclopaedia*, vol. 15 (Edinburgh).

1938   Palmer, W. M., 'The Fen Office Documents', *Proceedings of the Cambridge Antiquarian Society*, 38: 64–157.

1967   Rich, E. E. and Wilson, C. H. (eds.), *The Economy of Expanding Europe in the Sixteenth and Seventeenth Centuries* (Cambridge).

1972   Seymour, J., *The Companion Guide to East Anglia* (London).

1973   Finch, R., *Coals from Newcastle. The Story of the North East Coal Trade in the Days of Sail* (Lavenham).

1976   Wren, W. J., *Ports of the Eastern Counties* (Lavenham).

1993   Oosthuizen, S., 'Isleham: a medieval inland port', *Landscape History*, 15: 29–35.

1997   Barney, J. M., *The Merchants and Maritime Trade of King's Lynn in the Eighteenth Century* (Ph.D. thesis, University of East Anglia).

1999   Barney, J. M., 'Shipping in the port of King's Lynn 1702–1800', *Journal of Transport History*, 20: 126–40.

2002   Skempton, A. W., Chrimes, M. M., Cox, R. C. *et al.* (eds.), *A Biographical Dictionary of Civil Engineering in Great Britain and Ireland*, vol. 1, 1500–1830 (Chichester).

2003   Chisholm, M., 'Conservators of the River Cam: 1702–2002', *Proceedings of the Cambridge Antiquarian Society*, 92: 183–200.

2005   Chisholm, M., 'Locks, sluices and staunches: confusing terminology', *Transactions of the Newcomen Society*, 75: 305–16.

2005   Franklin, W., *Burwell. The History of a Fen-edge Village* (King's Lynn).

2006   Chisholm, M., 'Navigation and the seventeenth-century draining of the Fens', *Journal of Historical Geography*, 32: 731–51.

2007   Chisholm, M., 'Re-assessing the navigation impact of draining the Fens in the seventeenth century', *Proceedings of the Cambridge Antiquarian Society*, 96: 175–92.

2008   Chisholm, M., 'The Old Plough: a neglected property of Ely Porta Manor', *Proceedings of the Cambridge Antiquarian Society* (autumn).

Reconstructing the National Body: Masculinity, Disability and Race in the American Civil War[1]

SUSAN-MARY GRANT

Newcastle University

What man has nerve to do, man has not nerve to hear. (Harriet Beecher Stowe, *Uncle Tom's Cabin*)

It was winter soon and already soldiers were beginning to come back—the stragglers, not all of them tramps, ruffians, but men who had risked and lost everything, suffered beyond endurance and had returned now to a ruined land, not the same men who had marched away but transformed . . . We were afraid. We fed them; we gave them what and all we had and would have assumed their wounds and left them whole again if we could. But we were afraid of them. (William Faulkner, *Absalom, Absalom!*)

* * *

PRIOR TO THE CIVIL WAR, it was once observed, the 'mass of Americans read [history] not for truth so much as for confirmation'. The point bears repeating, not least because of who made it: the man who conceived and

Read at the Academy 4 October 2007.

[1] The author wishes to acknowledge the support of the Leverhulme Trust (RES/0333/7225) for funding the research that went into the final version of this article and, for helpful advice, the anonymous reader for the British Academy and the members of the University of Edinburgh American History Seminar, at which an early version of this paper was presented, especially Rhodri Jeffreys-Jones, Robert Mason, and Fabian Hilfrich.

Proceedings of the British Academy **154**, 273–317. © The British Academy 2008.

inaugurated this lecture series, Carl Bode, in his study of *The Anatomy of American Popular Culture*. The antebellum American public, Bode argued, 'patently appreciated only the books that conformed to its image of America'. The same might be said, however, of the modern-day reader interested in America's most brutal conflict to date. Works on the Civil War are hardly in short supply. ABC-CLIO estimates some 50,000 books on the subject exist so far, or, to put it another way, at least one a day since Lee surrendered to Grant at Appomattox. In the absence of any sign of war weariness among either scholars or the American general public, the Civil War will be a safe bet for publishers for many years to come and with the sesquicentennial of the war approaching we can expect the rate of output to increase. The centrality of the Civil War to America's national story seems assured, but numbers, in this case, may not be telling us everything. Familiarity with the subject may not have bred contempt but, as leading Civil War scholar Edward Ayers recently suggested, it may have bred complacency. 'It may be', he has argued, 'that we like the current story too much to challenge it very deeply and that we foreclose questions by repeating familiar formulas. The risk of our apparent consensus is that we paper over the complicated moral issues raised by a war that left hundreds of thousands of people dead. The risk is that we no longer worry about the Civil War.'[2]

In raising this point, it is notable that Ayers, in common with many Civil War scholars, references the number of dead. Prominent Civil War historians are rarely called upon to defend their subject but, on the occasions when they do feel prompted to explain its significance, it is the dead to whom they turn. So C. Vann Woodward, in his introduction to the *Oxford History of the United States* volume on the Civil War, James M. McPherson's *Battle Cry of Freedom*, highlights the 'simple and eloquent measurement' of the war's magnitude that the casualty figures provide. By casualties, however, he means the mortally wounded, and quotes the author's reckoning that American 'casualties at Antietam numbered four times the total suffered by American soldiers at the Normandy beaches on June 6, 1944', before observing—as so many have and still do—that 'American lives lost in the Civil War exceed the total of those lost in all

---

[2] Carl Bode, *Antebellum Culture* (originally published in 1959 as *The Anatomy of American Popular Culture, 1841–1860* (Carbondale and Edwardsville, IL, 1970)), p. 249; figures for number of works published given in David Stephen Heidler *et al.* (eds.), *Encyclopedia of the American Civil War: A Political, Social, and Military History* (New York and London, 2002); Edward L. Ayers, 'Worrying about the Civil War', in Karen Halttunen and Lewis Perry (eds.), *Moral Problems in American Life: New Perspectives on Cultural History* (New York, 1999), pp. 144–65.

the other wars the country has fought added together, world wars included.'[3]

The significance of the Civil War dead, of course, should not be, and has not been, underestimated. Specifically, the role of the dead in the construction both of Northern/Union nationalism and the Southern 'civic religion' that was the Lost Cause has been examined at length in studies that explore, from various angles, the American variant of the 'cult of the fallen soldier', a cult through which, David Blight has observed, the 'nineteenth-century manly ideal of heroism was redefined for coming generations' and within which 'the Union dead—and soon the Confederate dead with them—served as saviours and founders, the agents of the death of an old social order and the birth of a new one'.[4]

Certainly the Civil War had brought home to the American public, in the North and South, the most extreme physical consequence of war; both Southerners proximate to the battlefields and Northerners who visited Matthew Brady's photographic exhibition of 1862, 'The Dead of Antietam', could hardly avoid looking death, and the war that produced it, in the face (Fig. 1). Commenting on Brady's exhibition, the *New York*

---

[3] C. Vann Woodward, Editor's Introduction to James M. McPherson, *Battle Cry of Freedom: The Civil War Era* (New York and Oxford, 1988), pp. xviii–xix; in fact, the total of the Civil War dead exceeded that of all other American wars up to Vietnam. On this point, see Maris A. Vinovskis, 'Have social historians lost the Civil War? Some preliminary demographic specula-tions', in Vinovskis (ed.), *Toward a Social History of the American Civil War: Exploratory Essays* (New York, 1990), pp. 4–9; Paddy Griffith, *Battle Tactics of the American Civil War*, new edn. (Ramsbury, Wiltshire, 1996), pp. 19–20; and Susan-Mary Grant, 'Patriot Graves: American national identity and the Civil War dead', *American Nineteenth Century History*, 5:3 (Fall 2004), 74–100, esp. 77–8.

[4] David Blight, *Race and Reunion: The Civil War in American Memory* (Cambridge, MA, 2001), p. 72; the amount of work on the Civil War dead specifically and war memorialising generally is vast, but see, among others: William Blair, *Cities of the Dead: Contesting the Memory of the Civil War in the South, 1865–1914* (Chapel Hill, NC, 2004); Drew Gilpin Faust, *'A Riddle of Death': Mortality and Meaning in the American Civil War* (Pennsylvania, 1995); and, most recently, *This Republic of Suffering: Death and the American Civil War* (New York, 2008); Susan-Mary Grant, 'Patriot Graves' and 'Raising the dead: war, memory and American national identity', *Nations and Nationalism*, 2:4 (Oct. 2005), 509–29; Robert Pogue Harrison, *The Dominion of the Dead* (Chicago, IL, and London, 2003); Edward Tabor Linenthal, *Sacred Ground: Americans and their Battlefields* (Urbana and Chicago, IL, 1991); Monro MacCloskey, *Hallowed Ground: Our National Cemeteries* (New York, 1968); Carolyn Marvin and David W. Ingle, *Blood Sacrifice and the Nation: Totem Rituals and the American Flag* (New York and Cambridge, 1999); John R. Neff, *Honoring the Civil War Dead: Commemoration and the Problem of Reconciliation* (Lawrence, 2005); Michael Sledge, *Soldier Dead: How We Recover, Identify, Bury, & Honor Our Military Fallen* (New York, 2005); Garry Wills, *Lincoln at Gettysburg: The Words that Remade America* (New York, 1992); and Kenneth E. Foote, *Shadowed Ground: America's Landscapes of Violence and Tragedy* (Austin, TX, 1997).

Figure 1. Antietam, MD, bodies of Confederate dead gathered for burial. (Library of Congress Prints and Photographs Division, LC-DIG.cwpb-01093.)

Times famously observed that if the photographer had 'not brought bodies and laid them in our door-yards and along the streets, he has done something very like it', and in the process brought 'home to us the terrible reality and earnestness of war'. Such disturbing representations of war and the physical destruction it wrought on men's bodies, it has been argued, 'symbolized the righteousness of the Union cause—the large numbers of young northern soldiers slaughtered on the fields of battle became evidence of Union patriotism and virtue'.[5]

Towards the end of the conflict, Northern preachers had already established the terms through which Union sacrifice, at least, would be contextualised, stressing the 'new birth of freedom' that Abraham Lincoln had invoked at Gettysburg, a freedom purchased at the price of some 600,000 lives. So Congregationalist theologian Horace Bushnell, in his 1865 oration to the alumni of Yale who had served in the war, chose to stress 'Our Obligations to the Dead' who were, he declared, 'the purchase money of our redemption'. It 'is the ammunition spent that gains the battle', he advised his audience—survivors, we must recall, of the battles concerned—and it was that ammunition, their terminal 'shedding of blood' that had 'cemented and sanctified' the unity of the nation. The establishment of the nation was Bushnell's main point in this funeral oration, in which the Civil War was deemed to have accomplished what the Revolution had failed to achieve: 'The sacrifices in the fields of the Revolution united us but imperfectly. We had not bled enough to merge our colonial distinctions . . . and make us a proper nation. And so, what argument could not accomplish, sacrifice has achieved', Bushnell declaimed, and 'now a new and stupendous chapter of national history' awaited the American people.[6]

---

[5] *New York Times* review of Matthew Brady's Broadway exhibition, 'The Dead of Antietam', *New York Times*, 20 Oct. 1862; Gary Laderman, *The Sacred Remains: American Attitudes Toward Death, 1799–1883* (New Haven, CT, and London, 1996), p. 98; on reactions to Civil War photographs, see also Alan Trachtenberg, *Reading American Photographs: Images as History, Matthew Brady to Walker Evans* (1989, repr. New York, 1990), pp. 74–5; and Lisa A. Long, '"The corporeity of heaven": rehabilitating the Civil War body in *The Gates Ajar*', *American Literature*, 69:4 (Dec. 1997), 781–811, esp. 791.

[6] Horace Bushnell, 'Our obligations to the dead' (1865) in Mary Bushnell Cheney, *Life and Letters of Horace Bushnell* (New York, 1905), pp. 485–6. As Laderman has argued, 'In many ways for Bushnell . . . the organic life of the nation required the destruction of human life; the spiritual bonds of nationhood relied on the real, material blood of individual soldier-martyrs', but Bushnell was not unique in promulgating this interpretation of the war, which was a common theme both during and for long after the conflict. See Laderman, *The Sacred Remains*, p. 129.

The notion of redemptive sacrifice is hardly unique to the American Civil War, yet in an internecine conflict that had, by its end, taken on the obligation of a 'new birth of freedom' in the emancipation of some four million slaves, it acquired a particular resonance. As leading African-American spokesman Frederick Douglass had put it, the 'mission' of the Civil War was nothing less than 'National regeneration'. The problem for many historians, however, is that this ambition was never realised, or imperfectly realised at best. For African-Americans, in particular, the new social order bore disturbing resemblances to the old, and so one of the most dominant elements of the 'current story' of the Civil War—and it is far from a positive one—is represented by what might be termed the historiography of betrayal, of hopes raised and dashed, opportunities glimpsed but unattained, a mirage of equality that faded as northern and southern whites moved closer to that significant handshake across the stonewall at Gettysburg in 1913 that symbolised the final cessation of hostilities (Fig. 2). This was the ultimate compromise reached between former Union and Confederate foes at the expense of African-American hopes for equality. The story, so eloquently and comprehensively traced by Blight, is of the 'emancipationist vision' of the war giving way, over time, to the 'reconciliationist vision', of 'sentimental remembrance' winning over 'ideological memory'. In short, it is a story of opportunity missed, of the triumph of ethnic/exclusive over civic/inclusive nationalism, of a backward step taken at a time when, by all accounts, Americans had established firm sacred ground, sanctified by the bodies of the fallen, for a forward-looking future promising equality for all. Here, too, the dead play a central role. 'The most immediate legacy of the war', Blight asserts, 'was its slaughter and how to remember it', and it was in the name of the dead, to a great extent, that the South's 'white supremacist vision' came to dominate.[7]

Yet, to return to numbers for a moment, slaughter was not the war's only legacy; the scale of death in the Civil War was almost matched by the scale of non-fatal casualties—some half a million—among those who

---

[7] Blight, *Race and Reunion*, pp. 2–4; 64; Douglass quoted, p. 18. Other studies that focus on the process of reconciliation between North and South and the betrayal of African-American hopes for equality include: Paul Buck, *The Road to Reunion, 1865–1900* (Boston, 1937); Nina Silber, *The Romance of Reunion: Northerners and the South, 1865–1900* (Chapel Hill, NC, 1993); Cecilia Elizabeth O'Leary, *To Die For: The Paradox of American Patriotism* (Princeton, NJ, 1999); and Edward J. Blum, *Reforging the White Republic: Race, Religion, and American Nationalism, 1865–1898* (Baton Rouge, LA, 2005).

Figure 2. Gettysburg Fiftieth Reunion, 1913. Courtesy of the Pennsylvania State Archives.

returned home.[8] Along with commemorating the dead, the most pressing, and surely even more immediate, legacy of the war was how to reincorporate into civil society men who had not made the ultimate sacrifice, yet who had suffered, and who would continue to suffer in many cases, in the process of establishing the American nation. This aspect of the conflict's legacy is not yet part of the 'current story' of the Civil War, and its absence is revealing, perhaps even worrying, since the issue of how to respond to, and heal, the wounded war veteran remains of contemporary concern.

The figure of the wounded veteran is a discomfiting one to contemplate; a stark reminder of the cost of war, the violence that attends the birth of many nations, the veteran exists on the margins of the 'current story' of the Civil War, at least as historians tell it. The literary image of the veteran is, of course, rather different. The figure of the mentally or physically scarred veteran weaves through the Western canon. Examples as diverse as Sophocles' account of 'Poor Philoctetes, Poeas' wretched son', and Pat Barker's novel *Regeneration*, a fictional version of the time First World War poet Siegfried Sassoon spent at Craiglockhart Hospital, reveal how literature has portrayed the tragedy of war through the struggles of its living victims to come to terms with both conflict and, more crucially, peace. In the American case, the examples range from Civil War veteran Ambrose Bierce's disturbing tale, 'A Resumed Identity', of a soldier whose mind remained forever fixed in the time and place of the war, through Walt Whitman's prose and poetry in which the physical effects of conflict are quite graphically presented, the Native American Second World War veteran Tayo in Leslie Marmon Silko's *Ceremony*, and, beyond that, to the outpouring of personal accounts of social disengagement and dislocation produced in the aftermath of the Vietnam War.[9] With few exceptions, however, this literary fascination with the reintegration of the soldier and society in war's immediate aftermath has not been shared either by American historians or nationalism scholars, who seem more interested in the development of Civil War battlefields and their

---

[8] Figures from Lisa A. Long, *Rehabilitating Bodies; Health, History, and the American Civil War* (Philadelphia, 2004), p. 67; on this topic, see also Frank R. Freemon, *Gangrene and Glory: Medical Care During the American Civil War* (Cranbury, NJ, 1998).

[9] Sophocles' play is available in many editions, but a version is available at: <http://etext. library.adelaide.edu.au/mirror/classics.mit.edu/Sophocles/philoct.html> (accessed 10 Oct. 2006); Pat Barker, *Regeneration* (1991, repr. London, 1992); Ambrose Bierce, 'A resumed identity', in *Tales of Soldiers and Civilians and Other Stories* (1892, repr. New York, 2000), pp. 143–8; Leslie Marmon Silko, *Ceremony* (1977, repr. New York, 1986).

evolution into what Jay Winter identified, in a different context, as 'sites of memory, sites of mourning'. The physical landscape of the battlefield, the 'sacred patriotic space where memories of the transformative power of war and the sacrificial heroism of the warrior are preserved', takes precedence, in large part, over the living physical survivors of war.[10]

The scholarly, and public, preference for the sacrificial dead over the living veteran as far as war memorialisation is concerned may be understandable, even as it has been condemned as 'fundamentally dishonest. By materialising memory in statues and parks', Seth Koven has charged, 'we satisfy our sentimental and nationalist cravings and allow ourselves to displace bodily pain and ignore the presence of the tens of thousands of disabled victims of war.'[11] Koven's point was made in the context of the First World War, but it is equally applicable to the American Civil War. In 1944, the imminent demobilisation of American forces from the Second World War prompted Dixon Wecter to contemplate some of the issues and problems that arise when 'Johnny Comes Marching Home', but there has been little development of his findings since. No more did David Donald's 1975 edition of the diary of Alfred Bellard, wounded at Chancellorsville and mustered into the Invalid Corps, produce any upsurge of interest in the role of the disabled soldier, either during or after the war. With the notable exceptions of Eric Dean's *Shook Over Hell* and Fred Pelka's work on another member of the Invalid Corps, Charles F. Johnson, only a handful of articles to date have explored the physical and mental impact of the Civil War on the soldiers who fought it. The most important study to date of the Union veterans' organisation, the Grand Army of the Republic, does not engage directly with the disabled veteran, in whose name and for whose benefit so much GAR activity was undertaken. An implicit presence rather than the explicit subject, the veterans who populate studies of the soldier's homes constructed either under the auspices of the National Home for Disabled Volunteer Soldiers (NHDVS) or by individual states in the South in the war's aftermath remain shadowy

[10] Jay Winter, *Sites of Memory, Sites of Mourning: The Great War in European Cultural History* (1995, repr. Cambridge, 2003); Linenthal, *Sacred Ground*, p. 3.
[11] Seth Koven, 'Remembering and dismemberment: crippled children, wounded soldiers, and the Great War in Great Britain', *The American Historical Review*, 99:4 (Oct. 1994), 1167–1202, quotation at 1169. On this point, see also: Elaine Scarry, *The Body in Pain: The Making and Unmaking of the World* (New York and Oxford, 1985, repr. 1987), pp. 64, 80; Fred Pelka (ed.), *The Civil War Letters of Colonel Charles E. Johnson, Invalid Corps* (Amherst and Boston, MA, 2004), p. 203; and Rosemarie Garland Thomson, *Extraordinary Bodies: Figuring Physical Disability in American Culture and Literature* (New York, 1997), p. 6.

figures, gathered together in grainy photographs taken in their old age, their younger selves rendered invisible; in visual terms, Civil War veterans are plucked from the past into modern memory most notably on commemorative occasions, such as the fiftieth reunion of the Battle of Gettysburg, but only as a form of living tableaux, representing that part of American history that was the Civil War. The image of the Civil War veteran with which we are most familiar, and with which we may be most comfortable, is that of a man disabled not by conflict, but by age; a warrior no longer capable of waging war.[12]

The Civil War veteran, however, is the key not only to understanding how Americans in the mid-nineteenth-century resolved what Lisa Herschbach has described as 'the paradoxes of a conflict in which the preservation of national unity required the mutual destruction of its citizen-soldiery' but why the form that national unity eventually took became as exclusive as it did.[13] By exploring the broader military, medical, social and cultural contexts within which Americans conceptualised and came to terms with the extreme physical and mental destruction that the conflict had wrought on the bodies and minds of the fighting troops one

[12] Dixon Wecter, *When Johnny Comes Marching Home* (Boston, 1944); Dabid Herbert Donald (ed.), *Gone For a Soldier: The Civil War Memoirs of Private Alfred Bellard* (Boston, 1975); Eric T. Dean, *Shook Over Hell: Post-Traumatic Stress, Vietnam, and the Civil War* (1997, repr. Cambridge, MA, 1999); Fred Pelka (ed.), *The Civil War Letters of Colonel Charles E. Johnson, Invalid Corps* (Amherst and Boston, MA, 2004); Frances Clarke, '"Honorable Scars": Northern amputees and the meaning of Civil War injuries', in Paul A. Cimbala and Randall M. Miller (eds.), *Union Soldiers and the Northern Homes Front: Wartime Experiences, Postwar Adjustments* (New York, 2002), pp. 361–94; William Etter, 'Cripple, soldier, crippled soldier: Alfred Bellard's Civil War memoir', *Prose Studies*, 27:1 & 2 (April–August 2005), 80–92; R. B. Rosenburg, '"Empty sleeves and wooden pegs": disabled Confederate Veterans in image and reality', in David A. Gerber (ed.), *Disabled Veterans in History* (Ann Arbor, 2000), pp. 204–28; John D. Blaisdell, 'The wounded, the sick, and the scared': an examination of disabled Maine Veterans from the Civil War', *Maine History*, 41:1 (July 2004), 67–92; Ansley Herring Wegner, 'Phantom pain: Civil War amputation and North Carolina's maimed Veterans', *North Carolina Historical Review*, 75:3 (1998), 277–96; James Marten, 'Nomads in blue: disabled Veterans and alcohol at the National Home', in Gerber, *Disabled Veterans*, pp. 275–94; Theda Skocpol, *Protecting Soldiers and Mothers: the Political Origins of Social Policy in the United States* (Cambridge, MA, 1992); Stuart McConnell, *Glorious Contentment: the Grand Army of the Republic, 1865–1900* (Chapel Hill, NC, and London, 1992); Patrick J. Kelly, *Creating a National Home: Building the Veterans' Welfare State, 1860–1900* (Cambridge, MA, and London, 1997); Larry M. Logue, 'Union Veterans and their government: the effects of public policies on private lives', *Journal of Interdisciplinary History*, 22:3 (1992), 411–34; R. B. Rosenburg, *Living Monuments: Confederate Soldiers' Homes in the New South* (Chapel Hill, NC, and London, 1993).

[13] Lisa Herschbach, '"True clinical fictions": medical and literary narratives from the Civil War Hospital', *Culture, Medicine and Psychiatry*, 19:2 (1995), 183–205, quotation at 196.

can better understand the form and function, and limitations, of the new national body that emerged from the Civil War.

Context: a symbol, and a story

The Civil War is frequently seen and described as a watershed in America's development. In historiographical terms, however, it too often functions as a formidable barrier to understanding since only infrequently do persistent trends come into focus. The tendency to compartmentalise history in general exacerbates this situation; in mid-nineteenth-century America we have the antebellum era, the Civil War, and Reconstruction, and although they are clearly linked they are too often seen as separate entities. The role of the veteran in American society is a case in point. Space does not permit a detailed examination of America's war veterans from the colonial era onwards, but two early examples of how war and its survivors were conceptualised before the Civil War may suffice.

In 1861, Abraham Lincoln was faced with the pressing, and far from theoretical, issue of the perpetuation of America's political institutions, a topic that was of perennial interest to him. In 1838, he gave an address on the subject to the Young Men's Lyceum of Springfield, in which he touched on subjects that, in future years, he certainly had cause to contemplate afresh. He began by assuring his audience of America's geographic inviolability; no foreign armies could ever threaten the nation's safety, nor 'take a drink from the Ohio' by force. The only danger to America, Lincoln asserted, came from within: 'If destruction be our lot, we must ourselves be its author and finisher. As a nation of freemen, we must live through all time, or die by suicide.' Lincoln scholars are primarily interested in this speech because of the insight it provides into the future president's political thinking, his belief in the importance of law, his sly digs at the Democrats. Of less interest to them is the influence that Lincoln identified as important in the maintenance of those political institutions; what counteracted 'the jealousy, envy, and avarice, incident to our nature' and 'the deep rooted principles of *hate*' that Americans could so readily turn on each other was 'the powerful influence which the interesting scenes of the revolution had upon the *passions* of the people as distinguished from their judgment'.[14]

---

[14] Abraham Lincoln, 'Address before the Young Men's Lyceum of Springfield, Illinois', 27 Jan. 1838, in Roy P. Basler (ed.), *The Collected Works of Abraham Lincoln* (New Brunswick, NJ,

If the Revolution provided the emotional glue that held the nation together, it was through its living survivors that the message was conveyed, the lesson learned, and the memory kept alive. The revolutionary war's veterans had functioned as *'living history'* in this respect and, as Lincoln pointed out, 'every family' had,

> in the form of a husband, a father, a son or a brother . . . a history bearing the indubitable testimonies of its own authenticity, in the limbs mangled, in the scars of wounds received . . . a history . . . that could be read and understood alike by all, the wise and the ignorant, the learned and the unlearned.

Yet Lincoln recognised that the national sentiment produced by the Revolution, what he termed 'this state of feeling *must fade, is fading, has faded*, with the circumstances that produced it'. As the veterans died off, the histories they represented *'can* be read no more . . . They were a fortress of strength', Lincoln asserted;

> but what invading foemen could *never* do, the silent artillery of time *has done* . . . They are gone. They *were* a forest of giant oaks; but the all-resistless hurricane has swept over them, and left only, here and there, a lonely trunk, despoiled of its verdure, shorn of its foliage; unshading and unshaded, to murmur in a few more gentle breezes, and to combat with its mutilated limbs, a few more ruder storms, then to sink, and be no more.

The revolutionary war's veterans represented, for Lincoln, the 'pillars of the temple of liberty; and now, that they have crumbled away, that temple must fall, unless we, their descendants, supply their places with other pillars, hewn from the solid quarry of sober reason'.[15]

That Lincoln should identify not just veterans but visibly wounded veterans as the 'pillars of the temple of liberty' privileges the physical and physiological evidence of war over the oral or written narrative; the Revolution is quite literally written on the bodies of its former soldiers. Lincoln also privileges age over youth: the veterans he invoked were not the youthful 'citizen-soldiers' of America's revolutionary past—which might have been a more resonant image to employ—but those men in later maturity, and damaged maturity at that. Perhaps the intimidating 'masculinity of disorder and unruliness' of the colonial and revolutionary-era militias, identified by Stefan Dudink and Karen Hagemann, made the youthful warrior too unsettling a figure to reference for Lincoln's pur-

---

1953), 1. 108–15, quotations at 109, 114. For a brief discussion of this speech see, for example, Allen C. Guelzo, *Abraham Lincoln: Redeemer President* (Grand Rapids, MI, and Cambridge, 1999), pp. 90–1.
[15] Lincoln, 'Address before the Young Men's Lyceum of Springfield', p. 115.

poses, given that his main concern in this speech was the rise of what he termed 'this mobocratic spirit ... now abroad in the land'. Lincoln's visible veterans were certainly long past posing a threat; crippled both by war and by age, the purpose they served was ruminative rather than revolutionary; their mangled limbs were proof of the nation's 'authenticity'. Through the destruction of many individual bodies, Lincoln suggested, the national body's existence was both validated and protected.[16]

The year after Lincoln delivered his Lyceum Address, a very different image of the war veteran was presented to the American public. In 1839, Edgar Allan Poe published one of his most challenging short stories, 'The Man That Was Used Up'. In this story, the narrator meets a veteran— Brevet Brigadier General John A. B. C. Smith—whom he describes as in every respect 'remarkable'. Much attention is devoted to the General's physical attributes: his hair is described as glossy and 'jetty black', his whiskers—which the narrator cannot speak of 'without enthusiasm'— were 'the handsomest pair of whiskers under the sun', and his teeth 'the most brilliantly white of all conceivable teeth' while his shoulders, and indeed most of his body, 'would have called up a blush of conscious inferiority into the countenance of the marble Apollo'. At the same time, the narrator detects 'a primness, not to say stiffness, in his carriage—a degree of measured ... of rectangular precision, attending his every movement', which puzzles him. His interest is further aroused by the (over-)insistence of several of his companions that the General 'was a *remarkable* man—a *very* remarkable man—indeed one of the *most* remarkable men of the age', and by the General's, and just about everyone else he meets, frequent references to 'the rapid march of mechanical invention' in America. His curiosity aroused, the narrator determines to visit the General, but at first the famous war hero appears not to be at home. On being shown into the General's bedroom, he observes 'a large and exceedingly odd-looking bundle of something which lay close by my feet on the floor', which he kicks out of the way.[17]

---

[16] Lincoln, 'Address before the Young Men's Lyceum of Springfield', pp. 115, 111; Stefan Dudink and Karen Hagemann, 'Masculinity in politics and war in the age of democratic revolutions, 1750–1850', in Stefan Dudink, Karen Hagemann and John Tosh (eds.), *Masculinities in Politics and War: Gendering Modern History* (Manchester, 2004), pp. 3–21, quotation at 9.

[17] Edgar Allan Poe, 'The Man That Was Used Up: A Tale of the Late Bugaboo and Kickapoo Campaign', first appeared in 1839 in *Burton's Gentleman's Magazine*, has been reprinted in several collections of Poe's short stories and is available on-line via several sites: this paper used the version available at: <http://www.web-books.com/Classics/Poe/Stories/Man_Used_1.htm> (accessed 10 Sept. 2007).

The bundle on the floor, however, turns out to be the General, not so much in a state of undress as one of complete corporeal dismemberment. As the narrator looks on in horror, the General, aided by his black servant, proceeds to put himself together, pulling on his legs, screwing on his arms, and all the time conducting a running commentary both on the battles that had reduced him—literally and rather dramatically—to his current (non-)physical state and on the relative merits of the makers of the many prosthetic devices that he is in the process of fitting. Finally the narrator, as he concludes, had 'a perfect understanding of the true state of affairs . . . a full comprehension of the mystery which had troubled me so long. It was evident. It was a clear case. Brevet Brigadier General John A. B. C. Smith was the man—was *the man that was used up.*'[18]

Clearly, Poe's fantastical tale is not supposed to represent in any accurate way the image of the war veteran in Jacksonian America. Literary critics tend to read it as a satire on 'the nationalist ideology of American exceptionalism', composed in response to the Seminole War and subsequent forced removal of the Cherokee to Oklahoma conducted by General Winfield Scott, who may be the figure represented by General Smith. Specifically, the destruction of the General's body by Native Americans and its reconstruction by his black valet is understood as a commentary on the racial exclusiveness of the nation. The General, it has been suggested, was 'dismembered by his own racial hatred', and Poe's story was designed to highlight 'the prosthetic nature of the national narrative in its concealment of inglorious acts and unjust cruelties'. In its representation of a man who is, in effect, a cyborg, Poe's tale prefigures aspects of the fiction—and, indeed, real inventions—of the later nineteenth-century; in its representation of the veteran as a symbol of racial injustice it adds an unsettling dimension, and possibly even a challenge, to Lincoln's representation of the veteran as the emotive symbol of American nationalism. If the wounded veteran was, for Lincoln, a blasted oak, for Poe he is a mechanical man whose wounds, so far from being visible and therefore 'authenticating', are disguised, and so the man himself is deemed inauthentic. In both cases, however, it is through the physical body of a veteran that the nation—in both a positive and negative sense— is figured. In a nation where the body itself had clearly understood political connotations, these early—and contradictory—representations of

---

[18] <http://www.web-books.com/Classics/Poe/Stories/Man_Used_4.htm> (accessed 10 Sept. 2007).

the veteran must be factored in to our understanding of the conflict that began in 1861.[19]

Dismembering the nation

Prior to the Civil War, the American nation itself was frequently conceptualised in corporeal terms, a physical and spiritual body politic. In their desire to secede from the Union, Southerners, according to New York lawyer George Templeton Strong, were in danger of 'dismembering the country'. Secession, Strong believed, 'would do fatal mischief to one section or another and great mischief to both. Amputation weakens the body', he argued, 'and the amputated limb decomposes and perishes. Is our vital center North or South?', he inquired, 'Which is Body and which is Member? We may have to settle that question by experiment. We are not a polypoid organism that can be converted into two organisms by mere bisection.' Approached in this context, the Civil War itself took on medical connotations; war, announced surgeon and author Oliver Wendell Holmes 'is the surgery of crime . . . the disease of our nation was organic, not functional, calling for the knife, and not for washes and anodynes'.[20]

The utilisation of medical metaphors involving disease and dismemberment was a common trope of the time. Strong perceived the growing sectional crisis in relatively straightforward terms as posing a risk to the national body, and during the war itself 'the metaphor of the injured body politic' was, as Elizabeth Young has shown, a fairly typical 'rhetorical strategy' employed by both Union politicians in particular and northern elites in general as a means of condemning secession. Others, such as Holmes, believed that the national body was already diseased, and that secession was simply the logical presentation of an illness that had been attacking the nation's vital organs for many decades. His solution was

---

[19] J. Gerald Kennedy, '"A mania for composition": Poe's Annus Mirabilis and the violence of nation-building', *American Literary History*, 17:1 (Spring 2005), 1–35, quotations at 8 and 9; on this aspect of the story, see also David Haven Blake, '"The Man That Was Used Up": Edgar Allan Poe and the ends of captivity', *Nineteenth-Century Literature*, 57:3 (Dec. 2002), 323–49, esp. 346.

[20] George Templeton Strong, diary entries 20 Nov. and 31 Oct. 1860, in Allan Nevins and Milton Halsey Thomas (eds.), *The Diary of George Templeton Strong* (4 vols.), 3, *The Civil War* (New York, 1952), pp. 64, 56; Oliver Wendell Holmes, 'Doings of the sunbeam', *Atlantic Monthly*, 12:69 (July 1863), 1–16, quotation at 12.

perhaps a touch terminal, relying as it did on death: 'through such martyrdom must come our redemption', he wrote, having viewed Brady's photographs from Antietam, and it must be remembered that this was a man who had, in desperation, tramped that very battlefield in search of his missing son. Holmes hardly needed Brady's photographs to bring home to him the realities of a war that had its origins, as he perceived it, in a national sickness; slavery.[21]

Slavery, indeed, was the subject most likely to call forth the metaphor of disease, and a concomitant radical surgical solution. On Thanksgiving Day, 1860, Henry Ward Beecher, one of the North's most popular and influential preachers, delivered a sermon in the course of which he described slavery as like 'an ulcer, this evil eats deeper every day. Unless soon cauterized or excised, it will touch the vitals, and then the patient dies.'[22] The patient, in Beecher's view, was, crucially, not the South, but the nation, a significant point in light both of the war to come and its aftermath. In this context Lincoln, too, was prone to employ the medical metaphor in discussing the national crisis, and no more forcibly than when he was defending the Emancipation Proclamation. Writing to Albert Hodges in 1864, Lincoln traced his thinking on slavery, and in particular his reasons for taking a step—the issuance of the Emancipation Proclamation—that he had once believed to be unconstitutional. 'By general law', he explained, 'life *and* limb must be protected; yet often a limb must be amputated to save a life; but a life is never wisely given to save a limb. I felt that measures, otherwise unconstitutional, might become lawful, by becoming indispensable to the preservation of the constitution, through the preservation of the nation.' On another occasion he explained:

> I have sometimes used the illustration . . . of a man with a diseased limb, and his surgeon. So long as there is a chance of the patient's restoration, the surgeon is solemnly bound to try and save both life *and* limb, but when the crisis comes, and the limb must be sacrificed as the only chance of saving the life, no honest man will hesitate.[23]

---

[21] Elizabeth Young, *Disarming the Nation: Women's Writing and the American Civil War* (Chicago, IL, 1999), pp. 88; Holmes, 'Doings of the sunbeam', 12; Holmes published his account of his (successful) search for his son—the future Supreme Court Justice, Oliver Wendell Holmes, Jr.—in 'My hunt after "The Captain,"' *Atlantic Monthly*, 10:62 (Dec. 1862), 738–64.

[22] Henry Ward Beecher, 'Against a compromise of principle' (1860), repr. in Beecher, *Freedom and War: Discourses on Topics Suggested by the Times* (Boston, 1863), p. 53.

[23] Abraham Lincoln to Albert G. Hodges, 4 April 1864, in Basler (ed.), *Collected Works of Abraham Lincoln*, 7. 281; Lincoln quoted in Francis Bicknell Carpenter, *The Inner Life of*

It is important to bear in mind that, in 1861, these rhetorical flourishes were all-too brutally made flesh, that, for many Civil War troops, metaphorical national amputation translated into their personal dismemberment. The full impact of this physical mutilation on both the individual soldier and the nation has been downplayed, however, in part because we lack a full appreciation of the processes involved, in part because of the quite natural reluctance to disseminate widely the most disturbing images from the war, and in part, too, because of the historiographical positioning of America's Civil War as a conflict apart.

The fact that American Civil War soldiers were more likely to succumb to disease than die on the battlefield is a well-known and, as with the scale of death, frequently cited aspect of that conflict. The surgeon general's office estimated 53.4 disease-induced deaths per 1,000—yellow fever, smallpox, malaria and diarrhoea were the main culprits—but in the context of nineteenth-century wars this was not a particularly high percentage. Thomas Livermore offered overall figures—which remain accepted currency today—of 110,000 Union battlefield fatalities, but 250,000 deaths from disease; for the Confederacy, the figures were 94,000 and 164,000 respectively. 'Compared with male civilians of military age', Richard Shryock concluded, 'servicemen were five times as likely to become ill and experienced a mortality which was five times as high as that of those who remained at home.'[24]

Less well understood is the relative—to other conflicts—scale of amputations during the Civil War resulting from either direct wounding, disease or, often, a combination of the two. It has been asserted, for example, that the 'First World War led to amputations on a scale never seen before, or since', with over 41,000 men losing one or more limbs. This 'unusually high proportion of amputations', it has further been argued, 'was due to the fact that the mutilations in this war tended to be more severe than they had been in previous wars. This was partially due to the use of more effective instruments of dismemberment, such as

Abraham Lincoln: Six Months at the White House (1866, repr. Lincoln, NE, and London, 1995), pp. 76–7.
[24] See Michael A. Flannery, 'Another house divided: Union medical service and sectarians during the Civil War', *The Journal of the History of Medicine and Allied Sciences*, 54 (1999), 473–510, figs. 479; Charles Smart, 'On the medical statistics of the war', in *The Medical and Surgical History of the War of the Rebellion*, 3 vols. (Washington, DC, 1870–88), 3. 1–33; Freemon, *Gangrene and Glory*; Thomas G. Livermore, *Numbers and Losses in the Civil War: 1861–1865* (New York, 1901), pp. 5–8; Richard H. Shryock, 'A medical perspective on the Civil War', *American Quarterly*, 14:2:1 (Summer 1962), 161–73, quotation at 164.

artillery fire, hand grenades and small firearms.'[25] Yet this conclusion
does not bear scrutiny, indeed is flatly contradicted by the figures from the
American Civil War which, according to Laurann Figg and Jane Farrell-
Beck, far exceed 41,000. 'Approximately 60,000 amputations were performed during the Civil War', they assert, a figure representing
'[t]hree-quarters of all operations' performed during that conflict. Indeed,
a greater number of Civil War troops—45,000—survived the experience
of amputation than First World War troops, apparently, underwent it.[26]

Physical mutilation, of course, hardly tells the whole story of the Civil
War's impact on its soldiery, but even simply exploring that dimension
reveals that the Civil War, no less than the First World War, utilised
weaponry capable of inflicting a range of injuries on the human body that
resulted in the need for amputation. In the case of the Civil War, the most
common cause of battlefield wounds was the minié ball, an expansive
bullet used in the rifled muskets of the period. Devised by Captain Claude
Etienne Minié for the French army, this was a conical projectile with a
hollow base that, being narrower than the gun's barrel, was easily loaded,
but expanded on firing to engage with the rifling producing both a faster
and more accurate trajectory. Not only did such bullets penetrate flesh
to produce fracturing of bone but they blunted on impact, frequently
causing a shattering of bone and subsequent damage over a wider area
and, often, carried both 'skin and clothing into the wound'. In any case,
the nineteenth-century bullet, unlike modern variants, did not travel fast
enough to be sterilised by the air; even had they not introduced alien
matter into the body on impact, the bullet itself could cause corporeal
contamination, as well as producing wounds that 'were large, ugly, and
gaping'. Bullets from unrifled muskets, although less accurate, could result
in even larger wounds since their trajectory was less stable, and artillery fire

[25] Bourke, *Dismembering the Male*, pp. 33–4.
[26] Laurann Figg and Jane Farrell-Beck, 'Amputation in the Civil War: physical and social dimensions', *The Journal of the History of Medicine and Allied Sciences*, 48 (1993), 454–75, figs. 454,
458–60. Figg and Farrell-Beck acknowledge the difficulty in stating a definite number of amputations North and South. They cite the *Medical and Surgical History of the War of the Rebellion*, by
General Joseph Barnes, which gave a figure of 29,980 Union amputations which Barnes had noted
was a minimum; their estimate of a similar number for the Confederacy is supported by Wecter,
When Johnny Comes Marching Home, p. 209; I have not found the figure of 60,000 contradicted,
and have found it repeated, in, for example, the *Journal of the American Medical Association*,
JAMA, 281:5 (4 Aug. 1999), 491. On this point see also Shryock, 'Medical perspective', 161–2; and
Jennifer Davis McCaid, 'With lame legs and no money: Virginia's disabled Confederate Veterans',
Virginia Cavalcade (Winter 1998), 14–25, esp. 16.

similarly produced extensive wounds often resulting in the loss of limbs, as these contemporary surgical photographs reveal (Fig. 3).[27]

The sheer scale of the Civil War produced its own problems when it came to the treatment available for the wounded, and 'the inefficiency of

Figure 3.   Surgical Photographs. (Library of Congress Prints and Photographs Division, LC-DIG-ppmsca-10105u.)

[27] Figg and Farrell-Beck, 'Amputation in the Civil War', 455; Blaisdell, 'The wounded, the sick, and the scared', 81; Frank R. Freemon, *Gangrene and Glory: Medical Care during the American Civil War* (1998, repr. Urbana and Chicago, IL, 2001), pp. 48–9.

the Medical Bureau' was condemned at the war's outset by George Templeton Strong as nothing short of 'criminal and scandalous. Its superannuated officials are paralyzed by the routine habits acquired in long dealing with an army of ten or fifteen thousand', he averred, 'and utterly unequal to their present work.'[28] Given the speed with which armies on both sides were raised this shortage of professional physicians and surgeons with battlefield experience of the kind called for by the Civil War is unsurprising. Of the 115 regular Army staff surgeons available in 1861, twenty-four left to join the Confederacy and three refused to be involved at all. Support staff and facilities were also lacking, and in the absence of ambulance services and field hospitals—a situation that only began to be rectified on the Union side toward the end of 1862—many troops suffered and died unnecessarily. As Civil War surgeon John Lewis recalled: 'Although attempts were made as early as the summer of 1861 to organize and drill an ambulance corps, yet I never saw any effective service from it until a year or more had elapsed.'[29]

Civilian volunteer organisations, of course, most notably the United States Sanitary Commission (USSC) but also the Christian Commission and the Western Sanitary Commission, provided additional aid and, in the case of the USSC, a wealth of advice—not all of it welcome—for both the individual soldier and those responsible for treating him. The USSC, in particular, valued uniformity and organisation above all else but, given that medical care in the Civil War era lacked both 'unanimity in theory and practice', this was impossible to achieve. The consequences for the soldier of the unsettled state of American medical practice in the mid-nineteenth-century were not uniformly negative, but the care troops received was 'provided in a complex environment of therapeutic contention and professional animosity, much of which rested upon positions of political power and authority rather than on issues of scientific standing and credibility'. This proved especially critical as far as surgical procedures were concerned; the allopathic opposition to sectarian physicians, and the virtual exclusion of the latter from the battlefield, amounted to, in Michael Flannery's phrase, 'rank partisanship' which ultimately 'worked to the detriment of the average soldier's health care'.[30]

---

[28] Strong, *Diary*, 3. 181.

[29] Figures for US Army surgeons, Flannery, 'Another house divided', 483; Shryock, 'Medical perspective', 161; John B. Lewis in Stanley B. Weld and David A. Soskis (eds.), 'The reminiscences of a Civil War surgeon, John B. Lewis', *The Journal of the History of Medicine and Allied Sciences*, 21 (1966), 47–58, quotation at 51.

[30] Flannery, 'Another house divided', 510, 509.

Amputation was, of course, a dramatic—the word most commonly used at the time was 'heroic'—surgical procedure, and not a first resort response to wounding. The USSC certainly advised amputation as a suitable procedure for both compound fractures and serious laceration, but with a few over-enthusiastic exceptions most surgeons—allopathic and sectarian—were committed to 'conservative surgery' and sought alternative treatments in the first instance, even for serious wounds. This was not necessarily a good thing; in recalling his war experience, surgeon William Keen acknowledged the 'popular opinion that the surgeons did a large amount of unnecessary amputating', but had 'no hesitation in saying that far more lives were lost from a refusal to amputate than by amputation'. Nevertheless, amputation was at the time, and has remained since the symbolic wound of the war, highlighted by historians but mainly by literary critics as expressive both of the damage to the national/masculine body done by the war and, crucially, of the reconstruction of the nation after it.[31]

Reconstructing the human body

'The limbs of our friends and countrymen are a part of the melancholy harvest which War is sweeping down with Dahlgren's mowing-machine and the patent reapers of Springfield and Hartford', observed Oliver Wendell Holmes in 1863. 'It is not two years since the sight of a person who had lost one of his lower limbs was an infrequent occurrence. Now, alas! there are few of us who have not a cripple among our friends, if not in our own families' (Fig. 4). Those historians who have explored directly the reactions of Civil War amputees to their injuries and the concomitant response of the wider society to disabled veterans present, by and large, a positive image of the disabled Civil War combatant, even a positive image of amputation. 'If the war's legacy of crippled men was a burden of unprecedented magnitude', Herschbach suggests, 'it was seen by some as an opportunity.' Mostly, it was seen as an opportunity by the manufacturers of prosthetic devices, as Holmes recognised: 'A mechanical art which provided for an occasional and exceptional want has become a great and active branch of industry', he observed: 'War

---

[31] Figg and Farrell-Beck, 'Amputation in the Civil War', 455; William Williams Keen, 'Surgical reminiscences of the Civil War' (1905), quoted in Flannery, 'Another house divided', 508.

Figure 4. Winslow Homer, 'Our Watering Places—The Empty Sleeve,' *Harper's Weekly*, 26 August 1865.

unmakes legs, and human skill must supply their places as it best may'
(Fig. 5).[32]

Human skill was quick to oblige: almost 150 patents for prosthetics
were issued between 1861 and 1873, which 'represented nearly a 300 per
cent increase over the previous twelve years' (Fig. 6). 'For the nascent
industries of rehabilitative medicine', Herschbach has shown, 'the destruction of the soldier's body held new opportunities for rehabilitation—of
body, soul and society—along improved lines that could wed techno-
scientific knowledge with humanistic visions of reform and progress.' Yet
it went further than this, Herschbach argues, since 'the logic of prosthesis in the nineteenth century reaffirmed Northern ideologies of free
labour and industrial manufacture'. She suggests that Southern veterans
were less inclined to hide their wounds via the use of artificial limbs. 'If
the prosthetically reconstructed worker was the symbolic repository of
Northern ideologies of industry, progress and social mobility', she argues,
'the visibly disabled veteran was likewise an important symbolic repository
of Southern identity, one framed as much by defiance as defeat.'[33]

It was not such a straightforward sectional divide, however. In 1862,
the Federal government had provided for Union veterans who required
prostheses; seventy-five dollars for a leg and fifty for an arm were the
amounts allocated. However, towards the war's end and in its immediate
aftermath the Confederacy sought to match this programme, initially via
the Association to Purchase Artificial Limbs for Maimed Soldiers, established in 1864. What is remarkable, indeed, is the effort expended by many
Southern states, including North and South Carolina, Georgia and
Mississippi, to supply prostheses to former Confederate soldiers. In 1866,
for example, North Carolina passed a resolution to aid amputees 'with
the common funds of the State to procure necessary limbs, and thus to
restore them, as far as is practicable, to the comfortable use of their
persons, to the enjoyment of life and to the ability to earn a subsistence'.
Initially only legs were provided, but in 1867 artificial arms, too, were
made available. In the same year, the state of South Carolina set aside
$20,000—a considerable sum given the post-war economic position of
that state—for the same purpose, although it restricted the available

[32] Oliver Wendell Holmes, 'The human wheel, its spokes and felloes', *Atlantic Monthly*, 11:61
(May 1863), 567–80, quotations at 567–8, 574; Lisa Herschbach, 'Prosthetic reconstructions,
making the industry, re-making the body, modelling the nation', *History Workshop Journal*, 44
(1997), 25.
[33] Herschbach, 'Prosthetic reconstructions', 48.

Figure 5. Clement Patent Leg Advert (prosthesis). Image courtesy of the South Carolina Department of Archives and History.

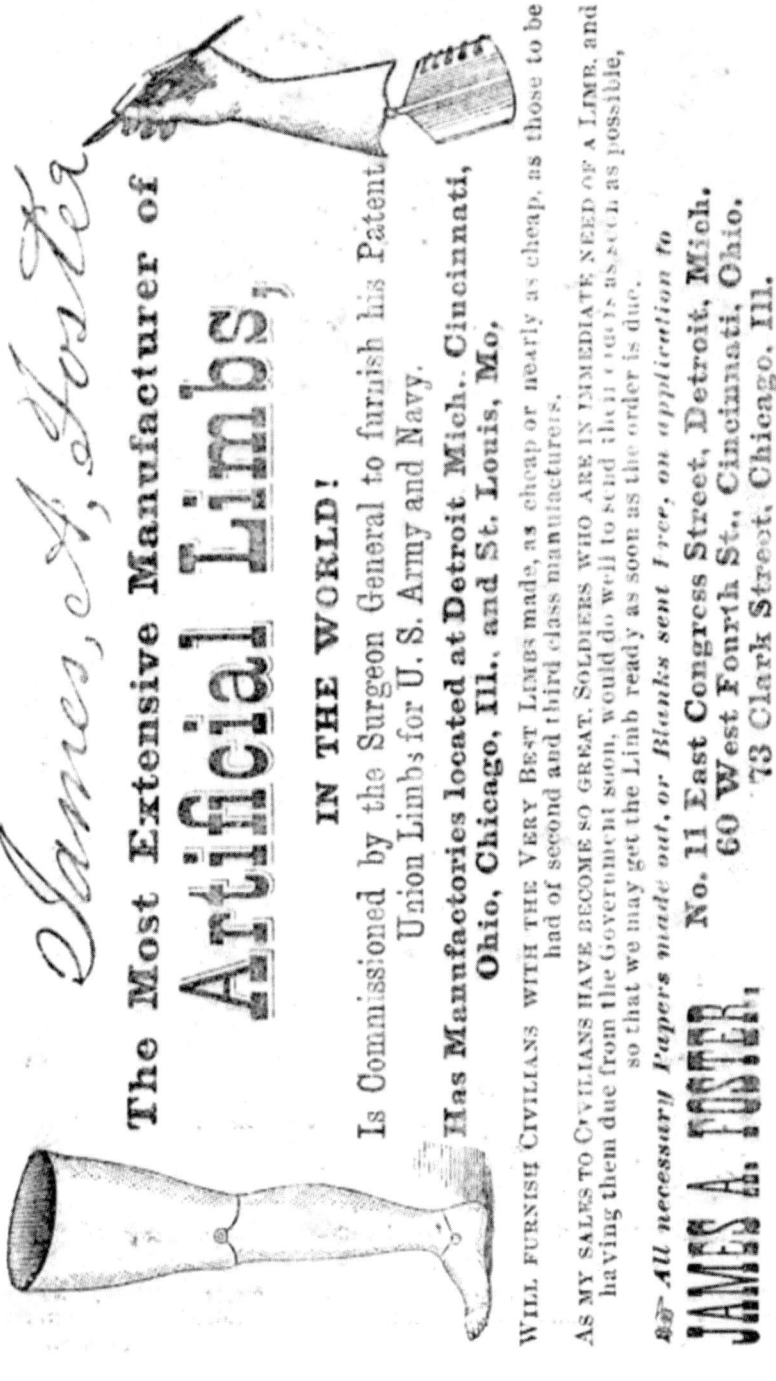

Figure 6. Advert for prosthetic leg. Image courtesy of the South Carolina Department of Archives and History.

prostheses to legs (Fig. 7). South Carolina, too, as North Carolina and the Union did, arranged free rail transport for veterans who needed to travel for medical examination or to have their prostheses fitted. There was no obvious reluctance on the part of disabled veterans to accept such support, but rather a great deal of interest in the programmes.[34]

If Confederate veterans welcomed the opportunity to acquire prostheses—not, perhaps, to disguise a wound but simply to achieve greater mobility and, as many contemporary social commentators hoped, economic self-sufficiency—Union veterans sometimes rejected them. Frances Clarke, for example, has uncovered in the evidence provided by a left-handed writing competition for Union veterans that many of them considered their wounds as 'honorable scars', and had no desire to disguise them, nor 'improve' themselves via the use of prostheses. Charles Coleman, who lost an arm, was just one example of a veteran who declared himself gratified by the response of the government who 'paid my board, transportation, and for my arm, and is now paying me eight dollars per month'; Coleman concluded that 'the pleasure in all this consists in knowing that my feeble efforts for the benefit of our common country are remembered and appreciated and . . . I cannot but feel happy to think that I lost my arm in so good a cause and for so just a government.'[35]

Taking issue with scholars who 'anticipate the literature on post-World War I wounds, which interprets the loss of a limb as a mark of feminization or humiliation', Clarke proposes that Civil War veterans felt no such shame. Many northern veterans, she argues, rejected the use of artificial limbs, and instead responded to their loss as to the death of a family member, 'sacrificed to maintain the integrity of home and nation'. By personifying 'their limbs and rendering their loss in terms of a death scene', Union veterans were able 'to grieve without relating grief to a permanent condition, inherent in the nature of their injuries, for the mourning and melancholy associated with funerals were liminal states. In their portrayal of grief, writers often explicitly made this transition from initial sadness or revulsion to reconciliation and acceptance of their loss.' Above

---

[34] On 'the Association to Purchase Artificial Limbs for Maimed Soldiers' see the *Confederate States Medical and Surgical Journal* (April 1864), 59, and Wegner, 'Phantom pain', 289; Resolution of 23 Jan. 1866, General Assembly [North Carolina] Sessions Records, quoted in Wegner, 'Phantom pain', 290; Statutes at Large/No. 4829/20 Dec. 1866, *Acts of the General Assembly of South Carolina, 1866* (Columbia, SC: State Printer, 1866): p. 433. See Thomas J. Rills to Governor [James Lawrence] Orr, 8 Sept. 1867; Jasper J. Hiers to Orr, 24 May 1867; and J. P. Marco to Orr, 1 July 1867, all in Miscellaneous Papers, 1866–1908, State Archives, South Carolina.

[35] Clarke, 'Honorable scars', pp. 363–4.

ORIGINAL

The State of South Carolina, [CERTIFICATE.]

Sumter DISTRICT.

I Lucius P. Loring Clerk of the Court of General Sessions and Common Pleas for the District and State aforesaid, do hereby certify that James E. Noyes has exhibited to me satisfactory evidence that he is a citizen of this State, and resides within this District. That he lost his leg during the recent war in the service of the Country, and that he is entitled to the benefit of the provisions of the Act of the General Assembly, "To provide Artificial Legs to all citizens of the State who have lost their legs during the recent war," approved December 20th, 1866.

Given under my Hand and Seal of Office, the 13th day of August 1867.

L P Loring

Clerk of the Court for Sumter District.

Figure 7. Surgeon's certificate, SC, for prosthetic leg. Image courtesy of the South Carolina Department of Archives and History.

all, they offered a narrative in which their personal dismemberment had held the nation together, and frequently approached their loss from a religious perspective that stressed the transient nature of life and of suffering and the belief that 'this body entire shall rise from the grave'.[36]

By establishing a link between their sacrifice and the nation's continued existence, Clarke's Civil War soldiers were writing in the context of the rhetoric of national sacrifice and redemption as expressed by northern preachers, in a way, perhaps, seeking to remind their audience—and they were absolutely clear that they were writing for an audience, and, incidentally, a substantial financial prize—that physical survival did not mean that there had been no physical sacrifice. Figg and Farrell-Beck also find that disabled veterans did not feel compelled to hide their disabilities. They find from their analysis of how amputees chose to present their injuries—either disguising these or highlighting them by visibly pinning empty sleeves—that those 'soldiers who returned from the war with amputations received such a positive response, first from the nurses and then from the civilian public, that they were not motivated to disguise their injuries'. Later in the century, by which time, they suggest, public interest in and support for the disabled veteran had diminished, it became both 'physically convenient and socially advantageous to men proud to show that they had given an arm or a leg in the war'.[37]

There certainly came a time when it was politically advantageous for veterans to remind the public of their sacrifices during the war, but the enthusiasm of Civil War nurses and the pride expressed by amputees themselves notwithstanding, the disabled veteran was an unsettling figure in the immediate post-war period as, indeed, he had been during the war itself. Veteran status was not something that was achieved only at the war's conclusion in 1865. In the context of the Civil War, 'veteran' was applied to anyone who had joined up in 1861, and a great many men, severely wounded in combat, became veterans between 1861 and 1865 but did not leave the army; instead they were assigned to the Invalid, or Veteran, Corps, established in 1863. By this stage in the war, desperate for any man it could get, the Union was offering generous financial inducements to those willing to join up or re-enlist. Only two groups were excluded from this largesse: the Invalid Corps, and the troops of the newly formed African-American regiments comprising the USCT. There was, as one contemporary report observed, 'inequality and injustice in

[36] Clarke, 'Honorable scars', pp. 389–90, 393.
[37] Figg and Farrell-Beck, 'Amputation in the Civil War', 468.

this distinction', but there is also a clue to the form that post-war American nationalism took; even as the Union fought for its very existence, it defined both black troops and disabled men as in significant ways separate from the nation that it was committed to saving. White soldiers' suspicion of African-American troops has been well-documented; less so their suspicion of and hostility toward their disabled comrades, black and white.[38]

The motivation behind the establishment of the Invalid Corps was, as for African-American regiments, far from straightforward, and highlighted the contradictory issues surrounding the disabled veteran, issues that in some respects are surprising although not unique to the American Civil War. During the Revolutionary War, disabled soldiers—those men who would mature into the 'pillars of the temple of liberty' according to Lincoln—were viewed with suspicion and some fear. Writing to William Shippen in 1777, George Washington had expressed his concern at wounded soldiers '[s]troling about the country at their own option, to the great detriment of the Services'. Washington's solution to what he described as 'this evil' was a Corps of Invalids to which such troops could be assigned, thereby securing much-needed support for the Continental Army but also, and crucially, saving society from whatever threat these disabled troops were deemed to pose. A similar attitude, reinforced by the mid-nineteenth century's general suspicion of the needy, can be detected in the reaction to the Invalid Corps. Seen as separate from the main body of the army—which in some senses they were—the troops of the Invalid Corps endured a degree of ridicule and suspicion both from their former comrades and from society at large.[39]

Negative attitudes toward veterans generally, but wounded veterans in particular, were most cogently—and repeatedly—expressed by the northern elite leaders of the USSC, but it was not specific to them; it found a resonance in wider society, North and South. President of the USSC, Henry Whitney Bellows, had been 'much exercised with the subject of the future of the disabled soldiers of this war' since 1862, but almost equally concerned by what he saw as 'a tide of another hundred thousand men,

---

[38] Report of J. W. De Forest, 30 Nov. 1865, *Official Records of the Union and Confederate Armies in the War of the Rebellion* (ORA), Series III, Vol. 5: 543–67, 543–4; see also, on preference for veteran regiments, ORA, III. 3: 1131–2; Bell Irvin Wiley, *The Life of Billy Yank: the Common Soldier of the Union* (1952, repr. Baton Rouge, LA, and London, 1978), pp. 342–3.

[39] George Washington to William Shippen, Jr., 26 March 1777, in Fitzpatrick (ed.), *Washington Papers*: <http://memory.loc.gov/ammem/gwhtml/gwhome.html> (accessed 10 May 2007); for further elucidation of this point see Susan-Mary Grant, 'Reimagined communities: Union Veterans and the reconstruction of American nationalism', *Nations and Nationalism*, 14(3): 498–519 (2008).

demoralized for civil life by military habits' threatening 'the order, industry, and security of society'. Returning soldiers, Bellows believed, would 'be not only physically but morally disabled, and will exhibit the injurious effects of camp life in a weakened power of self-guidance and self-restraint'.[40]

There is, of course, an obvious contradiction here as far as the relationship between men and war is concerned but, again, it is not one specific to the American Civil War. Within an American context, the Revolution has been identified as 'the first modern experiment in the creation of a form of masculinity peculiar to the modern nation-state, in which the citizen must carry within himself the qualities of a warrior, but the warrior must also remain the citizen he will become again at conflict's end'. For western warfare in general, Robert Nye has proposed, 'the business of mobilizing men to fight has been a greater challenge than putting the warrior genie back in the bottle at a war's end'. In the particular case of the American Civil War, however, the opposite was true; the Civil War, according to Eric Dean, had ' "let the genie out of the bottle" as the violence of the war years spilled over into civilian life in the postwar era', a point supported by the observation that 'two-thirds of all commitments to state prisons were men who had seen service in the army or navy'. Some of these men, of course, would have seen prison with or without the war factoring in to the equation; however, contemporary accounts of veteran crime statistics lent weight to the warnings of men such as Bellows that the returning soldier was a little too far from the 'citizen-soldier' ideal for comfort.[41]

The American Civil War, indeed, challenged the 'citizen-soldier' ideal on several levels. The return from war of so many disabled men unsettled many of the assumptions on which this ideal was predicated. Even if Civil War soldiers did not regard their wounds as in any sense emasculating or feminising, nevertheless a great many of them had returned from the battlefield in rather a different corporeal form than they had approached it. Amputation was, too, only the most obvious alteration; for men such as Bellows, the suspicion that the soldier had undergone a significant psychological shift, one not obviously written on the body but rather

---

[40] Sanitary Commission Report, No. 49, 15 Aug. 1862; No. 90, 1865 (Henry Whitney Bellows).
[41] Robert A. Nye, 'Western masculinities in war and peace', *The American Historical Review*, 112:2 (April 2007), <http://www.historycooperative.org/journals/ahr/112.2/nye.html> (accessed April 2007), 1, 3; Dean, *Shook Over Hell*, pp. 98–100; see also McConnell, *Glorious Contentment*, p. 20; and for contemporary crime figures see, for example, 'The reformation of prison discipline', *North American Review*, 105:217 (Oct. 1867), 556–91.

more insidiously hidden in the mind, was a far more unsettling thought. Equally unsettling for many veterans and non-combatants alike, however, was what the war had altered in terms of the national body. As Lisa Long has pointed out, by 1863 the war had effected what amounted to a role-reversal as far as masculinity was concerned; as African-American soldiers became 'able-bodied' as officially accepted combat troops, many white soldiers became disabled. This was a national corporeal shift too far, and one that no prosthetic device, however sophisticated, could disguise. The response was as brutal as it was simple; in reconstructing the national body, many whites simply left black troops out, and turned away, in emotional terms at least, from the reality of disabled veterans, black and white alike.[42]

Reconstructing the national body

For African-Americans, what worked against the rhetoric of equality was, ironically, the very route that they had taken to achieve it—military service—and the context in which they had done so; a civil war. Again, Long highlights one of the great difficulties facing Americans, especially northerners, seeking to come to terms with an internecine conflict 'ostensibly geared toward reuniting the estranged regions (at least on the North's part), the racial slurs, ethnic stereotypes, and general hate-mongering typical during foreign wars was not as attractive or effective as it might have been'. Also, and crucially, the outcome was almost irrelevant: whichever side was victorious, Americans had lost a war. In this climate, Long suggests, 'the rhetoric of race' became reanimated, in part through what she describes as 'the language of sanitation', the efforts on the part of the USSC to inculcate a stronger and more robust nationalism premised, in large part, on the experiences of the war. In this sense, the efforts of the USSC, their determination to impose order, their desire to measure and quantify not just supplies but men—indeed, Long argues that the USSC regarded these as virtually interchangeable—merged with the ambitions of the prosthetic limb manufacturers. Together they constructed a nationalist narrative that positioned both nation and person at the forefront of a brave new world of mass production, in which individuals, as well as goods, could be organised, rationalised and nationalised to produce a

---

[42] Long, *Rehabilitating Bodies*, p. 219.

new national body that emerged from the war stronger and better than what had gone before.[43]

Yet when one factors the Civil War's veterans, especially but not exclusively, its disabled veterans, into the equation, doubts arise as to either the popularity of such ideas or their acceptance by the mass of veterans and non-combatants, North and South. Without underestimating the influence that the nineteenth-century 'rhetoric of race' had, and without diminishing its insidious impact, historians need to probe more deeply the paradoxes involved in achieving national unity at the cost of so many lives and limbs. Not the least of these paradoxes involved the apparent failure of antebellum radicals, the strongest supporters of a new, inclusive American nationalism based not on ethnic signifiers but on civic precepts, to hold out for the 'emancipationist vision' for America that so many had given their lives to make real.

When historians encounter, for example, a man such as Thomas Wentworth Higginson, a fervent abolitionist, an officer in an African-American regiment, and a strong advocate of equal rights, they struggle to understand what appears to be his post-war apostasy. The explanation for a man such as Higginson's apparent change of heart, Scott Poole has recently argued, lies in a 'profound cynicism among American radicals', not regarding their ideals, but 'about the possibility of fulfilling them within the American national experiment'. In 1865, however, when Union victory had been achieved, and the possibility for equality—a fully civic nationalism—was within reach, it is hard to see why, and with such speed, Americans let it slip past them, especially given the visual representations of the veteran that were produced in the immediate post-war period.[44]

Given the fact that some of the most sharply political cartoons and paintings of the day drew disability and the USCT together by portraying a disabled African-American veteran, it is clear that many northerners knew what was at stake. Thomas Nast's political cartoon that appeared in

[43] Long, *Rehabilitating Bodies*, pp. 154 and 88; Herschbach, 'Prosthetic reconstructions', passim. On the USSC, see also Melinda Lawson, *Patriot Fires: Forging a New American Nationalism in the Civil War North* (Lawrence, KS, 2002), p. 19 and George M. Fredrickson, *The Inner Civil War: Northern Intellectuals and the Crisis of the Union* (1965, repr. New York and London, 1968), esp. pp. 98–112.

[44] W. Scott Poole, 'Memory and the Abolitionist heritage: Thomas Wentworth Higginson and the uncertain meaning of the Civil War', *Civil War History*, 60:2 (2005), 202–17; see also John Stauffer, *The Black Hearts of Men: Radical Abolitionists and the Transformation of Race* (Cambridge, MA, 2002).

Harper's Weekly in August of 1865 represented an overt challenge to the nation to pay its debt, not just that owed to black troops but also to disabled veterans; a message reinforced in Thomas Waterman Wood's famous triptych, 'A Bit of War History' (Figs. 8–11).[45] Ultimately, the message was ignored, mainly due to the unwillingness on the part of Americans, North and South, to confront fully the true costs, and as a consequence fail to grasp with both hands the opportunities, of the Civil War, to turn away from the disabled veteran, and from the black soldier, and focus instead on the dead. Those who had made the ultimate sacrifice were deserving of commemoration, of course, but equally it cannot be overlooked that they represented the ideal citizen-soldier, raising no awkward questions about how to effect the (re)transformation of the soldier into the citizen, nor how to face the future with a disabled body. By that point, however, both black and disabled veterans were already beginning to be sidelined in favour of a different narrative, a different understanding of the war, a return, in effect, to antebellum understandings of the national body.

In the war's immediate aftermath, this narrative did not yet dominate. The prejudice experienced by both African-American and disabled troops was, initially at least, obscured by the rapturous welcome home that Union soldiers received in 1865. The parades and ceremonies marking the cessation of hostilities placed the veteran—wounded and whole, black and white—centre-stage, and established a precedent, in some respects, for future ceremonial state occasions, such as presidential inaugurations, that included an obvious veteran presence. The veteran involvement at the inauguration of William McKinley, himself a Civil War veteran, was even captured on one of the earliest newsreels of such events, but by the turn of the century the ceremonial role of the veteran was already working to obscure the immediate post-war reality of many veterans' lives.[46]

The reality was that the disabled veteran remained a controversial and unsettling figure, similar in many ways to that of the former slave. In fact, the two were more closely linked than has been appreciated, with many officers and men of the Invalid Corps—some 40 per cent—assigned duty in the Freedmen's Bureau. Both, too, were accorded symbolic roles in the pageantry that accompanied Union victory in the Civil

---

[45] For a discussion of Thomas Waterman Wood's work, see Franny Nudelman, *John Brown's Body: Slavery, Violence, and the Culture of War* (Chapel Hill, NC, and London, 2004), pp. 155–6.
[46] The McKinley Inaugural Parade (1901) can be viewed through the Library of Congress, at: <http://memory.loc.gov/cgi-bin/query/D?papr:18:./temp/~ammem_Kxgo> (accessed 3 April 2008).

Figure 8. 'Franchise. And not this man?/Th. Nast, *Harper's Weekly*, 1865 Aug.5'. (Library of Congress Prints and Photographs Division, LC-USZ62-102257.)

Figure 9.   Thomas Waterman Wood, 'A Bit of War History: The Contraband'. (The Metropolitan Museum of Art, Gift of Charles Stewart Smith, 1884 (84.12a). Image © The Metropolitan Museum of Art.)

Figure 10. Thomas Waterman Wood, 'A Bit of War History: The Recruit'. (The Metropolitan Museum of Art, Gift of Charles Stewart Smith, 1884 (84.12b). Image © The Metropolitan Museum of Art.)

Figure 11.   Thomas Waterman Wood, 'A Bit of War History: The Veteran'. (The Metropolitan Museum of Art, Gift of Charles Stewart Smith, 1884 (84.12c). Image © The Metropolitan Museum of Art.)

War: African-American troops accompanied Lincoln on his visit to Richmond once the Confederate government had fled; members of the Invalid Corps were selected as the president's honour guard in the planned Grand Review (Lincoln was assassinated before it took place). Both wounded veterans and African-American troops were prominent in the president's funeral procession to the Capitol; the 22nd US Colored Infantry, indeed, were at the head of it, even if only by accident. If neither African-American regiments nor the Veterans' Corps took part in the Grand Review on 23 and 24 May 1865, it was partly because many remained in the South.[47]

Memorial Day, too, in both the North and South, provided an opportunity for veterans to gather, and for a more racially inclusive version of the war to be made prominent. In the war's immediate aftermath, it was by no means certain that black and white veterans be driven apart, nor that segregation become, in time, the norm even for the main Union veterans' organisation, the Grand Army of the Republic (GAR). Wallace Davis made this point fifty years ago, and it has been reinforced many times since. Black GAR members were accorded prominent roles in Memorial Day and Lincoln Day parades in Southern cities such as Richmond and Savannah until the First World War, in itself 'an explicit refutation of racist interpretations of the Civil War's legacy' and a reminder that the symbolism of sacrifice, even in the Southern heartland, could convey a racially inclusive message.[48]

Developing this point, Andre Fleche has recently enhanced our understanding of the black–white veteran relationship by highlighting the ways in which in 'their memoirs, publications, and memorial celebrations, black and white Union veterans formulated a joint vision of the war at

---

[47] For details of Lincoln's funeral procession and the black role in this see Neff, *Honoring the Civil War Dead*, pp. 75–7.

[48] On Memorial Day, see Gaines M. Foster, *Ghosts of the Confederacy: Defeat, the Lost Cause, and the Emergence of the New South* (1987, repr. New York and Oxford, 1988), pp. 42–6, quotation at 43; Caroline E. Janney, *Burying the Dead But Not the Past: Ladies' Memorial Associations of the Lost Cause* (Chapel Hill, NC, 2008), pp. 62–3; William Blair, *Cities of the Dead: Contesting the Memory of the Civil War in the South, 1865–1914* (Chapel Hill, NC, 2004); and David Blight, *Race and Reunion: The Civil War in American Memory* (Cambridge, MA, 2001), pp. 64–97; Wallace E. Davies, 'The problem of race segregation in the Grand Army of the Republic', *Journal of Southern History*, 13:3 (Aug. 1947), 354–72; W. Fitzhugh Brundage, 'Race, memory, and masculinity: Black Veterans recall the Civil War', in Joan E. Cashin (ed.), *The War Was You and Me: Civilians in the American Civil War* (Princeton, NJ, 2002), pp. 136–58, quotation at 145–6; see also Kathleen Ann Clark, *Defining Moments: African American Commemoration and Political Culture in the South, 1863–1913* (Chapel Hill, NC, 2005).

odds with the more reconciliationist, segregationist, and racist trends found in post-war society as whole'. Most Union veterans, he stressed, did 'not abet such trends by preferring reconciliation with ex-Confederates to recognition of the role blacks played in the war'. Yet in the context of commemorative events such as Memorial Day, the veteran's voice proved unable to rise above the 'rhetoric of race', since this found a more persistent expression beyond a single day. In some ways this is unsurprising; the emphasis of Memorial Day 'remained on the process of bereavement: the creation of cemeteries, the erection of funereal monuments, and the springtime decoration of the graves'. Although veterans were an obvious part of this ceremony, the link between memorialisation and the care of the disabled veteran, it has been argued, served only to 'delay' the implementation of programmes designed to support the returning soldier, certainly in the South. 'How voiceful the graves of those who died for freedom and country', declared former slaveholder Charles Colcock Jones, Jr. in 1880; but these voices from the tomb took precedence, to a large extent, over the conflict's living survivors in the immediate post-war period. Memorial Day certainly was an occasion when veterans were socially prominent, but they were there to bear witness; in the nineteenth-century Memorial Day, that most overt of American sacred ceremonies, belonged to the dead.[49]

Additional evidence for the complexity of this move away from civic and toward a reinvigorated ethnic nationalism lies not so much in how northern society, in particular, treated black veterans, but in what they did to white. In an attempt to deny, or at least avoid confronting, the sheer scale of destruction, some northerners attempted to make the Civil War veteran conform to Lincoln's image of the aged and safe Revolutionary exemplar. In effect, they avoided looking at what was before them, and instead gazed into a distant future. As early as 1867 the *New York Times* was already musing on the speed with which 'a heroic generation seems to be gathered away from life. It is the universal experience of history that almost before a nation has made ready to do justice to its heroes, the majority of them are gone, and it is the minority of survivors or another race of heroes who reap the benefits of the intended bounty'.[50] Civil War

---

[49] Andre Fleche, '"Shoulder to shoulder as comrades tried": Black and White Union Veterans and Civil War memory', *Civil War History*, 60:2 (2005), 175–201, quotations at 201, 177; on memorialisation and veterans' programmes, Wegner, 'Phantom pain', 289; Jones quoted in Foster, *Ghosts of the Confederacy*, p. 46.
[50] *New York Times*, 8 Dec. 1867.

troops, it seems, were barely out of uniform before being written into history, and out of the living nation.

Oliver Wendell Holmes, Jr., Civil War veteran and one of the most famous justices of the United States Supreme Court, would not have been surprised by this apparent desire to fast-forward a soldier's life to its conclusion. In the course of what is perhaps his most famous speech on the war, delivered at Harvard in 1895, he admitted to his audience that when he 'went to the war [he] thought that soldiers were old men'. Of course, as Holmes had found out thirty years before, the Civil War soldier was far from old; indeed, in the first year of the war, the 'largest single age group' among both Union and Confederate troops was eighteen, the next largest twenty-one. As conscription in the Confederacy drew on a wider sample of the Southern population, and as the more mature troops in both armies grew older, the average age for the Civil War soldier rose over the course of the conflict, but even at its mid-point, 'three out of every four Yanks were under thirty years of age and less than half of them had celebrated their twenty-fifth birthday'. In light of this, it is perhaps surprising to read the description offered by Colonel Robert G. Ingersoll in 1862 of '[o]ld gray-haired veterans with lips whitening under the kiss of death'.[51]

Yet Ingersoll's comment and the *New York Times*'s apparent impatience to age these young men who had given so much of their youth and health for the Union highlights the ambiguity attendant on the return of the citizen–soldier from war, an ambiguity rooted both in nineteenth-century understandings of masculinity and in the transformative impact of the conflict on the individual men and, beyond them, on the post-war nation. The controversy over veterans' pensions offers further elucidation of the ways in which this ambiguity was expressed. Despite elite suspicions of returning soldiers, Civil War veterans did not face the battle over pensions that Revolutionary soldiers had; in large part, the precedent had been established by the generation of '76. Through the General Pension Act of July 1862 the Union established the 'baseline' of pension legisla-

---

[51] Oliver Wendell Holmes, Jr., 'The Soldier's faith', An Address Delivered on Memorial Day, 30 May 1895, in Oliver Wendell Holmes, Jr., *The Essential Holmes: Selections from the Letters, Speeches, Judicial Opinions, and Other Writings of Oliver Wendell Holmes, Jr.*, ed. Richard A. Posner (Chicago, IL, 1992), p. 81; figures for average age of troops are taken from Wiley, *Life of Billy Yank*, pp. 301–4; and *The Life of Johnny Reb: the Common Soldier of the Confederacy* (1943, repr. Baton Rouge, LA, 1978), pp. 330–2; Ingersoll quoted in Fredrickson, *Inner Civil War*, p. 86.

tion that lasted until 1890, providing support for disabled veterans and for war widows. Between 1861 and 1885, 555,038 individuals claimed pensions, of which 300,204 were granted. After 1890, an extension to pension provisions resulted in some 63 per cent of Union veterans receiving assistance from the state; a big jump from the 2 per cent that had received support in 1866. By 1893, veterans' benefits accounted for over 40 per cent of the federal budget.[52]

Yet federal generosity in the case of war pensions did not necessarily translate into a general acceptance of or support for the recipients of these very necessary funds. Indeed, as Civil War veterans aged, and as pension legislation expanded after 1890 to include compensation for infirmities that, whilst deriving from the war, only became a problem in old age, the costs of veteran support soared. With rising costs came increased concern over the financial impact of the Union veteran on the nation. Concerns over fraudulent claims—not entirely groundless—undermined the image of the Civil War veteran as deserving citizen-soldier of the republic.

Revealingly, negative cartoon images of the grasping veteran that appeared, for example, in *Puck* magazine in the 1880s and early 1890s did not portray the Civil War veterans as most of them were by that point, old men; somewhat bizarrely, yet revealingly, whilst during and after the war both individuals and the media had prematurely aged the young soldier/veteran, by the early 1880s the by then aging veteran got his youth back (Fig. 12). It was the young Union soldier, not the 'grey haired' veteran, who was presented as draining the Federal coffers in one contemporary cartoon. Simultaneous with what Stanley Hirshon described many years ago now as the 'Northern abandonment of the Negro' in the 1890s was the process of abandoning the Civil War veteran; not economically, entirely, as pension payments did not cease and even former Confederates became eligible, but emotionally. As African-American veterans began to disappear from the public memory of the war, if not yet entirely from commemorative ritual, so the wounded veteran gained a new political prominence; yet the contradictory image of the veteran persisted. Presented by turns as both aged exemplar and youthful threat, by the start of the new century it was clear that many of the paradoxes involved in national reconstruction had been resolved only at the expense of both black and disabled veterans; removing them from the 'story' of the Civil

[52] Skocpol, *Protecting Soldiers and Mothers*, pp. 106–9; Vinovskis, 'Have social historians lost the Civil War', pp. 21–2, 24, 27.

THE INSATIABLE GLUTTON.

Figure 12. Cartoon of Union soldier, from the cover of *Puck* (New York) magazine, 20 December 1882.

War enabled a nation to heal, even as those who had fought in its name could not.[53]

Conclusion

It is fitting that, as the sesquicentennial of the Civil War approaches, a monument to America's disabled veterans is, finally, planned for 2010.

---

[53] Skocpol, *Protecting Soldiers and Mothers*, pp. 122–4; Stanley P. Hirshon, *Farewell to the Bloody Shirt Northern Republicans and the Southern Negro, 1877–1893* (1962, repr. Gloucester, MA, 1968), p. 255.

The American Veterans Disabled for Life Memorial, which will be situated in Washington, DC, represents a rather more immediate response to and recognition of the some three million living disabled American veterans, but its impact may well resonate in the study of America's more distant past, and in particular the Civil War. Designed, in the words of the Executive Director of the American Veterans Disabled for Life Memorial project, Victor Biggs, as 'a never-ending reminder to all of the human costs of war and conflict', its design incorporates—perhaps for the first time on any memorial—a representation of the human cost of war in the form of four bronze relief panels designed to render 'corporeal the challenges of life with physical and mental loss' (Fig. 13).[54] In the aftermath of the Civil War, a great many Americans had to face this challenge, but any overt, monumental recognition of that fact was not made tangible; the nationalist implications of Reconstruction, as much as the sentiment of the age, made such recognition impossible.

In the nineteenth century, the enthusiasm of America's prosthetic manufacturers notwithstanding, the reconstruction of the national body did not present a new, improved civic cyborg to the nation but, in the best tradition of the prosthetic limb industry, offered a new body that was virtually indistinguishable from the old; presented with the opportunity to make it better, more racially robust than before, imagination failed. Nineteenth-century Americans needed their war heroes, but the war heroes they needed were not the ones they had before them. The veterans they wanted were damaged, certainly, but time had removed the rawness from their wounds, and it was hard to say whether ammunition or age was the decisive factor in their infirmity. In the last decade of the nineteenth century, it certainly became advantageous for some veterans to remind the American public of the sacrifices of the Civil War generation: 'Many a Democratic candidate in the late nineteenth century called on his fellow southerners to stand with him now as he had stood with those at Gettysburg . . . If he could substantiate his claim by displaying an empty sleeve, his chances of victory improved', Gaines Foster observed, 'unless of course he campaigned against a one-legged veteran.' In the North, too, there was political capital to be made out of veteran status, and 'waving

---

[54] Victor Biggs quoted in 'A nation in support', the American Veterans Disabled for Life Memorial magazine, *Honor Earned*, Vol. 4 (Summer 2006) at: <http://www.avdlm.com/newsletter.php> (accessed 21 April 2008); second quotation from 'From design to destiny: building an American memorial', ibid.

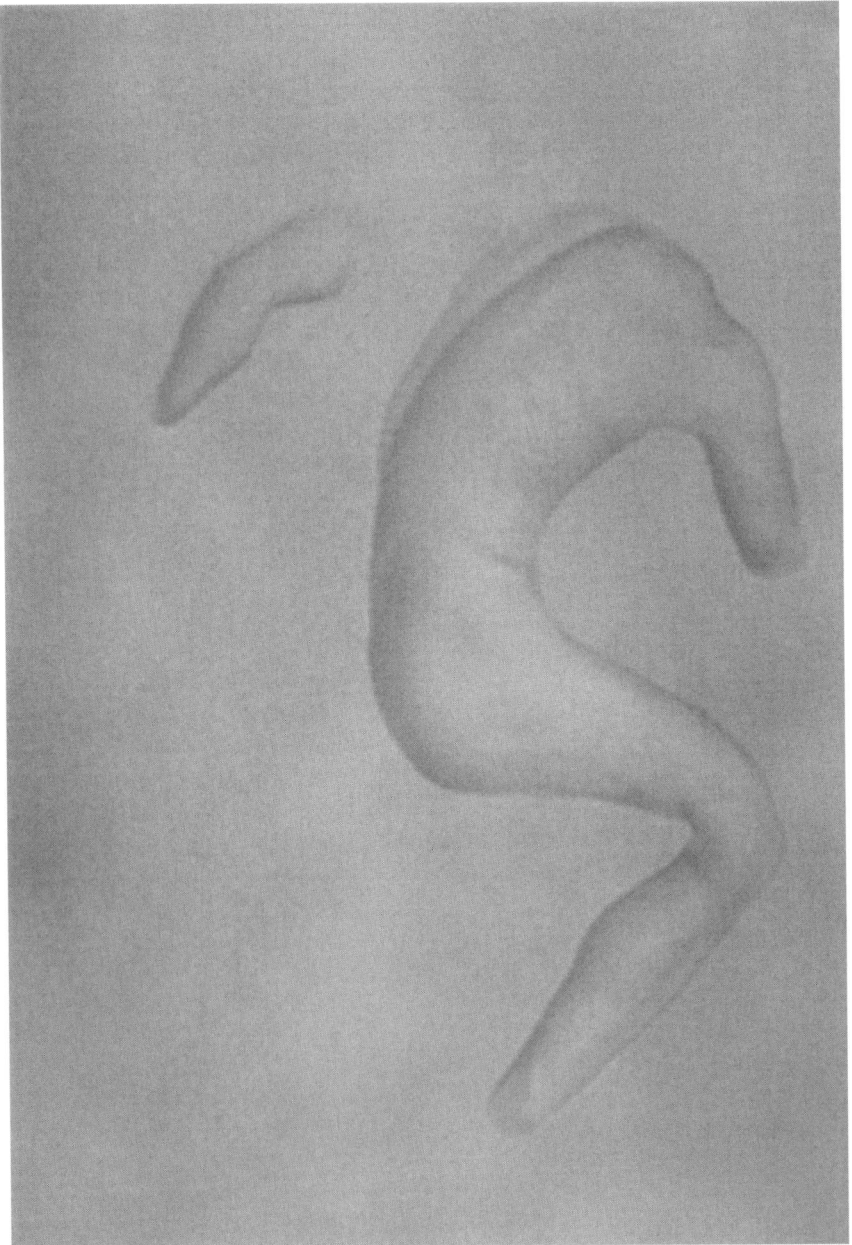

Figure 13. Bronze relief panel from American Disabled Veterans for Life Memorial. Image courtesy of the Disabled Veterans LIFE Memorial Foundation.

the bloody shirt' was a standard Republican tactic to remind voters who had been on the winning side in the Civil War.[55]

By the election of 1896, when cartoons of William McKinley in his Civil War uniform were juxtaposed with those depicting William Jennings Bryan in his cradle, 'the wartime memories used by bloody-shirt Republicans' had become 'as familiar as the scriptures'. By this point, however, the 'emancipationist vision' of the Civil War was already fading, although not yet quite invisible.[56] Working from the pattern established during the antebellum era and threatened, perhaps, by the implications of altering the colour of the nation's symbolic veteran, post-Civil War Americans effected their 'retreat from reconstruction', a process exemplified by their unwillingness to engage fully with the war wounded, to look beyond them, in effect, to a future that was, in its nationalist topography, bleakly familiar. In the end, in the aftermath of America's most (self-)destructive conflict to date, Americans indicated their preference for the safe and sanitary, aged and unthreatening image of the war veteran; in every sense, a man that had been used up.

---

[55] Foster, *Ghosts of the Confederacy*, p. 195.
[56] Patrick J. Kelly, 'The election of 1896 and the restructuring of Civil War memory', *Civil War History*, 49:3 (2003), 254–80, quotations at 254.

A Minority Opinion?

BARONESS HALE OF RICHMOND
Fellow of the Academy

THE PREVIOUS MACCABAEAN LECTURE in Jurisprudence, in 2005, was given by the Senior Law Lord, Lord Bingham of Cornhill.[1] It would have been given by the late Professor Peter Birks, had it not been for his untimely death. Each is a hard act to follow. Each is an outstanding exemplar of the two very different senses in which we commonly use the word 'jurisprudence'.

To law students, 'jurisprudence' means the one (usually compulsory) subject that has nothing at all to do with the nuts and bolts of what the law is: it is, as the *Oxford English Dictionary* puts it, the science or philosophy of human law. It is usually taught by the brainiest scholars in the department and requires students to read some important works of moral and political philosophy. Professor Birks was a jurisprudent of the science of human law rather than of legal philosophy.[2] Such scholars study and try to make sense of 'jurisprudence' in another sense: the corpus of judicial decisions on a particular subject or in a particular court or by a particular person. Lord Bingham is our longest serving senior judge. He is and has long been an exemplary provider of jurisprudence in its second sense.

Read at the Academy 13 November 2007.

[1] 'The Judges: active or passive?', *Proceedings of the British Academy*, 139 (2006), 55.
[2] As in *An Introduction to the Law of Restitution* (Oxford, 1985), a title which is universally recognised as an understatement.

Proceedings of the British Academy, **154**, 319–336. © The British Academy 2008.

My theme was prompted by his Maccabaean lecture of two years ago: 'The Judges: Active or Passive?' In this Lord Bingham addressed the traditionalist view of judging: that the judges' role is confined to giving effect to the terms which Parliament has enacted and to declaring what the common law has always been. Anything more is to usurp the law-making role which properly belongs to Parliament. In his view, the traditionalist view 'captures very important elements of the truth but does not express the whole truth'.[3] He accepts that judges have always made the law. The difficulty is how to find the 'elusive boundary between legitimate judicial development of the Law on the one hand and impermissible judicial legislation on the other'. He suggests that the acid test is whether the decision is 'legally motivated', which is permissible even if the judge has got it wrong, or whether it is 'not in truth legally motivated. This will be so if the decision is motivated not by legal but by extraneous considerations, as by the prejudice or predilection of the judge or, worse, by any personal agenda of the judge, whether conservative, liberal, feminist, libertarian or whatever.'[4] On this view, I take it, the decision should be predictable on the basis of precedent and legal principle, but not on the basis of the judge's personality or philosophy.

With huge respect, I question whether this view too, although it captures important elements of the truth, expresses the whole truth. I have three main reasons for questioning it. First, the business of judging, especially in the hard cases, often involves a choice between different conclusions, any of which it may be possible to reach by respectable legal reasoning. The choice made is likely to be motivated at a far deeper level by the judge's own approach to the law, to the problem under discussion and to ideas of what makes a just result. Secondly, an important project of feminist jurisprudence has been to explode the myth of the disinterested, disengaged, and distant judge. As Patricia Cain commented long ago,[5]

> I take it that 'bias'—in addition to being 'a line diagonal to the grain of a fabric'[6]—can be both good and bad. To the extent that a bias is a personal preference, something a person has affection for, it is something we want to acknowledge and celebrate about human personality. Can you imagine a person

[3] Bingham, 'The Judges: active or passive?', 60.

[4] Ibid. 70.

[5] 'Good and bad bias: a comment on feminist theory and judging', *Southern California Law Review*, 61 (1988), 1945, at 1946.

[6] She is commenting on Judith Resnik, 'On the bias: feminist reconsiderations of the aspirations for our judges', *Southern California Law Review*, 61 (1988), 1878.

with no preferences? On the other hand, to the extent that a person's bias constitutes bigotry, prejudice or intolerance, we certainly do not want to celebrate it. . . . We want the good bias, but not the bad one. . . . The trick, of course, is to be able to say which is which.

Thirdly, the judicial choice will be guided, not only by the judge's own views of what is right and just, but also by his or her personal philosophy of judging. Cass Sunstein has developed this point by reference to the United States Supreme Court.[7] There is a tendency to equate judicial 'activism' with a liberal or reforming agenda, such as that shown by the Warren Court of the 1950s and 1960s when racial segregation in schools was struck down[8] and women given some control over their own reproductive capacity.[9] Judicial passivity, if that is the right word, tends to be linked to a more conservative philosophy. But Sunstein has shown that, at least in the contemporary United States, there is no such connection. Judges with a particular view of what the law should be, whether to the left or to the right, are equally 'active'. He identifies four different approaches to judging in the Supreme Court.

First, there are the 'perfectionists' who want to make the Constitution the best it can be: they want to interpret the Constitution so as to give the people the rights that they think the people should have: the Warren Court were mainly perfectionists. Then there are the 'fundamentalists' who also want to make the Constitution the best it can be, but to do so by returning to the original understanding. They want to interpret the Constitution to mean what it meant at the time that it was ratified: Justices Scalia, Thomas and Alito on the present court are fundamentalists. In the middle he identifies two more moderate positions. 'Majoritarians' wish to defer to the will of the elected legislature unless it is quite clear that the Constitution has been violated. This leaves Congress and the States free to reflect the will of the people of the day, whether liberal or conservative, within their different spheres. This is a conservative position on judging, but one which would respect the right of the people to legislate for programmes which are very far from conservative: Justices Frankfurter and Holmes were of this view.

'Minimalists' are the ones that Sunstein likes best. They may be either conservative or liberal, willing to nudge the law in one direction or

---

[7] *Radicals in Robes: Why Extreme Right Wing Courts are Wrong for America* (Cambridge, MA, 2004).
[8] *Brown* v. *Board of Education*, 349 US 294 (1955).
[9] *Griswold* v. *Connecticut*, 381 US 479 (1965); *Roe* v. *Wade*, 410 US 113 (1973).

another. But they prefer nudges to earthquakes. They refuse to promote a broad agenda. Their distinguishing feature is that they believe in narrow, incremental decisions, not broad rulings that the nation may later have cause to regret. By their very nature, minimalists are not too sure that they are right.[10] Interestingly, in his view, the only two women who have been on the court are minimalists. Justice Ruth Bader Ginsburg is a (mostly) liberal minimalist, whereas Justice Sandra Day O'Connor was a conservative minimalist: 'minimalism is a method and a constraint; it is not a program and it does not dictate particular results'.[11] This cautious approach to judging could explain why Justice Anthony Kennedy, although a Republican and a Roman Catholic, has now replaced Justice O'Connor as the 'swing' vote on the Court.[12]

Most judges in this country never have occasion to own up to a personal philosophy, whether of life or of judging. Because of my unusual professional career, however, I have had to develop and express some sort of personal philosophy, and even, at one stage, a reform 'agenda'. I have been a legal scholar and later a law reformer, rather than a legal practitioner, before becoming a judge. It is difficult to be a legal scholar, still less a professional law reformer, without developing a point of view about what the law both is and should be.

Legal scholarship is, of course, a relatively recent development. Some people may still be reluctant to accept that it exists. Neil Duxbury, in his charming discussion of the relationship between judges and academic lawyers,[13] reminds us of Lord Annan's view that the retention of law 'which (as taught in England) is the most flagrantly vocational of all traditional subjects' on the academic syllabus 'remains mysterious'.[14] That was in 1963. But the fact that some knowledge may actually be useful in real life does not prevent its being a proper subject of academic study. The problem with law was always to explain to non-lawyers what we did apart from teaching students the rules. It is non-lawyers who tend to have the most 'traditionalist' view of what the law is and what judges do.

---

[10] Sunstein, *Radicals in Robes*, p. 252; after Learned Hand, 'the spirit of liberty is that spirit which is not too sure that it is right', in Irving Dilliard (ed.), *The Spirit of Liberty*, see 3rd edn. (Chicago, 1960), p. 190.

[11] Sunstein, *Radicals in Robes*, p. 29.

[12] Although he considers that judges should avoid making policy, he has also identified the qualities of a good judge as 'compassion, warmth, sensitivity and an unyielding insistence on justice' (evidence to Senate Judiciary Committee, Dec. 1987): feminists might well consider this a good bias.

[13] *Jurists and Judges: An Essay on Influence* (Oxford, 2004).

[14] Ibid., p. 69; quoting Noel Annan, 'The Universities', *Encounter*, 20(4) (1963), 3 at 10.

There are many different kinds of legal scholarship, all of which would be worthy academic endeavours, irrespective of whether there were any undergraduates sitting at the scholars' feet, anxious to gain the knowledge which will enable them to obtain riches or glory in the big wide world outside. All of them lead to, if they do not begin with, a particular point of view. The first, and in many ways the most important, is to make sense of the great undigested mass of judicial decisions: to find out what they are, to discover and lay bare the underlying principles, and to deduce what the principled answer to a new problem would be. This is what judges do on a case by case basis. But the great scholars of the law were and are able to do it over a whole subject: to see how it all fits together and to discover the concepts and principles which make it a coherent whole. As Peter Birks put it, 'there is no body of knowledgeable data which can subsist as a jumble of mismatched categories. The search for order is indistinguishable from the search for knowledge.'[15] Some, like Peter Birks himself, do it synoptically. Others do it in comprehensive detail. In my own subject, family law, the prime exponent of this brand of legal scholarship was Peter Bromley: he managed to bring together the common law of husband and wife, parent and child, and the ecclesiastical-turned-statute law of divorce and matrimonial causes, into a single coherent whole.[16] But pride of place should probably go to the late Sir John Smith; with Brian Hogan, he wrote the first comprehensive academic account of the criminal law.[17] Such authors, having a deep understanding of the underlying principles and of the bigger picture, usually have views about what the next case should decide. Increasingly those views are influential with the judges.[18]

Hence these treatise writers will tend to have a consistent view of what the subject is about, what the law is trying to achieve in the particular area, and what, therefore, will amount to the just result of any particular case. The criminal lawyer will have a theory about the justifications for

---

[15] P. Birks (ed.), *English Private Law* (Oxford, 2000), Preface.

[16] P. M. Bromley, *Family Law*, 1st edn. (London, 1957).

[17] J. C. Smith and B. Hogan, *Criminal Law*, 1st edn. (London, 1969); Glanville Williams had earlier published *Criminal Law: The General Part*, 1st edn. (London, 1953), but his *Textbook of Criminal Law*, 1st edn. (London, 1978) came after Smith and Hogan.

[18] Duxbury would give pride of place to Sir John Smith, whose case notes in the *Criminal Law Review* were undoubtedly influential; but some may think that Dr David Thomas, in expounding the principles of sentencing which had been previously locked in the judges' bosoms, was even more influential: his *Principles of Sentencing*, 1st edn. (London, 1970) was developed at the judges' insistence into *Current Sentencing Practice*, now a four volume loose-leaf encyclopedia (London, 1982).

imposing punishment which will guide his view about the justice of a particular rule of law. Subjectivists will tend to think that people should only be punished for the harm that they mean to do. But there is a respectable point of view that people can be expected to take more responsibility for their actions than that: for example, that the State is justified in requiring its citizens to take care not to purchase goods from an unconventional source without satisfying themselves that the goods have not been stolen;[19] and many feminists would argue that the State is justified in requiring men to take care to ascertain that they have the other's consent before engaging in certain sexual acts. Or to take an example of a similar issue from my own subject:[20] should a woman who has suffered brutal cruelty at the hands of her husband be expected to return to live with him if it is unlikely that he will do it again? All sorts of moral and empirical considerations come into answering a question like that: about the nature of marriage, the purpose of matrimonial relief, the autonomy and equality of the spouses, and the reliability of predictions of future behaviour. Such academic debates will often be mirrored in disagreements between the judges: between the subjectivists and the pragmatists in the criminal law; between the privacy of the family and the protection of the vulnerable in family law. But it is rarer for a judge to put pen to paper to give a systematic account of his point of view.

Then there are the legal scholars who ask, not about the law in the law reports, but about the law as it is experienced by the people or the organisations it affects. Sometimes this will involve empirical research, or at least the systematic study of other peoples' research and policy discussions. This is the direction in which family law went, after the reforms which took effect in 1971 destroyed so much of the conceptual coherence which Peter Bromley had discovered. A new breed of family law textbook came along.[21] The impact of the law upon real people with real problems is what made the subject interesting. The policy arguments flow from evaluating those impacts against a moral and political framework: what are the respective roles of the family and the State in looking after and supporting those who cannot look after themselves? How best can the law

---

[19] As Justices O'Regan and Cameron in the South African Constitutional Court pointed out in their dissenting opinion in *State* v. *Manamela*, CCT 25/99, Judgment of 14 April 2000, citing A. Honoré, *Responsibility and Fault* (Oxford, 1999), pp. 34–7 and 122–5.
[20] On which Peter Bromley and I have disagreed: cf. *Family Law*, 5th edn., 1976, p. 193 (but not repeated in the 6th edn.) and S. Atkins and B. Hoggett, *Women and the Law* (Oxford, 1984), p. 128.
[21] Exemplified by Stephen Cretney, *Principles of Family Law*, 1st edn. (London, 1974).

define and enforce the responsibility of individual family members towards one another, their children and their old folk? Once again, these academic debates are often mirrored in disagreements between the judges: there is no doubt that current views in the Court of Appeal on the economic relationship created by marriage are at odds with those of the House of Lords.[22] Once again, however, judges rarely enter into extra-curial debate with one another about such questions.[23]

There are many other kinds of legal scholarship. Legal philosophers ask the underlying questions about what law is. But they also ask questions about what it should be: or at least about an organising principle which would help us to decide what it should be. Their whole project is to develop a personal philosophy. A further development involves subjecting either the 'law in books' or the 'law in action', or both, to a penetrating critique from a particular theoretical perspective. The most obvious examples in recent years have been 'law and economics', critical legal studies, and feminism. Although there are many different perspectives in feminism, as Judith Resnik has said:[24]

> Feminist theories share a view that much of women's experiences of their lives has been omitted in the standard scholarly and popular descriptions of the world. A major shared premise is that knowledge of the world is constructed from one's viewpoint and that what has been assumed (by some) as a universal viewpoint is, in fact, a viewpoint of some men, who have articulated a vision of reality and claimed it to be true for us all.

The legal scholar is also expected to instruct and inspire her students. Because we know that the law is not a set of rigid rules, but is contingent and negotiable, we want to imbue our students with a sense of the excitement of discovery: discovery, not only of how to 'do' law in the technical sense, but also of how to think about the law and the purpose of law, either in general or in the particular subject under discussion. There have always been excellent teachers who can communicate a 'good set of notes' which the students can take away and learn in order to pass the examinations. But the real jurists are those who can communicate something more: and that something more is a point of view. The point of view may

---

[22] Witness the call for reform from the Court of Appeal in *Charman* v. *Charman* [2007] EWCA Civ 503, [2007] 1 FLR 1246, [2007] 2 FCR 217, paras. 106 ff., after the House of Lords' decision in *Miller* v. *Miller; McFarlane* v. *McFarlane* [2006] UKHL 24, [2006] 2 AC 618, [2006] 3 All ER 1.
[23] A recent exception is the debate between Lord Hoffmann and Lord Steyn on the relationship between the judiciary and the other branches of government: see J. Steyn, 'Deference: a tangled tale' [2005] *Public Law* 346.
[24] 'On the Bias', p. 1906.

be very hazy and undeveloped when the jurist starts the intellectual journey. It may go down some blind alleys or take some wrong turnings along
the way.[25] It may even experience a Damascene conversion when the light
dawns. But on the whole it will develop along consistent and foreseeable
lines. It will be transparent and articulated. Legal scholar A should be
able to write a learned piece on the legal philosophy of legal scholar B. In
such a world, consistency and predictability are a virtue, not a criticism.

The same goes for the other legal world which I have inhabited. The
Law Commission is a statutory body whose mission is the reform of the
law.[26] It looks to over-turn ancient anomalies and injustices, to promote a
coherent and principled body of law. It requires a vision of what the law
should be. It was meant to deal in so-called 'lawyers' law', those parts of
the common (and some statute) law which were important to lawyers
and their clients but not to government departments. From the start,
however, it dealt in family law and long before my time had developed a
collective point of view: a point of view which tried to redress centuries
of inequality between the rights of husband and wives, between the children of married and unmarried parents, and latterly between the able
minded and people with mental disorders and disabilities. This translated
into something I would describe as recognisably feminist, with its concern
to see the world through other eyes than those of the traditionally
empowered.

It was a point of view entirely in tune with my own earlier academic
work, on mental health,[27] on children,[28] on the family,[29] and on women
and the law.[30] In the academic world, and even in the Law Commission, I
never had any qualms about describing myself as a feminist.[31] Feminism
is quite a new word, let alone a new idea. The 1928 edition of the *Oxford
English Dictionary* called it 'rare' and defined it as 'the qualities of
females'. Obviously, it was not then thought of as a philosophy or a point

---

[25] As Jack Beatson observed in his obituary of Peter Birks, 'Birks coupled the clarity and certainty with which he advanced his ideas with a willingness to reconsider, even radically alter, his
position, and to state his new position with equal firmness . . .', *The Guardian*, 16 July 2004.
[26] Law Commissions Act 1965, s 1(1); fleshed out in s 3(1).
[27] B. M. Hoggett, *Mental Health Law*, 1st edn. (London, 1975, 4th edn., 1996).
[28] B. M. Hoggett, *Parents and Children*, 1st edn. (London, 1976, 4th edn., 1994).
[29] B. M. Hoggett and D. S. Pearl, *The Family, Law and Society: Cases and Materials*, 1st edn.
(London, 1982); 6th edn., by B. M. Hale, D. S. Pearl, E. J. Cooke and D. Monk (forthcoming
2008).
[30] Atkins and Hoggett, *Women and the Law*.
[31] Others might describe me as a pretty lukewarm and under-educated feminist but that is beside
the point.

of view but as a state of affairs. Feminism was not something which people, whether women or men, might believe in but something which women, and presumably only women, had. By 1933, however, things had moved on. The 'rare' was deleted and a new definition added: 'The opinions and principles of the advocates of the extended recognition of the achievements and claims of women; advocacy of women's rights.'[32] By 1972, however, this second definition has been refined to: 'advocacy of the rights of women (based on the theory of the equality of the sexes)'. That is the definition repeated in the current 1989 edition. It also defines a 'feminist' as 'an advocate of feminism'.

These definitions have several layers. The first is a theory that men and women are equal (whatever that complex concept might mean). The next is a belief in that theory. The next is the recognition that the equality of men and women is not adequately provided for in human institutions. And the final layer is translating that belief and that recognition into advocacy of the rights of women. Feminist scholars would have no difficulty in acknowledging all of that—though they might differ in their definitions of equality, in their analyses of the inequalities of human institutions, and in their prescriptions, if any, for a more equal world.

But in the light of Lord Bingham's lecture, I am bound to ask myself, how far is it possible to hold such a point of view and do a proper job as a judge? It will be understood that I am using feminism here simply as an example of all the other points of view of the kind listed by Lord Bingham—conservative, liberal, libertarian or whatever. I choose it because it is the one which I know best and the one which I try to espouse. There is another reason, most eloquently voiced by Sandra Berns: 'Why . . . is it still suggested that, in some matters at least, a black judge or a woman judge would be somehow biased while a white male judge would be impartial and neutral?' In a footnote she observes: 'To have one's identity transformed into a source of bias, of partiality is to be excluded, not only from the judiciary but from all forms of normal human intercourse. The silencing inherent in such claims is, it seems to me, a casting out, a sense of thrownness, an absolute exclusion from even the possibility of being authoritative.'[33] The very notion of objectivity is suspect but liable to drown out what is seen as a minority opinion.

---

[32] How intriguing that the first source quoted, from *Athenaeum*, 27 April 1895, reads: 'Her intellectual evolution and her coquettings with the doctrines of "feminism" are traced with real humour.' Apparently women flirt with theories as well as with men.

[33] *To Speak as a Judge: Difference, Voice and Power* (Aldershot, 1999), p. 8 and n. 20. For a review of cases of allegations of bias against Australian, Canadian and American female judges, see

Let me begin with the easy answers. There can be nothing wrong with a judge believing in the equality of the sexes. Indeed, I suspect that all my colleagues would say that they do so and so they should. Democracy itself is founded in the belief in equal freedom: 'democracy values everyone equally even if the majority does not'.[34] But whereas freedom is an idea which has been around for a long time and which the judges think they know well,[35] equality is a much more recent arrival on the legal scene. It found its way into the United States Constitution through the Fourteenth Amendment but it cannot be said that the Supreme Court revealed any real understanding of what it might mean until after the Second World War.[36] The equal rights of men and women were proclaimed in the pre-ambles to the Charter of the United Nations in 1945 and to the Universal Declaration of Human Rights in 1948. They were given legal force in international law in Article 3 of the International Covenant on Civil and Political Rights and of its sister Covenant on Economic, Social and Cultural Rights in 1966. They were fleshed out in the Convention on the Elimination of All Forms of Discrimination against Women (CEDAW) in 1979. This acknowledges that some differences of treatment may be necessary to redress historic disadvantage. The United Kingdom is a party to all of these, although they are not directly incorporated into domestic law.

However, equality of the sexes was a founding principle of what has now become the European Union, and this was a large part of the motivation for our domestic Equal Pay Act 1970 and Sex Discrimination Act 1975. It is also explicit in the European Convention on Human Rights, Article 14 of which guarantees to everyone the enjoyment of the rights and freedoms it defines without discrimination on grounds, among other things, of sex. The European Treaties do, in their different ways and different spheres, form part of the domestic law of the United Kingdom. I do not say that it would be impossible for a person who did not believe in the equality of the sexes to be a judge under our modern legal system. But it is not only acceptable but also easier to be a judge if one's fundamen-

---

R. Graycar, 'The gender of judgments: some reflections on "bias"', *University of British Columbia Law Review*, 32 (1998), 1. For the story of a woman judge treated in a way in which it is said that no man would have been treated, see Rosemary Hunter, 'Fear and loathing in the Sunshine State', *Australian Feminist Studies*, 19 (2004), 145.

[34] *Ghaidan* v. *Godin-Mendoza* [2004] UKHL 30, [2004] 2 AC 357, [2004] 3 All ER 411, para. 132.
[35] See e.g., *A and Others* v. *Secretary of State for the Home Department* [2004] UKHL 56, [2005] 2 AC 68, [2005] 3 All ER 169, *per* Lord Hope of Craighead, para. 108.
[36] R. Singh, 'Equality—the neglected virtue?' [2004] *European Human Rights Law Review* 141.

tal beliefs accord with the fundamental principles of the Constitution and legal system one is there to serve.

Are there some beliefs which it would be impossible for a judge to hold and still do a proper job as a judge? Today, for a judge publicly to profess a belief in witches and witchcraft might well raise eyebrows as well as doubts about his fitness for office. But in 1665, my far more learned and distinguished namesake, Sir Matthew Hale, told a jury 'that there were such creatures as witches he made no doubt at all; For first, the scriptures had affirmed so much. Secondly, the wisdom of all nations had provided laws against such persons, which is an argument of their confidence of such a crime. And such hath been the judgement of this kingdom, as appears by that act of Parliament which hath provided punishments proportionable to the quality of the offence.'[37] The last ground is sufficient in itself, then and now. The task of judging frequently requires the judge to uphold a law in the wisdom or justice of which he does not believe. In these days, the persistence of the death penalty in countries which also preserve a right of appeal to the Judicial Committee of the Privy Council presents a problem for at least some of the judges in that court. We were all appointed after the death penalty had in practice been abolished in the United Kingdom and most of us were appointed after the United Kingdom had ratified the Sixth Protocol to the European Convention on Human Rights of 1983, concerning the abolition of the death penalty. When Christmas Humphreys became an Old Bailey judge more than fifty years ago, it was agreed that he should be excused from trying cases in which he might have to impose the death penalty because he was a devout Buddhist. But generally speaking there is no conscience clause for judges. We have no right to opt in and out of particular cases in accordance with our conscientious objections to particular laws. The Employment Appeal Tribunal has recently held that a magistrate was not entitled to be excused from hearing cases in which he might be obliged to place a child with a homosexual couple even if this was contrary to his religious or philosophical beliefs.[38] We have all sworn impartially to administer justice according to law. As Lord Bingham put it in the first Pilgrim Fathers' lecture (before we had the Human Rights Act to give us

---

[37] Trial of Rose Cullender and Amy Duny, *State Trials*, Vol. VI, cols. 687–702, at 699–701. Alan Cromartie, suggests that he may have had 'a certain subsequent uneasiness': *Sir Matthew Hale, Law, religion and natural philosophy* (Cambridge, 1995), p. 239.

[38] *McClintock* v. *Department for Constitutional Affairs*, Appeal No. UKEAT/0223/07/CEA, handed down 31 Oct. 2007.

a more nuanced answer): 'If Parliament were clearly and unambiguously to enact, however improbably, that a defendant convicted of a prescribed crime should suffer mutilation, or branding, or exposure in the public pillory, there would be very little a judge could do about it—except resign.'[39] It is the connection between the judge's beliefs and how she goes about her judging which is what matters, not the beliefs themselves.

Nor can there be anything wrong in a judge believing that there should be more women judges, especially in the higher, law-making, ranks of the judiciary. Not long ago, it was thought regrettable that there were so few, but inevitable because there were so few in the senior ranks of the legal profession from whom the judges were recruited. A former Lord Chief Justice, Lord Taylor, said in his Dimbleby lecture of 1992, 'I have no doubt that the balance will be redressed in the next few years.'[40] Fifteen years later, however, women are still less than 10 per cent of the senior judiciary. To provoke more effort for change, it is necessary to make the positive case for judicial diversity: specifically, that a more diverse judiciary becomes a *better* judiciary.

There are both symbolic and substantive aspects to this. In a democracy, the people should be able to look to the judiciary as 'their' judges, not some alien aristocracy set to rule over them. Such a view comes naturally to the peoples of republics such as the United States of America, with a Constitution which opens with the words 'We the people . . .'. It may come less naturally to the people of a monarchy with an unwritten Constitution such as ours. Hierarchy still plays a much greater part in our lives than we would like to think. I have argued elsewhere that, however much some people may rail against the old fashioned, out of touch judges with their wigs and gowns and their glasses on the ends of their noses, others instinctively feel more comfortable with the judicial stereotype— anonymous, dehumanised, impartial, authoritative and intrinsically male.[41] But we too are a constitutional democracy. If equality is an important democratic principle, then one section of society should not be set in judgement over everyone else.

The substantive argument is more difficult: I have also argued that we should not expect individual women or minority judges to 'make a

---

[39] Sir Thomas Bingham, 'Anglo-American Reflections', Inaugural Pilgrim Fathers Lecture, 29 Oct. 1994; published in Tom Bingham, *The Business of Judging: Selected Essays and Speeches* (Oxford, 2000), part 6, chap. 2.
[40] Taylor of Gosforth, 'The Judiciary in the Nineties', Dimbleby lecture, BBC, 1992.
[41] 'Equality and the Judiciary: Why should we want more women judges?' [2001] *Public Law* 489.

difference'.[42] Along with many other senior women judges from around the world, however, I do believe that a more diverse judiciary will be a better judiciary.[43] Diversity of background and experience enriches the law. Women lead different lives from men, largely because we have visibly different bodies from men. This is not to say that all women are the same, any more than that all men are the same. Some women may lead lives which are very close to men's and (less plausibly) vice versa. But by and large, the interaction between our own internal sense of being a woman and the outside world's perception of us as women leads to a different set of everyday and lifetime experiences.[44] The same is true for other visible minorities. It is just as important that these different experiences should play their part in shaping and administering the law as the experiences of a certain class of men have played for centuries. They will not always make a difference but sometimes they will and should. This is all the more important at present, when equality principles are by no means fully embedded or achieved. People who have experienced their own personal humiliations can bring that experience to the humiliations of others.

This is only an aspect of the argument for diversity of judicial 'mentality', for background and experience are part of what goes to shape that mentality.[45] As Justice Felix Frankfurter of the United States Supreme Court accepted, a person 'brings his whole experience, his training, his outlook, his social, intellectual and moral environment with him when he takes a seat on the supreme bench'.[46] And as Justice Cardozo argued, 'out of the attrition of diverse minds there is beaten something which has a

---

[42] Ibid.; also Kate Malleson, 'Justifying gender equality on the bench: why difference won't do' (2003) 11 *Feminist Legal Studies* 1.

[43] e.g. Justice Claire L'Heureux-Dube. 'Making a difference: the pursuit of a compassionate justice', Address to the International Bar Association, Amsterdam, 20 Sept. 2000; Chief Justice Beverley McLachlin, 'Promoting gender equality in the judiciary', Seminar to the Association of Women Barristers, 2 July 2003; Brenda Hale, 'Making a difference? why we need a more diverse judiciary' (2005) 56 *Northern Ireland Law Quarterly* 281.

[44] Justice Albie Sachs, of the Constitutional Court of South Africa, tells how his colleague, Justice Yvonne Mokgoro, remarked in the course of argument in a case about whether the police owed a duty of care to later victims of a dangerous man given bail, 'if I get into a lift, I'm on my own and a man gets in, and we are alone together, I feel apprehensive': speech to the Sixth National Conference of the Discrimination Law Association, London, Dec. 2005.

[45] Basil Markesinis, 'Judicial mentality: mental disposition or outlook as a factor impeding recourse to foreign law', *Tulane Law Review*, 80 (2006), 1325.

[46] Ibid. 1333, quoting Philip Elman (ed.), *Of Law and Men: Papers and Addresses of Felix Frankfurter* (Hamden, CT, 1956), pp. 40–1.

constancy and uniformity and average value greater than its component elements'.[47]

This is, of course, a particular feature of appellate courts, where groups of judges come together to decide the hard cases. They may try to reach consensus or at least a plurality view. But in the common law world there is also a thriving tradition of judicial dissent: we do not pretend that the answers are always easy and clear cut. We explain why we have difficulty agreeing with the answers given by our colleagues.[48] Introducing different perspectives may help to develop new understandings. My view of the law of duress, speaking as a 'reasonable but comparatively weak and fearful grandmother',[49] was slightly different from my colleagues'—I would have allowed the battered wife who stays with her husband although she expects to be forced to cook the dinner, wash the dishes, iron the shirts and submit to sexual intercourse to plead duress when she is unexpectedly forced to handle stolen goods, store illegal drugs, or commit some other crime. I may have been a minority opinion on the court but I wonder whether I was a minority opinion in the country? A minority opinion may be tempered by the views of the majority,[50] but sometimes it must be voiced. Out of today's minority opinion can sometimes come the orthodoxy of tomorrow.[51]

Nor should one underestimate the importance of diversity in the body of trial judges. Trial judging, whether in criminal trials where the jury and not the judge is the finder of fact or in civil cases where the judge is also the finder of fact, is a much under-researched area.[52] A judge who understands relative powerlessness can bring that understanding to her task. This is not the knee jerk assumption that the alleged victim must be telling the truth. But it could be a deeper understanding of her behaviour, both in and out of the witness box. It could be a refusal to rely upon stereotypical assumptions about the relations between the sexes: is it really the case (as a senior circuit judge told me when I was starting out

---

[47] Benjamin Cardozo, *The Nature of the Judicial Process*, first pub. 1921 (New Haven, CT, 1961), p. 177.

[48] The virtues of the common law tradition are eloquently explained by Justice Michael Kirby in 'Judicial dissent—common law and civil law traditions' (2007) 123 *Law Quarterly Review* 379.

[49] *R v. Hasan* [2005] UKHL 22, [2005] 2 AC 467, [2005] 4 All ER 685, para. 73.

[50] A perception I owe, among many other things, to my legal assistant, Corinna Ferguson.

[51] See that great feminist judge Claire L'Heureux-Dube, 'The dissenting opinion: voice of the future?' (2000) 38 *Osgoode Hall Law Journal* 495.

[52] But see T. Bingham, 'The Judge as juror: the judicial determination of factual issues', in *The Business of Judging*.

on my judicial career) that a wife who has had an accident in her husband's car will always be covering up the truth? Such a judge could also
bring a more determined effort to ensuring that the trial itself is fair: that
a fair opportunity is given to the witnesses on both sides to give their best
evidence. Judge Learned Hand wrote this of the process of judging:[53]

> Of course, you must have impartiality. What do I mean by impartiality? I mean
> you mustn't introduce yourself, your own preconceived notions about what is
> right. You must try, as far as you can—it's impossible for human beings to do
> so absolutely, but just so far as you can—not to interject your own personal
> interests, even your own preconceived assumptions and beliefs.

Patricia Cain rewrote this advice from a feminist perspective:[54]

> When you listen as a judge, you must transcend your sense of self, so that you
> can really listen. Listen to the story that is being told. Do not prejudge it. Do
> not say this is not part of my experience. Find some small part of your own self
> that is like the Other's story. Identify with the Other. Do not contrast. Only
> when you have really listened, and only then, should you judge.

Of course, that means that women judges, who have not had the experience of being male, to whom the male is the Other, should listen just as
carefully to the male stories as they do to the female. The message is a universal one: do not reject a story out of hand because it does not conform
to your own experience or assumptions. If there are judges whose experiences are those of the Other, that can in time reduce the power of the
dominant stories.

In criminal trials, properly protecting the prosecution witnesses while
allowing the defence properly to deploy its case is a hugely demanding
task. It is so much easier to sit back and let defence counsel rip. It is also
much safer: appellate courts do not usually have the opportunity to criticise trial judges for failing to protect vulnerable witnesses properly; but
they have plenty of opportunities to criticise trial judges for 'descending
into the arena' and intervening too much. Enabling all the witnesses, on
either side, to give their best evidence is a much more radical idea than
one might think. I am not at all surprised that Professor Rosemary
Hunter's feminist trial judge friend, spending her working life presiding
over rape, sexual assault and child abuse cases, suggested that a feminist
judge is 'bloody tired'.[55] But the process of enabling witnesses to give

---

[53] *The Spirit of Liberty*, pp. 309–10.
[54] Cain, 'Good and bad bias', 1955.
[55] Rosemary Hunter, 'What (or who) is a feminist judge?', Paper presented at the Joint Annual
Meeting of the LSA and RCSL, Humboldt University, Berlin, 25–8 July 2007.

their best evidence, of listening carefully to the stories being told even if alien to one's own experience, can only enhance the fairness of the trial. A feminist trial should be a fairer trial.

Diverse judges can also make a difference in their interaction with their fellow judges. It becomes harder to give voice to sexist or racist views if there is a woman or a minority ethnic judge around the lunch table, no longer a servant but an equal. Better still, perhaps, if they are voiced and can then be challenged. A real virtue of diversity, as Justice Kate O'Regan of the South African Constitutional Court has put it,[56] is that one can begin to interrogate one another's prejudices and assumptions.

So, ideally, here we are with a collection of judges, diverse in their gender, ethnicity, background, experiences both in and out of the law, their mentality and approaches to judging; but alike in their knowledge of and training in the law and legal reasoning, and true to their judicial oaths, to 'do right to all manner of people after the laws and usages of this realm, without fear or favour, affection or ill-will'. Learning from one another, they can become a more complete judicial body than they were before.

But all those advantages do not tell us whether it is permissible to bring a feminist, or any other kind of '-ist', approach to the result of the case. As with the trial process, this cannot be a problem if all it entails is a deeper understanding of what the case is about. If a family judge understands how difficult it will be for a particular woman to re-establish herself in the labour market (and conversely, how easy it will be for another woman to do so), then she can quite properly exercise her discretion to award ancillary relief accordingly.[57] If an employment tribunal chair understands what it feels like for a school dinner lady to receive a letter warning her that to pursue her entirely justified equal pay claim may threaten not only her colleagues' jobs but also the school meals service offered to disadvantaged children, she may quite properly decide that it has crossed the border between permissible attempts to settle the case and impermissible victimisation.[58] This does not mean relying only upon one's own experiences, but taking steps to try and learn more about the experience of the Other generally. That is why the Judicial Studies Board publishes an *Equal Treatment Bench Book*. As Rosemary Hunter says, 'such

---

[56] Miriam Rothschild and John Foster Human Rights Trust Lecture, 'The challenge of change: judging under South Africa's new Constitution', London, University College, 23 Oct. 2007.

[57] *Barrett* v. *Barrett* [1988] 2 FLR 16, [1988] FCR 707; *SRJ* v. *DWJ (financial provision)* [1999] 2 FLR 176, [1999] 3 FCR 153.

[58] *Derbyshire* v. *St Helen's Metropolitan Borough Council* [2007] UKHL 16, [2007] ICR 90, [2007] 3 All ER 81.

an approach to fact finding arguably would perfect rather than violate judicial norms of fairness and impartiality'.[59]

This brings us to that part of judging which requires the judge to decide what the law is before deciding how it applies to the particular case. In the hard cases this is mostly the task of appellate courts, although first instance judges, especially in the High Court, are not exempt. What part can personal philosophy play here? By this I mean something more than the 'mentality' which is the product of the judge's background and experiences. I mean a consistent and coherent point of view. It seems to me that this too should present no problem, provided that two conditions are fulfilled: first that the point of view is consistent with the fundamental principles of the law one is sworn to apply; and secondly that it is carefully and cautiously applied to the issues in the case.

That brand of feminism which simply believes in the equality of the sexes is entirely consistent with fundamental principles. But most feminists would go beyond formal equality and look to the context in which the question arises, would understand that substantive equality involves accommodating difference,[60] and would also take account of historic and systemic disadvantage. That too is simply a deeper understanding of the complexities of equality. Sometimes it is possible to apply that understanding to the case in hand. An example is a case (in which I was not involved) concerned with discrimination against widowed fathers in the social security scheme.[61] Widowed mothers received several benefits which were not available to widowed fathers. The Government had promoted legislation to remove the discrimination: in some cases levelling up to give both the same benefits and in some cases levelling down to deny them to either. Did this mean that the earlier discrimination could not be justified? The Court of Appeal decided that it did. The House of Lords, however, accepted that the discrimination had been justified on the basis of the historical disadvantage of mothers in the market place and that it was a matter of judgement when that disadvantage had sufficiently disappeared. But that was a case under Article 14 of the European Convention on Human Rights; domestic anti-discrimination law may not always permit such sensitive accommodation to inherited difference.

---

[59] 'What (or Who) is a Feminist Judge?', 14.

[60] Perhaps more readily understood in the disability discrimination context, see *Archibald* v. *Fife Council* [2004] UKHL 32, [2004] ICR 954, [2004] 4 All ER 303.

[61] *R (Hooper)* v. *Secretary of State for Work and Pensions* [2005] UKHL 29, [2005] 1 WLR 1681, [2006] 1 All ER 487.

Outside the realms of formal equality and discrimination law, there are issues on which it is entirely permissible to look for substantively equal treatment: allowing women the same autonomy as men in sexual and reproductive choices, recognising that to cause a woman to have a child she never meant to have is not only a gross invasion of her autonomy and bodily integrity but also imposes upon her long term caring obligations towards the child;[62] realising the harmful effect which violence towards the mother can have, not only on the mother, but also on the child;[63] and calculating the real life time costs of time away from the labour market for child and other family care.[64] In cases such as these, it is possible to give voice to a distinctively female point of view without in any way transgressing the norms of judicial behaviour. These are all examples of using permissible and accepted forms of judicial reasoning to arrive at a conclusion which accords with permissible and acceptable underlying principles. All judges select from the available and permissible sources what factors they will rely upon in reaching their judgments. In the truly hard cases legal reasoning can take us in more than one direction. The direction we choose is bound to be guided by some deeper level of principle. If a female judge also chooses to tell the same story in a different way from the male,[65] this can also enrich the collective mix.

But alongside consistency with legal principle, I would suggest that the reasoning used in support of a result which reflects one's own point of view should be of the minimalist rather than the perfectionist or fundamentalist variety. I am with Sunstein here. Most of the time, it is dangerous to do more than is required to decide the case in hand. It is even more dangerous if that is done in pursuit of some grand design. A point of view is not the same as an agenda. If that makes me a feminist minimalist, I am in some very good company. Like Learned Hand, I try not to be too sure that I am right.

---

[62] *Parkinson v. St James and Seacroft University Hospital NHS Trust* [2001] EWCA Civ 530, [2002] QB 266, [2001] 3 All ER 97.

[63] *Re D (contact: reasons for refusal)* [1997] 2 FLR 48, [1998] 1 FCR 147; *Re L (a child) (contact: domestic violence)* [2001] Fam 268, [2000] 4 All ER 609.

[64] *Miller v. Miller, McFarlane v. McFarlane* [2006] UKHL 24, [2006] 2 AC 618, [2006] 3 All ER 1.

[65] As Erica Rackley has suggested that I did in the harrowing case of *N v. Secretary of State for the Home Department* [2005] UKHL 31, [2005] 2 AC 296, [2005] 4 All ER 1017.

'We keep the bread and wine for show'[1]— Consistent Irony and Reluctant Faith in the Poetry of Dannie Abse

TONY CURTIS

University of Glamorgan

DANNIE ABSE had his first collection of poetry accepted by Hutchinson in 1946 when he was a medical student in London. Although he wishes few of those early Dylan-esque pieces to survive, he has gone on to publish poetry, fiction and creative non-fiction for sixty years, mainly with Hutchinson. Despite that fact, despite the continuing success of his autobiographical novel *Ash on a Young Man's Sleeve*,[2] which has remained in print since 1954, Dannie Abse is a writer who has not received the critical attention which he deserves. I will talk about Abse's early activities as editor of the magazine *Poverty and Poetry* in the 1950s and as a member of the 'Mavericks' group of poets; also his roles as doctor and poet; wearing both 'the white and purple coat';[3]

White Coat, Purple Coat

White coat and purple coat
  a sleeve from both he sews.
That white is always stained with blood,
  that purple by the rose.

Read at the Academy 25 October 2007.

[1] *New and Collected Poems 1948–98* (London, 2003).

[2] London, 1954.

[3] The poet talks of his nearly giving up on his medical studies to pursue a full-time literary career in *The Presence* (London, 2007).

Proceedings of the British Academy **154**, 337–360. © The British Academy 2008.

And phantom rose and blood most real
   compose a hybrid style;
white coat and purple coat
   few men can reconcile.

White coat and purple coat
   can each be worn in turn
but in the white a man will freeze
   and in the purple burn.[4]

That final image undercuts those traditional strategies of the inversion of syntax and the end-focusing of the main clause: this emphasises those issues of 'duality' which the poet himself recognises:

The first voice cries: 'He's not what he seems,'
but the second one sighs: 'He is what he is,'
then one shouts 'wine' and the other screams 'bread',
. . . Now, now, I hang these masks on the wall.
Oh Time, take one and leave me all
lest four tears from two eyes fall.[5]

I will discuss the tensions between those roles and examine the ways in which the writer's identity as Londoner and a Cardiff Welshman also underpins his work.[6] In 1986, no doubt on a visit to support both his family and Cardiff City Football Club, Abse 'popped in' to Llandaff Cathedral: 'Inside soaring spaces of worship—Jewish, Muslim or Christian—I feel not just secular but utterly estranged like one without history or memory.' He stops before 'Epstein's dominating aluminium resurrected Christ' and admires the Lady Chapel's reredos and its 'gold-leafed wreaths of wild flowers'. But it is later that weekend, standing in his pyjamas under the 'opera-dramatic clouds' at Ogmore-on-Sea, with the knowledge that from the east 'a cancer sailed in from Chernobyl', that 'my own lips moved'.[7] Four years later he attended fellow poet John Ormond's funeral there and thought the Epstein to be 'a little less domi-nant'; it is the memory of the man which affects him, not the magnifi-

---

[4] *New and Collected Poems 1948–98* (London, 2003) Most of the poems quoted from are in this volume, though original collections are listed below. His *Collected Poems 1948–1988* (London, 1989) was, in fact, given the sub-title *White Coat, Purple Coat*. This poem is recited by the char-acter Pythagoras in the play 'Pythagoras (Smith)' *The View from Row G, Three Plays* Dannie Abse, introduction by James A. Davies (Bridgend, 1995).

[5] *Tenants of the House* (London, 1957).

[6] Abse subscribes to, amongst other publications, both *The London Review of Books* and the Cardiff City Football Club fanzine.

[7] Educated at a Cardiff Catholic Grammar, he returned home one day to ask, 'Who's Jesus Price, mama?' *A Poet in the Family* (London, 1974, later included in *Goodbye, Twentieth Century*).

cence of the cathedral.[8] Abse is a spiritual poet, not a poet of religion: '. . . the dull prayers of dead religious maniacs, symbols that have often lost their potency and restrictive disciplines . . . they are barriers, not bridges . . . I have said earlier that Auschwitz made me more of a Jew than Moses did . . .'.[9]

Dannie Abse's Jewish family background was part orthodox, part secular: from an early age he resolutely chooses to be secular:

> When Bernice Rubens attempted to enrol me in a Zionist youth movement I declined . . . We were both Jewish, both Welsh, though in her memoir Bernice Rubens judgmentally insists, 'Dannie Abse, a Cardiffian like myself, but far more Welsh than I . . . his Jewishness strictly secondary.'[10]

But in his writing he addresses those issues of faith, anger and compassion compelled by the events of the twentieth century, Abse's century, the century of particular Jewish tragedy:

> Goodbye, 20th Century.
>
> What should I mourn?
> Hiroshima, Auschwitz?
> . . .
> Goodbye, 20th Century,
> your trumpets and your drums,
> your war-wounds still unhealed.
> Goodbye, I-must-leave-you-Dolly,
> goodbye Lily Marlene.
> Has the Past always a future?
> Will there always be
> a jackboot on the stair,
> a refugee to roam?[11]

Though Abse is not simply a public poet: as he says, '. . . there is hardly an important occasion in my life that is not covertly profiled or overtly inhabited in my poetry'.[12] Dannie Abse was born in 1923 in Cardiff, the last of four children. His father, Rudolph, was the manager and part-owner of cinemas in the Valleys and his mother, Kate Shepherd, 'the prettiest girl in the Swansea Valley',[13] from a more orthodox family, was a fluent speaker of both Welsh and Hebrew. When his grandfather

[8] 'In Llandaff Cathedral', in *Goodbye, Twentieth Century: an Autobiography* (London, 2001).
[9] Ibid.
[10] *The Presence* (London, 2007), p. 44.
[11] 'A letter from Ogmore-on-Sea', in *Arcadia, One Mile* (London, 1998).
[12] Ibid.
[13] See *Contemporary Authors: Biographical Series* ed. D. Bryfonski (Detroit, 1984).

preached in Ystalyfera, 'David spoke to Dafydd'. Abse's childhood and family life are more reflected upon, more refracted, the subject of more variations of interpretation, than those of any other writer from Wales. Of his father he has written:

> When he was gay he told jokes; when moodily sad he would take down his violin and, with eyes closed like a lover, play Kreisler's 'Humoresque' until he became, for all the grey and green world of Wales, a model for Chagall.[14]

His family members, particularly the men, are larger-than-life, expressive, ebullient figures who become characters in his fiction and poetry and auto-biographical writings: Leo, the oratorical politician and writer; Wilfred, the successful psychoanalyst; Uncle Isidore, another Chagall-esque fiddler flying over grim roofs. Abse's family and upbringing are a destiny caught between the two poles of rational thought and medical skill and the dreams and ideals of politics, the music of words. Formal religious faith may have been dissipated in the dark mid-century, but to survive and prosper through that century an ironic sensibility and a deep need to believe in the greater purpose of life have been essential.

In *Ash on a Young Man's Sleeve*,[15] Abse fictionalised his boyhood and early manhood years in Cardiff. But he did grow up in a warm, support-ive and highly stimulating family: brothers Wilfred and Leo were exem-plars of energy and intellect in medicine and the law and politics. The clash of ideologies and the rise of Fascism in the 1930s were debated in that household. The two decades of *entre deux guerres* are haunted by horrors past and materialising threats. The young boy's Auntie Cecile and Uncle Bertie never lock their front door in case their son Clive should eventually return from the Great War: this is a figure that reappears as 'Cousin Sidney', actually missing in combat at Dunkirk, in a later poem.

The impressionable boy is taken by Leo to the Memorial Meeting for Jimmy Ford, a Cardiff man who has died fighting Franco in Spain. He hears that 'The Fifteenth Brigade, ragtime idealists, advanced; but Jimmy Ford lay horizontal, akimbo, on the dusty road near the tobacco fields, the vision of a white deserted farmhouse leaking out of his surprised eyes'.[16]

Despite his youth Dannie understands the significance of this loss and the political context of armed struggle; he wishes do something to help:

---

[14] *A Poet in the Family*.
[15] London, 1954.
[16] *Ash on a Young Man's Sleeve* (London, 1954).

If I was bigger perhaps I could go to Spain. It was worth fighting for. Maybe if I got killed they'd have a memorial meeting for me. It was very sad all these young men dying. One week Leo would show me a short story by Ralph Fox in *Left Review*. The next week there would be his obituary. There'd been an article by Christopher Caudwell, then a week later his obituary also. One week a poem by John Cornford, the next another obituary, and so on and so on. Nobody seemed to care except Leo and some of his friends.

He writes later of reading the Spanish poet Miguel Hernandez 'with rapt and growing anger',[17] though he also recognised that 'Righteous the rhetoric of indignation, | but protesting poems, like the plaster angels, | are impotent'. He remembers, too, his disaffection from 'the fashionable "pink" poets of the day—W. H. Auden, Stephen Spender, Louis MacNeice, and Cecil Day Lewis'—who 'were content to compose poems that were ordered carnivals of the interior life . . . to give readers pleasure'. Still, Spender's anthology *Poems for Spain*, published in 1940, had '. . . adult moral concerns and protestations [which] engaged my own schoolboy wrath and indignation'.[18] The young Abse 'owned no religious commitment', but, like the seventeenth-century divine, George Herbert, he 'wanted my poems to change the world'.[19] This was the impulse that would lead to his founding of the alternative poetry magazine *Poetry and Poverty* after the war.

Of course, Dannie Abse was too young to be engaged in active service during the war.[20] He followed his brother Wilfred into medicine and was training in Westminster Hospital as the war was drawing to a close. He speaks of being left out of the assignment of trainees who went to Germany to treat the victims of the death and concentration camps, possibly because he was a Jew. Ironically, after qualifying he was conscripted as a National Serviceman and that led, just as ironically, to his deployment and subsequent civilian career in Mass Radiography in London and his specialising in diseases of the chest. His experiences as a commissioned officer in the RAF were later fictionalised in *Some Corner of an English Field*.[21] The central character, Henderson, gives a confessional speech at his 'dining out' dinner:

---

[17] *A Poet in the Family*, pp. 6–8.
[18] *Contemporary Authors.*
[19] Ibid., pp. 10–11.
[20] For a more detailed examination of Abse's writing on wars see, T. Curtis, '"All Change!" Dannie Abse and the Twentieth Century Wars', in *Wales at War: Critical Essays on Literature and Art*, ed. T. Curtis (Bridgend, 2007).
[21] London, 1956.

> A doctor—but a National Serviceman nevertheless, who has not been quite at ease, quite at home . . . one had to face up to realities. I mean the external reality that is visible around us: the uniforms, the barrage balloons, the homesick faces—the internal reality: the longing to love someone and to be loved, the need for faith in each other and in God, and the terror of longing for something that one can't quite understand . . .

Dannie Abse rose, briefly, to be a Squadron Leader when his commanding officer fell sick, though his experiences of service, as might be expected, were underpinned by boredom and frustration. That slightly inebriated speech by Henderson with its confusion and the need to fix on some certainty beyond the predictable tedium of service life carries the weight of a post-war, post-Holocaust existentialist crisis; it is surely not too far removed from the writer's own feelings and the poems he was writing at that time. It is difficult not to read into Henderson's experiences and attitudes those of the writer.

> Somebody had written: a man's destiny is what he is. That was a lie. Fate was the accident that happened to one, a bomb falling, being called up, conscripted into boredom. It's not what you are that matters so much, thought Henderson, but where you are at a given time. One walked down a dark corridor, with all the vision and wisdom that one had, but if there was an open trapdoor there you fell right through, whoever you were. That was the morality of things, the biological morality of things.[22]

Actual conflict, experienced and imagined, was more acutely realised in the earlier novel: in *Ash on a Young Man's Sleeve* bombs fall in the young Abse's neighbourhood of Roath and his fictional friend Keith is carried dead from the debris. The character of young Abse walks away from that boyhood sobered by the loss: 'Near the air-raid shelters I heard, also, the waterfall crashing down into its disaster and saw, in the harp of wind, pools of rain-water trembling on the gravel pathway, reflecting shuddering fragments of sky. Pieces of sky, water leaves, hands all fallen, falling in the convalescent sunlight.' He strolls back to a 'home that was never to be home again'.[23]

There was no recourse to religious belief in these circumstances; the Abse family's religious observance had swung away from the Shepherds, his mother's family tradition of orthodoxy, to the rational application of medicine and law and the pragmatism of political action. Dannie Abse

---

[22] London, 1956, p. 82.

[23] The young Abse was himself injured when a bomb fell close to his house in Windermere Avenue, Cardiff. See *A Poet in the Family*, pp. 43–4.

has never committed himself to a religious belief: he says, 'As for religion, at sixteen I was happy to believe that when water spurts from rock or a bush spontaneously bursts into flame it is time to consult a physician.'[24] It is as if the dedication to a medical training had pre-empted the possibility of faith through mystery. However, as a writer he is constantly 'startled by the visible' and celebrates with irony and joy the peculiarities of our human world.

Clearly, a childhood spent in the shadow of Fascism and a young adulthood in blitzed Cardiff and London as a medical student would characterise and focus the professional man and the professional writer. The two ladies who occupied the room next to his student digs in Aberdare Gardens, NW6, Mrs Schiff and Mrs Blumenfeld, were refugees from Nazi Germany; only later would he fully realise the roots of their sadness:

> After the war years, I, like so many others, in Britain and elsewhere, learnt more and more about the death camps of Europe. I came to realise that what had happened to the relatives of Blumenfeld and Schiff was something that could not be irrevocably suppressed from consciousness, that in one sense I, too, was a survivor, that I could never encounter a German of a certain age-group without seeing him as a one-time inquisitor, that ordinary smoke towering over autumn gardens could trigger off a vision of concentration camps, false teeth, soap.[25]

Although he qualified after the war, Dannie Abse's training had been almost abandoned. The 'butcher's shop', as he called it, had sickened him; hospital life was 'beginning to feel like being in the First World War trenches', and it was much more exciting to read the poets he lists as 'new to me: Rilke and T. S. Eliot, Dylan Thomas and Alun Lewis' than Conybeare's *Textbook of Medicine*. It was only with Wilfred's support and through his obligation to his father that Dannie completed his training, rather than opting for the life of a full-time writer: the white coat was close to being discarded for the purple coat.

In 1949 Dannie Abse, now qualified as a doctor, started the magazine *Poetry and Poverty*; it had its roots in the Swiss Cottage society, '. . . a remarkably vivid cafe life because of the refugees, mostly Jews, from Austria and Germany',[26] and initially involved two friends, Molly Owen

---

[24] *The Presence*, p. 44.
[25] *A Poet in the Family*, p. 78.
[26] *Contemporary Authors*.

and Godfrey Rubens.[27] The two coffee bars, the Cosmo and the Cordial, were the haunts of Elias Canetti, who had a 'formidable aura and presence', Erich Fried, Lotte Lenya, Rudi Nassauer and others. *Poetry and Poverty* was always polemical and had the intention 'of publishing good poems (naturally) as well as focussing critically on the imaginative poverty of certain well known contemporary writers'. The first issue was duplicated roughly, but sold a thousand copies. It ran for six years and prefigured the *New Lines/Mavericks* rivalry and debate of the later 1950s concerning the form and subject-matter of contemporary poetry. Dannie Abse wanted to argue against what he described as 'The new choir . . . Proudly English they sing with sharp, flat voices | but no-one dances, nobody rejoices'; he preferred the 'Dionysian sin' of Dylan Thomas, the risk-taking of vision and language.[28]

> . . . I did not want to publish civilised, neat poems that ignored the psychotic savagery of twentieth-century life. Why, only the previous decade there had been Auschwitz and Belsen, Hiroshima and Nagasaki—so shouldn't poetry be more vital, angry, rough, urgent—in short, Dionysian? Should not poets write out of an urgent, personal predicament rather than compose neat little, clever exercises?[29]

There was an irony in Abse's and Howard Sergeant's organising of a counter movement to argue against the assumed clubbiness of The Movement and, ultimately, the *Mavericks* venture did not fulfil Abse's desire to promote poems 'written out of the heat of personal predicament and therefore imbued with a strong current of feeling'. He came to see that Alvarez's *The New Poetry* published in 1962 more effectively exemplified the aspirations which he had pursued in the previous decade.

Dannie Abse's work in the decades following the war had, close to its centre, a need to form an objective correlative, narratives and imagery for the mid-century's world war and its subsequent, consequent lurch into the Cold War. Over twenty years later he would characterise the poet's role in the world:

> They were the poems of a much-married man who was almost as happy as possible—yet felt threatened sometimes, and uneasy. For, as a doctor, he was clearly aware of other people's dissatisfactions and suffering. He was increasingly aware, too, of his own mortality—how the apple flesh was always turning

---

[27] Abse has written often of those years, of particular interest is 'a Meeting with Elias Canetti', in *Goodbye, Twentieth Century: an Autobiography* (London, 2001).
[28] 'Enter the Movement', in *A Poet in the Family*, pp. 150–4.
[29] Ibid., p. 153.

brown after the bite. In addition, there were those man-made threats: he took his wife to the Academy Cinema in Oxford Street only to be assaulted by a film about Auschwitz; or he would be exposed to the obscene, derelict war images of Vietnam. There was no running away. Writing poetry, too, was an immersion into common reality not an escape from it.[30]

That visit to the Oxford Street cinema is narrated in the poem 'A Night Out'.[31] Written in the 1960s, it tells of a visit to see 'a new Polish film' about the Holocaust. After the depiction of 'the spotlit drama of our nightmares: | images of Auschwitz almost authentic' and the 'trustful children, no older than our own, | strolling into the chambers without fuss, | while smoke, black and curly, oozed from chimneys'. Dannie and Joan Abse and their friends sip coffee 'in a bored espresso bar nearby' and return home to the comfortable surburbs, where the Abses make love 'in the marital bed'. That act may be phrasing a Kabbalistic belief in the need to rebalance the universe when moral chaos threatens; it is a clear, positive response to the negative images the film has planted in their minds.[32]

The world is healed, to an extent, to its only possible extent, by the union in marriage. 'A Night Out' is significant in the context of Dannie Abse's writing: having spent the war as a medical student, and his National Service in the comparative comfort of a Medic's commission, the writer is interrogating his right, any survivor's right, to re-enact the horrors of the Nazis' Final Solution. He asserts that right, that responsibility, more positively in other, later poems, including, 'Not Beautiful', 'Uncle Isidore', 'Case History', 'One of the Chosen' and 'No More Mozart—*Germany 1970*',[33] in which 'The German streets tonight | are soaped in moonlight . . . And twelve million eyes | in six million heads | stare in the same direction.'

Still, in the 1950s and 1960s the demobbed Dr Abse re-entered civilian life and began to build his professional career and family life; though this was done against the backdrop of the developing Cold War and the increasingly urgent threat of nuclear war. His experiences in the RAF, as well as the growing public discussion of the issues of atomic weapons as the wreckage of European cities and societies being reordered, must have meant that he was particularly aware of the fragile hope of the post-war

---

[30] Ibid., p. 198.
[31] All poems are to be found in *New and Collected Poems* (London, 2003).
[32] This is discussed in more detail by Joseph Cohen in his introduction to *The Poetry of Dannie Abse—Critical Essays and Reminiscences* (London, 1983).
[33] *Funland and Other Poems* (London, 1973).

period. As early as the third collection, *Tenants of the House*,[34] there is a poem which expresses that very real fear of imminent catastrophe, a second holocaust, a nuclear holocaust:

> Oh how much like Europe's Gothic Past!
>   This scene of my nightmare's protoplast:
>   glow of the radioactive worm.
>   Future story of the Blast?

The threat of an impending 'leukaemia in the soul of all' is at the core of a nightmare that, on this occasion, the presence of his wife by his side can not allay and the couplet form can not assuage:

> the grey skin shrivelling from the head
> our two skulls in the double bed,

'Verses at Night' records the deep insecurity of the post-war decade; that was to run in parallel in Dannie Abse's work across the genres with a need to revisit the Nazis' Holocaust; he needs to try again and again to make sense of what had happened in the Concentration and Death camps.

In the same collection 'The Emperors of the Island—*a political parable to be read aloud*' more successfully, because less specifically, creates a trope for the relentlessly destructive nature of humankind:

> There is the story of a deserted island
> where five men walked down to the bay.

One by one they dig a grave and each time one fewer returns until

> Four ghosts dug one grave in the sand,
>   four ghosts stood on the sea wet rock;
> five ghosts moved away.

It is polemical, but works both on the page and in performance because it has a lyrical pattern, and it remains as relevant and effective today as fifty years ago.

In Abse's next collection, *Poems Golders Green*,[35] in 'The Grand View' he deals specifically with the question of mysticism and faith:

> For I, too, am spellbound by the grand view,
> flung through vistas from this windy hill,
> am in pure love. I do not know who
> it is that I love, But I would flow
> into One invisible and still.

[34] London, 1957, repr. 1958 and pub. in the USA, 1959.
[35] London, 1962.

He is drawn to the mystics 'in their far, erotic stance', but has to remain rooted to the actual, to the real world. In natural surroundings particularly he is, Wordsworth-like, touched by the need to open himself to larger, more spiritual forces:

> There are moments when a man must sing
> of a lone Presence he cannot see.
> To undulations of space I bring
> all my love when love is happening;
> green directions flying back to me.
>
> There are moments when a man must praise
> the astonishment of being alive,
> When small mirrors of reality blaze
> into miracles; and there's One always
> who, by never departing, almost arrives.

Here he is close to the position of fellow Welsh poet R. S. Thomas, who bird-watching on the moor, or on the coast, also waits for God, for the small mirrors to blaze into miracles. However, the world in his and our century may have offered us more reality than we can bear and far too few miracles.

That collection also included a response to the release from prison of the collaborator and broadcaster for Mussolini, Ezra Pound—'After the Release of Ezra Pound'. Pound the poet, editor, mentor of T. S. Eliot, was, of course, also the collaborator, supporter of Mussolini. Abse's poem takes the form of a reply to a Paul Potts's poem and his forgiveness of Pound; Abse objects that 'Pound did not hear the raw Jewish cry, | the populations committed to the dark . . .' and that if his journey of release between prison cell and his coffin was surely short

> . . . that ticking distance between
> was merely a journey long enough
> to walk the circumference of a Belsen,
> Walt Whitman would have been eloquent,
> and Thomas Jefferson would have cursed.

He finds it impossible to forgive absolutely. In 'Ezra Pound and my father', a chapter in *A Poet in the Family*, Abse describes how his father would persevere with the crackling signals from Italy and Pound's 'gibberish and rhetoric and near obscenity' because they might glean some alternative news on the progress of the war in which brothers Leo and Wilfred were fighting. That 'lousy anti-semite' uttering the 'ravings of an eccentric poet, the paradox of a sensitive Fascist' and his irritating 'nasal harangue' made an impression in that summer of 1943 quite contrary to the enthusiasm which the young poet had had for the work in Pound's *Selected Poems* borrowed earlier from Cardiff Central Library.[36]

The 'Red Balloon' in the same collection presents an image of anti-semitism from Abse's boyhood and that sense of anger at such racism is continually expressed in his poetry; the most effective, shocking work is 'Case History' with its disarmingly conversational tone and avoidance of a pattern of rhyme:[37]

> 'Most Welshmen are worthless
> an inferior breed, doctor.'
> He did not know I was Welsh.
> Then he praised the architects
> of the German death-camps—
> did not know I was a Jew.
> He called liberals, 'White blacks',
> and continued to invent curses.
>
> When I palpated his liver
> I felt the soft liver of Goering;
> when I lifted my stethoscope
> I heard the heartbeats of Himmler;
> when I read his encephalograph
> I thought, '*Sieg heil, mein Fuhrer.*'
>
> In the clinic's dispensary
> red berry of black bryony,
> cowbane, deadly nightshade, deathcap.
> Yet I prescribed for him
> as if he were my brother.
>
> Later that night I must have slept
> on my arm: momentarily
> my right hand lost its cunning.

The two aspects of Abse the man—doctor and writer, the wearer of the 'white coat and the purple coat'—inform many poems and much of the fiction, autobiography and journal writing; however, there is too the dilemma of the professional doctor who trained through the 1940s and the Jew whose accident of birth meant that he was relatively safe in Britain while the Nazis embarked on their Final Solution to 'the Jewish problem'. At the point of initial qualification the young doctor was not included in the contingent from Westminster Hospital who travelled over to Germany to help with the victims of Belsen and other camps. One of

[36] *Poems Golders Green*, pp. 58–63.
[37] *Ask the Bloody Horse* (London, 1986).

this cohort would almost die as a result of contracting typhus while working to save the fragile survivors of Belsen.

> None of this I knew until much later when I guessed that I was not allowed to join the Belsen team because I was a Jew. Meanwhile, on May 8th, it was Victory Day. With Nan I joined the effervescent singing crowds in Trafalgar Square who were wearing paper hats as at a party.
> I often think about not going to Belsen.[38]

There is regret and an irrational guilt: the grim irony that because he was a Jew Dannie Abse was not a witness, did not almost share the fate of the camp inmates, as his fellow student Hargreaves did, whose month of May 1945 was, in retrospect, a dance macabre, a James Ensor painting. Abse the writer becomes a passionate and angry survivor; of course, the patient in 'Case History' is a collective personification of all those bigots, racists and revisionists who deny the Holocaust and would not stand in the way of another genocide. A doctor's role is to treat patients without prejudice; to treat the symptoms and the sick person in a concerned, but largely objective way. The moral dilemma holds too: at what point may the right hand 'lose its cunning'? And what exactly does that mean? It is ambiguous and deeply unsettling. A touchstone might be Psalm 137: 'If I forget thee O Jerusalem, | let my right hand forget her cunning.' Abse the doctor overrides Abse the Jew: some sort of movement towards healing the wounds of history must take place and the poem succeeds both in expressing his anger, the desire for retribution, and the need to be professionally detached. In both roles, doctor and poet, Dannie Abse wrestles with a moral dilemma, but in each finds resolution through his professional skill.

Perhaps more than any other fact, the wars of his century, our century, form the man and inform the writer. The First World War casts a shadow over the decade of Dannie Abse's boyhood, as does the rise of Fascism and the Spanish Civil War, then the Second World War and its aftermath. 'Three Street Musicians'[39] play '"Roses of Picardy"' and 'now, suddenly, there are too many ghosts about'. In 'Not Beautiful',[40] Doctor Abse gives the lie to a man who'd show optimism in the face of the twentieth-century horrors: '. . . all Hiroshimas, in raw and raving voices, | live skeletons of the Camp, flies hugging faeces, | in war, in famine, he'd

---

[38] *Goodbye Twentieth Century*, pp. 86–7.
[39] *Funland and Other Poems*.
[40] *A Small Desperation* (London, 1968).

find the beautiful.' It's better to feel anger, the poet says: '. . . to curse is more sacred | than to pretend by affirming. And offend.'

The other major elements in this writer's life, his Jewish heritage and his profession as a doctor, are, as I have indicated, implicated in his response to the wars, but, perhaps surprisingly, medicine is not a focus of his poetry until Dannie Abse is in mid-career. 'Case History' was published first in *Ask the Bloody Horse*, his ninth collection, but the first poems directly dealing with his profession and his experiences in hospital appear in his fifth book *A Small Desperation*, over twenty years into his career as a poet. 'Pathology of Colours', one of the strongest of these poems, in fact, is as much a poem of warfare as a poem of medicine:

> . . . the criminal, multi-coloured flash
> of an H-Bomb is no more beautiful
> than an autopsy when the belly's opened—
> to show cathedral windows never opened.
>
> So, in the simple blessing of a rainbow.
> in the bevelled edge of a sunlit mirror.
> I have seen, visible, Death's artefact
> like a soldier's ribbon on a tunic tacked.

It is a Sixties poem, a Cold War poem of trepidation which conflates the worries of Abse the family man, the man whose family members are protesting against The Bomb, with those of Abse the former RAF officer and the doctor who has dealt with disease and death professionally. The promise of a rainbow is the illusion of a refraction of angled glass. What is a rainbow in any case but a watery illusion, an airy phenomenon you can't touch?

> There are those . . . who wish to compartmentalise my occupations of doctor and poet. Oh there's a doctor, here he's a poet. I don't think I'm that divided. Of course I have conflicts, tensions and I do contradict myself. In that I'm like everybody else, and such oppositions within oneself do help to breed poems. Besides, though I start with the visible, I don't know where I'm going to end.[41]

The Maverick must sing with a scalpel in his hand; and Mavericks were 'poets writing from the centre of inner experience'.[42] Dannie Abse came to realise that the apparently opposed sides of his life were one whole: 'Pathology of Colours' proclaims that agenda in a striking and

[41] Interview with Joseph Cohen in *The Poetry of Dannie Abse*.
[42] From Abse's Introduction to the *Mavericks* anthology; quoted from 'Way out in the Centre', an essay by Daniel Hoffman in *The Poetry of Dannie Abse*, ed. Joseph Cohen (London, 1983).

memorable way. Wearing the white coat, but acknowledging the purple coat, 'The Doctor'[43]

> . . . will prescribe
> . . . the clearest water
> ever, melting ice from a mountain lake;
> sunlight from a waterfall's edge, rainbow smoke;
> tears from eyelashes of the daughter.

After all, when 'The Magician' is at work, 'Sometimes something he cannot understand | happens.'[44] Later poems of medicine also involve the whole of the man, the whole of the poet: in 'In Llandough Hospital'[45] Dannie Abse's dying father is 'thin as Auschwitz in that bed'. It is a moment which changes the poet's life and his view of the world:

> And as a child can't comprehend
> what germinates philosophy,
> so like a child I question why
> night without stars, then night without end.

And in a poem from the same collection, 'Interview with a Spirit Healer',[46] the rational, sceptic Dr Abse dismisses the charade of the healer:

> Let him, in faith stare on. I loathe his trade,
> the disease, and the sanctimonious lie
> that cannot cure the disease. My need,
> being healthy, is not faith; but to curse the day
> I became mortal the night my father died.

The unsettlingly imperfect rhymes underpin the fact that faith is not to be so easily won for Dannie Abse. Some five years later *Funland and other Poems*[47] includes his most successful poem in performance, 'In the Theatre'. This recounts an experience his older brother Wilfred had when training in medicine. He was present 'in 1938, in Cardiff, when I was Lambert Rogers' dresser'. The patient needed to be conscious during the operation and was aware, if distantly, of what was being done to him, of the limited state of surgery at the time: 'more brain damage because of

---

[43] *Way Out in the Centre* (London, 1981).

[44] *Poems, Golders Green* (London, 1962): also, the play 'Pythagoras Smith'—in *The View from Row G* (Bridgend, 1990)—examines the fine distinction between madness and magic and scientific argument.

[45] Ibid.

[46] *A Small Desperation.*

[47] *Funland and Other Poems.*

the probe's braille path'. When the patient speaks, with 'a ventriloquist voice that cried', it is not his brain that he feels has been violated; he cries out, '. . . You sod | leave my soul alone, leave my soul alone', over and over until

> . . . the antique
> gramophone wound down and the words began
> to blur and slow, 'leave . . . my . . . soul . . . alone . . .'
> to cease at last when something other died.
> And silence matched the silence under snow.

That final line's iambic pentameter secures the gravitas of the poem's effect. If there is a soul in the rational world of practical medicine, in the theatre of surgery, then it materialises as the mess of blood and grey matter. And there is little hope of an afterlife, simply a cold silence.

After his father's death and with his mother in old age, Dannie Abse decided to 'Return to Roots',[48] and bought a house in Ogmore-on-Sea, some twelve miles along the Glamorganshire coast from Cardiff. He says, 'There were pebbles on the beach of Ogmore and perhaps sermons were hidden in some of them.' However, when his mother is dying there is a sense of helplessness: he writes in the poem 'Exit'[49] that she is in 'this concentration camp for one'. It as if our own natural mortality (and by implication God or the gods) can deal us a blow as terrible as that of the Nazis' victims: the practice of medicine brings one up against that realisation more acutely than reading. So where does one find the faith to carry on when life's persistent irony undercuts one's ideals, one's professionalism? May Dr Abse be no more learned and capable than the notorious Dr Mesmer of Vienna and his pseudo-medical magic tricks?[50] Still, the doctor through his stethoscope hears both 'the sound of creation' in the 'young woman's abdomen . . . and, in a dead man's chest, the silence | before creation began'.[51] The poet's visions are eventually informed by the doctor's experiences, though the stethoscope is no relic to be held in awe and included in 'a procession of banners' in 'a cold, mushroom-dark church'. The poet celebrates 'when men become philosophers' not 'priest or rabbi'. The poem ends with one of the strongest verses in Abse's work as he hears, amplified:

---

[48] The title of a chapter in *Goodbye, Twentieth Century.*

[49] *Ask the Bloody Horse.*

[50] Mesmer is referred to many times by Dannie Abse: see also *The Two Roads Taken* (London, 2003), and *A Poet in the Family* and his novel *Dr Simmonds and Dr Glas* (London, 2002).

[51] 'The stethoscope' from 'Poems 1973–1976', in *Collected Poems 1948–1988* (London, 1989).

> night cries
> of injured creatures, wide-eyed or blind;
> moonlight sonatas on a needle;
> lovers with doves in their throats; the wind
>   travelling from where it began.

The alliteration and assonance, the internal rhyme and para-rhyme launch the poem into a music that is both celebratory and unsettling.

And in that poem from the time of his mother's death, 'Exit',[52] Dannie Abse tried to take solace in the story of David and Bathsheba,[53] for 'out of so much suffering | came forth the other child | the wise child, the Solomon'. The Old Testament story would inform a later, longer poem, one of his mature, significant achievements: 'Events leading to the Conception of Solomon, the Wise Child.' It is Abse's most direct response to the continuing crisis in the Middle East.[54]

Here Dannie Abse reworks the Bible story—a king's infatuation, pursuit and seduction of one of his military commander's wives, Bathsheba the wife of Uriah. The implications of this act for the central characters are echoed in a demotic chorus in the manner of T. S. Eliot's Chorus in *Murder in the Cathedral.*

> Since scandal's bad for royal business
> the King must not father the child;
> so he called Uriah from the front,
> shook his hand like a voter. Smiled.

The language of this long poem swings from the Biblical to the ballad, from lyrical poetry to wise-crack innuendo. The narrative progresses from Ancient Israel to the present day. Tribes still fight over the same land; lives, personal and public, are enacted against a constant backdrop of violence. Prayers and pleas rise from all sides, all cultures and beliefs:

> Allah Akbar!
> Sovereign of the Universe!
> Our father in Heaven!
> Father of Mercies!
> Shema Yisroael!

And then the hush of the land, the desert land:

---

[52] *Ask the Bloody Horse.*
[53] One of many raids on the Old Testament for narrative inspiration rather than Biblical truth.
[54] *Arcadia, One Mile.*

after the shadow of an aeroplane
   has hurtled and leapt
below the hills and on to the hills
   that surround Jerusalem.

The position which a British Jew takes on the Middle East may be problematic: this is the only piece by Dannie Abse to deal with the issue. Through the previous decades and other collections, however, there has been a number of writings which engage with the Cold War and the Vietnam War. Joan Abse and their daughter Karen were involved in protests at Britain's nuclear arsenal. CND and specifically the Greenham Common Women's demonstration are mentioned.[55] His 'Ham & High' journals record a 'die-in' organised by the Hampstead branch of CND in which 'everybody would lie down signifying that the Heath was planned as Hampstead's Mass Grave' in the event of a nuclear holocaust; at which event he, reluctantly, agrees to read a poem from the 1950s—though he insists, 'I dislike participating in public protests, especially if one is asked to be ostentatious in them. I wish I did not feel that way, but I do.'[56] More explicit and showing more direct anger is his piece about the Chemical Warfare Centre at Porton Down in Wiltshire where he writes: 'I confess that such facts [the shooting of animals in wounding tests] remind me of the medical atrocity experiments of the Nazis in 1942 in Ravensbrück Concentration Camp for women.' Both experimenters used the justification of research into saving the lives of their own army's casualties. And Abse's play 'The Dogs of Pavlov' memorably explores the moral dilemmas of experimentation and manipulation.[57]

The Vietnam War was also a continuing concern for Dannie Abse, expressed in poems such as 'On the Beach', 'Give me your Hands', 'Forgotten', and others. He witnessed that war because it was the first televisual war, recorded, observed, mediated, at a distance from us. It was a decade-long, increasingly absurd conundrum which Britain's natural ally, the USA, had been drawn and then plunged fully into.

I know the geography of the great world
has changed; the war, the peace, the deletions
of places—red pieces gone forever,

[55] 'April 1984', in *Journals from the Ant-Heap* (London, 1986, repub. in *Intermittent Journals*, Bridgend, 1994).
[56] Dannie Abse wrote a regular column for the 'Ham and High'—the popular name for the *Hampstead and Highgate Express*.
[57] For a fuller discussion of Abse's plays see T. Curtis, *Dannie Abse: Writers of Wales Series* (Cardiff, 1985), and James A. Davies's introduction to *The View from Row G, Three Plays*.

and names of countries altered forever:
Gold Coast Ghana, Persia become Iran,
Siam Thailand, and Hell now Vietnam.[58]

The world has changed, as its map has changed from the simplicity of his boyhood atlas.

In Vietnam, beneath scarred trees,
unreal the staring casualties.
Of course I care. What good is that?[59]

But it is a distant war, someone else's war, about which we are powerless.

Yawning, I fold yesterday's newspaper
from England, and its news of Vietnam
which has had, and will have, a thousand names.
Then I lie back on the tourist sand.[60]

That is the dilemma: the professional man, the happily married man, the successful writer must needs be unsettled, deeply disturbed by the world's conflicts and the inevitable turning of the apple's core to rottenness. So how may faith survive?

In 'The Abandoned', a poem first collected in 1957 but reworked through over forty years and republished in 2001,[61] one may see Dannie Abse's abiding concerns and also his greater skill and confidence in handling imagery and verse forms. In the later version the poet gives two inscriptions; unlike the earlier version in which both quotations were from the seventeenth-century poet George Herbert, the revised poem substitutes one from the Talmud:

There is no space unoccupied by the Shekinah—Talmud.

. . . thy absence doth excel
All distance known. —George Herbert.

The poem in its four parts addresses God directly, but in the later version it is with a lower-case 'you', rather than the upper-case 'You', as a more direct address:

---

[58] 'Forgotten', in *The Yellow Bird* (New York, 2004).

[59] 'Give me your Hands'.

[60] 'On the Beach'.

[61] This was first published in *Poems, Golders Green*, but reworked and extended for inclusion in *Poems, New and Selected*.

> God, when you came to our house
>   we let you in. Hunted,
>   we gave you succour,
>   bandaged your hands
>   bathed your feet.
>
> Wanting water we gave you wine.
> Wanting bread we gave you meat.
>
>   . . . We have to hold our breath to hear you breathing.

In the second section the simile of waiting for a sign, an intervention by God, as if waiting in a train stuck at a station, is dropped. And in the third section of this poem he writes a villanelle whose key couplet is:

> God in the end you had to go
> We keep the bread and wine for show.

It is both a sadness and a celebration. In one reading we celebrate the passing martyr, the son of god with the communion mass; in the other we ourselves have passed that stage in our evolution when we need such solace, such symbolism, such a belief in transubstantiation. Also in that villanelle the image of a failed connection as a fused light is replaced by the white horse galloping across the snow 'leaving no hoof-marks in the rain'. The location of the poem is thus moved away from the urban—trains and electricity—towards the rural: in all probability fixing itself in Ogmore-on-Sea in Wales rather than Golders Green and the suburbs of London. Dannie Abse's life in 1957 was offering a different set of images from that of 2001.

In the fourth and final section, particularly in the revised version, he seems completely dismissive of organised religion, specifically the Catholic Church, which is nailed to its responsibilities by the hard, full rhymes[62]

> Absurd saints search for the rack.
> Plumed Popes begin to doubt, lose track.
> 'Did the shadow answer back?'

The revised poem edits some of the over-blown images and that final section has three five-line verses, rather than six; it loses the imagery of senility and the somewhat excessive 'do not blaspheme | cursing man'. The climax is reached more clearly; and more forcefully focuses on the white coat experiences in opposition to the purple robes of the high church. The

---

[62] The poet was educated in a Catholic secondary school, St Illtyd's, in Cardiff.

doctor poet knows that in our bodily suffering we are pushed closer to the need for an Almighty; in the hospital bed, on our death bed, pain and despair may push us to prayer, exhortation, a quick and desperate faith, the insistence of rhyme:

> Listen. Can't you hear again
> an idiot desperate in a house,
> the strict economy of pain,
> a voice pleading and profane
> calling you by name?

The rational man of medicine can agree with Richard Dawkins, Jonathan Miller and others that God the idea has served its purpose and that we are now strong enough to form and accept our own destiny, be shaped by our own actions. And yet, the smells and bells, the music and poetry of religion have a power which may stir for us old yearnings. Again, Abse says in his recent, confessional memoir, *The Presence*,[63] these must be resisted, even in our darkest hours:

> To pray, though, to the gods, or to the God—what arrogance! It is like address-ing the vast sky behind the stars and saying, 'Here I am.' Reversed thunder, indeed! As George Herbert indicated, along with other definitions of prayer;
>
> > . . . Prayer, the Church's banquet, Angel's age,
> > God's breath in man returning to his birth, . . .
>
> > Engine against th'Almighty, sinner's tower
> > Reversed thunder . . .

It is poems not prayers that are central to Dannie Abse's life and they appear liberally in this journal/memoir, both his own poems and others'. He writes:

> When I was a child I believed that God could read even my secret thoughts, my velleities. Later . . . I became agnostic and certainly knew that if God existed he could not be shut within the confines of synagogue, chapel, church, or mosque with all their crazy prescriptions, their regulated liturgies and rites and dead schedules. Later still, on rare occasions, when I have, as it were, fallen through a hole in the air into wonder I have been persuaded that, as Thomas Aquinas wrote, 'The truths of revelations are not the same as the truths of reason.' But I have used these experiences not in the moral realm but in an attempt to write poems while sitting comfortably in my study far from the thistle-eating donkey and the desert of religion.[64]

---

[63] *The Presence* (London, 2007).
[64] Ibid., pp. 16–17.

He deals with the guilt of losing, of consciously leaving, one of the great religions; he sees his role as a poet fulfilling spiritual needs by articulating the mysteries and truths which present themselves in his life. He proves as unconventional in his relationship with God as that other great post-war poet from Wales, the Reverend R. S. Thomas. Abse has little regard for organised religions, Jewish or Christian:

> So let both ministers propound
> the pathology of religions,
> and pass my gate you zealots of
> scrubbed, excremental visions.[65]

The biblical truths may be no more than 'two drab tablets of stone'.[66] Though the Old Testament is valued for the music of Solomon and 'the beautiful rod of Aaron | first with its blossom | then with its ripe almonds', ancient deities are far in our past: 'The gods, old as night, don't trouble us.' For they have outgrown their usefulness, their power:

> All the old gods have become enfeebled,
> mere playthings for poets. They doze
> or, daft, frolic on Parnassian clover.
> Sometimes summer light dies in a room but only
> a bearded profile in a cloud passes over.[67]

What significance we strive for in our lives must be found in human resources. The young boy at the Seder meal goes to the door to answer the guest's knocking and finds no one. He returns and the glass of wine has been drunk—'a shadow flies | when a light is shone'. And 'The mystery named | is not the mystery caged.'[68]

Dannie Abse's latest book, the memoir *The Presence*, closes with 'Lachrymae' which was included in his latest collection *Running Late* and then 'Postscript January 7th 2007', in which he recalls his uncle Isidore, a colourful character who appeared first in *Ash on a Young Man's Sleeve*. Isidore, 'long after a string had snapped' on his old violin, would say, 'Little boy, who needs all the lyric strings? | Is the great world perfect?', 'Uncle Isidore',[69] 'smelly | schnorrer and lemon-tea Bolshevik', has one

---

[65] 'Even', from *A Small Desperation*.
[66] 'Apology', from *Ask the Bloody Horse*.
[67] From 'The Old Gods', an unpublished poem sent to the author as 'a playful, inconsequential poem' on 30 Aug. 2007.
[68] Ibid.
[69] *New and Collected Poems*.

answer for the sufferings of the world, though: he plays on, after the pogroms and the camps, after the doctor's visit, through the thunder and rain on his violin, 'some notes wrong, all notes wild'. That practice is a model for the writer, too: 'The unutterable, at best, becomes music.'[70]

Dannie Abse has always known that the great world is not perfect. In his practice as a doctor and in his work as a writer, he has for over sixty years found ways of regretting the world's imperfections and celebrating our responses in the face of that. Now, bereaved, but determined, he plays with one string less. It is a sad and important music. In Dannie Abse's 'running late' years, in the years of bereavement, there is no lessening of the writer's powers or his publishing success. But the faith remains reluctant and the sustaining irony, life's grim metaphor, underpins all that happens and all that is written. Having declared that he felt he might write no more poetry after Joan's death, Dannie Abse has, in fact, once more taken and examined the 'spiritual X-rays' that are poems.[71]

The only poem to have survived the poet's critical eye from his first collection, that book drowned by the 'noisy echoes' of Dylan Thomas and other writers, *After Every Green Thing*, sixty years before, is 'The Uninvited', a poem stimulated by his reading of Rilke's eighth letter to Kappus: 'When we are open to important moments of sorrow, then our future "sets foot in us . . ." our destiny begins and "we have been changed as a house is changed into which a guest has entered."'

> They came into our lives unasked for.
> There was light momentarily, a flicker of wings,
> a dance, a voice, and then they went out
> again, like a light, leaving us not so much
> in darkness, but in a different place
> and alone as never before.
>
> So we have been changed
> and our hopes no longer what they were;
> so a piece of us has gone out with them also,
> a cold dream subtracted without malice,
>
> the weight of another world added also,
> and we did not ask, we did not ask ever
> for those who stood smiling
> and with flowers before the open door.

---

[70] 'Between 3 and 4 a.m.', in *On the Evening Road* (London, 1994).
[71] Joan Abse died in a car accident in 2005: see the obituary by Tony Curtis in *The Independent*, 17 June 2005.

We did not beckon them in, they came in uninvited,
the sunset pouring from their shoulders,
so they walked through us as they would through water,
and we are here, in a different place,
changed and incredibly alone,
and we did not know, we do not know ever.

Strung between irony and faith, perhaps reluctant irony, perhaps with the consistent search for faith, the word comes alive in us and we live through words. The poet Dannie Abse speaks for all of us when he says, 'Though I start with the visible, I don't know where I'm going to end.'

Theopoesis:
the Contest of Priest and Poet

GEOFFREY HARTMAN
Fellow of the Academy

I DO NOT KNOW when it began, the contest or conflict between priest and poet; and I am not enough of an intellectual historian to research the issue by a thematic inquiry. Prophet versus King or Priest would be a more familiar antithesis, and the point William Blake insisted on is the identity of Prophet and Poet. So let me begin with Blake's apodictic pronouncements, also because the persuasive entry of the topic into the present literary consciousness, at least in England and America, is mainly, I think, due to the feistiness of his polemical pamphlets and verse.

Blake's contribution is most succinct in *All Religions are One* (*c*.1788). I quote the 5th Principle from this pamphlet that has a subtitle suggesting the poet identifies with Isaiah's 'The Voice of One crying in the Wilderness':

> The Religions of all Nations are derived from each Nation's different reception of the Poetic Genius, which is everywhere called the Spirit of Prophecy.[1]

This perspective excludes any creative role for priestly intermediaries or administrators. But Blake goes further in Plate 11 of *The Marriage of Heaven and Hell*. He blames the priesthood for having limited our reception of the poetic–prophetic spirit, and so joins the anticlerical polemic of

---

Read at the Academy 3 October 2007.

[1] Blake neatly reverses Robert Lowth's opinion in *Lectures on the Sacred Poetry of the Hebrews*, tr. G. Gregory, 2 vols. (1787), 1. 37, and which may have been widespread, that 'If the actual origin of Poetry be inquired after, it must of necessity be referred to Religion.'

Proceedings of the British Academy **154**, 361–373. © The British Academy 2008.

many Enlightenment thinkers.[2] He also elaborates a genealogy of corruption that attacks the Priest in the name of the Poetic Genius.

The institution of priesthood is accused of enslaving the vulgar 'by attempting to realize or abstract the mental deities from their objects'—objects, Blake claims, which the 'enlarged and numerous senses' of the ancient Poets had animated with Gods and Geniuses. Humanity originally viewed divine beings as emanations of its own imaginative powers, stimulated by and engaging in ideal converse with the external world. But the clerical establishment, refusing to acknowledge the human source of that relationship, instituted and coerced the worship of reified abstractions. Consequently, 'men forgot that all deities reside in the human breast'. To enlarge our sensibility once more and take back what was alienated, Blake composes his own revisionary epics about First and Last Things.

I choose Blake for his clarion qualities, and the audacity of his imagination, not for any consonance with look-alike opinions found among the deists, whom he denounced,[3] and who had little use for an exalted view of poetry. The manner in which Blake equates Poetic Genius with 'the universal Humanity' does not conform to deism's formulations concerning a 'natural [that is, innate and universal] religious sentiment'.[4] Neither is religion, for Blake, dependent on either scientific (Newtonian) or pseudo-empirical arguments from the wondrous system of the universe. Both of the pamphlets accompanying 'All Religions are One' bear the title 'There is no Natural Religion'.[5]

What I wish to do in this lecture is to chart, in a series of close readings, the complexity of the relation between poetry and both natural and revealed religion in Addison, Blake, and Coleridge, authors who in very different ways did not give up, or not entirely, the rights of poetry at a time when the imagination, and in particular the enthusiastic imagination, was being curtailed and even repressed.[6] Political sensitivities cer-

---

[2] See Frank E. Manuel, *The Eighteenth Century Confronts the Gods* (Cambridge, MA, 1959), and *The Changing of the Gods* (Hanover, NH, and London, 1985).

[3] Sometimes, unfortunately, by a rant like that in 'To the Deists,' Plate 52 of *Jerusalem*.

[4] Cf. Frank Manuel, *The Broken Staff: Judaism through Christian Eyes* (Cambridge, MA, 1992), pp. 179 ff.

[5] David Hume's *Dialogues on Natural Religion*, with its effective attack on arguments invoking intelligent design, had been published, finally, in 1779.

[6] For the persistence, nevertheless, of metrical paraphrases of Scripture, but also of many kinds of visionary poetry in eighteenth-century France, see especially the chapter on 'Le sacre du poète' in Paul Bénichou, *Le sacre de l'écrivain 1750–1830* (Paris, 1973), pp. 79–91.

tainly played a part in the repression; but my emphasis will be on how visionary poetry strove to maintain itself, and even retain its initiative, in a climate of opinion generally hostile to its imaginative claims.

* * *

One of the neatest short poems of the eighteenth century is Addison's 'The Spacious Firmament on high'. I will call it a Sky poem; officially, however, it would have been classified, in addition to being a titular ode ('such a bold and sublime manner of Thinking', the author comments in his introductory remarks, 'furnishes very noble Matter for an Ode'), as a 'metrical paraphrase' of Psalm 19, the granddaddy of Sky poems.

> The Spacious Firmament on high,
> With all the blue Ethereal Sky,
> And spangled Heav'ns, a Shining Frame,
> Their great Original proclaim.
> Th'unwearied Sun, from Day to Day,
> Does his Creator's Pow'r display,
> And publishes to every Land
> The Work of an Almighty Hand.
>
> Soon as the Evening Shades prevail,
> The Moon takes up the Wondrous Tale,
> And nightly to the list'ning Earth
> Repeats the Story of her Birth;
> Whilst all the Stars that round her burn,
> And all the Planets in their turn,
> Confirm the Tidings as they roll,
> And spread the Truth from Pole to Pole.
>
> What though in solemn Silence all
> Move round the dark terrestrial Ball?
> What though nor real Voice nor Sound
> Amidst their radiant Orbs be found?
> In Reason's Ear they all rejoice,
> And utter forth a glorious Voice;
> For ever singing, as they shine,
> 'The Hand that made us is Divine'.

How regular a structure: rhymes proceeding two by two in stanzas of eight lines of eight syllables each. A *square* poem, except it has only three stanzas. But that increases its snap and compactness. A large proportion of adjective and noun pairings ('Spacious Firmament', 'spangled Heav'ns',

'Shining Frame', 'great Original') confirms not only our sense of regularity but of an economy arising from the intelligibility rather than mystery of what is described. No great personal amazement is expressed, no lo! or behold! For this is a universe so naturally eloquent, so clear in its message. It 'publishes' day and night the good news, an evangel drawn from the world of nature. The fact, then, that the poem was first published in one of England's early proto-newspapers, *The Spectator* (no. 465, 26 August 1712), is only apparently a coincidence.

The ode makes no secret of its dependence on Psalm 19. Indeed, it proclaims, as it were, that 'great Original' too—imitating rather than emulating it. Addison's poem does not claim the virtue of Original Composition and paraphrases the first six verses of the psalm, a portion often subtitled in hymnals 'The Book of Nature'.

Addison's ode is, in effect, a Letter to England's contemporary Augustans. Paul's famous pronouncement in his *Letter to the Romans* (1: 19 ff.) on the *invisibilia* being clearly discernible through the *ea quae facta*—by which he specifically meant that what can be, indeed must be, inferred from the natural world is a Creator both all-powerful and wise, so that even without a special revelation there is no excuse for unbelief— Paul's pronouncement became a standard cosmological proof-text for what Blake denounced as the 'Religion of Nature'.

The passage from Romans was used to support not only a variety of Deisms but also the natural sciences and descriptive nature poetry. Newton, at the end of the *Principia*, alludes to Paul's sentences.[7] And Addison introduces his ode in *The Spectator* with a long comment that includes the following: 'The Supream Being has made the best Arguments for his own Existence, in the formation of Heaven and the Earth, and these are Arguments which a Man of Sense cannot forbear attending to, who is out of the Noise and Hurry of human Affairs.'

Thus his ode too makes a natural theology argument, reminding Mr Spectator's busy worldly correspondents, in town or country, and with the least condescension and pretension on his part, of a Sky News within easy reach.

The modesty of such a poem, its compact secondariness, the prevailing mode of a religious poetry that tries to maintain a neoclassical type of decorum, does not exclude certain surprises. True, the shift from the first to the second stanza is as smooth as the poem's sustained theme of

---

[7] See Newton's 'General Scholium': 'This most beautiful system of the sun, planets, and comets, could only proceed from the counsel and dominion [*consilio et dominio*] of an intelligent Being . . .'. The Vulgate has 'virtus, et divinitas'.

what Christopher Smart, in a hymn published some fifty years later, calls 'sounds and objects' that 'reason | In behalf of praise and pray'r'.[8] But Addison's third stanza shows a breach, a doubt, an unexpected reading of the void as a void, and silence as silence.

The breach takes up precisely half of the last stanza and is followed by a counterturn recovery. All's well, or seems to be so, at the end. The downturn, however, even if it lasts but a stylised moment, deserves further consideration.

The turn did not have to occur, despite the fact that Addison's faithful paraphrase acknowledges in this manner the contradictory third verse of Psalm 19. Yet most poets found a smoother way of circumventing the problem. Smart's solution, in a later paraphrase, is both standard and ingenious. He moots the problematic third verse by filling hypothetical lacunae, just as the King James Bible did, which reads '[There is] no speech nor language, [where] their voice is not heard'. Smart, in turn, writes:

> There is no nation, clime or tongue,
> Where their first mattins are not sung
>   And in the spirit caught;
> There is no language, sound or speech,
> But their melodious vespers reach,
>   And warble to the thought.[9]

Instead of untuning the sky, Smart acknowledges the non-presence of literal sound while asking that it be interpreted by the spiritual or thoughtful observer.

This may be Addison's understanding as well. 'In Reason's Ear they all rejoice', the final stanza's recovery begins. Yet the tone, the placement, and overall tightness of Addison's poem lead to a surprise.

If this is an ode, it must be what was called at the time a Minor rather than a Great Ode; that is, its model would have been Horace rather than Pindar. Perhaps Addison chose the Horatian model thinking of his poem as a picture of the world in little, a microcosm. His strophic turn, however, opening the third stanza, is reminiscent of the Greater Ode, where abrupt, antithetical transitions were allowed. The first two lines of that

---

[8] Hymn XII, 'ST. PHILIP AND ST. JAMES', ll. 11–12. As in *The Poetical Works of Christopher Smart, Vol. 2. Religious Poetry 1763–1771*, ed. Marcus Walsh and Karina Williamson (Oxford, 1983), p. 57.

[9] Psalm XIX in *A Translation of the Psalms of David, Attempted in the Spirit of Christianity, and Adapted to the Dinve Service* (1765). As in *The Poetical Works of Christopher Smart Vol. 3*, ed. with introduction and commentary by Marcus Walsh (Oxford, 1987), p. 42.

turn, moreover, sharpen the antithetical mood by the contrast of their adjective–noun sequences with those in the poem's opening: 'solemn Silence' instead of 'Spacious Firmament', 'Dark terrestrial Ball' as against 'blue Etherial Sky'. And the 'What though' need not strike the reader as dismissive: it could be defiant. Rhetorical the turn certainly is, yet it suggests emotion breaking through as an adverse thought is overcome. Was Addison, like Pascal, alarmed by 'the eternal silence of infinite space', by the suggestion of a terrible rather than benevolent sublimity, even horror at a sheer, vacuous mechanism?

What is most remarkable is that Addison tries to raise a 'glorious Voice' from that silence at the same time as he downplays his own voice. From the ode's beginning, the theme of an intelligible cosmic chorus is central. But when the figure of these luminous cosmic voices ('Forever singing, as they shine')—when this figure suddenly gives out, it is restored in a coda and reinforced by the only instance of *direct* speech the poem offers: 'The Hand that made us is Divine'.[10]

Hence the drama of Addison's poem resides in its double turn. A fear reflected by the last stanza's downturn (the cata-strophe) is almost at once absorbed into the ana-strophe of the poem's symmetrical lineaments. Yet, on closer reading, what is subdued in this formal manner returns in the very statement declaring reason's victorious intervention. The ode's explanatory finale, 'In Reason's Ear they all rejoice', does not show forth a rational worshiper: what it shows is the poet in the poet, since at the very moment he denies a figure, the figure strikes back. A metaphor bleeds through, and grotesquely so. For, can you picture 'Reason's Ear,' this catachresis of a personification, without it evoking a grotesque image?

Addison's rebound from his moment of doubt is either bravado or conformist. Probably both. It demonstrates, in any case, how skilfully he uses the genre of paraphrase to subordinate his 'hand' to the divine 'hand' that guided the composer of the 'great Original' he imitates. The glorious voice comes, if at all, solely from the Creator via the things created. The poet's own creativity is closely guided by a sanctified text and celebrates reason. Reason as the light of nature within and upon us leads to a twofold conviction: that a Creator exists, and that He is wise and Almighty.

As a hymn, then, Addison's ode keeps religion within the bounds of reason. Miracles and other mysteries of faith, as well as moral and cultic

---

[10] 'He made us', the *res creatae* likewise inform Augustine in what the Tenth Book of his *Confessions* admits is a figurative move.

prescriptions, require supplementary legitimation; and this comes through the revealed law, whose perfection is celebrated in the latter portion of Psalm 19 (verses 7 ff.) not covered by Addison's paraphrase.

Because of this delimitation, it is not possible to tell from Addison's poem what role poetry could play with respect to positive rather than natural religion. Stylistically, however, everything points away from an originating, revelatory power of the kind Blake will arrogate. Except that the final stanza, in one insubordinate flash, discloses poetry's constructive unreason.

For the more we scrutinise 'In Reason's Ear they all rejoice' the more peculiar it is. First of all, its focusing vigour depends on the sound-values that precede: 'real' and 'radiant', both of them disyllables, one extended to be such, the other contracted. These r-plus words (as well as 'Ear-th') seem to flow into the core expression 'Reason's Ear', a verse that turns out to be a near palindrome. 'Ear' is doubly present in it, backwards and forwards, a grapheme scrabbling to be integral to the word 'reason' itself. The hand of the poet declares itself after all in this eary moment.

* * *

While Blake's early 'To the Evening Star' remains a Sky poem, and specifically a Night Piece similar in kind to Addison's second stanza, it deploys a mythopoeic imagery that is not in the service of attesting the existence of a Supreme Artificer. 'The Spacious Firmament on high', Addison begins; but for Blake, an anti-globalist in the era of Newton, 'The Sky is an immortal Tent built by the Sons of Los' and 'every Space larger than a red globule of Man's blood | Is visionary, and is created by the Hammer of Los'. I quote from *Milton*, a much later work; yet Blake's early poem (from *Poetical Sketches*, 1788) already conveys the importance of a homely yet visionary perspective.

The contrast with Addison is heightened by the eloquent paradox 'speak silence', a paradox perhaps inspired by Psalm 19's crux. In context, 'speak silence' ('with thy glimmering eyes') magnifies not only the silence of the stars but contrasts with the poet's speech-act. Blake creates his own semblance of an 'Omnific Word'[11] or 'glorious Voice'.

---

[11] Milton's Christ (*Paradise Lost*, 7. 216 f.) hushes and pacifies Chaos with a proto-Logos uttered before the beginning of the Beginning.

Yet though 'To Evening' is not part of a traditional cosmological argument, neither is it, despite sensuous effects, a naturalistic description of nightfall's gradual advent in the Western hemisphere, a theme that comes into its own in the eighteenth century.[12] The poem exists as a vocative instrument, and a remarkably imperious one. Its speaker is a *magister ludi* who rejoices in a logos-power able to summon light from the dark so strongly that the evening star is close to being, as in a heavenly marathon, a sun succeeding the sun:

> Thou fair-haired angel of the evening,
> Now, while the sun rests on the mountains, light
> Thy bright torch of love! Thy radiant crown
> Put on . . .

Blake, however, does station himself in the Evening Land, in what *Poetical Sketches* calls 'our western isle'. He does so to assert the West's capacity for a Progress of Poetry. He re-animates the evening-star motif of Bion's well-known minor lyric by adding a geopolitical element—a 'prophetic', or intensely wishful, dimension alluding to Britain's genius loci. A rising poetic star rivals that of the East, and potentially recaptures the aura of the 'universal Poetic Genius' who in ancient time walked upon England's mountains green. Moreover, since Hesperus is not eclipsed by an epiphanic moon, as in many Night Pieces, the star becomes a forerunner to itself, a guardian spirit anticipating the dawn.

Exactly what this dawning signifies for the British and Hesperian muse is hard to tell from a blank verse sonnet that remains a neoclassical pastiche—subverted somewhat by its supple use of the blank verse measure. Yet its diction, in contrast to the purgative path Wordsworth will take, strives to recover something of the original unity of poetic and prophetic.[13] The inert phraseology is rescued from a silver mediocrity that lingers, as if to purge itself, in the very repetition of 'silver':

> While thou drawest the
> Blue curtains of the sky, scatter thy silver dew
> On every flower that shuts its sweet eyes
> In timely sleep. Let thy west wind sleep on
> The lake; speak silence with thy glimmering eyes,
> And wash the dusk with silver.

---

[12] See Christopher R. Miller, *The Invention of Evening: Perception and Time in Romantic Poetry* (Cambridge, 2006).
[13] Cf. Geoffrey Hartman, *Beyond Formalism: Literary Essays 1958–1970* (New Haven, CT, 1970), p. 194.

Now, whether or not 'To Evening' is about the poetic vocation, it transforms, like Addison's ode, a minor genre into a greater one. Even in a sonnet's condensed space it not only hails a divine personification but mimics the 'turn' and 'counter-turn' of a Great Ode. So that, after having magnified the star's idyllic, Venusian power, Blake depicts, in equally stylised terms, a power vacuum, one that breeds 'terrific' images:

> Soon, full soon,[14]
> Dost thou withdraw; then the wolf rages wide
> And the lion glares through the dun forest.

As in Addison, then, the mood suddenly turns.[15] Also, as in Addison, an anastrophe immediately follows in the form of a coda. Blake's fiat-mode changes into a petition and dispels nightmare by offering the apotropaic image of starry dew:[16]

> The fleeces of our flocks are covered with
> Thy sacred dew: protect them with thine influence.

It has become commonplace to view poems as about other poems or about poetry as such. But 'influence', surely, that strongly placed, last word, points here to a material if mythic influx of 'stellar virtue'. Blake's further career confirms that he is reluctant to abandon a richly allusive idiom. He preserves and redirects a tradition that has survived both neoclassical refiners and priestly reifiers. As yet, however, not Romanticism so much as a restored pastoral Classicism is the aim.[17]

Blake will go past the juvenilia of *Poetical Sketches* to epic-length Prophetic Books. His 'enlarged and numerous senses' will transform the Sky poem into extravaganzas with their deceptive assortment of visionary figures: gods, giants, geniuses of all kinds, drawn mainly from non-Classical

---

[14] The literal meaning is not only 'soon, very soon' but also 'soon full, like a full moon'. See also below, n. 15.

[15] As I have mentioned, the Night Piece would ordinarily depict a steady progress, often culminating in the image of a majestic Moon. Cf. '*Hesperus* that led | The starry host, rode brightest, till the Moon | Rising in cloudy majesty, at length | Apparent Queen unveiled her peerless light'. *Paradise Lost*, 4. 605–8.

[16] Cf. *Paradise Lost*, 4. 667–72 on the stars: 'these soft fires | Not only enlighten, but with kindly heat | Of various influence foment and warm, | Temper or nourish, or in part shed down | Their stellar virtue on all kinds that grow | On Earth . . .'. Also, for the connection of dew and morning star, see *Paradise Lost*, 5. 745–7.

[17] See, also in *Poetical Sketches*, 'To Morning', a companion piece to Blake's Night Piece, though it is more of a residual schoolboy exercise. Writing his Evening Star sonnet in blank verse could be another indicator of Blake's Classicist ambition fused with what through Shakespeare and Milton had become a native measure.

sources, Nordic or pseudo-Nordic, folkloric, 'Oriental'. Milton's War in Heaven and the Book of Revelation serve as major templates. Blake must have decided that to renounce the formulas of visionary literature would sacrifice too much. It might lead to poetry's recession ('The languid strings do scarcely move | The sound is forced, the notes are few'[18]), and risk the voiceless, prayerless state Coleridge depicts in 'The Ancient Mariner'.[19]

* * *

Coleridge always journeys to the heart of loss, including that despairing, prayerless acedia. 'Night is my hell', he writes in his *Notebooks*: it torments him with unnatural dream-images and deepens his fear that a Wordsworthian nature sensibility is out of reach. The natural world cannot mediate or console. When he uses the word 'soul' it carries with it an echo of 'sole'. Mediation becomes urgent and its absence haunts his poetry:

> O Wedding-Guest! This soul hath been
> Alone on a wide, wide sea:
> So lonely 'twas, that God himself
> Scarce seeméd there to be.

That simple 'O' (echoed in 'soul' and 'alone') reappears by itself in a serious mock of the Night Piece genre and 'Caeli enarrant' paraphrases:

> The stars that wont to start, as on a chace,
> Mid twinkling insult on Heaven's darken'd face,
> Like a conven'd conspiracy of spies
> Wink at each other with confiding eyes!
> Turn from the portent—all is blank on high,
> No constellations alphabet the sky:
> The Heavens one large Black Letter only shew,
> And as a child beneath its master's blow
> Shrills out at once its task and its affright—
> The groaning world now learns to read aright,
> And with its Voice of Voices cries out, O![20]

---

[18] 'To the Muses', *Poetical Sketches*.
[19] Looking at Blake's career as a totality, his 'speak silence' is a timely imperative that turns Addison's orthodox rationalisation of a poetic figure (the voicing of the heavens) into a protest on behalf of a poetry that has been or is in danger of being silenced.
[20] *Poetical Works of Samuel Taylor Coleridge 1772–1834*, ed. E. H. Coleridge (Oxford, 1912), p. 486. The editor quotes Coleridge's notes on the poem from the MS: 'I wrote these lines in imitation of Du Bartas as translated by our Sylvester.'

What the stars declare is some sort of confidence game, or satanic plot (cf. *Paradise Lost*, 5. 700 ff.). Yet this dark reading of heavenly portents is better than not being able to decipher anything, to have a 'blank on high'. Poets must be capable of reading the void, must preserve the belief that everything is 'Symbolical, one mighty alphabet | For infant minds' (*Destiny of Nations*, 19–20). Though what is left is only a large Black Letter, that is, an undecipherable ancient ballad, to attempt its reading at least forces a voice from the void. The entire world's groaning condenses as the vocative sign that often stands at the beginning of an ode or of heightened speech generally. That O, in an Omega rather than inaugural position, and itself so close to the symbol for nothingness, voices the labour-pains from which the poet's own invocations are born.

To find a charm to counteract the power of blackness, to get a voice out of silence and the dark, even if it is the groan or scream of his own agony that wakes the terrified sleeper—this is behind the tenor of Coleridge's most peculiar poem, his 'Hymn Before Sunrise in the Vale of Chamouni', a 'Hymn in the Manner of the Psalms', as it is identified on first publication (1802).

Of this complex and strangely deceptive hymn (Coleridge had never been to Chamounix), I will only emphasise its longing for a star, or starry voice, amid the massive blackness of the silent mountain called 'Blanc' (recall: 'all is blank on high'). The star is Hesperus; but now as morning star it seems to have been halted in its course by the benighted mountain. Coleridge describes his imaginative exertions to free the star, so that it, indeed all of nature, can move toward dawn and dissolve a nightmare stasis.

Yet Coleridge's poetic voice, as it amplifies itself, and calls repeatedly on nature, is, like the locale itself, based on a fake mimesis. Not just because its high-pitched religious rhetoric has only the force of a frustrated fiat when it asks all nature to 'Utter forth God' as creator (58 ff.), validating once again the proof-text from Romans.[21]

Coleridge's mimesis involves self-falsification because, instead of writing a nature poetry equal to Wordsworth's, which earlier lyrics like 'Frost at Midnight' and 'The Nightingale' (also poems of the night) showed him capable of doing, he chooses the artifice of a near-hysterical, declamatory sublimity concocted from a hyperbolic blend of Milton (see, especially,

---

[21] But can one overlook that to 'utter forth God' suggests a logos power creating God?

Paradise Lost, 5. 153 ff.) and Klopstock, the latter via a minor ode by Friederike Brun. The self-deviance here is astonishing.

To be fair, though: is Coleridge's effusive hymn any more archaising and artificial than other benevolent—or desperate—forgeries aspiring to a glorious voice in emulation of the ancient Bards? Can even Blake be exempted? Consider also MacPherson's *Ossian*, or 'The Ancient Mariner' with its antique as well as Eastern Tale patina—although that poem differs by not presenting itself as more than an imitation. In 'Hymn before Sunrise' the sun does not rise, and what we hear is the death-rattle of a sublime style on life-support.

* * *

My subject has been the struggle for survival of a visionary or enthusiastic poetry. That struggle, evaded by Addison's delimitation of poetry's authority, yet deepened by Blake's bardic, and Coleridge's tormented sublimities, displaces 'the primeval Priest's assumed power' (as Blake called it in the opening line of *The [First] Book of Urizen*) by an investiture of the Poet–Prophet ('le sacre du poète'). The Poet Priest antithesis I have adopted, and which is resolved in favour of the poet, almost literally so by Keats's vow to Psyche, 'Yes, I will be thy Priest', is no more than shorthand for a complex literary and historical issue. The Romantic Enlightenment, as it should be called, recognised that the fate of the poetic spirit in human affairs was intertwined with an inventiveness previously expressed through traditional visionary categories, whether pagan or Christian.[22] Blake claimed that his *Jerusalem: the Emanation of the Giant Albion* preserved the Divine Vision in a time of trouble (Plate 95), as if he had heard Hölderlin's famous cry: 'What are poets for in a needy time?'

Today the hold on the imagination of theopoetic themes and figures remains firm. Whatever presently motivates belief, a suspension of disbelief is habitual when conceptions are underwritten by a long literary history. Problems arise mainly if this inheritance is neglected, or codified and doctrinally restricted, or taken so sternly that we forget, as Blake wrote, 'that all deities reside in the human breast'.

---

[22] I have already mentioned that the persistence, however precarious, of both orthodox and heterodox (perhaps better described as multidox) religious poetry is extensively recorded in Paul Bénichou's famous study of *Le sacre de l'écrivain*. In England, however, the movement toward a 'pouvoir spirituel *laïque*,' the secular investiture of the writer, was less politicised.

In the later eighteenth century, after Lowth, Eichhorn and Herder sidestepped the Biblical criticism of Enlightenment thinkers—the latters' skeptical dissection of the text and mocking dismissal of Scripture's unity and authority—the Bible was re-presented and valued (Elinor Shaffer has shown this) as a chrestomathy of Oriental literature.[23] A proliferation of stylistic imitations ensued, accompanied, however, by a heightened anxiety about original composition. Was there a chance for a second Renaissance, for a new, distinctively Nordic or Western visionary genius, a 'homebred glory' as Keats called it in *Endymion* (4. 13)?

Milton's *Paradise Lost* was central to this question: not because of an earlier concern, best expressed by Marvell, that the poet's very strength might 'ruin . . . | The sacred truths to fable and old song', but because Milton, while magically absorbing into the Biblical narrative a humongous weight of myth and theology, might hinder new epic ventures aiming for a more indigenous mode of representation, for a style closer to actual sense perception, phenomenological insight, and the directest possible reflection of human concerns. Hence also Coleridge's encouragement of Wordsworth's favourite quest, a 'philosophic Song | Of Truth that cherishes our daily life' (1850 *Prelude*, 1. 229–30).

The good news is that once Church and State stop enforcing an established *imaginaire*, the poetic potential of every individual can respond and even contribute to the moving, ingenious, but also hazmat fantasia not only of popular but also dogmatic religion. If there exists a 'universal poetic Genius' inspiring all Bibles and other divinely glued epic fragments, then theology is well on its way to becoming one of the liberal arts. This statement, of course, puts me squarely in Matthew Arnold's camp: 'The strongest part of our religion to-day is its unconscious poetry.'[24] But is that poetry, or our recognition of it, all that unconscious?

---

[23] E. S. Shaffer, *'Kubla Khan' and The Fall of Jerusalem: The Mythological School in Biblical Criticism and Secular Literature 1770–1880* (New York, 1975).
[24] *The Study of Poetry* (1880).

'But I, that knew what harbred in that hed': Sir Thomas Wyatt and his Posthumous 'Interpreters'

CATHY SHRANK

University of Sheffield

IN NOVEMBER 2003, the body of Francesco Petrarca was disinterred. This was not the first time the bones of this famous poet had been disturbed. Nineteenth-century scientists had already exhumed them, but Italian pathologists were now eager to apply modern technology to reconstruct the poet's face and create a definitive portrait for the seven hundredth anniversary of his birth.[1] This lecture examines our impulse to pick over the bones of our dead poets by looking at the case of Sir Thomas Wyatt the Elder, a translator and imitator of Petrarch, long credited with being the first English poet to introduce the sonnet into our vernacular. It explores why it is that Wyatt's commentators have recurrently excavated his poetic remains, searching for answers about the man who wrote them. It does so by analysing the seemingly confessional nature of Wyatt's poetry, before proceeding to argue that—rather than being self-revelatory—Wyatt's works actually resist and evade such self-exposure, especially when compared to the Petrarchan tradition on which he was drawing.

Read at the Academy 31 October 2007.

[1] <http://books.guardian.co.uk/news/articles/0,6109,1186654,00.html> [accessed 17 Sept. 2007].

Proceedings of the British Academy **154**, 375–401. © The British Academy 2008.

Thomas Wyatt died in October 1542, from a fever contracted whilst hurrying to meet a Spanish envoy at Falmouth.[2] His untimely passing— in his late thirties or early forties—prompted a flurry of elegies.[3] Strikingly, two appeared in print, at a time when printed obsequies were rare and seem to have been reserved for the death of royalty.[4] Funeral verses by John Leland and Henry Howard, Earl of Surrey mourn a mere gentleman.[5] They do so—above all—because he is a poet, elevated alongside Dante and Petrarch, revered above Chaucer.[6] Despite their shared project, however, there are revealing differences between the two elegists. Leland's twelve-page pamphlet commemorates Wyatt's varied roles. Its thirty Latin verses focus on different aspects of his life, praising him—in separate poems—as a friend, ambassador, soldier, local landlord, or bearded bald man.[7]

Where Leland presents external evidence for Wyatt's character, Surrey, in contrast, anatomises the dead poet, breaking him down into constituent body parts. He performs a blazon, a standard poetic technique whereby the qualities of the object under perusal—usually a woman—are listed. Such catalogues of female virtue are generally restricted to what can be seen or heard: coral lips, golden hair, white skin,

---

[2] Colin Burrow, 'Wyatt, Sir Thomas (c. 1503–1542)', *Oxford Dictionary of National Biography*, <http://www.oxforddnb.com> [accessed 18 Dec. 2007].

[3] These include verses by Sir Anthony St Leger, Sir Thomas Chaloner and John Parkhurst, see Kenneth Muir, *Life and Letters of Sir Thomas Wyatt* (Liverpool, 1963), p. 220.

[4] The two extant printed elegies before 1542 are on Henry VII and his uncle and surrogate father, Jasper Tudor, Duke of Bedford: [*Elegy on the death of Henry VII*] (London, Wynkyn de Worde, 1509), *The epitaffe of the moste noble & valyaunt Iasper late duke of Beddeforde* (London, Richard Pynson, 1496). Henry was born at Jasper Tudor's castle in Pembroke after the death of his father. R. S. Thomas, 'Tudor, Jasper, duke of Bedford', *ODNB* [accessed 18 Dec. 2007].

[5] [Henry Howard *et al.*], *An excellent Epitaffe of Syr Thomas Wyat, with two other compendious dytties* (London, John Herford for Robert Toye [n.d.]); John Leland, *Naeniae in mortem Thomae Viati equitis incomparabilis* (London, Reyner Wolfe, 1542).

[6]   Bella suum merito iactet florentia Dantem.
           Regia Petrarchae carmina Roma probet.
           His non inferior patrio sermone Viatus
           Eloquij secum qui decus omne tulit.
           (Leland, *Naeniae*, sig. A3ᵛ; for a translation, see Muir, *Life and Letters*, p. 264.)

           A Hand that taught what might be saide in rime
           That refte Chaucer, the glorye of his wytte [. . .]
           ([Howard], *Excellent Epitaffe*, sig. A1ᵛ.)

[7]   Caesariem iuueni subflauam contulit: inde
           Defluxit sensim crinis, caluumque reliquit.
           Sylua sed excreuit promissae densula barbae.
           (Leland, *Naeniae*, sig. A5ʳ; for translation, see Muir, *Life and Letters*, p. 267.)

an angelic voice.[8] Surrey's blazon of Wyatt, however, peels back the flesh, exposing each body part as the site of a different attribute: his breast, virtue; head, wisdom; visage, a certain blend of Stoic morality; hand, his poetic talent. He presents Wyatt as a figure whose inner qualities can be laid bare, an open book in death as in life, when his 'persinge looke dyd represent a mynde | Wythe vertue fraught, reposed, voyde of guyle' (sig. A1ᵛ). Surrey stabilises Wyatt's posthumous image, removing its contours and rough edges; there is no evidence here, for example, of his imprisonment for killing a man in a brawl eight years earlier,[9] or of his membership of what Susan Brigden has called a 'high-rolling gambling fraternity at court'.[10] By the end of Surrey's elegy, Wyatt has become Christ-like, dying for the sins of his fellow men, who have failed to realise his worth: 'Sent for our welthe, but not receavyd so. | Thus for our gylte this Juell have we lost' (sig. A1ᵛ). Circulating beyond a coterie of manuscript readers, the printed elegy thus serves to monumentalise Wyatt, fixing his reputation.

Certainly Surrey's saintly Wyatt sets the pattern that others followed: Leland's elegies celebrate 'spotless Wyatt' ('candido [. . .] Viato', sig. A3ʳ) and his 'severer studies' ('seueriora', sig. A3ᵛ)—a tendency to highlight the moral seriousness of Wyatt's poetry that we find fifteen years later in Richard Tottel's preface to *Songes and sonettes* (1557). In this first major printed collection to contain Wyatt's poetry, the printer praises 'the weightinesse of depewitted sir Thomas Wyat the elders verse'.[11] The nineteenth-century clergyman G. F. Nott was to cling gratefully to these posthumous eulogies when faced with the task of discussing his subject's sexual probity. 'We hear of no charges against him by his enemies on account of immoral conduct', he insists, suppressing Wyatt's self-accusations in his letters to his son in 1537: 'on the contrary he was universally spoken of as a man whose life was irreproachable; and as the tenor of his writings shews him to have been of a pious and an eminently religious turn of mind, we may fairly conclude that his behaviour never at any time occasioned public scandal.'[12]

---

[8] See, for example, Shakespeare's parody of this convention in Sonnet 130, 'My mistres eyes are nothing like the Sunne', *Shake-speares Sonnets* (London, G. Eld, 1609), sig. H4ʳ.

[9] In May 1534, Wyatt had been imprisoned in the Fleet for his part in a fight in which one of the London sergeants was killed. Burrow, 'Wyatt, Sir Thomas'.

[10] Susan Brigden, '"The Shadow that You Know": Sir Thomas Wyatt and Sir Francis Bryan at Court and in Embassy', *The Historical Journal*, 39:1 (1996), 1–31 (at 17). As Brigden notes, 'both Bryan and Wyatt were listed in Edward Seymour's accounts of his gaming debts'.

[11] Henry Howard et al., *Songes and sonettes* (London, Richard Tottel, 1557), sig. A1ᵛ.

[12] G. F. Nott (ed.), *The Works of Henry Howard, Earl of Surrey and of Sir Thomas Wyatt the Elder*, 2 vols. (London, T. Bensley, for Longman, Hurst, Rees, Orme, and Brown, 1816), 2. xvii.

The twin legacy of Surrey's elegy is thus the enduring image of 'vprighte' Wyatt, and a Wyatt whose personality is readable—not through his 'persinge look' (as it was for Surrey)—but through his work, 'the tenor of his writings'.[13] Surrey's claim in another commemorative poem—'I [. . .] knew what harbred in that hed'—is one that generations of critics have sought to emulate.[14] From the first edition of Wyatt's collected poems, produced by G. F. Nott in 1816, critics and editors have confidently asserted their ability to find the writer in the work.[15] Nott, for example, buttressed his text of the poems with historical evidence. The work is prefaced by a 'memoir' of Wyatt; his notes on the poems recurrently posit biographical readings;[16] and the collection ends with a hodge-podge of historical documents, including deeds of exchange; Wyatt's account books from his embassy in Spain; and the description of a Christmas joust in 1525. These appear in a string of appendices, left to stand without commentary, as if the connections between the poems and the historical detail were obvious. Indeed, such is Nott's reliance on the poetry for biographical evidence that he cannot believe that Wyatt ever

---

Cf. Nott on his whitewashing of Wyatt's sexual mores in his observations on l. 13 of 'They flee from me' ('sweetly she did me kiss'): 'The propriety of this image depends in great measure on a circumstance which grew out of the manners of the days of chivalry, and which is now forgotten' (2. 546). The commentary on the ending of 'So feeble is the thread' (when the poetic speaker imagines the woman placing the poem between her breasts) strikes a similar, if strained, note: 'Wyatt seems so confident that his strains would be graciously received that it will be pleasing to believe they were addressed to his wife.' For Wyatt's letter to his son, see Muir, *Life and Letters*, pp. 38–41 (at p. 40). Wyatt was also accused of consorting with courtesans by Edmund Bonner (see Muir, *Life and Letters*, p. 67), but Nott probably did not know of this, since Bonner's accusations were not made widely available until J. Bruce printed them in *Gentleman's Magazine* (June 1850), pp. 565–8. However, as Nott reprinted Wyatt's letters to his son, he must have been aware of his confession that 'foly and unthriftnes that hath as I wel deseruid, broght me into a thousand dangers and hazards, enmyties, hatrids, prisonments, despits and indignations' (Muir, *Life and Letters*, p. 40).

[13] Howard, *Excellent Epitaffe*, sig. A1ᵛ; Nott (ed.), *Works*, 2. xvii.

[14] Howard, 'Dyuers thy death doe diuersly bemone', *Songes and sonettes*, sig. D2ʳ.

[15] Unlike subsequent nineteenth-century editions—such as *The Poetical Works of Sir Thomas Wyatt* (London, William Pickering, 1853)—Nott's edition does not simply reproduce Tottel's text, but also draws on manuscript sources (mainly BL MS Egerton 2711, 'the Egerton Manuscript', and BL Add. MS 17492, 'the Devonshire Manuscript'). Nott is here indebted to some extent to the lost edition prepared by his uncle, John Nott, four copies of which survive in proof (all copies of the finished edition were lost in a printer's fire).

[16] Nott suggests, for example, that 'The answer that ye made' is one of a group of poems 'written on the occasion of [his] separation from Anne Boleyn', a 'circumstance [that] would account for their being both obscure and unfinished. They might have been hastily written on the first impulse of feeling: though prudence had suggested afterwards the propriety of not finishing or making them public', Nott (ed.), *Works*, 2. 549.

went to Italy: 'it is extraordinary that if Wyatt did indeed travel into Italy, [. . .] that he himself should not have made some allusion to it in his poems', he writes, scoffing at Isaac Walton's claim that Wyatt knew Italy first-hand, proof of which—surviving in Henrician letters—has subsequently been pieced together by Susan Brigden and Jonathan Woolfson.[17]

That Wyatt's life-story should have captured critical attention is hardly surprising. It is the stuff of adventure. Imprisoned three times (narrowly avoiding execution on the latter two occasions, in 1536 and 1541); connected romantically with Anne Boleyn; sent abroad as the king's ambassador: the repeated rise and fall and rise of Wyatt's fortunes epitomise our perception of the cruel uncertainty of life at the court of Henry VIII, who seems to have grown increasingly irascible with the passing years and his mounting illnesses. It is therefore quite understandable that from the nineteenth-century 'rediscovery' of Wyatt onwards, consistent attempts should have been made to read his poems biographically, tying specific lyrics to key events in Wyatt's life—most notably the king's courtship of Anne Boleyn, her subsequent disgrace and execution. These attempts to *chercher* the poet (and with him, *la femme*) are exemplified by W. E. Simonds's endeavours in 1889 to produce a complete chronology of Wyatt's poems on the basis of crude analyses of metrical form and content. He divides the poems into periods of 'Protestation and Entreaty', 'Prosperity or Attainment', 'Disappointment or Deception', 'Disillusion and Recovery' and—more prosaically—'late poems', when an older, wiser poet finds more serious topics on which to write.[18] As Simonds writes:

> We may remark that it was very natural for Wyatt, with his head full of the poetry of Italy, and possibly that of France, [. . .] to cast his eye around for another Laura or Diane, to whom he might dedicate the verse he was beginning to translate and to compose. If his choice happened to fall upon the brilliant and fascinating Anne Boleyn—and what thing more likely?—his verse would prove not at all unwelcome to this young coquette fresh from the Court of France.[19]

Wyatt is thus cast as an English Petrarch, and the woman at the heart of this narrative is, of course, Anne Boleyn.[20] The tenacity of this tradition

---

[17] Nott (ed.), *Works*, 2. xi; Susan Brigden and Jonathan Woolfson, 'Thomas Wyatt in Italy', *Renaissance Quarterly*, 58 (2005), 464–511.
[18] W. E. Simonds, *Sir Thomas Wyatt and his Poems* (Boston, 1889).
[19] Ibid., p. 128.
[20] Cf. Sergio Baldi: 'Nineteenth-century scholars persuaded themselves that all of Wyatt's love poems were written for Anne Boleyn, though there is no evidence at all for this belief, and it is

is evident today on <www.luminarium.org>, a web resource—now ten years old—much used by students, where a portrait of Anne Boleyn appears, without qualification, above the text of Wyatt's 'They Flee from Me', probably his best-known poem.

Simonds is undoubtedly an extreme case. However, he is not alone in either his desire to produce a chronology of Wyatt's poems,[21] or in reading the poetry as being 'intimately connected with Wyatt's own experience'.[22] As A. K. Foxwell wrote in 1913, Wyatt's verses 'attest [his] actual standard of life, and are the outcome of his convictions'; his *'life and work* is a song of harmony'.[23] Even after Roland Barthes announced the 'Death of the Author' in 1967, the search for Wyatt in his poetry has continued, a persistent trend highlighted in David Rosen's observation in 1981 that 'for the last fifteen years critics have tended to find in Wyatt's verse an expression of his personality'.[24] As Stephen Greenblatt wrote in 1980, in his still-influential *Renaissance Self-Fashioning*, Wyatt's poetry invites its 'audience [. . .] to experience the movement of the poet's mind through assurance, doubt, dread, and longing', in a 'painstaking rendering of the inner life'.[25]

---

inspired only too obviously by Victorian romantic idealism. The intention was to make the poet almost into another Petrarch, with Anne Boleyn as his Laura', *Sir Thomas Wyatt*, translated by F. T. Prince (London, 1961), pp. 13–14.

[21] The literary 'cursus' Simonds constructs, as Wyatt moves from love lyrics to graver, more moral matters (i.e. his satires) then religious poetry (his psalms) is similar to that found in a milder, but persistent, form in the work of many Wyatt critics and editors, including Kenneth Muir and Patricia Thomson (eds.), *The Collected Poems of Sir Thomas Wyatt* (Liverpool, 1969), where—despite the ostensible reliance on the order of the poems in the Egerton Manuscript—the satires are gathered into a discrete group placed after the lyric poetry (whereas in the manuscript they are interspersed with these poems).

[22] Simonds, *Sir Thomas Wyatt*, p. 124.

[23] A. K. Foxwell (ed.), *The Poems of Sir Thomas Wiatt*, 2 vols. (London, 1913), 2. xiv, xx. Compare W. J. Courthorpe in 1897 on 'the vehement individuality and character of W's poetry' and E. M. W. Tillyard in 1929, describing Wyatt as 'a man of remarkable character, part of which has been made accessible to us through the medium of a number of short poems'. Courthorpe, *History of English Poetry*, cited by Patricia Thomson (ed.), *Wyatt: the Critical Heritage* (London, 1974), p. 13; Tillyard (ed.), *The Poetry of Sir Thomas Wyatt: a Selection and a Study* (London, 1929), p. v.

[24] David Rosen, 'Time, identity, and context in Wyatt's verse', *Studies in English Literature, 1500–1900*, 21 (1981), 5–20 (at 5).

[25] Stephen Greenblatt, *Renaissance Self-Fashioning: from More to Shakespeare* (Chicago, 1980), p. 159. Alistair Fox's much-cited chapter on 'The unquiet mind of Sir Thomas Wyatt' acknowledges the gap between Wyatt and the 'selves' asserted in his poetry ('in an attempt to bolster his shattered ego'); however, his readings of the poems are still predominantly biographical/psychological: the fragmented selves projected in Wyatt's poetry are seen as a response to the 'metaphysical panic' 'unleashed' by 'Anne Boleyn's defection'. Like most biographical readers, Fox focuses in particular on Wyatt's relationships with Anne Boleyn and Thomas Cromwell, and on

So why is it that Wyatt's poetry lures us into these biographical readings, identifying poetic speakers with the poet himself, even in a critical
climate—post-Barthes—where first-year undergraduates are gently dis-
suaded from doing likewise? The answer lies, in part, in the stylistic and
structural features of Wyatt's poetry. First and foremost of these stylistic
tics must be the way in which the poems are punctuated by the appearance of the first person singular; 'There is no more insistent expression of
the "I" in Tudor literature', Greenblatt notes.[26] The amount to which
Wyatt's poems are preoccupied with the self can be illustrated by measuring his adaptations of Petrarch against the Italian originals. Repeatedly,
Wyatt's translations transform an address to a third person into a poem
about the self. Petrarch's *Rima* 103, for example, advises Stefano Colonna
the Younger to take heed from Hannibal's inability to press his advantage.
'Hannibal was victorious, but he did not know later how to make good
use of his victorious fortune', Petrarch states: 'therefore, dear my Lord,
take care that the same does not happen to you' ('Vinse Annibàl, et non
seppe usar poi | ben la vittoriosa sua ventura; | però, Signor mio caro,
aggiate cura | Che similmente non avegna a voi', ll. 1–4).[27] This is
remoulded by Wyatt into a lament for his own protracted embassy in
Spain in the late 1530s (one of the few Wyatt poems which does seem to
suggest a precise location and therefore potential date). 'At Mountzon
thus I restles rest in spayne', it complains (l. 8), identifying with
Hannibal's failure, rather than instructing someone else to learn from it.[28]
So too in Wyatt's translation of *Rima* 98, the external addressee—Orso
dell'Anguillara—is replaced by the speaker's self. Where Petrarch's Orso
cannot be reined in (unlike his horse),[29] Wyatt's speaker aligns himself
with that horse, announcing that 'I my self be bridilled of my mynde'—
a characteristic reworking of the Petrarchan source not only because

---

his experiences in prison in 1536 and 1541. Fox, *Politics and Literature in the Reigns of Henry
VII and Henry VIII* (Oxford, 1989), pp. 257–85; quotations from pp. 265, 264.

[26] Greenblatt, *Renaissance Self-Fashioning*, p. 155.

[27] Robert M. Durling (ed./trans.), *Petrarch's Lyric Poems* (Cambridge, MA, 1976), pp. 206, 207. As
discussed below, Wyatt was almost certainly using Vellutello's edition of Petrarch's poems, which
reorders the poems; however, for ease of reference for twenty-first-century readers, Petrarch's *rime*
will be cited by the now standard numbering (as used by Durling) and all subsequent quotations
of Petrarch will be from Durling's parallel text edition.

[28] Thomas Wyatt, 'Off cartage he', BL MS Egerton 2711, fol. 54ᵛ. Unless otherwise stated, all
subsequent quotations of Wyatt's poetry will be from the Egerton Manuscript. In transcriptions,
i/j and u/v have been retained, superscript letters have been lowered and contractions silently
expanded.

[29] Durling (ed./trans.), *Petrarch's Lyric Poems*, pp. 200, 201.

Wyatt intensifies the presence of the first person, but because he also renders that (male) speaker curiously passive.[30] An examination of subjective emotions is thus substituted for Petrarch's more objective address to a third person. The tone—like much of Wyatt's oeuvre—consequently appears confessional. This feeling is heightened by the seemingly conversational nature of his poetry. Critics such as E. M. W. Tillyard have drawn attention to the 'touch of drama' in his lyrics, which are likened to Donne's poetry over half a century later.[31] This same sense of performance is conveyed by F. M. Padelford:

> The poems are like monologues snatched from intense situations, like chance sparks from an anvil all aglow. There is no stopping for introduction or setting, and it is as if we were to enter the theatre at a moment when a situation is critical, and passionate utterance is at its height. The molten words, as if too long repressed, overflow from highly-wrought emotion. The language is direct, familiar, and unadorned; a case left to stand or fall by the bare truth of it.[32]

As Tillyard's or Padelford's words indicate, Wyatt's poems have a strong sense of a poetic speaker, who is either talking to a third party, or working through his own experience in language which is deliberately—often awkwardly—colloquial. This awkwardness is found, for example, in Wyatt's metrical roughness, which the compiler of *Songes and sonettes* felt moved to correct in 1557, amending Wyatt's lines to by-then more conventional pentameters. This discordance is also found in the way Wyatt allows words to rub up against each other, rather than striving to achieve a more eloquent, copious style: 'Ther was never File so half well filed | to file a file for every smythes intent', he writes; or 'And I my self my self always to hate.'[33] Nott, for one, failed to appreciate this stylistic quirk, objecting to it in his note on 'Love and fortune and my mynde'. 'This is one of Wyatt's worst sonnets', he complains: 'How very inelegant is the second line, in which the word "*that*" occurs four times.'[34] Since we can see Wyatt consciously avoiding monotonous vocabulary in many of his revisions to the Egerton Manuscript, this repetition would appear to be choice, rather than accident or the limitations of Tudor English, the

---

[30] Wyatt, 'Though I my self be bridilled of my mynde', BL MS Egerton 2711, fol. 21ʳ.

[31] Tillyard (ed.), *Poetry of Sir Thomas Wyatt*, pp. 34–6.

[32] Frederick Morgan Padelford (ed.), *Early Sixteenth Century Lyrics* (Boston, 1907), pp. xlv–xlvi. For a similar conjunction of an appreciation of the affective power of Wyatt's poetry with attention to its dramatic quality, see Fox, *Politics and Literature*, p. 264.

[33] Wyatt, 'Ther was never File', ll. 1–2, BL MS Egerton 2711, fol. 14ᵛ; Wyatt, 'The piller pearisht is', l. 13, Muir and Thomson (eds.), *Collected Poems*, p. 238.

[34] Nott (ed.), *Works*, 2. 542.

'lack of diuersyte' of which Wyatt lamented in the dedicatory epistle to *The Quyete of mynde*.[35] That is, as we can see from these examples, Wyatt's poetry eschews an obviously polished or ornate style, potentially placing it closer to the registers of everyday speech.

Wyatt's poems further achieve a conversational style through their interruption with sighs, exclamations, direct questions, proverbs, and oaths (as in the rondeau 'What no perdy'). Wyatt's 'Farewell Love' is a useful example of his technique.[36] The sonnet opens with a direct address, 'Farewell Love' (l. 1), the orality of which is reasserted at the beginning of the third quatrain: 'Therefor farewell goo trouble yonger hertes' (l. 9). Avoiding ornament and employing stock descriptions ('bayted hookes', 'blynde errour', 'sherpe repulce', 'idill yeuth', 'brittil dertes', ll. 2, 5, 6, 11, 12), the language rarely strays from conventional, early sixteenth-century idiom, culminating in the biting note of the concluding proverb: 'me lusteth no lenger rotten boughes to clyme' (l. 14). The emphatic nature of this maxim is further strengthened by its appearance in a final couplet (the development of which was to prove one of Wyatt's most influential innovations in his Englishing of the sonnet form).

'Farewell Love' is also characteristic of Wyatt's poetry in its seeming dramatisation of a moment or event. Thomas M. Greene has observed Wyatt's tendency to 'linearise' his translations, 'transforming a circular plot to a unique, unrepeatable plot'.[37] As Greene points out, Wyatt makes small changes, removing 'talor' (sometimes), altering the plural 'estremi' to a singular 'extremitie'.[38] The cumulative effect is that Wyatt's verse is made to articulate a single event (rather than the perpetual state which is found in Petrarch's *rime*). Coupled with the ordinariness of Wyatt's diction, this process of linearisation helps increase the sense that his poetry is confessional, describing an actual occurrence. This impression is enhanced by the fact that Wyatt tends to avoid allegory, which had been a dominant mode of medieval poetry. Greg Walker, for example, notes how 'the difference between Wyatt's anxieties and the allegorical trepidations of the figures in a previous generation's anti-curial satires, such as Drede in Skelton's *Bowge of Courte*, lies precisely in the sense that these words were written to explore a felt condition rather than to exemplify a

---

[35] Thomas Wyatt, *The Quyete of mynde* (London, Richard Pynson, [1528]), sig. a2[r].
[36] BL Egerton MS 2711, fol. 13[r].
[37] Thomas M. Greene, *The Light in Troy: Imitation and Discovery in Renaissance Poetry* (New Haven, CT, 1982), p. 251.
[38] Ibid., p. 251.

universal truth'.[39] With great economy, with a smattering of concrete nouns and simple adjectives, Wyatt can evoke a sense of real place, or occasion: such as the Kentish home in 'Myne owne John Poytz', where 'in fowle weder at [his] booke [he] sitt[s]' (l. 81).[40] The erotic encounter in 'They flee from me' is similarly captured through deceptively simple diction and syntax, such as the series of noun phrases and active verbs that are evenly distributed across the lines:

> in *thyn aray*, after a *pleasant gyse*
> when her *lose gowne* from her *shoulders* did **fall**
> and she me **caught** in her *armes long and small*
> therewithall swetely did me **kysse**
> and softely *saide dere hert*, howe like you this?[41]

Atmosphere is further conveyed by the pair of sensory adverbs introduced as the situation intensifies ('swetely', 'softely', ll. 13, 14) and that snippet of direct speech: 'dere hert, howe like you this?' (l. 14). The choice of the proximal deixis *this* (rather than the distant *that*) further draws us in to the moment, whilst a retrospective irony is resonant in the fact that the blandishment 'dere heart' is the only non-concrete noun phrase in the description of the episode.

The betrayal that this poem records is also characteristically Wyatt, as is the barbed *politesse* of its closing line: 'I would fain knowe what she hath deserued' (l. 21), an ability to hide a sting in the tail that recurs across his writings, including in his letter to his son in April 1537, where he acknowledges—of his failed marriage to Elizabeth Brooke—that 'the faulte is both in your mother and me', before snatching this away with the coda 'but chieflie in her'.[42] A sense of a consistent outlook, or a coherent body of experience, is thus created by the repetitive nature of the scenarios depicted in Wyatt's poems and by the recurrence of a similar voice or register across his writing—a tone that is described as 'subdued sarcasm' by Greene, 'blame-style' by Reed Way Dasenbrock, in contrast to Petrarch's *stile de la loda*, or praise-style.[43] Repeatedly, we find Wyatt's

---

[39] Greg Walker, *Writing under Tyranny* (Oxford, 2005), p. 428.

[40] BL MS Egerton 2711, fol. 49ᵛ. For a brief discussion of the 'solid[ity]' of Wyatt's nouns in 'Myne owne Poytz', see Colin Burrow, 'Wyatt and Sixteenth-Century Horatianism', in Charles Martindale and David Hopkins (eds.), *Horace Made New* (Cambridge, 1993), pp. 27–49 (at p. 37).

[41] Ibid., fol. 27ᵛ (italics added).

[42] Muir, *Life and Letters*, p. 41.

[43] Greene, *Light in Troy*, p. 251; Reed Way Dasenbrock, 'Wyatt's transformation of Petrarch', *Comparative Literature*, 40:2 (1988), 122–33 (at 129).

speakers locked in despair or self-loathing, a state which he often adds or embellishes in his translations. So, for instance, in his version of *Rima* 189, he switches Petrarch's 'i'ncomincio a desperar del porto' ('I begin to despair of the port') to 'I *remain* despering of the port'.[44] This sense of emotional paralysis is typical of the endings of many of Wyatt's poems, including his translation of *Rima* 269, rendered as 'The piller pearisht is whearto I Lent'.[45] Wyatt excises Petrarch's shift into philosophical gener-alisation ('Oh our life that is so beautiful to see, how easily it loses in one morning what has been acquired with great difficulty over many years!'; 'O nostra vita ch'è sì bella in vista, | com' perde aggevolmente in un matino | quel che 'n molti anni a gran pena s'acquista', ll. 12–14).[46] Wyatt's sonnet instead concludes, still focused on the self, predicting a life of self-hatred, a stalemate hammered home by the masculine rhyme of the final couplet: 'And I my self my self alwayes to hate | Till dreadful death do ease my dolefull state' (ll. 13–14). The reiterative nature of the situations found in Wyatt's verses thus helps create the sense that there is a unified body of experience behind, and expressed through, these poems. Wyatt's speakers are constantly striving for stasis, bruised by change, dis-appointed by transience.[47] The proverbial wisdom cited often refers to the futility of seeking to hold the wind in a net, or capture water in a sieve.[48] Alterations and additions to Petrarch's lines highlight a sense of perpet-ual and unwanted change or motion: 'vita' ('life', l. 47) is expanded to become 'vnesy life' (l. 37);[49] a contrast between 'pace' and 'guerra' ('peace' and 'war', l. 30) is tellingly redescribed by Wyatt as the difference between 'rest' and 'errour' (l. 28), error holding within it a sense of wandering,

---

[44] Durling (ed./trans.), *Petrarch's Lyric Poems*, pp. 334, 335; Wyatt, 'My galy charged with forgetfulnes', BL MS Egerton 2711, fol. 21ᵛ (italics added).

[45] Wyatt, 'The piller pearisht is whearto I Lent', in Muir and Thomson (eds.), *Collected Poems*, p. 238.

[46] Durling (ed./trans.), *Petrarch's Lyric Poems*, pp. 442, 443.

[47] Other recurrent preoccupations include 'doubleness' (the word appears in three of the first six poems in the Egerton Manuscript) and waste, especially the 'wast' of words (see, for example, 'What nedeth these thretning wordes and wasted wynde?'). For a discussion of the impact of instability on Wyatt's poetic voice, see John Kerrigan, 'Wyatt's selfish style', *Essays and Studies*, 34 (1981), 1–18. This essay also draws attention to Wyatt's poetry as 'secretive' (p. 8), a quality discussed below.

[48] Wyatt, 'Whoso list to hounte', l. 8; 'A spending hand', l. 91.

[49] Petrarch, *Rima* 37, Durling (ed./trans.), *Petrarch's Lyric Poems*, pp. 98, 99; Wyatt, 'So feble is the threde', BL MS Egerton 2711, fol. 67ᵛ; 'thvnsesy' is spelt 'thvnsesy', but I have amended the spelling, to aid the sense, in line with versions of the poem elsewhere (in *Songes and sonettes*, sig. I4ᵛ, as well as the Devonshire and Arundel Manuscripts).

derived as it is from the Latin *errare*.[50] Motion, in other words, offers Wyatt a ready metaphor for dissatisfaction, as demonstrated by two lines (again translated from Petrarch) in Wyatt's own hand in the Egerton Manuscript: 'From thowght to thowght from hill to hill love doth me lede, | Clene contrary from restfull lyff these common pathes I trede', the couplet reads, the regularity of the metre and the predominant monosyllables in the first line in particular capturing the enforced tedium of this unlooked-for journey.[51] In this uncertain, shifting world, the word *stay* holds dual promise, able to mean both 'stop' and 'support'.[52]

The desire for fixity, and the sense of bewilderment or frustration in the face of transitoriness, extends to the portrayal of human relationships. Little attention has been paid to Wyatt's habit of translating *speranza* (and its related terms) not as *hope*, but *trust* (the exception being Elizabeth Heale, in her discussion of Wyatt's poem 'Love and fortune and my mynde').[53] This small change entirely alters the dynamic depicted, and is not a mistranslation on Wyatt's part: he translates *spero* as 'I hope' in his translation of Petrarch's *Rima* 134 (l. 2).[54] The choice of 'trust' over 'hope' both imposes expectations—about standards of behaviour required from the addressee—and sets up the speaker for inevitable disappointment when that involuntary contract is broken. As Wyatt himself wrote, in his *Defence*, designed to exonerate himself from the charge of treason in 1541, 'yt is a smale thynge in alteringe of one syllable ether with penne or worde that may mayk in the conceavinge of truthe myche matter or error. For in thys thynge "I fere", or "I truste", semethe but one smale syllable chaynged, and yet it makethe a great dyfferaunce.'[55]

When read together as a body of poetry, then, the consistency of attitude, tone, and scenario help create the impression that the experiences and emotions voiced are those of the poet himself, especially when combined with the plain, colloquial style, the focus on inwardness, and the

---

[50] Petrarch, *Rima* 360, Durling (ed./trans.), *Petrarch's Lyric Poems*, pp. 560, 561; Wyatt, 'Myne olde dere enmy', BL MS Egerton 2711, fol. 8ʳ. The first three stanzas are missing from the Egerton MS, and have here been derived from *Songes and sonettes*, sig. F3ʳ.

[51] BL MS Egerton 2711, fol. 65ʳ; Petrarch, *Rima* 129, Durling (ed./trans.), *Petrarch's Lyric Poems*, pp. 264, 265.

[52] 'Stay, v¹', sense 1, and 'stay, v²', sense 1; 'stay, n²', sense 1a, and 'stay, n³', sense 1, *Oxford English Dictionary Online*, <http://dictionary.oed.com> [accessed 20 Dec. 2007]. See Wyatt, 'If waker care', l. 13, 'my hert alone wel worthie she doth staye', BL MS Egerton 2711, fol. 66ᵛ.

[53] Elizabeth Heale, *Wyatt, Surrey and Early Tudor Poetry* (London, 1998), p. 99.

[54] Wyatt, 'I fynde no peace', BL MS Egerton 2711, fol. 20ᵛ; Durling (ed./trans.), *Petrarch's Lyric Poems*, pp. 272, 273.

[55] Muir, *Life and Letters*, p. 197.

evocation of time, place and—occasionally—actual people (poems are addressed to the courtiers John Poyntz and Sir Francis Bryan, for example).[56] Here the way in which we tend to receive Wyatt is significant: Wyatt's poetic voice—the features of which I have been mapping—is one created out of the experience of sitting down to read a substantial body of his work, presented *en masse*, be it in modern or Victorian editions; imprints of *Songes and sonettes* from the sixteenth to the twentieth centuries; or the Egerton Manuscript, where—unusually for a miscellany—the work of one poet dominates (albeit versifying which was ignored and overwritten by generations of the Harrington family into whose possession it came).

The potentially cohesive nature of Wyatt's idiom can be illustrated by examining 'So feble is the thred', one of Wyatt's more critically neglected poems. A translation of Petrarch's *Rima* 37, it is also a piece which unleashes C. S. Lewis's scorn. Particularly regrettable in Lewis's view is Wyatt's choice of metre, 'the terrible poulter's measure'. 'The thudding verbiage [. . .]', Lewis complains, 'raises a wonder why the man who thought Petrarch could be translated so, also thought Petrarch worth translating.'[57] Both Lewis's term *verbiage* and Patricia Thomson's phrase 'lumbering poulter's measure' hint at the reasons underlying their dissatisfaction with Wyatt's selected metre: written in alternating lines of twelve and fourteen syllables, poulter's measure is somewhat wordier than we tend to expect from our poetry, accustomed as we are to pentameters, which came to dominate English verse.[58] Yet—as well as allowing an investigation of Wyatt's accustomed style and techniques—proper reconsideration of the poem also shows Wyatt to be a much more accomplished poet than Lewis suggests.

'So feble is the thred' is rare within Wyatt's oeuvre because it is one of the few poems which we can situate chronologically. Written in Wyatt's hand and entitled at a later date 'In Spayne' (possibly by his son),[59] the poem originates from his protracted embassy between April 1537 and April 1540. The circumstantial dating is collaborated by Jason Powell's

---

[56] 'Myne owne Iohn Poyntz' and 'My mothers maydes' are addressed to Poyntz (who is named in ll. 70, 103); 'Syghes ar my food' and 'A spending hand' are addressed to Bryan (who is named in l. 7 and l. 9 respectively).

[57] C. S. Lewis, *English Literature in the Sixteenth Century Excluding Drama* (Oxford, 1954), p. 225.

[58] Patricia Thomson, *Sir Thomas Wyatt and his Background* (London, 1964), p. 187.

[59] I owe this suggestion to Jason Powell (private correspondence, Oct. 2007), who sees the title as evidence of Wyatt's family attempting to place and categorise his poetry after his death.

work on the ink in the Egerton Manuscript, whereby the uneven fading would indicate the use of dry ink, ideal for use when travelling.[60] In this instance, there would thus seem to be a plausible autobiographical motive on Wyatt's part for translating Petrarch's canzone: *Rima* 37 laments separation from Laura, and at this time Wyatt had left behind his own long-term mistress, Elizabeth Darrell. The long lines of poulter's measure, far from being 'lumbering' (Thomson's phrase), are entirely suited to a poem which marks the long days of enervating absence, the duration of which becomes all the more unbearable for being set against the brevity of human existence:

> the lyff so short so fraile that mortal men lyve here
> so gret a whaite so hevy charge the body that we bere
> that when I thinke apon the distance and the space
> that doth so ferr devid me from my dere desired face
> I know not how tattayne the wynges that I require
> to lyfft my whaite that it myght fle to folow my desyre [.]   (ll. 21–6)

These lines are far from being metrically inept. The predominant monosyllables capture the sheer heaviness of the physical body, while the marked caesuras in those first two lines imitate the faltering flight of a bird failing to rise from the ground. The halting rhythm is then in tension with the yearning for contact, resonant in the frequent attempts at enjambment (three out of these six lines—ll. 22, 23, 25—run on in a grammatical sense). The transformation of Petrarch's canzone into an English form (poulter's measure) is enhanced by Wyatt's subtle—but characteristic—use of alliteration, which provides an alternative to the patterning of sound achieved in the Italian with its greater number of similar rhymes (Italian words having a much smaller pool of endings than English).

The poem is also unusual for Wyatt in that it celebrates love. The experience might be painful, but for once it is not the woman's fault. Yet even as the poem traces a different trajectory, it does so in terms that can be found elsewhere in the Wyatt canon. Recurrently, for example, love is seen to require the self-abnegation common to much Tudor love poetry, as in Wyatt's line elsewhere: 'I love an other and thus I hate myself.'[61] What in Petrarch's poem are contradictory but simultaneously held emotions— 'in odio me stesso, et amo altrui' ('I hate myself and love another') are

---

[60] Jason Powell, 'Thomas Wyatt's poetry in Embassy: Egerton 2711 and the production of literary manuscripts abroad', *Huntington Library Quarterly*, 67:2 (2004), 261–82.
[61] Wyatt, 'I fynde no peace', l. 11, BL MS Egerton 2711, fol. 20ᵛ.

here transformed into one being the consequence of the other ('and thus').[62] In 'So feble is the thred', however, this self-abandonment is portrayed as welcome, even necessary, if we consider the metaphor of the ship, which needs someone at the helm if disaster is to be averted: 'those handes those armes that do embrace | me from my sellff and rule the sterne of my poor lyff' (ll. 82–3). The speaker here places himself, gladly, under the woman's guiding hand.

As we saw earlier, enforced motion—and the search for stasis—are familiar motifs of Wyatt's poetry. Wyatt's Kent, for example, celebrated in 'Myne owne Iohn Poyntz', offers the speaker more than simply freedom from courtly corruption; Wyatt's speaker is 'at home' (l. 80), unlike Luigi Alamanni, who wrote the Italian original whilst exiled in Provence.[63] Within 'So feble is the thred', it is the woman—'my swete wele' (l. 6)—who becomes emblematic of home, situated in 'that plesant place | where she doth lyve by whome I lyve' (ll. 95–6). The repetition of 'lyve' here acts as a tribute to the woman's sustaining powers, a lovely equilibrium established in the simple symmetry of that phrase. Where Laura, honoured by Heaven, is someone 'in whom virtue and courtesy dwell' ('alberga onestate et cortesia', l. 111), Wyatt's poem depicts the woman's virtue as active, not simply lodging, but flourishing in her, capable as a consequence of inspiring or infusing the man whose love she nurtures: she is 'the restyng place of love where vertu lyves and grose' (l. 93).

Besides its unusually positive treatment of the woman, 'So feble is the thred' also stands out because it forms a sequence in the Egerton Manuscript which can potentially be read as a narrative. The poem is preceded by a sonnet, 'If waker care', revised in Wyatt's hand in the darker ink which is characteristic of ordinary ink, rather than the dry ink used when travelling.[64] It is followed by 'Tagus fare well', an obvious allusion to Wyatt's longed-for departure from the Iberian peninsula, penned in Wyatt's own hand and also headed 'In Spayne'.[65] This physical evidence, suggesting a triptych of poems ranging from before the embassy ('If waker care') to the end of that period abroad ('Tagus fare well'), is supported by internal echoes of sentiment and idiom. 'So feble is the thred' depicts the woman as a healing refuge, whose 'pleasant word & chere' did

---

[62] Petrarch, *Rima* 134, l. 11, Durling (ed./trans.), *Petrarch's Lyric Poems*, pp. 272, 273.
[63] 'Sono in Prouenza', Luigi Alamanni, Satire 10, l. 97, reproduced in Muir and Thomson (eds.), *Collected Poems*, pp. 337–9.
[64] BL MS Egerton 2711, fol. 66^v.
[65] Ibid., fol. 69^r.

'bryng [. . .] redresse off lingred payne' (ll. 74–5). This builds on the preceding poem, which cherishes 'thunfayned chere of phillis' (l. 9). In both poems, love necessitates self-abandonment. However—as we saw earlier—this is not abhorred, but relished: Phillis 'from my self now hath me in her grace | she hath in hand my witt my will and all'. '[A]nd all'— the sigh at the end of the line in which the lover surrenders himself, bodily, to his beloved—hints at a bawdy reading. 'Will' can assume its meaning of 'desire', and the 'grace' the lover receives—courtesy of a hand-job—would thus be the sexual grace for which Sidney's Astrophil would sue, some fifty years later.[66]

This sexualised reading is entirely consistent with Wyatt's tendency to make Petrarch's Laura a much more tangible figure. Over and over in his translations, Wyatt removes Petrarch's heavenly register: 'anima' and 'alma' are habitually translated as 'heart' or 'mind', not 'soul'.[67] As Sergio Baldi observes, both Wyatt and Petrarch's speakers 'describe their lady as "cruel", but by this word they mean different things: for Petrarch's lady is hard and immovable only because of her virtue, and in the cause of virtue, while Wyatt's is merely fickle, unfeeling, or ungrateful'.[68] More particularly, though, this sensuality has an immediate resonance with Wyatt's eroticisation of *Rima* 37. Petrarch's canzone merely imagines looking at Laura's 'noble arms and gestures sweetly haughty' (le braccia gentili | et gli atti suoi soavemente alteri', ll. 100–1); the very adjective cho-sen—haughty (*alteri*)—reminds us that he is allowed to look, not touch. Wyatt's poem in contrast evokes a sense of contact, in 'those handes those armes that do embrace' (l. 82); the asyndeton, omitting the construction *and*, emphasises that tactility, as if recording the sensation of now hands, now arms. Continuing this erotic vein, the poem ends with the speaker imagining the paper on which the poem is written nestling between the woman's breasts, an image absent from the Italian original: 'By twene her brestes she shall the put there shal she the reserve' (l. 98), a physical favour

---

[66] 'Will, n¹', sense I.1.a, *OED* [accessed 21 Dec. 2007]; Philip Sidney, *Astrophil and Stella*, in *Sir Philip Sidney*, ed. Katherine Duncan-Jones (Oxford, 1994).

[67] See Wyatt, 'Such vayn thought' (a translation of Petrarch, *Rima* 169), l. 6; 'The piller pearisht is' (a translation of Petrarch, *Rima* 269), l. 10; 'So feble is the thred' (a translation of Petrarch, *Rima* 37), l. 7; cf. 'The lyvely sparks' (a translation of Petrarch, *Rima* 258, where *alma*, l. 9, is omitted entirely).

[68] Baldi, *Sir Thomas Wyatt*, pp. 31–2. The much more earthbound nature of Wyatt's women pos-sibly explains why he was drawn to translate poems from the 'In Vita' section of Petrarch's *Rime*, rather than those from 'In Morte', where the dead Laura becomes yet more heavenly and untouchable; Wyatt only translates two poems from 'In Morte': 'The pillar pearisht is' and 'Whoso list to hounte'.

which—like the lover's situation in 'If waker care' (l. 11)—is tellingly described as 'grace' (l. 96). Wyatt's trio of verses—moving in the Egerton Manuscript from requited love and sexual fulfilment to enforced separation—is completed by 'Tagus fare well', which shares the sensuality of the preceding poems, as London 'like bendyd mone doth lend her lusty syd' (l. 6). Further to that, it carries over a pivotal image from 'So feble is the thred'. The final line of 'Tagus fare well', at long last, anticipates the 'winges' (l. 8)—painfully lacking in the previous poem—which will bear him homeward.

The rarity of 'So feble is the thred'—but also its rootedness within Wyatt's oeuvre—is further exemplified by the role played by the puns within it. Wyatt's poetry frequently plays on words. Habitually, this serves to highlight the sliding meaning or deceptiveness of language. So, for example, the 'love' inspired by 'her lokes lovely' in 'For to love her' proves unfounded (l. 1), and the lady less than lovable, despite her beauty; 'trusting by trought to have had redresse' thus transpires to be a foolish delusion and a misplaced trust (l. 3).[69] Similarly, 'They flee from me' depends for much of its power on its interrogation of what Greene has called 'wobbly words', not least among them the terms 'kindly' and 'gentill'.[70] However, 'So feble is the thred' does not deploy word-play to expose the instability of language; rather, how meanings concur. Amending the original translation from 'viage' to 'Iornei' (l. 20), Wyatt's description of the sun's course from East to West puns inter-lingually on the French *journée* (day); the 'whaite' (l. 22) which causes the body to fail is both the extended *durée* of the lovers' separation and the weight of the lover's body, too heavy to 'fle to folow [his] desyre' (l. 26); the ambiguous spelling of 'faytfull hert' (l. 36) contains a sense of both fateful and faithful; and the 'wofull cace' he moans (l. 81) is both the 'cace or skyn' of l. 64 and the pitiful condition of the speaker.[71]

'So feble is the thred' and its companion pieces are thus both unusual within the Wyatt canon and emblematic of it: emblematic because they display Wyatt's characteristic voice and techniques; unusual because they invert them—because they seem to be specific; because they hang together as a narrative; because they (tentatively) air the possibility of a love that is both reciprocated and curative; because they celebrate puns, rather than revile them; and finally because they seem on the verge of

[69] BL MS Egerton 2711, fol. 14[r].
[70] Greene, *Light in Troy*, p. 257.
[71] 'Case, n[1]', sense 5a, *OED* [accessed 21 Dec. 2007].

achieving that longed-for repose, although that yearning—as yet-unfulfilled—is in itself also typically Wyatt. As the case of the 'In Spayne' section of the Egerton Manuscript would seem to show, in other words, Wyatt's poetry does present us with an alluring sense of a cohesive, or at least recurrent, persona. Certainly this is the case in the form in which we tend to read him, one poem after another. Yet I also want to suggest that his poems—whilst hinting at biographical readings—also prove resistant to them, eluding readers who try to pin them down to historical event, place, person. This is particularly so because—despite their seemingly confessional tone—the poems recurrently withhold specific references. Take Wyatt's translation of Petrarch's *Rima* 269. Petrarch's opening line remembers both his patron (Cardinal Giovanni Colonna) and Laura, both of whom had died in the plague which swept across Italy in 1348–9. Wyatt's opening line—'The piller pearisht is whearto I Lent'—has no equivalent to the commemorative function of Petrarch's 'Rotta è l'alta colonna e 'l verde lauro' ('Broken are the high Column and the green Laurel'), recording as it does both Colonna's and Laura's names. Wyatt's poem, however, is invariably read by critics and editors as a lament for his dead patron, Thomas Cromwell, who was executed in 1540. But such interpretations, whilst possible, can only remain speculative, based on two bits of purely circumstantial evidence: first, that the poem Wyatt translates was in part about death of a patron; secondly, that Wyatt is said to have wept at the foot of Cromwell's scaffold, a scene famously described in the Spanish *Chronicle of Henry VIII*:

> And amongst all those gentlemen, Cromwell saw Master Wyatt [. . .] and called to him, saying, 'Oh, noble Wyatt, God be with thee, and I pray thee, pray to God for me!' (He had always had a great love for this Master Wyatt.) And Wyatt could not answer, so many were the tears that he shed. All those gentlemen marvelled to see how deeply Master Wyatt was moved. And as Cromwell was a very wise man, he reflected on it, and said out loud, 'Oh, Wyatt, do not weep, for if I were no more guilty than you were when you were arrested, I should not have come to this!'[72]

The habitual opacity of Wyatt's Petrarchan translations—about whom they are referring to, when they were written—is all the more noteworthy when we consider the form in which Wyatt was reading Petrarch: namely, Alessandro Vellutello's *Il Petrarcha*, first printed in 1525 with extensive commentary. Patricia Thomson seems to have been the first to note Wyatt's use of Vellutello in an article printed in 1959, which high-

---

[72] Cited in Muir, *Life and Letters*, p. 173.

lights Wyatt's debt to Vellutello's exposition on *Rima* 190, 'Una candida cerva' (which Wyatt translated as 'Whoso list to hounte'), although Wyatt's borrowings go much further and deeper than this.[73] The neglect of Thomson's discovery is exemplified by the amount of critical ink that has since been spilt, pondering what led Wyatt to transform Petrarch's 'Nessun me tocchi' (l. 9) into the Latin of the Vulgate: 'Noli me tangere' (Christ's words to Mary Magdalene at his resurrection). The immediate answer is that those are the words used in the commentary. This does not take away from the fact that Wyatt's decision to follow Vellutello's Latin, rather than Petrarch's vernacular, leads to an intriguing juxtaposition of two biblical allusions—the second being Christ's words to the Pharisees: 'give therefore to Caesar, that which is Caesar's'.[74] Nevertheless, it is true that we as critics need to attend to the version in which Wyatt was reading Petrarch, not least because Vellutello's edition marked a decided shift in the reception of the Italian poet. Vellutello reordered the poems, so that they fitted known events in the author's life, a sequence he then bolstered with the prefatory 'Life of Petrarch' and an accompanying commentary, which knitted the poems tightly together, frequently stressing how one leads on from that preceding it. Vellutello presents himself as a historical detective, poring over Petrarch's letters and writings, visiting Petrarch's old haunts in Avignon and the Vaucluse, even interviewing descendants of his known associates.[75] Great care is spent establishing the historical 'truth' about Laura, in a prefatory 'Life' which follows that of Petrarch. Vellutello's supporting material also includes a map of the Vaucluse, which focuses 'in exaggerated detail upon the region where the Sorgue river passes through Cabrières', where Petrarch was supposed to have met Laura.[76] Petrarch's *rime* are thus presented as a record of the poet's life. As William Kennedy notes, the extensive prefatory material and dense commentary surrounding each poem 'draw attention to biographical relationships between the poet and his poetry' and 'imply a closer connection between the voice of the speaker and that of the historical writer than earlier readers were likely to assume'.[77]

Vellutello's *Petrarcha* went through twenty-seven editions in the sixty years between 1525 and 1584, making it by far the 'most popular and

---

[73] Patricia Thomson, 'Wyatt and the Petrarchan commentators', *Review of English Studies*, NS, 10:39 (1959), 225–33.

[74] Matthew 20. 20–1, in Tyndale's translation.

[75] See William Kennedy, *Authorizing Petrarch* (Ithaca, NY, 1994), pp. 47–51.

[76] Ibid., p. 49.

[77] Ibid., p. 51.

influential' of the sixteenth-century commentaries.[78] Not only was it the work which Wyatt was probably using, therefore; it was also the means by which his Tudor readers were likely to receive their Petrarch, a Petrarch whose poetry was being read as a narrative of his own life. Wyatt's poems play on this. Translating Petrarch, he is engaging with what had become a biographical tradition. Yet he also disrupts that narrative. He plucks individual sonnets out of Vellutello's carefully arranged and interwoven sequence, often further denuding them of external reference points (as we saw with his translation of Petrarch's *Rima* 269, 'Rotta è l'alta colonna e 'l verde lauro'). This tendency to strip out specific referents extends beyond Wyatt's Italian translations. We can see him removing them in the Egerton Manuscript, for example, notoriously altering the line 'her that did set our country in a rore'—generally read as referring to Anne Boleyn—to '*Brunet* that set *my welth* in such a rore' (l. 8, italics added).[79] This caution—in removing potential allusions to affairs of state—is possibly also reflected in the cancelling of the word 'tyranny' in two places in the same manuscript (corrections made in Wyatt's hand). Wyatt substitutes 'crueltye' in the first line of 'Who hath herd of such crueltye before?', and 'what reson' in the poem 'Desire alas' (l. 5).[80] This second example in particular looks decidedly unguarded in its original form, which had read 'tyranne it is to reule thy subiectes | by forcyd law and mutabilitie' (ll. 5–6). By the mid-1530s, a number of acts extending royal powers, including the Act of Supremacy, had been steered through parliament to further the split from the Church of Rome. By this time, therefore, lines juxtaposing 'tyranne' and 'forcyd law' were probably best avoided, even in a poem ostensibly about love, particularly when coupled with a suggestion of 'mutabilitie', which might be interpreted by hostile readers as alluding to religious change.

Admittedly, the sense of exclusion created by our inability to know for sure whom or what is being hinted at in Wyatt's poetry is in part produced by the fact that these poems are coterie poems, written for circles of acquaintances, not primarily intended for a print audience. Yet that

---

[78] Thomson, 'Wyatt and the Petrarchan commentators', 227.

[79] Wyatt, 'If waker care', BL MS Egerton 2711, fol. 66[v].

[80] i.e. the line originally read 'Who hath herd of suche tyranny before', BL MS Egerton 2711, fol. 29[v]; in 'Desire alas', the line is amended to read 'What reson is to rewle thy subiectes so', fol. 50[r]. Cf. Wyatt's translation of Serafino's strambotto 'Sio son caduto'; Wyatt initially follows Serafino's first person pronouns, translating l. 1 as 'I ame not ded allthough I had a fall'; this is corrected in the Egerton Manuscript in Wyatt's hand to '*He is* not ded *that somtyme hath* a fall', fol. 40[r] (italics added).

inscrutability runs deeper, permeating Wyatt's metaphorical language. Throughout Wyatt's poetry, there is a horror of exposure. Where Petrarch writes how his cares 'show' ('mostrò') more clearly than a colour through 'crystal or glass' ('cristallo o vetro'), Wyatt talks instead of crystal 'bewray[ing]' the colour beneath.[81] Wyatt's choice of verb is all the more striking because he altered it from 'declare' during revisions. Similarly, in 'The piller pearisht', Wyatt postpones Petrarch's allusion to the laurel until the second quatrain, where he transforms Petrarch's commemorative gesture to ''l verde lauro' into a nightmarish vision of uncasing. Note here a move characteristic of Wyatt's translations, where words spoken about another—in this case Laura—are transferred to the poetic self (the same technique we saw earlier, in relation to Orso's horse). As Wyatt writes in 'The piller pearisht', fortune—'happe' (l. 5)—has 'rent' away 'of all [his] ioye the vearye bark and rynde' (ll. 5–7). Petrarch's equivalent— the loss of his double treasure ('il mio doppio tesauro', l. 5)—has none of this sense of violent exposure, the stripping of a tree that ensures its utter destruction. The bare, unprotected tree is here the inverse of the refuge offered by 'the hertes forrest' in Wyatt's translation of *Rima* 140 (l. 9), where Wyatt freely embellishes on Petrarch's plain 'core', or heart, giving safety a sense of a physical location—'the hertes forrest'—that is absent from Petrarch's poem, or Surrey's alternative translation ('Coward Loue then to the hart apace | Taketh his flight', ll. 9–10).[82] Habitually, then, Wyatt's speakers endeavour to maintain a layer of protective opacity, withholding necessary points of reference or evading committing to definite statements. 'If', 'yet', 'but' are favourite conjunctions. Tellingly, the description of the ideal woman in 'A face that shuld content me' is undercut by the recurrent use of conditional verbs: '*shuld*' the face be 'cumley to behold' (l. 2); '*shuld*' it be able to 'Speke withowt wordes' (looks presumably proving more reliable than verbal communication, ll. 4–5); '*shuld*' the hair 'be of cryspyd goold' (l. 6), then 'these *myght* chance I *myght* be tyed' (l. 7).[83] Yet even as the speaker offers the tentative possibility of commitment, this is destabilised by the revelation in the last line

---

[81] Petrarch, *Rima* 37, ll. 57–8, Durling (ed./trans.), *Petrarch's Lyric Poems*, pp. 98, 99; Wyatt, 'So feble is the thred', l. 50.

[82] Wyatt, 'The longe love', BL MS Egerton 2711, fols. 5ʳ⁻ᵛ; Petrarch, *Rima* 140, Durling (ed./trans.), *Petrarch's Lyric Poems*, pp. 284, 285; Howard, 'Loue, that liueth, and reigneth in my thought', *Songes and sonettes*, sig. A4ᵛ.

[83] Wyatt, 'A face that shuld content me', Muir and Thomson (eds.), *Collected Poems*, pp. 132–3 (italics added).

that the knot which 'shuld not slyde' needs to be 'knytt agayne' (l. 8); that is, it has slid before.

That Wyatt's poetic speakers should be evasive is perhaps unsurprising, considering that it is commonplace to say that their creator lived in a world of surveillance, both watched himself and required to watch others. As Cromwell instructed Wyatt in 1537, his role as ambassador to the emperor, Charles V, required him to 'fishe out the botom of his stomake'.[84] Yet it was not just foreigners that Henry's courtiers were expected to spy upon, but each other, a habit of espial that we glimpse through the lens of Thomas Elyot's *Pasquil the playne* (1533), where Harpocrates casually reveals towards the end of the text that he had been eavesdropping at a window as Pasquil and Gnatho converse; his covert observation is all the more sinister because Gnatho has already warned Pasquil that 'if [he] wolde be a reporter, it mought tourne the to no littell displeasure'.[85] As Muriel St Clare Byrne shows in her analysis of the Lisle Letters, 'every man in the King's service was a potential spy and informer, which was probably [. . .] why Marillac [the French ambassador] spoke so enviously of the English intelligence service'.[86] Wyatt himself was included in this web: while he was required to watch the Holy Roman Emperor, Bonner was sent to watch Wyatt, almost to Wyatt's undoing, since it was Bonner's accusatory letters to Cromwell which formed the basis for Wyatt's arrest for treason in 1541, when they were found among the former chancellor's papers.[87]

As mentioned earlier, Wyatt's response to the charge of treason was to compile his *Defence*. The document, a feat of rhetorical prowess, is described by Walker as 'so honest in its admissions'.[88] Walker also observes that 'it is tempting to conclude that here, at bay, we see the true Wyatt emerge'.[89] As I hope to show in the final section of this lecture, the document is indeed 'honest', and I think it does show 'the true Wyatt', but perhaps not quite in the sense that Walker's words suggest. This is not to take issue with Walker's central argument that Wyatt's *Defence* is remarkable for its bravery in mounting a critique of the 1534 Treason Act and daring to assert that a subject can disagree with his monarch's policy

---

[84] Cromwell to Wyatt, 10 Oct. 1537, Roger Bigelow Merriman (ed.), *Life and Letters of Thomas Cromwell*, 2 vols. (Oxford, 2000), 2. 92.

[85] Thomas Elyot, *Pasquil the playne* (London, Thomas Berthelet, 1533), fols. 28^v, 4^r.

[86] Muriel St Clare Byrne (ed.), *The Lisle Letters*, 6 vols. (Chicago, 1981), 6. 240.

[87] Muir, *Life and Letters*, p. 175.

[88] Walker, *Writing Tyranny*, p. 349.

[89] Ibid., p. 348.

without being disloyal or seditious; that you can 'myslyk[e]' a law and still obey it.[90] Nevertheless, the *Defence* is not straightforwardly 'honest', in the way in which we would primarily understand 'honest' today (that is, as 'truthful').[91] Wyatt does not actually confess anything (wisely, no doubt). Like his poetic speakers, much hangs on hypothetical utterances. The key charge against Wyatt is that he made a treasonous remark over dinner in 1538. Wyatt's mission at this point was to ensure that Henry VIII was not excluded from any league between the Emperor and French king. By 1538, this looked set for certain failure, not least because Henry omitted to build on the amicable relationship Wyatt had established with Charles V. Bonner reports that during this period Wyatt had burst out, 'By goddes bludde, ye shall see the kinge our maister cast out at the carts [arse], and if he soo be serued, by godds body, he is well serued.'[92] Since pushing criminals out of the back of a cart was a usual way of hanging them in the period, Wyatt therefore stands accused of imagining the death of his monarch, in breach of the 1534 Treason Act. This central accusation is then bolstered by several other complaints, among them that Wyatt associated with courtesans; that Wyatt allowed and encouraged his servant, John Mason, to meet Cardinal Reginald Pole (deemed a traitor to Henry VIII); and that Wyatt repeatedly complained about both his previous imprisonment in the Tower in 1536 and his current position as the king's ambassador. 'Gods bludde! was not that a prety sending of me ambassadour to thempereour, first to put me in the Tower, and then furthewithe to send me hither?' Bonner recounts Wyatt exclaiming: 'By godds preciouse bludde, I had rather the king shuld set me in Newgate than soo doo' (p. 66).

Wyatt never denies any of the charges outright. His treatment of the 'carts arse' accusation exemplifies his method. At no point does he proffer a single version: 'this is what happened'; 'this is what I said'. Instead, he posits a series of hypotheses: first, why, *if* he had said these words, they would not necessarily have been spoken 'falcely, maliciouslye, and traitorouslye' (p. 196). Secondly, he asks that attention be paid to the exact wording attributed to him—be it 'fall', 'caste', or 'left owte'—and proposes that any variation between the witnesses' accounts, however small,

---

[90] Wyatt, *Defence*, in Muir, *Life and Letters*, pp. 187–209 (at p. 205).

[91] 'Honest, a', sense 3c, *OED* [accessed 21 Dec. 2007].

[92] Muir, *Life and Letters*, p. 67. Muir here quotes a Victorian transcription, which coyly changes 'arse' to 'tail'. Bonner originally wrote 'arse'; the term has therefore been restored here. Thanks to Jason Powell for clarifying this point and thus explaining the discrepancy between Bonner's letter (as printed in *Life and Letters*) and the phrase in Wyatt's *Defence*.

points both to their unreliability and their malice (p. 197). His third line of argument is to stress the unlikelihood that he would have been so 'veri a foole' to have exposed himself as a traitor to Bonner and his companion Simon Haynes, 'with whome [he] had no great acquayntaunce and myche les truste' (p. 197). The fourth strategy is to suggest that his alleged words were merely 'a commen proverbe', and that this proverb (should he have spoken it), far from compassing the king's death, instead regrets that—like a parcel 'negligently' 'lefte owte of the cartes ars'—Henry VIII might be omitted from the imminent 'union of moste parte of Christendome' (p. 198). Fifth, Wyatt returns to close reading in order to try again to expose the unreliability of Bonner's testimony, arguing that logically he would not have said what he apparently said at the time alleged because, knowing that Henry had already been excluded from the league: 'is yt now lyke that after this I wolde vse the future tens in that was paste? and "shall"? "Ye shall see"? And then "yf he be so, by goddys bloude he is well servyd"; and then "I wolde he were"' (p. 198). 'Consyder the place and tyme where my accusares sayethe that I shulde speake yt and therby ye shall easily perseave that ther theie lye and mysreporte my tale, or els that I cane [not] speake Inglyshe', Wyatt reasons. Since Wyatt is clearly more than proficient in his own tongue, by framing the matter as a choice between these two options (that they lie, or he cannot speak English), he manoeuvres the auditor/reader into agreeing with his claim that Bonner and his supporters bear false witness. Wyatt's sixth tactic is also designed to suggest that Bonner has concocted the evidence, artfully appropriating Wyatt's accustomed style to authenticate the accusation. As Wyatt explains,

> [b]y cawse I am wonte some tyme to rappe owte an owthe in an earnest tawlke, looke how craftylie theie have put in an othe [by goddes bludde] to [. . .] make the matter seme myne; and bycawse theie have garded an nowghtitie garmente of thers with on of my nawghttie gardes theie wyll swere and face me downe that that was my garment.   (p. 199)

A rough, plain style—marked by exclamations and oaths—is not necessarily sincere, in other words; it can be imitated, assumed like a cloak. Wyatt's eighth and final method deployed to rebut the charge, insists simply upon his lack of treasonable intent: even 'yf I had so saide, I mente not that nowghtie interpretation that no Devell wolde have imagined vpone me', he states (p. 199), before proceeding to cite his own actions as evidence of his loyalty.

The means by which Wyatt seeks to assert his innocence on this matter are thus consistent only in their collective aim to discredit or disprove
Bonner's testimony. This same evasiveness, this reluctance to commit to
one definitive statement, is also found in Wyatt's attempt to refute the
charge that he conspired with the Catholic Pole. Wyatt resorts to ridicul-
ing the suggestion, falling back on the question of his religious allegiance.
Yet even this confesses nothing. It substitutes for a statement of faith the
opinions of others: 'I thynke I shulde have more adoe with a great sorte
in Inglande to purge my selffe of suspecte of a Lutherane then of a
Papyst' (pp. 195–6). We do not learn what Wyatt *is*; rather what others
think he is (which is *not* what he is accused of being). Negative definition
of this type in fact reveals little, just as in 'Myne owne Iohn Poyntz' we do
not hear what qualities and ambitions the speaker holds, but what he
refutes: 'I cannot I no no it will not be' (l. 76).

The shifting argument of the *Defence* is a rhetorical *tour de force*. The
truth of Wyatt's position—and the untruth of Bonner's—is demonstrated by the mutability of Wyatt's argument, adapting to meet the
charges posed. Truth is not equated with, or achieved by, fixity of position, no more than it is in Wyatt's poem 'Vnstable dream', which dissoci-
ates the two qualities: 'be stedfast ons or els at least be true', the speaker
pleads (l. 2).[93] The Wyatt displayed in the *Defence* is, thus, in many ways,
as Walker suggests, the 'true' Wyatt, because it is here that we see him
at work, deploying the 'oratory' and 'prudence' for which Thomas
Warton would commend the poet in the 1770s.[94] Warton's choice of the
term *prudence* here holds appropriate—if probably inadvertent—
resonances with Machiavellian *prudenzia* (copies of whose works were
already circulating at the English court during Wyatt's lifetime).[95]

The 'true' Wyatt, then, is a man of judicious circumspection, mould-
ing his words to suit the circumstances at hand. As such, he is entirely
concordant with early modern conceptions of honesty, which encompassed more than simply truth-telling. As Jennifer Richards's work on the
translation of the Latin term *honestas* has shown, it includes having the

---

[93] BL MS Egerton 2711, fol. 54ʳ.

[94] Thomas Warton, *The History of English Poetry*, 4 vols. (London, J. Dodsley and others, 1781),
3. 28.

[95] Cromwell received copies of *Il Principe* and the history of Florence from Lord Morley in 1537,
James Carley, 'Parker, Henry, tenth Baron Morley', *ODNB* [accessed 21 Dec. 2007]. For evidence
that Henrician courtiers were reading Machiavelli from the mid-1530s, see also Sydney Anglo,
Machiavelli—The First Century: Studies in Enthusiasm, Hostility, and Irrelevance (Oxford, 2005),
pp. 97–102.

ability to restrain yourself, and to tailor what you say to the occasion and audience.[96] Certainly 'honesty' has little to do with the plain speech for which Wyatt was known in life—and which is characteristic of both his poetry and his speech; indeed, as we saw Wyatt suggest in his *Defence*, the plain style is no less available than the ornate for imitation and appropriation. Apparent openness or sincerity in Wyatt's world was yet another tool for probing (or framing) others, used as bait for drawing out the unwary. As Cromwell instructed Wyatt in October 1537, 'You must in your conference with themperour take occasion to speake of all those matiers, and soo frankely to speake of them as you may feale the depenes of his harte.'[97] The primary meaning of honesty in the period, however, was *honour*, as found in Bonner's complaint that Wyatt—in suffering Henry's embassy to 'ride on such spittell jades'—regards 'neyther the kings honour or his honestie or ours'.[98] In his letters to his son, Wyatt protests against this superficial sense of honesty: 'I meane not that honestye that the comen sort callith an honist man.'[99] Rather, for Wyatt, real honesty goes beyond a 'reputation for riches, for authoritie, or some like'. Instead, it displays exactly the sort of self-moderation detailed by Richards, as can be seen through his commendation of his father in the same letter. Wyatt holds up Sir Henry Wyatt as an example of an 'honest' man for his own son to emulate; the qualities he draws attention to are his reverence, his pity, his truth, his loyalty, his diligence, and his circumspection.[100] No man was 'more circumspect', we are told. Whilst qualities such as truth and loyalty fit easily with modern conceptions of honesty, its connection to prudence or circumspection is rather less familiar to us, and a convenient reminder that early modern perceptions of the term encompassed this variety of meaning. Wyatt's 'persinge eye' (to return to Surrey's elegy) might indeed be as watchful as it was honest: the two meanings do not necessarily conflict in this period. Like the Wyatt of Surrey's elegy, the 'true' Wyatt is composed of, and able to reconcile, seeming opposites, a visage 'sterne and mylde': a Wyatt who can adapt—chameleon-like—to the varied roles for which he is celebrated in Leland's *Naeniae*. For all their seeming interiority, Wyatt's poems are similarly anchored in a public world. His poetic speakers are intensely conscious of

---

[96] Jennifer Richards, *Rhetoric and Courtliness in Early Modern Literature* (Cambridge, 2003).

[97] Merriman (ed.), *Life and Letters of Thomas Cromwell*, 2. 92.

[98] Muir, *Life and Letters*, p. 68.

[99] Ibid., p. 41.

[100] Ibid., p. 202; cf. Wyatt's grouping of 'honestie, wyt or discretion' in his *Defence*, pointing to their use as synonyms (p. 139).

their audience, as they recurrently endeavour to justify, protect or reclaim their speakers' 'honesty' (that is, their honour), which has been damaged by the women who have deserted them.[101]

And here I want to state the wider implications of this study of Wyatt. Tudor poets played fast and loose with the apparent intimacy of lyric poetry, both evoking and disrupting the assumption that it would reveal an autobiographical narrative, if only we as readers could decode it. This tantalising license with biography is glimpsed in embryonic form in Wyatt's selectivity, wresting individual items from Vellutello's poetic life. It emerges, in more ludic and developed form, in later texts, such as George Turberville's *Epitaphes, Epigrams, Songs and Sonnets* (1567), where the tale of Tymetes' unsuccessful pursuit of Pyndara is woven sporadically through the text, the reader given only occasional clues as to which poems relate to that story. It erupts more strikingly still in George Gascoigne's *Adventures of Master F. J.* (1573), where a narrative of seduction is teasingly presented under a plethora of initials, prefaced as it is by an exchange of letters between Master H. W. and G. T., reflecting on the doings of F. J., which H. W. has arranged to have published by the printer, A. B. This playfulness is all but lost on us now. Attempts to find Wyatt—and his women—are but one piece of the jigsaw, part of a wider tradition, where Vellutello-like, we endeavour to track down the 'true' story of our lyric poets, as witnessed by the hunt for Shakespeare's dark lady, W. H. or—most recently—Mrs Shakespeare.[102] However, the remains of our poets can prove reluctant to reveal their mysteries, as those Italian scientists, disinterring Petrarch, discovered in 2003. The skull contained within the sepulchre turned out not to be his at all, but that of a woman. We now know Petrarch's mitochondrial DNA and genetic haplotype, or at least those of the male skeleton deposited in his grave:[103] but we are still very far from knowing what he looked like, and staring at him, face-to-face.

Note.   I am extremely grateful to all those who read—or listened to—earlier drafts of this paper, especially Alan Bryson, Mike Pincombe, Jason Powell, Goran Stanivukovic and Phil Withington. Thanks also to Abi Brundin, for our useful chats about Petrarch and disinterred poets.

---

[101] See, for example, Wyatt, 'Blame not my lute' or 'In aeternum'.

[102] Germaine Greer, *Shakespeare's Wife* (London, 2007).

[103] This probably is Petrarch's skeleton; damage to his ribs is consistent with that inflicted by a donkey, and it is on record that Petrarch was once kicked by such a beast. For details of Petrarch's DNA, see <www.isogg.org/famousdna.htm> [accessed 30 Oct. 2007].

Mind the Gap; or Why Humans Are Not Just Great Apes

R. I. M. DUNBAR

Fellow of the Academy

Introduction

EVOLUTION HAS HAD a poor press in the social sciences and the humanities over the past century, though it has not always been so: the nineteenth century witnessed considerable interest among the nascent social sciences in the ideas propounded by the new evolutionists within biology. This is neither the time nor place to delve into the history of why evolutionary ideas subsequently came to be so vehemently eschewed by social scientists. Instead, my aim here is simply to underline the claim that an evolutionary perspective is not, as seems often to be supposed, a competing paradigm for conventional explanations in the social sciences. Rather, an evolutionary perspective should function, as it does in biology, as a framework theory that allows all the disparate subdisciplines to be integrated in a way that they can talk to each other on a level playing field. Biology has benefited enormously from an evolutionary perspective over the past half-century in particular, since an evolutionary framework has allowed ethologists and ecologists to integrate their work with physiologists and molecular geneticists (even though the former still grumble about the latter's molecularisation of biology). I argue that Psychology— a notoriously fractionated discipline at the best of times—could benefit

Read at the Academy 11 October 2007.

Proceedings of the British Academy **154**, 403–423. © The British Academy 2008.

in the same way, since an evolutionary approach would allow neuroscientists to talk to social and developmental psychologists in a way that, hitherto, they have conspicuously failed to be able to do.

I do not wish to defend this proposal in detail here. It simply stands as a framework for my lecture. Instead, I will try to demonstrate the value of an evolutionary framework by example. My aim in this lecture is to sketch out an argument as to why humans are so different from other apes and monkeys, despite the fact that we share so much of our evolutionary history with them. My point is that, in doing so, I will have to draw on many different subdisciplines of Psychology (as well as other disciplines like anthropology) whose integration into this story is only possible because evolutionary theory provides us with an overarching framework within which to combine them.

We share a long evolutionary history with the great apes, in particular: the human lineage (including all the many fossil species that have existed over the last six million years or so since our lineage parted company with that of the chimpanzees) is firmly embedded within the African Great Ape family and shares with them many aspects of their biology, genetics, psychology and behaviour. More trivially, we also share a very high percentage of our DNA with chimpanzees (though *quite* what this means is open to question). Yet, it is surely obvious to everyone that we are not 'just great apes'. In several conspicuous ways, we are very different. That difference does not really seem to concern the kinds of anatomical or cognitive differences—our bipedalism and tool-making abilities—that anthropologists have tended to emphasise in the past. Rather, I want to argue that the real difference lies in a much more intangible set of competences—the ability to live in the virtual world of the mind. In a word, this is the world of culture. I will focus on two aspects of human behaviour that are, in many respects, archetypal of human culture: story-telling and religion. Both require us to be able to imagine worlds that do not physically exist. I shall argue that, apes' much-vaunted capacities for cultural learning notwithstanding, no other living species is even on the same page as humans in this respect—because all other animal species lack the neuronal computational power required to make it possible. The key to understanding why this is so lies in the reasons why our brains have evolved.

The evolution of the social brain

The social brain hypothesis was first mooted in the late 1980s by Byrne and Whiten (1988) as an explanation for the fact that primates have much larger brains for body size than any other taxonomic group (a point first noted by Jerison 1973). Most of this increase in brain size is the result of an enlarged neocortex (Finlay and Darlington 1995; Finlay *et al.* 2001), and especially an enlarged frontal lobe (though some other subcortical areas such as the cerebellum are also differentially enlarged in humans: McLeod *et al.* 2003). Primates rely on sociality as a tool for solving the everyday ecological problems of survival and successful reproduction rather than solving these problems by individual trial and error. So the proposal was that primates' more complex social lives imposed significantly greater cognitive demands on them than was the case for other non-primate species.

Since this suggestion was originally proposed, considerable evidence has been adduced in its support (for recent summaries, see Whiten and Byrne 1997; Emery *et al.* 2007; Dunbar and Schultz 2007*a*, 2007*b*). One of the core findings was a quantitative relationship between social group size and relative neocortex size in primates (Fig. 1). On a double-log plot, mean species group size is linearly related to relative neocortex size (indexed as the ratio of neocortex volume to the volume of the rest of the brain). This has been interpreted as implying that some aspect of cognition imposes a constraint on the number of relationships that an individual can maintain as a coherent social network.

Although the essence of the social brain hypothesis is really about social complexity and its cognitive demands (and considerable evidence is now available to show that various indices of behavioural complexity correlate with neocortex size: see Dunbar and Shultz 2007*a*), it is this quantitative relationship with group size that has mainly attracted attention. Indeed, it seems that the social brain hypothesis is often seen as being synonymous with this one core finding. However, it is important not to lose sight of the fact that this group size effect is really only an emergent property of the underlying relationship which focuses on the cognitive demands of behavioural complexity.

This has recently been given added emphasis by new findings that have emerged from attempts to test the social brain hypothesis on non-primate species. Shultz and Dunbar (Shultz and Dunbar 2007; Dunbar and Shultz 2007*b*) have shown that, across a wide range of bird and mammal species (specifically carnivores, ungulates and bats), the social brain

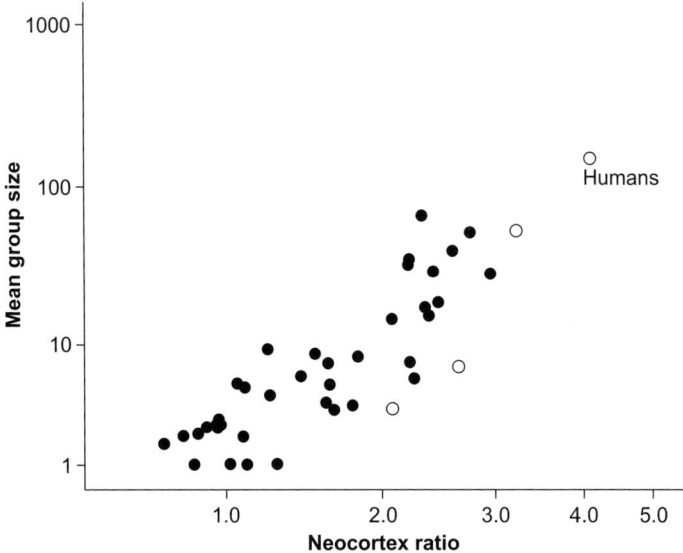

Figure 1. Mean social group size for different species of primates (prosimians, monkeys and apes) plotted against relative neocortex size (indexed as neocortex ratio, the ratio of neocortex volume divided by the volume of the rest of the brain), Ape species are distinguished as open symbols (lower left to top right: gibbons, gorillas, chimpanzees and modern humans). The point labelled for humans is that predicted by the ape regression equation. Redrawn from Dunbar (2008).

hypothesis takes a qualitative rather than a quantitative form. In all these taxonomic groups, it is pairbonded (i.e. reproductively monogamous) species that have disproportionately large brains. Anthropoid primates contrast strikingly with this pattern in that they, and they alone, exhibit a quantitative relationship between group size and brain size.

These results suggest that it is the cognitive demands of pairbonding that underpin the social brain (thereby leading to the initial enlargement of brain size in several animal families), and that anthropoid primates (and maybe one or two other numerically small groups such as elephants and the horse family) have extended the use of these pairbond-like relationships to other non-reproductive group members—thereby creating the quantitative relationship that we observe in their case (Shultz and Dunbar 2007). In effect, they have developed what we might well refer to as 'friendships' (Silk 2002; Smuts 1985), relationships that have all the characteristics of pairbonds but without the sexual connotation— although perhaps this may explain why friendships can so easily acquire sexual overtones in humans. In anthropoid primates, friendships function as alliances—reciprocal coalitions whose members reliably come to each other's aid (see for example, Dunbar 1980, 1989). These serve the important function of buffering individuals against the costs of group-living— competition during foraging, and the persistent forms of low-level harassment consequent on living in close proximity to others that results in infertility in females in both captivity and the wild (Abbott *et al.* 1986; Dunbar 1980).

Because pairbonding is often associated with bi-parental care, it is not intuitively obvious whether the cognitive load is imposed by the demands of pairbonding as such or by those of bi-parental care. Birds allow us to sort this out because some species have one without the other: this disso- ciation demonstrates unequivocally that it is species with pairbonds, irre- spective of whether or not they have bi-parental care, that have large brains. Birds also emphasise a second point: it is species that have *lifelong* pairbonds that have unusually large brains, not those that have annual pairbonds (i.e. those that find new partners each year), indicating that it is something about the costs of long term relationships that is cognitively demanding.

This raises two important issues. One is why pairbonds (and pair- bond-like relationships) are so costly in cognitive terms. The other is the more difficult question of just what pairbonds actually are. It is well understood that pairbonds (and especially lifelong pairbonds) incur sig- nificant risks for their members: a poor choice of partner will have a massive effect on an individual's fitness because of the opportunity costs of having to start all over again with the business of mate-finding. Such circumstances can arise either because a mate is less fertile than other members of the population or because it is less reliable (either in terms of providing care for the young or in terms of infidelity, or both). The fact that poor judgement could have catastrophic consequences for the indi- vidual's fitness—literally by reducing its lifetime reproductive output to zero in the worst case—will inevitably impose intense selection for the ability to make fine judgements about the suitability of prospective mates. However, the need to maintain a high level of behavioural coordination and synchrony must also impose significant demands on cognition. This is particularly obvious in those cases where the pair has to share rearing duties, as in many bird species where one member of the pair has to stay on the nest while the other feeds. If the pair do not coordinate their behaviour effectively, the individual left sitting on the eggs may eventually be forced to choose between starving and abandoning the eggs. In effect, pairbonds are cooperative alliances for joint reproduction and the pair members have to be willing to recognise and accommodate the partner's interests. In effect, they have to be able to second-guess the partner's needs and factor these into the scheduling of their own requirements. It seems likely that it is this specific need that may have provided the trigger for the evolution of those social cognitive skills associated with theory of mind in humans.

This does, however, raise a serious question: just what is a pairbond? We tend to recognise pairbonds by virtue of the fact that joint reproduction is a key component. But in reality, that is not the animals' experience of it any more than it is ours. Pairbonded species of birds have pairbonds in order to be able to engage in bi-parental care, thereby generating significant reproductive benefits. Bi-parental care is the ultimate goal, but to achieve this they must find an effective solution to the proximate goal of creating and maintaining a functional pairbond. Their perception of what is involved (and hence the underpinning cognitive mechanisms) is the rather intangible unknown. Indeed, we have difficulty trying to specify exactly what is involved even in our own case: we know a relationship when we see or experience one, but we do not have any adequate metric by which we can define it operationally. Relationships of this kind are something we *feel* rather than cognise directly.

This much is perhaps obvious from the social psychology literature on friendships: here, several decades of research have identified two key dimensions to relationships—being close and feeling close (Sternberg 1997; Berscheid *et al.* 1989). The first of these is easy to specify, because it simply has to do with time spent together (in effect, spatial proximity) or the frequency of interaction. The second is more difficult, because it has something to do with our inner emotional experiences and we have great difficulty verbalising these. We intuit them as a form of 'hot' cognition, but they are not as accessible to conscious verbal description as 'cold' cognition. And for that reason, we face a double dilemma in the case of animals, since we lack any means of describing the inner experiences in other species. The time may now have come to grapple directly with the thorny issue of animals' mental experiences: we may not be able to push it quietly under the behaviourist carpet any longer if we want to make any progress in understanding the nature of relationships in humans or other animals.

The bonds that bind

The social brain hypothesis, then, argues that maintaining and servicing the kinds of intense relationships found in pairbonds (in most birds and mammals) and friendships (among anthropoid primates) involves serious cognitive work, which in turn is reflected in the size of a species' brain. But it is, at the same time, apparent, both from the human social psychology literature on friendships and from the ethological literature on how primates service their relationships, that cognition is only part of the story. There is a deeply emotional component to relationships that derives in both cases from doing things together. This leads us, perhaps inevitably, into the issue of how primates bond their social groups.

For Anthropoid primates, and in particular Old World monkeys and apes, social grooming is the principal mechanism used for social bonding. Grooming is an intense activity in which one individual leafs through the fur of another, removing bits of vegetation, dead skin and other debris. It is very much a one-on-one activity, in which the groomer is often deeply concentrated on its task. Grooming lowers the heart rate in the groomee and reduces the frequency of signs of tension and stress (yawning, scratching, etc.: Goosen, 1981; Castles *et al.* 1999), to the point where the recipient of grooming can become so relaxed it actually falls asleep. Many species devote considerable proportions of their day to social grooming—in the limiting case, as much as one fifth of the waking day. Grooming shares many of the features of massage: it is physically stimulating and mildly painful, and thus triggers the release of endorphins (the brain's own painkillers) (Keverne *et al.* 1989). It is endorphins that are probably responsible for these soporific effects.

However, the real significance of this is that these psychopharmacological effects mediated by grooming seem to play a crucial role in the process of building the trust and reciprocity that form the basis of primate social relationships. We have no real idea how endorphins give rise to bonded relationships, but one possibility is that they simply allow two individuals to feel relaxed enough in each other's company to spend time together. Time is a commodity that we have to invest to create a relationship, and there seems to be a more or less linear relationship between time spent together and the strength of a relationship—at least in terms of functional consequences such as willingness to come to a grooming partner's aid (see Dunbar 1980, 1984, 1989). It may be that endorphins simply provide the proximate reinforcer that makes it worth spending time with someone else, or it may be that these neuroendocrines are themselves intimately involved in the bonding process. Either way, it seems that their role is critical.

Humans and the social brain

Modern humans have much larger brains (and especially neocortices) than other primates, and we can legitimately ask what the relationship between neocortex size and group size in primates can tell us about human group sizes. As Figure 1 suggests, there are quite distinct grades in this relationship within the primates: apes lie to the right of monkeys, and monkeys lie to the right of prosimians, suggesting that servicing groups of a given size requires proportionately more computational power as you pass from prosimians through monkeys to the apes (Dunbar 1998). Hence, the appropriate regression line from which to predict human group sizes is that for apes. Interpolating the modern human neocortex ratio into the ape equation yields a predicted group size of ~150 (Fig. 1).

A search of the ethnographic literature revealed that this is in fact the typical size of hunter-gatherer communities (Dunbar 1993; Hamilton *et al.* 2007). More remarkably perhaps, this figure of ~150 appears frequently in many aspects of historical and contemporary human organisation (Table 1). It was the mean village size recorded for almost all English counties in the Domesday Book as well as during the eighteenth century, and is the typical size of the company in most modern armies, the number of recipients of a typical Christmas card distribution list in Britain, and the size of the social network in reverse 'small world' experiments, amongst others. Thus, a wide range of contemporary social phenomena seem to yield much the same kinds of grouping patterns, despite marked differences in both scale and organisation. The only substantive difference between social networks in traditional hunter-gatherer and agricultural societies and modern post-industrial societies seems to be that, in traditional societies, everyone in the community has more or less the same network of 150 acquaintances, whereas in modern urban societies our networks are highly fragmented—my 150 consists of a set of subnetworks that barely overlap. You and I may share one small set of friends, say through work, but there is no overlap at all in the remaining subsets—we do not share any relatives, nor do we share hobby circles, church networks, spouses' friends, schoolgate friends (the often temporary friendships built up through one's children's school friends) or sports club friends. Networks in modern societies are fragmented and dispersed

Table 1. Examples of human social groupings that conform to the predicted size of ~150 individuals[a].

Grouping	Typical size	Source
Neolithic villages (Middle East, 6500–5500 BC)	150–200	Oates (1977)
Maniple ('double century') (Roman army: 350–100 BC)	120–130	Montross (1975)
Domesday Book (1085): (average county village size)	150	Hill (1981), Bintliff (1999)
Eighteenth-century English villages (mean of county means)	160	Laslett (1971)
Tribal societies (mean and range of communities; $N=9$)	148 (90–222)	Dunbar (1993)
Hunter-gatherer societies (mean clan size; $N=213$)	165	Hamilton et al. (2007)
Hutterite farming communities (Canada) (mean, $N=51$)	107	Mange and Mange (1980)
'Nebraska' Amish parishes (mean, $N=8$)	113	Hurd (1985)
Church congregations (recommended ideal size)	200	Urban Church Project (1974)
E. Tennessee rural mountain community	197	Bryant (1981)
Social network size (mean, $N=2$ 'small world' experiments)	134	Killworth et al. (1984)
Goretex Inc: factory unit size	150	Gladwell (2000)
Company (mean and range for 10 Second World War armies)	180 (124–223)	MacDonald (1955)
Christmas card distribution lists (mean total recipients: $N=43$)	154	Hill and Dunbar (2003)
Research specialities (sciences and humanities) (mode, $N=13$)	100–200	Becher (1989)

[a] Confidence intervals around the predicted mean are 100–200 (Dunbar 1993).

(often over considerable geographical distances), whereas in traditional societies they typically form a single cohesive community—even though that community itself may be distributed over a wide geographical area (as in many contemporary hunter-gatherers).

This figure of ~150 seems to mark a distinct limit for relationship quality: there seems to be a marked difference in the quality of the relationships we have with those who are inside the chosen circle versus those who are outside. My informal definition for this limit to our social world is that it is everybody whom we know as persons, everyone with whom we have a definable personal relationship. Those inside this circle are individuals towards whom we feel some sense of obligation, whom we trust would help us out if we so requested, who would reciprocate our sense of personal commitment. We know where these individuals fit into our network of relationships, they know where we fit into theirs, and our knowledge in both cases is based on personal acquaintance. Sometimes, that knowledge can be indirect (friends of friends, or a shared grand-parent), but it defines those to whom we owe personal obligations; if we offend them, or spurn them in some way, that offence will come to haunt us through the effect it has on the relationships that link us. In contrast, beyond this circle of 150, people cease to be individuals, at least in so far as our relationships are concerned. Even though we recognise them as individuals (i.e. we can put names to faces), our relationships with them are less personal and more typological. We need rules of thumb to guide our interactions with them rather than being able to rely on personalised knowledge. In such cases, the rule is usually cued by some appropriate badge that signifies the status of an individual and how we should address them, and this often requires that we formally badge them in order to recognise them—uniforms, badges of rank, styles of speech, and so on.

As with all primate social groups, human social networks are highly structured. We do not interact equally with all members of our immedi-ate social world. Rather, it seems that our social world consists of a series of hierarchically inclusive circles of acquaintanceship that are reflected in both the perceived intimacy of the relationship and the frequency of interaction (Hill and Dunbar 2003). These circles of acquaintanceship seem to have a very consistent structure: each annulus includes about twice as many people as the one immediately inside it, so that the cumulative numbers of individuals included in successive circles exhibit a constant scaling ratio of approximately 3 (Zhou *et al.* 2005; see also Hamilton *et al.* 2007). Roughly speaking, they progressively include 5, 15, 50, 150, 500 and 1500 individuals (see Dunbar 1993; Zhou *et al.* 2005), and, for all we know, may extend beyond that in a further series of circles that have the same ratios.

The role for cognition

The fact that brain size correlates with social group size implies that this involves a cognitive limit. However, we know surprisingly little about the kinds of cognition that might be involved in managing social relation-ships. Although everyone probably agrees that this is some form of 'social cognition', quite what that entails remains unclear. The only aspect of this that we know much about is what has become known as theory of mind (Leslie 1987; Perner 1991). Theory of mind is the ability to reflect on another individual's mind states. As such, it is one level in a potentially endless reflexive series of mind states and beliefs about mind states known as the levels of intentionality (Dennett 1987). We know a great deal about theory of mind (second-order intentionality) because developmental psychologists have explored it in considerable depth. In simple terms, it is the cognitive rubicon that children pass through at about the age of 4–5 years, although some individuals (autistic people) never achieve this even as adults (Baron-Cohen *et al.* 1985). However, the problem with theory of mind is that we know a great deal about its natural history but, as Roth and Leslie (1998) have pointed out, we have almost no idea what it actually involves in cognitive terms.

Nonetheless, even though the exact processes involved may be somewhat opaque, we can perhaps use the notion of intentionality to give us some purchase on the problem of how humans differ from other primates since the orders of intentionality form a natural scale, and thus seem to provide us with an index of social cognitive competence. The claim that intentionality itself is no more than some aspect of executive function (Ozonoff 1995; Mitchell 1997; Barrett *et al.* 2003; Stylianou 2007) would provide a justification for this. My concern here is less with the debates about whether or not theory of mind (or, more generally, intentionality) is modular or the outcome of executive function (although my inclination is towards the latter) than with the simpler claim that the intentionality scale seems to provide us with a metric of social cognitive competence (as indexed by the ability to hold several individuals' mental states in mind at the same time).

This being so, our main interest at this point is what the natural limits of intentional reasoning might be in humans. We have assayed normal adults in a number of separate studies, and it seems that the limits of function for adults are consistently fifth order ('I *believe* that you *suppose* that I *imagine* that you *want* me to *believe* that . . .') (Kinderman *et al.* 1998; Stiller and Dunbar 2007). Around two-thirds of individuals have their limit at or below fifth-order intentionality, and three-quarters have their limit at or below sixth order. There is considerable individual variation around this (Stiller and Dunbar 2007), and we have shown that the higher levels are lost during the active phase of at least two well-known clinical conditions (bipolar disorder: Kerr *et al.* 2003; paranoid schizophrenia: Swarbrick 2000). These competences develop over a period of time between age 5 (when children first acquire theory of mind, or second-order intentionality) and the early 'teens (when they finally acquire fifth-order adult-level competences; Henzi *et al.* 2007).

Intentionality and the virtual world

The issue of interest here is what can be achieved with different levels of intentionality. If intentional competences allow us to hold several different individuals' mind states in mind at the same time, then it seems likely that they will impose constraints on cultural phenomena that require us to think intentionally. This is perhaps most obvious in the case of imaginative play. Leslie (1987) noted that theory of mind may be crucial for children to be able to engage in fictive (i.e. pretend) play where they have to imagine that the world is other than it really is (i.e. dolls can drink tea, the steering wheel on the back of a chair is a real car). Leslie's point can be extended to drama. Consider the case of the audience watching Shakespeare's *Othello*. They have to believe that Iago intends that Othello imagines that Desdemona is in love with Cassio, an activity involving four levels of intentionality. However, notice that, at this point, the kind of story they are dealing with is not especially demanding (or, for that matter, particularly enthralling). Why should Othello care if Desdemona fantasises about Cassio? The bottom line of everyday life is that very few of us would be anything but mildly bemused by such a trivial phenomenon, and the story would end there as a dull narrative. What gives Shakespeare's play its bite is the fact that Iago is able to persuade Othello that Cassio reciprocates Desdemona's feelings, thereby creating a romantic triangle and raising the stakes high enough for all of us to be gripped by the drama (especially when, with the benefit of spectator-sight, we are aware of Iago's scheming plan). At this point, of course, the audience is having to work at fifth-order intentionality, and is thus at the natural limits for the great majority of the population.

But, in putting this story together, Shakespeare himself has to go one level higher than his audience, to sixth order: he has to *intend* that the audience *believes* . . . I suggest that this might explain why the capacity to enjoy good literature is a widespread human universal, but the ability to *compose* good literature is not—storytelling demands social cognitive competences that are beyond the normal range for the great majority of the population. Thus it is that, when we sit down to write those novels we have so long aspired to write, our natural limits at fifth-order intentionality constrain most of us into writing dull narratives.

We can use the same framework for exploring the cognitive demands of religion, because this too requires us to work with an imagined world—a world that we cannot see or feel directly because it exists only in our heads. The transcendental experiences that we have during religious events are undoubtedly very real, but they are not the stuff of real physical experiences created by the world impinging on our senses. They belong, rather, to an inner virtual world of the imagination.

A task analysis of the mentalising demands of religious beliefs suggests that it is perfectly possible to have religion with any order of intentionality; however, the *form* of religion depends on the levels of intentionality at which you can work (Table 2). Crucially, there appears to be a critical difference between the forms of religion possible at fourth- and fifth-order intentionality. At fourth order, you can have what I refer to as social religion: I can enjoin you to believe what I believe to be true about some deity's interests in us, but you do not have to agree with that claim even though you may accept that I am convinced by the truth of what I believe: there is no compulsion on you to believe. I can only make you agree with me by using a police force (of either a secular or a heavenly kind). But, in that case, your level of personal and intellectual commitment to the project is likely to be very limited. However, fifth order seems to represent a crucial rubicon: at fifth order, it seems that, when I accept that you believe this claim to be true, I *ipso facto* also commit myself to the veracity of your claim. We now have what I term 'communal religion'—a set of beliefs that bind us into a single community whose members share the same world view. At this point, we have a very powerful mechanism enforcing the communal will, for making us all sign up to

Table 2. Forms of religious belief made possible by different levels of intentionality.

Intentionality Level	Possible statements of belief	Form of Religion
First	I *believe* that god [. . . exists]	none
Second	I *believe* that god is *willing* [. . . to intervene if you disobey his laws]	supernatural fact
Third	I *intend* that you *believe* that god is *willing* [. . . to intervene . . .]	personal religion
Fourth	I *intend* that you *believe* that I *want* god to be *willing* [. . . to intervene . . .]	social religion
Fifth	I *intend* that you *believe* that god *understands* that I *want* him to be *willing* [. . . to intervene . . .]	communal religion

the communal project (whatever that may happen to be). We do not need a police force to make us behave in a religious way: we are all deeply and personally committed to it and adhere to these beliefs of our own free will.

What makes us so different?

I return to my opening question: why are humans not just great apes? I have suggested that the answer lies in our capacity to live in a virtual mental world. We can engage in activities that are well beyond the competences of even the great apes. Indeed, they are so far beyond the competences of other species that there is no chance that the proverbial chimpanzee sitting at a typewriter will ever produce the works of Shakespeare within any reasonable length of time (and I speak on the scale of millennia here). The one remaining question is why we humans should have needed such extraordinary cognitive abilities.

From an evolutionary point of view, this is especially puzzling because brain tissue is exceptionally expensive. Aiello and Wheeler (1995) pointed out some time ago that brain tissue is among the most expensive matter in the body to maintain, and that this provides a very steep gradient up which natural selection has to drive brain evolution if it is to increase brain size (their 'expensive tissue hypothesis'). There is some tentative comparative evidence (Dunbar 2003*a*, 2003*b*) given some additional support by recent as yet unpublished human neuroimaging studies—that intentional competences are correlated with some aspects of brain volume. If so, then it follows that the selection pressure for the capacity to manage the higher orders of intentionality incurs a very significant energetic cost to the individuals concerned. The advantages to be gained from investing in such capacities must thus be considerable. What might these be?

Primate societies are implicit social contracts. Like all social contracts, their stability and functionality depends on the members trading off short and long term benefits. As with pairbonds, a group will only remain stable as a coalition providing members are willing to compromise on some of their short term benefits in order to gain in the long run through group-level effects. These group level effects come in the form of increased survival, and hence higher reproductive rates, mainly as a result of reduced predation rates (Dunbar 1988; Shultz *et al.* 2004) though there may also be more direct benefits in terms of the survival of individual offspring (Silk *et al.* 2003; Silk 2007).

However, all social contracts of this kind face the same problem: freeriders. There is always a significant benefit to be gained by individuals who take the benefits of sociality but do not pay all the costs (Enquist and Leimar 1993; Nettle and Dunbar 1997; Dunbar 1999). Since the intrusiveness of freeriders is proportional to the size of the population, the large communities that characterise humans face a significantly greater challenge in this respect than those of our primate cousins. As a result, more sophisticated mechanisms are needed to ensure that freeriders do not overwhelm the community. While there is a number of cognitive mechanisms for managing freeriders (Dunbar 1999), the absence of grooming on a large scale means that we inevitably lack the endorphin-based mechanisms that lie at the root of primate sociality. This is a serious issue, because it creates a 'bonding gap' of quite significant proportions (Dunbar, in press) that could seriously destablise the fragile basis on which group-level collaboration depends. Something was needed to fill that gap.

In fact, the pattern of brain size evolution suggests that this really only became a serious issue in the later stages of human evolution following the appearance of archaic humans (*Homo heidelbergensis* and allies) around half a million years ago (Dunbar, in press). At this point, brain size took off with a rapid rate of increase, implying a corresponding increase in the size of communities that had to be bonded. Nonetheless, our capacity to create the large communities that were presumably needed to ensure survival (and the reasons why we needed such large communities remain unclear) must have depended on solving the bonding issue satisfactorily. While social conformity and 'good behaviour' can always be imposed by punitive action on backsliders (Orstrom *et al.* 1994; Clutton-Brock and Parker 1995; Fehr *et al.* 2002), there are limits to which such action can really enforce social cooperation. Since there are always benefits to be gained from freeriding and there is a significant chance that any one freerider will escape detection and/or punishment, the temptation to freeride will mean that some proportion of individuals will always do so, no matter how effective punishment is in reducing the absolute frequency (for an identical problem in relation to poaching and conservation, see Cowlishaw and Dunbar 2000). Social cooperation is far more effective when individuals act willingly because they all voluntarily sign up to the communal project (Orstrom *et al.* 1994). Mechanisms that create a sense of communality are, thus, more likely to result in the required levels of altruism than the use of social control.

As has long been appreciated in the social sciences, both religion and story-telling play an important role in social bonding in all human cultures (Durkheim 2001). Religion does so through the capacity of rituals to trigger the release of endorphins, since many of these are of just the kind of mildly stressful activities that are especially good at releasing endorphins. Religion, of course, also has the advantage of having an intellectual dimension, and here the cognitive demands become important in creating the kind of dual-process bonding mechanism that we find in primate social grooming. To the extent that the intellectual component of religion is a form of story-telling, story-telling itself enters the frame as an important mechanism for community bonding. However, story-telling goes beyond mere religious explanations for the way the world is and should be; it offers its own kind of opportunity to develop a form of entertainment that can be just as powerful a bonding mechanism in its own right.

One could argue that both of these are mere epi-phenomena—non-adaptive by-products of the fact that we have big brains. Exactly this claim has, of course, been made for music (Pinker's (1998) 'music as evolutionary cheesecake' argument). However, such a claim rests uncomfortably with the time, money and effort that, irrespective of culture, humans invest in all three of these phenomena. In fact, all human societies value story-telling for itself as a form of entertainment, and many of these stories are intimately involved in creating a sense of community: origin stories, tribal histories, and moral tales are among the commonest of campfire 'tellings', and all contribute directly to providing a sense of community. Indeed, the very performance itself often contributes directly, not least through laughter (another powerful releaser of endorphins: Dunbar 2004). By way of confirmation, van Vugt *et al.* (submitted) have recently demonstrated experimentally that laughing together causes strangers (but not existing friends) to be significantly more generous towards each other in public goods games. It is important to note that religion and story-telling both acquire their community-enhancing properties through language: without language, it would not be possible to tell a 'big enough story' to create the bonding effects or to persuade people to take part in religious rituals on a regular basis. It seems that regular participation in these community-bonding exercises is essential, almost as though it was a form of inoculation requiring boosters at set intervals to maintain a consistent level of performance.

But aside from the trivially obvious answer of language, what is it that limits these 'activities of the mind' to humans alone? One answer has to be that only humans can cope with the fifth-order intentionality that is necessary to allow these phenomena to produce the effects they do. The best that any non-human species can do seems to be second-order intentionality—and even that is probably true only of great apes (O'Connell and Dunbar 2003), since the consensus is that all other animal species can aspire only to first order. If mentalising skills really are an emergent property of executive function competences (Barrett *et al.* 2003) and these in turn are a function of the computational power (and hence size) of the brain (Dunbar 2003*a*), then the simple explanation for this striking difference between ourselves and all other species lies in the size of our brain (and, perhaps more specifically, the frontal lobes, since these are generally considered to be the *locus operandi* for those capacities that we conventionally refer to as executive functions). In effect, the differences between us and all other animals come down to the fact that the size of our brain allows us to do something that is simply not possible with a smaller brain. While brain organisation and aspects of neural efficiency (see for example Burki and Kaessmann 2004) must, of course, play a role, there are good arguments for thinking that it is simply the size of the computer that may be important (see for example Duncan 2001). No matter what the differences in structure and organisation may be, we do have a size issue to explain away and our over-large brains cannot be there merely by accident or as a trivial by-product of something else. In sum, the difference between us and our nearest cousins is not simply a matter of having greater intelligence (however we want to measure that) but what that greater intelligence allows us to do (namely, live in a virtual world), and why we need that emergent capacity at all (i.e. to enable us to bond much larger communities than would otherwise be possible for a monkey or an ape).

References

Abbott, D. H., Keverne, E. B., Moore, G. F. and Yodyinguad, U. (1986), 'Social suppression of reproduction in subordinate talapoin monkeys', *Miopithecus talapoin*, in J. Else and P. C. Lee (eds.), *Primate Ontogeny* (Cambridge), pp. 329–41.

Aiello, L. C. and Wheeler, P. T. (1995), 'The expensive tissue hypothesis: the brain and the digestive system in human evolution', *Current Anthropology*, 36: 199–221.

Baron-Cohen, S., Leslie, A. M. and Frith, U. (1985), 'Does the autistic child have a theory of mind?', *Cognition*, 21: 37–46.

Barrett, L., Henzi, S. P. and Dunbar, R. I. M. (2003), 'Primate cognition: from "what now?" to "what if?"', *Trends in Cognitive Sciences*, 7: 494–7.

Becher, T. (1989), *Academic Tribes and Territories* (Milton Keynes).

Berscheid, E., Snyder, M. and Omoto, A. M. (1989), 'The relationship closeness inventory: assessing the closeness of interpersonal relationships', *Journal of Personality and Social Psychology*, 57: 792–807.

Bintliff, J. (1999), 'Settlement and territory', in G. Barker (ed.), *Companion Encyclopedia of Archaeology* (London), pp. 505–45.

Burki, F., Kaessmann, H. (2004), 'Birth and adaptive evolution of a hominoid gene that supports high neurotransmitter flux', *Nature Genetics*, 36: 1061–3.

Bryant, F. C. (1981), *We're All Kin: a Cultural Study of a Mountain Neighbourhood* (Knoxville, TN).

Byrne, R. and Whiten, A. (eds.) (1988), *Machiavellian Intelligence* (Oxford).

Castles, D., Whiten, A. and Aureli, F. (1999), 'Social anxiety, relationships and self-directed behaviour among wild female olive baboons', *Animal Behaviour*, 58: 1207–15.

Clutton-Brock, T. H. and Parler, G. A. (1995), 'Punishment in animal societies', *Nature*, 373: 209–16.

Cowlishaw, G. and Dunbar, R. I. M. (2000), *Primate Conservation Biology* (Chicago).

Dennett, D. (1987), *The Intentional Stance* (Cambridge, MA).

Dunbar, R. I. M. (1980), 'Determinants and evolutionary consequences of dominance among female gelada baboons', *Behavioural Ecology and Sociobiology*, 7: 253–65.

Dunbar, R. I. M. (1984), *Reproductive Decisions: an Economic Analysis of Gelada Baboon Social Strategies* (Princeton, NJ).

Dunbar, R. I. M. (1988), *Primate Social Systems* (London).

Dunbar, R. I. M. (1989), 'Reproductive strategies of female gelada baboons', in A. Rasa, C. Vogel and E. Voland (eds.), *Sociobiology of Sexual and Reproductive Strategies* (London), pp. 74–92.

Dunbar, R. I. M. (1993), 'Coevolution of neocortex size, group size and language in humans', *Behavioral and Brain Sciences*, 16: 681–735.

Dunbar, R. I. M. (1998), 'The social brain hypothesis', *Evolutionary Anthropology*, 6: 178–90.

Dunbar, R. I. M. (1999), 'Culture, honesty and the freerider problem', in R. I. M. Dunbar, C. Knight and C. Power (eds.), *The Evolution of Culture* (Edinburgh), pp. 194–213.

Dunbar, R. I. M. (2003a), 'Why are apes so smart?', in P. Kappeler and M. Pereira (eds.), *Primate Life Histories and Socioecology* (Chicago, IL), pp. 285–98.

Dunbar, R. I. M. (2003b), 'The social brain: mind, language and society in evolutionary perspective', *Annual Review of Anthropology*, 32: 163–81.

Dunbar, R. I. M. (2004), 'Language, music and laughter in evolutionary perspective', in D. K. Oller and U. Griebel (eds.), *Evolution of Communication Systems: A Comparative Approach* (Cambridge, MA), pp. 257–74.

Dunbar, R. I. M. (2008), 'Cognitive constraints on the structure and dynamics of social networks', *Group Dynamics*, 12: 7–16.

Dunbar, R. I. M. (2008), 'Why only humans have language', in R. Botha and C. Knight (eds.), *The Prehistory of Language* (Oxford).

Dunbar, R. I. M. (in press), 'Mind the bonding gap: constraints on the evolution of hominin societies', in S. Shennan (ed.), *Pattern and Process in Cultural Evolution* (Berkeley, CA).

Dunbar, R. I. M. and Shultz, S. (2007a), 'Understanding primate brain evolution', *Philosophical Transactions of the Royal Society of London*, 362B: 649–58.

Dunbar, R. I. M. and Shultz, S. (2007b), 'Evolution in the social brain', *Science*, 317: 1344–7.

Duncan, J. (2001), 'An adaptive coding model of neural function in prefrontal cortex', *Nature Neuroscience*, 2: 820–9.

Durkheim, E. (2001 [1900]), *Elementary Forms of Religious Life* (Oxford).

Emery, N., Clayton, N. and Frith, C. (2007), *Social Intelligence: From Brain to Culture* (Oxford).

Enquist, M. and Leimar, O. (1993), 'The evolution of cooperation in mobile organisms', *Animal Behaviour*, 45: 747–57.

Fehr, E., Fishbacher, U. and Gächter, S. (2002), 'Strong reciprocity, human cooperation and the enforcement of social norms', *Human Nature*, 13: 1–25.

Finlay, B. L. and Darlington, R. B. (1995), 'Linked regularities in the development and evolution of mammalian brains', *Science*, 268: 1578–84.

Finlay, B. L., Darlington, R. B. and Nicastro, N. (2001), 'Developmental structure in brain evolution', *Behavioral and Brain Sciences*, 24: 263–308.

Gladwell, M. (2000), *The Tipping Point* (London).

Goosen, C. (1981), 'On the function of allogrooming in Old-World monkeys', in A. B. Chiarelli and R. S. Corruccini (eds.), *Primate Behaviour and Sociobiology* (Berlin), pp. 110–20.

Hamilton, M. J., Milne, B. T., Walker, R. S., Burger, O. and Brown, J. H. (2007), 'The complex structure of hunter-gatherer social networks', *Proceedings of the Royal Society, London*, 271B: 2195–202.

Henzi, P., de Sousa Pereira, L., Hawker-Bond, D., Stiller, J., Dunbar, R. I. M. and Barrett, L. (2007), 'Look who's talking: developmental trends in the size of conversational cliques', *Evolution and Human Behavior*, 28: 66–74.

Hill, D. (1981), *An Atlas of Anglo-Saxon England* (Oxford).

Hill, R. A. and Dunbar, R. I. M. (2003), 'Social network size in humans', *Human Nature*, 14: 53–72.

Hurd, J. P. (1985), 'Sex differences in mate choice among the "Nebraska" Amish of central Pennsylvania', *Ethology and Sociobiology*, 6: 49–57.

Jerison, H. J. (1973), *Evolution of the Brain and Intelligence* (London).

Kerr, N., Dunbar, R. I. M. and Bentall, R. P. (2003), 'Theory of mind deficits in bipolar affective disorder', *Journal of Affective Disorders*, 73: 253–9.

Keverne, E. B., Martensz, N. and Tuite, B. (1989), 'Beta-endorphin concentrations in cerebrospinal fluid of monkeys are influenced by grooming relationships', *Psychoneuroendocrinology*, 14: 155–61.

Killworth, P. D., Bernard, H. P. and McCarty, C. (1984), 'Measuring patterns of acquaintanceship', *Current Anthropology*, 25: 385–97.

Kinderman, P., Dunbar, R. I. M. and Bentall, R. P. (1998), 'Theory-of-mind deficits and causal attributions', *British Journal of Psychology*, 89: 191–204.

Laslett, P. (1971), *The World we have Lost* (London).

Leslie, A. M. (1987), 'Pretense and representation—the origins of "theory of mind"', *Psychological Review*, 94: 412–26.

MacDonald, C. B. (1955), 'Company', *Encyclopedia Brittanica*, 14th edn., pp. 143–4.

McLeod, C. E., Zilles, K., Schleicher, A., Rilling, J. K. and Gibson, K. E. (2003), 'Expansion of the neocerebellum in Hominoidea', *Journal of Human Evolution*, 44: 401–29.

Mange, A. and Mange, E. (1980), *Genetics: Human Aspects* (New York).

Mitchell, P. (1997), *Introduction to Theory of Mind* (London).

Montross, L. (1975), 'Tactics', *Encyclopedia Britannica*, 15th edn.

Nettle, D. and Dunbar, R. I. M. (1997), 'Social markers and the evolution of reciprocal exchange', *Current Anthropology*, 38: 93–9.

Oates, J. (1977), 'Mesopotamian social organisation: archaeological and philological evidence', in J. Friedman and M. J. Rowlands (ed.), *The Evolution of Social Systems* (London), pp. 457–85.

O'Connell, S. and Dunbar, R. I. M. (2003), 'A test for comprehension of false belief in chimpanzees', *Evolution and Cognition*, 9: 131–9.

Orstrom, E., Gardner, R. and Walker, J. (1994), *Rules, Games and Common-Pool Resources* (Ann Arbor, MI).

Ozonoff, S. (1995), 'Executive functions in autism', in E. Schopler and G. B. Mesibov (eds.), *Learning and Cognition in Autism* (New York), pp. 199–218.

Perner, J. (1991), *Understanding the Representational Mind* (Cambridge, MA).

Pinker, S. (1998), *How the Mind Works* (London).

Roth, D. and Leslie, A. M. (1998): 'Solving belief problems: toward a task analysis', *Cognition*, 66: 1–31.

Shultz, S. and Dunbar, R. I. M. (2007), 'The evolution of the social brain: Anthropoid primates contrast with other vertebrates', *Proceedings of the Royal Society, London*, 274B: 2429–36.

Shultz, S., Noe, R., McGraw, S. and Dunbar, R. I. M. (2004), 'A community-level evaluation of the impact of prey behavioural and ecological characteristics on predator diet composition', *Proceedings of the Royal Society, London*, 271B: 725–32.

Silk, J. B. (2002), 'The 'F'-word in primatology', *Behaviour*, 139: 421–46.

Silk, J. B. (2007), 'Social components of fitness in primate groups', *Science*, 317: 1347–50.

Silk, J. B., Alberts, S. C. and Altmann, J. (2003), 'Social bonds of female baboons enhance infant survival', *Science*, 302: 1232–4.

Smuts, B. B. (1985), *Sex and Friendship in Baboons* (New York).

Sternberg, R. J. (1997), 'Construct validation of a triangular love scale', *European Journal of Social Psychology*, 27: 313–35.

Stiller, J and Dunbar, R. I. M. (2007), 'Perspective-taking and social network size in humans', *Social Networks*, 29: 93–104.

Stylianou, M. (2007), *Does Executive Function Training Improve Mentalising Ability?* Ph.D. thesis, University of Liverpool.

Swarbrick, R. (2000), *A Social Cognitive Model of Paranoid Delusions*. Ph.D. thesis, University of Manchester.

Urban Church Project (1974), *Let My People Grow!* Workpaper No. 1. Unpublished report to the General Synod of the Church of England, London.

van Vugt, M., Hardy, C., Stow, J. and Dunbar, R. I. M. (submitted), 'Laughter as social lubricant: a biosocial hypothesis about the pro-social functions of laughter and humor'.

Whiten, A. and Byrne, R. W. (eds.) (1997), *Machiavellian Intelligence II: Extensions and Evaluations* (Cambridge).

Zhou, W.-X., Sornette, D., Hill, R. A. and Dunbar, R. I. M. (2005), 'Discrete hierarchical organisation of social group sizes', *Proceedings of the Royal Society, London*, 272B: 439–44.

Classical Music and the Subject of Modernity[1]

JOHN BUTT
Fellow of the Academy

ON THE LAST day of 2006, *The Observer* published an article reporting Julian Lloyd Webber's plea that classical music be restored to its former privileged place in the classrooms of Britain. As he told *The Observer*, 'You have to be able to walk before you can run . . . Classical music is the grammar of music; it is the harmony, the melody, the notation . . . It is wrong for teachers to focus on "youth music" such as R&B instead of the likes of Mozart and Shostakovich . . . because classical music is the root of all other styles.'[2]

Much as we might sympathise with at least some of Lloyd Webber's general intentions, there is, I believe, a fundamental misunderstanding of classical music, if it is seen as 'the grammar of music' or 'the root of all other styles'. Much as one might hear some rock and pop superstars— from *The Beatles* to *Tenacious D*—as occasionally playing off, debasing, or even purposely contradicting classical practice, surely one cannot say that classical music stands at their root, even if we bear in mind that it had much to do, historically, with the development of notation and the

Read at the Academy 6 November 2007.

[1] I borrow part of my title from Anthony J. Cascardi's *The Subject of Modernity* (Cambridge, 1992), which has influenced some of the conceptual background for this study. It is impossible to list the number of readers and listeners who have helped me make this study less incoherent than it might otherwise have been, but my warmest thanks are due to Reinhard Strohm, who worked extremely hard to help me refine the final version.

[2] Anushka Asthana (education correspondent), 'Out with Classroom Rap, in with Mozart', *The Observer* (Sunday, 31 Dec. 2006).

tonal system. And, if we were to consider the history of world music, this too has seldom engaged with western classical music, even when it has had any exposure to it. Of course, it might well be that Lloyd Webber's point works far better in reverse: classical music has often absorbed many other forms of music into its vocabulary and performative gestures, somehow transforming them into a music that is quite distinct from the sum of its parts. In this way, classical music may have something of the quality of an enzyme—to borrow a metaphor from Stephen Greenblatt;[3] perhaps it is a practice that absorbs many elements (including those indigenous to its own traditions), but somehow changes their meaning and content in ways that cannot necessarily be predicted in advance. Perhaps, then, in terms of the broader culture and histories of world musics, this function renders classical music more an exception than the norm to which all the others aspire. But would such exceptionality necessarily define it as a universal, transcending all other forms of music, or is it rather an exception in the sense of being a temporally (and culturally) bound deviation from the broader environment of world musics? This is one of the main questions I will be trying to address in this paper.

What about the voices opposed to Lloyd Webber in the same article from *The Observer*? Tina Redford, project manager at MusicLeader North West (an organisation addressing the professional development of music teachers), states that 'Music education and teaching methods have to modernise . . . A music leader in a classroom has to have an intrinsic sense of liking and valuing young people, listening to their ideas and responding to them. The only way to do that is to engage with the kind of music they want to make, not what others want to prescribe to them. We are trying to get away from a didactic teaching style and classical music is seen as didactic.'

Again, one may agree with some of the sentiments here, such as the desirability of a diversity of music within the educational environment. But there are surely some things here that will jar for anyone sceptical of the many recent applications of the word 'modernise'. This is a word that has become particularly prevalent since the 1980s, especially in the last decade or so (at least in the UK). Seldom does it now refer to such laudable aims as, for instance, the redressing of historic inequalities, the eradication of poverty, or even, necessarily, the sort of progress in science that

---

[3] See, for instance, Stephen Greenblatt, *Renaissance Self-Fashioning—from More to Shakespeare* (Chicago and London, 1980), p. 230, or *Marvelous Possessions—the Wonder of the New World* (Oxford, 1991), p. 4.

unequivocally brings an improvement in the human condition. As Fredric Jameson has recently quoted from Oskar Lafontaine's memoir of his fate under Schroeder in Germany, '"modernizers" today understand little other than the economic and social adaptation to the supposed constraints of the global market . . . Modernity has simply become a word for the conformity to such economic constraints—the question of how we want to live together and what kind of society we want has become a completely unmodern question and is no longer posed at all.' Indeed, as Jameson goes on to suggest, 'people like Lafontaine are unmodern because they are still modernists—it is modernism that is unmodern— "modernity" however in the newly approved positive sense is good because it is postmodern'.[4]

That Tina Redford is using the term 'modernise' in this 'postmodern' sense is perhaps substantiated by the implication that schoolchildren are essentially customers with their pre-given interests and desires. This is part of a trend in education towards an insipid sort of naturalism that sees each person or group as a ready-made particular, best left unscarred by any didactic universals. It further suggests that everything good about music is fundamentally natural, latent in all its dimensions within the human psyche. If there is some symmetry between the premodern and the postmodern, one might wonder whether this represents a return to the old scholastic prohibition against curiosity in the unknown or unfamiliar, against changing the order at hand and violating our inborn place within that order.[5] But the religious order that was previously protected against violation is now reoccupied by that of the global market, often posing as an ideal democratic principle. If this sort of attitude is hardly conducive to the cultivation of classical music, it is surely barely any better for the health of popular music, since it tends to efface the resistant or oppositional elements of any music whatsoever.

Given that what we call 'classical' music has seldom generated profits, even at the times of its greatest influence, it does not seem to fit so naturally into a world where, increasingly, everything must have its economic cost (again, the same doubtless applies to many other musics). Therefore, it is difficult to cultivate it as an art available to all, whether in terms of its audience or its creation, if it is not afforded some degree of privilege

---

[4] Fredric Jameson, *A Singular Modernity—an Essay on the Ontology of the Present* (London and New York, 2002), pp. 9–10.

[5] Hans Blumenberg, *The Legitimacy of the Modern Age*, translation by Robert M. Wallace of *Die Legitimät der Neuzeit*, 2nd rev. edn. 1976 (Cambridge, MA and London, 1983), esp. pp. 325–9.

in education and the allocation of public or charitable resources; it requires far more in terms of general effort and time than most other forms of music. If it is left to take its place, equally, beside the other forms of music, it follows that the personal choice to indulge in classical music becomes increasingly expensive. The claim that classical music is essentially elitist and therefore does not belong to the ordinary person, becomes a self-fulfilling prophecy. In an environment where the only generally agreed index of value is that which can be quantified—this is the essential assumption lying behind John Carey's recent polemic, *What Good are the Arts?*[6]—there is no way that anyone can unarguably claim that classical music has any particular value at all, especially if the only way to find out is for us all to fill in an endless chain of questionnaires.

Most significantly—and this is perhaps the factor that has changed most over the last few decades—classical music culture has traditionally involved substantial amateur participation in music making, whether this be in large choral societies, amateur instrumental groups, or simply performance alone at home. Roland Barthes and Edward Said, as ardent amateur classical musicians, stood out as part of a dying breed of intellectuals who felt that their hobby developed their thought and perception in ways that could not otherwise have been acquired. But nowadays it is clear that many capable people—outstanding intellectuals included—get by perfectly well without any encounter with classical music, that the demise of civilisation so often predicated on the advent of Rock and Roll still seems yet to materialise and, most tellingly, that august journals such as the *London Review of Books* are more likely to review monographs about Bob Dylan than about Beethoven.

Does this all suggest that classical music essentially belongs only to the past? This will be another question underlying much of what I have to say, although at this stage my provisional answer is—frustratingly perhaps—yes and no. To begin with, we do need to guard against the assumption that all was somehow rosy for classical music over the last two centuries, that scores of respectable, decent citizens queued up in an orderly fashion for endless concerts and operas. Moreover, if classical music were indeed to have been so directly complicit in oiling the wheels of the industrialised west, we might indeed be correct in seeing it as of its time and now to be superseded by music more conducive to our age of diversity and equality. While classical music clearly has to carry the bur-

---

[6] John Carey, *What Good are the Arts?* (London, 2005).

den of a few threads of respectability in its genealogy—don't we all?—
its history is surely much more varied and ambiguous. Funding was never
straightforward or even ubiquitous, nor was universal education in the
art, whether for composers, performers or listeners. Indeed, many of the
inherited traditions within classical music, at least in the UK and the US
—such as its privileged place in education or the public provision of
orchestras—were the product of a particular high modernist mindset
that reached its peak only in the middle of the twentieth century.

The status of classical music in western society thus seems to be highly
ambiguous. Indeed, perhaps one of the strengths its tradition has had lies
in the way it sits between the establishment—confirming the status quo
in sound, as it were—and that which opposes or subverts it, challenging
its secure assumptions. If I understand it aright, it is an art that takes
inherited orders as its starting point (thus its reliance on a particularly
strong pedagogy of harmony and counterpoint), but can also act as a critique of our assumptions. What I am beginning to imply is that classical
music is of a piece with the fundamental attitudes and reflexes of modernity itself. My argument will now need to proceed by trying to define what
both classical music and modernity might be, in order ultimately to give
more flesh to that 'yes and no' answer (to the question, does it belong only
to the past?). After that, the question would be, does classical music still
belong to us and do we still belong to modernity? Inevitably, much of this
latter line of enquiry will have to remain sketchy here.

Is there anything substantial that can unequivocally identify classical
music as more than merely an example of 'music' in the more general
sense? After all, it is hard to dispute that there is much that classical music
and most other forms of western music have in common in terms of
melody, tonality, mode, rhythm and harmony. *Greenday's* 'Basketcase' is
a song that in its harmonic frame is essentially identical to Pachelbel's
canon. Whether or not this latter is a genuine example of the Lloyd-
Webberish flow from the classical to the more popular, surely what is
more significant is the fact that the similarities between these two pieces
lie in the basics of the tonal system that is common to both genres. The
bass line of Pachelbel's canon is one of the generic expansions of the
perfect cadence (chords V–I), which is the most fundamental dynamic
impulse of the tonal system. It is not surprising, then, that this crops up in
a variety of music—indeed, the same pattern underlies 'Puff the Magic
Dragon' as well. Given that much classical and virtually all popular and
traditional music share common tonal underpinnings, it does not take
much to turn a classical piece into one that sounds more popular, and to

'classicise' a popular one. More challenging is the fact that a piece of unadulterated classical music can take on an entirely different ethos if it is used in a way outside its customary home in the concert hall (or, increasingly, personal sound system): Vivaldi's *Four Seasons* becomes a different, not always welcome, animal when a company switchboard puts us on hold for half an hour, and Wagner's 'Ride of the Valkeries' is somehow translated into another language when heard as part of the sound track to *Apocalypse Now*.

Perhaps, then, the safest way of distinguishing classical music from competing musical languages is to suggest that it tends to display a combination of certain tendencies or attitudes rather than essential qualities: e.g. it tends towards more complexity than most surrounding music; it usually requires the cultivation of a specific, and somewhat abstract method—performance technique or compositional theory—before it can be created; it displays a degree of 'written-ness', that is, the development of the sort of sound structure that is sometimes best created and recorded in notation; it has a tendency to subsume diverse musical gestures within a broader, dialogic argument. But it is perhaps a mistake to identify it solely in terms of its specific musical substance. We surely have to take into account at least some of the attitudes and tendencies of the cultures that accompany it, and of which it may well also be a constitutive ingredient.[7] These might include the ideal of listening to the music in dedicated spaces where the listener's attention is as fully engaged as possible (and usually without direct physical participation); a culture in which the musical practices designated as classical are seen as beneficial in terms of education and continuing personal development. Again, a specific method is usually cultivated and practised, prior to the musicmaking proper. It also presupposes a society in which there is a sufficiently numerous paying public to finance both the space and the performances. In short, classical music is a particular historical construct that includes a menu of performative and receptive practices as much as specific compositional structures; it is an ensemble of things that came

---

[7] This is part of the overriding argument of Lydia Goehr's *The Imaginary Museum of Musical Arts* (Oxford, 1992), by which the 'work concept' dating from around 1800 is defined in terms of a 'regulative concept'. Reinhard Strohm suggests, rather, that this concept originated in fifteenth-century humanism, in 'Looking back at ourselves: the problem with the musical work-concept', in Michael Talbot (ed.), *The Musical Work—Reality or Invention?*, Liverpool Music Symposium, 1 (Liverpool, 2000), pp. 128–52; and '"Opus": an aspect of the early history of the musical work-concept', in Tomasz Jez (ed.), *Complexus effectuum musicologiae*, Studia Miroslavo Perz septuagenario dedicata (Kraków, 2003), pp. 309–19.

together at a specific historical juncture and therefore could equally well dissolve if the historical conditions accompanying its emergence begin to dissipate.

When, then, might classical music actually have emerged? If it is essentially to be connected with concert-hall practice and the sense of moral self-improvement that the Germans termed 'Bildung', then its emergence would unequivocally have to belong to the late eighteenth century. This is the conclusion of Karol Berger's recent searching study of musical modernity, where he identifies the classical style specifically with a new form of human autonomy, distinct from the order of the cosmos; one in which God becomes a metaphor for harmony rather than, as before, harmony a metaphor for God.[8] But, if this account is correct, then Pachelbel's *Canon*, Vivaldi's *Four Seasons* and the entire works of Bach and Handel would have to count as preclassical (as indeed they do in traditional historical categories of western music, where the term 'classical' tends to be more strictly reserved for the generation of Haydn to Beethoven). One way out of the problem of excluding music predating the 'classical' era (if indeed it is a problem) is somehow to 'retrofit' it as classical music. The obvious example of this is Bach's *Matthew Passion*, which was 'rediscovered' by Mendelssohn in 1829 and received by the German public as one of the greatest of all classical works, a sort of Old Testament to the New of Beethoven and his followers.

Another strategy might be to note how earlier music may have provided one or more of the vital strands that contributed to an eventual 'full-blown' culture of classical music: the development of an official 'canon' of music within the plainchant repertory; the successive emergence of modality, polyphony and rhythmic complexity; the implications of using notation. The place of music in the Middle Ages as one of the scholastic seven liberal arts (indeed on the more prestigious, theoretical side: the *quadrivium*) meant that music—as theory, at least—retained the aura of its Pythagorean links to the essential order of the cosmos. The eventual emergence of classical music might well be a sort of reoccupation of the prestigious position music had retained throughout the Middle Ages, both in terms of cosmic theory and its ubiquity in liturgy, court and civic life; this gave some of the music concerned a sense of canonic identity. Therefore, there is no obvious point at which 'early

---

[8] Karol Berger, *Bach's Cycle, Mozart's Arrow—an Essay on the Origins of Musical Modernity* (Berkeley, Los Angeles and London, 2007), see esp. pp. 14, 127.

music' ceased and 'classical music' began: as one model moved to the other, strands of the older and newer conceptions lay side by side.[9]

Nevertheless, it is striking that the roots of this continuum clearly lie in the Middle Ages. Most other western arts and intellectual traditions comprise a canon stretching back into antiquity. However much music was cultivated in the ancient world, even as something with striking affective powers, it never developed in any sense as a body of exemplary works; and, like the majority of world music, it seems to have been primarily monophonic. This therefore gives support to my claim that classical music (together with its direct historical precedents) is something exceptional even among the western arts in general, and is more directly connected with the history of modernity.

Some aspects of classical music culture may have been partly accidental, though. At the outset of the seventeenth century, music that was specifically geared towards human emotion and expression was very much in vogue; this was a product of a humanism that seemed to forsake the lofty cosmic ideals of the Platonist tradition in favour of a type of music that mimicked, stirred and stilled the human passions (thus following the alternative, Aristotelian, strand in the conceptions of music inherited from the ancients).[10] This new idiom was soon to be heard in church, court and the newly emerging public venues, particularly those associated with opera. Yet music's direct connection with a specific text did not seem as secure as the reformers might initially have imagined: for, as new formalising procedures emerged from an interplay of traditional techniques of musical construction, dance patterns and newly expressive gestures, music seemed somehow capable of pursuing a life of its own, certainly paralleling human emotion and the implications of text, but not necessarily confining itself to these. In other words, however much humanist reformers at the end of the sixteenth century (together with many music critics of the eighteenth and nineteenth centuries) might have prized music for its supposedly 'natural' qualities, what was becoming increas-

---

[9] For Reinhard Strohm the most crucial root of musical modernity lies in the humanists' artificial derivation of musical ideas from ancient precedents, beginning in the fifteenth century; see 'The Humanist idea of a common revival of the arts, and its implications for music history', in Maciej Jablonski and Jan Steszewski (eds.), *Interdisciplinary Studies in Musicology*, Report from the Third Interdisciplinary Conference, Poznan (Poznan, Society for the Advancement of the Arts and Sciences, 1997), pp. 7–25; and 'Music, Humanism, and the idea of a "rebirth" of the Arts', in Reinhard Strohm and Bonnie J. Blackburn (eds.), *Music as Concept and Practice in the Late Middle Ages*, New Oxford History of Music, vol. 3/1 (Oxford, 2001), pp. 346–405.

[10] Berger, *Bach's Cycle*, pp. 35–7.

ingly effective were precisely its independent aspects, its deviation and modification of supposed natural principles. With this potential for autonomy came the sense that musical works were individuals, following their own implications and potentials, and thus almost of a piece with the individuality of those who created them. Discrete musical works also began to adopt a series of internal laws, checks and balances that paralleled Hobbes's theory of the artificially structured state—in other words, something that eschewed the immediate dictates of nature in order to mediate between the competing forms of power and authority.

Perhaps the most dynamic aspect of this developing musical culture was the tension between a sense of the universal and the particular: music could articulate, represent, or even actualise both a more conservative sense of an established order—that which corresponds to pedagogic method—and a radical sense of individuality. It could develop a feeling of alienation, resistance or even opposition to the surrounding orders. In other words, it worked dialectically in the sense that it could lead to results that could never quite accurately be predicted. If this thumbnail sketch is accurate, it describes a world of music utterly remote from that of the supposedly 'modernised' classroom, which mirrors the choices of its students or engages them in a range of practices cleansed of didactic, methodical, content. The idea of a music that has to do with human, spiritual or moral order and that—simultaneously—challenges, subverts or utterly opposes such orders, seems to be an ontological category entirely foreign to a conception of music that expresses the self with the apparent spontaneity of an unmediated bodily function.

Having sketched the way classical music developed within specific historical parameters, what do these same conditions tell us about the western modernity that I propose is of a piece with classical music? First, modernity itself is—in the wider course of humanity—the exception rather than the rule, however much we might today use terms like 'modern' and 'modernise' as normative categories of unlimited progress. The concept of modernity, which I am trying both to define and co-opt, might seem unorthodox to some in the field of musicology. This latter has tended to avoid the term as a broad historical category and generally associates the 'modern' with the specific stylistic category of 'modernism', as applied to progressive music from the late nineteenth century to the last decades of the twentieth. It may well be that musicologists have avoided engagement with 'modernity' and all the broader cultural issues that this implies because of the autonomy that western music seems to have acquired through that very modernity, and specifically through the intensified ideology of modernism (thus something relatively recent); namely, a sense that music stands apart from all other considerations, that it is somehow more 'true' than the messy contingencies of politics, society and, specifically, cultural history.

Historians, on the other hand, have long used the broad categorisation by which the Ancient World is separated from the Modern World by the Middle Ages.[11] Modernity thus has its beginnings in the era of the Renaissance and Reformation and is fed by the scientific revolution of the sixteenth and seventeenth centuries. Culturally, it surely has some real presence in Montaigne, Shakespeare and Cervantes, the philosophy of Locke, Hobbes, Descartes and Spinoza. It reaches both a peak and a crisis at the time of the Enlightenment and French Revolution and thereafter forges ahead with the industrial revolution and the increasing dominance of capitalism. It is thus tempting to divide it into three historical phrases, the first dating from the sixteenth century to the end of the eighteenth; the second, from the time of the French Revolution to the late nineteenth century; and the final phase characterised by modernism. By this model, the second phase would neatly coincide with what Karol Berger characterises as the inauguration of 'our' modernity, which is associated with the type of music traditionally termed 'classical' and 'romantic'.[12] However, it is impossible to give the concept of modernity hard and fast chronological markers. While the Renaissance, with its restoration of a lost antiquity, could not be considered 'modern' in itself, its new oppositional mechanism—beating the immediate past with the stick of the ancient world—could well have been significant, since this was indeed something that was soon to be engaged against the very antiquity it previously envied. In other words, many aspects of modernity were inaugurated within earlier traditions, their eventual effects being entirely unanticipated when they first arose.

Much also depends on particular views or national traditions, which might prioritise different starting points: the Reformation, for instance,[13] or Descartes' concept of the self-conscious, reflexive ego, unmediated by

---

[11] Habermas traces this conception back to Hegel's designation of the 'new age' as coinciding with the Renaissance, Reformation and the discovery of the new world, in his *Lectures on the Philosophy of History*; Jürgen Habermas, *The Philosophical Discourse of Modernity—Twelve Lectures*, translated by Frederick Lawrence of *Der philosophische Diskurs der Moderne*, 1985 (Cambridge, MA and London, 1987), pp. 4–5.

[12] Berger, *Bach's Cycle*, pp. 5, 14.

[13] This is certainly true of German conceptions of modernity, beginning with Hegel and taken further in art criticism by Jacob Burckhardt. See also Jameson, *A Singular Modernity*, p. 31.

any light other than its own, or the political revolutions of the late eighteenth century. Some theoretical traditions usefully define modernity as primarily a qualitative category—as a sort of attitude—rather than as chronologically bounded, thus allowing that elements of it might well appear in periods long before the 'Modern' age.[14] This also allows that there can be considerable strength in 'non-modern' traditions within the age when modernity seems to dominate. Indeed, it may well be that modernity is liveliest when it interacts with traditions that it is either trying to surpass or that, in turn, challenge it. This sort of modernity thus retains a dynamic quality that could become ossified when that which is modern finds no resistance. In all, the precise bounds of modernity are dependent on the sort of narrative one adopts to explain it, as if it contains the seeds of a story that can be unfolded in several ways.[15]

Well-worn theories associate modernity with various developments in the way the cosmos was believed to cohere: foremost is perhaps the concept of 'disenchantment' (Max Weber's famous term), a retreat from the magical significance of the world and human practices, the 'extirpation of animism'.[16] With this came the view that the cosmos was not necessarily constructed entirely for mankind's benefit, so that a new form of human initiative was required to render the natural world amenable to human purposes. This is what Hans Blumenberg terms the 'burden of self-assertion'. With the new development of scientific method, it became necessary to adapt man to the impersonal reality uncovered by repeatable experimentation. But this distinction between reality and the human condition also brought with it the contrary tendency: to adapt that reality to the needs and purposes of man.[17] The most positive aspect to arise from this is the potential to see reality as that which is most actual and immanent, rather than as something that must always remain beyond our immediate experience; this might be what gives modernity its restless and ongoing energy.[18] On the other hand, this development tends to drive a wedge between the natural world and human civilisation, to suggest that

---

[14] The classic text for this approach to modernity (or rather that which is termed 'Enlightenment') is Theodor W. Adorno's and Max Horkheimer's *Dialectic of Enlightenment* (*Dialektic der Aufklärung*, 1944), translated by John Cumming (London and New York, 1997).

[15] Jameson, *A Singular Modernity*, pp. 31–3. For Jameson, modernity is a narrative category rather than a concept as such, see p. 40.

[16] Adorno and Horkheimer, *Dialectic of Enlightenment*, p. 5.

[17] Blumenberg, *The Legitimacy of the Modern Age*, pp. 137–8, 209.

[18] Harvie Ferguson, *Modernity and Subjectivity—Body, Soul, Spirit* (Charlottesville, VA and London, 2000), pp. 3, 66.

humankind is progressively alienated from the secure and harmonious place in the natural order that our cultural memories always seem to evoke. Hans Robert Jauss usefully relates this line of thinking to a trajectory leading from Rousseau to Adorno, thus suggesting an intellectual epoch that coincides directly with the era of modernity as I am trying to outline it.[19] However, the sense of a growing rift between western humanity and nature did not necessarily prevent the re-invention of the transcendent hidden reality to give human orders support and justification. While the birth of the nation state is one of the most palpable inventions of modernity—deriving from its tendency to divide phenomena into manageable units (which are then rationally governed as efficiently as possible)—such units are invariably buoyed up by the reinvention of myths relating to their identity and cohesion. Again, modernity is almost always something which works in counterpoint with non-modern elements, the interaction often resulting in a change on both sides, an unpredictable synthesis that is itself rarely stable.

Roughly simultaneous with the beginnings of self-assertion in the Renaissance and Reformation was the breakdown of the medieval chivalric tradition and the complex customs and interactions of various classes, dominated by aristocratic and military etiquette. Cervantes' satire on the old order, *Don Quixote*, clearly demonstrates that this had irrevocably declined by the early seventeenth century.[20] What is less certain is what the disintegration in this order actually led to, although it clearly left a space for new ways of defining the self. Some commentators point to the steady breakdown of the assumption of resemblance and interconnectedness between all facets and dimensions of the world and universe (something also central to Cervantes' satire). This has been most famously theorised by Foucault in recent years, but is already clearly evident in Descartes' critique of inherited modes of thought: 'Whenever people notice some similarity between two things, they are in the habit of ascribing to the one what they find true of the other, even when the two are not in that respect similar.'[21] The concept of resemblance has undergone many forms of

[19] Hans Robert Jauss, 'Der literarische prozess des modernismus von Rousseau bis Adorno', in Reinhart Herzog and Reinhart Koselleck (eds.), *Epochenschwelle und Epochenbewusstsein* (Munich, 1987), pp. 243–68.
[20] Cascardi, *The Subject of Modernity*, pp. 72–124.
[21] René Descartes, *Regulae ad Directionem Ingenii* (c.1628), trans. John Cottingham, Robert Stoothoff, Dugald Murdoch, (Cambridge, 1985), Rule 1, p. 9. For the most ubiquitous study of these issues in recent times, see Michel Foucault, *The Order of Things—an Archaeology of the Human Sciences* (*Les Mots et les choses*, 1966), unattributed translation (New York, 1994). See

revival within even the strongest eras of modernity, most significantly in the various forms of musical Romanticism. Thus, again, modernity cannot be thought of as a monolithic movement, uninflected by survivals from the past and restorations in the present. Older elements often become spheres of knowledge and practice developed along their own trajectories. Moreover, the inevitable tensions between the various practices, ancient and modern, generate a sense of movement, whether positive and progressive or negative and alienating.

The breakdown in the system of resemblance during the seventeenth century may well have led to the increasing autonomy of different activities and practices, developed more for their own sense of coherence than for the way they might automatically relate to other things.[22] The development of different activities independently of one another could, technically, be infinite and ongoing, thus engendering a sense of openness in terms of both reality and the human mind.[23] Something of the excitement at the opening of new horizons is captured by the print of the Pillars of Hercules on the title page of Francis Bacon's *Instauratio Magna* of 1620.[24] One gets the sense of the possibility of breaking out of an enchanted circle of interconnected elements and that, having chosen a direction in which to sail, the journey could be potentially endless. Pragmatically, separation could also be exercised in the name of efficiency, something most obviously demonstrated in the concept of division of labour necessary for industrialised societies. It was precisely this same division of labour that facilitated the development of the modern symphony orchestra, where every player has a specific place and a single instrument to perfect to the highest possible level, through methodical practice of an approved pedagogical system. Modernity is thus frequently related to the development of instrumentalised rationality, the ability to

---

also Dalia Judovitz, *Subjectivity and Representation in Descartes: the Origins of Modernity* (Cambridge, 1988), p. 41. Judovitz is sceptical of reductionism on the part of both Foucault and Descartes, observing that writers from Plato to Montaigne were well aware of the way resemblance could produce illusion, and suggesting that Foucault merely relied on Descartes' opinion, which itself lacked a systematic critique of resemblance.

[22] Foucault tends to associate this process with a second stage of modernity, beginning in the late eighteenth century, although others would see it as already seeded in Descartes' conception of the separation of subject and object. What links them is perhaps the notion of 'method', which overrides assumed connections between things. Jameson, *A Singular Modernity*, pp. 73–4, 86.

[23] Eric Voegelin, *Religion and the Rise of Modernity*, Collected Works, vol. 23; History of Political Ideas, vol. 5; ed. with an introd. by James L. Wiser (Columbia, MO and London, 1998), pp. 136–7.

[24] Blumenberg, *The Legitimacy of the Modern Age*, p. 340.

adapt rational principles from one situation and apply them in another, thus progressing the material comforts of humankind. Max Weber's conception of equal temperament in music as an essential element of rationalisation is, of course, particularly telling here.[25]

If, in one sense, modernity led, through the division of labour, to a sense of alienation, of being separated from some intuited organic whole, in another way it led to a consolidation of the individual. Given that reality has to be constructed, as much as it is duplicated or mirrored, the question of how it is represented from each individual viewpoint becomes more pressing, something obvious in the development of perspective in painting. The standard accounts of the development of the human subject within modernity tend to stress its sense of autonomy and its freedom from the constraint of the inherited orders into which it was born; yet this has to negotiate with other subjects in order to achieve a society that is both harmonious and progressive. This approach immediately risks a level of generalisation, though; after all, were there not recognisable human subjects before the mythical dividing line between modernity and premodernity? Is not the variety of subjecthood within modernity so extremely great as to render the concept of a 'modern subject' meaningless? Charles Taylor provides a useful starting point by linking the growing sense of internalisation with the turn against an external, pre-existent order that is 'found' and that determines our station and role in life, towards a form or order that is made with our own minds; this is something made overt in Descartes' work on subjectivity, particularly in the *Discours de la Méthode* (1637).[26]

Of course, something of this inward turn was evident in Augustine, but with him it was coupled with a sense of the moral sources as lying outside us, which are by definition good (like Plato's cosmos). Descartes' move was to make such moral sources internal to the individual.[27] This by no means excluded the divine origin of such internal moral sources, but made these independent of the order of the external world and cosmos. Thus the essence of modern ethical and political thought was to lie in the subject's sense of his or her own dignity, something to be enhanced and

[25] Max Weber, *The Rational and Social Foundations of Music* (*Die rationalen und sozialen Grundlagen der Musik*, appendix to *Wirtschaft und Gesellschaft*, written 1911, published Tübingen, 1921), trans. and ed. Don Martindale, Johannes Riedel and Gertrude Neuwirth (Carbondale, IL, 1958).
[26] Charles Taylor, *Sources of the Self—the Making of the Modern Identity* (Cambridge, 1989), p. 124
[27] Ibid., p. 143.

developed over and above the disenchanted matter of the world. This was seeded in Descartes' conception of the subject and later developed much more overtly in the moral system of Kant.[28] This is not to say that the modern subject is to take a reckless attitude towards the external world as something that is merely the plaything of subjectivity, but rather that the orders of nature do not automatically determine our inner nature, that our rationality demands that we accept the outside world in relation to the evidence it offers, our models for understanding it always being subject to modification and improvement. Rationality is thus procedural rather than a substantive, ready-perfected vision of reality.

Before turning more directly to the way that music might relate to this sense of modern subjectivity, I will briefly propose another contextual element that arose at precisely the same time that classical music came into being. I suggest that the sort of music emerging with modernity acquired much of its apparent power precisely through doing musically what the modern novel was doing textually, in other words, as a sort of fiction that brought its own, new form of 'truth'. Catherine Gallagher relates the development of the 'true fiction' of the novel specifically to modernity, to that attitude of speculation and scepticism which led the reader of novels to entertain speculations about the believability of the characters and actions, to hypothesise about motives and outcomes. This sort of fictionality challenged the reader in gauging the likelihood of possible outcomes, something vital in negotiating new forms of commerce and enterprise.[29] As she perceptively puts it, ordinary people had to exercise the ability to suspend literal truth claims even in order to accept paper money. Thus, most of the developments associated with modernity required precisely the kind of 'cognitive provisionality' developed in the novel, a sort of fiction that was accepted and fostered for some sort of practical convenience. The characters of novelistic fiction are open, inviting the reader to bring them to life, internalised in a way that would be impossible were they to represent actual people. This sort of internalisation is not necessarily the direct identification that many critics of the bourgeois sensibility of the novel have assumed, but something much more open and flexible, enabling the reader to reflect on his or her own unfathomability in contrast to the knowability of the novelistic character. It is thus more an exercise in flexible self-creation than one of recognising

---

[28] Ibid., p. 152.
[29] Catherine Gallagher, 'The rise of fictionality', in Franco Moretti (ed.), *The Novel, Vol. 1: History, Geography, and Culture* (Princeton, NJ, 2006), pp. 336–63.

a completed model of oneself behind the text. Moreover, as Descartes tried to show in *Le Monde* (1664), the notion of fictional worlds becomes the prototype for the way we gain our knowledge of the real world, as if we were imitating God's creative capabilities, trying them out on a fictional world in order to adapt them to the real one. The representation of the world becomes a form of metaphor, a representation of what things ideally should look like, rather than something essentially of a piece with nature, as metonymy.[30]

Having brought up the relation of music, not only to modernity as a broad cultural attitude but also to the novel, I am perhaps beginning to fall victim to a very common problem in recent music scholarship. This is the tendency to translate music into other phenomena, to reduce it to more concrete and readable models, particularly the verbal. However, having used such models as analogies in order to bring music out of its habitually autonomous territory, I now suggest that the type of music I am addressing is specifically important because it also helps to constitute modernity in the very process of reflecting it. Taking the novelistic analogy as a starting point, it is clear that most forms of music relate to narrative in the broadest way (that is, to a human sense of organisation in time, rather than necessarily to the specific implication of a storyline) and also to some sort of voice.[31] Indeed, the latter can—as in novels—be quite multiple, but, given the way lines and gestures may be combined simultaneously in music, this can present multiple voices and associated viewpoints in a way that is entirely unique. While some forms of musical narrative can come closer to the novelistic than others—sonata form, for instance, in its relation to novels of the Enlightenment era—what is significant is that a narrative element is palpable in music precisely because it is performed in time. A 'modern' listener will try to piece together elements of narrative in any music which contains a plethora of events and gestures (even if the emerging temporality is relatively static or circular). Indeed, it is the implication of a stronger form of listenership—akin to the reader of a novel—that makes classical music so significant in the development of the modern subject. In hearing relationships both between figure and ground—if the music profiles a specific melodic

---

[30] Judovitz, *Subjectivity and Representation*, pp. 92–4, 189–90.

[31] I use the term 'narrative' here in its broadest sense, as covering the way human understanding is organised in relation to time, thus implying that most music evokes a sort of temporality, even if this may be relatively cyclical or even static. This broader concept of narrative is theorised at exhaustive length by Paul Ricoeur, in *Time and Narrative*, trans. Kathleen McLaughlin and David Pellauer, 3 vols. (Chicago, 1984, 1985, 1988).

line—and between events passing in time, one is not just testing out a possible world, as one might in reading a novel, but exercising a form of consciousness over time. And what is specifically significant about this form of consciousness is that it is purposely artificial, based on fictional musical events (rather than—say—an exercise in coordinating one's listening with an assumed harmony of the spheres or one that amplifies one's prior sense of identity).

Let me suggest some of the ways in which this form of artificial (i.e. constructed) consciousness is different from that of a premodern experience. One of the most perceptive accounts of experience of the self in time from the ancient world is Augustine's self-analysis of the recitation of a psalm—thus something that could well have been as much a musical experience as a verbal one.[32] He overcomes the problem of the pinpoint subjectivity of the present (i.e. the fact that our consciousness at any particular moment is gone as soon as it comes) by noting the persistence of the mind's attention and how it is through this that what is expected passes into the memory. Before beginning a psalm, his faculty of expectation engages the whole, but, as he begins to recite, this future expectation pours through the consciousness into the memory (perhaps rather like the sand in an egg-timer). From the experience of reciting a psalm, Augustine abstracts the way we encounter both small durations and longer, including life itself and the whole history of mankind. Music, in this sort of consciousness, thus helps to attune us to a greater reality that is entirely pre-given and to which the state of attention aligns us. There are, of course, many other ways in which music can exercise our sense of being in ways that are not specifically 'modern' (by which I do not mean that they are by any means irrelevant to our own condition). Dance music can regulate a predictable flow of physical movements in space as well as time; music can also be used to express precisely the feelings we are experiencing at any particular time, the type of person we believe ourselves to be or the cultural group to which we belong or aspire to belong. None of these modes—and more—are necessarily to be excluded in the culture of classical music, as I have been outlining it. Where would it be, if it did not in some ways resonate with our emotions, confirm our beliefs or sometimes make us want to dance? Rather, I would suggest its crucial element is that of fictionality, of the implication of a form of consciousness that is *not* merely an amplification or confirmation of what is already given or expected.

[32] St Augustine, *The Confessions*, book 11.28, trans. R. S. Pine-Coffin (Chicago, 1990), p. 125.

I do not have time to do anything more than sketch out what I mean by this relationship between classical music and modern subjectivity. My current work specifically addresses the Passions of Bach, which are significant in this regard since so much about the intention lying behind them is surely of a premodern mindset: texts concerning the universal sinfulness of mankind, as a state dating back to the beginnings of human time; or the sovereignty of Jesus as something wound into the very fabric of the world and all creation. Musically, too, the textures tend towards a consistent web of harmonic certainty, music that is so technically confident that it might be understood to reflect the very unseen structure of the cosmos that surrounds us and of which we are a symptom. Yet, in practice, the results can be entirely surprising. When Jesus speaks only three lines in the long second half of the *Matthew Passion*, we hardly notice his absence since the large number of emotionally charged arias, sung by personages constructed in our present rather than in the past of the story, together point to him in their varied ways. Following Hobbes, we might infer that the monarch is constructed through the very authority of his free subjects, who together 'authorise' him through their own intensified subjectivity. Moreover, in the arias themselves, there is a constant dialectic between the singers as personages entirely dependent on the material of the music that brings them to presence and their melodic independence from this web of musical connections.

It is obviously impossible to gauge what all listeners—from whatever period or background—are likely to experience when listening to Bach's Passion arias. All I can suggest is something of the possibilities of what a listener attuned to imperatives of modernity, as I have outlined them, might intuit (whether consciously or not). What we might be able to hear are abstract but emotionally charged personages emerging in the course of their ariosos and arias, as musical characters who are built up through conformity to a pattern, or deviation and repetition. Sometimes, these characters acquire a sense of themselves through a subject–object duality, by which we hear a quaking heart or flow of tears represented in the music, but viewed at a distance by the singer (since she might sing patterns independent of the pictorial figuration). This same subject–object relationship can work at the level of listening: we can observe the construction of a musical subjectivity in time as an object from our own position, or we can make the same musical event part of our own subjectivity as we map the vocal line onto our own consciousness. Following the musical events of a Bach aria can have a sense of directional narrative, although this is much more a feature of later music, as Berger has shown.[33] But, in the way so much of the music is the manipulation and creative elaboration of an initial body of sound, there is almost the sense that our expectation is exercised through an increasing enlargement of our initial experience. The progress of the piece both confirms and expands an initial burst of musical consciousness, deepening our experience as if in concentric circles. This form of subjective consciousness is quite different from that performed by coordinating oneself with a given external reality, like Augustine's recitation of a psalm. Neither does it necessarily have a specific aim in mind, such as the anticipated resolution of opposing elements: it is a sort of exercise in consciousness in and for itself, born of the specifically Protestant imperative to develop personal responsibility for the cultivation of faith.

Of course, my study of Bach relates to what I would call the earlier stages of musical modernity. But similar issues would emerge for the study of 'classical music' proper and later types. The period of the later eighteenth century brings in the obvious linear features of sonata form, by which the free and open dialectical elements of earlier music are now directed towards a level of synthesis and resolution, precisely in the way many contemporary novels might be structured. Again, it is not the 'truth' of the individual elements that counts, but the way they relate, both combining and inflecting one another in a process we can both view objectively and map as subjects in time. This is precisely the type of music that can absorb other musical influences, which thereby become something entirely different within the course of the musical fiction. In typically 'modern' fashion, much music around the turn of the nineteenth century appropriates elements of folk music, dance, or even ancient church polyphony, stripping them of their supposedly natural 'truth' and constructing something that is a new type of fiction. This is equally true of music that aspires to be more naturalistic or popular, such as Italianate opera, all of which presupposes expert singers who have undergone rigorous institutional training in voice production and coloratura. As we map any of this music with our consciousness we might find ourselves facing particular moral quandaries. How are we to take it, for instance, when Mozart writes some of his most ravishingly beautiful music in his operas for characters we know are being flattering, dishonest or downright evil? Does the beauty of the music represent some sort of truth that belongs to us as listeners and which the singer does not directly

---

[33] Berger, *Bach's Cycle*, esp. pp. 45–129.

hear? Or does the music teach us that fiction is all we have, but it is up to us whether we use it for good or ill? The crucial thing is that this music might encourage us to ask questions, feel ambiguities, try out characters, ones that we might not otherwise have been able to experience.

Later music might radicalise the subject–object relations by rendering the music quite alien to our own feelings or sensations, an independent entity that is neither the continuous cosmos of premodernity nor the idealised bourgeois subject of the early nineteenth century. But there are countless ways in which this process might work; what they all have in common is the tendency for the music concerned not to take its elements at face value, as a form of truth continuous with the rest of existence. They all mostly presuppose a form of attention that is bounded by a time frame. Many within the modernist mindset tend to assume that supremely autonomous music's fictional truth is so refined and honest in its own integrity that it in fact outdoes any other kind of truth. It is supremely true because it is so distanced from the messy ambiguity of the rest of reality. With this in mind, it is easy to see how the later culture of classical music has so much contributed to its own sense of exceptionality—as something totally separate from the mundane—that the modernist outlook is thus assumed to apply to the whole of this art of modernity (as I claim for it). From this point of view, the advent of a postmodern mindset, or at least that part of it that undoes the dichotomy of high and low culture, has provided a healthy corrective. But, one could ask, might we not also have lost a sort of productive tension between different types of culture?

If we accept my thesis of classical music as not only reflective of modernity but also part of its very constitution, then we have to accept that it also brings with it both the positive and negative elements of that modernity. Human autonomy as something cultivated away from what seems to be naturally inherited is both wonderfully liberating and fulfilling, but also potentially oppressive and cruel. Artificiality enables us to escape naturalising prejudices and achieve things in technology, art and thought that we might never have believed possible. Yet it can also take us so far away from our necessary grounding in the world that we are in danger of destroying the environment that sustains our very existence. Universality, in the sense of bringing differences together and synthesising them into something new, can both surpass the best qualities of the contributing factions or intensify the worst. Moreover, it is very easy for a dominant faction to claim successful synthesis of all the others and exterminate anything that remains, the cultural equivalent of colonialism, perhaps. I would claim that it is classical music and its supporting culture that expresses, represents and even constitutes all these things in musical time (with all the caveats that music cannot do these things 'on its own', without a certain range of preconceptions on the part of those receiving it). One can easily think of examples where classical music seemed to be co-opted as a force for the good—Beethoven's evocation of the free human subject liberated from hierarchy or domination, the various forms of musical resistance to Stalinist oppression—or for the worst—the co-option of Beethoven, Wagner and Bruckner by the Nazi regime. In its historical use, then, classical music might be associated with as many dangers as advantages, although it belongs to a modernity that is—on balance—ultimately more successful than disastrous. If it were entirely a 'safe' sort of art, I doubt if it would have the importance that I am trying to attribute to it.

But, if we are to believe that classical music contains a specific kernel of cruelty—its origins in barbarism, as Horkheimer and Adorno would have said[34]—this could hardly refer to specific aspects of musical content, since this would be to read a meaning into something that can really carry no stable meaning. Scepticism towards the habit of finding a literal meaning in anything from human culture is surely one of the greater achievements of modernity, but one that has frequently been eroded, even in some of the writing of self-proclaimed postmoderns. I suggest that it is rather the sense of mechanism that is the central issue: music in modernity combines elements, plays them off against one another within an artificial construction, and in such a way that the listener is invited, as never before, to intuit meanings, resonances and significance. This is music that seems positively to welcome a diversity of reception, since it can work in both rhetorical and dialectical relation to virtually anything we bring to it.[35] In a rhetorical mode of listening it will confirm our assumptions, beliefs or prejudices with remarkable conviction and certainty; in the dialectical, it will put everything we assumed into question, leading us to thoughts and sensations that could not necessarily have been predicted. If what is powerful about this music is essentially its mechanisms—its sense of 'method'—in other words, its relation to the thought

[34] Adorno and Horkheimer, *Dialectic of Enlightenment*, pp. 111–12.
[35] I borrow this distinction between rhetoric and dialectic from Stanley Fish's study of seventeenth-century English literature (which is itself grounded in Plato's *Gorgias*). See Stanley E. Fish, *Self-Consuming Artifacts—the Experience of Seventeenth-Century Literature* (Berkeley and Los Angeles, 1972), see esp. pp. 1–29.

processes of modernity, then one can begin to understand how such mechanisms can be put to a variety of uses.

So what is the fate of this culture in our own time? First, it is impossible that the conditions of, say, the early nineteenth century can be recreated in such a way that the music has exactly the same, seemingly beneficial effects and cultural aura that it supposedly had then. The notion of 'restoration' is a sterile one if it is believed to take us back to exactly where we were once before. On the other hand, as I have argued elsewhere, the concept of restoration in the present is considerably more promising if it becomes a part of our own creative practice.[36] There is also a sense in which restoration of past practices, values or ideas helps to ground us in a feeling of historical continuum that replaces some of the roots that the more aggressive forms of post/modernism have tended to efface. Such roots might be entirely false or, for some people, entirely alien to their actual genealogy. But in many ways these roots are all we have, synthesised as they are in the wake of the alienation resulting from late modernity's purposive erasure of the past.[37] Putting this more positively, historical roots of this kind are there for all to share, particularly for those who have benefited directly from some of the inclusive processes of western modernity and can now claim a stake in a cultural inheritance to which they were formerly denied access. Thus, if there is any time to break with the truism that classical music is essentially a bourgeois phenomenon, now is that time.

Another point to consider is that what I have called 'classical music' has always had the tendency to absorb and transform gestures and vocabularies from other types of music. The dialectical nature of this music as a process heard in real time means that it has the potential to inflect whatever presuppositions we bring towards it in new stages of reception. In this sense, it is not necessarily worn out as historical conditions change, since its counterpoint of elements renders it always already something that is changing whenever it is sounded. This is one way in which the music is, in a sense, separable from the wider culture from which it derived, although it is impossible to predict what sort of effect it might have.

But there is surely no doubt that classical music has completed a certain trajectory in terms of the music created today (which is now often

[36] John Butt, *Playing with History—the Historical Approach to Musical Performance* (Cambridge, 2002), esp. pp. 165–217.

[37] Ibid., pp. 158–63. See also Fredric Jameson, *Postmodernism, or, the Cultural Logic of Late Capitalism* (Durham, NC, 1991).

called merely 'new music', thus distinguishing it from popular or contemporary music, but also distancing it from the classical canon). Until,
say, the 1960s there was still the sense that classical music had gone
through a sense of progress stretching back to the late sixteenth century.
The tonal harmonic language seemed to develop in ways that built upon
conventions of the previous generation, but broke certain rules in order
to push the musical language forwards, usually towards more complexity
and expressive nuance. To Schoenberg and his circle, the development of
tonality towards free and, later, structured atonality was an historical
inevitability. If we admire certain composers—say Tchaikovsky and
Elgar, or those in the Italian opera tradition from Rossini to Puccini—
partly because they remained purposely resistant to certain aspects of
musical progress, and thus quite 'modern' in their own oppositional way,
today it is exceptionally difficult to tell whether a contemporary composer
is progressive, conservative, reactionary or avant garde. Ironically, composers who adopt the technical complexities of 1950s high modernism, or
indeed the aleatoric procedures of experimental music, might sound curiously old-fashioned, while some of those who write music in a simple,
modal or neo-tonal style can seem somehow authentic to the present
(particularly if they somehow cross over with the broader culture of popular music). Whether or not we take 'authenticity to the present' as the
highest possible cultural accolade does of course betray the extent to
which we are still wedded to the concept of a 'classical' art, but the essential point here is that 'the progressive' now seems to point more to the past
than to the future.

With the demise of its specific trajectories, then, the culture of classical music has clearly changed; but this is something it shares with most
of the arts. It is difficult to claim that this music is part of a culture that
is still fully present in all its substantive aspects and unquestioningly to
be justified as the most authentic cultural sound available. Indeed, the
broader modern narrative of progress and historical destiny (as was evident from at least the end of the eighteenth century) is surely untenable
as something that can simply continue uninterrupted, as if all we have to
do is step back onto the pathways established by the Enlightenment.
Now, creative restoration of past practices together with interaction with
other forms of music are not merely options in ensuring the survival of
classical music in any form, they are absolutely imperative. Perhaps, like
some of the most unequivocal achievements of modernity itself (universal justice, equality of rights, freedom of the individual, etc.), classical
music is not going to endure—as if it were *the* natural order—without

some form of positive effort. Thus, contrary to the protestations of Julian Lloyd Webber, its universality is hardly self-evident and definitely not self-sufficient.

If classical music's integrative tendencies can still somehow operate in our time, even without its original sense of historical trajectory, we might also reconsider its traditional forms of resistance to the societal norm of its time (the same could be said of popular music, which is perhaps only in danger of becoming 'too popular' to preserve its counter-cultural credentials). Learning to play an instrument, applying this technique to a sometimes alien repertory, developing a coordination of the physical and the intellectual—all these are somewhat counter to much of the culture we currently experience, since none of these activities has an immediate purpose in our world of targets and measurable goals. But bringing up a new generation that works towards ends that cannot, by definition, be measured, might perhaps help us creatively to regenerate one particularly crucial strand of modernity: its striving for a world that continually challenges inherited prejudices and subverts the literalism of convenient, unthinking beliefs.

Abstracts and Notes on Lecturers

Palace or Powerstation? Museums Today
DUNCAN ROBINSON

In 1965 Isaiah Berlin delivered the A. W. Mellon Lectures at the National Gallery of Art in Washington DC. With his inimitably rich blend of philosophy and intellectual history he sketched for his audience not only 'Some Sources of Romanticism' but also the mixed blessings that that movement, born of the European Enlightenment, bestowed upon the world in the twentieth century. Careful though he was to maintain his distance from contemporary politics and ideologies, Berlin nonetheless implicated the museum, as the site of his discourse, in a wider discussion of art and society.

In this lecture, I have outlined the development of the art museum in the later twentieth century, using recent architectural interventions to illustrate some of the changes that have taken place in attitudes and expectations. I go on to discuss both the opportunities and challenges which face cultural institutions in Britain today, arguing that the curator's task is to rise to these challenges to ensure that the museum operates as both a palace and a powerstation, preserving the past and generating new ideas.

Isaiah Berlin Lecture

Duncan Robinson, FSA, is the Master of Magdalene College, Cambridge, and a Deputy Vice-Chancellor of the University of Cambridge. He is a graduate of both Cambridge and Yale Universities and an Emeritus Fellow of Clare College, Cambridge. He worked at the Fitzwilliam Museum as Assistant Keeper then Keeper of Paintings and Drawings, 1970–81. He then became the Director of the Yale Center for British Art in New Haven, Connecticut, USA, 1981–95, before returning to Cambridge to take up the Directorship of the Fitzwilliam Museum, which he held until his retirement in 2007.

Mr Robinson served as a member of the Arts and Humanities Research Board (1998–2003). He was a Governor of the South Eastern Museums Service, 1997–9, of the Museums Service, East of England, 2002–3, and of its successor body, East England Museums, Libraries and Archives Council, 2003–4. In 1998 he became President of the Friends of the Stanley Spencer Gallery, Cookham, and from 2000 to 2006 he served as a Vice-President of the National Association of Decorative and Fine Arts Societies. He is a Trustee of The Burlington Magazine Foundation, The Royal Collection, and Yale University Press (London), and chairs the Trustees of the Henry Moore Foundation and The Prince's Drawing School.

Architectural Politics in Renaissance Venice
DEBORAH HOWARD

Over the past few decades Venetian historiography has highlighted architecture as one of the means of expression of the so-called 'Myth of Venice'. It has become an accepted tenet among architectural historians that the Republic sought to project its ideology to the public through the patronage of public buildings, and that architecture helped to define the polity of the ruling patriciate by framing its state ceremonial. Architectural historians have sought to identify political and religious affiliations in both executed and unexecuted designs. This lecture questions the validity of this assumption through a close examination of decision-making procedures in the major public building projects of the sixteenth century.

It attempts to define where the power base lay in the implementation of state building projects. What were the relative roles of the Doge, the Procurators of St Mark's, the Council of Ten and the Senate in the defining of architectural policies? Where and by whom were the crucial design decisions made? What was the effect on the constant rotation of officers on project management? How did non-noble employees such as chancery secretaries and *proti* (masters of works) participate in the political decisions? How closely were public building sites monitored? What were the relative roles of technology, funding issues and the theories of classicism of the printed treatise? The lecture suggests that 'democratic' processes often impeded the formulation of coherent ideologies of state, while technological innovation on the building site earned as much respect as classical erudition.

Italian Lecture

Deborah Howard is Professor of Architectural History in the Faculty of Architecture and History of Art and a Fellow of St John's College, Cambridge. She is the present Head of the Department of History of Art. A graduate of Cambridge University and the Courtauld Institute of Art, she previously taught at University College London, Edinburgh University and the Courtauld Institute, returning to Cambridge in 1992.

Her principal research interests are the art and architecture of Venice and the Veneto; music and architecture in the Renaissance; and the relationship between Italy and the Eastern Mediterranean.

Anthropology is *Not* Ethnography
TIM INGOLD

Anthropology and ethnography are endeavours of quite different kinds. Radcliffe-Brown was the first to insist on this distinction, in terms of a contrast between nomothetic and idiographic modes of inquiry. For Radcliffe-Brown, social anthropology was a nomothetic science that aimed at theoretical generalisation. But his idea of anthropology as a generalising science was disputed by Kroeber who held, to the contrary, that anthropology was an idiographic endeavour closely allied to history, the aim of which was the descriptive integration of phenomena. This view was subsequently taken up in British social anthropology by Evans-Pritchard. But what then becomes of the distinction between anthropology and ethnography? Defending Radcliffe-Brown against the charges of his critics—including Evans-Pritchard, Leach and Lévi-Strauss—I argue that his basic idea of the social as a life-process is one that we can take forward, though only by taking the word 'social', in a sense quite different from Radcliffe-Brown's, to signify an order that is implicate rather than explicate. Linking the distinction between explicate and implicate orders to that between theoretical and descriptive integration, I show that what truly distinguishes anthropology is that it is the study not just *of* but *with* people. While in its sensibilities anthropology thus resembles art, in its working practices it is more like a craft. The anthropologist's craft of engaged observation, however, differs from the ethnographer's of writerly description. It is the ethnographer, and not the anthropologist, who must turn away in order to write. The questions that anthropologists address are philosophical ones, but they are better answered thanks to their observational engagements with the world and their collaborations with its inhabitants.

Radcliffe-Brown Lecture in Social Anthropology

Tim Ingold is Professor of Social Anthropology at the University of Aberdeen. He has carried out ethnographic fieldwork among Saami and Finnish people in Lapland, and has written extensively on comparative questions of environment, technology and social organisation in the circumpolar North, as well as on evolutionary theory in anthropology, biology and history, on the role of animals in human society, and on issues in human ecology. His recent research interests are in the anthropology of technology and in aspects of environmental perception. He is currently writing and teaching on the comparative anthropology of the line, and on issues on the interface between anthropology, archaeology, art and architecture. His books include *Evolution and Social Life* (Cambridge, 1986), *Companion Encyclopedia of Anthropology* (ed.) (London, 1994), *Key Debates in Anthropology* (ed.) (London, 1996), *The Perception of the Environment* (London, 2000), *Creativity and Cultural Improvisation* (ed. with Elizabeth Hallam) (Oxford, 2007) and *Lines* (London, 2007).

Visions of European Unity since 1945
NOËL O'SULLIVAN

From the outset Europhile élites have deliberately avoided public debate about the kind of European identity the integration project aims to create, relying on pragmatism in order to avoid provoking resistance to the project. Beyond the confines of the élites, however, there has in fact been a wide-ranging debate about the nature of European unity ever since the Second World War. Now that the earlier generation of confident European leaders has disappeared and uncertainty about the nature and future of the integration project has emerged, especially since the rejection of the Draft Constitution in the French and Dutch referenda of 2005, this debate has acquired renewed interest.

The present lecture seeks to illuminate the debate in three ways. The first is by identifying the various models of European unity which have figured in the debate. The second is by outlining the principal lines of attack used by Eurosceptics to discredit all of them. The third is by considering which models are likely to prove most relevant for the future. It should be added that the lecture is only concerned with intellectually substantial contributions to the debate, so that brief ones like Winston Churchill's call for the establishment of a United States of Europe in 1946, for example, will not be considered. Attention will mainly be restricted, moreover, to models of West European integration, with only passing reference to the discussion of pan-European integration which has occurred since the end of the Cold War.

Elie Kedourie Memorial Lecture

Noël O'Sullivan is Professor of Political Philosophy at the University of Hull. His research has been on the sources of extremism and instability in modern European politics and political thought. His most recent monograph is *European Political Thought since 1945* (2004). Others include *The Philosophy of Santayana* (1992), *Conservatism* (1976) and *Fascism* (1983).

Byzantium and the Limits of Orthodoxy
AVERIL CAMERON

Byzantium is commonly approached through the lens of Orthodoxy, and indeed its role as the exporter of Orthodoxy and the ideas on which it was based to a string of countries which include Russia has had an important effect on how Byzantium itself has been perceived. This lecture questions whether Orthodoxy is indeed the best framework for understanding Byzantium; it suggests that Byzantine Orthodoxy was deeply contested at all periods, and Byzantine society more pluralistic than has often been supposed. The lecture also raises questions about the nature and place of religion in this largely centralised but still pre-modern society. Within the rhetoric of east and west, or of Catholic Europe and Islam, Byzantium occupies an uncertain middle space. Given the resurgence of nationalist religion in several post-Soviet countries, and the frequent appeal to Byzantine origins, as well as the ever-expanding mass of publication on the Crusades, in which the place given to Byzantium remains contested, it seems more necessary than ever to ask how Byzantine society actually worked, what was the (changing) structure of the state, and how far it was sustained by a distinctive Orthodox ideology. The lecture seeks to open up some of these important issues and to lay out some of the necessary parameters.

Raleigh Lecture on History

Averil Cameron is Warden of Keble College, Oxford and the author of many books and articles on late antiquity and early Byzantium. Her research interests include the relation between Byzantium and early Islam and she is currently engaged in a study of the working of religion in the Byzantine state. She was the editor of *Fifty Years of Prosopography: Rome, Byzantium and Beyond*, Publications of the British Academy (Oxford, 2003), and her most recent publications include *The Byzantines* (Oxford, 2006); 'Enforcing Orthodoxy in Byzantium', in Kate Cooper and Jeremy Gregory (eds.), *Discipline and Diversity*, Studies in Church History 43 (Woodbridge, 2007), 1–24, and 'Roman studies in sixth-century Constantinople', to appear in Philip Rousseau and Emmanuel Papoutsakis (eds.), *From Inheritance to Bequest: the Transformations of Late Antiquity* (in press).

Celtic Origins, the Western and the Eastern Celts
WOLFGANG MEID

In the first part of the lecture the concept of 'Celtic'—primarily a linguistic one—and its extension to nonlinguistic uses—the source of various misconceptions—is discussed. The second part refers to the various Celtic movements and settlements. The ancestors of the Celts—as speakers of an Indo-European dialect—came from the East, but established themselves in Western Europe. Later, from the fifth century BC onwards, Celtic groups migrated eastwards again, settling in Noricum and Pannonia, overlaying an autochthonous population of equally Indo-European linguistic origins. The linguistic evidence for the Eastern Celts, consisting mainly of personal and tribal names, is presented, and inferences are drawn as to the survival of Celtic speech, social structures and cultural habits into Roman times.

Sir John Rhŷs Memorial Lecture

Wolfgang Meid is Emeritus Professor of Comparative Linguistics at the University of Innsbruck (Austria). His main research interests are methodological aspects involved in the reconstruction of the Indo-European proto-language, the original home-land and the culture of Proto-Indo-European society, and Celtic studies (in particular the interpretation of the linguistic remains of ancient Celtic languages). He has published more than forty monographs and 130 contributions to periodicals and edited volumes. His publications in Celtic studies include a commented text edition of the Old Irish tale *Táin Bó Froích* in two versions (Dublin 1967, Innsbruck 1970), *Gaulish Inscriptions* (1992), *Celtiberian Inscriptions* (1994), *Keltische Personennamen in Pannonien* (2005) and *Die Kelten* (2007). Wolfgang Meid was awarded the honorary degree of D.Litt. Celt. in 2005 by the National University of Ireland.

Hamlet's Two Fathers
DAVID BEVINGTON

A familiar and cliched notion persists that Hamlet delays in avenging the murder of his father because he is in the grip of a psychological paralysis of the will. The idea is deeply flawed. Ernest Jones's formulation of the idea in his *Hamlet and Oedipus*, based on the work of Sigmund Freud, argues that Hamlet cannot bring himself to punish his uncle for committing an act that Hamlet himself unconsciously longs to do: namely, to possess his mother sexually. This essay argues that Hamlet is indeed caught up in an oedipal crisis of epic proportions, but that he responds to it intelligently, forthrightly, and nobly. His problem is not that he is unable to act, but that the corrupted world in which he finds himself poses intractable problems. Once he has determined that his uncle really has murdered Hamlet's father, Hamlet proceeds swiftly to kill a man hiding in his mother's chambers. The assumption that this man is the hated uncle is entirely plausible, and yet the slain man turns out instead to be the counsellor Polonius acting as a spy. Hamlet immediately perceives that he has killed the wrong man and that he will have to suffer the consequences of this insufficiently considered act. Other characters in the play, notably Laertes, similarly illustrate how fatally easy it is to act rashly and wrongfully on what seem to be sound assumptions: Laertes plots to kill Hamlet, who has indeed killed Laertes's father Polonius, but Laertes fails to recognise that the real villain in the case is Claudius. Hamlet's rightmindedness is further vindicated by his contrastive view of his two fathers. His natural father, now dead, appears to have been a brave warrior, a caring husband, and a wise and noble figure of authority. Hamlet's stepfather Claudius is an able diplomat and a master of political rhetoric, but he is also the murderer of his brother, an adulterer in the sense of having stolen his brother's wife, and a committer of incest for having coveted his sister-in-law. He represents what is so corrupted with the modern world. Hamlet's hatred of Claudius is of course intensely personal, but the negative judgement of Claudius is vindicated in the play itself. So is Hamlet's determination to win his mother away from the sexual embraces of her one-time brother-in-law. Hamlet's longing to reclaim her is oedipal, and is reflective of Hamlet's own deep personal revulsion at sexuality, but it is also defensible in Hamlet's terms because what Gertrude is doing is morally offensive and potentially soul-destroying. Hamlet succeeds at least partly in winning her away from Claudius. She disobeys and lies to her husband for Hamlet's sake, and dies (it would seem) reconciled to her son. The memory of Hamlet Senior has been vindicated, and Hamlet has fulfilled his task of vengeance in a providential way that neither he nor anyone else could have foreseen. In dying bravely, not as a suicide but as the avenger of his father, Hamlet finds surcease from an existence that he has understandably found to be unendurable.

Shakespeare Lecture

David Bevington is the Phyllis Fay Horton Distinguished Service Professor Emeritus in the Humanities at the University of Chicago. His books include *From 'Mankind' to Marlowe* (1962), *Tudor Drama and Politics* (1968), *Action Is Eloquence* (1985), *Shakespeare: The Seven Ages of Human Experience* (2005), *This Wide and Universal Theater: Shakespeare in Performance, Then and Now* (2007), and *Shakespeare's Ideas*

(2008). He is the editor of *Medieval Drama* (1975), *The Bantam Shakespeare*, and *The Complete Works of Shakespeare* (6th edn. 2008). He is a senior editor of the Revels Student Editions, the Revels Plays, *The Norton Anthology of Renaissance Drama*, and the forthcoming Cambridge edition of the works of Ben Johnson.

Artists and Craftsmen in the Late Bronze Age of China (Eighth to Third Centuries BC): Art in Transition
ALAIN THOTE

Major social changes occurred in China in the Late Bronze Age, in particular during the fourth century BC. As the article intends to show, they are mirrored in the artistic production and in the organisation of the workshops. Until the turn of the fourth century BC, the arts were mainly of a religious nature and were dominated by bronze production. In the workshops this production was the result of a collective effort in which each person intervened at a particular moment of the process. In the late fifth century BC, the influence of bronze decoration on other media began to be challenged by new artistic interests. In less than a century, the nature of artistic production changed completely. After having been mainly limited to religious expression, art turned to categories in which new forms of sensibility could be expressed. The fourth century BC is a key period in the development of the arts for these dramatic changes. In particular, lacquers (and few other media) became the main source of inspiration for bronze decoration. The article explores these interactions in terms of creativity and their consequences on the artistic production seen as a whole.

Elsley Zeitlyn Lecture on Chinese Archaeology and Culture

Alain Thote has been Directeur d'études at the École Pratique des Hautes Études, Paris since 2001, and he holds the chair of Art and Archaeology of Pre-Imperial China. He is currently director of the Centre de recherches sur les Civilisations chinoise, japonaise et tibétaine, a joint research centre supported by four institutions. A graduate of École des Hautes Études Commerciales (Management), École du Louvre (Art History, MA) and Université Paris 7 (Sinology, Ph.D.), Professor Thote began his career as a researcher in 1986 at the Centre National de la Recherche Scientifique (CNRS). He participated in the first archaeological excavations jointly conducted by Chinese and French Archaeologists in China, in the desert of Taklamakan (1993, 1994, 1996), and has been co-director of the excavations of the site of Gongying in Central China since 2000. Professor Thote contributed to several exhibition catalogues and is the author of numerous articles on Chinese archaeology. In 2003 he curated an exhibition entitled 'Chine, l'énigme de l'homme de bronze' in Paris. As a visiting professor, he taught at Heidelberg University in the spring of 1996, and at the Institute of Fine Arts, New York University, in the fall of 2005 and 2007.

Seventeenth-Century Draining of the Fens and the Impact on Navigation
MICHAEL CHISHOLM

Draining the Fens in the seventeenth century was an enterprise of national significance, spawning a large literature. According to many authors, little attention was paid to the needs of navigation, with the result, so it is said, that river commerce was seriously compromised. This assessment is wrong. Recently published work shows that trade continued, even flourished, after Denver Sluice was built across the Ouse in 1652. Consequently, what is now needed is a dispassionate review of original sources to determine how water depths were managed and how inland shipping practices changed, together with numerous related matters. Only then would it be possible to make a rounded assessment of how competing needs for land drainage and for maintaining navigable waterways were juggled in the context of limited, and often inadequate, resources.

2008 British Academy Special Lecture

Michael Chisholm, Sc.D., FBA, read Geography at Cambridge (1951–4) and went straight to a research and teaching post in Agricultural Economics at Oxford, publishing *Rural Settlement and Land Use. An Essay in Location* in 1962. He held posts successively at Bedford College London, Ibadan (Nigeria), Bristol, and Cambridge before retiring in 1996. His research and writing interests have focused mainly on contemporary issues of regional economic development, the latest book being (with Steve Leach), *Botched Business: The Damaging Process of Reorganising Local Government 2006–2008* (2008). Among his public appointments have been: Social Science Research Council (1967–72); Local Government Boundary Commission (1971–8); Rural Development Commission (1981–90); and the Local Government Commission (1992–5). His interest in the Fens was triggered by being Chairman of the Conservators of the River Cam, a statutory navigation authority established in 1702.

Reconstructing the National Body: Masculinity, Disability and Race in the American Civil War
SUSAN-MARY GRANT

The debate over the reconstruction of the American nation and the reconfiguration of American nationalism in the aftermath of the Civil

War has, to date, focused mainly on the subjects of race and reconcilia-tion within the context of Reconstruction politics. The war's disabled vet-erans, however, are frequently left out of the discussion: uncomfortable reminders of the sectional conflict at the time, they have been all-but ignored since. Exploring the ways in which the disabled veteran was incor-porated into the revived national body within the broader context of nineteenth-century concepts of masculinity, particularly as these related to race, challenges the somewhat one-dimensional view of the conflict, and the nationalism arising from it, that still prevails. The contradiction involved in commemorating the whole but dead white soldier with an almost equally strong desire to downplay, or render invisible, both the black and the disabled veteran, goes to the heart of post-Civil War American national identity: the new national body could not be con-ceived of as damaged, or even much altered by the war, but was presented as arising intact from the struggle, if anything stronger than before.

Sarah Tryphena Phillips Lecture in American History

Susan-Mary Grant is Professor of American History at Newcastle University. She is the author of *North over South: Northern Nationalism and American Identity in the Antebellum Era* (2000) and *The War for a Nation: the American Civil War* (2006), and has edited several volumes on the Civil War. She was co-founder, in 1992, of the British American Nineteenth Century Historians' association (BrANCH) and is currently editor of the Routledge journal, *American Nineteenth Century History*.

She serves on the international advisory board of *Nations and Nationalism* (Blackwell) and on the steering committee of the Association for Research into Ethnicity and Nationalism in the Americas (ARENA), which is based at the Walker Institute, University of South Carolina. Her present research project focuses on disabled Civil War veterans between 1861 and 1917.

A Minority Opinion?
BARONESS HALE OF RICHMOND

One difference between 'academic' and 'real' law is that academic lawyers are expected to give their opinions, not only about what the law is, but about what it should be. A consistent philosophy is a virtue rather than a drawback. Judicial decisions, on the other hand, should be 'legally moti-vated' and not influenced by 'any personal agenda of the judge, whether conservative, liberal, feminist, libertarian or whatever' (Tom Bingham, 'The Judges: active or passive?', *Proceedings of the British Academy*, 139 (2006), 55). This lecture explores the extent to which it is possible for a judge to bring her personal perspective, in this case feminism, to the business of judging and concludes in favour of 'feminist minimalism'.

Maccabaean Lecture in Jurisprudence

Brenda Hale, Baroness Hale of Richmond, became the United Kingdom's first Lord of Appeal in Ordinary in 2004 after a varied career, first as an academic lawyer at the University of Manchester, next as a member of the Law Commission leading its programme for the reform of family law, and then as a Judge in the Family Division of the High Court from 1994, the Court of Appeal from 1999, and now in the appellate committee of the House of Lords (next year to become the United Kingdom Supreme Court). She is President of the United Kingdom Association of Women Judges, President-elect of the International Association of Women Judges and Chancellor of the University of Bristol.

'We keep the bread and wine for show'—Consistent Irony and Reluctant Faith in the Poetry of Dannie Abse
TONY CURTIS

This lecture examines and evaluates some of the central themes and tropes of one of the most significant post-war British poets. It places that poetry in the wider context of Abse's fiction and creative non-fiction, from the 1954 *Ash on a Young Man's Sleeve* to the confessional and elegiac *The Presence* of 2007, and by so doing emphasises the constant interweaving of the poet's life and his re-imaginings of that life. Professor Curtis shows how Abse's roots as a Welshman, his determination to remain a secular Jew and his responses to the challenges of war, the Holocaust and personal loss all serve to strengthen his resolve as a writer and direct his imagination.

Warton Lecture on English Poetry

Tony Curtis was born in Carmarthen in 1946. He was educated at Swansea University and Goddard College, Vermont. He is Professor of Poetry at the University of Glamorgan where he established and runs the M.Phil. in Writing. He has published over thirty books, including nine collections of poetry. He won the National Poetry Prize in 1984 and a Cholmondeley Award in 1997. He was elected a Fellow of the Royal Society of Literature in 2001 and in 2004 was awarded a D.Litt., the first such, from the University of Glamorgan.

Theopoesis: the Contest of Priest and Poet
GEOFFREY HARTMAN

The essay contains a reconsideration of the contest between religion and poetry in the eighteenth century and Romanticism. It charts in a series of close readings the complexity of the relation between poetry and both natural and revealed religion in Addison, Blake, and Coleridge, authors who in very different ways did not give up, or not entirely, the rights of poetry at a time when the imagination, and in particular the enthusiastic imagination, was being curtailed and even repressed. At issue is the poet's vocation as it asserts itself in a freer visionary poetry and seeks to displace 'the primeval Priest's assumed power' (Blake) by reappropriating, recreating, or forging anew an ancient, /logos/-powered voice.

British Academy Special Lecture

Geoffrey Hartman is Sterling Professor of English and Comparative Literature (Emeritus) and Senior Research Scholar at Yale. He has held distinguished visiting appointments at many universities in the US and abroad, is a Corresponding Fellow of the British Academy and a Chevalier, Ordre des Arts et Lettres of the French Ministry of Culture. Among his other awards are the Christian Gauss Prize for *Wordsworth's Poetry*, the René Wellek Prize for *The Fateful Question of Culture*, and the 2006 Truman Capote Prize for *The Geoffrey Hartman Reader*. He is also a co-founder of the Fortunoff Video Archive for Holocaust Testimonies and continues as its Project Director.

'But I, that knew what harbred in that hed': Sir Thomas Wyatt and his Posthumous 'Interpreters'
CATHY SHRANK

Elegies on Sir Thomas Wyatt the Elder by Henry Howard, Earl of Surrey, and John Leland equate his poetry and his character, transforming him and his verses into moral exempla, a move indicative of later trends of Wyatt editing and criticism, with their tendency towards biographical readings and frequent attempts to fit his poems into a narrative. With their insistent use of the word 'self', plain style and evocation of a particular event, place or occasion, it is perhaps inevitable that Wyatt's poems have invited such interpretations, yet this lecture suggests that Wyatt's works resist biographical readings, thanks to their deliberate opacity, recurrent removal of specific referents, and extraction (in the case of his Petrarchan translations) from a biographical narrative which is forcefully set out in Wyatt's likely source (Alessandro Vellutello's *Il Petrarcha*). It argues that the honesty articulated in his letters and poetry is modulated by 'circumspection', and his constancy achieved by an ability to change.

Chatterton Lecture on Poetry

Dr Cathy Shrank is a Reader in Tudor Literature at the University of Sheffield. She is the author of *Writing the Nation in Reformation England* (Oxford, 2004) and is currently co-editing *The Oxford Handbook of Tudor Literature, 1485–1603* (Oxford, forthcoming). Her research is focused on sixteenth-century poetry and prose, and she is particularly interested in non-dramatic dialogue and the intersection between the literature and politics of the period.

Mind the Gap; Why Humans Are Not Just Great Apes
R. I. M. DUNBAR

Although we share many aspects of our behaviour and biology with our primate cousins, humans are, nonetheless, different in one crucial respect: our capacity to live in the world of the imagination. This is reflected in two core aspects of our behaviour that are in many ways archetypal of what it is to be human: religion and story-telling. I shall show how these remarkable traits seem to have arisen as a natural development of the social brain hypothesis, and the underlying nature of primate sociality and cognition, as human societies have been forced to expand in size during the course of our evolution over the past five million years.

Joint British Academy/British Psychological Society Lecture

Robin Dunbar, FBA, is Professor of Evolutionary Anthropology and Director of the Institute of Cognitive and Evolutionary Anthropology at the University of Oxford. He read Psychology and Philosophy at Oxford, after which he gained a Ph.D. in Psychology at the University of Bristol. He has held research fellowships at Cambridge, Stockholm and Liverpool Universities, before being appointed as a lecturer, and later Professor, of Anthropology at University College London, following which he held chairs in Psychology and then Biology at Liverpool University. He is co-Director of the British Academy's Centenary Research Project ('Lucy to Language: The Archaeology of the Social Brain'), a multi-disciplinary collaboration involving five UK universities whose aim is to determine what it is to be human and how we came to be that way.

Classical Music and the Subject of Modernity
JOHN BUTT

Classical music seems to fit increasingly awkwardly into our culture today. Its practice is more expensive and time-consuming than most other forms of music and many call for it to be afforded no particular privilege in funding and education. However, its defenders are not necessarily doing it a service by declaring it to be of universal significance, the fount of all other forms of music. In this paper, I argue that the culture of 'classical music' (which is something much broader than the content of 'the music itself') is of a piece with the wider historical context of western modernity. While there is considerable leeway as to how modernity might be defined and when it took hold, it can be related to the tendency in the West to question inherited systems on a continual basis, and no longer to assume that the cosmos was designed for the benefit of humankind. In order to progress in the modern world, a certain degree of artificiality, of necessary fictional construction, became necessary. I suggest that it is exactly this sense of 'fictional construction' that marks out the emerging culture of classical music, particularly in its relation to the stronger modern sense of self and the subject. In its very turn away from its connection to an assumed natural order, classical music could have been partly constitutive of western modernity. It may well be that current issues about the status of classical music are directly related to the fate of modernity itself, the latter being challenged and supposedly superseded from a number of viewpoints. While a direct restoration of the past is out of the question, there may be some real ways in which something of the critical energy of classical music could be of considerable value in our current climate.

Aspects of Art Lecture

John Butt, FBA, is Gardiner Professor of Music at the University of Glasgow. He is the author of several major studies of Bach and the Baroque era and has also written on the modern culture of historically informed performance (*Playing with History*, Cambridge 2002, which was shortlisted for the 2003 British Academy book prize). He will shortly be publishing his study of the Bach Passions and their relation to issues of modernity. As a performer, he is a noted organist and harpsichordist and has recently enjoyed considerable success as director of the Dunedin Consort, with whom he won the 2007 Classic FM/Gramophone award in Baroque vocal music for a recording of Handel's *Messiah* in its first performed version (Dublin, 1742).

Lecture series published in the *Proceedings of the British Academy*

The holding of academic lectures, and their publication in the *Proceedings*, have constituted a key activity of the British Academy since its foundation.

There are currently twenty-four established series of lectures. Some are of long standing, but there are several recent additions which have extended the range of the programme. Distinguished speakers are invited on the recommendation of the Academy's subject-based Sections or specialist nomination committees.

There are ten annual lecture series, eleven biennial series. Another three series have become incorporated in the Academy's programme of symposia. The Academy also organises occasional special lectures.

The lecture series are detailed below in the order in which they were inaugurated. Recent published lectures are listed (with *Proceedings* volume and page numbers).

Lectures published in print in the *Proceedings of the British Academy* are also available in PDF format via www.proc.britac.ac.uk

Warton Lectures on English Poetry   *Annual; first delivered* 1910

Mrs Frida Mond endowed this lecture series as a tribute to Thomas Warton, 'the first historian of English poetry, whose work not only led the way to the scientific study of English Literature, but also stimulated creative genius, and played no small part in the Romantic Revival'.

Recent published lectures:
2004   David Womersley, 'Dulness and Pope' (**131,** 229–50)
2005   Margaret Reynolds, 'The Child in Poetry: Foundlings, Lostlings, Changelings' (**151,** 1–52)
2006   R. F. Foster, ' "Now Shall I Make My Soul": Approaching Death in Yeats's Life and Work' (**151,** 339–360)

Shakespeare Lectures   *Annual; first delivered* 1911

In 1910 Mrs Frida Mond provided for a lecture to be delivered 'on some Shakespearean subject, philosophical, historical, or philological, or some problem in English dramatic literature and histrionic art, or some study in literature of the age of Shakespeare'. Delivered on or around 23 April.

Recent published lectures:
2004   Michael Pennington, 'Barnardine's Straw: The Devil in Shakespeare's Detail' (**131**, 205–27)
2005   Alan C. Dessen, 'Staging Matters: Shakespeare, the Director, and the Theatre Historian' (**139**, 35–54)
2006   Ian Donaldson, 'Shakespeare, Jonson, and the Invention of the Author' (**151**, 319–338)

Philosophical Lectures   *Symposia; first delivered* 1914

The will of Miss Henriette Hertz made provision for a lecture 'on a philosophical problem or some problems in the philosophy of Western or Eastern Civilisation in Ancient or Modern times or discussions of theories of the Phenomena of life to Eternity'. Since the early 1990s, the lectures have been grouped together to form symposia, which are published in their own *Proceedings* volumes.

2001   *Bayes's Theorem* symposium:
Elliott Sober, 'Bayesianism—its Scope and Limits' (**113**, 21–38)
Colin Howson, 'Bayesianism in Statistics' (**113**, 39–69)
A. P. Dawid, 'Bayes's Theorem and Weighing Evidence by Juries' (**113**, 71–90)
John Earman, 'Bayes, Hume, Price, and Miracles' (**113**, 91–109)

Aspects of Art Lectures   *Biennial; first delivered* 1916

Established by the Henriette Hertz Trust, the lecture is intended to be 'on some problem or aspect of the relation of Art in any of its manifestations to human culture; Art including Poetry and Music as well as Sculpture and Painting'.

Recent published lectures:
2003   Stephen Banfield, 'Scholarship and the Musical: Reclaiming Jerome Kern' (**125**, 183–210)
2005   Joseph Leo Koerner, 'Everyman in Motion: from Bosch to Bruegel' (**139**, 297–328)

Master-Mind Lectures   *Biennial; first delivered* 1916

Miss Henriette Hertz provided for a lecture on 'some Master-Mind considered individually with reference to his life and work especially in order to appraise the essential elements of his Genius: the subject to be chosen problem in English dramatic literature and histrionic art, or some study in literature of the age of Shakespeare'. Delivered on or around 23 April.

Recent published lectures:
2004   Michael Pennington, 'Barnardine's Straw: The Devil in Shakespeare's Detail' (**131**, 205–27)
2005   Alan C. Dessen, 'Staging Matters: Shakespeare, the Director, and the Theatre Historian' (**139**, 35–54)
2006   Ian Donaldson, 'Shakespeare, Jonson, and the Invention of the Author' (**151**, 319–338)

Philosophical Lectures   *Symposia; first delivered* 1914

The will of Miss Henriette Hertz made provision for a lecture 'on a philosophical problem or some problems in the philosophy of Western or Eastern Civilisation in Ancient or Modern times or discussions of theories of the Phenomena of life to Eternity'. Since the early 1990s, the lectures have been grouped together to form symposia, which are published in their own *Proceedings* volumes.

2001   *Bayes's Theorem* symposium:
       Elliott Sober, 'Bayesianism—its Scope and Limits' (**113**, 21–38)
       Colin Howson, 'Bayesianism in Statistics' (**113**, 39–69)
       A. P. Dawid, 'Bayes's Theorem and Weighing Evidence by Juries' (**113**, 71–90)
       John Earman, 'Bayes, Hume, Price, and Miracles' (**113**, 91–109)

Aspects of Art Lectures   *Biennial; first delivered* 1916

Established by the Henriette Hertz Trust, the lecture is intended to be 'on some problem or aspect of the relation of Art in any of its manifestations to human culture; Art including Poetry and Music as well as Sculpture and Painting'.

Recent published lectures:
2003   Stephen Banfield, 'Scholarship and the Musical: Reclaiming Jerome Kern' (**125**, 183–210)
2005   Joseph Leo Koerner, 'Everyman in Motion: from Bosch to Bruegel' (**139**, 297–328)

Master-Mind Lectures   *Biennial; first delivered* 1916

Miss Henriette Hertz provided for a lecture on 'some Master-Mind considered individually with reference to his life and work especially in order to appraise the essential elements of his Genius: the subject to be chosen from the great Philosophers, Artists, Poets, Musicians'.

Recent published lectures:
2004   Terence Cave, 'Montaigne' (**131**, 183–203)
2005   John Stachel, 'Einstein' (**151**, 423–59)
2006   Lorraine Daston, 'Condorcet and the Meaning of Enlightenment' (**151**, 113–134)

Italian Lectures   *Biennial; first delivered* 1917

In 1916 Mrs Angela Mond offered funds for a lecture series 'to be on some subject relating to Italian literature, history, art, history of Italian science, Italy's part in the Renaissance, Italian influences on other countries, and any other theme which the Council may consider as coming within the scope of such a Lecture'.

Recent published lectures:
2003   Brian Pullan, 'Charity and Usury: Jewish and Christian Lending in Renaissance and Early Modern Italy' (**125**, 19–40)
2005   Carlo Ginzburg, 'Dante's Epistle to Cangrande and its Two Authors' (**139**, 195–216)

Raleigh Lectures on History   *Annual; first delivered* 1919

In 1918 Sir Charles Wakefield (formerly Lord Mayor of London) offered the Academy the sum of £500 a year for at least five years to commemorate the tercentenary of Sir Walter Raleigh; from this fund, a history lecture was founded. Since 1974 the subject has rotated between the medieval, early modern and modern fields.

Recent published lectures:
2004   Alexander Murray, 'The Inquisition and the Renaissance' (**131**, 91–126)
2005   Keith Wrightson, 'Mutualities and Obligations: Changing Social Relationships in Early Modern England' (**139**, 157–194)
2006   R. J. Evans, 'Coercion and Consent in Nazi Germany' (**151**, 53–81)

Sir Israel Gollancz Memorial Lectures   *Biennial; first delivered* 1924

Endowed by Mrs Frida Mond in 1924, this lecture deals with 'Old English or Early English Language and Literature, or a philological subject connected with the history of English, more particularly during the early periods of the language, or cognate subjects, or some textual study and interpretation'. The lecture series was subsequently named after Sir Israel Gollancz (Secretary of the Academy 1902–30).

Recent published lectures:
2002   Ralph Hanna, 'Yorkshire Writers' (**121**, 91–109)
2004   Joyce Hill, 'Authority and Intertextuality in the Works of Ælfric' (**131**, 157–81)
2006   James Simpson, 'Bonjour Paresse: Literary Waste and Recycling in Book 4 of Gower's *Confessio Amantis*' (**151**, 257–284)

Sir John Rhŷs Memorial Lectures   *Biennial; first delivered* 1925

In May 1924 a memorial fund was offered to the Academy 'for the promotion of Welsh and other studies', to commemorate the services of the Rt Hon. Sir John Rhŷs, FBA, Professor of Celtic, and Principal of Jesus College, Oxford.

Recent published lectures:
2001   Ralph A. Griffiths, 'After Glyn Dŵr: An Age of Reconciliation?' (**117**, 139–64)
2003   Fergus Kelly, 'Thinking in Threes: "The Triad in Early Irish Literature"' (**125**, 1–18)

Albert Reckitt Archaeological Lectures   *Biennial; first delivered* 1951

The Reckitt Archaeological Trust, established by the late Mr Albert L. Reckitt for the furtherance of archaeological research, was transferred to the Academy in 1950; it was decided to establish a lecture series in memory of the founder.

Recent published lectures:
2002   Charles F. W. Higham, 'The Origins of the Civilisation of Angkor' (**121**, 41–89)
2004   Joan Oates, 'Archaeology in Mesopotamia: Digging Deeper at Tell Brak' (**131**, 1–39)
2006   Norman Hammond, 'Recovering Maya Civilisation' (**151**, 361–385)

Chatterton Lectures on Poetry   *Annual; first delivered* 1955

Established in 1954 under the will of E. H. W. Meyerstein of Gray's Inn, this annual lecture is to be given by a lecturer under the age of 40 on the life and works of a deceased English poet (interpreted as 'a deceased poet writing in the English language').

Recent published lectures:

2004   Fran Brearton, 'Robert Graves and *The White Goddess*' (**131**, 273–301)
2005   Jane Stabler, 'Byron, Conversation and Discord' (**139**, 111–35)
2006   Robert Douglas-Fairhurst, 'A. E. Housman's Rejected Addresses' (**151**, 83–111)

Dawes Hicks Lectures on Philosophy   *Symposia; first delivered* 1955

Established in 1954, under the will of George Dawes Hicks (Professor of Philosophy at the University of London), these lectures were to be given on 'subjects relating to the History of Philosophy, either ancient or modern'. Since the early 1990s, the lectures have been grouped together to form symposia, which are published in their own *Proceedings* volumes.

2004   *Rationalism, Platonism and God* symposium:
        John Cottingham, 'Plato's Sun and Descartes's Stove: Contemplation and Control in Cartesian Philosophy' (**149**, 15–44)
        Michael Ayers, 'Spinoza, Platonism and Naturalism' (**149**, 53–78)
        Robert Merrihew Adams, 'The Priority of the Perfect in the Philosophical Theology of the Continental Rationalists' (**149**, 91–116)

Maccabaean Lectures in Jurisprudence   *Biennial; first delivered* 1956

This lecture series, which may be on any aspect of Jurisprudence, was endowed in 1956 by the Maccabaeans, a society of Jewish professional men with a strong interest in the law, to mark the tercentenary of the Jewish resettlement in England under Cromwell.

Recent published lectures:
2003   Brian Simpson, 'The Rule of Law in International Affairs' (**125**, 211–63)
2005   Lord Bingham of Cornhill, 'The Judges: Active or Passive?' (**139**, 55–72)

Sarah Tryphena Phillips Lectures in American Literature and History
Biennial; first delivered 1961

Dr Carl Bode, Cultural Attaché at the US Embassy in London 1958–9, proposed a series of lectures on American Literature. In 1960 a lecture series was endowed by the Ellis L. Phillips Foundation—the scope of the series to include American history, though the emphasis was to be on literature.

Recent published lectures:
2003   Eric Foner, 'Abraham Lincoln: The Great Emancipator?' (**125**, 149–62)
2005   Richard Gray, '"They Worship Death Here": William Faulkner, *Sanctuary* and Hollywood' (**131**, 251–71)

Thank-Offering to Britain Fund Lectures   *Biennial; first delivered* 1966

In 1965 the proceeds of a 'Thank-you Britain' appeal, initiated by the Association of Jewish Refugees, were presented to the Academy as a token of gratitude from the people who had sought refuge in this country from the oppression of the Nazis. One of the purposes of the fund was to establish a 'Thank-offering to Britain' Lecture.

Recent published lectures:
2002   The Right Honourable Lord Woolf, 'Human Rights: Have the Public Benefited?' (**121**, 301–14)
2004   Lord Moser, 'The Future of Our Universities' (**131**, 303–30)

Keynes Lectures in Economics   *Annual; first delivered* 1971

Proposed by the economists within the Academy, these lectures are devoted to an up-to-date survey of theoretical research and trends of thought in the field of economics. In recent years, the lectures have been followed by formal discussion.

Recent published lectures:
2003   John Vickers, 'Economics for Consumer Policy' (**125**, 287–310)
2004   Timothy Besley, 'The New Political Economy' (**131**, 371–95)
2005   Stephen Nickell, 'Practical Issues in UK Monetary Policy, 2000–2005' (**139**, 1–33)
2006   Ken Binmore, 'The Origins of Fair Play' (**151**, 159–193)

Mortimer Wheeler Archaeological Lectures   *Symposia; first delivered* 1971

On the proposal of Council a lecture series was established to commemorate the eightieth birthday (in September 1970) of Sir Mortimer Wheeler (Secretary of the Academy 1949–70). Since the early 1990s, the lecture has been subsumed within a number of Academy symposia on archaeological subjects, published as distinct volumes of the *Proceedings*.

Recent published lecture:
2001   Robin Osborne, 'Urban Sprawl: What is Urbanization and Why does it Matter?' (**126**, 1–16)

Radcliffe-Brown Lectures in Social Anthropology   *Biennial; first delivered* 1972

This series was established in 1972 by the Academy and the Association of Social Anthropologists and named after the Association's first

President, A. R. Radcliffe-Brown, FBA, who was also the first Professor of Social Anthropology in the University of Oxford.

Recent published lectures:
2003   Gillian Feeley-Harnik, 'The Geography of Descent' (**125**, 311–64)
2005   Philippe Descola, 'Beyond Nature and Culture' (**139**, 137–55)

Elie Kedourie Memorial Lectures   *Annual; first delivered* 1996

In 1993, a Fund was set up by appeal, in memory of the modern historian and political philosopher Elie Kedourie, FBA, in order to establish a lecture in modern history, preference being given to subjects in Middle Eastern and modern European history.

Recent published lectures:
2004   James Piscatori, 'Imagining Pan-Islam: Religious Activism and Political Utopias' (**131**, 421–42)
2005   Dominic Lieven, 'Empire, History and the Contemporary Global Order' (**131**, 127–56)
2006   Anthony D. Smith, 'Nation and Covenant: The Contribution of Ancient Israel to Modern Nationalism' (**151**, 213–255)

British Academy Lectures   *Annual; first delivered* 1998

Established to mark the Academy's move to Carlton House Terrace in 1998, the keynote British Academy Lecture is intended to address a wide audience and to promote understanding of the humanities and social sciences.

Recent published lectures:
2003   Gillian Beer, 'Revenants and Migrants: Hardy, Butler, Woolf and Sebald' (**125**, 163–82)
2004   Mervyn King, 'What Fates Impose: Facing Up to Uncertainty' (**131**, 397–420)
2005   Colin Renfrew, 'Becoming Human: the Archaeological Challenge' (**139**, 217–38)
2006   Ian Hacking, 'Kinds of People: Moving Targets' (**151**, 285–318)

Isaiah Berlin Lectures   *Annual; first delivered* 2001

Established under the will of Sir Isaiah Berlin (President of the Academy 1974–8), the lecture is intended to appraise the contemporary condition of any one of the fields of learning with which the Academy is concerned.

Recent published lectures:
2004   Lord Sutherland, 'Nomad's Progress' (**131**, 443–63)
2005   Marilyn Strathern, 'Useful Knowledge' (**139**, 73–109)

2006 Bernard Bailyn, 'The Search for Perfection: Atlantic Dimensions' (**151**, 135–158)

Elsley Zeitlyn Lectures on Chinese Archaeology and Culture
Annual; first delivered 2001

Through a bequest from Miss M. H. Zeitlyn in memory of her father, this lecture series was established 'to support the understanding and appreciation of Chinese Archaeology and Culture and to stimulate new programmes of high quality research in this field'.

Recent published lectures:
2004 Robert Bagley, 'The Prehistory of Chinese Music Theory' (**131**, 41–90)
2005 Lothar von Falkenhausen, 'The Inscribed Bronzes from Yangjiacun: New Evidence on Social Structure and Historical Consciousness in Late Western Zhou China (*c*.800 BC)' (**139**, 239–95)

Joint British Academy/British Psychological Society Lectures
Annual; first delivered 2001

In 2001 the Academy held a lecture to mark the centenary of the British Psychological Society. The Academy's Psychology Section subsequently recommended that a joint lecture should be added to the Academy's lecture programme.

Recent published lectures:
2003 Susan E. Gathercole, 'Working Memory and Learning During the School Years' (**125**, 365–80)

British Academy Law Lecture
Biennial; first delivered 2004

In 2003 the Academy approved the proposal of the Law Section for an additional Law Lecture, to complement the Maccabean Lecture.

2004 Edwin Cameron & Jonathan Berger, 'Patents and Public Health: Principle, Politics and Paradox' (**131**, 331–69)
2006 Neil MacCormick, 'Judicial Independence: Who Cares?' (**151**, 195–211)